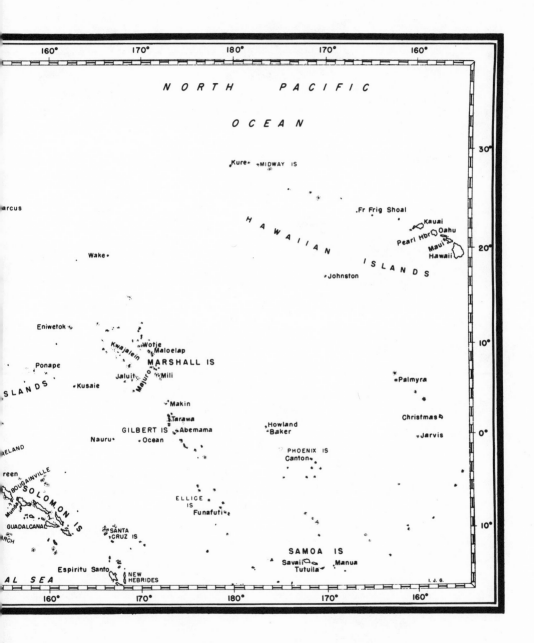

JAPAN'S
WAR
THE GREAT
PACIFIC
CONFLICT

JAPAN'S
WAR
THE GREAT
PACIFIC
CONFLICT

BY EDWIN P. HOYT
with a new preface

Cooper Square Press

First Cooper Square Press Edition 2001

This Cooper Square Press paperback edition of *Japan's War* is an unabridged republication of the edition first published in New York in 1986, here supplemented with a new preface. It is reprinted by arrangement with the author.

Book design by Liney Li

Published by Cooper Square Press
An Imprint of the Rowman & Littlefield Publishing Group
150 Fifth Avenue, Suite 911
New York, New York 10011

Distributed by National Book Network

Library of Congress Cataloging-in-Publication Data
This book was previously cataloged by the Library of Congress as follows:

Hoyt, Edwin Palmer
   Japan's war.
   1. World War, 1939–1945— Campaigns— Pacific Area. 2. World War, 1939–1945— Japan. 3. Japan— History, Military— 1868-   . 4. Japan— Politics and government— 1868-   . 5. Pacific Area— History. I. Title.

   D767.H653 1986
   940.54'26
                                                                            85-24192

ISBN— 0-8154-1118-9 (pbk : alk. paper)

⊖™ The paper used in this publication meets the minimum requirements of American National Standard for Information Sciences— Permanence of Paper for Printed Library Materials, ANSI/NISO Z39.48–1992.
Manufactured in the United States of America.

This book is for Arleigh Burke, who is famous in postwar Japan as the father of the Self-Defense Forces. As a professional naval officer, Admiral Burke fought the Japanese all during the Pacific War as bravely and hard as he could, and then, once victory was in hand, exhibited that compassion for which Americans are justly known and turned about to become one of the best and most effective friends in the world of the New Japan.

Preface to the Cooper Square Press Edition

Much has occurred in the world since the first publication of *Japan's War*, and since we have entered the twenty-first century, but Japan is a nation that seems to be mired in the past. The political hacks who have governed the country since Prime Minister Tanaka have offered no leadership, but neither has the opposition. The result is a political quagmire, marked by corruption and confusion, in which the Japanese people, wanting change, have rejected the half-measures of the opposition and retained the ineffectual coalition that has been in power in recent years.

A bright light seemed to appear on the horizon when Morihiro Hosokawa of the famous Konoye family became prime minister. But he proved to be a comet flitting across the landscape and has since retired to political obscurity. His great accomplishment was to initiate the debate about Japan's responsibility for the Pacific War. Japan has never properly come to grips with its grisly past, and what is certain is that until this failure is addressed it will continue to hinder Japan's international progress.

The ultra-nationalist mindset still exists in Japan, as exemplified by the Prime Minister and the governor of Tokyo. The Prime Minister, Yoshiro Mori, has made so many gaffes as to become a national laughingstock. He has declared Japan to be a special example of a holy state, and, although the Shinto religion was divorced from Japan by the 1947

Constitution, the Prime Minister has invoked its shadow again. Members of his own party began to call for his resignation.

By early November 2000 the Mori cabinet's approval rate had fallen under fifteen percent, the lowest in post WWII history.

The governor of Tokyo, Shintaro Ishihara, has insisted on making and carrying out his own China policy, to the embarrassment of the Foreign Ministry.

Internationally, Japan is still dependent on its alliance with the United States, yet hampered by the Constitution that General Douglas MacArthur thrust upon the nation in the first months after the defeat in World War II. Economically, the surge of prosperity labeled as the "economic miracle" vanished in the bursting bubble of speculation and gave way to a serious and lingering recession that is just now beginning to diminish. The Japanese banking system, which once led the world, has collapsed. Japan was famous for its industrial allegiances: workers entered the work force and almost always stayed with the same company until retirement. This is no longer true. The "lifetime employment" dream turned out to be just another myth, and in 2000 the unemployment figures surpassed those of the past. Young people coming out of high school and college found it hard to get jobs. Many had to settle for *arubaito*—part-time work.

Additionally, other problems have begun to appear. Random criminality, once virtually unknown in Japan, has increased alarmingly, particularly violent crimes committed by the young. Women's place in the work force grows stronger, but they do not seem to be very happy. *Ofisuredii*—office ladies—often opt against marriage, preferring their independence.

All this makes for a bewildered and bewildering Japan whose future—which once appeared so bright—seems threatened. One thing is certain: at the dawn of the 21st century, Japan is waiting for a leader. The direction in which this unknown, potential leader will take the country remains to be seen.

生者必滅

Preface: "He who is born must die"

Meditation on inevitable death should be performed daily. Every day when one's body and mind are at peace, one should meditate upon being ripped apart by arrows, rifles, spears, and swords, being carried away by surging waves, being thrown into the midst of a great fire, being struck by lightning, being shaken to death by a great earthquake, falling from a thousand foot cliff, dying of disease, or committing seppuku at the death of one's master. And every day without fail one should consider himself as dead.

Hagakure
(*The Book of the Samurai*), Chapter 11, Tsunetomo Yamamoto,
Eighteenth century[1]

A Japanese newspaperman in 1975 said it one way. One night, when he and an American confrere had put away most of a bottle of Scotch whisky and were arguing amiably over world affairs, he looked at his American friend appraisingly.

"You'll never understand," he said. "The trouble with you is that white skin of yours."[2]

Yasuhiro Nakasone, prime minister of Japan, said it another way in the winter of 1984, as he probed the road that Japan was to follow in her future relations with Asia and the world. Japan, he said, represented the leadership of Asian culture, which was moving with America, the heir to European culture, to bring together two great cultures that would thereafter dominate the world.[3]

Note that no mention was made of the Soviet Union. Despite the USSR's position as one of two major powers in the 1980s, the Japanese prime minister treated that power almost as if it were a transitory phenomenon, not to be considered in the great scheme of world affairs. And the Japanese, in the century and a quarter since Commodore Perry opened the Pandora's box in Tokyo Bay and forced the Japanese to deal with the outside world on the West's terms, have never lost sight of the fundamental aim of dominating their environment.

Japan in the 1980s is following a destiny laid down long ago by the leaders of the kingdom, a destiny that demands for the Japanese the leadership of Asia and perhaps the world. Inherently the Japanese believe in this destiny just as they believe in the superiority of their civilization over all others, including the Chinese, from whom they borrowed literature, art, and a written language, and Western society, particularly American, from whom they borrowed technology.

The kingdom of Japan is the oldest self-perpetuating government. Since the beginning of the Christian Era by which we Westerners measure time, the kingdom of Yamato has been independent, and, until 1945, for nearly two thousand years had not once been defeated in battle, nor had any foreign boot ever trod the land since the Yamato race came down from Korea to conquer the scattered clans in those islands and establish the line of authority that has basically endured ever since the second century A.D.[4]

It was to follow that destiny that in 1931 the ill-fated and ill-advised leaders of Japan plunged the nation into a struggle to dominate China and then, in desperation, extended that effort to all of East Asia and the Pacific basin. The result, as the world knows, was the war Westerners call the Pacific War, but which Japanese have always referrred to as *Dai-Toa Senso,* the Great East Asia War. It began in China, and until the very end the leaders of Japan believed that if they could solve "the China question" it would not be difficult to disengage from the West and achieve a modus vivendi, one which would maintain a satisfactory Japanese empire. That belief was held down to that furious fortnight in August 1945, when the atomic bombs were dropped and the Soviets began their march into Manchuria.

This book is the story of that Japanese pursuit of destiny, from the opening of Japan by the West until the two great antagonists, the United States and Japan, made their peace in 1951, and forty-seven other nations signed the treaty. In fact, the struggle did not actually end, but in 1952 entered a new phase which brought Japan to a power she had never before enjoyed, and which, in the 1980s, raised many questions about the future. This book is concerned with the events of 1853 to 1952 and the lessons that may be learned from them.

Contents

Once when a group of half a dozen young samurai were traveling to Edo in the same boat it happened that their boat struck a ship in the night. Half a dozen seamen from the ship leaped aboard the boat and demanded retribution, which in this case meant taking the boat's anchor. One of the young samurai came running up, shouting.

"Do you think that we samurai are going to let you take equipment from a boat carrying warriors? We will cut you down and throw you into the sea."

On hearing that, the seamen turned and fled back to their ship.

Hagakure, Chapter 2[5]

JAPAN'S WAR

THE GREAT PACIFIC CONFLICT

八紘一宇

1. "All eight corners of the world under one roof"

The two tales from the *Hagakure* are offered here to prepare Western readers of this book to understand a philosophical approach to life so much different from our own that some Westerners are inclined to believe the concept invalid or pertaining only to a small class of Japanese. The willingness to accept death without a whimper and to commit suicide with the thought that by so doing one is advancing a lofty cause are not Western concepts. Most of us in the West do not live every day prepared to die. And neither do most Japanese. But deep in the Japanese consciousness is acceptance of this philosophy of life, and in times of trial it emerges and can dominate the thinking of the entire nation. As for the tale of the young samurai facing down the rough sailors, it tells of another aspect of Japanese philosophy. The samurai is with Japan yet, beneath the black suit and white shirt of the *sarariman* who goes about his business daily so much in the manner of his Western counterpart. Let events tear away the Western clothes and from beneath will emerge the warrior of old, no matter how long he has been submerged. Doubters may examine the development of the "Imperial Way" in the 1920s and 1930s when a shrewd group of army leaders instituted a system of *bushido,* which had lain dormant since the Meiji Restitution, and an "Emperor Worship" that had never existed to the extent to which it was brought in the 1930s.

From the beginning the Japanese considered themselves to be the natural rulers of their world. The *Nihon Shoki (Chronicles of Japan)* say that in 660 A.D. the Emperor Jimmu (who could have been no more than a tribal chief) decreed laws to govern his people. He ordered the building of a palace. He promised to "extend the line of the Imperial descendants and foster rightmindedness."

"Thereafter, the Capital may be extended so as to embrace all of the six cardinal points [of the compass] and the eight cords may be covered so as to form a roof."

This was the policy of *hakko ichiu,* which meant all eight corners of the world under one imperial roof, or rule of the world that Jimmu knew.[1]

This was the first declaration of *polity,* a term the Japanese borrowed from the British and came to revere. It meant a form of government and a social organization all in one—a way of life.

Jimmu's ambition was the result of the movement of Chinese civilization into Japan. Travelers returned from the continent bringing a religion (Buddhism) and a language (Chinese). The religion joined the Japanese Shinto nature worship and the two existed side by side. The written language was converted to Japanese purposes, using the Chinese ideographs to make Japanese words. For example, the Japanese adopted the ideograph for *kuo,* which in Chinese means country. But the Japanese word for the ideograph is *koku.*

Neither Jimmu nor his immediate successors achieved their goal. They did gain control of more and more territory and grew arrogant, until Prince Shotoku wrote a letter to the emperor of China, whom he addressed as Emperor of the Setting Sun and signed himself Emperor of the Rising Sun.

The Japanese tribal chiefs were extremely independent and quarrelsome.[2] In Japan the soldier was always superior to the scholar although, when Kyoto was made the capital and peace reigned in the land for a time, the emperors turned to scholarship. But in so doing they lost power, and in 1192 the warrior Yoritomo Minamoto captured the emperor and forced from him the military command of Japan. The title was shogun, and his command was called the *bakufu* (military camp). To get away from the softness of court life Yoritomo Minamoto moved the *bakufu* to the little town of Edo, and this place became the functioning capital of Japan. The shogun declared the emperor to be so holy that it would be insulting to ask him to stoop to govern. Thus Kyoto and the emperor were left to live in a fairyland, while the shogun ruled. This is the very practical origin of the "Emperor Worship" of the 1930s.

The shogun's rule was maintained by force. He gathered around him thousands of warriors. These were the samurai, and they were held together by the code of *bushido,* which was a more stringent version of the Western chivalry. All this was ingrained in Japan by the thirteenth century and would persist as the Japanese way for five centuries more.

Japan was finally united and the warlords all subdued by Ieyasu Tokugawa in the sixteenth century. He moved the capital of Japan from Kyoto to Edo, which later was called Tokyo. He gathered around him 250 barons, who held their offices by his command. One requirement of each baron was that he maintain a large force of samurai at the disposal of the shogun, and thus the warrior class controlled Japan. The samurai had two occupations, war and scholarship. They were forbidden to engage in trade or professions. They spent their days writing poetry and practicing calligraphy. The most belligerent swaggered about the countryside terrorizing the farmers and artisans; the rule was to bow down when a samurai or a noble's procession passed. Anyone who did not bow down was likely to have his head cut off summarily, as a traveler might step on a bug.

In the Tokugawa days the laws were strict and the death penalty was often invoked. Usually it meant cutting off the head with a long samurai sword, and sometimes pages, samurai in training, were assigned these executions for practice. It was not unusual for a young samurai to cut off ten heads, one after the other. The idea of execution by head-cutting, seemingly so barbarous for those of us who forget sixteenth century English practices in the Tower of London, was constantly reinforced in Japanese society. Torture, which was also practiced by Westerners as late as the eighteenth century (and still is, in the "intelligence community" and the East-West struggle, if we are to believe the stories), was an acceptable means of extracting information and a successful deterrent to crime.

A man was caught robbing the Edo warehouse of the Baron Nabeshima, and because the crime of robbing a lord of the realm was so grave he was sentenced to death by torture. All the hairs of his body were burned off, and his fingernails and toenails were pulled out. His tendons were cut, and he was bored with drills and sliced, stretched, and squeezed. In the end, his back was split in two, and he was boiled to death in soy sauce.[3]

The laws were enforced and order maintained by an intricate

system of secret police and spies, who moved around constantly looking for wrongdoing.

By the seventeenth century the European navigators had discovered Japan. Portuguese, Spanish, and Dutch adventurers came bringing the cross and the sword. The sword availed them nothing against the fierce Japanese samurai. The cross did begin to make an impression and Ieyasu tolerated the Christians. Ieyasu saw that the foreigners' firearms could be useful to the warriors. So Nagasaki was declared to be "the foreigners' port," and an island in the harbor was set aside for trade. The foreigners were not allowed off the island without special permission.

After Shogun Ieyasu's death in 1616 his successor, Hidetada, was heavily influenced by the Buddhist priests. Buddhism had been brought into Japan from China to compete with the native Shinto nature religion. The priests of these two oriental religions could agree on one policy: the Western religion must be driven out. Hidetada reversed the policy of toleration, and the Christian priests were exiled from Japan. Then began a period of persecution that ended in the deaths of some 280,000 Japanese Christians, hunted down like animals. Every Japanese had to take a loyalty oath to Buddhism. To prove that they were not Christians, they had to trample on an image of Christ and on one of the Virgin Mary.

The persecution reached its zenith in Shimabara, where an enemy of the Tokugawas, Masuka Tokisada, gathered 33,000 people in the fortress of Amakusa and prepared to resist a siege. A third of those inside were women and children. The Tokugawa forces could not dislodge the Christians, so they called on the Dutch whose ships came up and bombarded the fortress until the walls were breached, and the inhabitants were then massacred by the Tokugawa men.[4]

But instead of furthering the Dutch cause, this and similar actions made the Japanese contemptuous of these weak Europeans who had turned against their own kind. That lesson ought to have been learned just then; to the Japanese all white-skinned foreigners were alike. It was a concept that would endure.

Through the years, the Tokugawas continued to hold power and the kingdom remained peaceful, all the dissenters kept in check by the shogun's armies of samurai. The eighth Tokugawa gave way to the ninth, then the tenth. The eleventh shogun was Ienari, whose health indicated what was happening to the line: he was an epileptic. The twelfth shogun was his son Ieyoshi who was so weak that his ministers actually ruled.

One of the most important of these ministers was Masahiro Abe, entrusted by Ieyoshi with the defense of the coast, and thus with the dealings with foreigners who approached that coast. The policy was *uchi harai*—shell and repel, drive the foreign ships away. Abe, realizing that Japanese coastal defenses were not adequate to withstand Western naval attack, temporized with the French and gave them trading concessions in the Ryukyus, which, after all, were not really Japan proper.[5]

The Americans arrived in Japanese waters in the 1820s, when some American vessels en route to China were cast up on Kyushu's shore, and so were some whaling vessels out of New England, wrecked while scouring the seas for sperm whales. *Uchi harai* was very much in force. These seamen were treated roughly; they had broken Japanese law by being washed ashore. Some were killed for that reason. Some were killed for no reason that the Americans could understand; they could not conceive of the samurai code, which let a warrior cut down any ordinary person who annoyed him, any more than an American flier in World War II could understand why he was being executed by the sword. It would be in the twentieth century, as in the seventeenth, a part of the samurai mystique. The Japanese understood this; in the seventeenth century the samurai swaggered through the streets. In the revived *bushido* of the twentieth century, the policeman as well as the soldier would become the symbol of authority, and he would swagger through the streets.

In the nineteenth century these were concepts the Westerners did not understand. American shipowners began protesting to the government in Washington, and in 1846 Commodore James Biddle anchored two American warships in Tokyo Bay. But when the Japanese sent a boat, and Commodore Biddle got down into it, he was pushed and insulted by a Japanese sailor. If Biddle had then cut the man down with his sword, or ordered a subordinate to shoot him, he would have won Japanese respect. Instead, Biddle practiced Christian forbearance, he smiled and ignored the incident. The word immediately reached the capital: these Americans were weaklings of no account and need not be taken seriously. So Abe refused to deal with Commodore Biddle and the American mission failed. The worst part of it was that the Americans did not even know why it failed.

A new problem arose in 1848. The Japanese were holding as prisoners a number of shipwrecked Americans. Captain James Glynn in the warship *Preble* was dispatched to Nagasaki to get those seamen, and he was not willing to take no for an answer. When he appeared and stated his demand, the Japanese sent dozens of junks into the harbor, loaded with armed samurai. Captain Glynn let it be known that he was prepared to back up his demands with the force of his guns. This was the sort of talk the Japanese could understand. They delivered the prisoners, and Captain Glynn sailed away. Here was an object lesson, in the fashion of Stephen Decatur's bombardments of Tripoli, that could even have implication for the 1980s and the vexing matter of aircraft hijacking. This confrontation by a determined American captain did something to correct the bad image of Americans left by Commodore Biddle.

Among the other humiliations visited on the Dutch, who would do anything to maintain their trade concession at Nagasaki, was the submission of an annual report to the shogun about events abroad that concerned Japan. In 1852 the Dutch chief Donkier Curtius reported to Edo that the Americans were sending an expedition and that it would be powerful enough to land troops on the Japanese shore. The Japanese now made every attempt to build up their defenses. But by the spring of 1853 they had not managed to create any adequate defense of Edo, the capital, which could be reached by steaming up Tokyo Bay. They had learned enough about foreign munitions and ordnance to begin building foundries and making bullets and cannonballs, but they were still unable to cast a gun large enough to fire successfully on a big ship. Therefore, if they were to have guns, they would have to get them from some European power.[6]

For this second American mission to Japan, quite by accident, the Americans chose just the right man, Commodore Matthew Calbraith Perry, brother of Oliver Hazard Perry, the hero of Lake Erie. Matthew Perry had made his name in the Mexican War, and his success there had convinced him that he was another Nelson. He was overbearing, brusque, and opinionated. When he was assigned this mission of opening Japan to trade, at first he believed it was beneath his dignity. When otherwise apprised by the navy department he undertook the task reluctantly, but thoroughly. As he prepared he gathered botanists, naturalists, and artists, to study the land to which he was going, and as large a fleet as he could manage, including two of the new steam frigates.[7]

In July 1853 these black ships arrived off the coast of Japan and began moving toward Tokyo Bay, belching smoke from the engines that turned the paddle wheels.

From the Dutch, from Hongkong contacts, and from his chief interpreter, a missionary, Commodore Perry had a clear picture of the attitude of the Japanese. He decided to meet it with an unmatched arrogance of his own. He stopped off at Naha, Okinawa, the capital of the Ryukyus, which Abe had opened for trade, and tried out the procedure, knowing that word of what he did there would swiftly reach the Japanese capital. He insisted on being entertained officially at the palace by the governing regent. He insisted on having a house for his seamen on the shore. He staged landing maneuvers with plenty of sight of cannon and rifles to give the Japanese an idea of what they could expect if they gave him any trouble.

And as he expected, news of all this activity did get back to Edo before Perry left in June 1853 for Tokyo Bay. He steamed to Uraga, the port at the entrance to Tokyo Bay. As the black ships came fuming up, Japanese guard boats headed out from shore to warn them off, but the Americans blithely ignored the guard boats and steamed right by, dropping anchor outside Uraga. Commodore Perry then let it be known that he had a letter from the President of the United States, which he would give only in person to the shogun, as the first minister of the emperor of Japan.

This demand caused consternation in the shogun's palace in Edo. A council of the barons was called and Perry was informed that it would take time to assemble the advisors from across the land. Perry gave them three days. He also sent boats out to look for another anchorage closer to Edo. This move caused consternation.

The shogun knew his defense guns had only ten rounds of ammunition each, and that the guns themselves were too small to harm the big ships. Perry landed on the beach with a full armed guard and delivered his letter. The Japanese said it was time for the Americans to leave; Perry saw that to leave would be to accept a rebuff, so he went back to his ship, and the squadron steamed up to within sight of Edo's suburbs and anchored again. The Japanese were thoroughly frightened; they sent emissaries and presents were exchanged. Satisfied that he had made his impression, Perry announced that he was leaving and would return in one year for an answer to the letter. Then he sailed away.[8]

Eight days after Commodore Perry left Japan, Shogun Ieyoshi died. The gossips said he had been struck down by the gods for yielding to the foreigners' demands. Iesada succeeded, but the real power now lay in the hands of Councillor Abe and the barons. Abe circulated the letter from American President James Fillmore and asked for advice. Fifty-nine barons were consulted, and nineteen said to reject the demands.

They knew what had happened to China, forced to open her ports to foreign trade, then humiliated in the Opium War of 1840, and forced to make more concessions to the hated foreigners.

But forty of the barons said either to trade with the foreigners as they demanded, or to stall and pretend to open trade until the Japanese defenses could be perfected and the foreigners driven out. They advocated a crash program of rearmament along European lines. The debate raged, and beneath it was another question: the recognition by many of the barons that the Tokugawas had lost their drive, and a growing movement among them to restore the power of the emperor.[9]

As the year came to an end, Perry learned that the Russians were preparing to move to open Japan; in fact, the Russian naval expedition commander, Admiral Putiatin, called on Perry to join forces with him. Putiatin had gone to Nagasaki and from there requested a trade treaty between Japan and Russia. The Japanese had refused, but the pressure was on them.

As promised, Commodore Perry returned in 1854, but not in the summer. Afraid that the Russians would get there first, he came in March. This time he had ten ships, not four, and he let it be known that he had fifty ships nearby and fifty more ships in California. If the Japanese did not get down to negotiating, he was going to act.

Perry was bluffing. He had with him about a fourth of the total U.S. naval strength of the day. He could have bombarded the Japanese harbor, but had his 1600 men landed they would have been overwhelmed by the Japanese warriors. It never came to this because the Japanese were truly awed by Perry's recalcitrance and the power he indicated. The Japanese agreed to allow American ships to call at

Nagasaki, to aid American seaman and treat them properly, but stopped short of a trade treaty. American vessels could also come to Shimoda, on Honshu, and Hakodate, on Hokkaido. Perry did hold out for appointment of an American consul who would come to Shimoda to negotiate a trade treaty. The Japanese agreed, but there was a definite misunderstanding: the American version of the clause read that consuls should be appointed to reside at Shimoda at any time that either of the two governments found it necessary. The Japanese version said only if "conditions make it necessary," and their interpretation was that nothing had been given away, that the whole matter of consuls would have to be the subject of more negotiation and more delay. This agreement, which was really not an agreement, was signed and sealed at Kanagawa on March 31, 1854. Some of the Japanese were much impressed by the American presents: a small railroad train circling at twenty miles per hour on its tracks; telegraph sets, which sent messages through wires; pistols and muskets of the newest design. The Japanese already knew about weapons; here were other fruits of the foreign culture. Perhaps, said some, there was something to be gained. But the council of elders was not ready to admit that Japan's whole existence was now to be changed and let it be known that no concessions had been made to the foreigners. The truth would have to out later.[10]

The American success was followed by frantic European action. The British sent Sir James Sterling to secure a treaty, and he did. The Russians sent Admiral Putiatin back to Japan, and he got a treaty in 1855. Then came the Netherlands, and then came France, all jumping on the bandwagon. The result was a powerful reaction among the barons to throw all the rascally foreigners back out, and thus began a new struggle for power in Japan, with the foreigners at the center of it, and the barons lining up either with the Tokugawa shogunate or the Imperial Restoration party.

In 1856 American consul Townsend Harris arrived at Shimoda. The Japanese ignored him on the pretext that his coming was outside the agreement because they had not felt any need for him. For a while he was under house arrest. For a while he was spied upon and guarded constantly to see that he did not move about. But by showing a determination to remain and create trade, Harris impressed the Japanese, who realized he did have the power of the black ships behind him. And after almost a year he began to make progress toward trade. A big sticker was extraterritoriality, which, in effect, put the Americans above Japanese law, which the Americans demanded (in the European colonial pattern), and the Japanese refused for months. Finally, however, Harris got his treaty and the extraterritoriality, and in the end Japan was astounded to learn that he would be received in the palace behind the moat at Edo (now the Imperial Palace). He was accorded the treatment given princes, brought in a sedan chair in a procession, the roads cleared before him, the people prostrating themselves alongside the road as the procession passed, and every night the train stopping at the best of Japan's inns for the best of Japan's entertainment. On December 7, 1857, Townsend Harris walked into the audience room at Edo palace, presented to the shogun in person his credentials from the President of the United States, and spoke of his hopes for the future of Japanese-American relations.[11]

Shogun Iesada then did the unthinkable: he addressed the barbarian. The shogun was pleased, he said, to have the letter sent with the ambassador from a far distant country and was pleased with the discourse. Intercourse would be continuous from that point on forever.

For better or for worse, the change had been made. Japan had become a part of a world the Japanese knew virtually nothing about. Now they would have to learn and learn very quickly if they were not to suffer the fate of China, India, Indochina, the East Indies, the Malay Peninsula, and the Philippines. The foreigners had their feet inside the door. But what the foreigners, Americans and others, did not understand was the degree of Japanese arrogance.

One of the Japanese officials most responsible for the treaty was the shogun's chief councillor, Masayoshi Hatta, who spent four years on the problem of foreign affairs, which meant dealing with the Westerners. In 1858 he went from Edo to Kyoto to try to enlist the support of the emperor. He submitted a memorial stating his arguments for the treaty:

> In establishing relations with foreign countries, the object should always be kept in view of laying the foundation for securing hegemony over all nations. The national resources should be developed in military preparations vigorously carried out. When our power and national stand-

ing have come to be recognized we should take the lead
... declare our protection over harmless but powerful
nations. . . . Our national prestige and position thus en-
sured, the nations of the world will come to look up to
our Emperor as the Great Ruler of all the nations, and
they will come to follow our policy and submit to our
judgment. . . .[12]

The emperor had rejected the memorial and refused to approve
the treaty, but the shogun signed it anyhow. Japan's foreign policy
was set. Her method would be to bide her time until she could rule
her world.

柳の枝に 雪折れなし

2. "The willow branch but bends beneath the snow" OLD JAPANESE SAYING

*L*ike the willow branch, the leaders of this new Japan were willing to bend beneath the weight of foreign influence—for a while. Who were these people, and how did they go about changing an Oriental nation with a thousand-year-old tradition of feudalism into a modern industrial state?

The signing of treaties between the shogun and the foreigners was one thing, but securing the approval of the royal court at Kyoto and the nobles who backed the emperor was another matter. The foreign treaties became an issue and also they made an issue between the Japanese factions. Those nobles who had been outside the shogun's circle now began to move toward the party of Imperial Restoration, and it was not long before Japan was rocked by something very close to civil war; clans lined up either for or against the shogunate. The real issue was modernism.[1]

The shogun government recognized the need of Japan to turn to Western technology if she was to avoid the fate of China. The Dutch sold a warship to Japan, which was christened the *Kanko Maru,* and Dutch engineers and seamen taught a chosen group of samurai how to run the ship. Thus in 1855 was born the Imperial Japanese Navy. Soon schools were opened in Edo, where young Japanese warriors began to study foreign languages, and then to attend lectures given by foreigners in engineering, physics, chemistry, and other technologies and sciences. In 1860 an official Japanese mission left for the United States to celebrate the ratification of the trade treaty.

They were accompanied by the *Kanko Maru,* now manned by a Japanese crew. These were men of the new Japanese navy, samurai converted to the sea.[2]

The Japanese visitors to America were astounded by Western cultural practices such as ballroom dancing, and public mingling of "nice" women with men. But when they came home, this part of the trip was relegated to social gossip, for what they really had to say was that they had seen railroads connecting thousands of miles of territory, steamships by the score, tall buildings made of iron and stone, public water and sewer systems, shoe factories, cotton mills, iron and steel foundries, modern newspapers turned out by huge presses, street railroads, and hundreds of other manifestations of a complex mechanical society that was completely strange to them. This, they told the shogun, was the challenge that must be met.

There were men among the samurai who accepted the need to learn from the West, but did not accept anything else Western. Sanai Hashimoto was one such. He came from a family of physicians, and his youth was spent in the Confucian education that was typical of the upper-class Japanese. He learned medicine and took over his father's practice when he was twenty years old. He went on to study and then become an instructor in the new school of Sugita Seikei at Edo, where the Western subjects were being taught: physics, chemistry, mathematics, military science. In 1855 he achieved full samurai status, honored by the shogun.

But like many of the upper class Sanai was not content to accept any Western claims of superiority.

"If we continue to proclaim our own way of benevolence and righteousness and our own doctrine of loyalty and filial piety, and if we begin to take the skills of machinery and techniques from them, it will come to the point when they must be very careful of us," he said. What he meant was: learn from the West, then challenge the West.

How modern! Yet, soon Sanai found himself on the side of the Imperial Restoration group, whose motto was: Revere the Emperor and Repel the Barbarian. Deeply involved in the struggle for succession to the shogunate, Sanai was arrested back in Edo by the shogun's men and executed by the sword. The problem was that the issues of traffic with foreigners and the succession became inextricably bound together. By 1863 the Imperial Court at Kyoto had enough power to force the shogun to accept as advisors the feudal barons of the

Satsuma and Tosa clans, who were adherents to the emperor. In 1865 the Choshu clan rebelled against the Tokugawas. Their Choshu army was the first of the new forces, trained in Western ways and equipped with Western weapons. When the shogun sent an army of the old-style samurai against them, the Choshu slaughtered them.[3]

In 1862 the emperor was powerful enough to order the shogun to expel the foreigners by the summer of the next year.

When the shogun returned to Edo to post the Imperial Decree the European and American government representatives were prepared for a showdown because attacks on Europeans had caused a number of deaths, with the most publicity given that of an Englishman. C. L. Richardson was riding along on horseback near Yokohama with two friends when they encountered a party of samurai from Satsuma, returning from Edo, having delivered to the shogun the imperial order to expel the foreigners. The British, feeling secure in their extraterritoriality, and as arrogant as the British could be in a colonial environment, refused to give way to the Japanese party and kept the road, where, by Japanese custom, the foreigners should have dismounted and bowed to the samurai. So the samurai attacked and cut off Richardson's head. The British demanded indemnity and the Japanese refused. The British then brought in a naval expedition and bombarded Kagoshima, the Satsuma capital. They destroyed the shore guns, the local arsenal, and all the brand-new Japanese steamers in the harbor. The Japanese were mightily impressed and paid the indemnity. Then, in one of those apparent turnabouts that they did so well, the Japanese asked the British to help them build such warships and teach them to operate them.[4]

Next came an incident involving the Satsuma's enemies in the barony of Choshu in the northwest, who adhered to the imperial point of view against the foreigners. Choshu controlled the Shimonoseki Straits, and when an American ship, the *Pembroke,* tried to go through the straits in June 1863, it was fired on and driven off by the shore batteries. Dutch and French ships received the same treatment. Warships were sent from these countries, and they silenced the shore batteries. The same happened again. Finally a combined fleet attacked, landed and destroyed the batteries, then demanded that the straits be kept open.

At Kyoto the emperor began to listen to advisors who had traveled in Europe and America and warned that Japan did not have the resources to conduct military operations against the Westerners. Force would not work, until Japan had entered the industrial revolution and had become as modern as these foreign states.

Conditions began to favor an imperial restoration. The Tokugawas, with no strong man emergent, continued to lose prestige and the support of the barons. Little by little the Imperial Court regained the powers it had granted the shoguns six hundred years earlier: the right to allocate territory in particular.

The shogun turned to France, Britain's natural enemy in Europe, and the competition was on. But the shogunate was rent with internal strife, the country was suffering from inflation and from an exchange rate accepted by the shogun, which allowed a foreigner to bring silver in from China, and make a 50 percent profit by simply changing money back and forth.

The samurai, long idled from war, had been increasingly drawn into court life, and their expenses far outweighed their pay, so they went into debt. Some became merchants. The old social structure tottered. By 1866 the shogunate was in deep trouble, bankrupt financially and morally, and the military efforts to suppress the rebel clans were failing. On February 3, 1867, Emperor Komei died and was succeeded by his fifteen-year-old son, Meiji. The leaders of the Satsuma and Choshu clans moved into Kyoto. The clans presented a united front, in behalf of the new emperor against the shogunate, and on January 3, 1868, the Imperial Palace announced that all power was restored to the throne. Takamori Saigo, the leader of the Satsuma army, secured the surrender of the shogun.

So, power had been restored to the throne. Now what?

At first all went well. For five years the new emperor learned about his country and its problems and learned modern European ways under foreign teachers. The main point, to become outwardly like the Westerners, was not lost. Meiji addressed himself to the building of lighthouses, port facilities, and industries so that Japan would not have to import her capital goods. Railroads began to move across the countryside. Spinning mills were built and foundries and shipyards. Foreigners were brought in to supervise these plants, and the Japanese understudied them and learned. A naval shipyard was built by the French at Yokosuka. Government technical schools sprang up. The best students were sent abroad to learn the foreign ways first hand. The government put up huge sums for construction and then sold the industries off. The real secret was that the industries were sold only to Japanese; unlike China, no concessions were given to the foreigners, so control of things Japanese was vested in Japanese hands. A number of rich trading families began to acquire enormous power through industrialization: the Mitsuis, Mitsubishis, Sumotomos, and Yasudas, the Kawasakis and Tanakas and Asanos. These names would continue to be prominent in Japan from that time on until today.[5]

The samurai found it hard to abandon the old ways, and some held out for the stipends their class had received for hundreds of years. The peasants suffered from hardship and food shortages in the inflations, and rice riots were not uncommon in these formative years.

But the imperial government persisted on its course: industrialization, modernization, and education, all aimed at catching Japan up to the Westerners. Japan was the only nation in Asia so determined, and by being determined managed to escape the fate of China and the other countries: political and economic colonization.

The foreigners came and taught and managed, but as the Japanese learned, they eased the foreigners out. Subtly they resisted all foreign encroachment.

The emperor moved to Edo, whose name was changed to Tokyo. In the summer of 1871 the old clan boundaries were wiped out by Imperial Decree, and the clan holdings became prefectures within the empire, under direct imperial rule. Feudalism was nearly dead. Previously the samurai had been enjoined by decree to wear their swords at all times. Now it became optional. People could travel for the first time from one end of Japan to the other without seeking permission from a dozen governments. The old social classes of daimyo, samurai, farmer, artisan, and the hated merchants were abolished. The new kingdom consisted of a nobility, who were the old barons and courtiers, the warriors, who became the gentry, and commoners, without distinction.

The samurai lost their identity. They were not included in the new military forces, there was no place for knights in armor in a modern army. If they wanted to survive, they had to conform. One of their leaders, Aritomo Yamagata, went to France and Germany to learn Western military ways and came back to Japan to be second vice minister of war. The minister was an imperial prince and there was no first vice minister, so, in effect, Yamagata ran the army. In

1870 he secured the first conscription law, which made every Japanese subject to military service, three years active duty and two years in the reserve. Soon 10,000 men were being called annually and trained in the new military ways.[6]

Farmers began to buy their land with clear title. The entire tax system was changed. To eliminate the samurai their old rice allotments were converted to their value in government bonds, and all the feudal payments were commuted. The railroads up and down the country were completed, and telegraph lines ran alongside them. Interisland shipping by steamship made up the rest of a modern communications system. Spinning and weaving mills had established a major textile industry. Japan was building her own ships, her own guns, her own munitions. She was approaching self-sufficiency in manufacturing.

A new dispute now settled over Japan, between those who wanted to consolidate and build up the country's resources and those who wanted to move out immediately in a program to acquire colonies in Asia as they saw the European powers doing. The Japanese eye was on Korea, which Yamato had dominated in the early centuries of the Christian Era.

One leader of the expansionist group was Takamori Saigo, who had done so much to return the Imperial party to power. He was very unhappy about the degradation of the samurai class and the establishment in power of men he regarded as bureaucrats. The issue came to a head in October 1873, when the young emperor (obviously instructed by his "bureaucratic" advisors) ordered Saigo and the others to stop agitating for movement into Korea and to concentrate on internal improvements. To divert attention from Korea, the emperor authorized a "punitive" expedition against China's offshore island of Formosa, where a number of Ryukyuan islanders had been mistreated by the Formosans. The expedition consisted of thirteen ships with 3600 soldiers. They went to Formosa, they conquered, and they came home. The Japanese ambassador at Peking protested loudly, and the Japanese set in motion wheels that would lead to the annexation of the Ryukyus in a few years and the seizure of Formosa in a few more. But Saigo and his friends were not appeased by this adventure. They wanted Korea and employment for the samurai. When they did not get it, Saigo was furious. He resigned from the government and went home to Satsuma. Thus, by the default of some of the nobles was established the oligarchy that would run Japan until the army took over in the 1930s. The reader will see these names time and again: Hirobumi Ito, Tomomi Iwakura, Koin Kido, Toshimo Okubo, Shigenoba Okuma, and Aritomo Yamagata. The oligarchy by clever maneuvering kept its control against pressure for representative government of the sort Japanese travelers had seen in England, France, Holland, and America.

Out in the provinces, the dissident young samurai, no longer so very young, soon gave up wasting their time complaining about the government in Tokyo and set about plotting to overthrow the oligarchy.

They were ignored, but they were not silenced.

An attempt was made to silence them in 1875 with the enactment of severe press and publication laws that forbade criticism of the government's policies. All this was done by the oligarchy in the name of the emperor and the people.

Takamori Saigo had more or less washed his hands of active politics and had established a school in the Satsuma capital of Kagoshima. He was training young men for government service. But the young men were samurai; it was his intent to preserve the samurai and the samurai traditions, while changing their function. The final disestablishment of the samurai class in 1876 was almost enough to sever Saigo's remaining loyalties to the system he had helped establish. The relationship between Satsuma Prefecture and Tokyo became extremely strained, and finally in 1877 the oligarchy ordered the military authorities in Satsuma to transfer guns and ammunition to a safer district, lest the Satsumans rebel and overthrow the government.

Saigo regarded this move as the final insult, and he ordered the seizure of the supplies, then led a force of 15,000 men north. He was in open rebellion against the Tokyo government.

The rebellion lasted nine months and forced the government to commit its entire army of 32,000 men, plus 10,000 reserves. In the end, Saigo was trapped in his fort near Kagoshima, and he and his men died there. Thus finally ended the old samurai tradition and the last opposition to the modernization of Japan.[7]

But no sooner had this relict been disposed of, than a new challenge faced the oligarchy. More and more Japanese were learning the way of the West, and their exposure to the political institutions of the Western democracies brought agitation for a liberalized Japan.

The Japanese best-seller of 1869 was a book called *Seiyo Jijo* (*Conditions in the Western World*), which described daily life in Britain and America and came out flatly in favor of a parliamentary democracy of the British sort for Japan. Radicals were translating Rousseau and Montesquieu and talking about "people's rights." Everywhere the Japanese, even the farmers, were becoming politically conscious, and this put new pressure on the oligarchy for reforms. Memorials, riots, speeches, books, all advocated liberalization of the government. There was nothing to match the Satsuma rebellion, but there need not be. The oligarchy was worried about the future, and when a friend of Saigo's assassinated Prime Minister Toshimishi Okubo in revenge, the oligarchy nearly panicked. It so happened that in this hour of crisis retired United States President Ulysses S. Grant was in Tokyo, and the councillors called on him to ask his advice: how much freedom should the people have?

President Grant was not a great democrat. In a meeting with Emperor Meiji he advised great caution in the granting of popular democracy, for, as he warned, once given, the institutions would be hard to take away. What about an elected legislature with full power? Very dangerous, said U. S. Grant. The emperor and his councillors were greatly impressed by this advice about the potential threat of too much freedom. So, an American politician on a world tour had a great deal to do with the sort of government that came out of the Meiji restoration.[8]

From 1881 until 1889 the oligarchs quarreled among themselves, jockeying for personal position and maneuvering to achieve their political and moral goals. At the same time various popular movements sprang up, died, consolidated and split. The Liberal and Progressive parties emerged from this amoeba atmosphere. The Liberals wanted popular democracy, the Progressives also wanted democracy, but to a lesser degree. The oligarchs, however, held on and these parties disappeared. Their major gift to Japan was the discovery by the Mitsui and Mitsubishi families that they could make good use of political movements. These families, first rice merchants, then bankers, and now industrialists, had become the two most important economic entities in Japan. One might liken them to huge corporations, although that was not their form. Mitsui took over the Liberals, and Mitsubishi supported the Progressives. And thus was born the *zaibatsu*, the political-economic cartel that was to play so large a part in the future of Japan.

In the middle of the 1880s partisan politics took an ugly turn, resulting in riots and tax revolts, and even plans for assassination of high government officials. The government then enacted serious restrictive laws, and the Mitsui and Mitsubishi families backed away from the dangerous radicalism that had developed, for it threatened their relationship with the government. So in a few months, deprived of their financial backing, the Liberal and Progressive parties disappeared completely.[9]

Emperor Meiji was determined to give Japan a modern government, and in 1882 he had sent commissioners abroad to study the various forms of European and American governments. The result of these studies was the establishment of a two-tier system of government. On February 11, 1889, at the Imperial Palace behind its moat in Tokyo, Emperor Meiji proclaimed the new constitution from his throne. This document was to control the history of Japan until 1945, and, through the unique pressures that could be exerted by the emperor's advisors, to enable a powerful group of men to subvert the strength of the emperor and seize power for themselves in his name.

The Meiji Constitution was designed to preserve the absolute power of the monarch, yet to give a degree of power to the people. The underlying motive was to allow the people play as long as all went all right, but to preserve the imperial rule at all costs. The emperor was "sacred and inviolable." He must be revered, his actions must not be the subject of debate, nor would any derogatory comment about the imperial family be tolerated. The emperor had supreme command of the army and the navy. He could make war and peace and conclude treaties of alliance. He initiated any amendments that would be made to his constitution. So there was no way to limit the power of the emperor under the constitution his advisors had devised.

The most important lawmaker in the government was the emperor. The most important body was the Privy Council, which advised him. Separate was the Imperial Household, which involved other councillors and the emperor could play one group against the other. His ministers counseled with the emperor, and every Imperial Rescript (law) had to have the signature of a minister of state on it. But were a minister to make so bold as to refuse to sign an edict, then the emperor would simply have him removed and appoint a new minister.

Outside the constitution was the *Genro,* an unofficial senate of elder statesmen, whose function was to advise the emperor; the purpose was to preserve a balance against the ministers who were expected to be political, while the *Genro* were old servitors: generals, admirals, diplomats, who had become "statesmen."

A legislature was created called the Imperial Diet. It consisted of a House of Peers (Lords) and a House of Representatives. The peers were hereditary or appointed by the throne. The House of Representatives was elected. Theoretically all money bills had to originate in the lower house, but even that power was in effect denied the house because of a provision that if the budget was not enacted then the previous year's budget was simply repeated. Thus the House had no control over the prime minister.[10]

As it turned out the most important provision of the constitution was the paragraph which made the emperor chief of the civil government on one hand and commander in chief of the military on the other. The military was separate from the civil government, and the chiefs of staff had direct access to the emperor. The provision that the emperor could make law by edict controlled everything. Later one such edict announced that the army and navy ministers had to be active duty officers of the army and navy, and they, too, had direct access to the throne.

The Meiji Constitution was called "democratic," but in fact it retained absolute power in the hands—or, to put it more succinctly—in the name of the emperor. The right to vote was limited to property owners, which meant 1.25 percent of the population of Japan, or about 500,000 men. Freedom was limited by edict and laws passed by the legislature. The judicial system considered a man guilty if arrested, unless he could prove his innocence.[11]

Japan had always been a military society. The Emperor Meiji and the men around him really did hope to give more power to the people, but the emperor reserved for himself the right to stop immediately any swings in the political pendulum. With the addition of the Ryukyus Japan became an empire, and Emperor Meiji would make sure it stayed that way, with imperial power paramount. His constitution, proclaimed in 1889, would remain unchanged until 1946, and the underlying principle uttered by Lord Hatta in 1858 remained as well. Japan was acquiring the machinery for world conquest.

身を捨ててこそ 浮かぶ瀬もあれ

3. "He who would get ahead must brave the current" JAPANESE PROVERB

*I*f Takemori Saigo had been more patient, perhaps his hopes would have been fulfilled, for Emperor Meiji had never abandoned the dream of empire, he had only taken the counsel to delay until Japan was ready.

In 1882 Japan had three shipyards, fifty-one merchant ships, five arsenals, fifty-two factories, ten mines, seventy-five miles of railroad, and one telegraph system. By 1890 all these assets had increased manyfold; the army had increased to 73,000, with a reserve that would bring it to 274,000 men in time of war. The navy was building twenty-three ships. Army and navy together accounted for a third of the Japanese government budget. No one was threatening Japan, so the enormous defense expenditures could be justified only because Japan wanted to come to parity with the European nations that had established colonies all around her. Emperor Meiji knew that only by assuming the character of a porcupine could Japan stave off the voracious colonists. But that was not the only reason. The Europeans looked upon colonialism as a natural development of the industrial revolution and excused it as necessary to bring the benighted Oriental and African peoples of the world to enlightenment. The Japanese, by leaping into the industrial revolution so furiously, not only forestalled the Europeans but adopted their view of the need for colonialism; Japan must gain colonies of her own.

The argument of need had an apparent validity: virtually every hectare of arable land in Japan was in cultivation, and by 1890 when the land yielded 183 million bushels of rice and other grains, it had just about reached its limits. The modernization of Japan, improvement of public health and sanitation, was bringing a rise in population, which meant that Japan would have to produce enough manufactured goods to trade for foodstuffs. She would need markets. Japan learned fast; she had soon adopted all the European arguments favoring colonial adventure. Monkey see, monkey do! An examination of Japan's attitudes in these formative years gives a mirror view of the excesses of the Europeans and Americans abroad that should give the reader a sense of cultural shame. Whatever excuses were necessary to justify colonial adventures were there to be made. In Japan's case the whole adventure was supported by the ancient concept of *hakko ichiu,* the determination of Japan to be first among nations.

In 1890 Japan's empire consisted of the home islands, the Ryukyus, which they had occupied after a long haggling with China that came to nothing, and the Kurile Islands north of Hokkaido, which they had acquired in a compromise with Russia by giving up claim to the southern half of Sakhalin Island.

These territorial changes had left scars: the Chinese still laid claim to the Ryukyus, and some Japanese still thought they ought to have Sakhalin Island. But these questions were as nothing compared to the depth of feeling in China and Japan over Korea. At one time or another Korea had been a vassal of Japan and of China. Her history as a Chinese appendage was much longer, and in 1890 the Chinese claimed that the king of Korea was a minister of the emperor of China, and so told the Japanese. The Koreans tried to play both sides by paying tribute to Tokyo and to Peking, but all this did was reinforce the claims of both sides.

What happened in the next quarter century was a prelude to all that has happened in this corner of the world since 1945:

In 1876, Japan copied Commodore Perry's technique and sent a naval survey squadron along the Korean coast, with a warning that the next force would be a fleet of warships and that the way to prevent trouble was to open Korea to trade with Japan. This foray resulted in the Treaty of Kanghwa in 1876, which opened two ports to Japanese shipping. From that point on China and Japan struggled for control of Korea. Up above, watching and waiting, were the Russians. Their interest in Korea was to get a warm water port. The one they chose was Wonsan, which they called Port Lazaroff. In the 1880s when Korea sought to modernize its army the Russians offered to send officers to train the Koreans, in exchange for use of this port. China and Japan leaped in to prevent that agreement, and together they succeeded. They did not, however, wipe out Russia's interest in the area, which has continued ever since.[1]

By 1890, Japan had advanced so far in its industrialization and modernization that the government and the upper class considered their country to be on par with European nations. Less than forty years had passed since the black ships entered Tokyo Bay; men who had been adults in 1853 when Japan was a feudal state were now at the height of their powers. Japan had met the challenge and adopted Western ways. She had a strong central government, a powerful citizen army and navy, a system of universal education, a growing industrial society, and a steady agricultural industry. Looking around from their islands, the Japanese saw the Europeans everywhere: the Russians had moved into Manchuria and controlled the Liaotung Peninsula. Germany had bitten off the Shantung Province of China, which was called the colony of Kiaochao. England had taken Hongkong and had concessions at Shanghai and Weihaiwei. Singapore and the Malay Peninsula were also in British hands. The Dutch held all the scattered islands of the East Indies down to New Guinea, which was German. France was also ensconced in Shanghai and had moved into the old empire of Annam.[2]

In Tokyo each new foreign acquisition brought a wave of imperialist spirit, and Korea, whence the Yamato rulers of Japan had sprung, was the center of Japanese attention.

Japan in 1889 was undergoing enormous social and political tension. The major issue was extraterritoriality of the Europeans in Japan, and so strong was the feeling that when Foreign Minister Shigenoba Okuma did not show enough pugnacity in negotiations to suit the extremists, an attempt was made on his life. This plot so shocked the government that the whole cabinet resigned. It was replaced by a government under General Aritomo Yamagata, as result of an agreement among the oligarchy: the Choshu and Satsuma clans would alternate with prime ministers. Thus also was established a principle that abides to this day: *sodan,* or group consultation, before any important decision is taken. That means the reaching of a consensus, for which no person assumes total responsibility.

Sodan began as a protective device for the emperor's counsellors, a matter of survival in a harsh feudal society wherein the penalty for almost any breach of propriety was self-inflicted death. If an advisor to the shogun or a daimyo advocated a certain policy, and that policy failed, then the advisor was honor bound to commit *seppuku*. Obviously it was best not to be personally responsible for error, and the way to avoid it was the group decision, reached by consensus. Individual opinions had to be sacrificed for the general good. This system has remained virtually unchanged.[3] Thus when foreigners have tried to fix the causes of Japan's actions of the years, for the most part they have missed the point. Consensus is *the* essential part of the Japanese *polity,* and the exceptions to the rule are hereafter noted.

The new Japanese constitutional government was controlled by the military as had been the shogun government although the elections resulted in victory for the Liberal and Progressive parties against the cabinet's choices; in the first Diet these parties held 171 of 300 seats in the lower house. But the reins of control were firmly held by the oligarchs, under Prime Minister Yamagata. He rode roughshod over the elected representatives for over a year. When his government fell, the oligarchs chose a member of the Satsuma clan, Masayoshi Matsukata. He lasted only another year, and then back went leadership to the Choshu. In 1894 the House of Representatives passed a vote of no confidence by 253 votes to 17; but the government remained, for the emperor so ordained. The principle of government by the oligarchs, as opposed to the legislature, would continue until 1945. Faced with popular dissent, the oligarchs in, they dissolved the parliament in June 1894 and governed without legislators.[4] Nearly half a century later, General Tojo would repeat the performance.

The summer of 1894 was notable as the season in which Japan came of age among nations: a new treaty was negotiated with Britain, one that eliminated the hated extraterritoriality. The given reason was that Japan had shown itself amenable to modern Western judicial processes. The fact was that this was not in almost any sense true. The real reason for the elimination of the colonial relationship was Britain's realization that the Japanese were about to rebel against extraterritorialism and throw it off anyhow and had so reduced foreign influence in Japan that there was nothing the foreigners could do about it. Britain's leaders also wanted a powerful ally in Asia in view of Russian expansionism.

The British lead brought all the other European nations to

follow. So in thirty years Japan achieved a status of equality with the colonial powers, the only nation in Asia to do so.[5]

Japan's government now turned seriously to empire building. The dispute with China over control of Korea had dragged on for twenty years; in 1894 Japan was looking for an excuse to act. It came when a band of anti-Japanese Koreans called the Tonghaks rebelled against the Korean government. China sent troops to help quell the rebellion. Japan's military and political leaders said this was intolerable; China could not be allowed to interfere thus with the sovereignty of Korea. For "sovereignty of Korea" read Japanese influence. So Japan sent troops also. By July the Tonghaks had been quieted down, but the Chinese and Japanese troops remained. On July 23 the Japanese invaded the king of Korea's palace in Seoul and at gunpoint forced him to sign an agreement expelling the Chinese. Two days later the Japanese navy sank the Chinese troopship *Kowshing*. The war was declared officially on August 1. This series of events, the strike before the declaration, is a historic Japanese method of making war; it dates from the days of the samurai. As with the Israelis, the preemptive strike is celebrated by the Japanese in song and story.[6]

The outbreak of war with China healed the political differences in Tokyo so completely that cynics claimed Prime Minister Ito had arranged the war to cement his political control of Japan. The reality, of course, was the pressure from the emperor to further the empire.

No one could have asked for a military exercise better to show off the stunning results of Japan's Europeanization than the war against China. The Chinese armies and the Chinese navy were in the state that Japanese forces had been forty years earlier. By mid-September the Japanese navy controlled the Gulf of Chihli, which meant the Chinese could not ship reinforcements to Korea by sea. They captured Port Arthur on November 21. By February they held all Korea and the Liaotung Peninsula of Manchuria.

Having proved their military prowess and having control of Korea, the Japanese suggested a peace treaty. Viceroy Li Hung-chang came from China to Shimonoseki to negotiate. The Japanese wanted Shanhaikwan, the gateway through the Great Wall to Mongolia, and Tientsin and Tangku. They were prepared to be very hard-nosed.

But all this was changed when a Japanese assassin tried to kill

Viceroy Li after he reached Japan. The Japanese government was enormously embarrassed by this breach of hospitality. Much of what they had been doing was done to impress Westerners that Japan was thoroughly modern and civilized. This event, even though Li was unhurt, caused the Japanese to "lose face." The emperor sent his personal physician to visit the Chinese envoy. The prime minister made personal apology. And the harsh peace treaty terms were scaled down in order to retrieve Japan's reputation abroad.[7]

But by any standards, the terms had to be satisfactory to a nation just embarking on the road to imperialism. Japan took Taiwan, the nearby Pescadores Islands, and the Liaotung Peninsula of Manchuria. China promised to pay 360 million yen in indemnity, or about three times the Japanese national budget of 1894. The Japanese also secured an entry into China for trade at Weihaiwei on the northern shore of the Shantung Peninsula. And China renounced all claims to Korea, which gave Japan a free hand to move in the future. It was a very small war for a very big gain.

Japan lost no time in beginning the takeover of Korea. First the post office went into Japanese hands and gave them control of mail and telegraphic communication. The Japanese taxation system was installed. The Korean army was to be "trained" by the Japanese, they said, so they removed the Korean officers and installed Japanese officers.

All Japan was exultant. Japan had proved, had she not, that she was the equal of any country in the world? The press became boastful and so did Japanese diplomats. But now came a bitter lesson in international politics. The Japanese had moved too far, too fast, and had irritated the Western powers. It had been interesting to watch one nation in Asia pulling itself up to the standards of the West. But Japan had gone further, and now she threatened the special privileges and ambitions of the Europeans in Asia. This could not be allowed; the Japanese had to be put in their place.

The Russians were the first to show the shock. As noted, they wanted a warm water port, or more than one, if possible. They had been eyeing Korea. They had also been looking at the Liaotung Peninsula and Port Arthur in particular. Even more important than the warm water port was the continuation of Manchuria in hands friendly to Russia. The Czar's government was building the Trans-Siberian Railway, and the plan called for one section to go through

Manchuria to Vladivostok. It was intolerable to the Russians to see Manchuria fall under Japanese influence.

The Russians approached Britain, but alone among the European powers with interests in China, Britain was not worried by the thought of Japan in Manchuria. Better the Japanese, said the British, than the Russians. But the Russians enlisted the support of France and Germany with the argument that they must show a united front or Japan would gobble up Asia. So hardly was the ink dry on the treaty of Shimonoseki than the Russians began making warlike noises. A formal note was sent to Tokyo "advising" the Japanese that they had best give up the Liaotung Peninsula.

The Russians had a Pacific fleet at Vladivostok. The Japanese minister at St. Petersburg reported that Russia was ready for war.[8]

Japan was not. The war with China, no matter how easy it seemed, had strained her every resource. She needed time and that cash indemnity from China to build up her army and navy.

On receipt of the Russian note, Emperor Meiji called an Imperial Conference to discuss the Russian demand. With only the objection of Foreign Minister Munemitsu Mutsu, it was agreed that Japan must practice *enryo*—the polite obeisance that hid the inner fury. The humiliation shocked Japan, but it must be borne temporarily. The emperor announced that it was not important, but the country *knew*. Politicians of every view joined together in condemnation of the European interference in Japan's affairs. A wave of antiforeign sentiment and intense nationalism swept the country. Newspapers clamored for the extension of Japanese territory, and the idea of the annexation of all Manchuria was brought into the open in political discussions. Shojiro Goto, the minister of agriculture, submitted a memorial to the throne, pointing out that possession of Manchuria and Korea would solve Japan's agricultural problems for generations to come. He proposed their acquisition. How, he did not say.[9]

Thus, unwittingly, the Russians, Germany, and France brought an end to a division within Japan which represented the last of the pre-Perry days. Until now the large conservative segment of the Japanese leadership had advocated the preservation of the old ways and the limitation of contact with the outside world. Now the conservatives switched to another policy: aggressive nationalism. The world would not let Japan alone, so Japan must surround herself with protective territory and the means to total self-sufficiency. The

Japanese isolationists of 1895 did an about-face to become the most ardent expansionists. *Nippon shugi* became their new doctrine: Japanism.

And so, one does not have to be a Japanophile to understand the Japanese confusion, and then anger at being told by the Europeans that the right of colonial aggression belonged only to white faces. The seeds of the Pacific War had been sown in the threat of force used by the Americans to open Japan to outside influence. The seeds had been watered and were now growing steadily.

In 1887 at the height of the debate over Japan's proper course of action, Viscount Tani had stated the view of the expansionists:

". . . Improve our government affairs, make our country secure by military preparation, and then wait for the time of confusion in Europe, which must eventually come sooner or later; . . . such an event will agitate the nations of the Orient as well, and hence, although our country is not mixed up in the matter so far as Europe is concerned, we may then become the chief nation of the Orient."[10]

Japanese growth in the late 1890s was slowed by internal dissension until the Progressive and Liberal parties finally joined in the Constitutional (Kenseito) party to challenge the oligarchy of ministers around the emperor for control of the parliament. The struggle was for a meaningful legislature that could not be ignored by the prime minister. During this struggle, until 1904, Japan turned an apparently placid face to the Western powers. That face, however, did not mean that the Japanese were not completely aware of what was happening in Asia.

The decay of the Chinese empire was speeded by the foreign encroachments on her territory. Whereas Japan adopted the Western ways, the Chinese rejection and the weakening of the empire led to European scrambling for chunks of China.

Having apparently stopped the Japanese in Manchuria, the Russians began moving in there. They also moved to replace China in control of Korea. Here they came up against the Japanese again. The Japanese minister, Goro Miura, plotted with antigovernment forces in Korea in an attempt to bring to power a pro-Japanese government. The plot caused the king of Korea to flee to the Russian ministry for protection and increased Russian influence in Korea.

The Russians also moved in China. They lent the Chinese the money to pay the Japanese reparations, but they took a lien on

China's customs revenue for repayment. This new influence in China was increased when the Russians secured the right to build the rail link through Manchuria and secured control of the Liaotung Peninsula.

The Germans saw what the Russians were doing and decided to cut off a piece of China for themselves. In 1897 two German missionaries were killed by Chinese bandits, and the German government used this as an excuse to seize Kiaochao Bay on the southern coast of the Shantung Peninsula. Here they built the German city of Tsingtao, and here they based the German East Asia Cruiser Squadron, the most powerful European navy force in north China.

The Japanese turned to industrial and commercial development of Korea, and this brought no Russian recriminations at the moment. The Russians had temporarily put aside their ambitions in Korea. Too much was happening in the rest of Asia and in China.

The United States joined the frantic grab for colonies, rapidly taking over Hawaii, Midway Island, Guam, Samoa, and then declaring war on Spain and getting the Philippines. At almost the same time, 1898, in China, the Boxer Rebellion endangered the foreign diplomats in Peking, and a relief force was organized among the European nations. The United States sent troops and ships, and so did Japan. The result was another humiliation for China and the loss of more territory. The Europeans and Japan demanded reparations. England secured a tighter hold on Weihaiwei on the north side of the Shantung Peninsula; she got control of more territory in Hongkong, and concessions in the Yangtze River valley. Her merchants were everywhere and British shipping controlled the China trade. There was really nothing left for the Americans, and besides they were completely occupied trying to digest the Philippines, where they discovered that the Tagalog independence movement was real and not just an outcry against Spain. They spent the next five years suppressing the rebellion. So in China, hoping to achieve trade advantages, they heroically declared an open-door policy, turned over their Boxer reparations to scholarships for the Chinese, and adopted a highly moral tone of criticism of the colonial powers. The American open-door policy sought to assure the rights of all countries to invest in all parts of China, no matter which power had control of that area. At the same time the United States closed its new colonial acquisitions to foreign investment. The Japanese, seeing that, considered the American position to be selfish and hypocritical. But they said nothing. Japan's international manners were impeccable. Japan was the first of the powers to withdraw its troops after the suppression of the Boxers along the Peking–Tientsin rail line.[11] The government was following Viscount Tani's advice: lie low and wait.

勝つ 前もって

4. "The phrase 'Win first, fight later' can be summed up in the two words 'Win beforehand.'" SAMURAI NOTES ON MARTIAL LAW

Sen ri no michi mo ho ippo yori hajimeru. A journey of a thousand miles still begins step by step. That was the policy of Japan in the years 1895–1904. The dream of empire was not abandoned, it was simply submerged while the nation gathered strength and solved its internal problems. The main problem was the struggle for control between two factions within the Choshu clan, which would last until 1932, the year the army healed its internal differences to prepare to seize power. The Satsuma clan was no longer that important, for they had lost their power in the army with the Saigo rebellion. A Satsuma prime minister might be chosen to relieve intolerable tension between the two Choshu sides. If this seems an overly detailed view of internal Japanese politics, still it must be considered because this balance continued through 1945.

One Choshu faction was led by General Yamagata, who said it was the intent of the emperor that the military should rule. Prince Ito was of the modern school of constitutionalists: ultimate power should be in civil hands. The one unifying factor between these disparate philosophies was the reverence of the emperor.

General Yamagata had the support of the Kenseito party and Ito formed the Seiyukai party to oppose him. The divisions were not healed by the differing perceptions of the Russian threat. Yamagata, the militarist, saw a Russia trying to gain more control over China. It also seemed to him that the Russians were now ready to reopen their attempts to control Korea. He wanted military action.

Ito believed that the best course was to seek Japan's ends through diplomacy.

In 1901 the Ito government fell, and the new prime minister was General Taro Katsura, a protégé of General Yamagata. Katsura began planning for a war to be fought before the Russians could complete the Trans-Siberian Railway.[1]

The Japanese government negotiated a treaty with Britain, while the ex-premier, Ito, was abroad in Russia trying to work out a deal with the Russians to guarantee a Japanese noninterference in Man- churia if the Russians would not interfere with the Japanese in Korea. The Anglo-Japanese alliance of 1902 effectively immobilized Britain; in case of war with any power over Korea Britain would remain neutral. So the way was paved for Japan to get belligerent with the Russians.

The Japanese army and navy by this time had been built up to first-class strength. The compulsory military training program had been in effect for thirty years. All Japanese men between seventeen and forty years of age were subject to call-up in time of war. On January 10 of each year all young men twenty years old reported to their local military authorities for two years' duty.

Most of these young men went into the army, which, as noted, was dominated by the Choshu clan. The Satsuma clan did continue to dominate the Imperial Navy. And in the Sino-Japanese War of 1894 the navy had made its mark. Indeed, the hero of that war was the son of a Satsuma samurai, Heihachiro Togo. This young man had been encouraged by his father to join the Satsuma navy in 1866. During the struggle between the shogun and the emperor the Sat- suma navy had joined the Choshu clan and the Tosa clan armies to fight on the imperial side. Gunner Togo fought aboard the warship *Kasuga,* a 1200-ton paddle wheel steamer armed with six guns. The sailors wore the kimono and the officers carried the two swords of the samurai. Neither Admiral Enemoto, the shogun commander, nor Admiral Atatsuka, the Satsuma commander, knew very much about naval warfare.[2]

At the end of the civil war, the emperor ordained development of a modern army and a modern navy, and the Satsuma navy was disbanded. Officer of The Third Class Togo then joined the Imperial Japanese Navy as a midshipman. Off went the kimono and away went the swords. The new uniform of the Imperial Navy was a copy of that of the British Royal Navy, the most powerful in the world.

Before he went to sea, Togo went to school in Yokohama to learn English. In 1871 he went aboard the warship *Ryogo* as a midshipman, and a few months later he was among twelve midshipmen sent to England to learn the British navy way. After two years at the Thames Nautical Training College he went to sea in the training ship *Hampshire,* and then went back to his books. He had to learn seamanship, mathematics, navigation, all from the ground up, in English.

While Togo was in England the Japanese government ordered several warships built by British shipyards. He was lucky to be abroad when the Satsuma rebellion scoured Japan, for his loyalty remained unquestioned, although his brother died as one of the rebels.

As the Japanese navy burgeoned, Togo was promoted rapidly. By 1882 he was a lieutenant commander and first officer of the warship *Amagi,* then commander of the *Daini Teihu.* The Japanese navy was involved in a number of punitive expeditions against the Chinese and Indochinese who "violated" Japanese rights. It was good training for the sailors of the new navy. Togo sailed to Hongkong, Taiwan, Korea, and Shanghai. In 1890 he was chief of staff to the commander of the Kure naval base and a captain. When the sons of the American missionaries seized Hawaii, Captain Togo was sent in the warship *Naniwa* to protect Japanese lives and property. Then it was back to Japan and shore duty again as commander of the Kure naval base.[3]

In July 1894, Togo was again at sea as commander of the *Naniwa.* To him belongs the distinction of firing the first shots of the Sino-Japanese War and sinking a Chinese-chartered British ship, with 1100 Chinese soldiers aboard. It was an act of war, committed when no war existed, but Togo was never reprimanded, for he had done precisely what his seniors wanted: "win first, fight later."

He later distinguished himself in the one real naval battle of the war, the fight the Japanese call the Battle of the Yellow Sea, on September 17, 1894, and he participated in the occupation of Port Arthur. In January 1895 he became a rear admiral and a member of the Council of Admirals. From this point on he would make Japanese naval policy.[4]

In 1896 Togo became head of the Japanese naval war college, responsible for teaching officers tactics and strategy. He was instrumental in achieving a basic change in naval policy: Japan began building her own warships. After several years in shore jobs, Togo was appointed Admiral of the Fleet. In 1900 he took the Japanese naval contingent to Taku Bar during the Boxer Rebellion.

In October 1903 Admiral Togo was summoned to the admirality, where Admiral Ito, chief of the Naval General Staff, informed him that war would soon break out between Japan and Russia, and that Togo would command the Imperial Navy fleet. In the next two months the fleet was prepared for battle, and on December 28 Togo went aboard the flagship *Mikasa*. In January, a hundred Japanese warships lay at anchor and moorings in the naval base at Sasebo. Soon they would face the Russian fleet, the third largest in the world. Of course, not all the Russian ships were in the Pacific, but they could be.[5]

The Japanese strategy was laid down in Tokyo by Emperor Meiji. It was very simple: Japan would attack without warning. This attitude, so unseemly to Westerners, was and is, as noted, an essential of Japanese military strategy from the earliest days.

On February 4 the Japanese negotiators at St. Petersburg were warned. "We now find Ourselves obliged to conclude that the Russians do not want peace," the emperor said. On February 5 Admiral Togo received the imperial order. At nine o'clock on the morning of February 6, he sailed against Port Arthur. His plan of attack was simplicity itself: move up to Port Arthur vicinity and then send his torpedo boats into the port to attack the Russian fleet. If they succeeded, the victory was won. If they failed, the main elements of the fleet remained intact. Meanwhile they would bombard the Russian fleet from outside.

The attack was carried out in the early hours of February 8 by the torpedo boats, and they were singularly successful. Two battleships and five cruisers were put out of action. Another unit of the fleet attacked Russian ships at Chemulpo, Korea, and then landed elements of the Japanese army. The surprise was complete. Only then did the Japanese declare war.[6]

General Nogi, the admiral's opposite number in the land battle for Manchuria, did just as well. The Japanese soldiers, trained and toughened under the sharp discipline of officers themselves trained in the Prussian pattern, took heavy casualties but kept forging on against the Russians. Nogi did not flinch at sending five thousand men to fall in a diversionary attack against Port Arthur's High Mountain; that was what troops were for, to be sent to fight and die. Two of the general's sons were among those to die.

In May 1905 Admiral Togo also defeated the Russian Baltic fleet in the Battle of Tsushima Strait. It was a great victory, and Togo, who was already the hero of the Japanese people, was even further exalted. There could be no question that next only to the emperor, "the Son of Heaven," Heihachiro Togo was the most revered man in Japan. He was appointed chief of the Imperial General Staff, the highest office a naval man could achieve. From 1905 to 1909 he held the strings of power of the Japanese naval establishment.

These were years of tension for Japan. The Japanese army had never wavered from the conviction announced by General Yamagata that Japan's security depended on controlling the land areas around her. The army demanded a twenty-five division force, with another twenty-five divisions in reserve. Admiral Togo and the navy held that Japan needed no colonies, but that, like England, she was a trading nation, and her future lay in maintaining a strong naval force. Specifically, Japan must be prepared to overpower the United States and prevent her from carrying out her open-door policy in Asia. Let the nation never forget, the navy reminded, that only because of the alliance with Great Britain had Japan been able to wage war against China and against the Russians without interference. What Admiral Togo wanted was a two-fleet navy. Immediately the navy moved to get a dozen new battleships built.[7]

From the international point of view, the major result of the Russo-Japanese War was the development of enmity between Japan and the United States. Having won the war, the Japanese army and navy expected to share in the victory as they had after the Sino-Japanese War. Cash indemnification was high on the list, enough cash to build battleships and tanks and big guns. Theodore Roosevelt, the President of the United States, had offered America's good offices to secure peace from the ashes of the war in Manchuria. The Russians and the Japanese met at Portsmouth, New Hampshire, with the Americans as referees. The Japanese removed the last of the Russian obstacles to their suzerainty over Korea, the Russians were pushed out of Manchuria, and the Japanese took over the concessions the Russians had secured from the Chinese. After a delay of a decade the Liaotung Peninsula was theirs to hold, if not to have. They took the southern half of Sakhalin Island. But when it came to cash, the Russians jibbed, and the Americans supported them. In the end, the cash indemnity was lost, despite the spirited arguments of the Japanese army and navy. The Japanese public was so angry with the terms of the treaty that many people demanded the resignation of the government. The normally sedate *Asahi Shimbun,* largest newspaper in the land, said that the politicians had turned military victory into political defeat. Some newspapers suggested the assassination of the cabinet ministers and the emperor's close advisors. Riots broke out in Tokyo, and the government had to declare martial law and bring in soldiers to restrain the violent.[8]

So while Portsmouth brought an end to the Russo-Japanese War, it watered the seeds of enmity between the Japanese and the Americans.

Those seeds had been aided twenty-five years earlier by the Americans. In the 1860s when Leland Stanford and his associates were building the western section of the trans-continental railway across the United States, they had discovered that by employing Chinese laborers they moved faster and cheaper than by using the usual combination of German and Irish laborers who had been building American railroads for years. The Orientals drank tea instead of whiskey, and if they fought, they kept their quarrels to themselves.

Once the railroad was finished, the thousands of Chinese laborers were cast upon the western labor market, and the "working men" of America began to object. The result was the Chinese Exclusion Acts, which forced most of the Chinese to go home, not only from the United States but from Hawaii, where they had congregated to work in the cane fields.

Meanwhile, some Japanese had come to the United States and many more to Hawaii, encouraged by the planters. The American labor movement led the discrimination against the Japanese as well and was joined by farm groups, for American farmers soon saw that Japanese farmers were harder working and more skillful than themselves. So agitation against the Japanese grew apace in the American west.[9]

The Japanese had been trickling into America at the rate of about a thousand a year. But in January 1900, after the annexation of Hawaii to the United States, 12,000 Japanese suddenly appeared on the American shore. The result was panic in San Francisco. Mayor James Phelan quarantined the oriental section of the city on the excuse that bubonic plague had begun there. It was not true. The Japanese protested, but the San Francisco Labor Council began agitating for laws similar to the Chinese Exclusion Acts. Furious, the Japanese government stopped issuing passports to contract laborers bound for America, even if American employers wanted them. In 1904 and 1905 the American Federation of Labor began agitation for anti-Japanese laws. The sensational press of California took up the cry and made it constant. Virtually every day the public was bombarded with tales of "the yellow peril."

The first newspaper to take up the cudgels against the Japanese was the San Francisco *Chronicle*.

"Japanese a Menace to American Women" was a typical scare headline. "Brown Asiatics Steal Brains of Whites," said the newspaper. Not to be outdone in a circulation race William Randolph Hearst's San Francisco *Examiner* took up the cry. Soon all San Francisco papers were knuckling under to the feeling of working-class and farmer whites that the Japanese were a threat to their livelihood. Hearst took it much further, for he had built a journalistic empire with newspapers in Seattle, Los Angeles, New York, Washington, D.C., Boston, Baltimore, and many other cities. The outcry against the Japanese became national and ever more vocal.

The California legislature voted *unanimously* to demand that Congress exclude all Japanese. A Japanese and Korean Exclusion League enlisted thousands of members. And, the unholy racists of the west and the unholy racists of the south united in an unholy alliance. In 1906 all Orientals in San Francisco were ordered to attend a segregated school.[10]

To the Japanese it was at first flabbergasting, and then insulting, to learn that these red-necked Americans whose culture seemed so barbaric had the gall to look down upon the children of Yamato, a civilization that flourished when California was populated entirely by savages and bears.

Tokyo's *Mainichi Shimbun* called upon Admiral Togo to send Japanese warships to California to protect Japanese citizens!

President Roosevelt tried to stop the developing racism, but could not, and being a politician, he yielded to the public demand for racism. The United States and Japan began to negotiate a Gentleman's Agreement which left Japan seething: she was called upon to place sharp limits on the travels of her nationals to the western hemisphere.

As chief of the Imperial General Staff, Admiral Togo had one warning to make to his countrymen:

"The gods soon take the crown away from those who relax in the pleasures of peace. The Ancients said, 'After a victory, tighten the straps of your helmet.' "[11]

The admiral did just that. The discipline within the Imperial Navy was never relaxed. Japan continued to build. Under the Emperor Meiji's Imperial Rescript to Soldiers and Sailors (see Appendix), the responsibilities of the military man were laid out as definitely as they had ever been in the days of the samurai's *bushido*.

In Tokyo newspaper editors gritted their teeth and fulminated against the United States. The Japanese navy was convinced that the one nation in the world that meant Japan harm was the United States of America. Drawing a new defense program for the first time since the defeat of Russia, the Imperial Navy set up the United States of America as "the enemy." This perception was to last for the next thirty-five years.

Navies were changing drastically in the early years of the twentieth century. The major weapon with which Admiral Togo had surprised the Russians, the torpedo boat, was on its way out, superseded by the destroyer and the submarine. With the building of the British warship *Dreadnought* came a whole new era, of the armored battleship, a huge floating gun platform, virtually impervious to attack by the warships of the day. After 1900 all major nations were building battleships.

The United States was far behind England, Germany, and Japan in this building program. But by 1906 so concerned was Theodore Roosevelt about the anti-American feeling that had developed in Japan that it became the central factor in his foreign policy. He consulted everyone who knew anything about Asia. Was Japan capable of attacking and defeating the United States?

No, said Roosevelt's experts. Japan was still suffering from the enormous cost of the Russo-Japanese War, and her failure to secure the cash indemnification she had demanded had set her back several years.

Roosevelt was comforted but not totally reassured. He decided that the United States would make a show of force in the Pacific that should frighten the Japanese into silence. He would send the American battle fleet on a "goodwill mission" across the wide ocean.

So "The Great White Fleet" set out, sixteen battleships and four admirals. First it went south in the Atlantic, then down around Cape Horn and up the West Coast of the United States. Some months were spent impressing Americans, and then the fleet set out across the Pacific, to New Zealand and Australia. The Americans were greeted with hysterical approbation, for the Australians were nearly as anti-Oriental as the Californians. All the while, Tokyo observed the American jingoism sourly. *Mainichi Shimbun* was more than astringent: let Admiral Togo make a preemptive strike against the U.S. fleet to destroy it and "save civilization" from the barbaric Americans.[12]

When the fleet reached Manila in the fall of 1908 it was not quite certain how much farther it would proceed. Political affairs had gone from bad to worse. The "Gentleman's Agreement" had been finally reached earlier that year but the result had been continued fury among the Japanese people, egged on by their press. Admiral Togo sent the Japanese fleet to sea. Was there some reason for that? Did this action mean that Japan was ready to attack the American fleet when it moved into Japanese waters? For months American and Japanese diplomats had been working to ease the tensions, but the publicists of the two nations continued to snarl across the Pacific like angry dogs.

And where was the Japanese fleet? That was the question asked by Washington, as the American fleet prepared to up anchor at Manila, Tokyo bound. As a precaution the U.S. Pacific Fleet was sent from the West Coast to Samoa, to be within reach in case of trouble.

Admiral Togo had prepared a surprise for the Americans. All 160 of Japan's warships were going to be prepared to greet the Americans, at sea, just off the Japanese shore. Admiral Togo not only believed in the preemptive strike, but in preemptive bullying, so his naval force was ordered to make a good show of Japanese naval might for the Americans as they came.

Fortunately for faint hearts, a typhoon interrupted the greeting procedure, and the two fleets never met at sea.

With this sort of buildup, the Americans were noticeably nervous as they came up Tokyo Bay toward the Yokosuka naval base. But the Japanese, so angry beneath, put on their brightest smiles. Tokyo was alive with bunting when the Americans appeared, and the editors of *Mainichi Shimbun* concealed their fury beneath warm greetings and great praise for the "white ships." The newspapermen were practicing, as was all Japan, the combination of courtly courtesy for which the Japanese are noted and *enryo*, that wonderful restraint that leads the Japanese to smile beatifically when his real desire is to cut your throat.

The greeting was helped along considerably by imperial orders that no one was to get out of line when the barbarians were in town. The reception was managed completely by the imperial government, down to the instructions posted by the police in every district of Tokyo and Yokohama warning the public to behave themselves on pain of swift and awful punishment. No worry about the Americans understanding the meaning of the posters on the lamp posts; not one American in a hundred thousand could read Japanese.

Admiral Togo gave a party for the American officers, and Emperor Meiji came to the party, which was a hitherto unknown honor for foreigners. The party was marked by toasts and pledges of friendship—all totally meaningless—and was followed by an American party for the Japanese, which meant more toasts and more pledges, and naught else.[13]

The Americans soon went away, and nothing had changed. Admiral Togo did not relax his guard for a moment, although a look at the American fleet had convinced him that he really had nothing to fear from that direction, particularly because the Anglo-Japanese alliance effectively precluded the Americans from action in the Far East. Japan was free to continue her empire building.

The first paragraph of the Treaty of Portsmouth had guaranteed Russian recognition of "Korean independence" and the paramount nature of Japan's political, military, and economic interests in Korea. A few months after the treaty was signed, Prince Hirobumi Ito appeared in Seoul to negotiate a treaty with Korea under which this new dependency of Korea on Japan would be recognized. The Koreans tried to escape the net, the king even appealed to President Roosevelt for help. But Roosevelt knew that any attempt by the Americans to interfere in Japanese affairs would end only in disaster. Suddenly his advisors had pointed out that the Philippines were a lot closer to Tokyo than to Washington. America had everything to lose and nothing to gain by befriending the Koreans. The President's answer to the king was to close down the U.S. legation in Seoul, which meant that in the future American dealings with Koreans would be conducted through Tokyo.

So Japan's quest for empire surged on. In the summer of 1907 Korea was made a "protectorate" of Japan. Shadow officials from Japan joined all the Korean ministries and lesser government agencies. Japanese police joined the Korean police force. The Oriental Colonization Company was organized to exploit Korean resources for Japan.

By 1909 all the preparations were made. Japan controlled the police, the government, transportation, and every public aspect of

Korean life. All that was needed was an excuse to make Korea a part of the empire. It came in October, when Prince Ito took a trip to Harbin, representing the Privy Council of Japan, to talk to the Russians about "mutual problems." He was assassinated, and the Japanese police arrested a Korean nationalist. The suspicion was raised that it was a put-up job by the extremist Yamagata element in the army, to get rid of a thorn in their side. But this could not be proved and it was the excuse used by the Katsura government to annex Korea. The army moved into Seoul. A hard-line military man, General Masatake Terauchi, became the resident general and a force of Japanese marines moved in to preserve order. The country was placed under martial law. The Koreans were informed that now they were Japanese. A special throne room was set up in the capital for the use of the Japanese emperor.[14]

Forty years earlier the Emperor Meiji had refused the demands of his hotheaded friends to go to war to take Korea. Wait, he had said, and it would come. Now, forty years later, the emperor had made of Japan a great empire. Taiwan, Korea, Sakhalin, the Ryukyus, the Bonins, the Kuriles had all become Japanese. South Manchuria had been brought within the Japanese orbit; Japan controlled the railroads, and Japanese were beginning to build up the industries to benefit Japan. In forty years the emperor had brought his country out of feudalism and to the forefront of Asian nations. *Hakko ichiu* no longer seemed so wild a dream.

郷 に 入って は 郷 に 従え

5. "When you enter a village, join the villagers"

*B*y the opening of the Russo-Japanese War Japanese politics had
assumed a pattern. On the one side was the military party, led
now by Taro Katsura, and on the other side was the civil party,
headed by Prince Kimmochi Saionji, after the death of Hirobumi
Ito.

Emperor Meiji, having accomplished his major aims by 1910,
gave ever more responsibility to the men around him. This change
created new difficulties, for the Japanese government was two-headed.
As long as the emperor led personally there was no conflict, for he
was supreme ruler of the military *and* of the civil government. But
as his will to rule waned, the military expressed constant dissatisfaction with any attempt to harness its expansion. Unfortunately for
the civil rule advocates and for the world, as it turned out half a
century later, Japanese tradition had a peculiar quirk that worked
for the military. It was *niju seifu,* or dual government. It had existed
for a thousand years.[1]

In 1900, in one of those continual quarrels with Prince Ito,
General Yamagata persuaded the Privy Council (and the emperor)
to rule that only generals and admirals *on active duty* could hold office
as ministers of war and navy. Thus was established a precedent which
was to make possible an army revolution in the 1930s.

In 1912 when Prince Saionji was prime minister he sided with
the majority in the Diet who wanted to restrict military spending.

So the Choshu leaders persuaded the Imperial Army and Imperial Navy general staffs that they must intercede.

In the quarrel that followed, the war minister resigned, and when Prince Saionji tried to appoint a new war minister, no active duty officer would take the post so the cabinet could not be organized, and Saionji had to give up the premiership.

This shortcoming of the constitution might have been rectified by Emperor Meiji, who had managed all these years to strike a balance between the militarists and the advocates of civil power. But Emperor Meiji died that summer at the age of sixty, and left a constitution tailored to his personality and a son who was in no way fitted to rule Japan. The prince, who took the imperial name Taisho for his rule, never ruled in any sense; he was physically weak and he also suffered from mental illness, and the entire function of government devolved to the councillors and political and military leaders. Thus immediately on Meiji's death, a totally new political situation emerged. The emperor was still the ultimate authority of Japan, and all power resided in his name. It was power to be used by someone. Immediately it was used by the *Genro,* the council of elder statesmen. The new emperor was too weak to ever think of objecting. The Taisho period began with the emergence of the Lord Keeper of the Privy Seal and the Imperial Household Agency as the fonts of power, backed by the Privy Council. In military affairs, Admiral Togo still retained enormous influence, and he was the teacher of the young prince Hirohito who would some day ascend the throne. Togo supervised seventeen instructors who taught the prince Chinese and Japanese literature, French, English, chemistry, physics, calligraphy, law, and politics. The admiral himself took care of the prince's military education. But the crown prince was merely an heir in waiting with no voice in public affairs.[2]

The navy saw this army play for power in the Saionji difficulties of 1912 and when a new prime minister selected his cabinet, no naval officer would serve as navy minister. General Yamagata then contrived to secure a rescript from the throne, ordering appointment of a navy minister, and the navy submitted. But the damage was done. By not consulting the navy first, the militarists had driven a deep rift into the defense community, one that would not be healed until the Japanese armed forces were reorganized under American influence in the 1950s.[3]

With the eruption of war in Europe in the summer of 1914, Japan was constrained by her alliance with Britain to take the side of the Triple Entente. The Japanese were delighted to do so because it gave them a new opportunity to seize territory. It took only two months for the Japanese to seize the German colony of Kiaochao in China's Shantung Province.[4] Japan then moved into the German Pacific colonies. They took the Mariana Islands and the Marshalls without much trouble. They moved into the Caroline Islands. They coveted German New Guinea, but the Australians got there first, and the New Zealanders moved into German Samoa before the Japanese could.

The Japanese navy cruised the Pacific in search of German warships, but Admiral von Spee's German East Asia Cruiser Squadron had headed to Cape Horn to try to cross the Atlantic and make the run back to Germany, a gamble that failed. Japan then had no further part in the great war except to provide supplies, and she could enjoy her captures.[5]

Japanese expansionists in the army, navy, and foreign office then concentrated their efforts to colonize China in furtherance of Lord Hatta's Memorial to the Throne of 1858. The time had come: the European powers were preoccupied as Hotta had said they would be. In 1915 Japan presented the infamous "Twenty-One Demands" to the Chinese government. These demands would give Japan a ninety-nine-year lease on the southern Manchuria railroads, economic control of Manchuria, the old German colony of Kiaochao, the German rights in Shanghai, economic control of mines at Hankow, and the employment of political advisors to the Chinese government and special concessions in China, which would have made China a colony of Japan.[6]

The Chinese flatly refused to discuss any interference with their government. The Japanese government then ordered mobilization of the troops and gave China an ultimatum: the other demands of the troops would be accepted or . . .

The Chinese capitulated. Japan moved her army into Manchuria and outer Mongolia. She established a military presence in Shanghai. She held onto Kiaochao. Now she had Korea, economic control of Manchuria, Taiwan, the Kuriles, Ryukyus, and a string of islands in the Central and South Pacific that would provide naval bases, and the Marianas which were valuable agriculturally as well. Japan had taken one more giant step in her drive for empire and preeminence in Asia.

What happened next is vital in the history of Japan's drive in the 1930s, and in the current situation between Japan and the USSR in the 1980s:

So preoccupied with the war in Europe were the Allies, and ultimately the United States, that the Japanese were able to consolidate their territorial gains between 1915 and 1919. All this was done very quietly, through secret agreements signed with all powers but the United States.

The Japanese tried to come to a similar agreement with the Americans, but failed: Washington had the "Open Door" to think about, which meant American businessmen insisted on keeping their options to trade with China open.

Meanwhile, the Japanese became China's bankers, and in exchange for their loans, they secured new areas of economic exploitation, all the while claiming loudly that they stood for nonintervention in the affairs of China.

In 1917 as Russia crumbled into revolution, Britain urged the United States and Japan to mount a joint expeditionary force that would land in Siberia and secure the Trans-Siberian Railway all the way to Moscow. The Japanese army opposed the plan. But when the Japanese realized that Siberia was loaded with military supplies, which might fall into the hands of the revolutionary government, the army and the navy moved. In January 1918, two Japanese warships appeared at Vladivostok to "protect" the foreign consular corps.

General Giichi Tanaka, a specialist in Russian affairs, recommended that the question of the foreign residents be used as an excuse to send two divisions of Japanese troops to Siberia to wipe out the Bolshevik forces. The foreign ministry supported the plan but said it had to be "self-defense." So "self-defense" it became. The Japanese assembled a force to operate in northern Manchuria, Mongolia, and Siberia. Their rear would be protected by the Kwantung (the Japanese name for Liaotung) Army in southern Manchuria. The American government, preoccupied with the desire to create a new Europe, suggested that the Japanese send troops to help the Czechslovak legions—Austrian prisoners of war captured by the Russians, who had broken out of their prison camps and moved along the Trans-Siberian Railway to Siberia. It was just the excuse Japan wanted, and the occupation of Siberia was on.[7]

The Japanese cabinet promised the Allies that only 12,000 troops would be sent. The army was furious. Here had been a chance to saw off Siberia and add another chunk of empire, a chance muffed by the civilian government. Ultimately the army triumphed and three and a half divisions were sent to Siberia.

The presence of this huge force in Siberia became a Japanese lever at the Paris Peace Conference.

The Allied powers approached the surrender of Germany with the high hope that they could outlaw war as an instrument of national policy. In Japan, too, there was a strong peace movement, welling from the universities and the political parties. Not so in the inner circle of Japan's leadership. The aspirations of the oligarchy and of the army had never changed. Japan was to build more empire and take the leadership of Asia first of all. *Hakko ichiu.*

Now that Japan had joined the exploiters, the colonial nations of the world in pursuit of prestige and power, the Japanese wanted to be treated as equals in all ways. *Asahi Shimbun,* the largest Japanese newspaper, noted at the opening of the conference that racial inequality was the greatest issue among nations and called upon Japan to lead all the colored peoples of the world in seeking equality.[8]

But the race prejudice of the Westerners, and particularly of the Americans and the British, was so deep-seated that the concession that "all men are brothers" could not be made at the Paris peace talks, although Japan fought to the end for provisions that would provide for racial equality.

When the Americans stalled and wriggled on the issue, even the most open-minded Japanese lost faith in the sincerity of the Westerners. The issue became intermingled with the color issue in America and bogged down completely. Japan had agreed to participate in the League of Nations, but it became a matter of national honor that they do so on an equal basis with all others. The issue was sloughed off, but, in fact, it was the most important aspect of the peace conference. Everything that happened toward the end was influenced by the Japanese perception of Western powers trying to misuse her and even cheat her of the fruits of her "victory" over Germany. To this was added fuel to the growing distrust of the United States when the Americans, having done so much to manage Pacific affairs in the peace conferences, refused to join the League of Nations.

One of the reasons for this refusal was the American feeling that Japan had mistreated China in her drive for empire. Another was the racism that played into the hands of the isolationists and took America on a solo course in foreign policy that meant isolationism for the next twenty years.[9]

The Versailles Treaty, rejected by the United States, gave Japan virtually all she had asked for in China and the Pacific. Her troops remained in Siberia until 1922, the last to leave Soviet Russia. She occupied northern Sakhalin and remained there until 1926.

Meanwhile, the American diplomatic initiative in Asia was designed to stop Japanese expansion, a fact that certainly did not escape the Japanese. American bankers tried to put together capital for China, to keep Japan away. America fought the Japanese occupation of Siberia and Sakhalin. The Americans opposed the continued Japanese presence in Shantung Province.

By 1920, then, American-Japanese relations were already in a critical state. The Japanese resented American racism enormously and held the United States responsible for the failure of the Paris peace talks to guarantee equality of all peoples. The Japanese military saw the United States as its major potential enemy, and the American navy returned the compliment in Plan Orange, which was the generic name of a series of fleet plans for war in the Pacific.[10]

The end of World War I saw Japanese industry burgeoning. The percentage of people employed in industry had risen from 20 percent in 1877 to 49 percent. The expansion of empire meant expansion of markets for industrial goods, and the expansion of industrial markets encouraged the expansion of empire. The army and the *zaibatsu,* the great industrial combines, were traveling on converging courses. The *zaibatsu* had gotten their start under Emperor Meiji's policy of organizing Western-style industry. All these industries were sold off to private capital, providing instant fortunes. By 1920 the family firms of Mitsui, Mitsubishi, Sumitomo, and Yasuda each controlled a virtual economic empire. There were others: Furukawa, the copper kings; Shibusawa, banking and engineering; Kawasaki, shipbuilding, railroad equipment, and steel; Asano, cement and steel; Okura, mining; Kuhara, engineering.

All of these industrial empires were basically family concerns. Sumitomo in those days was run by one man. Mitsubishi was controlled by two families, the Iwasakis. Mitsui was one big family, eleven branches, functioning under rules laid down in 1900 that still served.[11]

Mitsui and Mitsubishi had their eyes once again on the political arena. Mitsui was the most powerful of the trusts: Mitsui Gomei, the holding company, supervised Mitsui Bank, Mitsui Trading Company, Mitsui Mining, Mitsui Textiles, Mitsui Shipping, and warehousing, sugar, metals, and heavy machinery companies. Mitsui set the pace for the others.

The industrial combines had prospered enormously during the 1914–18 war. Imperial Steel Works, for example, made profits enough between 1915 and 1918 to cover the initial capitalization of the company. By 1918 Japan's steel industry had more than doubled from 250,000 tons of output to 580,000 tons. Other industries showed the same pattern, which continued until after 1921, when the European countries and the United States settled down to a peacetime industrial footing. Then reaction set in, which meant serious economic problems for Japan in the glutting of industrial and agricultural markets.

The industrialization of Japan brought radical political movements and an industrial labor movement to the country, in an atmosphere that seemed to welcome change. Prime Minister General Masatake Terauchi was forced to resign in 1918 as a consequence of riots by the peasants against shortages of rice. Some liberal thinkers believed that the era of the generals had passed, and that from this point on the people would begin to rule. That feeling was enhanced by the reluctant approval by the oligarchs of the *Genro* of Kei Hara as prime minister in 1918. Hara was a commoner and president of the Seiyukai political party. The elder statesmen had to swallow hard to accept a politician as prime minister but they did. He came to office with the cry that "militarism is extinct."[12]

For the first time Japan had a partisan government; all the members of the cabinet except the ministers of war and navy were Seiyukai men. In the elections of 1920 the Seiyukai won 60 percent of the vote, and the country seemed more stable than it had ever been.

But early in the 1920s labor organizers and radicals began fomenting strikes and disturbances, and the government responded with repressive legislation. In 1921 Premier Hara was assassinated by a railroad worker. Although Finance Minister Koreikiyo Takahashi took over, the party had lost its chance. He resigned in a little more than a year, and the government resumed its nonpartisan, elite nature.

On the surface, the Meiji Constitution seemed to the outside world to be an instrument, albeit an imperfect one, of a constitutional monarchy. But the appearances were deceptive. The Japanese people had never enjoyed "democracy." The equivalent of the American Bill of Rights in the Japanese constitution was contained in fourteen articles dealing with "rights and duties of subjects." Most of the attention was to duties. For example:

Article XXVIII. Japanese subjects shall, within limits not prejudicial to peace and order, and not antagonistic to their duties as subjects, enjoy freedom of religious belief.

Article XXIX. Japanese subjects, shall, within the limits of law, enjoy the liberty of speech, writing, publication, public meeting, and associations.[13]

What those articles meant was that Japanese citizens could have as much freedom as the government in power at the moment wanted them to have. The constitutions of such nations as England and the United States provide for the freedom of individuals against the government. No such concept ever entered the minds of the men who had drawn the Japanese constitution. The constitution gave them the illusion of liberty, not the reality. The only inviolable right a Japanese citizen was guaranteed was the right to own property. To the Japanese, the ownership of property was the key to the good life, respectability, and freedom from the oppression of the authorities. It had always been so. From the earliest days, Japan had been economically upwardly mobile, the most capitalistic of all societies.[14]

The basic instrument for oppression of the Japanese people was the Peace Preservation Law. Such law had been in effect in Japan since 1887 and had been revised several times to meet conditions. By the 1920s the law provided for suppression of anything that threatened "peace and order." That law was used to quell riots, to put down demonstrations, to control labor union activity and radical political activity. The daimyos of old Japan ruled their provinces through their samurai. The modern Japanese state began to rule its cities and provinces through the police network. The police were enforcers, and judge and jury. Citizens could be thrown into jail and kept there without explanation. The police were everywhere. The *koban* (police box) was visible in every district. The police knew who lived where, and the citizens were responsible to the police who kept law and order in their little areas. Men and women bowed to the police box when they went by.

The police were controlled by the Ministry of Home Affairs, which also controlled censorship, and any material deemed subversive to law and order was censored.

What was not accomplished in the matter of guiding popular thought by the police and the censors was accomplished by the Ministry of Education, which decided what was going to be taught in the schools.

By the beginning of the twentieth century, education was compulsory throughout Japan. The government sensed the need for a people who could be trained, and education meant training. The army could not have agreed more. For in this system the army saw its chance to extend its influence through all Japan.

The Japanese army, oddly enough, was in its way the most democratic organization in the country. With the establishment of military conscription at the beginning of the Meiji Era, Japan needed soldiers and officers. They came from the farms for the most part; poor farm boys, previously relegated to lives of poverty, discovered that through the army they could rise high, even to cabinet rank. Thus the relationship between the army and the peasantry of Japan was very close.

In the bad economic years of the early 1920s, the army began to rebel against political rule. The young officers would go home to the farms and hear the stories of the difficulties of their parents and come back to camp furious with the authorities who permitted the people to suffer. Thus was born a new military class, not the Field Marshal Yamagatas and the General Katsuras but soldiers with the mud of the farms fresh from their feet. These men were not nobles who chose soldiering, but commoners who were rising to power through the military and through the military alone.

The army and the navy continued to spend huge sums of money to build divisions and ships. The army's excuse was the need to police Korea and Manchuria. The Kwantung Army by 1920 had become the strongest and most powerful military force of Japan. Situated so far from Tokyo the Kwantung Army command enjoyed a greater freedom than any other unit of the Japanese military. When the Japanese forces were withdrawn from Siberia in 1922, the problem arose as to what was to be done with these divisions. Japan had more troops than could be profitably employed, and with the necessary evacuation of northern Sakhalin that would come soon enough, the problem would be increased. These thoughts worried the generals, who had no intention of allowing the army buildup to be reversed.

Two years after the Paris Peace Conference Japan's situation seemed once again perilous. The United States led a movement to form a four-power consortium to finance China. To be sure, Japan was to be a part of the consortium, but only a part, along with the United States, France, and Great Britain. Were this to be successful it would threaten Japan's hand in China. And in another area, Japan's military expansion was already under threat. The Americans in the summer of 1921 called an international disarmament conference to meet in Washington. The object was obviously to obstruct Japanese colonial expansion. The problem in Tokyo was that many of the politicians believed in disarmament, and so did a growing segment of the public. The men around the emperor, and particularly the militarists of the army and the navy, had no intention of allowing Japan's teeth to be pulled, on the eve of what they could see as the triumph of empire. Japan had joined the colonial club and now rivaled Britain as an Asian colonial power. The militarists had no intention of giving up strength or territory. *Hakko ichiu.*

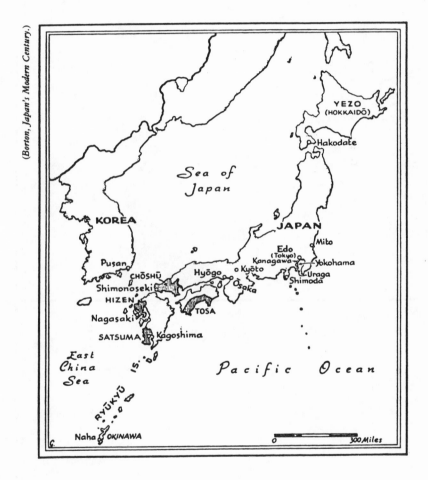

Japan in 1868.

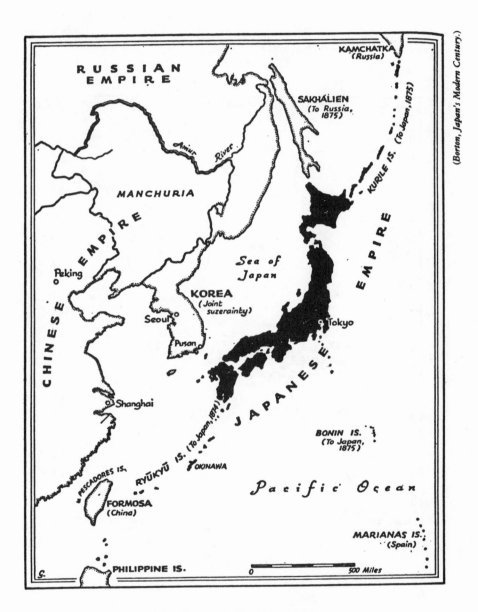

(Borton, Japan's Modern Century.)

The Japanese Empire, 1890.

Japanese Empire and European Concessions in China, 1900.

Japanese Empire, 1915.

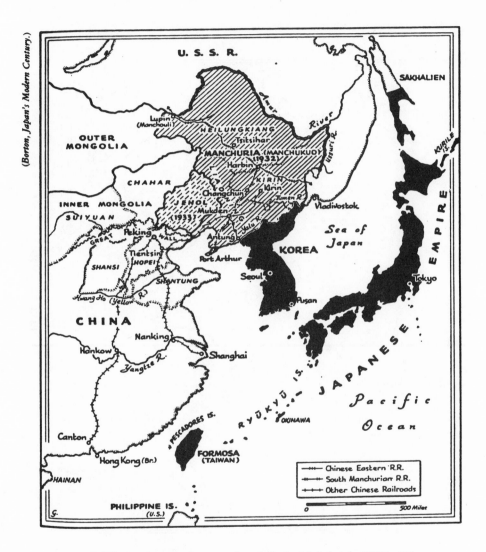

Military Aggression on the Asiatic Mainland, 1931–37.

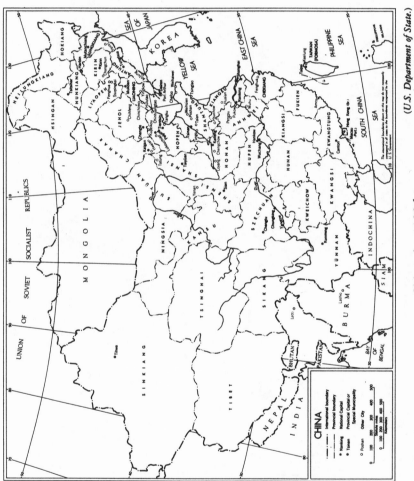

China circa 1936.

(*U.S. Department of State.*)

内弁慶　外味噌

6. "Braggart at home, flatterer abroad"

*T*he Washington armament conference of 1921 is commonly mis-
understood to have been an idealistic American attempt to stop
the international naval arms race that threatened after World War I.
It is true that at the end of 1920 Senator William E. Borah of Idaho,
a Progressive Republican and pacifist, did introduce a resolution into
Congress for that reason, and the resolution was appended to the
Naval Appropriations Bill, which made it hard to ignore. Nor was
there any great inclination to ignore the resolution, because the
Republicans had campaigned in 1920 on a platform of international
peace through disarmament. They still believed that they had gone
through "the war to end all wars," and had "made the world safe for
democracy."

But by the time the idea had been worked over by the State
Department and the Republican administration that had just taken
power, the whole reasoning had changed. The Washington conference was enlarged to include more: an attempt to limit Japanese
expansion in Asia.[1]

All the powers with interests in the Far East, except Soviet
Russia, were invited to attend the conference.

When the invitation came to Japan, the cabinet saw it as a ploy
to take away Japan's gains of the war. So Japan asked for further
information and indicated that she did not wish to discuss Sino-
Japanese relations, the Twenty-One Demands, or Shantung Province. France, Italy, and Great Britain all agreed unconditionally, and

U.S. Secretary of State Charles Evans Hughes blithely ignored Japan's conditions and announced that she, too, had accepted the invitation. The scope of the conference was extended to include naval disarmament, the U.S. open-door policy of unrestricted trade for all nations, Japan's possession of Shantung Province, the integrity of China and Russia (Japanese troops were still in Siberia and gave no signs of leaving, and they still held northern Sakhalin Island), the Anglo-Japanese alliance, the status of the old German colonies, Pacific communications, and narcotics in China.[2]

Japan then faced a serious dilemma. Should she ignore the conference and proceed with her own plans? On the army side, the plans called for continued expansion wherever opportunity arose. On the navy side, the plans called for the building of eight more battleships and eight more cruisers, which would give Japan a fleet powerful enough to defeat the United States in case of trouble. The catch was that projected naval budget for 1922 was a third of the national budget. The navy's plan would raise total military expenditure to 60 percent of the budget. The army opposed it, and Prime Minister Hara did, too, for other reasons. He really favored international disarmament and, so, persuaded the navy that if all countries cut their naval spending, Japan could get by with less. Some of the admirals objected, but Navy Minister Tomasaburo Kato agreed that it was worth a try. After conversations with the army and the politicians, Kato realized the political climate in Japan was such that he would not get his 8–8 fleet. The Washington conference, in that sense, gave him an excuse to give it up, although he did not say so to the Americans and British.[3]

Hara's dispatch of the delegation to Washington was just about his last important act; he was assassinated a week before the conference convened.

The Washington conference lasted from November 1921 until February 1922. Minister Admiral Kato was convinced during these discussions that the United States and Britain were really trying to seek agreement and not just hamstring Japan. Agreeing were advisors Teikichi Hori, Isoroku Yamamoto, Seizo Sakonji, Mitsumasa Yonai, and Shigeyoshi Inoue. This group returned to Japan to be known as "the treaty faction." They disagreed with Fleet Admiral Kanji Kato, who wanted a powerful fleet at all costs and went home to lead "the fleet faction."[4]

The Japanese at the Washington conference were very conciliatory. Seven treaties came out of the conference. One set the fleet ratio among Britain, the United States, and Japan, at 5–5–3. Japan was to have a fleet 60 percent as powerful as that of Britain and the United States. The rationale was that Britain had the Atlantic, the Pacific, the Indian Ocean, and the Mediterranean to worry about; the United States had the Atlantic and the Pacific, and Japan had only the Pacific. The Americans and British agreed to limit their Pacific naval bases and not to fortify them further. They agreed that Japan could keep the old German Pacific colonies under mandate for another twenty-five years, but Japan would not fortify them. Thus the Japanese could feel secure against attack. In a peaceful world no alliances were necessary, so the Anglo-Japanese alliance was scrapped. The Americans wanted a "Board of Reference" to oversee the open door for trade in China. Japan objected strenuously to having the Western powers looking over her shoulder, and, in the interest of amity, this idea was also scrapped. Japan agreed then to get out of Shantung Province, to withdraw her troops from Siberia and also from northern Sakhalin, and the air of amity was increased.[5]

The immediate result of the Washington conference was a general feeling of relief by all parties in the Pacific. Minister Admiral Kato came home to say that war with the United States was not inevitable, and would, on the contrary, be suicidal for Japan, given America's industrial potential. His advisors agreed with him, but Admiral Kanji Kato did not.

Minister Admiral Tomasaburo Kato died in 1923, but the argument over the direction of Japan's navy continued within the naval establishment, with admirals Sakonji and Yonai leading "the treaty faction" and Admiral Kanji Kato leading "the fleet faction."[6]

The year 1924 was fateful in Japanese modern history. All the original oligarchs of the *Genro* had died off, Field Marshal Prince Yamagata, the last, in 1922. Prince Saionji, a transitional figure, was the only one left with connections to the Meiji years, and he favored political party control of the government rather than oligarchy. So the old was dead and the new rung in. In elections that year the political parties won the vast majority of Diet seats, and Kenseikai was the leading party. Thus President Komei Kato of the Kenseikai party became prime minister. Representative democracy seemed to have triumphed in Japan. The next year universal male suffrage was enacted. But even as the forces of democratization surged forward, so did one force of tyranny: the growth of the radical parties (Communist and Socialist) in Japan had brought about violent clashes and even street fighting that worried the authorities. Prime Minister Kato then backed a new Peace Preservation Law, which gave almost unlimited power to the police to deal with "dangerous thought." Just to join a society or party that advocated changing the constitution could cost a person ten years' imprisonment. Thus the new "people's era" brought no more freedom but paved the way to restrict freedom even more than in the past.[7]

For example, Professor Sakuzo Yoshino wrote an article criticizing the military for trying to influence political decisions. He was branded as a "radical," and in order to save his neck he resigned his post at Tokyo Imperial University and moved into obscurity.[8]

There was no question about the truth of Yoshino's charges. The army was growing restless and more political every year. In 1923 and 1924 the Japanese army was reorganized. The withdrawal from Siberia and the cuts in defense budgets enacted by the Diet made it necessary to reduce the army from twenty-one to seventeen divisions. The officer corps was not reduced, however. For even when the cuts were made, the army secured a quid pro quo: compulsory military training was introduced at the middle school level and carried on through university. Thus the officers of the disbanded divisions were assigned to teaching. This move gave the military a foothold in the schools.[9]

The old samurai generals were going fast. The new leaders of the army who came from the farms and the small towns were professionals. What was good for the army, from their point of view, was necessary for the country. They were frugal, patriotic, and intensely loyal to the Imperial Way. The Meiji Rescript to Soldiers and Sailors was a bible to them.

In the 1920s the elements of control in the Imperial Army were:

1. The Supreme Military Council (*Gunji Sangi In*), which consisted of the senior field marshals and admirals. Their deliberations could deal with any sort of issues that in any way affected defense.

   It was convened at the call of the emperor.
2. a. The minister of war.
   b. The chief of the Imperial Army General Staff. He directed the employment of the army units.
   c. The inspector general of military training. He was responsible for the readiness of the army.

These three men were considered to be all on a par as far as authority was concerned, for all had access to the throne.[10]

Two rising stars in the army were General Kazushige Ugaki, son of a samurai from a lesser fief, and General Sadao Araki, the son of a Buddhist priest. Each was developing his own faction within the army.

Ugaki was following the conservative way, a level below that old Choshu aristocracy of the military services. Sadao Araki belonged to the new class of military men, those who had come up from poverty.

In the early 1920s, a number of cliques were forming within the Japanese army and attracting groups of younger officers. In October 1921, majors Nagata, Kobatake, and Okamura, all classmates from the Japanese military academy in Tokyo, all students in Europe, met in Baden Baden, Germany, to make a secret agreement. They vowed to reorganize the Japanese army and purge the old Choshu, or aristocratic, elements. They formed the Double Leaf Society, which was the first of the young officers' groups. The next year, General Taro Utsonomiya, an ultranationalist leader of the army, summoned to his deathbed his most valued follower, Sadao Araki, who was then a colonel. The dying general ordered his aide to mark out with a red pencil on the map of Asia the longitudes of the area that Japan must conquer in the future: Siberia, China, India, Southeast Asia, Indonesia, Australia, and New Zealand. Araki gave his promise, and the general died happy.[11]

The Araki faction came to be known as *kodo ha*—action group. Here, from an analysis made by a Japanese is what they stood for:

One hundred per cent soldier. Hardboiled sort yet warm-hearted. Ready to sacrifice rules for personal sympathy. The cause of the Emperor is higher than the law of the land. Must make extreme sacrifices today to achieve the "direct rule of the Emperor." Very strongly believes in divine origin of the Imperial House, and "manifest destiny." Bitter foe of communism. In private association, hail fellow well met; general associating with private. Battle field commanders; no peace time men. Death in battle the highest honor that can befall a Japanese. Consider politicians no better than so many "frogs in the well" (narrow-viewed persons). Believes argument useless. "I will knock him down" type. No compromise. White or black. No

grey. In organization like a steam roller. Very restless.
Unhappy in sustained peace. National socialistic in their
thinking but confused. Not logical. Two and two do not
make four.[12]

The army opposite number, generally the followers of General
Ugaki, were the *tosei ha*—control group. Here is the analysis of their
character:

Law abiding. Not so pious. Outward observance of national
policy but not fanatical. War minister type rather than
battle commanders. Capable administrators, diplomats, suave
in manner. Businesslike, possessing relatively clear ideas
of figures. Realistic. Watch their step. Lay stress on merit
rather than personal sympathy. Respect "status quo." Believe in evolution rather than revolution. Pay due consideration to the present happiness of an individual. Individual
just as important as the state. The present life as important
as the future. Common sense sort. Pay due consideration
to private property. Believe in wisdom of cooperating with
capitalists and politicians. Consider international cooperation important. Two and two make four.[13]

In these years, however, the army was anything but popular.
The public resented the enormous military expenditures of the past,
and army officers took to changing to civilian clothing when they
left their bases, so they would not get involved in arguments.

The navy did not suffer quite as much, since its leaders had
shown more respect for the public purse in the Washington disarmament treaties. But in 1925 Admiral Kanji Kato became vice chief
of the Naval General Staff. He and his assistant, Admiral Nobumasa
Suetsugu, began organizing the young naval officers behind the "fleet"
concept of a strong and aggressive Japanese naval power. Their ploy
was to attack Britain and the United States as untrustworthy, and
America, in particular, as racist and anti-Japanese. For that reason,
they said, Japan had to grow much stronger on the sea.

The civilian governments of the 1920s infuriated the army and
the navy time after time. In 1924 the Minseito party held the strings
in the Diet, but the cabinet was known as "The Mitsubishi Cabinet,"
because four members were closely connected with the Iwasaki fam-

ilies, which ran Mitsubishi enterprises. Similarly in this period, it was common knowledge that the Mitsuis had the Seiyukai political party in their pocket.

A general or an admiral earned 550 yen per month, which was then about $125. Rumors of payoff and wild entertainments (a costly geisha charged 50 yen for an evening) made the military men seethe against the crooked politicians.[14]

On December 25, 1926, a wrenching change came to Japan. Emperor Taisho died. As a leader of the country, Taisho had been nothing, and, the people were sure, more than a little bit crazy to boot. They told the story of the day he opened the Diet with the annual Imperial Address and then rolled up his Imperial Rescript like a telescope and peered through it at the Dietmen. That story made the rounds of the teahouses to general guffawing. And yet, the Imperial Presence was not to be laughed at in Japan. The three Sacred Treasures, the Sword, the Jewels, and the Mirror represented two thousand years of Yamato, and the Emperor was a God.[15]

There was, even in this serious moment of transition between eras, however, a sign of the clash between tradition and reality. When it was apparent in December that Emperor Taisho was not long for this world below, newspaper reporters had besieged the Imperial Household to try to get a "scoop" on the name of the new era. *Mainichi Shimbun* had discovered that the secret commission appointed to choose the name for the era had chosen *Kobun*—"light and literary attainment"—and the new emperor, Hirohito, approved. The newspaper so reported on the day of Taisho's death. But next day, when the official notice was handed out, the name was *Showa*—Enlightenment and Peace. Thirty years later the facts came out: the name chosen actually had been *Kobun,* but when *Mainichi* revealed it, the Privy Council had made a quick change. Such important matters as the choice of a new era's title were not to be subject to journalistic acrobatics. The president of *Mainichi* resigned, and so did the executive editor.[16]

Immediately, Crown Prince Hirohito ascended to the throne. Actually, in the indisposition of his father, Hirohito had been prince regent for the past four years. *Sho* and *wa,* meaning enlightenment and peace, were ideographs that did, indeed, represent Hirohito's character. His greatest admiration was reserved for the British crown, and after a trip to England he had determined that when he came to the throne he would reign as a constitutional monarch, not rule behind the *Genro* as had his grandfather and father.

The sense of well-being and peace deserted Japan in 1927 when a financial panic was followed by severe economic depression. The Japanese slump was then followed by the international collapse of 1929 and the subsequent world depression. One of the most severe trials to the Japanese was the death of the raw silk market in America and Europe. Silkworm culture was the province of most farm wives in Japan, and sale of silk meant the difference in the best of times between subsistence and a little luxury. In the late 1920s hardship hit the farmers of Japan. University graduates, coming out of their own cocoons, found that only a fifth of them could get jobs. The others roamed the streets and in bitter desperation began joining radical political groups. The police began staging raids on radical organizations and jailed thousands of dissenters.

As the country wallowed in depression, the soldiers and the sailors learned of the plights of their families and grew ever angrier. Among the military men, the civilian government of Japan was thoroughly discredited, and the "democracy" spoken of so glowingly after the defeat of Germany had now become little more than a dirty word. The solution to Japan's woes, said the generals of the *kodo ha,* was to take over Manchuria. This fabulous grain bowl, with its water power and coal and iron ores, was the colony that would solve all Japan's economic woes and provide the base for expansion into Mongolia and China.

In 1927 General Giichi Tanaka became prime minister of Japan. He was president of the Seiyukai party, but his principal advisor on foreign affairs was Kaku Mori, a civilian, the real power of the party. General Tanaka now came out openly with a policy designed to take over Manchuria. He made a trip to Mukden, to meet with all the officials of the various Japanese enterprises in Manchuria and Mongolia. A report that purported to be an account of this meeting was later published by a Shanghai newspaper, but the Japanese denied it.[17]

It *was* real. Tanaka announced an eight-point program, two of the points concealed from the public. One of these said that Japan would support any regime in Manchuria that would guarantee Japan's special economic and military positions there. The other said that if any problems arose in Manchuria or Mongolia that affected Japanese interests, Japan would act.

Noyuboshi Muto, a moderate general who attended the meeting, asked Prime Minister Tanaka if he was sure of what he was saying:

> Muto: If this program is carried out, it is bound to precipitate war between Japan and the United States. Are you prepared to risk a war with the United States, or even a World War?
>
> Tanaka: I am determined to cope with whatever consequences this policy may bring.
>
> Muto: Are you sure that your determination will not falter?
>
> Tanaka: I will not falter.
>
> Muto: Since the government has the determination, we will obey orders and say nothing.[18]

1927. Mukden. The army knew precisely where it was going. The only question was, when?

嘘も方便

7. "A little lie doesn't hurt"

Now came the first overt acts of the supernationalists who were determined to colonize Manchuria and other parts of China. There could be no question by this time that the Tanaka memorial was real. It was just too good a copy of what Prime Minister Tanaka had said and what the supernationalists had been saying for months to be otherwise. Japan was preparing to surge forward on her drive for empire. The stage was set and the characters knew their roles.

Kaku Mori was the éminence grise of Japan. His official title was only Parliamentary Vice Minister of Foreign Affairs, which previously had been of very little importance. But Mori was the power of the ruling Seiyukai party and he controlled General Tanaka. When Mori assumed his insignificant office he called the foreign ministry's officials together and announced that he intended to "get tough with China." How could that be, when Prime Minister General Tanaka was in charge? For one thing, Mori had connections with many supernationalists who wanted Manchuria. These included General Tei-ichi Suzuki, the prime minister's right-hand man, and Yosuke Matsuoka, then an official of the South Manchurian railway. Many of the *zaibatsu* were taking an interest in exploitation of Manchuria in the middle 1920s, too. Mori, the power of the Seiyukai, was in touch with all these people, and with the leaders of the Kwantung Army, and was conducting machinations to take over Manchuria. In the spring of 1927 Mori had forced General Tanaka to send troops of the Kwantung Army to Shantung Province, "to protect Japanese life and property." Tanaka had objected.

"If Tanaka will not assent to sending the expeditionary force," said Kaku Mori, "I'll make him resign from the presidency of the Seiyukai."[1]

So Tanaka sent the troops. Kaku Mori, from his seat of obscurity, was, in effect, running not only the Ministry of Foreign Affairs but also the government.

General Tanaka was trying to negotiate with Marshal Chang Tso-lin, the warlord of Manchuria, for further Japanese control of railroads and enterprises. The marshal was, however, bemused by his own problems, chief of which was the steady march northward of Chiang Kai-shek's expeditionary force, which aimed to unite China under the Nationalist flag. The marshal, along with several other warlords of the north and west, was going to have to join up or fight.

Prime Minister General Tanaka had seen the trend—that Chiang was sweeping the warlords away. He was really interested in maintaining the marshal as ally and instrument in Manchuria, and he sent emissaries to Peking, where the old marshal lived, to persuade him to give up the ancient northern capital of China and retreat to Mukden, in the hope that Chiang would be satisfied to conquer north China and would not move beyond the Great Wall.

Marshal Chang refused to retreat.

Negotiations and machinations continued. In the spring of 1928 Chiang Kai-shek's expeditionary force moved up into Shantung Province, augmented by the armies of warlords Feng Yu-hsiang and Yen Hsi-shan, who had joined up. Some 19,000 Japanese were still living in Tsingtao, along the railroad and in Tsinan.

Major Takashu Sakai, the Japanese military attaché at Tsinan, cabled Tokyo demanding troops be sent to protect the Japanese citizens. The war ministry in Tokyo had reservations, and so did General Tanaka. Generalissimo Chiang Kai-shek had visited Tokyo that previous winter and had assured the Japanese that he was breaking off his relations with the Communists and the Soviets, who had been supporting his revolution but who had now become troublesome. General Tanaka believed that and did not see that there was any immediate danger.[2]

But Mori insisted, and so once more troops were dispatched to China, 5000 soldiers of the Kwantung Army. They were supposed to remain in Tsingtao, but Japanese military attaché Sakai informed Colonel Fukuda, commander of the force, that hundreds of Japanese had been killed in Tsinan. The real figure was thirteen Japanese, but

Major Sakai did not mind a little lie. Colonel Fukuda put his troops on the Tsingtao-Tsinan railroad and brought them inland. On the morning of May 3 the Japanese consul, Koichi Nishida, called on Generalissimo Chiang at his headquarters and praised the conduct of the Chinese troops. Ten minutes after the Japanese left, Chiang heard machine gun fire. The Japanese were attacking the Chinese troops. Chiang ordered his troops to cease fire and demanded the same of the Japanese authorities. The Japanese called for a meeting. Chiang set the meeting for the office of his commissioner for foreign affairs, Tsai Kung-shih. The minister of foreign affairs, Huang Fu, was also there at the time.[3]

Later in the day, Foreign Minister Huang Fu returned to Chiang's headquarters. Here is his story:

When Chiang had heard those machine guns firing, so had the people at the office of the commissioner for foreign affairs. Soon they discovered the office was surrounded by Japanese troops. Foreign Minister Huang went into the courtyard and identified himself to a Japanese officer and asked what was happening. The officer invited him to accompany him to Japanese headquarters. Huang went. He was escorted to a small room with a chair and table and left there. After some time another Japanese officer came in and demanded that Huang sign a statement they had prepared. It said that the clash between Chinese and Japanese troops had occurred because the Japanese caught the Chinese looting. Huang refused to sign.

The Japanese officer drew his pistol, placed the muzzle against Minister Huang's head and told him that if he wanted to live, he would sign.

Huang reprimanded the officer for insolence.

The Japanese became red-faced and abusive, but he did not shoot. Finally, Huang agreed only to sign that he had read the charges. The Japanese let him go.

Huang went back to the office of the commissioner for foreign affairs. The Japanese delegation came and demanded that the Tsingtao-Tsinan railroad not be used to move Chinese troops. The Chinese forces must withdraw twenty miles outside Tsinan. The Chinese delegate then said they could only report to Generalissimo Chiang, they could not act. So they went back to Chiang's headquarters. When they told their story, Chiang realized that the Japanese were trying to create an incident that would bring an opportunity to the Kwantung Army to attack Chiang. That night he moved his troops out of Tsinan. The next day, the Japanese attacked the city and bombed it. Thirteen thousand Chinese were killed.[4]

Major Sakai and his friends were furious that Chiang Kai-shek had escaped the trap. They captured Tsai Kung-shih, Chiang's commissioner for foreign affairs in Tsinan, bound him, took him to Japanese headquarters and "tried him." He was ordered to kneel and would not. To frighten him, they brought in a dozen Chinese, whom they charged with looting and shot to death on the spot. Tsai still would not kneel. They broke his legs with rifle butts. He collapsed but continued to shout his defiance. They tore out his tongue, and then they shot him.[5]

These were the young officers of the Kwantung Army. No Japanese record was ever made of these proceedings, and Prime Minister Tanaka knew nothing of what had happened in Tsinan. But a Chinese had been hiding in the closet while the Japanese were torturing Tsai. When they left for the night, he sneaked out and made his way to the Chinese camp. Chiang Kai-shek, who just a few months earlier had been assured of the benevolence of the Japanese government toward his revolution, now knew the truth. He would not be gulled again.

Chiang then swung his force around to the west, and then pushed north.

Prime Minister Tanaka did not know what had happened in Tsinan, but in a cabinet meeting he was persuaded to issue a warning to the old marshal and to Chiang. If Chiang came up into Manchuria after warlord Chang Tso-lin, the Japanese would "take appropriate action."[6]

This warning was given Marshal Chang on May 18. The Japanese wanted him to retreat from Peking to Mukden. The old marshal said he would rather die than see Peking in the hands of his enemy, Feng Yu-hsiang.

The Kwantung Army, primed by Mori and his friends, and the priming reinforced by General Tanaka, now decided that what was wanted was a show of force. General Chotaro Muraoka, the new commander of the Kwantung Army, moved the headquarters from Port Arthur, the terminus of the South Manchurian Railway, up to Mukden, the main city and rail center.

From the American embassy in Nanking, and from the American consulates at Harbin and Shanghai, the Americans had been watching with concern the movement of Japanese military forces in Manchuria and China proper.

With the feeling that Japan was preparing to act, Secretary of State Frank B. Kellogg called Japanese Ambassador Matsumoto to the State Department and warned him officially that in the United States view Manchuria belonged to China, and any attempt by Japan to seize Manchuria would be regarded by the United States as a most serious matter. At this point, said the Secretary of State, the United States wanted to know Japan's intentions regarding Manchuria. The ambassador cabled the message to Tokyo, where it electrified the foreign office and was transmitted immediately to Prime Minister Tanaka.[7]

Prime Minister General Tanaka now had to recall his word to General Muto at the Mukden conference:

The question was about Point 8, which said that should "chaos" arise in Manchuria and Mongolia, thereby endangering Japan's special interests, Japan would take action.

"Are you sure your determination will not falter?" General Muto had asked.

"I will not falter," said Tanaka.[8]

And so Muto had said no more except that he would obey orders. Now, Muto was no longer in command. The new leader had the same orders, however.

On May 20 the Imperial General Staff at Tokyo prepared secret mobilization orders. Three Japanese columns would converge on Mukden. Other Japanese troops would move to Chichow, Ichou, Shanhaikwan, and Chao Yang-chen, Hsinmintun, and Hsinchiatun. Marshal Chang Tso-lin would be disarmed and the Kwantung Army would take over.

The general staff and the Kwantung Army agreed that the imperial order authorizing the mobilization would take effect on May 22.

Now the crisis had arrived. What was to be done in view of Washington's warning?

From Washington Ambassador Matsumoto cabled that the U.S. State Department had warned Japan officially that Manchuria belonged to China. Other than an outright threat to use military force against Japan if she acted in Manchuria, the message could not have been more clear.

Kaku Mori called a meeting to discuss the American reaction, and from the chair insisted that Japan must plunge forward to follow the plan made at the Mukden conference. Some of the military men urged caution. Others urged Mori on. General Araki asked why all the delay, since the government had already made and announced its plans?

Mori said yes. Go ahead. The navy said no, stop. Prime Minister General Tanaka wavered.[9]

From Mukden came queries from the Kwantung Army. What were the orders? At Mukden on May 21 Major General Tsune Saito, chief of staff of the army, advised his commanders that the orders would come at any hour. They waited. No orders. The unit commanders, ready to act, were growing restless and critical of Tokyo.

On May 22, General Muraoka came up from Port Arthur and waited. No orders. At midnight came the word that the move had been postponed.

On May 23, Colonel Kanichiro Tashiro arrived from Tokyo with the news that the cabinet had changed its mind. Chang Tso-lin would be allowed to remain in power.

General Muraoka sent a telegram of protest to the war ministry.[10]

On May 25 Kaku Mori said the cabinet must carry out the plan to take over Manchuria. He sent envoys to Prime Minister Tanaka, who was at his country house in Kamakura. Tanaka said no. There would be no occupation of Manchuria.

The envoys went back to Tokyo and told Kaku Mori. He was indignant. So were many of the officers in Imperial Army Headquarters, and so were the officers of the Kwantung Army, but General Tanaka had ultimately decided not to risk war with the United States, for that was the issue at hand.[11]

Here Kaku Mori and General Tanaka parted company. Tanaka would soon lose the support of the Seiyukai party. But more important, having been encouraged by the highest officials in the land to "think Manchuria," the officers of the Kwantung Army felt let down and morose, when the coded cable of rejection arrived. Here was the recollection of one officer:

"Colonel Komoto clutched the telegram in his hand and bit his lip. . . . General Muraoka and Chief of Staff Saito hardly spoke the rest of the day . . . Colonel Seishiro Itagaki and Lieutenant Colonel Kanji Ishihara were silent. . . ."[12]

The officers of the Kwantung Army now had a new worry. There were about 12,000 Japanese soldiers in and around Mukden. Chang Tso-lin's troops had begun the retreat towards that city, and they were concerned about being outnumbered. Colonel Daisaku Komoto decided to go to Tokyo and see what could be done. He revealed his plans to Itagaki and Ishihara, and they encouraged him to go. But General Muraoka said no.[13]

On June 3 the Nationalist column neared Peking and prepared to take command of that old northern capital city. Chang Tso-lin began to retreat northeast toward Mukden.

General Muraoka decided to take matters into his own hands. He ordered Lieutenant Colonel Yoshiharu Takeshita to go to Peking and find an assassin who would kill Chang Tso-lin. Colonel Komoto got wind of the plot and told Takeshita that was the wrong thing to do. The onus would be on Japan if he did it. So he took over the assignment, and sent Takeshita to Peking to identify the train on which the marshal would be riding.

Komoto then sent Lieutenant Yasunosuke Kanda to find a place for action. Kanda reported that the best place was at Huangkutan, where the tracks of the South Manchurian Railway passed over those of the Peking-Mukden Railway. The only guards were a handful of Japanese railroad guards. A Major Tomiya, head of the railroad guards in that area, became aware of the activity and was enlisted in the plot. The details were turned over to him, and Komoto provided the money.[14]

Enlisted men from the engineer corps brought explosives to the overpass. A demolition expert installed the detonator. Komoto engaged three dissident Manchurians to lurk near the crossing. If the train was derailed, but Chang Tso-lin still lived, they were to rush into his car and kill him. Nothing was to be left to chance.

The marshal's train left Peking at 1:15 A.M. on June 4. At 5:20 A.M. the train crossed the tracks at Huangkutan. In the marshal's car a mah jong game had just ended, and the marshal was still sitting at the mah jong table when his car blew up. He was struck in the nose by a fragment of steel and fell unconscious under the table. He was taken out of the train and to a Mukden hospital, where he died.[15]

The three Manchurians who had been ordered to stand by were regarded by the plotters as too dangerous to let live. They were to be killed immediately. Here is what happened next:

"Immediately after the incident," said the official Kwantung Army announcement of the tragedy, "our garrison troops spotted three suspicious looking Chinese attempting to clamber up the embankment of the South Manchurian Railway. Our troops at once approached and questioned them. Whereupon, the Chinese attempted to hurl a bomb at our troops. Our men promptly stabbed and killed two of them. The third man fled."[16]

When that report reached Tokyo it had been amplified. The three Chinese had two bombs and three letters addressed to Chinese revolutionaries.

It was true, the third man did escape. He made his way to the headquarters of Chang Hsueh-liang, the old marshal's son and heir, and told the true story of the Japanese plot.[17]

The colonels had even greater plans. They hoped that the Kwantung Army would mobilize and take control of Manchuria. But General Saito said this was impossible. The colonels then set up a reign of terror, bombing the homes of Japanese residents of Mukden and meeting houses. They then called the Japanese consulate to ask if the consul really felt the local police force could protect Japanese residents. But the consul was too smart; he knew what was happening and refused to take the bait. He refused to accept the army's offer to mobilize.

Meanwhile, General Tanaka back in Tokyo was appalled at the insubordination of the Kwantung Army, but in no position to do anything about it because so many officers in Tokyo were sympathetic, and Tanaka had now lost the support of Kaku Mori.

Chang Hsueh-liang was accepted by the Japanese as the new marshal of Southeastern Manchuria. But the Japanese in Manchuria were now split into several factions: the Kwantung Army, the South Manchurian Railway, and the Okura *zaibatsu* interests. Yosuke Matsuoka was vice president of the South Manchurian Railway and he announced his contempt for Kaku Mori.

The war ministry announcement about the Chinese plot did not convince many people in Tokyo or anywhere else. The opposition Minseito party began to raise a fuss in the Diet. With Emperor Hirohito's coronation near, many politicians thought it a terrible time to raise trouble and agreed that the matter should be hushed up.

In the summer General Tanaka heard that the Kwantung Army had murdered Chang Tso-lin, and he sent an investigator to Mukden. In the fall the prime minister learned that the death of Chang Tso-lin was without doubt the result of a plot by the Kwantung Army colonels. Tanaka's faith in the Kwantung Army then was destroyed, and he moved all negotiations with the Chinese relative to Manchuria to Nanking to keep them out of the reach of Kwantung Army influence.

As the news seeped through Tokyo men around the Imperial Throne expressed dismay and demanded that the offenders be punished. Prince Saionji told Tanaka he must inform the emperor. But the leaders of the Seiyukai party insisted that Tanaka be quiet for if the guilty were punished, Japan would stand accused in the eyes of the world. Still Prince Saionji persisted, and finally Tanaka did go to the emperor and named Colonel Komoto as the leader of the plot. Emperor Hirohito said that the guilty must be punished. Tanaka promised.

Then, however, the army objected, and so did Tanaka's own cabinet. He temporized and announced punishment by "administrative action." General Muraoka and Colonel Komoto were involuntarily retired for failing to guard the route of the old marshal. That was all. The army said the incident was closed. There was no evidence of any army participation in the plot, the generals lied.[18]

When Tanaka took this information to the emperor, Hirohito accused his prime minister of contradicting himself. Tanaka said he would explain. The emperor looked at him coldly.

"No need to explain. Just leave your report as you go out."

Tanaka walked out of the audience room sweating. He asked Grand Chamberlain Kantaro Suzuki for another audience. The emperor refused it. The next day Tanaka told his cabinet that it was time to resign. On July 1, 1928, the Tanaka cabinet resigned in disgrace. The emperor commanded Osachi Hamaguchi, of the Minseito, to form a new cabinet.[19]

The affair was a triumph for Hirohito. He had acted in the tradition of his grandfather, ruling, forcing the resignation of a prime minister who had lied to him. General Tanaka's disgrace was greater than that of any leader of modern times. His spirit was broken and not long afterward he died.

But Tanaka's disgrace was as nothing to what the incident had done to Japan: the colonels of the Kwantung Army had defied the Japanese government and the emperor and had gotten away with it. The first long step in the campaign of the *kodo ha,* the activist faction, had been taken, and the young officers saw how easy it had been. They were now ready for the next move.

油断大敵

8. "Negligence is a powerful enemy"

*I*n Tokyo after 1928 the struggle between the advocates of parliamentary government and peaceful change and the expansionists bent on conquest held the center of the political arena. The only member of the old oligarchy was Prince Saionji, who was committed to peace and civilian government through the Diet. But the Tanaka government of 1927–29 had shown the new danger that threatened Japan—the *kodo ha* members.

At this time, the *zaibatsu* families were taking a new interest in politics, with the Mitsuis backing the Kenseikai and the Mitsubishis supporting the Minseito. Tanaka was replaced by the emperor, in July 1929, as prime minister by Osachi Hamaguchi, president of the opposition Minseito party. The program of the government called for retrenchment of expenditures, reforms that would increase the power of the civilian government, and a friendly policy toward China. It was a positive effort to improve Japan's economic and political stability, and it might have succeeded if the world's economy had remained prosperous and stable as it seemed to be in the summer of 1929. In national elections the voting public showed confidence in the Minseito party by giving it an absolute majority in the House of Representatives. But then came the collapse of the American and British stock markets, and an international depression that hit Japan's foreign trade very hard.

Silk prices fell by 50 percent. Exports dropped 27 percent.

In the autumn of 1930 as the cold economic winds were gathering, Japan was called to attend a new naval armament conference in London, and Prime Minister Hamaguchi agreed to send a delegation if Japan was not going to be asked to weaken herself below the point of adequate self-defense.

Some naval officers were contemptuous of the Western attempt to cut armaments further. Admiral Kanji Kato dismissed the invitation to him to be a delegate to the new conference by saying it was his duty to fight wars, not prevent them.[1]

Minister of the Navy Admiral Takeishi Takarabe did attend, however, along with the politician Reiijiro Wakatsuki, who was chief of the delegation. For six weeks the conferees sparred without getting anywhere. The Japanese were holding out for an increase to 70 percent of the strengths of the American and British fleets.

At London the Americans and British held out for the same old ratio and would not budge. They also wanted a six-year moritorium by all powers on the building of battleships.

The Japanese delegation was primed to demand an increase from three-fifths to seven-tenths of the American and British naval strengths, with no limitation on submarines. This demand represented a compromise within the navy, where the "fleet faction" and "treaty faction" were still arguing basic Japanese naval strategy. Admiral Teikichi Hori, the chief of the Naval Affairs Bureau, was a "treaty" man. So were Admiral Mitsumasa Yonai, Admiral Shigeyoshi Inoue, and a rising captain, Isoroku Yamamoto. They held that there was no way Japan could win a war against the potential power of the United States and that such a war must be avoided. That view was held in contempt by the "fleet faction," led by Admiral Kato Kanji and Admiral Nobumasa Suetsugu. They continued to boast about Japan's "invincible fleet" and continued to demand that it be strengthened.[2]

In London the delegates struggled with the problem. When it looked most hopeless, the emperor let it be known, through the Keeper of the Privy Seal, that the conference must not fail or Japan would be in trouble.

In the end, the Japanese naval delegation to London could not budge the Americans and British on the ratio. Finally, U.S. Senator David Reed and the Japanese ambassador to London, Tsuneo Matsudaira, were selected to meet privately. Without benefit of naval experts they reached a compromise, and this was initialed by the delegates and sent back to Washington and Tokyo.

Overall, Japan seemed to have gotten nearly what she wanted: 69 percent of the strength of the Americans and British. But the catch was that she could keep only 60 percent of the cruiser force of the Americans and British, and as for submarines, she would have to actually reduce her force by a third to maintain parity with the Americans and British.

Delegate Wakatsuki knew there would be trouble over the draft treaty, but he assured Tokyo that he had secured every possible concession from the British and Americans.

The Japanese foreign office immediately advocated acceptance; its policy was to seek accommodation with the West, as well as with China.

The real trouble came from the growing "fleet faction." Admiral Suetsugu gave the text of the draft treaty to the newspapers, hoping it would rouse such a public storm that the treaty would be abandoned. It did arouse a storm, but the Hamaguchi cabinet stood firm in its approval. Five days later Suetsugu was getting ready to hold a press conference to announce his opinion, when he was restrained by official order. Still, he managed to tell his views "unofficially" to some reporters and these were published. Admiral Kanji Kato, the chief of the Naval General Staff, called on Prime Minister Hamaguchi and complained.

The offended admirals got together and drew up their own proposals. But when they took them to Hamaguchi he told them the London draft treaty would relieve the financial burden on the Japanese people in these depressed times, and that not to sign would be to bring on an arms race which would be enormously expensive and very dangerous.[3]

The admirals finally seemed to accept the draft treaty if the government would use other means, such as the buildup of naval aviation, to strengthen the navy's defenses. This was generally agreeable.

Admiral Kato, relying on that privileged position of *niju seifu*, sent a complaint directly to the emperor. Hirohito did not give him any satisfaction. In the Supreme War Council of army and navy leaders Kato objected to the treaty and clashed with Admiral Takarabe. He said the treaty limited Japan's powers of defense. Also in disagreement were the leaders of the army. The schism between "treaty" and "fleet" men then broke into the open. Admirals Saito,

Okada, Kiyoura, and Yamamoto came out for the treaty. Kato and Suetsugu were backed by a large number of younger officers, who were in touch with the Araki *kodo ha* of the army. The argument had now been made public, and a large segment of the press and public announced objections to the treaty, although *Asahi Shimbun,* Japan's largest paper, backed the government.[4]

In this atmosphere of strain, Prime Minister Hamaguchi sought an audience with the emperor, who approved his efforts to get the treaty through. Hamaguchi came away from the palace with new resolution.

In the summer of 1930, Prime Minister Hamaguchi presented the treaty to the Privy Council for approval. The constitution provided for treaty making by the cabinet, with the approval of the emperor, and Hamaguchi had already sent a private memorial to the emperor. The Privy Council was split; some members suggested that the disapproval of army and navy factions ought to make the treaty a dead issue. But Hamaguchi reminded them that foreign policy was not the province of army and navy.

Miyoji Ito, chairman of the Treaty Examination Committee of the Privy Council, did all he could to sink the treaty. He packed his committee with members who were hostile and ignored the diplomatic community which was for the treaty.

But, backed by the throne, Premier Hamaguchi was obdurate. He let it be known that if the Supreme War Council continued to be obfuscatory, he would intercede with the throne to shake up the membership and secure a council willing to listen to reason.

Prince Saionji backed the treaty. The Grand Chamberlain, Kantaro Suzuki, kept Prince Fushimi from siding with the naval dissidents. Admiral Keisuke Okada, who came from the same prefecture as Admiral Kato, persuaded Kato to tone down his objections. He did, but a few weeks later he resigned.[5]

Reluctantly the Privy Council approved the treaty; this was the high point of civil authority in the Japan of the Meiji Constitution. The conflict stirred up by the debate brought violence. On November 14, while boarding a train on the platform at Tokyo station, Prime Minister Hamaguchi was shot. The assassin was a young man named Tomeo Sagoya, a member of *Aikoku-sha* (Love of Country Association), one of the superpatriotic secret societies that had sprung up in the past few years. Hamaguchi did not then die but was incapacitated for four months and had to turn over his duties to Foreign

Minister Kijuro Shidehara. He came back in March 1931, but resigned in April because of continued physical difficulty following the
shooting. Reiijiro Wakatsuki of Minseito became the new prime
minister.

No one could see at the moment the enormous effect that the
London Naval Conference of 1930 would have on Japan. Actually,
it had not much changed the naval ratios. Under the terms of the
Washington treaties, Japan could not go to war with the United
States. But one difference between 1922 and 1930 was that the
thought of opposing America was stronger in the later year.

The real damage to Japan, however, was probably inevitable,
and it came to a head at this time. The argument between "treaty"
and "fleet" factions of the Imperial Navy ceased to be an argument
any longer; the talking was over; the sides were chosen. From this
point on officers had to decide which clique they would favor.

Also the treaty came at a time when the expansionists in the
Japanese army were becoming extremely worried about the success
of Chiang Kai-shek in pulling China together. Chang Hsueh-liang,
the new warlord of Manchuria, was leaning towards Chiang's national
government, despite every effort of the Japanese to stop him. A few
weeks after the 1928 assassination of the old marshal, Japan had sent
a trained diplomat, Gonsuke Hayashi, to ascertain the young marshal's attitudes. Hayashi reported that Chang Hsueh-liang gave indication of being pliable. He had suggested that he would probably
stop negotiations with Chiang Kai-shek. But later the young marshal
began to show other signs, as one discussion indicated:

> Hayashi: The Nanking government is seething with
> internal dissension, and is also Communist-oriented. Ja-
> pan's rights in Manchuria might be impaired. Therefore it
> would be best to take a wait-and-see attitude. Should you
> disregard Japan's warning we are resolved to exercise free-
> dom of action. We hope you will therefore try to suppress
> undesirable elements. Japan will give you every help you
> may need.
>
> Chang: Being Chinese, I must proceed from the
> Chinese viewpoint. The only reason for my desire to co-
> operate with the Nanking government is that I want to
> see a unified China. Although I am willing to consider

Japan's advice, nevertheless ultimately my course will depend on the will of the people of Manchuria. I do not understand why time and again Japan has threatened me so severely.

Hayashi: Japan has already decided that even if she has to interfere in China's affairs she will do so. I hope you will soon make your decision.

Chang: My decision is that I must abide by the will of the people of Manchuria.[6]

In fact, Chang Hsueh-liang was warned, and he delayed his decisions. He also began concealing his ideas from the Japanese.

In the south, Chiang Kai-shek had also learned his lesson about the Japanese from the Tsinan incident. The winter before, in Tokyo, General Tanaka had assured Chiang that if he threw the Communists out of his government and banished the Russians he could count on Japanese support. Tsinan had shown him what Japanese promises meant. The Japanese had added insult to injury by insisting on keeping their troops in Tsinan pending settlement of all issues, especially Manchuria. The Chinese had responded with a boycott of Japanese goods that cost Japan millions of yen in trade losses.

At the end of December 1928, Chang Hsueh-liang announced that the three provinces of Manchuria would adhere to the Chinese Nationalist government. After that, the signs went from bad to worse for the Japanese. They had secured from the old marshal, just before his murder, the right to build new railroads in Manchuria. But the young marshal now said that would be up to the Nanking government.

Such talk did not please the Kwantung Army or the expansionists of the army *kodo ha* in Tokyo. Two quite separate elements were involved within the military: Japan's overall defense pattern and the future of Manchuria.

Following the Tsinan incidents of 1927 and 1928 and the murder of Chang Tso-lin, the failure of the government to punish the offenders as they ought to have been punished showed a weakness in the government. Although Prime Minister Tanaka was a general himself, he had proved unable to control the army in time of crisis. The young militants in the Japanese army became ever bolder. General Araki was commandant of the Army War College in 1928, and his teaching followed the general strategic line first laid down by General Yamagata and Admiral Togo in 1907: the three potential enemies of Japan were the United States, the USSR, and China. In the years that followed those two leaders, the general strategic picture had changed from time to time; one potential enemy would be at the top, and then another. But the Japanese strategy was unchanged. For war with the USSR, Japan must be prepared to destroy enemy ground forces in a campaign in Manchuria, Siberia, and Sakhalin. Against the United States, the Japanese navy would have to command the western Pacific. In case of war with China, Japan would occupy key areas in the north and central areas of China. But only one of these wars would be fought at a time.

In 1918 the United States had gone to the top of the list of enemies—and stayed there. Additions to the war plan included the capture of Guam and the Philippines, and the Hiroshima infantry division was trained for occupation of the Philippines.[7]

But the army's principal interests lay in China and Manchuria, a fact that caused the young officers to begin dreaming of the day that positive action would follow the failed plan of General Muraoka and Colonel Komoto. Various staff officers began making "studies," which were passed around among the young officers: Colonel Kanji Ishihara's "Plan for Acquiring Manchuria and Mongolia" was one of the best read. A plan for a "Showa Reformation," which would take government out of the hands of the politicians, was also very popular reading. This agitation had its equivalent among the civilians in Manchuria; the Manchuria Youth League demanded the establishment of a Manchuria-Mongolia state.[8]

Led by such senior officers as General Araki, the young officers were encouraged to unify their various secret societies and act in unison. And in 1929 a conspiracy to use the army to seize Manchuria was set in motion by a gang of "young" officers, most of them lieutenant colonels or colonels, between thirty-five and forty-five years old.

After Colonel Kanji Ishihara had begun his "study" of the manner of wrenching Manchuria away from China, in the summer of 1929 China and the USSR fell into disagreement on many issues, and one result was a quarrel about the Chinese Eastern Railway. The USSR ended up breaking diplomatic relations with Chiang's government over this matter.

This struggle encouraged the Japanese officers to believe that the time was near. Colonel Ishihara went to Harbin to ascertain the possibility of military operations there. He went to the south to study the military situation at Chinchow. Finally, he made a third trip to Manchuria, and the plot for the Mukden incident was complete.

Ishihara and the other conspirators knew that any Japanese attempt to annex Manchuria would run counter to the League of Nations and to prevailing sentiment in the Western world. It could not be chanced, because of the internal political storm it would create in Tokyo. An "incident" had to be manufactured. Some "atrocity" had to be "perpetrated" by the Chinese, to enable the Japanese to react immediately and with great force.

The incident must be planned so carefully that world opinion would be divided; this was not as difficult as it seemed, for the Japanese army men had observed the great truth: there are always people in the Western countries who are eager to believe the worst of their own government and the best of any other. Given half a chance, an incident in Manchuria could be made to glorify Japan and heap obloquy on the Chinese. More planning had to be done for that.

The plotting began in 1929, as the officers of the Kwantung Army saw that Chang Hsueh-liang was not going to be readily controllable by the army. Then, after the London Naval Treaty of 1930 showed the strength of the emperor and the feelings of the men around him, the army plotters extended their plans. They would also seize political power in Japan and eliminate all the people around the emperor who might stand in the way of the army's ambitions in Manchuria and China. By isolating the emperor they could control the throne as they wished; it had been done before; the example of the shoguns stood before them.

Altogether twenty-four officers were directly involved in the Manchurian conspiracy, ranging from Lieutenant General Shigeru Honjo, commander of the Kwantung Army, and Major General Kuniyaki Koiso, chief of the Military Affairs Bureau of the war ministry, and Major General Yoshitsugu Tatekawa, of the Japanese general staff, down to First Lieutenant Suemori Kawamoto, a minor regimental officer of the Kwantung Army. The lieutenant would plant the explosives that would start the chain reaction, and all else would be done by various officers assigned, up to the legitimization of the incident by General Honjo.

Lieutenant Colonel Ishihara was the planner. Colonel Seishiro Itagaki would actually supervise the operations.[9]

While Colonel Ishihara traveled and plotted, and while Colonel Itagaki assembled his trusted conspirators, similar thinking was going on in Japan among other groups. Among the supernationalists was Ikki Kita, a philosopher of sorts, who wanted state socialism for Japan and planned it all out in a program that called for army and an awakened citizen corps to rebel against the government. The organization was *Yuzonsha,* the Society to Preserve the National Essence. The chosen instrument was General Ugaki. This group functioned at the same time as Shumei Okawa's society, an offshoot of which was led by General Araki within the army.

The army organization was the Cherry Blossom Society. It included a number of highly placed lieutenant colonels and majors. In fact, membership was restricted to officers below the rank of colonel, "who seek the reform of their country without any ulterior selfish motive."[10]

By the winter of 1931 the Cherry Blossom Society had only about a hundred members, but their posts were in such places as the Ministry of War, the Imperial General Staff, and the Tokyo Garrison Headquarters.

Their plan, put together in January, called for coordination with Shumei Okawa's group, to gather 10,000 people in Hibiya Park near the Imperial Palace on March 20, 1931, and organize a demonstration that would deteriorate into a riot.

Because of the riot, the conspiring higher army officers would call out the First Division of the army, but its real function was to seize the Diet, not far away from the park, and cut off all communication with the outside world.

Next, the general officers who were secret supporters of the Cherry Blossom Society would reorganize the army. Three generals would break into the Diet and announce the army's nonconfidence in the cabinet and demand its resignation immediately. Other officers would call on Prince Saionji and Prince Kanin to recommend the immediate appointment of General Ugaki as prime minister.[11]

General Ugaki seems to have listened to those who approached him on the subject with only half an ear, for when he learned the extent of the plot and the utilization of the army to overthrow the elected government, he balked. No, he said. No. And so the March incident never came off.

It was not a joke, however, nor a half-hearted effort. The young officers had planned three incidents, and they had not known which to try first. The March incident failed, and it was decided that the country was not ready for government overthrow just yet. The priority was placed on the Manchurian incident.

During the late spring and early summer Major Isamu Cho circulated a "Manifesto Concerning Manchurian Problems" among a selected group of young officers in Japan.[12] Shumei Okawa went around the country making speeches in twenty major cities.

In Manchuria, Lieutenant Colonel Ishihara arranged with the Ministry of War to have two large howitzers moved up from Port Arthur to Mukden. A shed was built within the garrison compound to hide the guns. One was trained on the North Barracks and the other was aimed at hangars on the airfield, which housed Chinese fighter planes.[13]

By midsummer, the three main activists of the plot had virtually taken charge of the Kwantung Army. The army had switched commanders of the Kwantung Army, and Lieutenant General Shigeru Honjo was new in the job. Honjo was located in Port Arthur, miles away. Major General Mitsuharu Miyake, the chief of staff, soon discovered that when Colonel Itagaki, Lieutenant Colonel Ishihara, and Major Tadashi Hanaya expressed insolence or insubordination, they were backed by General Honjo. Since Miyake could not control them, he left them alone.[14]

Then came July 1931, and an incident called the Wanpaoshan Affair: The Koreans, as Japanese nationals, had special treatment in Manchuria, a fact resented by the Manchurians. That summer the resentments boiled over after a group of Koreans dug a ditch several miles long across land occupied by Chinese farmers, in order to irrigate some leased land at Wanpaoshan. The Chinese tried to fill in the ditch, the Koreans called on the Japanese authorities, who sent the special police of the Japanese consulate. The police fired on the Chinese and dispersed them. The Koreans had their ditch, but the Japanese had riots—in Korea rioters killed about three hundred Chinese. In China the Chinese attacked Japanese residents and stormed a Japanese hospital. The Chinese government protested that the Koreans were living outside the Chientao district, the only one the Japanese had leased.[15]

Then came another shocking matter.

Captain Shintaro Nakamura was a Japanese army officer stationed at Harbin. Early in June he secured travel permits from the Chinese government in Harbin to go into Inner Mongolia. He used a false name and declared that the object of the trip was to make an agricultural survey.

He then set out, with a Japanese assistant and Russian and Mongolian interpreters, along the Chinese Eastern Railway. On June 27 they arrived at a solitary eating place on the road near Solun, in the Hinganling Mountain range. There they were stopped and questioned by Chinese soldiers. When the Chinese discovered that they had a Japanese army map, they grew suspicious and arrested the party. They found surveying instruments, six revolvers, and a large supply of narcotics, which the Japanese obviously were preparing to use for trade or bribes. They were taken to the Chinese barracks and held there for several days. Then they were marched out to a hill in back of the barracks and shot as spies. Their bodies were cremated.[16]

Word of the incident reached the Japanese, who began an investigation. So did the Chinese, who announced that the men were spies. The Japanese began raising a furor. Chang Hsueh-liang sent an emissary to Tokyo to say that he wanted to settle the matter amicably. He also sent an ambassador to have talks with Foreign Minister Shidehara and War Minister Jiro Minami to see if the differences between Manchuria and Japan could not be resolved. But, by this time the Japanese army was determined to have absolute control of Manchuria, and the talks got nowhere. The Nakamura incident was prolonged to keep Japanese "Manchuria fever" at a high pitch.

By August, the "Manchuria fever" had permeated the War Office of Tokyo and the army. Minister of War General Jiro Minami made a speech to a gathering of division commanders in which he virtually called for the use of force to take over Manchuria.[17] In only slightly veiled language he spoke insultingly of Prime Minister Wakatsuki and the civilian cabinet. By this time, largely for economic reasons, so great was the influence of the radicals in the army and the navy, and so badly deteriorated the influence of the civilian politicians with the press and public, that Wakatsuki felt unable to make a public issue of the war minister's insulting remarks. For if Minami resigned from the cabinet, then the chance of getting the budget through the parliament seemed very slight.

In the meantime, the scandalous behavior of the Kwantung

Army in Manchuria had become a serious issue in Tokyo. Prince Saionji buttonholed General Minami and assailed him for the brutality of the army against Chinese civilians. The army in Manchuria, he said, was no better than a gang of hoodlums and "fascist gangsters."[18] He cited chapter and verse of atrocities, and Minami could not but agree. Then the war minister went back to his office and did absolutely nothing to stop or even to discourage the Kwantung Army. It seems obvious that he knew what was going to happen next.

There were other signs in Tokyo of trouble to come. One night Okawa got drunk and told several friends that he and a number of officers of the Kwantung Army were about to do something great in Manchuria. Lieutenant Colonel Masaichi Shimamoto, just transferred to the Railway Guard Battalion at Mukden, announced that he, too, was about to participate in something great in Manchuria. The secretary of the Lord Privy Seal at the Imperial Palace learned from the secretary of Prince Saionji that the young officers of the Kwantung Army were about to create an incident. Too bad, he said. *Shikata ganai.* (It can't be helped.) There was nothing to be done.[19]

Around September 12, it became apparent in Mukden that something serious was stirring. Young officers were asking for military supplies to be stockpiled in strange places. Eiichi Kimura, a director of the South Manchurian Railway, told Consul General Hisajiro Hayashi that he was worried about the army creating an incident. Hayashi sent a message to General Honjo, but it was intercepted by members of his staff and held up. The conspirators were now growing extremely nervous, all the more so because of reverberations reaching them from Tokyo.

On September 11 War Minister Jiro Minami was summoned to the Imperial Palace by an angry Emperor Hirohito, who had heard that the Kwantung Army's young officers were out of control. He warned Minami to restore order to the army. The next day, Foreign Minister Shidehara had a worried cable from Consul General Hayashi, reporting that a junior officer had told him an incident would break out within the week. Shidehara called Minami and told him that if this happened the nation's security would be in jeopardy.[20]

Minami spoke then to General Hanzo Kanaya, the chief of staff of the army. A meeting of senior Imperial General Staff officers was then called at the war minister's residence. Minami spoke:

"You don't think there is any chance that the Kwantung Army would take action without consulting army headquarters do you?"

Various officers spoke up, most of them saying that it was impossible. Then Major General Yoshitsugu Tatekawa looked up from scraping his pipe:

"There is no need to worry. The Kwantung Army is not that stupid."

There was something in his tone that alerted Kanaya.

"Oh? It seems that you have some inside information . . ."

"No, that I don't. No. No."

The vehemence of Tatekawa's denial made Chief of Staff Kanaya suspicious.

"We had better advise Honjo of the emperor's warning of the 11th by telegram."

General Kuniyaki Koiso, chief of the Military Affairs Bureau, interrupted.

"We'll be taking chances with a telegram. It might be misinterpreted. Let Tatekawa deliver in person letters from the minister of war and the chief of the general staff."[21]

So right there the two generals wrote the letters and handed them to General Tatekawa. He went to his office and sent a telegram announcing that he would arrive in Mukden on September 18. That was all. But then his assistant, Colonel Kingoro Hashimoto, who was in contact with the plotters, sent another secret message to Colonel Itagaki: "Tatekawa is expected to arrive Mukden tomorrow. Hospitable treatment will be appreciated. His mission is to prevent the incident."[22]

Those odd words about hospitable treatment were not accidental. The idea was to get Tatekawa out of the way, for good reason: he knew about the plot and had no intention of interfering, but he had to be covered. "Hospitality" meant to take him to an inn or geisha house and be sure he saw nothing.

When General Honjo had the official message, it suggested that either Itagaki or Ishihara be chosen. He and Ishihara exchanged a few words, assured each other that the plot was on for that night, and parted. Itagaki then went to Penhsisu where he waited for General Tatekawa's express train to stop and then got on. The general immediately warned Itagaki that Tokyo was worried about the recklessness of the young officers. He said he would wait for a meeting to discuss the whole matter, and that would be the next day. The train arrived at Mukden at 1:00 P.M. and was met by Major Hanaya. Tatekawa allowed himself to be persuaded to go to an inn.[23] The young officers left him there to be entertained. He spent the night with the geishas, drank a lot of sake, and was sound asleep by nine o'clock, while Hanaya and Itagaki went about their night's business.[24]

On September 18 a formal conference was held in Mukden between Chinese General Yung Chen, representing Marshal Chang Hsueh-liang, and Consul General Hisajiro Hayashi, who really had the power of an ambassador. General Yung admitted Chinese guilt in the Nakamura affair and said he hoped they could soon settle the matter and let the ashes rest.

Since it was an army affair, Consul Hayashi decided he had best consult with the Kwantung Army officer in charge of the matter for the army before saying much more, and he called a recess in the conference at 8:00 P.M. so he could send for the man. He dispatched Morita Morishima of his staff to bring the officer, Colonel Kenji Doihara, chief of the army Special Affairs Section at Mukden. Morishima could not find Doihara. He then looked for Major Tadashi Hanaya, the colonel's assistant, but could not find him either. Both officers were already on their way to the stations assigned to carry out the plot.[25]

So the wheels were in motion, moving hurriedly, because the plotters had just learned that Major General Tatekawa was in Mukden, dispatched from Tokyo by the Imperial General Staff to stop the plot. Too much was known by too many people about the plans.

The sound of shooting awakened the drunken General Tatekawa. He got into his uniform and staggered up to the reception desk of the inn, but there he was met by soldiers who surrounded him and escorted him back to his room. "We were ordered to guard you and stop you from walking outdoors, since it is dangerous," said the noncommissioned officer in charge. The general staggered back to his room and collapsed on the futon. He was held there until morning and then escorted to a room above the Special Affairs Bureau of the Kwantung Army in Mukden headquarters, where he found another captive, General Honjo.[26]

At three o'clock in the morning of September 19, 1931, Minister Minami was awakened by the night duty officer of the war department in Tokyo.

"Now what?" demanded the war minister.

The young officer then read him a telegram from Japanese Intelligence Chief Colonel Kenji Takihara in Mukden, which announced that at ten-thirty on the evening of September 18 a unit of the Northeastern Frontier Defense Army of the Republic of China had dynamited part of the South Manchurian Railway and attacked the Japanese railway guards in their barracks northwest of Mukden. An atrocity, the colonel called it. Thereupon the second battalion of the Mukden garrison had raced in to annihilate the enemy. . . .[27]

This time the young officers of the Kwantung Army and the Imperial General Staff had not failed.

無理が通れば道理ひっこむ

9. "When one walks the path of iniquity righteousness disappears"

*T*he rebellion of the young officers on the night of September 18, 1931, was not just a local Mukden affair. Before dawn a message purportedly from General Shigeru Honjo, commander of the Kwantung Army, reached Lieutenant General Senjuro Hayashi, commander of the Korea army at Seoul, asking for immediate reinforcements of the Kwantung Army. Early in the morning a detachment of Japanese air force planes at Pyongyang suddenly took off for Mukden.[1]

This action seems to have been unauthorized, of a piece with the Mukden incident.

Troops of the Twentieth Division at Seoul and Pyongyang left by train for the Korea-Manchuria border, to stay there and await instructions. General Hayashi wired Tokyo, awaiting imperial orders to move farther. There was no immediate reply. On that morning of September 19 the Ministry of War and the Imperial General Staff were trying to stop the rebellion. General Minami wired General Hayashi back that he was absolutely forbidden to cross the border. He sent orders to three units in Manchuria to stop wherever they were and report their position.

At 7:00 A.M. Chief of Staff General Kanaya was at his desk in Tokyo. The press was already bedeviling the army, but they got no information. General Minami called a meeting with General Sugiyama, the vice minister of war and General Koiso, the chief of the Military Affairs Bureau of the war ministry. They were also tight-lipped. The prime minister called a meeting of the cabinet at 10:00 A.M. After that meeting, General Minami emerged to give the reporters a statement, which said nothing in six paragraphs.[2]

At army headquarters, the young members of the Imperial General Staff were still trying to secure imperial sanction for further military action in Manchuria. General Kanaya said no, not until he had secured imperial approval. It was apparent that most of the leaders of the army approved of what had been done, but were afraid of imperial disapproval. Through his household staff, the emperor was well aware of the activities at Imperial General Headquarters. When General Kanaya approached the Imperial Household for an audience with the emperor, on September 20, he was told that Hirohito was "indisposed." In the absence of imperial approval, Kanaya had to order General Hayashi to stay on the Korean side of the border.[3]

In this crisis, Prime Minister Wakatsuki failed to take immediate, strong action. He complained to Prince Saionji's secretary that he had not received reports from the Ministry of Foreign Affairs or the Ministry of War about what had been going on in Manchuria, and when he called the minister of war and rebuked him for taking military action without imperial order, General Minami referred back to the incident at the time of the murder of Chang Tso-lin, when General Tanaka had been prepared to move in Manchuria but was restrained only by the warning from the United States. There, said General Minami, was the precedent. So by calling one illegal action the precedent for another, the military men justified their disloyalty to the throne.[4]

The Japanese public still knew virtually nothing about what had happened. On September 21 the newspapers reported that sporadic fighting was still going on. Only one Japanese soldier had been killed, Private Rokuro Niikuni of the special railway detachment. If any of the newspaper readers wondered how an "attack" by the Chinese would kill only one soldier, no one in authority was ready to enlighten them.[5]

Prime Minister Wakatsuki told the press that he had virtually no information about the events, which was probably the only truthful statement made by a politician or military man in Tokyo that day. Baron Wakatsuki had heard that troops from Korea were moving, but he could say no more than that. He spoke of his "great hopes for peace" and settlement of the new problem. Here again, the prime minister's statements were revealing; he could not attribute a cause, or a motive to the action; he did not even say that the Chinese had attacked, but only that he had reports that they had attacked. So he was not lying to the public. Of course, he could not tell them that he had learned of the young officers' plot unless he was willing to take a stand on the issue.

With the prime minister showing such weakness, Prince Saionji tried to stop the rot from his palace in Kyoto. He sent word to Emperor Hirohito that under no circumstances should he approve the army's actions. If one of the military men succeeded in getting an audience, Hirohito was advised to withhold his word on the subject.[6]

At this time, the army's attitude was hardening in support of the seizure of Mukden. The young officers seemed to have gotten away with their plot; the results were what the senior army officers had wanted for years. General Minami informed the foreign office that the army believed the troops should enlarge the area of capture. The feeling was growing among most of the generals that since the die was cast, all Manchuria should now be seized.

Cabinet approval was requested before troops in Korea would move; but it must be swift, or they would move anyhow, said General Minami. Had Prime Minister Wakatsuki secured an audience and requested imperial support to stop the rebellion right there, it probably could have been done. The military men were still so shocked by their own temerity that a powerful thrust might have disarmed them. But the thrust did not come and with every hour that passed the self-justification of the army men increased. Everything they were doing, they told one another, was in the interest of Japan.

By the end of September 20, a new military oligarchy had seized control of the army, and War Minister General Minami was its captive.

In Manchuria, the Kwantung Army's troops were moving out and engaging the Chinese. There were only 12,000 troops assigned to the Kwantung Army at this point. That is why General Honjo had sent the call for reinforcements from the much larger Korea army. Tokyo was also worried lest Chang Hsueh-liang stage a strong counterattack and wipe out the Japanese. No serious effort was made from Tokyo to stop the fighting. General Tatekawa, the emissary sent from the war ministry to stop the incident, encouraged the enlargement of the field of action. Lieutenant Colonel Ishihara now proposed to move the army north, take Harbin, and settle once and for all the future of all Manchuria. Even Tatekawa could not swallow that, and he forced delay.[7]

Next, the Kwantung Army troops attacked Kirin, captured it without incident, and forced the local general, Hsi Ch'ia, to proclaim "independence." General Tamon, commander of the Japanese force, held a revolver to Hsi Ch'ia's head as he did so. Immediately the Tokyo newspapers began running laudatory articles about Hsi Ch'ia.

Without waiting further for imperial sanction, the Korea army moved across the border into Manchuria and joined the revolt, on the excuse that Mukden needed protection. When Tokyo's Imperial Army Headquarters learned of these moves, even the cabal of generals began to fear that the armies in Korea and Manchuria had gone too far. What if they could not control them at all?

At this point, the generals tried to obtain imperial sanction for what had been done so improperly. General Kanaya secured an audience and asked the emperor for his approval. Hirohito refused and sent him away. War Minister Minami pleaded with Prime Minister Wakatsuki to seek imperial approval. Wakatsuki refused him.[8]

American Secretary of State Henry L. Stimson awoke on Saturday morning, September 19, 1931, to the shock of the Manchuria incident.[9]

"The situation is very confused," he wrote in his diary that day, "and it is not clear whether the army is acting under a plan of the government or on its own."

But Stimson learned quickly enough that the Kwantung Army had run amok. By September 21 the U.S. State Department policymakers had concluded that Baron Kijuro Shidehara, the Japanese foreign minister (and the other civilians in the government) had been taken almost as much by surprise as had the world. "The presumption was strong that he had not been a party to it and that it was contrary to his entire policy." This was a conclusion, but in this case the U.S. Department of State was absolutely correct.

By September 23, Secretary Stimson felt that the United States was facing a dilemma: how to refrain from agitating America's friends in Japan, and yet warn the militarists. And it was here that American policy failed. Three years earlier, the Kwantung Army had been poised for just such a coup, which was planned by General Tanaka.

When the United States had warned Tokyo not to do it, that had been enough to frighten Tanaka out of acting. Had the United States issued a similar warning in 1931 the effect would have been the same, because Japan's naval force was in no shape to counter a threat by the United States. From that point on, American policy bogged down in bureaucratic technicalities. "My problem," wrote Secretary of State Stimson in his diary on September 23, "is to let the Japanese know that we are watching them and at the same time do it in a way which will help Shidehara who is on the right side, and not play into the hands of any nationalist agitators."[10]

What would have helped Shidehara and the forces of reason in Japan just then would have been the sort of threat that would have forced the militarists to subside. But the leaders of the Western world were preoccupied with their own muddled economic affairs. On September 21 the British government announced that it was going off the gold standard, a bit of news that rocked the financial communities of Paris, Washington, and Tokyo. Prices crashed on the New York Stock Exchange in what Dow Jones called "one of the most disastrous breaks of the year."[11]

Instead, the signals that went from Washington to Tokyo indicated that the Americans were unwilling to take any action. A journalist asked a State Department spokesman if it was not time to invoke the Kellogg-Briand peace pact (renouncing war) and for the United States, Britain, and France to consult. The State Department spokesman said no. He admitted that "the situation [as of September 21] is more widespread than it was on Saturday" (two days earlier), but he expressed optimism because of reports that the Japanese cabinet "had moved to stop the aggressive action of the army."[12]

Far more important in Washington that week was the news that the United States Steel Corporation had cut the wages of its employees by 10 percent in reaction to the deepening economic crisis.

U.S. Senator Hiram Johnson of California, a leader of the American isolationist bloc, expressed his disgust with the State Department:

"Where now is the bugle call? Where is the sacrosanct Kellogg Pact?"[13]

The Washington *Evening Star,* then the national capital's most important newspaper, demanded that the world's statesmen intervene to end the dispute and stop the Japanese movement toward China.

The New York *Herald Tribune* called the crisis "a real emergency," but with one of those "on the other hand" flips for which editorial writers are famous, said, "The Chinese are by no means free from blame and others cannot too hastily pass judgment."

No one asked the editorial writer to delineate the blame that should fall on the Chinese for their resistance to Japanese aggression in Manchuria. "On the other hand" was always a good ploy.

The New York *Post* was more forthright and more prescient. Its editorialist saw "the yellow man, solidified and equipped, at last challenging the white man—the West may as well shudder at its lack of power to meet them."

The Scripps-Howard New York *World Telegram* accused Japan of violating the Kellogg-Briand peace pact. "If the United States wishes to save its honor, it will demand jointly with other powers, or alone, if necessary, that Japan withdraw and make restitution."

William Randolph Hearst's New York *Mirror* said, "the wily Japan is doing her stuff," and other Hearst newspapers suggested that the United States do something about it.

Colonel Robert McCormick's Chicago *Tribune* said, "Japan will cover her action with mollifying formulas and emerge from the scene with substantial profits from her military coup."

And, that is what happened. Immediately, Japanese Ambassador Katsuji Debuchi informed the Americans that what they were reading about Manchuria was highly exaggerated. Many Americans read that news with only half an eye, for on September 24 American stocks crashed again.

Secretary Stimson sent identical notes to Japan and China urging a cessation of hostilities. The Chinese, of course, had no control whatsoever over what was happening.

Later, much later, much too late, the Americans proposed a strong position be taken by the United States and Britain, and Britain refused.

Secretary of State Stimson was reduced to the folderol of diplomacy and sent a note to Tokyo. Baron Shidehara replied:

> I have the honor to acknowledge receipt of your note of September 25, in which you were so good as to convey to me the views of the American Government on the

subject of the actual conditions of affairs in Manchuria.

The Japanese government is deeply sensible of the friendly concern and the fairness of attitude with which the American government has observed the recent course of events in Manchuria. Sharing with the American government the hope expressed in your note under acknowledgement, this government has already caused the Japanese military forces in Manchuria to refrain from any further acts of hostility unless their own safety as well as the security of the South Manchurian Railway and of Japanese lives and property within the Railway zone is jeopardized by the aggression of Chinese troops and bands. . . .[14]

The Manchurian situation had bogged down in the mud of diplomatic linguistics.

Once more, between September 21 and 23, the arrest of the conspirators, including those high in the ranks of the military, might have turned the tide. On September 23 the emperor summoned Prime Minister Wakatsuki and told him to see that the Manchurian situation was not aggravated. As commander in chief of the armed forces, if the emperor had then demanded strong action, he could hardly have been refused. But Hirohito failed the test. In his defense it must be said that his advisors also failed him: Prince Saionji, Prime Minister Wakatsuki, the Grand Chamberlain, Baron Kantaro Suzuki, the Lord Keeper of the Privy Seal, and the minister of the Imperial Household. These last three were almost daily confidants of the emperor and their influence on him was enormous. None had the courage or the foresight to stop the military juggernaut when there was yet time. The deterioration of civil government was already so advanced that the only way to save it would have been through imperial intervention.[15]

In the last days of September temporization lost the cause. The cabinet approved of funds to support the Korea army's illegal adventure after the fact. The prime minister reported this move to the emperor, who was not pleased, and who told General Kanaya, at his next audience, "Take Heed," which was as serious a reprimand as the emperor could make personally.

The imperial problem at this point in history was bound up in the changed nature of the emperor's position, as it had developed since the days of Hirohito's grandfather. The Meiji Constitution (see

Appendix) established the emperor as the absolute chief of state. But as noted, in Meiji's declining years he had leaned heavily on his Privy Council and Imperial Household and had seldom taken action without consulting them. This attitude and chain of events established precedents. After Meiji's death, the almost complete incompetence of Emperor Taisho had meant that the councillors ruled in the name of the emperor, and this was the situation that existed when the young Hirohito had come to the throne. He was surrounded by veils of tradition and ceremony, and he found it extremely difficult to get accurate information on political subjects, and also to act. Hirohito added to this dissipation of imperial power. In his youth as prince imperial, he visited England and was so impressed by the solid, orderly working of the British government that he said he would reign as emperor of Japan in the manner that George V reigned as emperor of the British Empire. By 1931, then, this philosophy had been so firmly established that Hirohito had sacrificed a great deal of power. Still, his power was such that if he expressed displeasure, then careers could be wrecked in a moment. His whole life was spent exercising restraint and yet trying to impose the force of his will on the Japanese government. By this time, obviously he had failed. The acceptance of the Kwantung Army's seizure of Mukden was an enormous blow to the prestige of the emperor within army circles. They knew, after this, that they could have their own way ultimately.

After the failure of prime minister and emperor to roll back time and force the army to evacuate Mukden, there was no stopping the Kwantung Army in Manchuria. The South Manchurian Railway was pressed into service to move troops, and its leadership, in cahoots with the Kwantung Army from the beginning, was only too eager to cooperate. China protested to the League of Nations. When War Minister General Minami learned that, he said, "Why in the world do we not withdraw from the League?"[16]

The general's remark represented the views of the *kodo ha* of the army and the "fleet faction" of the navy. International cooperation had been tried by the civilians since 1918, and all it had brought Japan, from the point of view of the militarists, was loss of empire. The Shantung Peninsula had been theirs, and was gone. Siberia had been theirs and had to be returned; Sakhalin, too.

In October, the Kwantung Army ran completely amok. The Japanese government in Tokyo had replied to international questioning with announcements of Japan's peaceful intentions. The statements were true as far as the civilian government was concerned. But on October 8, the Kwantung Army bombed Chinchow, the headquarters of Marshal Chang Hsueh-liang. General Honjo announced to army headquarters that he was going to move against Chang's troops. No one even dared censure Honjo. The big three of the army, generals Minami, Kanaya, and Muto, met and agreed on new demands to be made of the cabinet: the Manchuria issue must be settled in Manchuria, not by the League of Nations or with China. What they meant was that the seizure of Manchuria must be legalized by the Japanese government. All this was counter to the civil government's policies, but no one did anything. Prime Minister Wakatsuki told Baron Kumao Harada that he had lost control:[17]

> I would summon the Minister of War to explain to him at great length the necessity of maintaining orderly conduct of our troops abroad. He would then agree. . . . Then what would happen? The troops stationed abroad would commit acts which would run completely counter to the agreement that the Minister of War and I had just made. . . .[18]

October brought another dreadful shock. A new group of conspirators of the army had planned yet one more rebellion. So 1931 was marked by three moves by three sets of conspirators: the March rebellion, which had failed, the September rebellion of the Kwantung Army, which succeeded, and a third October rebellion, which was to bring the government completely under the army. Lieutenant Colonel Kingoro Hashimoto and Major Isamu Cho were to lead the Cherry Blossom Society in a coup that would seize power on October 24. Troops would be brought into the streets of Tokyo, and army and navy planes would fly over to show military support. The Wakatsuki cabinet would be wiped out by a bomb during a cabinet meeting at the prime minister's house. The opportunity would be taken to eliminate a number of "undesirable" military officers. General Ugaki would be offered the prime ministership, and the plotters would take over his cabinet.[19]

But the principal plotters were already flushed with success, beguiled by the easy way in which the Kwantung Army had defied authority, and drunk with anticipation of their coming victory. Large sums of money were made available to the plotters, some of it from the Manchurian Kwantung Army. Hashimoto and Cho began throwing extravagant geisha parties for officers they wanted to attract to the cause. They got drunk and boasted. This evidence of corruption caused many of the young officers to turn away from the Cherry Blossom Society to other extremist groups that were more spartan in their approach.[20]

It became common knowledge around the war ministry and army headquarters that such a plot was afoot. The crisis came one day when Colonel Hashimoto, sure of his success, bearded General Hajime Sugiyama, the vice minister of war, and insolently demanded his adherence. The plot was called the Revolution of the Imperial Flag. General Ugaki was to become military dictator of Japan. At about that same time General Sadao Araki went to a geisha party where he, too, was threatened. The plotters had gone too far for even the army leaders; the plot was about to break into an open political scandal. Fearing that such would wreck the army, General Minami and General Kanaya were afraid to order the usual sort of investigation; they could not trust their own junior officers to carry out their orders. At an all-night meeting at War Minister Minami's house with officers known to be loyal to him, the decision to act was made. A selected group of loyal officers and soldiers was assembled and in the small hours of the morning twelve major conspirators were arrested.

Of course not a line about the arrests appeared in the newspapers. There were no signs that anything unusual was happening in Tokyo. The front pages of the newspapers were filled with articles about fighting there. From Washington came a report of American attempts to go to Manchuria to find out what was happening, and, of course, Japanese stalling to prevent just that. At Geneva the League of Nations was talking. But the public of Japan had much more on its mind, a story given equal importance in the newspapers concerned the sinking of the Japanese steamer *Yunnan Maru* off the Oregon coast in a storm. Another heralded the sailing of a group of American baseball players heading for Japan after getting some advice from Ty Cobb about how to comport themselves.[21]

The degree of deterioration of the army's discipline was indicated by the punishments of the admitted conspirators. Under the Japanese constitution, they had committed treason, for which the penalty was death. The most severe punishment, however, was that given Colonel Hashimoto, who received twenty days in confinement.

The others received ten days. The sentences were carried out in geisha houses in the vicinity of Tokyo. The plot was hushed up by the generals. The most serious repercussions were those affecting General Minami, the minister of war, and General Kanaya, the chief of staff. They resigned.

Within thirty days another plot was discovered by the Japanese police. This new attempt was to involve the Azabu Regiment, 50,000 reservists, and the Imperial Guard, to establish a dictatorship under the emperor. The dictator was to be General Sadao Araki. This plot, too, was defused, but once again, so embattled were the army leaders and the civil government that they were afraid to bring the matter into the open and prosecute the plotters. The plots, the deception, the confusion all redounded to the serious embarrassment of Japan in the eyes of the world. Time after time the civilian government would make one statement, only to have the military contradict it by action. Until 1931 the Japanese had an international reputation for probity; it disappeared in that one year, and the world began to view Japan as dishonest and bent on aggression.

William Henry Chamberlin, who spent four years in Japan as correspondent for the *Christian Science Monitor,* summed up the situation thus:

"Japanese army and navy officers have never taken kindly to the idea that the Diet should control the activities of their services. Japan perhaps came nearest to civilian control over the fighting services in 1930 when Premier Hamaguchi, an unusually forceful personality for a Japanese civilian, pushed through the ratification of the London Naval Treaty."

But as a foreigner, Chamberlin was not privy to the materials that would let him understand what was occurring in Tokyo just then. Japanese scholar Tatsuji Takeuchi was.

"The actual authority for directing the nation's foreign policy was gradually shifting from the Ministry of Foreign Affairs to the Ministry of War by the middle of August [1931]," said Takeuchi. ". . . Towards the middle of October, however, even the last vestige of dual diplomacy appeared to be waning, with the Ministry of War in firm control of the government. . . ."[22]

In Manchuria the aggression of the Kwantung Army continued. There was no one to stop it after October 1931. The League of Nations tried, by demanding withdrawal of Japanese troops. The

Kwantung Army ignored the league. A commission was sent to investigate. By the time it was ready to go, the Japanese had conquered all Manchuria. On December 11, 1931, Prime Minister Wakatsuki resigned. In the forlorn hope that the return to power of the Seiyukai party would help matters, Prince Saionji persuaded the emperor to give the government leadership to Ki Inukai. It was little more than a facade. War minister of the new cabinet was General Araki, the beau ideal of the young officers of the army, aggressive backer of the Kwantung Army, and proponent of a Japan that would bring *hakko ichiu* to the world.

By the end of 1931 the army was in control of Japan's political life. The Kwantung Army had completed its conquest of Manchuria. Henry Pu-yi, the last of the Imperial Manchu dynasty, had been spirited away from his home in Tientsin by Colonel Itagaki, and virtually at gunpoint had been told that he was to be the head of a new country called Manchukuo, which is Chinese for Manchu Country. In February 1932, with Kwantung Army advisors on all sides, Henry Pu-yi solemnly declared the "independence" of Manchukuo from China. Japan now had a new colony.[23]

The army wasted little time in moving for more power, more expansion.

With the Japanese investment of Manchuria, and the threat to north China that was express in Japan's movements in the area, the response of the Chinese was to boycott Japanese goods. The boycott had long been China's one effective response to foreign aggression against the succession of weak governments of the nineteenth and twentieth centuries. In 1926, Secretary Stimson had visited Hongkong and had there seen what a Chinese boycott could do. The Chinese were protesting the British shooting of a number of Chinese student demonstrators in Shanghai. The Hongkong Stimson saw was virtually a ghost town.[24]

The Japanese had developed the China market until they sold more goods to the Chinese than to anyone but the Americans, so the boycott of Japanese goods by Chinese merchants was equally effective. The central point of the boycott was Shanghai, which lies on a peninsula bounded by the Yangtze River on the northeast and the Whangpoo River on the southeast. The waterfront is on the Whangpoo. The commercial city then consisted of the International Settlement and the French Concession, on the north side of the

Whangpoo. The Chinese city sprawled around this area. The population of the international concessions included foreigners of almost every nation, and the Chinese who did business with them. The Chinese city protruded at two points into this area, at Chapei on the north and in what was called the Old City, on the south. Operating under extraterritorial rules, the foreigners had their own "cities" in the international concession, with their own laws and police. Besides the police, the foreigners also maintained military forces to "protect their nationals." In 1931, there were 2500 Japanese marines, 2300 British marines, 1250 American marines, and 1050 French, plus a few Italians. The Japanese had a much larger force there, for they had the largest foreign population in Shanghai. They also had twenty-three warships in the harbor, while the British had five, the French, two, and the Americans, one. The great Japanese naval strength was a result of the Japanese policy of trying to break the boycott by show of force up and down the Yangtze.

The trouble began on January 18, 1932, when a clash between Japanese and Chinese occurred in front of a Chinese factory in Chapei. Two Japanese were seriously wounded, and one of them died. (Later it was learned that these Japanese were ultranationalist priests who had come to Shanghai specifically to provoke an incident.)

Two days later fifty members of this sect proceeded to the factory, set it afire, and fought the municipal police. Three Chinese policemen and three Japanese were wounded. One of each died.[25]

On January 20 the Japanese consul general in Shanghai demanded a formal apology from the mayor of Shanghai, arrest of everyone responsible for the attack of January 18 (he didn't say the Japanese), reparations, control of the anti-Japanese movement, including dissolution of all anti-Japanese organizations. The last two demands meant dissolution of the boycott. The next day the mayor said he could do all but the last two. This was what the Japanese had been waiting for. Admiral Koichi Shiozawa sent an ultimatum: if the mayor did not dissolve the boycott, the admiral would take the steps necessary to protect Japanese interests.

In Tokyo the navy was just then under the influence of the "fleet faction," led by Admiral Suetsugu. Beginning on January 14 a powerful Japanese naval force appeared in Shanghai, two cruisers, an aircraft carrier, and sixteen destroyers.

About 30,000 Chinese soldiers of the Nineteenth Route Army were stationed around the Chapei district of Shanghai. This was the headquarters of the Shanghai-Nanking defense area, and these were among the best trained of all Chinese soldiers.

The mayor of Shanghai greeted the arrival of the Japanese force with the promise that he would do all possible to avoid incidents. The Japanese, however, adopted a belligerent stance that would become ever more common in their dealings in China. The Japanese consul issued an ultimatum that the boycott had to end by 6:00 P.M. on January 28 or else. . . . On the morning of the twenty-eighth Admiral Shiozawa informed the commanders of other foreign defense forces that he intended to move on the morning of January 29.

The mayor of Shanghai capitulated to the threat, but that was not really what the Japanese wanted; the admiral wanted to make a show of force that would frighten the Chinese into accepting further territorial and trade concessions to the Japanese. That night Admiral Shiozawa announced at 11:15 that at 11:45 he would send Japanese marines on a sweep into Chapei, the Chinese quarter, and that the Chinese must remove all troops. It was impossible for the mayor to act in thirty minutes and the admiral knew it; the whole action was provocative to the utmost, staged to create an incident.

So the Japanese moved into Chapei, and fighting broke out. On the face of it the likelihood is that the first shot was fired by the Japanese, although, of course, they denied it.

Thus began the Shanghai incident, which lasted from January 28, 1932, until March 3. The Japanese found that they had taken on a tough nut in the Nineteenth Route Army. The Chinese held their positions. At 4:30 in the morning of January 29, Admiral Shiozawa ordered up his carrier bombers, and they sprayed the civil quarter of Chapei with incendiaries and burned that section of the city. The correspondent of Reuter news service reported that by 5:30 the flames were leaping from block to block, crawling toward the International Settlement, and rising seventy-five to a hundred feet in the air. Thousands of women and children were killed, and before the day was over 250,000 Chinese refugees streamed into the International Settlement. Here at Chapei was the first atrocity of the war that would last for fourteen more years.[26]

The irony was that the Nineteenth Route Army held firm in its positions and continued to do so for the next month despite all Japanese efforts to dislodge them.

The Japanese excesses and their failure to dislodge the Chinese troops with this enormous force caused a surge of bad publicity for Japan in foreign capitals. The Japanese were extremely sensitive to foreign opinion. They determined that they must win a military victory at Shanghai. They began pouring army and marine troops into Shanghai from Japan.

Admiral Shiozawa was disgraced, more for his failure to win than for his disgraceful action. Admiral Kichisaburo Nomura arrived to take over. By February 18 the Japanese had assembled a land force of 16,000 men, with howitzers, field guns, and tanks, supported by aircraft. General Kenkichi Ueda arrived from Tokyo with the Ninth Division to redeem Japanese military honor. The Japanese issued another ultimatum to the Chinese to withdraw and dismantle their defenses, and the Chinese refused. The Japanese attacked on February 19, and their attack was repelled. General Ueda was disgraced and replaced by General Yoshinori Shirakawa, who came up with the Eleventh Division, which was sent up the Yangtze and began an enveloping movement.

The Japanese threatened to pinch in the Chinese forces, which retreated about twenty miles and took up positions. The Japanese then announced that with the retreat of the Chinese, hostilities were at an end.

The incident had backfired completely. Instead of proving the enormous power of Japan, it had proved that one badly armed Chinese army without heavy artillery or air cover could hold off the well-equipped combat forces of Japan, supported by planes and naval artillery. Instead of destroying Chinese morale, the Shanghai incident had raised it and had helped Chiang Kai-shek in his drive to unite the Chinese.

As for Japan, the Shanghai incident was taken by War Minister Sadao Araki as a lesson for Japanese soldiers in the army's rejuvenation of the ancient *bushido* concept. The code of the samurai said that if a samurai withdrew his sword even two inches from its scabbard, it could not be replaced until it had shed blood. Thus an officer committed to an attack, as was General Ueda, should have committed suicide when the attack failed. But that would have been an enormously expensive policy in terms of army officers, so the Japanese invented a new military concept: strategic withdrawal. Japanese troops never retreated. Nor did they surrender; on this policy the army was hard as granite. There could be no defeat. The soldier won victory or he died. Japanese pilots in the China war were issued revolvers and swords, but no parachutes.

In the Shanghai incident the army made much of the story of one officer of the Ninth Infantry. In the attack on Chapei he was wounded and left on the field in the strategic withdrawal of the division. He was found on the field by a Chinese officer who knew him from university days when the Chinese had studied in Japan. The Chinese rescued the Japanese officer and took him to a Chinese hospital. Recovered, the Japanese officer returned to the Chapei battlefield and disemboweled himself on the spot where he had fallen. General Araki liked to tell that story as symbolic of the code demanded of the Japanese soldier.[27]

This army madness seemed to spread like fire after the Manchuria and Shanghai incidents.

For a time, the diplomats managed to stop the expansion. In March, the League of Nations was just getting down to debating the Manchurian question at Geneva. The Japanese foreign office, Ambassador to China Shigemitsu, and the other civilians in power still hoped to achieve some international legitimization of their activities in Manchuria. It did not turn out that way. Japan was roundly condemned, and in the course of the condemnation pressure arose from the nationalists to walk out of the league.

But time dragged on, and the Japanese troops and Japanese navy remained in Shanghai. On April 29, 1932, Emperor Hirohito's birthday, the Japanese staged a parade and demonstration that ended up in Race Course Park. Ambassador Shigemitsu, General Shirakawa, and Admiral Nomura were all on the platform, singing "Kimigayo," the Japanese national anthem, when a young Korean nationalist, desperate in his attempt to draw attention to the plight of his country under Japanese imperialism, hurled a bomb. General Shirakawa was killed. Ambassador Shigemitsu lost a leg. The bombing brought about a wave of terror in Korea by the *Kempeitai* (Japanese military police) and resulted in the flight to the West of such Korean nationalists as Syngman Rhee.[28]

Since the end of 1931 the military nationalists had moved fast inside the armed services. Now the navy as well as the army was deeply involved in what would earlier have been called treason: Japanese army and navy men were forbidden by law to take part in any political activity. But now supernationalism was affecting every aspect of life in Japan, civil as well as military. Even peasants were joining superpatriotic societies that pledged death to anyone who defied the military. Since the inception of modernism in Japan, the government and the people had paid great attention to creating a positive image of their country in the world. Suddenly, this concern for world opinion was cast off. Part of the reason had to go back to the racism of European and, particularly, American societies. Part had to be attributed to the fulminations of the religious groups, Buddhist and, particularly, Shinto, which detested foreign ways. Part had to be found also in the submerged yearning for the old Japan of the feudal days.

The whole of the reaction began concentrating to bring patriotism to a fever pitch, and each newspaper article about criticism from abroad or about opposition at home to the new way brought violent reactions.

Japan's attitude toward China hardened. The world's attitude toward Japan began to harden. Such were the fruits of the new imperialism.

憎まれっ子 世にはばかる

10. "A bad boy frightens everyone"

*T*he Manchurian incident marked the beginning of the end of the
League of Nations and put the finger on Japan as the bad boy
of world society. In the fall of 1932 Japan "recognized" the state she
had created single-handedly, Manchukuo, two weeks before the
League's Lytton Commission produced a careful report that a less
militant Japan could have lived with. The report condemned the
Japanese military intervention but admitted that Japan had special
rights and interests in Manchuria—it sounded like something the
emperor might have said. Britain, France, and the United States were
all restrained in their criticism of Japan. But the militarists could not
stand a word of criticism. In fact, Japan had already gone mad, as
the events of 1932 showed clearly:

February: In a military encounter in Shanghai, three Japanese
soldiers from Kyushu charged into a Chinese position with explosives
tied to their bodies. They were blown up but so was the Chinese
position. When the Japanese press got the story, it was spread across
the news pages for days. Poets, dramatists, novelists, and motion
picture producers seized upon this evidence of the Yamato spirit,
the supreme bravery of which "only Japanese are capable." This idea
moved across Japan like wildfire. Thousands of school principals used
the theme to open their patriotic morning speech to their pupils: let
every school child remember and emulate the divine Japanese spirit
of the "three human torpedoes."[1]

February: Junosuke Inouye, former finance minister and prominent member of the Minseito party, was shot to death by a peasant youth who was a member of one of the supernationalist organizations. Inouye's "crime" was to hold down the army budget during the Hamaguchi administration.[2]

March: Takuma Dan, managing director of the Mitsui *zaibatsu*, was assassinated. His "crime" was that as a member of the economic ruling class he was working against army control of Japan.[3]

The murder occurred on the street in front of the Mitsui building in Nihonbashi, downtown Tokyo. It shocked all Japan, for Baron Dan was the most powerful industrial leader in the country. The assassin made no attempt to escape, and when questioned by the police, he announced that he was a blood brother of the murderer of Inouye.

Working from this knowledge the *Kempeitai* unraveled a plot that led back to the army.[4] These two civilian killers were innocent dupes, young farm boys who had risen to the call because of the dreadful condition of the farmers. Crop failures of the past five years had wiped out the resources of millions of Japanese. The international depression had wrecked the silk market. Children were going to school in the villages with empty lunch boxes. In 1931 in one village in Yamagata Prefecture, the head man reported that 110 of the village's 467 girls between the ages of fifteen and twenty-four were sold to brothels and spinning mills. It was small wonder, then, that the people of the rural areas hated the government and the economic royalists such as Mitsui. Hundreds of thousands of the army's soldiers and young officers came from such families, and when they went home and learned that their sisters had been sold into prostitution so the rest of the family could eat for a few more months, their anger became a burning coal.

Such men were easily persuaded by the supernationalists that only direct revolutionary action could alleviate the misery of the working poor in Japan. Dr. Shumei Okawa, once chief propagandist for the South Manchurian Railway and one of the principal fomenters of Japanese imperialism in Manchuria, had come home to work. His *Book of the Tiger* was a call to arms and a manifesto for *Dai Nippon,* Great Japan, ruler of the world.[5]

The start, Dr. Okawa agreed with Colonel Kingoro Hashimoto, the founder of the Cherry Blossom Society, had to be rebellion within the army. The army would seize control, wipe out the crooked politicians, and set up an honest social-minded government for the benefit of all the people.

The activists had been working to this end for months. The plan, first set for February, but later changed to March 20, called for Dr. Okawa's followers to bomb the prime minister's house and the headquarters of the two political parties, Minseito and Seiyukai. Then, 10,000 civilian demonstrators were to converge on the Diet. This mob action would provide an excuse for the army to call out troops to guard the government buildings. Members of the Cherry Blossom Society were to be assigned to the strategic entries to the Diet. At the peak of the action, one of two generals would enter the Diet and go straight to the dais and demand the resignation of the whole cabinet. This general would be either General Tatekawa or General Kuniyaki Koiso, both implicated in the Manchurian incident. The army generals would then demand that General Ugaki, the head of the *tosei ha* of the army and minister of war, be appointed by the emperor to form a new cabinet.[6]

This plot was known to a number of high-ranking officers in the *tosei ha*. They included General Hajime Sugiyama, vice minister of war, General Koiso, who was then chief of the Military Affairs Bureau, which had become the political arm of an army that was forbidden by the constitution to have any political ties or to engage in political action.

General Koiso, who was deeply involved in this plot, had the assistance of his subordinates in the powerful Military Affairs Bureau. They were Colonel Tetsuzan Nagata, chief of the operational section, and his assistants, Colonel Hideki Tojo and Colonel Teiichi Suzuki.

The secret of the plot was to raise enough commotion by civilian activity to force the use of the army. But Dr. Okawa was unable to secure that sort of civil support, although he propagandized both right and left as heavily as he dared. Two trial runs in the first ten days of March failed to produce more than three thousand demonstrators. That was not enough to create the sort of impact the *tosei ha* had to have to justify the calling out of the troops without obviously committing a rebellious act against emperor and constitution. General Ugaki, fearful for his reputation if the plot were to fail, pretended that he had just heard of it and summoned Vice Minister Sugiyama and Military Affairs Bureau Chief Koiso and told them to put a stop to it.

"Do you think you can use His Majesty's troops for such a purpose?" he demanded of Koiso. That was the key; the whole plot had to look spontaneous, and that could not be managed in March 1932.[7]

So the March plot never got off the ground. But it left the army more divided than ever.

May: Sunday, May 14, was a sunny day in Tokyo. That afternoon, Prime Minister Tsuyoshi Inukai went into the tatami room of his official residence in central Tokyo. The simplicity of the straw mats, the low table, and the sliding paper screens were always calming. Since Baron Wakatsuki's resignation at the end of 1931, the task of running the government had grown increasingly difficult in the face of the arrogant generals. Prime Minister Inukai was pondering the next day's problems and looking over the Sunday evening newspapers. The prime minister had been having the usual trouble with the militant generals. He owed his office to the fact that he was regarded at seventy-six as an "elder statesman" who might be able to keep the growingly brutal military under control.[8]

At 5:30 two taxi cabs suddenly pulled up in front of the official residence. Out of the cars jumped a dozen junior naval officers and army cadets. Without stopping to remove their shoes, they pushed their way through the front door and headed for the prime minister's room, knowing precisely where to go. Prime Minister Inukai was sitting before the low table. They surrounded him. He reached out for a cigarette box on the table and passed it around. Not one of the military men took a cigarette.

The prime minister looked down at their feet. They had paid him a hateful insult by entering the tatami room in their military boots. Gently he pointed that breach out:

"Won't you at least remove your boots?"

"You needn't worry about our boots," shouted Lieutenant Taku Mikami. He pulled out his pistol and aimed it at the prime minister. "You know what's happening."

Inukai looked at the red-faced young officer levelly.

"There's no need to get excited. If we talk this over, we can come to an understanding."

The calm tone, the *enryo*—restraint—had the desired effect. Shamefacedly Mikami realized how badly he had breached etiquette. He lowered his pistol.

Another lieutenant looked at him angrily:

"No talking. Shoot! Shoot!"

Prime Minister Inukai raised his hand to calm the second noise-maker. Just then a third young lieutenant joined the group, rushing in from the hallway, brandishing his pistol. He pointed the weapon and shot.[9] Lieutenant Mikami then shot. The prime minister collapsed slowly, face down on the low table.

At almost that same moment other young officers and cadets were attacking Seiyukai party headquarters, and the house of the Keeper of the Privy Seal, Count Makino, the Metropolitan Police office, and the major electrical stations of Tokyo. All these attacks ended in dismal failure. It was a plot, not a spontaneous urge, that much was clear from the leaflets dropped around the city. The targets were the politicians and the *zaibatsu* who "squeeze sweat and blood out of the common people."

"Japan," said the plotters, "is on the verge of dying in a cesspool of depravity."[10]

Even the army was accused of corruption, a fact worrisome to War Minister Araki, who rushed back from the country to his office in civilian clothes. He was met there by grinning officers of the Cherry Blossom Society, who demanded that he seize power, declare martial law, and organize a military government—all, of course, in the name of the emperor.

Araki was relieved to see that this murder, the first attack on a prime minister in modern history, had been carried out by naval officers, not army. He was prepared to resign, but public opinion seemed to be on the side of the plotters. The newspapers lamented the assassination, but they also argued that the assassins had reasons to act. If a relatively free press was supposed to be a guardian of freedom, as Thomas Jefferson had said, then Japan's press failed the test this day. The generals watched public opinion for several days for signs of antimilitary sentiment. There was none. Soon even Araki was crying in public for the assassins:

"When I consider why these naive youths acted as they did, I cannot hold back my tears . . . what they did they did in the genuine belief that it would be good for the Empire."[11]

And when the navy court-martialed the killers, there was not a single death sentence. One by one the prison sentences were commuted. There was no public outcry. Japan had embarked on the road to chaos without public objection.

The Kwantung Army had by this time completed its military campaign in Manchuria and had to be restrained from marching across the Great Wall to north China and Mongolia. Within the army the Imperial Way faction, the *kodo ha,* had triumphed and was demanding power. But eighty-two-year-old Prince Saionji, the emperor's strongest advisor, was still hoping to head off the military oligarchy he could see coming. He faced an almost insoluble problem. The military was too strong to ignore. Almost every day some general expressed antipathy to a government led by politicians. The newspapers gave great prominence to these statements, and the public cheered. After all, for five years the public had been exposed day after day to newspaper stories of political corruption that coursed through the ranks of both major parties, each of which had *zaibatsu* connections.[12]

The army wanted General Araki for prime minister, but Saionji knew that to put Araki in would be the end of representative government. He persuaded the army to compromise on a naval prime minister; despite the Inukai murder the navy was far less riddled with militarism than the army. Admiral Makoto Saito became prime minister. He was one of the most liberal of the admirals, even though he was seventy-three years old and retired to the reserve list. Also, his integrity was unquestionable. Both political parties, recognizing the emergency, supported him. The army could find no reason to oppose him. General Araki remained as war minister.

The Saito government was in trouble from the beginning. General Araki made one demand after another for more money for army expansion. He was steadily opposed by Finance Minister Korekiyo Takahashi.

The army unabashedly extended its campaign of aggression in China. The Manchuria affair was not yet ended; Japan had recognized the new state but had not yet dealt with the matter in the League of Nations. Yosuke Matsuoka, from the South Manchurian Railway, was the special ambassador sent to Geneva to argue Japan's case. Along with him went General Tatekawa and Colonel Ishihara, two of the principal plotters in the Kwantung Army seizure of Mukden.[13]

Japan's new road was indicated by Privy Councillor Viscount Kentaro Kaneko, in a speech to an assembly of army officers on the last day of August 1932. Japan was to invoke a Monroe Doctrine in Asia. Viscount Kaneko said the idea had been urged upon him in 1905 by President Theodore Roosevelt.

The army men who assembled to hear this speech included General Araki, virtually all the high officers of the war ministry, and the army general staff. This speech was just what they wanted to hear; it reinforced their idea that Japan was going to lead Asia into a new era, with Japan controlling a vast Asian empire. This idea, of course, meant that the white man had to go. Japan had marked the Asian continent as its own.[14]

The Asian Monroe Doctrine was welcomed by the Japanese press. The next day *Asahi,* the largest newspaper, ran a long editorial pointing out the need for it.

This attitude permeated all Japan. The newspapers stationed permanent correspondents in Manchuria, as they had them in Seoul and Taihoku, capitals of other Japanese colonies. Only the form of Manchukuo's government was different, and everyone knew this was merely a pretext to try to confuse the outside world. The true masters of Manchukuo were the generals of the Kwantung Army.

Following the conquest of Manchuria, the Chinese soldiers who continued to resist became "bandits." The Japanese position in Manchuria had been "legalized" and now the interlopers were the Chinese.

This Monroe Doctrine for Japan in 1932 became the real foreign policy of Japan. Ambassador Matsuoka at Geneva explained this as the reason the Japanese would not accept the Lytton Commission's recommendation that Manchuria be placed under international rule by the League of Nations. That, said Ambassador Matsuoka, would mean a continuation and extension of Western imperialism in Asia. There was the rub. The only imperialism the Japanese were prepared to accept from this point on was their own.

"America's control of the destiny of Panama is no more essential to the safety of the United States than is Japan's control of Manchuria to the safety of her empire," said Scrutator, a columnist for the *Japan Times.*[15]

"The recognition of Manchukuo marks the first step toward an independent diplomacy," said the newspaper *Jiji Shimpo.*[16]

Westerners did not seem to come to grips with this announcement of a new Japanese imperialism to match their own. Americans, in particular, had never really considered the Monroe Doctrine to be imperialistic, so it was easy enough to toss off the Japanese claims as so much propaganda from Tokyo. But in Tokyo, America was seen for what she was, a truly imperialist power. The Japanese had no complaints to make about United States imperialism, as long as it did not affect Japanese interests. What the Japanese now insisted upon was the right to do what the Westerners had already done.

From Washington came the stern disapproval of Secretary of

State Stimson, but it was not matched by the same fervor from President Herbert Hoover. After all, 1932 was an election year in the United States, and Hoover's main concern was the American economy. As for Britain, her main concern was not only the economy but the unpleasant development of events in Europe. On the very day that Viscount Kaneko unveiled his Japanese Monroe Doctrine, off in Berlin Hermann Goering was elected speaker of the lower house of the German Reichstag in a smooth coup by Hitler, who had combined forces with the Catholic party to bring power to the minority National Socialist forces in the Reichstag. That day also, Dictator Mussolini, the strongest totalitarian leader in Europe, backed Hitler's demand for military parity with Britain and France. Britain had plenty to worry about within a thousand miles of home. Japan was a long way off.

Seeking approval for their behavior the Japanese found it where they wanted. A Hearst columnist, George E. Sokolosky, told a Williamsburg symposium that Japan had done just the right thing in seizing Manchuria. A Professor Dodd at the University of Chicago advocated the dumping of the U.S. constitution and its provisions for separation of executive, legislative, and judicial powers in favor of a more efficient system. Such material was meat and drink for the Japanese journalists and politicians. "See," they could say, "all the world is following the lead of the totalitarians. Our way is the way of the future."

馬鹿につける薬なし

11. "There is no medicine to cure a fool"

*B*y the end of September 1932, General Araki was talking about Japan forming her own "League of Nations."[1] To Araki it was a foregone conclusion that the League of Nations would reject Japan's coup in Manchuria, and neither he nor any of the other generals were prepared to back down. "A question of life or death for Japan," he called it. That was the army line: Japan must be imperialist or die.

Thus General Araki began the campaign that would turn Japan into a totalitarian militarist state.

The opening public move came in a press conference on September 23, 1932, when Araki digressed from a discussion of Manchuria and the League of Nations to discuss the Imperial Way.

"The principle of the Imperial Way is that the Emperor and the people, the land and morality, are one and indivisible."[2]

Araki was at this point beginning the transformation of the army. The method was *seishin kyoiku,* "spiritual training." It began even before the recruit reported for duty at his nearest army headquarters. A letter was sent to the family, telling them of the great honor the son was to have, to serve the emperor, and that from the day the youth entered the barracks the army would become father and mother to him.

On that day, the youths disappeared into the barracks in their civilian clothes and came out in a short while to parade before their admiring relatives in full uniform. The parades were never sloppy, for nearly all those young men had already been subjected to military discipline in the schools. When the army had retrenched after the retreat from Siberia, thousands of officers had become teachers, and here in the early 1930s was the result.

This invitation to families to watch their sons and brothers inducted was not just a polite gesture. It was a part of General Araki's plan for the nation. The army was the vanguard; the target was the nation of Japan; the goal was to build a nation of people dedicated to denial of self, with such ardent loyalty to the Imperial Way, that the citizen would feel that dying for the emperor was a privilege. The ultimate goal, said General Araki, was to instill into the nation the soul of the soldier.

"Whether I float as a corpse under the waters, or sink beneath the grasses of the mountainside, I willingly die for the Emperor." Every day, every morning for two years, that chant greeted the rising sun as the soldiers began their training.[3]

They marched for miles in the summer heat without helmets, and when they were completely exhausted and ready to drop, their officer would give the command for double time and they would run the last mile. That was proof, said the officer, that a man could always find a reserve of strength to do his best for the emperor. In the winter they trained in the cold, maneuvers were held without tents in subzero weather. The men bivouacked in the snow, and during a maneuver they were not allowed to sleep for three or four days.

If men dropped and died in this training, and they did, bits of hair and nail clippings were saved, the body was cremated, and a terse announcement to the family accompanied the personal effects; their son had died a hero's death for the emperor. Seldom did a family learn any more.

The soldiers were taught to be fierce as well as hardy. Bayonet training was all important. With masked helmet, padded apron, and padded gloves they learned to use a rifle-sized stick with a padded knob on the end, to charge their "opponents" with dreadful shrieks, to punish them, to relish close combat. Always, their officers told them, to relish close combat. Always, their officers told them, they must attack. Never must they think of defense.

> Under the falling blade there is a river of hell.
> Jump into it and you might float.

Let the enemy cut your skin
You cut his flesh
Let the enemy cut your flesh
You cut his bones.[4]

Such quotations, taught carefully to the officers, were dinned into the men. Take the offensive—surprise the enemy—death rather than surrender—no retreat—these were the rules of the Japanese army.

It took two years, the term of the youth in the military service, two years of harsh, hard training, where noncommissioned officers beat into the recruits the army law: obey without question. At the end of the two years, the soldiers were assembled, the Imperial Rescript to Soldiers and Sailors was read to them once again, as it had been on all important occasions during their service, and they were disbanded, to go home and join the reserve associations. They had no further responsibility, except if some crisis occurred, then they would come back to die for the emperor.

General Araki's rebuilding plan by the fall of 1932 had created a new religion for Japan: Emperor Worship. Officially the religion would be Shinto, the ancient Japanese nature worship. But it was becoming a new Shinto. "Not only the Imperial Army but the entire nation regard our Emperor as a Living God. For us it is not a question of historical or scientific accuracy. It is an article of faith."[5]

If there were Japanese, Buddhists, Christians, and others, who did not agree with this philosophy, after 1932 they had best be careful. For the powers of the Ministry of Home Affairs were strengthened year after year, and the home ministry ran the police. Soon there would also be the Thought Police, watching carefully for any deviation from the norm; the norm was unquestioned obedience to official command.

In 1932 the expansion of the Japanese army officer corps began. For the future that Araki and his generals saw, a much larger army was needed. Primarily this meant officers and noncommissioned officers; the cannon fodder could be whipped into shape quite quickly. Finance Minister Takahashi fought the military budget, but lost round after round of the battle.

The army expanded and expanded. The code was carefully reworked by General Araki and his officers, the *bushido* of the old samurai was improved. The twin swords of the samurai, the long battle sword and the short killing or suicide sword, had gone out of fashion with the modernization of the Japanese army and navy in the 1880s. They had been replaced by the European saber of the Prussian army and the light dress sword of the British navy. But in the 1930s Araki brought back the samurai sword to Japan.[6] Sword makers were encouraged to revive the art, and the Yasukuni Shrine, the Shinto shrine of heroes across from the Imperial Palace, housed the finest sword smithy in the empire. Sons of the samurai, of course, brought forth the family's historic treasures, the ancient weapons so carefully fabricated during the Tokugawa shogunate. Many had been lost, given up during the "sword hunt" when the samurai were forbidden to wear swords any longer and thousands were seized and melted down. Now the officer who had a sword with an ancient lineage was indeed envied; as for the others, a young lieutenant would give a half-year's pay for his new-made samurai sword.

After the *Yonen Gakko,* the beginning military school, the students could aspire to the *Shikwan Gakko,* Japan's military academy in Tokyo, in the former gardens of the Tokugawa shoguns. There the budding officers were exposed to a thoroughly military education. In fact, the great difference between the army and the navy began here; at the naval academy in Eta Jima, in Hiroshima Bay, the students were educated. That was the naval philosophy. At the *Shikwan Gakko,* the army students were trained. They came out of school full of *bushido* and enthusiasm for war. Their training had taught them to lead their platoons with drawn swords. Such action was worth the firepower of twenty rifles, the Japanese Field Service Manual said. "The Officer by his courage and coolness under a rain of bullets must inspire the soldiers and imbue them with unshakeable confidence in himself." This was almost pure samurai philosophy, as in this advice from *Hagakure,* the *Book of the Samurai:*

> When on the battlefield, if you try not to let others take the lead and have the sole intention of breaking into the enemy lines, then you will not fall behind the others, your mind will become fierce, and you will manifest martial valor. . . . Furthermore if you are slain in battle, you should be resolved to have your corpse facing the enemy.[7]

The training and the philosophy had serious flaws: they substituted courage for common sense. Unlike the navy officers, the Japanese army leaders knew virtually nothing about their potential enemies, the armies of the Soviet Union and the United States. They neither knew nor cared anything about the industrial potential of their enemies. They substituted faith for reason; Japan was in the right, they said, and faith and courage would conquer all. The leaders of the Imperial Army were by 1932 fanatic in this belief. They were so concerned with the development of the Japanese martial spirit that this program dominated all else.

The philosophy also led the army into dishonesty and arrogance in dealings with the outside world. "Walk with a real man a hundred yards and he will tell you at least seven lies," said the *Hagakure*. In the samurai tradition, lying to the outside world, as opposed to lying to your master, was not only permitted, it was regarded as intelligent. General Araki had no compunction about lying. At the end of September 1932, R. G. Marshal of the United Press Associations asked the general if Japan was not building up an enormous supply of munitions for war, and was moving into Jehol Province.[8] Absolutely not, said General Araki. Whereupon Japan's army, which had been stockpiling enormous amounts of munitions, moved into Jehol Province. By March 1933, the key area of Jehol had been occupied by the Kwantung Army.

After Japan walked out of the League of Nations in 1932 the military expenditures went higher and higher, until in 1934 they amounted to nearly a billion yen, or 43 percent of the total Japanese budget. Why? asked Finance Minister Takahashi. None of his business, said War Minister Araki. This arrogance brought no great public outcry. It was an indication of the speed of the march towards military oligarchy in Japan and where it was taking the army.

General Araki now supervised the preparation of a large number of "public affairs" pamphlets for distribution to the troops. They were also distributed to schools and the general public. The theme was *kodo,* the Imperial Way. The subjects were defense, the perfidy of the white men, the need for a Pan-Asian doctrine, and the need for a war to cleanse Asia of European colonialism. All this material was swallowed by the Japanese people without a choke.

The year 1934 opened on a more belligerent Japan that was warning the world not to help China in her effort to fight Japanese imperialism. By summer, a new international naval conference was on the world agenda. Japan had already decided that she was going to build an enormous fleet, one the "fleet faction" promised would be capable of defeating the British and the Americans when the time came. Some cooler heads still had influence in the navy, among them Rear Admiral Isoroku Yamamoto, who, because of his enormous prestige in the navy, was chosen as chief military delegate to the London Naval Conference of 1934. But he went there with specific instructions: he was to secure equal rights to arms in terms of total naval tonnage, or Japan would withdraw, abrogate the naval treaties, and go it alone.

The feeling of the general public was shown at Tokyo station as the delegation left for Yokohama and their ship: dozens of officers and civilians showed up, not to wish them well, but to harangue them on what was expected at London.[9]

The London naval talks went on through December. At the end of January, without an agreement, Admiral Yamamoto and his staff began the land journey across the Trans-Siberian Railway. They were going home. Yamamoto reported to the emperor that the talks had failed, but he suggested that they be kept alive. The sentiment within the navy opposed it; the "fleet faction" was basking in the reflected prestige of the Imperial Army's growing power.

The secret construction of a new navy had already begun while Yamamoto was abroad. Huge 18.1-inch guns had been tested and proved. These were two inches larger than the guns of any other navy in the world. Construction was beginning on the enormous new battleships *Yamato* and *Musashi,* the largest in the world at 72,000 tons. There was no way Admiral Yamamoto could stop the tide of the naval construction program. He devoted himself to the technicalities of his trade. He was a strong advocate of a big carrier force. He opposed the building of the big battleships. By the time they were ready to fight, he said, the science of naval warfare would have turned to the air. Such huge battleships would be of no use, said Yamamoto. With the powerful new aircraft under development, they would be easily sunk from the air. Many "battleship admirals" in the Japanese fleet disagreed with what Yamamoto had to say, and there was no way of showing proof. But Yamamoto argued with force and logic and in the fall of 1935 Yamamoto was appointed chief of the Aeronautics Department of the Imperial Japanese Navy.[10] He was to have his chance to prove his theories.

———

In 1934 the Japanese army continued to expand in China. From Jehol Province the troops moved into adjoining Chahar, which with Suiyuan makes up Inner Mongolia. They penetrated into Hopei Province, where the old northern capital of Peking is located. It was clear that they intended to take all of north China. The reason for this aggressive policy—and millions of Japanese believed ardently in the reasoning—was the need to protect Japan's investment in Manchuria. The continuation of the world depression had convinced those millions that the Japanese economy, without Manchuria, was no longer viable. The continued resistance of Chang Hsueh-liang's forces in northern Manchuria and north China and the refusal of the Chiang Kai-shek government to come to an accommodation with Japan over Manchuria and Inner Mongolia led the majority of the nation to believe that force was the only way.

Another part of the rationale was that Japan was doing only what Britain, France, Spain, Germany, and the United States had done in the Pacific and Asia before her. The Japanese had watched the big powers scrambling for territory and seizing it without regard for the wishes of the inhabitants. They were not impressed by Western arguments that this was not done any more. Having withdrawn from the League of Nations in 1932, after supporting it ardently for a dozen years, Japan felt that she was an outcast among nations and was prepared to go it alone. From that point on the sword would be her scepter.

As it was with Germany, where Hitler had just taken power and was beginning to move to create lebensraum, strong action by the big powers would have stopped Japan's expansion. But the big powers were unprepared and afraid. Soviet Russia was trying to create a viable economy and let Japan alone. The United States and Britain both supported China's position against piecemeal takeover, but neither was willing to risk war with Japan by doing anything about it.

Internally, however, there was another serious military problem in Japan. The army overseas, in Manchuria and China, was out of control. Following the success of the young officers' coup in the Manchurian incident, the officers overseas took the position that they were in charge of policy in their own area, without regard to Tokyo. The result was harsh repression wherever the Japanese army trod. Several times Emperor Hirohito noticed this failing, but nothing ever seemed to happen.[11]

The Imperial Way faction of the army (*kodo ha*) had taken control with the Manchurian incident. General Araki, the war minister, was a founding member of the *Kokuhonsha,* Society for the Foundation of the State. His associates were generals Mazaki, Ugaki, and Koiso and Admiral Saito, the premier. But while the *kodo ha* seemed to be riding high in the army and making inroads into the navy, the control faction *(tosei ha)* was far from dead, and with General Araki's moves to radicalize the army, a large number of officers turned from the *kodo ha* to the *tosei ha*. They did not accept Araki's view that a Showa Restoration was needed, in the same way that the Meiji Restoration had eliminated the shogunate. Araki and his fellows of *kodo ha* believed that only after political government was destroyed, and the villains around the emperor were replaced by army and navy officers, could Japan become stable. The *tosei ha* generals lamented the excesses of the army in Manchuria and Mongolia and vowed that they had to stop; the army must be brought under central control. The *tosei ha* looked to Europe and saw how rapidly Hitler was remaking a military Germany, under tight, central control. Until the Japanese forces in Manchuria and north China could be controlled, there was no chance of this happening in Japan, and the Araki faction was making no effort to control the Kwantung Army.[12]

This matter of control became more and more important. Several times the emperor expressed his dissatisfaction with the way the army overseas was behaving. In January 1934 General Araki was forced to step down as war minister and was replaced by General Senjuro Hayashi, leader of the control faction of the army. The emperor was extremely pleased because General Hayashi promised to abide by the spirit of the Meiji Rescript to Soldiers and Sailors, which, among other things, set down the rule that military men stayed completely out of politics.

The emperor was still worried. He observed in January to his aide, General Honjo, that the military men were doing entirely too much talking about political affairs.[13]

The factionalism of the army continued to be a major problem of Japanese government policy at home and abroad. Foreign Minister Koki Hirota told the emperor in the spring of 1934 that the factionalism made it hard to carry on foreign policy since what one group espoused the other army group immediately opposed.

The army, by this time, had begun lying regularly to the emperor. Prince Kanin, the army chief of staff, assured the emperor on March 17, 1934, that the army had no intention of taking aggressive action against China. Actually the army was taking aggressive action every day.

The emperor continued to watch carefully the activities of his government. He asked for a report from War Minister Hayashi about the state of mind of the young officers and was assured that they were "growing more tranquil."[14]

But turmoil continued. In the summer of 1934 Keisuke Okada succeeded Prime Minister Saito.

In the spring of 1935, Manchukuo troops (puppets of the Kwantung Army) drove Chinese troops out of Jehol Province. A Chinese newspaper editor friendly to Japan was assassinated when he wrote favorably about the Japanese. The Japanese insisted on the withdrawal from Hopei Province of all Chinese troops, and after a month Ho Ying-chin, the Chinese war minister, agreed to do so. The Kwantung Army increased its forces around Shanhaikwan and Kupeikou. Japanese army policy became more brutal. The emperor followed these events daily, but he was given a highly distorted picture by the people around him; he was reassured constantly that Japan was making no effort to enlarge the sphere of activity. The opposite was true.

Within the army the continued resistance of the Chinese brought demands of the young officers for stronger action to assure Japanese control in north China.

The Military Affairs Bureau of the army continued under the control of the conservative *tosei ha,* although the waves created by the Imperial Way group were swirling all around the Imperial General Headquarters. In 1934 General Koiso went to other duty, and so did Colonel Tojo. Tojo was rewarded in 1933 by promotion to major general and command of the military academy. From that vital post he went to command the 24th Infantry Brigade and, thus, he was out of the intensely political Tokyo atmosphere of the period.

Tojo's friend and military academy classmate, Tetsuzan Nagata, remained in the Military Affairs Bureau in Tokyo. He was also promoted to major general's rank. In 1934 he was in Tokyo when a number of young officers planned a new coup. The *Kempeitai* swooped down on them and prevented the series of political killings the officers had in mind. General Nagata and others hushed up the affair by holding the court-martial behind locked doors. This became another *kodo ha–tosei ha* struggle when General Mazaki, the inspector general of military training and a *kodo ha* man, managed to get the charges quashed and the young officers released.[15]

Some of them were sent to the Kwantung Army, which meant they would continue their revolutionary activity.

On July 13 the emperor remarked to Prime Minister Okada that the cabinet must be on guard against being led by the nose by the military forces stationed overseas.

The Kwantung Army had decided to have the South Manchurian Railway establish a major company in north China; this move was planned without any consultation with the government. Prime Minister Okada was upset, but he told General Honjo, who was at this time military aide to the emperor, that he could not stop it. Here was a prime example of army arrogance.

On July 15 the army matter came to a head. The triumvirate that ran the army, the war minister, the chief of staff, and the chief of military education, had been meeting to discuss personnel problems. The most serious was the continued recalcitrance of many young officers, and the emperor had asked the war minister to be sure that only officers willing to take orders were sent overseas. In these summer meetings the difficulties between the Imperial Way and the control faction came to a head. War Minister General Hayashi then went to the emperor and asked that Inspector General Jinzaburo Mazaki be relieved of command, since he was one of the most important leaders of the *kodo ha* and as such was destroying discipline within the army. Mazaki, said the war minister, had been one of those primarily responsible for several short-lived rebellions at the military academy over army policy. The emperor knew also that Mazaki had been responsible for the improper advance of the Japanese army into Jehol Province of China, and that Mazaki and Araki had recently been arousing more unrest in the army.[16]

So General Mazaki was kicked upstairs to become a member of the Supreme War Council, and General Jotaro Watanabe was appointed inspector general of military education. Watanabe was a control faction member.

A number of the young staff officers objected to the changes, and one of them, Lieutenant Colonel Saburo Aizawa, decided that Major General Tetsuzan Nagata, the director of the powerful Military Affairs Bureau, was responsible for the downfall of Aizawa's hero, Mazaki, and that the new administration was bent on turning the army over to the control of the *zaibatsu* and the politicians. He went to General Nagata and accused him and said that if Nagata were a loyal officer, he would resign his post. Nagata refused and ordered Aizawa transferred to Taiwan for insubordination. This was precisely the sort of excess by young officers that the *tosei ha* of the army wanted to bring under control.

A furious Lieutenant Colonel Aizawa then journeyed to the great national shrine at Ise, prayed there, and came back to Tokyo, walked into General Nagata's office and killed him. He was ordered up for court-martial, but his action was approved by hundreds of young officers drawn to the Imperial Way faction.

As a result of this affair, War Minister Hayashi resigned and was replaced by General Yoshiyuki Kawashima.

As the year progressed, the fortunes of the Imperial Way faction seemed to be heading steadily downward. In the fall the Seiyukai party, which backed Araki and his friends, lost prestige. In January the party miscalculated, because it still had a majority of seats in the Diet, and forced the dissolution of parliament. In the new elections, the Seiyukai met disaster, as did all the ultranationalist groups. The people had spoken against the extremism that the Kwantung Army and its followers in Japan had been exhibiting, in what would be the last backlash of public opinion in pre–World War II Japan. The Minseito party, which backed the control faction, became the strongest in Japan.

The Imperial Way faction had become so outspoken in its demands and was so well known that a time of crisis was approaching. No longer could the Imperial Way be achieved by parliamentary means, the leaders decided. The triggering incident was the order given to General Mazaki to testify at the murder trial of Lieutenant Colonel Aizawa. He appeared but refused to answer questions. It was obvious that he was going to be disciplined by the army.[17]

So, the Imperial Way faction of the army concluded that unless they staged a coup d'état, they were lost. On the morning of February 15 appeared a notice in the "personals" column of *Asahi Shimbun:*

> Current Issues Stabilized: There has been a crystallization of the correct judgment of you who are wise and can see into the meaning of things. Let us make every effort—all of us unitedly—to strengthen our national power and to make progress for the Empire by leaps and bounds.
> Leader of the Orient, Marunouchi
> Art Club, Half-Piercing Solid Star.[18]

That advertisement was the signal to the waiting troops of the Imperial Way. The plot was all laid out. The time was now set for the early morning hours of February 26, 1936. The instruments chosen by the ringleaders were the First Infantry Regiment, the Third Regiment, the Third Imperial Guard Regiment, and the Seventh Artillery Regiment. The leaders were Captain Shiro Nonaka and Captain Teruzo Ando.

Before dawn the assassin groups were on their ways, each numbering thirty officers and men, each given a specific target and as much information about the person as possible. Seven important government figures were targets for assassination.

One group hurried to the prime minister's official residence and broke into the house. An officer led them down a corridor. They opened the door and as the figure in the bed arose, they began firing.

Admiral Kantaro Suzuki, the Grand Chamberlain, was aroused by the noise of the intruders. He got up from his bed and faced them. The leader of the mob was a master sergeant.

"I want you, Lord Grand Chamberlain, to surrender your life for the sake of the Showa Restoration."

"What are you talking about? Who is your leader?" demanded the Grand Chamberlain.

The sergeant stopped. He did not answer.

"So you cannot say anything! Then shoot!"

Two shots were fired, and another assassin rushed forward with a samurai sword to cut off the admiral's head. But Mrs. Suzuki struggled with him and he put down the sword. The assassins left. Mrs. Suzuki called a doctor, and her husband survived.[19]

Another group went to the residence of Viscount Makoto Saito, the Lord Keeper of the Privy Seal. Altogether, 150 officers and soldiers burst into the house. The viscountess met them in her night robes and said they should kill her first. They pushed her aside and stepped into Saito's bedroom firing submachine guns. Saito died with forty-seven wounds.

Assassins found General Watanabe at home and killed him. Another group went to the hot springs at Yugawara where Count Makino was staying in a Japanese inn. They could not find him, he was warned and got away. Another group went to the house of Finance Minister Korekiyo Takahashi, and they, too, bungled. The finance minister was only wounded.

Other groups of revolutionaries seized the War Office, the new Diet building, and various communications centers.

All this destruction was accomplished by 4:30 in the morning. At *Mainichi Shimbun,* the overnight reporter on duty in the newsroom was dozing in his chair, wondering if the snow had stopped yet. A blizzard from Siberia had roared down on Tokyo that night, and the streets were covered with snow.[20]

The quiet of the room was broken by the ringing of the telephone. The reporter picked it up.

"The prime minister's residence is being raided. Our army is attacking *us,*" shouted a voice. And then the connection was broken.

The reporter put on his overcoat and went out into the snow. He got into his car and began driving toward Nagata-cho in central Tokyo. He passed Hibiya Park and went on, nearing the government section of the city. Suddenly a soldier in a brown overcoat and garrison cap stepped into the road ahead of him and waved him over with his rifle. The reporter slowed and stopped. He rolled down the window.

"I'm from *Mainichi Shimbun,*" he said.

"Who cares about the press? Turn back!" shouted the soldier, and he brought his gun around to point it at the car.

The reporter turned the car around and drove back to the newspaper office. He picked up the telephone. . . .

The plotters were thorough. Colonel Itagaki, the executioner of the Mukden plot, had been promoted to be chief of staff of the Kwantung Army. Naturally, the young officers group believed they could count on this proven successful rebel. But when Itagaki got the word, there was a complication: General Tojo could not be counted on to support the rebels. Quite to the contrary, Tojo's association with General Nagata warned Itagaki that he could count on Tojo *opposing* the plot with all the power of the *Kempeitai.* So instead of joining, as he might have been tempted to do, Itagaki informed Tojo of the message and told him to take all measures necessary to preserve order in the Kwantung Army. He need not have asked. Tojo was already moving. As a routine matter the *Kempeitai* opened the mail of suspicious figures, gathered information from police spies, and routinely tortured criminals to discover what they knew. Tojo had the dossiers of all the malcontents among the officers' corps of the Kwantung Army, all the South Manchurian

Railway employees, and other civilians. Within hours the *Kempeitai* had swooped down on military and civil suspects, taken them into custody, and Manchuria, the tinderbox, had been thoroughly wetted down.

Privately, Tojo was upset by the disturbance that rocked the army and he told his wife what a pity it was. Publicly he followed the line of duty, which led to the authorities of the war ministry and the chief of the Imperial General Staff.[21]

Behind the cordon of soldiers the greatest tragedy yet to befall a modern Japan was being played out.

General Honjo, the emperor's military aide, and one of the conspirators of the Mukden incident, was completely shocked at 5:00 A.M. when an officer from the First Infantry Regiment awakened him at his home with a message from his son-in-law, a regimental officer, who was one of the conspirators.[22]

Honjo called a car and hastened to the Imperial Palace, where he learned of the murders and the other attacks.

The fact was that it was hard for General Honjo to blame the young officers, for secretly he sympathized, as did nearly all the generals, with the Imperial Way group's yearning for untrammeled army power.

One person who did not sympathize in the least was the emperor. War Minister Kawashima showed up at the palace at about nine o'clock, having held his first meeting with the officers occupying the War Office. The war minister began talking, justifying the tragedy as the result of a weak cabinet; he had met with the young officers and was impressed by their deep sincerity, etc. etc. etc. He began to read the rebels' manifesto.

The emperor looked at him furiously. "You don't need to tell us that. Isn't it rather your duty to determine by what means this rebellion will be quelled?"

The word rebellion was the harshest that anyone in authority had yet used. The war minister was thunderstruck.

"I humbly beg your pardon," he said, and withdrew.[23]

The generals were hoping to quiet the matter down and proceed as though nothing had happened. The emperor would not have it.

When the small army of newspaper reporters and photographers from the Tokyo metropolitan press moved into central Tokyo that morning, they found that every street in the government district was blocked off by armed soldiers who appeared more than usually menacing. Field guns and machine guns were sitting in the intersections. The area round the Diet, the prime minister's house, the Metropolitan Police Headquarters, and the whole government area down to Akasaka was occupied by troops. The reporters were not allowed to pass.

What had happened?

No one outside the cordoned area really knew.

An army car accompanied by two trucks full of soldiers pulled up in front of the *Mainichi* building, and the officer in the back seat of the car thrust a leaflet into the hand of a reporter. The officer had a difficult time delivering the leaflet for he was clutching a samurai sword in one hand and a revolver in the other.[24]

The reporter looked down at the leaflet, as the officer held the gun on him. The truckloads of soldiers included other officers, all equipped with samurai swords and pistols. The soldiers in the trucks were pointing their guns at the windows of the newspaper building.

But finally they went away, and the leaflet could be read: "We have been compelled to annihilate those elder statesmen, military leaders, bureaucrats, political party leaders and other criminals who have been shamelessly hindering the Heavenly prerogative of the Supreme being from materializing the Divine Showa Restoration. . . ."[25]

Whatever that meant, obviously it was not intended to be funny. It was not funny. A rebellion was in progress, a rebellion of field troops of the Imperial Army. Not even the generals knew about this one. It came from the source, those peasant soldiers who had been growing more distressed each month with the knowledge that their parents and brothers and sisters back on the farm and in the villages were going hungry. Or was it as simple as that? The young officers and soldiers who had appeared at the newspaper offices were sincere enough. But were they instigators or pawns?

That day, Wednesday, February 26, the newspapermen sat idle. There was no news of the rebellion, and before the day was out the visit of the rebels was followed by a visit from military authorities, to *Mainichi* and every other newspaper. The newspapermen were told that they were forbidden to speculate on it. Nothing was to appear to signify that any disturbance had taken place that day. Nothing! It was 8:15 that evening before the newspaper editors and reporters had any real inkling of what was happening. The public, except for those people who saw the troops and were threatened in one way or another, knew nothing at all of what was going on.[26]

Since the War Office was occupied by the rebels, the war minister and the other officials gathered at the military police headquarters to plan their next steps. General Kawashima wanted desperately to gloss over the matter. General Mazaki led the others in preparing a proclamation that sounded like an endorsement of the rebellion. But it did not work this time. The emperor was enraged, and he did not completely trust the military men around him. His instructions were clear: quell the rebellion.

In a few more hours the newspapermen began to sort out what had happened during the early hours of the morning. The first facts, other than the sight of the armed men, came from the Ministry of War at 8:15 on Wednesday evening. It was a grim report of bloodshed, but with no indication of any resolution.

The rebels continued to hold the War Office, the various other vital points, and the prime minister's house.

That night the newspapers were published as usual, but with almost no indication that anything untoward had occurred. They did report that the Tokyo Stock Exchange had been closed all day Wednesday, but they did not say why. That was the only indication of any excitement.[27]

That night, the Supreme War Councillors met with the rebel officers at the war ministry and tried to persuade them to give up the rebellion. They read the strange proclamation that seemed so sympathetic, but did note that all depended on His Majesty's will. They did not tell the rebels the extent of His Majesty's anger or his insistence that the traitors be punished. War Minister Kawashima and Vice Chief of Staff Sugiyama were most concerned that the affair not develop into a confrontation between the Imperial Way faction and the control faction, which it threatened to do.

Meanwhile, the emperor's orders were being obeyed, reluctantly. A state of emergency was declared, and the First Division was directed to maintain order. The rebels, who surrounded the key points, were, in turn, now surrounded by loyal troops. The First and Second fleets were ordered up to Tokyo Bay and Osaka Bay. The marines at Yokosuka naval base were ordered to Tokyo. Since the assassins had killed the prime minister, Home Minister Fumio Goto held a cabinet meeting at the Imperial Palace and organized the government for action.[28]

The second day ran into the first. At 1:00 A.M. on February 27 the whole cabinet resigned. The emperor saw that War Minister Kawashima had not made any special gesture for his major responsibility in the disaster, and His Majesty was again furious. General Honjo tried to excuse his fellow general, but the emperor was not impressed.[29]

The emperor declared martial law and Lieutenant General Kohei Kashii was appointed to carry it out. The emperor told him to disarm the troops by force if necessary. The timing was left to the general, so he stalled.

General Honjo tried to excuse the actions of the officers involved, particularly since his son-in-law belonged to the rebel group. They meant well, he said, even if they were wrong.

"How can we not condemn even the spirit of these criminally brutal officers who killed my aged subjects who were my hands and feet?" said the emperor. "To kill old subjects whom I trusted in most is akin to strangling me with a silken cord."[30]

This was a Hirohito the palace courtiers had never before seen. In the fumbling, the excusing, the inaction, he was growing impatient. He told Honjo that something had better be done quickly by the military authorities.

"Otherwise," he said, "I shall personally lead the Imperial Guard Division and subdue them."[31]

There was a threat to frighten the generals! For if the emperor did indeed lead out the troops personally, all his generals would, for honor's sake, have to commit suicide. That word got to the generals quickly enough.

The severity of the moment was relaxed slightly by report of an almost comic development reported by the chief of the military police to the palace: the insurgent soldiers who had rushed to the prime minister's house to assassinate him had, in fact, mistaken Prime Minister Okada's brother-in-law, Colonel Matsuo, for the chief minister, and they had killed him. Okada had hidden in a closet.

The murderers had taken up station to occupy the house, and they stayed. Eventually they brought in a coffin and put the body in it. They let the prime minister's secretaries in to see the body; the secretaries looked at one another, and then retired discreetly, saying nothing.

One of the maids found one of the secretaries and asked him to come to her room. He did so, and there in a closet he found Prime Minister Okada, safe and sound.[32]

On this second day, the secretary negotiated with the officer in charge of the house to allow some family and friends to come to mourn over the corpse. The dead were to be treated gently, the officer knew, and he acceded to the request.

The secretary brought in friends, and they viewed the body, saying nothing. He also brought a white face mask, a pair of horn-rimmed glasses, and an extra morning coat. These were delivered to the maid's closet and out of it stepped a man in glasses, a mask, and a morning coat. They moved along the corridor to the porch off the mourning room. There a local police officer was directing the traffic. He had been let in on the secret, and when he saw the man in the mask he yelled at him:

"You fool, didn't I tell you that seeing the dead man would upset you?" He shouted at a soldier:

"Call a car! Quick!"

The soldier ran down to the courtyard and got a car. The man in the face mask and horn-rimmed glasses put a handkerchief to his face as well and was hustled down into the car and out of the premises, the rebels watching curiously.[33]

It was another two days before the prime minister could be spirited safely to the Imperial Palace to report to His Majesty. He resigned then, and Foreign Minister Hirota Koki became the new prime minister.

By that time, only because of the emperor's insistence, the rebellion had been squelched. For three days his generals had tried to ameliorate his stance. For three days he had repeated his demand that the rebels be arrested and punished severely. None of the comments about their spirit or their intentions swayed him.

The generals tried to temporize. They promised military action, then came to the palace and reported that the rebels were giving up so it would not be necessary. The rebels would then back away, and the emperor would again insist on action. Finally, on Friday, February 28, it became apparent to the generals that all their arguments were futile, the emperor would not budge, and that their own time was running out.[34]

General Kawashima made one last attempt to find clemency for the traitors. He came to the Imperial Palace and announced that the rebels were prepared to commit suicide for their crimes, but for honor's sake, they wanted an imperial agent sent to inform them to commit *seppuku*. The commander of the First Division said he did not want to tell his troops to fire on their fellow soldiers. There was no other way, said War Minister Kawashima, to resolve the incident.

The emperor snorted. He would not honor these traitors thus.

"If they wish to commit suicide, let them do as they please. It is out of the question to dispatch an Imperial agent to such men."[35]

The emperor then told Honjo in the strongest terms to see that the rebels were subjugated *at once.*

Honjo was petrified. He dared not utter a word as he backed out of the Imperial Presence.

Honjo's son-in-law called and said the imperial agent must come. Honjo gave his son-in-law the bad news. There would not be an imperial agent.

Finally, General Honjo summoned a representative from the Imperial War Council, the supreme military body of Japan. Ironically, the man who came was General Araki, who was more responsible than any other for what had happened. Honjo told him what the emperor demanded, and Araki, the promoter of the Imperial Way, had no recourse but to yield to the imperial command. Force would be used to subdue the rebels, he said. Immediately.

The generals were still loath to open fire. Planes came over Tokyo and dropped leaflets all around the government area, explaining the situation and demanding surrender. At six o'clock on Saturday morning, February 29, General Kashii was ready to open fire. The First Division was ordered to move at 8:00 A.M. to one area, and the Imperial Guard Division was ordered to move at the same time.[36]

At 8:30 the First Division troops were moving in, bayonets fixed, bullets in the chambers of the rifles. The rebels began surrendering en masse. By 11:30 only a handful of men at the prime minister's house and 200 soldiers under Captain Ando at the Sanno Hotel were still holding out.

At 2:00 P.M. Captain Ando tried to commit suicide, but botched it. By 2:30 the last troops had surrendered. General Kashii reported to the Imperial Palace and told the emperor that the incident was over. By 5:00 P.M. traffic was moving normally all over Tokyo.

War Minister Kawashima appeared at court that evening and

asked His Majesty's forgiveness. He had told all the rebel officers that they must now commit *seppuku*. None had, and they had all been arrested.

The young officers were still under the illusion that their actions had been heroic, not treason. They expected to have their day in court and to be treated as had the "heroes" of the Manchurian incident. But the public, on learning of the imperial attitude, turned against the army rebels this time. The officers were stripped of their commissions and honors. The war minister issued a statement apologizing to the emperor and the nation for the "indelible black mark" the army had smudged on the history of the Showa regime.[37]

For a week the *Kempeitai* moved through the army ranks making arrests of conspirators, including General Honjo's son-in-law. Five special courts were created. The rule was set: there would be no appeals. There would be no public sideshow, the trials would be held in secret.[38]

The army high command was shaken up. Generals Minami, Hayashi, Mazaki, Abe, and Araki were retired. A new commander was sent to the Kwantung Army. Kawashima was retired. General Honjo, disgraced by his son-in-law, also retired. A new inspector general of military education was appointed and instructed by the emperor to give the young officers some education in realities instead of so much *bushido*. In July, thirteen of the officers were convicted of treason and executed. Some prison terms were meted out. But, by and large, the army managed to keep punishment to a minimum and to subvert the imperial will regarding the future. The emperor had been able, almost single-handedly, to see that the rebellion was put down. But he could not administer the army and the government, and the rot that had set in was so far advanced that it could not be stopped. The army was still bent on achieving power and destroying the political government of Japan. In the autumn of 1936 the army was still lying low, but the generals continued to scheme.

Emperor Hirohito of Japan. His reign, called Showa (Bright Peace), brought Japan to the bloodiest war and her first defeat in history.

(Japanese Defense Agency.)

Japanese infantry training. A camouflaged soldier in gas mask. A machine gun nest high in a leafless tree. Soldiers moving forward in a truck.

(Japanese Defense Agency.)

A Japanese soldier, home for the first time since war began, greets his young son.
(Japanese Defense Agency.)

Manchuria, 1931. An officer reads orders from Tokyo to the troops.
(Japanese Defense Agency.)

The Japanese army was often called the best in the world. The men often marched through the Manchurian swamps for thirty or forty miles a day.
(Japanese Defense Agency.)

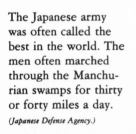

The Japanese seize another town. Manchuria, 1932.

(Japanese Defense Agency.)

1940. These Seaforth Highlanders left Shanghai on August 25, 1940, marching past the Cathay Hotel. They were almost the last line of protection of the British in China, and then they were gone.

(Imperial War Museum, London.)

The famous Betty Bomber (Mitsubishi Type 0) was the workhorse of the Japanese forces. A combination of what the B-17 bombers and C-47 transport were to the Americans.
(Japanese Defense Agency.)

A Japanese naval gun crew at work. Although the Japanese did not have radar, their gunnery was far better than that of the Americans at the outset of the war.
(Japanese Defense Agency.)

Japanese destroyers lay a smoke screen.
(Japanese Defense Agency.)

Prime Minister Tojo
and his war cabinet,
December 1941.
(Imperial War Museum.)

Battleship row,
Ford Island,
Pearl Harbor, Hawaii.
This photograph
was taken from one
of the attacking
Japanese aircraft on
December 7, 1941.
(Japanese Defense Agency.)

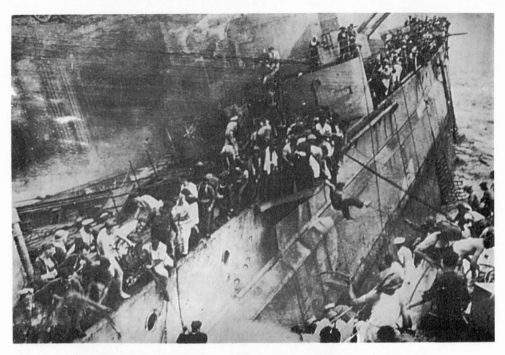

British sailors escaping the battleship *Prince of Wales* off Malaya after
she was bombed by Japanese aircraft on December 10, 1941. Not
long after this photo was taken she sank.

(*Imperial War Museum.*)

Japanese troops in the South Pacific. This photo was propaganda for
the home front.

(*Japanese Defense Agency.*)

Yasukuni Shrine, the spiritual home of 2.5 million Japanese servicemen who lost their lives in the Great East Asia (Pacific) War. The trees have now grown much higher in relation to the *torii*.

(*Japanese Defense Agency.*)

1942. The surrender of the British at Singapore, of February 15. Lieutenant General Yamashita (far side) and General Percival at the interview.

(*Imperial War Museum.*)

1942. Victorious Japanese cavalry parading through Hongkong.
(Imperial War Museum.)

1942. Defeated Australian troops sweeping the streets of Singapore.
This was part of the Japanese propaganda effort to destroy the "face"
of the white man in Asia.
(Imperial War Museum.)

小事は 大事

12. "A small matter can become a great one"

When the abortive rebellion of the young officers was over, it was referred to in Japan as the "2–26 Incident." Disgraceful as it had been, no one then realized that the failed rebellion was simply a convolution in the greater rebellion: that of the Japanese militarists against civilian control.

But from the moment that the rebellion was quelled, the militarists set out to subvert the will of Emperor Hirohito.

Prince Saionji, the most trustworthy of the emperor's advisors, had suggested that the next prime minister ought to be Prince Konoye, a strong figure who was respected by the army. But Prince Konoye refused the post, on the basis of his health. What he meant was the basis of what might happen to his health if he took the job. For in March 1936, the prime ministerial post was the hottest potato in Japan. Koki Hirota was a compromise candidate, a civilian who was known to be a nationalist. He was barely acceptable to the control faction of the army, which was now in charge of army headquarters in Tokyo, although not of the armies overseas.

When Hirota was summoned by the emperor he was given four missions: to govern Japan constitutionally, exercise restraint in foreign affairs, avoid upsetting the business world, and preserve the nobility. These injunctions represented the emperor's worst fears of what the army might try to do.[1]

Prime Minister Hirota immediately ran into trouble: the army was up to its old trick; unless he would agree to the army's veto power over cabinet ministers, no general would serve as war minister and he could not form a cabinet.

The army had now perfected this technique, through which it would force itself to power, and the Hirota cabinet was the proof positive.

The *tosei ha* generals were in complete charge of the army in Tokyo. When Prime Minister Designate Hirota was looking for a war minister, he sought advice from an old acquaintance, General Sugiyama. The general suggested General Hisaichi Terauchi, who had been commander of the army in Korea. Terauchi's great asset was his political naiveté, said Sugiyama.

Hirota could not have asked for advice from a worse source if he sought a restrained war minister. Sugiyama was at the heart of the *tosei ha,* he was vice chief of staff, and one of the most militant of the militarists. Hirota made the error of trusting him.

So Hirota appointed Terauchi, and the army was quite pleased. So was Hirota until he showed Terauchi his list of appointments. Terauchi produced an army blacklist, and five of the Hirota appointments were on it, all men appointed for their fair and liberal views. Terauchi said he could not join the cabinet.[2]

"This cabinet is characterized by the same old liberalistic approach as ever and devoted to compromise and retrogression," the general told the press.

So there could not be a cabinet. No other general would take the war minister's post.

To resolve the issue, the emperor asked questions, through General Honjo, his military aide. The army denied it was interfering, and like a little puppet, Honjo, who had to know the truth, since these men were his old associates, told more lies to His Majesty. The Military Affairs Bureau, which was no less than the army's political arm, was trying to dictate the nature of the new government. At that moment General Tomoyuki Yamashita and Major Akira Muto were at the prime minister's temporary headquarters, charging in on Hirota without notice as they wished, samurai swords at their sides, telling the prime minister whom he could appoint and whom he could not. The arrogance of the army was almost complete. It grew worse. After Hirota had finally winnowed out the names of the men objectionable to the army and made a cabinet, he gave the list to General Terauchi.

"No," said the general. "You have on this list two men from

the Minseito party and two from the Seiyukai party. The army will not accept more than one man from any party. I cannot accept the war ministry."[3]

Finally, Koki Hirota had enough. He sent word to the emperor that the army was dictating his choices. The emperor called General Honjo in again. The army was again interfering by trying to limit the politicians to one member from each party. Honjo tried to deny it, but was shocked to learn that His Majesty no longer trusted him, so he had made private inquiries through the new Lord Privy Seal, Kurahei Yuasa. Here was a loophole in army command that could not be plugged up: the emperor's right to have trusted people around him.

Honjo was quick to get in touch with Sugiyama and inform him of the development.

At about that time Prime Minister Hirota telephoned General Terauchi and told him he had decided to give up trying to form a cabinet because of the army's intransigence and was going to call the newspapers and give them that statement.

In so doing, Hirota took the one action that would save his cabinet. The army was not yet ready to show its steel fist.

"Just a minute," said General Terauchi. "Wait just a minute. . . . No, I'll call back."[4]

So Terauchi went into the Military Affairs Bureau's office and conferred with Sugiyama, Yamashita, and Muto. If Hirota announced his failure to form a cabinet, and if the emperor then criticized the army, all these men would have to resign, and their cause would be lost. They had to back down. So they did, giving full credit to General Terauchi for refusing to budge under pressure and insisting that two political party members from Minseito and Seiyukai be included.

So the cabinet was formed, General Honjo told the new lie to the emperor, and the army told it to the public.[5] The army came out of this struggle with one more great victory: the rules were again changed so that once more only active duty army officers could hold the post of war minister. The rationale was that this would prevent "factionalism" from again emerging. The truth was that this change put complete political veto power in the hands of the leaders of the army.

Despite the change in command of the Kwantung Army, that force continued to defy Tokyo and expand its operations in China as it pleased. In the fall of 1936, Colonel Ishihara, the planner of

the Mukden incident, was sent to Changchun, the capital of Manchukuo and headquarters of the Kwantung Army, on a special mission.

Colonel Ishihara had changed over the years. No longer was
he one of the hotheads who demanded change in the military. He
had joined the *tosei ha,* and now he came to Manchuria to admonish
the leaders of the Kwantung Army in the name of Imperial Japanese
Army Headquarters. In the future, he was to tell General Ueda and
his staff, they were to obey Tokyo's instructions without fail.[6]

When Colonel Ishihara arrived at Changchun, he was taken
immediately to the house of the chief of staff of the Kwantung Army.
And who was that? None other than Colonel Itagaki—Colonel Itagaki, the man who carried out the plot that Ishihara had planned
so expertly. He was General Itagaki now. He had been advanced up
through the ranks of the Kwantung Army, another sign of the Tokyo
military command's failure. The discussion was strained from the
beginning, for the men now found themselves on different sides of
the fence. Other officers at Itagaki's house that evening were Major
General Hitoshi Imamura, the new assistant chief of staff, and Lieutenant Colonel Akiro Muto, who had been transferred to Manchuria
after the 2–26 Incident because he had tried to dictate to the new
Hirota government in the name of the army. He was now staff officer
in charge of Kwantung Army operations in the troublesome and
delicate area of Inner Mongolia.

Colonel Ishihara spoke frankly to this group. Tokyo did not
like what they were doing in Inner Mongolia. It had to stop.

Colonel Muto interrupted.

"Are you merely voicing the opinions of your superiors or do
you yourself truly believe what you are saying?"

"That's enough!" Ishihara commanded. "I'm opposed to any
operations whatsoever in Inner Mongolia. Just when the building of
Manchukuo is finally under way, you want to risk stirring up Russia
and China with these clumsy plots. . . ."

Muto made a rude remark, reminding Ishihara of his own revolutionary past. The others laughed. The tensions grew. Ishihara
turned to his old ally Itagaki for support, but Itagaki was silent. The
embarrassment continued through dinner. The next day Ishihara
repeated his remarks to General Ueda and the others and saw that
he was getting nowhere. That day he left for Tokyo to report that
the Kwantung Army was no more under control than it had been
before.[7]

Later that year the results of Colonel Muto's mischief appeared. The Kwantung Army tried to set up a government in Inner Mongolia headed by Mongol Prince Teh. The Chinese reacted swiftly and sent a military expedition, which defeated the puppet army at Suiyuan and took control of the territory. It was an embarrassment to the Japanese government. General Itagaki was directly responsible for the plot, but he was not even censured.[8]

The government's policy in 1936 called for the careful treatment of the Western powers so as not to antagonize them at the moment, while Japan strengthened her naval forces. Japan would also increase her presence and influence in Southeast Asia, but again not militarily at the moment. The *zaibatsu*, with whom the military was reaching an accommodation, would build up the Japanese industrial position in Korea and Manchuria. By negotiation the government hoped to achieve an alignment with China against the Soviet threat perceived in the north. That's why Colonel Ishihara had gone to Changchun: Japan was trying desperately to push Chiang Kai-shek into fighting the Communists as the price of Japanese nonintervention in his affairs. The blackmail did not succeed, Japan's policy slid into a fragmented effort to create regional government entities in north and west China. The Kwantung Army's constant attempt to seek new military adventures was very embarrassing. The Soviets were not fooled by any statements. They knew the Kwantung Army and its ambition to swallow the maritime provinces of Siberia. The Soviet armed forces in the Far East by 1936 had been trebled.[9]

The anticommunism of Japan permeated the government and became a cornerstone of national policy. Out of it came the signing of the Anti-Comintern pact with Nazi Germany in November 1936.

The government was also busily engaged in building Japan's armed forces. The navy, once the naval agreements with Britain and the United States were junked, embarked on an accelerated shipbuilding program. The intent was to bring the navy to a point where it could guarantee control of the Western Pacific against the U.S. Navy. Thus in 1936 the Japanese national budget increased 22 percent over 1935.

The emperor approved all this. He had been persuaded that Japan must be self-sufficient now that her reliance on international agreements had failed. And the emperor, like Prince Saionji, recognized that the army had so much power now that the only way it could be stopped was to find a government powerful enough to stop it. But as long as the army could cause the fall of the government by withdrawing the war minister from the cabinet, there was no way to develop a government powerful enough to control the army. When the Meiji Constitution was written, this little clause had been envisaged as a protection of the military from the bungling of civilian amateurs. In fact, it had turned out to be the fatal flaw in the Meiji Constitution, which would finally bring about the destruction of the Japanese empire.

千里の道も 一歩より始まる

13. "The road of a thousand miles still begins with a single step"

The Japanese navy was preparing to beard the United States and Great Britain. If only those powers had been willing in 1934 to raise Japan's ratios as against the fleet units of Britain and America, the whole issue of naval strength might have been solved. But the British and the Americans had balked at giving Japan even a 10 percent increase and the submarine force she wanted. So the treaties came unraveled.

The Japanese government had given notice in 1935 that all naval agreements were off. Immediately, construction of the "new navy" had begun. In fact, all the plans had been made two years earlier, and the materials to build the huge new battleships were stockpiled at the Kure naval yard. Elsewhere a campaign to build destroyers, cruisers, aircraft carriers, and submarines began. The rationale of the "treaty faction" of the navy was that only by securing parity at sea could Japan negotiate with the big powers from strength.[1] The "fleet faction" needed no rationale. They had long proposed a powerful fleet to let Japan lead from strength in the diplomatic game. In fact, they had been building such a fleet within the terms of the international naval agreements for ten years. Ton for ton their warships were faster, more heavily armored, and better armed than their British and American counterparts. Their torpedoes were the best in the world, and their torpedomen the most efficient. The submarines built and planned, the RO class and the larger I class, were better fighting instruments than the American S class and Fleet class. The I-boats could cross the Pacific and return without fueling, an achievement the Americans did not manage until after 1945. From 1935 on, the Imperial Navy did a magnificent job with its resources to complete a naval force that could match up to the foreigners. By the end of the decade the navy would succeed beyond its dreams, bolstered by a partnership that transcended personalities to this point. Both naval factions agreed, for their own reasons, on the need for a powerful fleet. The philosophical question of how it was going to be used was not a major issue in the late 1930s.[2]

The Japanese army was preparing to fight the Soviet Union. In 1934 with the intelligence that the Soviets had deployed a large number of heavy bombers to the maritime provinces, the Japanese Imperial General Staff changed its plans for war with the USSR. Of its total force of thirty divisions, 80 percent were earmarked for war against the USSR. The army's air forces were increased and most of the increase went to Manchuria and Korea. The decision was made to attack and fight in Siberia, east of Manchuria, then north to the Lake Baikal district.[3]

Independently, the Kwantung Army was trying to swallow China. By 1935 the Kwantung Army had been increased to four divisions and eighteen air squadrons. The total manpower was 164,000 men. The Imperial General Staff wanted these forces concentrated in Manchuria for possible operations against the Soviets, but the constantly insubordinate Kwantung Army kept moving troops out into Inner Mongolia and China on its adventures.[4]

This was definitely *not* the thinking of the general staff. Colonel Ishihara was in 1936 promoted to major general and chief of the Operations Bureau of the general staff. His order to the China Garrison Army, stationed west of the Great Wall with its headquarters in Tientsin, was to leave the Chinese alone and prepare for operations against the USSR. The training programs of the army were directed to that end. As far as China was concerned, the Imperial General Staff's position was that the China Garrison Army occupied Chinese soil only to protect the borders of Manchukuo and stop Chang Hsueh-liang's raids there. The area of Mongolia and north China was referred to at home in Tokyo as the "neutral zone."[5]

The difficulties with the Kwantung Army caused the Tokyo high command to depend on less direct measures for control. They came to depend on Major General Hideki Tojo, who was sent to Manchuria to head the *Kempeitai*. The *Kempeitai* was far more than a simple unit of men who wore a band on their arms and picked up drunks and AWOL soldiers. The *Kempeitai* was a combination of military police and counterintelligence agency, entrusted with the internal security of the army. As such, no unit and no person of the Kwantung Army was above its inquiries. The *Kempeitai* had far more authority than such a unit in a Western army. The secret police units had the task of rooting out conspiracies inside the army and out. Thus, through the *Kempeitai,* the Tokyo authorities began to bring the Kwantung Army under control. General Tojo, an old friend of General Tetsuzan Nagata, the control faction leader assassinated by Lieutenant Colonel Aizawa, was regarded as one of the most stable members of the control faction.[6]

In Manchuria, General Tojo made the *Kempeitai* the most efficient secret police agency in Japanese history. After he completed the organization, virtually nothing happened in Manchuria that the *Kempeitai* did not know about. And there was a great deal to follow, for intrigue threaded throughout Manchukuo, the puppet kingdom whose nature fooled only those who wanted to be fooled.

Such problems occupied the Tokyo army authorities endlessly. The plotting of the Itagaki-Muto clique did not stop. The militants of the Kwantung Army spread their influence to the young officers of the China Garrison and created a growing atmosphere of unrest in Peking and Tientsin. The Hirota government, always struggling with the army faction, gave ground as slowly as possible, relying on diplomacy that contradicted the military actions, hoping that some miracle would enable the civilians to recapture control of the government.

But events were overtaking the Hirota government.[7] Following the Suiyuan incident, when Chinese General Fu Tso-yi thwarted Colonel Muto's plans to take over Mongolia, the Chinese became much more restless, thus proving General Ishihara's point that they should have been left alone. The fact was, however, that it probably would not have made much difference. The Chinese were gathering momentum under Chiang Kai-shek, with all action directed toward the unification of the country and the ejection of the Japanese. This impetus was given more power in December 1936, when Chiang Kai-shek was visiting the Suiyuan front. He was abducted by Chang

Hsueh-liang and taken to Hsian. Chang then demanded, as the price of the Generalissimo's freedom, that Chiang agree to an all-out war against Japan, to drive the Kwantung Army out of north China and Manchuria, and to fight alongside the Chinese Communists, who, after their break with Chiang in the 1920s, had marched to Yenan and had begun operations against the Japanese in Mongolia.

Following these developments, the Japanese position in China had become more and more difficult. One incident followed another. The murder of Japanese businessmen and soldiers became commonplace. Most of China was turning anti-Japanese.

In these difficult times, the generals in Tokyo felt the need for men they could trust in Manchuria and China. Colonel Ishihara had been promoted to major general, and the generals did not forget his report on conditions in the Kwantung Army after the visit to warn them about going slowly in China.[8] To try to control the extremists, the general staff promoted Itagaki and sent him to command the Fifth Division, located in Japan. This took Itagaki out of prominent position. Major General Tojo was also promoted to lieutenant general and made chief of staff of the Kwantung Army. For the first time since 1931, the generals in Tokyo felt that they had the Kwantung Army under control.[9]

Tojo did not disappoint his superiors in Tokyo. There were no more incidents involving the Kwantung Army. There were many reports from Tojo about the course of events that he felt must be followed. As a student of Soviet-Japanese military affairs he was one of the strong advocates of war with Russia. But before Japan could take on the USSR and wrench away the maritime provinces, she must first settle the China problem. Like many Japanese, Tojo expected this to be relatively easy, since China had never been given time to develop economically, and Chiang Kai-shek had the most tenuous control over his own armies. Tojo was not a great student of history or world affairs. His father had been a general before him. Hideki Tojo had fought in the Russo-Japanese War, he had participated in the occupation of Siberia, and he had spent much of his life behind a desk. His foreign experience had been limited to a stint as a military attaché in Germany where he had learned to admire the Prussians and, later, Hitler. He knew very little about the British, and his knowledge of the United States was confined almost entirely to his impressions when riding across the country on a train on his way home to Japan from Germany. The Americans he saw were noisy, informal, and seemed to be concerned about nothing but creature comforts and making money. He was not impressed.[10]

As a soldier's soldier, Tojo had the respect of his army superiors. His assessments of the China situation carried a good deal of weight.

The Hirota government fell in the winter of 1937 in a disagreement between the military and the politicians. In the days that followed it became apparent that the room for maneuver had been lessened, the army proved obdurate and would not accept as prime minister even one of their own, General Kazushige Ugaki, because Ugaki was not a member of the "club"—in the 1920s he had favored the reduction of the size of the army. No general would serve as his war minister, so he had to give up the idea of forming a government.[11]

For four months a government formed by General Senjuro Hayashi survived, but then it, too, fell. Prince Fumimaro Konoye was pressed by Prince Saionji to become the new prime minister, another sign of the narrowing of the political base. Konoye was hardly a figure that the moderates would like to endorse; his views were all too much like those of the army, favoring Japanese expansion in China. But the alternative was a government by General Gen Sugiyama, one of the leaders of the hard-line army faction. The army had proposed him for the job of prime minister; it was the first army move for total power. The alternatives were nearly all gone, Prince Konoye was the last hope of averting army takeover. So reluctantly, he agreed to accept the responsibility.[12]

Konoye was a very popular figure in Japan, handsome, debonair, highly placed, rich, and with the charisma associated with motion picture stars and popular entertainers more than political figures. It was said that while virtually all others so fortunate as to actually have the honor of an audience with the emperor observed the protocol of never looking the "God" in the face, Konoye would sit, with legs crossed, and chat with his emperor as though they *were equals.* He had been a member of the House of Peers for many years, and its president for four years.

Everyone, it seemed, welcomed the handsome prince, from the emperor to the common farmers, whose situation he had often lamented, and who looked to him for relief. The army expected him to espouse their views. He came to office, it seemed, with the hopes of Japan that he could be all things to all people. He appeased both factions of the army with appointments; General Araki, who had been serving quietly as military councillor to the emperor, suddenly was pressed back into political life as minister of education. It seemed innocuous on the surface, perhaps, but actually this appointment meant that not only the army was gaining power but that army control was now going to be exercised over the entire Japanese public from kindergarten on up.[13]

General Araki's influence and ideas had already permeated the corps of young officers of the army with *bushido*. When Lieutenant Colonel Aizawa murdered General Nagata he did it in a peculiarly bloody samurai fashion; he pulled out the samurai sword he was entitled to wear with his uniform, and hacked the general to death with it.

The bloody ways of *bushido* were indeed coming to the fore.

This aspect of the change in Japan came very quickly after General Araki was restored to public prominence. Japanese education became more and more military. *Bushido* became a national symbol of probity; school children began to learn the Imperial Rescript to Soldiers and Sailors handed down by Emperor Meiji. Small boys drilled at the schools with wooden rifles. The samurai sword became a national symbol of the mystique of Japan.

Whatever Prince Konoye might have accomplished in different times, a month after he took office, he was faced with another crisis.

Early in the summer of 1937 Tojo sent a new situation report to Tokyo. The Chinese were growing stronger, and Manchukuo's position was thus threatened. The Chinese had signed a mutual assistance pact with the Mongolian People's Republic (Outer Mongolia), and this was another threat to Japan. It might lead to a Soviet-Chinese pact against Japan. In the tradition of the Sino-Japanese and Russo-Japanese wars, Tojo advocated a preemptive strike against Nanking, to knock China out in a hurry. Tojo's assessments dovetailed with those of Tokyo. Britain and the United States were supporting Chiang Kai-shek, and that support threatened to make him even stronger. The foreign office did not agree, but the generals were of a single mind for a change.[14]

The Japanese army had maintained a presence in north China since 1901, a result of the Boxer Rebellion. But for that matter, so had Britain, France, Italy, and the United States. The other nations, however, had not been particularly expanding activities in north China. Some 2200 Japanese citizens lived in Peking alone, more in Tientsin and other cities of the north. To protect their interests the Japanese kept pouring troops into the China Garrison Army. The Chinese liked the Japanese less and less. Taking their cue from the old hands who had adopted the Kwantung Army view, the new junior officers and noncommissioned officers showed contempt for the Chinese and often mistreated common Chinese citizens. Any time Chinese and Japanese soldiers came near one another, an incident threatened. The incident came in July 1937. In Tokyo, Foreign Minister Kaki Hirota was half expecting it. He had heard rumors that the hotheads of the Kwantung Army had been at the garrison troops in north China and were planning an incident "around the time of the Festival of the Weaver."[15] That was July 7. Hirota had complained to the war minister, and an official of the Military Affairs Bureau of the army had been sent to north China to see that nothing happened. But the Tokyo man arrived too late. The Japanese garrison forces under General Koichiro Tashiro were conducting maneuvers along the Peking-Hankow railway on the night of July 7. This, in itself, was an arrogant and unwarranted act, for the area was the ground of the 29th Chinese Army. A single company of Japanese was moving right through Chinese military territory, when the soldiers came to the Lukouchiao across the Hu River, known in English as the Marco Polo Bridge. On the bridge, the Japanese passed a Chinese company. Somehow a shot was fired. So edgy were the men of both sides that one shot led to a volley and a pitched battle followed. It was broken off that night. The army headquarters in Tokyo was informed, and the foreign office was told. Foreign Minister Hirota heard about the affair before dawn on July 8 and was furious with the army for allowing such a matter to come up just then; he was making some progress in trying to come to an accommodation with the Chinese.[16]

At Tientsin, a senior staff officer counseled patience, lest the incident get out of hand. So did General Ishihara from Tokyo. A cease-fire was arranged.

On July 8, the Japanese garrison army in Tientsin sent reinforcements to Peking. For two days nothing but sporadic firing disturbed the air. Chiang Kai-shek did not want to fight the Japanese. He was much more interested in uniting China, and the Japanese presence in this area had been accepted since the Boxer Rebellion. Chinese General Sung Che-yuan, director of the Hopei-Chahar army, ordered his troops to hold, and he negotiated the cease-fire. But it had no been signed yet by July 9.[17]

Meanwhile, in Tokyo, with the army factional dispute now subdued, the generals were mostly of a mind to go to war. The rationale, composed almost entirely of Japanese yearnings, was that the Chinese had been murdering Japanese citizens for many months (true) and that the troops would continue to cause incidents (not necessarily true) unless the Chinese army was dealt a resounding defeat. That would mean mobilization of a large force to deal this punitive action to China.

The mood of the Japanese public, stirred for months by exaggerated news reporting of incidents and all anti-Japanese acts from China, was chauvinistic and anti-Chinese. Demonstrators came out by the thousands to support a military move.

War Minister General Sugiyama went to the emperor with the army's arguments. It would take less than a month, he said, to subdue Chiang's armies and create peace in China. He proposed the mobilization of five divisions in Japan, and the use of the Kwantung Army to carry out the "pacification."[18]

The prime minister was pessimistic about the possibilities. General Ishihara and General Shun Tada, assistant chief of the general staff, opposed the move. But General Sugiyama was his most persuasive with the prime minister. He said the mobilization did not necessarily mean war, but a show of force to prevent war.

All along, Chiang Kai-shek had been temporizing, to try to avoid any excuse for the Japanese to make another move in China. He had tried to localize every incident, including that of Suiyuan that same year. Now, with the Japanese mobilization, Chiang saw the handwriting on the wall. Even so, he tried to give the Japanese an honorable path of withdrawal. He told the Chinese people:

> Six years have passed since the loss of Manchuria, and now the battle is drawing near Peking. Should Peking become a second Mukden, our capital Nanking may well follow. The very fate of our nation depends upon how the Marco Polo Bridge incident is resolved. Should we be pushed to the point where no further concessions were possible, then sacrifice and resistance would be our only choice. Though our nation is weak, we must protect the lives of our people and sustain the burden of history passed down to us by our ancestors.[19]

In north China, the young hotheads of the Japanese army were in a position to make their influence felt at home. While the discussions in Tokyo continued and the last arrangements for the cease-fire were being worked out, the Tientsin reinforcements arrived, and the Japanese at the Marco Polo Bridge opened fire again. It was the afternoon of July 10. Once again, the Chinese fought back and held. They called for reinforcements and Chiang ordered them. A highly colored report of this activity reached Tokyo, and Prime Minister Konoye was persuaded, and so was the emperor. On July 11, Konoye authorized the dispatch of Kwantung Army units, Korea army troops, and three divisions from the homeland to north China.

The Japanese were not listening. War fever had suddenly seized the nation, and the three home Japanese divisions, including General Itagaki's Fifth Division, were prepared for departure in a carnival atmosphere.

Almost unnoticed was Chiang Kai-shek's reaction: general mobilization of the Chinese armies.[20]

In Changchun, General Tojo moved into action, with General Sugiyama's orders to send supporting troops. He personally led out a brigade north of Peking to outflank the Chinese and cut Inner Mongolia off from China.

The generals of the Imperial Japanese Army were more united than they had been since the First World War. They approached the China incident with the belief that they were ready now to fulfill Japan's destiny to become the leader of Asia.

窮鼠かえって 猫を咬む

14. "The cornered mouse will fight the cat all the harder"

Let the reader mark how easily war came to Japan in the summer of 1937, and how little the Japanese people and their leaders considered the consequences of their actions. So imbued had the military leaders of the nation become with the idea that Manchuria actually belonged to them, and that north China and Mongolia were spheres of Japanese influence, that it seemed only natural to send troops to protect what was Japanese. This total misconception was a result of six years of constant propaganda by the army, the South Manchurian Railway, and, more recently, the *zaibatsu*, who by 1937 had billions of yen invested in Manchuria and north China.

Once the incident began, and the first divisions were mobilized, the army bowed its neck and there was no turning back. Admiral Mitsumasa Yonai, the navy minister, was opposed to extending the Marco Polo Bridge incident, and he said as much in the cabinet. He usually discussed the day's events with his trusted assistant, Admiral Isoroku Yamamoto, who reinforced his views. But each day the chance of stopping the incident short of total war grew slimmer. Prince Konoye was persuaded that the best way to operate in crisis was to establish a supercabinet of five ministers: himself, the war minister, the navy minister, the foreign minister and the minister of finance. War Minister Sugiyama and the finance minister were whole-hearted supporters of expansion in China. Navy Minister Yonai opposed and so did Foreign Minister Hirota. Prime Minister Konoye swung with the winds, but almost always ended up on the side of the hawks.[1]

An indication of the army's machinations at this time of crisis was the Miyazaki affair. General Ishihara warned Prime Minister Konoye that the army threatened to push Japan into a long and expensive war. He suggested that Konoye go to China and meet with Chiang Kai-shek to try to resolve the difficulties through negotiation. What the conservative elements of the army wanted was primarily Chinese recognition of Manchukuo as an independent state and freedom to exploit Mongolia. Konoye vacillated toward going, but he knew the temper of the army, and he was afraid that if he did go, and did reach an agreement, and the army precipitated another incident, he would be faced with an internal crisis more serious than the 2–26 Incident. So Konoye tried another compromise: Ryusake Miyazaki was the son of Enten Miyazaki, who had been very close to Chinese President Sun Yat-sen and knew the Chinese and Chiang Kai-shek. Prince Konoye got the idea of sending Miyazaki to China to try to work out the problem face to face with Chiang. The five members of the supercabinet agreed, including General Sugiyama, and Miyazaki set out hastily for Kobe, where a steamer was leaving for Shanghai. On the pier he was arrested by the army's *Kempeitai* and prevented from going to China. The army was not going to allow anyone to stop its drive for power.[2]

From the vantage point of 1986 it seems clear that the Western powers, including the United States, have to accept some responsibility for the Japanese attitudes. During the League of Nations discussions of Manchuria at the time of the 1931 crisis, the Western powers indicated that Japan had a "special position" in Manchuria, and the Lytton Commission repeated the statement. Why should Japan have had any more special position in Manchuria in 1931 than she had in 1900 or in 1985? The statement represented the self-serving position of colonial powers; if they denied Japan a "special position" then, of course, they were denying themselves special positions and that they were not prepared to do.

In that sense then, one must understand the Japanese feeling that in China their country was continuing to follow the Europeans. The difference was that Japan's ambition, at the lowest level, was to replace the Europeans and the Americans as the colonial powers in Asia; at the highest level it was to eliminate colonialism and establish an Asian federation. At no time, of course, did Japan expect to be less than leader of the Asian bloc.

The dispatch of three divisions to north China from Japan might have been justified as a simple show of force by the Japanese government. But the movement of General Tojo's Chahar Expeditionary Force to Changpei and Changyuan, and then down toward Kalgan, to cut off Inner Mongolia from Peking, was something quite different and represented Japanese ambitions for Inner Mongolia. Tojo's own idea was to clear up north China and then attack the Soviet Union as soon as possible.

For two weeks after the Marco Polo Bridge incident, the situation in the Peking-Tientsin area still seemed possible to resolve. Japanese General Tashiro died suddenly of natural causes. He was replaced by General Kyoji Kotouki, and this change created a certain confusion among the Japanese. But on July 25, the three divisions from Japan began to arrive at Taku in Pohai Bay. That day Japanese troops attacked Langfang, about halfway along the Tientsin-Peking railroad. The Japanese had about two hundred aircraft assigned to this operation and on July 26 planes bombed Langfang. The Tanabe Brigade of the 20th Division tried to storm the Kuang An Gate in Peking, but the Chinese fought them off. The war had definitely expanded from a simple bridge incident between two companies.[3]

The outside world watched but did nothing of any importance to stop the fighting. Britain and France suggested that a serious attempt to interfere diplomatically might be useful. They approached the United States, but they were rebuffed by Secretary of State Cordell Hull, who mirrored the American position. The United States was still stagnant with depression, and the American people were still isolationist. America's concern with the world was extremely limited.

A taste of what was to come was felt in Japan that July when the puppet Hopei-Chahar government constabulary rebelled against the Japanese and massacred two hundred of them. The call of Chiang Kai-shek had raised the Chinese spirit and the will to resist foreign domination. In a sense, the Japanese were reaping the harvest of the European powers' years of influence. The Chinese bore a hundred years of resentment against foreign intrusion into their affairs and foreign seizure of their territory. The Japanese were shocked by the level of resistance, so much greater and more unified than anything they had seen before.

In the Peking area the Japanese attacked in force beginning July 27, supported by rotation bombing. The fighting was bitter around Nanyuan and two Chinese generals were killed in action. The Chinese counterattacked and drove the Japanese back near Langfang. A fight for the Fengtai railroad station raged back and forth. But the Chinese had already realized that they did not have the guns, tanks, or planes to stand up against a frontal assault by the Japanese. Their tactic was to fight by day and retreat by night. Having taken the Fengtai railroad station, they evacuated it that night and retreated to the far bank of the Yungting River. This tactic would be repeated a thousand times in the years to come.[4]

On July 30 the Japanese captured Tientsin, and the pattern of Japanese occupation was set: looting and burning destroyed much of the city. It was permitted by the Japanese officers as a weapon of war; they would show the Chinese it did not pay to resist the Imperial Japanese Army. What happened to Tientsin was not Japanese army policy; quite to the contrary, it represented a breakdown of army discipline at the command level. Once again the rebels of the Japanese army were defying the high command and running the army in the field the way they wanted to.[5]

On August 4 the Chinese 29th Corps evacuated Peking. Within a week, the Japanese had established a puppet government for the whole area. The commanders of the three Japanese divisions had no intention of stopping the fighting. It was their assigned task to seize territory. They spread out, moving in a great circle around Peking.

The Japanese were winning everywhere. The Chinese fought and retreated, but they fought again, and again. This was not what had been anticipated in Tokyo.

On August 7 the Chinese National Defense Council decided that the Japanese assault would be regarded as the opening of general war, and the council adopted a "sustained strategy of attrition," verifying the tactics of Chiang's generals. This was the only effective measure the Chinese could take, for they were hopelessly outclassed by the Japanese army and navy.[6] The Japanese had only seventeen army divisions, but they were modern divisions, trained in Western fashion. The Japanese generals had vowed to build the finest army in the world and there is indication that they had.

At this moment of the outbreak of war, the Japanese army's seventeen divisions, totaling 380,000 men, could soon be augmented by 738,000 members of the army reserve, all of whom had undergone the same rigorous training. And with the conscription system already in place, it was no trick to increase the troop number at the same high level of training in two years by increasing the draft.

Statistically the Chinese army looked much more powerful than it was: two million soldiers in Chiang Kai-shek's Nationalist forces. The Chinese had one hundred ninety-one divisions, compared to the Japanese seventeen, ready for action. But the Chinese only had weapons and equipment enough to employ eighty divisions, and at least half of these were ill-trained and ill-equipped. The ready reserve was only half a million men, and there was no system for replacement or training outside the active divisions. Conscription in China consisted of a patrol raiding a village and seizing any young men who had not run away or hidden. They were bound, strung together by ropes around their necks, and moved so far from their native villages that there was no hope of return. Then they accepted their status as soldiers, at least until an opportunity to desert presented itself. Their training was entirely the responsibility of the army commander, as was their outfitting and provisioning. Some units were well managed; some were unbelievably corrupt.[7]

The Japanese division was self-sustaining, with its own artillery, cavalry, engineers, tanks, and quartermaster troops. It numbered 22,000 officers and men.

The Chinese division numbered 11,000 men, a third the number of rifles of the Japanese and less than half the number of machine guns, no tanks, no trucks, and virtually no motorized vehicles at all.

From Tokyo it looked like a war that would be fought along the lines of the Sino-Japanese War, quick and easy.

One statistic was disregarded by the Japanese: the population of Japan was 105,000,000. The population of China was 450,000,000. And the Japanese missed the signal Chiang Kai-shek sent them with his announcement of the strategy of attrition.[8]

Militarily speaking the Japanese could in no way fault their forces in north China. They were advancing steadily and their casualties were light compared to those of the enemy. Their attitude, however, was something else. Since the Chinese were to be taught a lesson, the Japanese treatment of captives and wounded left something to be desired. Usually, except for captives needed by the intelligence officers, the prisoners and wounded were shot to death on the battlefield. The result of this policy on the China army was supposed to be instillation of fear and respect of the Japanese into the hearts of the Chinese. Instead, it created a fear and resentment that led to ever greater Chinese resistance.

The Chinese were fighting hard. At the battles of Chienpien

and Hengling, the Chinese forces suffered casualties of more than 50 percent, and still they fought on. The Japanese moved, but the Chinese kept coming.

Where was this great single defeat that was to end the Chinese resistance, according to War Minister Sugiyama?

The emperor asked that question of his prime minister. He was met by embarrassed silence.

Even as the fighting escalated, Foreign Minister Hirota continued to try to end the "incident" by negotiation. He and the other peacemakers of Tokyo were under a great disadvantage because of the nature of the reporting of the events of the war. For example, when those Japanese troops from the homeland had tried to storm their way through Peking's Kuang An Gate at the end of July, the attack was reported in Japan as an attempt by a convoy of military trucks to enter the gate to "protect local Japanese residents." The Japanese people and even the government were being given highly colored accounts of events in China, by the army and by reporters either sympathetic to the army or controlled by military censorship.

Thus the Japanese accounts spoke of "the illegal acts of the Chinese 29th Army" and of "countermeasures" and "retribution."[9]

At the beginning of the second week of August 1937, in Tokyo there seemed to be a ray of hope that the "incident" might be ended. The emperor had spoken strongly to Prince Konoye: the time has come now for a settlement of this matter by diplomatic negotiation, said His Majesty. Prince Konoye expressed his agreement. Foreign Minister Hirota expressed his high hopes. Even War Minister General Sugiyama and his hawks of the general staff were growing uneasy. Operations in China were not proceeding as they ought to have.

Foreign Minister Hirota drew up provisions for a cease-fire. It would establish a demilitarized zone, the Japanese would voluntarily reduce their forces in China. The Japanese would also disband the puppet government they had now established in north China.[10]

Certainly this proposal offered hope, its supplementary documents indicated the Japanese wanted to undo what they had done and "forget the past." Hirota's position was conciliatory. On August 7 he secured the approval of both War Minister Sugiyama and Navy Minister Yonai. The papers were sent to Shanghai by hand with a special envoy, who delivered them to Japanese Ambassador Kawagoe, who was just returning from sick leave.

Preliminary discussions were held in Shanghai with a high Chinese official, who then set out for Nanking. The date was August 10, 1937.[11]

The battles in north China had not yet spread south, but Shanghai was alive with tension. On July 20 the Japanese had only warned the Chinese not to fly their aircraft over Shanghai, perhaps not realizing what this meant: the Japanese were flying military aircraft in and out of Shanghai constantly. Now they were denying China the right to fly over Chinese territory. To underline their warnings, they moved troops about the borders of the international zone of Shanghai and conducted night exercises. After one such exercise they claimed that a sailor named Miyasaki was missing and accused the Chinese of abducting him. No proof could be obtained either way, and the matter was dropped.

On August 9, however, Japanese Marine Lieutenant Isao Oyama came speeding in a car up to the gate at Hungkou airfield. He was stopped by a Chinese guard. The lieutenant objected and began to move on. The Chinese guard tried to stop him and Oyama pulled out his pistol and shot the guard to death. Other guards then killed Lieutenant Oyama.[12]

So, while Foreign Minister Hirota's peace proposals were on their way to Nanking, at Shanghai the Japanese military was making other demands on China. The Chinese troops in Shanghai must be withdrawn. The Chinese defenses in Shanghai must be dismantled immediately.

That night the Chinese National Defense Council ordered three divisions up to Shanghai to attack the Japanese. They began moving to Chi Chi University, Pao-shan Bridge, and Shanghai University. The Japanese troops, army and navy, fought back and the casualties on both sides were heavy. Chinese planes bombed the Japanese marine headquarters and damaged the cruiser *Idzumo,* lying at anchor in the Whangpoo River. Japanese and Chinese planes clashed in air battles.[13]

Communications between Shanghai and Nanking were cut off. Hirota still had a thread of hope, and he sent a cable to the embassy at Nanking, asking that the peace proposal be offered direct.

It was too late. The Japanese had retaliated for the bombing of the *Idzumo* by bombing Nanking. Now, instead of peace, Hirota was faced with evacuating all the Japanese embassy staff from the Chinese capital.

On August 13 the Japanese cabinet authorized the sending of two more divisions of troops from Japan to "protect Japanese residents" in Shanghai. Four days later the Japanese cabinet stopped talking specifically about north China. They could not bring themselves to admit they had precipitated a war. To the Japanese the China war now became "The China Incident."[14]

General Iwane Matsui was given command of a new expeditionary force to central China, he was seen off at the Tokyo station by Prime Minister Konoye and War Minister Sugiyama, and his last words were that he was going to march to Nanking. The capture of the Chinese capital would certainly be the blow that would bring China to her knees and Chiang Kai-shek to his senses.

君子 危うきに近寄らず

15. "The wise man does not court danger"

*T*he "one month" General Sugiyama had said it would take to end "the China Incident" passed. August became September and Japan found herself ever more deeply immersed in the China war. The prowar faction in Tokyo continued stubbornly to insist that one clear-cut victory would force Chiang Kai-shek to seek a peace with Japan.[1]

Shanghai would certainly provide that victory, Shanghai the gateway city that symbolized China. In August, 10,000 Japanese marines, volunteers, and reservists were serving in Shanghai. That month, twenty warships escorted five troop transports to the city. Thirty ships of the Japanese fleet were anchored at Wusung. Two divisions of troops under General Sekikon Matsui arrived.

The Kwantung Army was engaged in Inner Mongolia, north of Peking. The three divisions sent from Japan in July were moving down the railroads south and west of Peking.

By September 1, the Japanese public was feverish in its support of the war. The newspapers were full of war stories:

"Japanese Troops Score Great Victory," said one headline. The Japanese had won another battle and had chased fleeing Chinese troops down the Tientsin-Pukow railway.

"Japanese Troops on Shanghai Front Capture Lotien," said another, talking about Japanese "reinforcements" that had caused many Chinese casualties. No one seemed to wonder why, if the "incident" could be managed so easily, it was necessary to send even more reinforcements.

"Japanese Planes Shoot Down Chinese Fighter." Other Japanese planes from a carrier bombed the South Station on the Shanghai-Hangchow-Ningpo railway. Three hundred Chinese troops were killed, said the Japanese report by Domei news agency.

"Japanese Warships in Whangpoo and Yangtze Open Fire on Chinese Positions in Shanghai" (and also on civilian areas).

"Chinese Fleeing Shanghai"; 200,000 had left by September 1, Domei reported.[2]

Japan's naval blockade of Chinese ports, begun early in the "incident," prevented the delivery of a steamer destined for Shanghai, Domei reported from Detroit.

Nanking was smarting from Japanese air raids, and Chinese Foreign Minister Wang Chung-hui was reported to have fled the city. "Chinese Leaders at Nanking Panic-Stricken," said the Japanese newspapers.

An aerial photograph of a great fire was said to show the burning of the Chinese arsenal at Nanking after Japanese bombing.

"Japanese Warships Shell Canton."

Also that day, the newspapers announced the appointment by the government of a new Resources Planning Bureau, necessary, said the War Office, to complete the mobilization of Japan for war.[3]

War? What happened to the "incident"?

"Full Annihilation Said In Sight for 29th Army," said the headline. The 29th Army had been annihilated several times already.

"Planes Bomb Canton Bases."[4]

It was clear that Japan was engaged in warfare with China from Mongolia to the south China border.

War Minister General Sugiyama's conversation with the emperor had discussed only three divisions moving to north China. Something had changed.

From Tientsin, captured at the beginning of the "incident," came a report that the two hundred schools would open on September 15, with revised textbooks prepared under Japanese supervision. This report revealed a good deal more than the Japanese might have intended: it showed their real ambitions in China.

The Nanking government tried to teach the children hatred of Japan by means of textbooks which contained false stories of the barbaric and illegal acts of Japan. The anti-Japanese textbooks were quite effective as the minds of little children are always influenced by what they are taught and told in schools.[5]

The revision of textbooks was complete. Now the Tientsin children would learn about the heroic Japanese. Perhaps, like Japanese children, they would learn about Navy Commander Kaoru Fujita, twenty-nine, who had fought and died a hero's death at the battle of Tan Shan, and how just before leaving Japan for the front he had divorced his wife in the old samurai tradition, so his mind would be on nothing but the battle ahead, and so his wife would be free of the enormous obligation of filial piety to his family, which could demand all her energies, because he knew he would die in China.

The revision of textbooks was certainly an attempt by the Japanese to make the Chinese think as they did. *Hakko ichiu!*

And what was this, by Domei from Los Angeles?

"$15,000 in Donations Sent from L.A. Japanese."[6]

Even the overseas Japanese were getting into the action, in support of the brave Japanese soldiers and sailors serving in China! A similar amount was collected in San Francisco. Did anyone in Tokyo wonder what Caucasian Americans, their sympathies traditionally with the Chinese (as long as they stayed in China), would think of that?

But what the Japanese did not do was tell the stories of heroic Chinese soldiers who marched into the Japanese heavy guns and died like flies. Nor did the Japanese newspapers print the photograph of a little child sitting amid the bodies and the rubble of the Shanghai railway station. They did not, but newspapers all over the world did, for this photograph symbolized what was happening in China, the unprovoked and vicious assault by the Japanese on a civilian society. This killing non-war in China was something new.[7] The world had not yet witnessed the blitz of London or the systematic destruction of the Warsaw ghetto, or the atomic bomb. What was happening in China symbolized a new low in man's inhumanity to man, and sympathy for Japan began to erode in the United States and Europe.

No one questioned General Sugiyama about what had happened to his "one month," no one but General Ishihara and a handful of his friends. Each new call for "reinforcements" buttressed Ishihara's argument that the Japanese army was dragging the country into a quagmire. No one suggested that the new Resources Planning Bureau, with the cabinet-level administrator at the top of it, was little more than a cover for what was actually happening: the government was ignoring the Diet. Japan was once again an oligarchy, but this time an oligarchy dominated by the military.[8]

No one questioned because they could not. The China incident had brought military censorship. The newspaper correspondents referred to "certain warships" and to the Ishiwara Unit or the Akashiba Unit of troops, not the Fifth Division or the Twentieth Division. At home the laws for preservation of the state were invoked and tightened. No one could question any government decision without running the danger of immediate jailing either by the police or the *Kempeitai*. Even foreigners were no longer immune.[9]

The members of the Diet did not dare complain about the erosion of their powers. Matajiro Keidzumi, leader of the Minseito party, dutifully traveled to the Peking front to visit the troops. He took down the names and addresses of the soldiers he met and brought them home so he could inform the families that their heroes were still alive. He watched the battle of Pataling, where, of course, the Japanese advanced and the Chinese retreated. He came home by military aircraft to Tokyo, and he said not one word of question about what all those soldiers were doing on Chinese soil, or what they intended to do.

If this was not war, it was at least a rough approximation of it.

But in Japan few cared. The headiness of victory after victory in China erased the miseries of the past. The emperor worshiped on September 1 at the Kashikodokoro, Koreiden, and Shinden shrines in the Imperial Palace, asking the blessing of his fellow Gods on the Japanese soldiers and sailors in China. No one, outside the palace inner circle, knew that he was still asking the question: what had happened to General Sugiyama's one-month-to-victory? The mobilization of the nation to build army and navy created more factories, and more factories meant more jobs. A good rice crop was predicted for 1937. Soon China would become a great market for more Japanese goods. Public support of the war was shown in the way donations were coming in to the sailors' and soldiers' relief funds at the war and navy offices. By August 31, Y 10 million had been received at the War Office and Y 6 million at the Imperial Japanese Navy office, almost all of it in small donations from average citizens.[10]

"The intense and fearful crisis of the second Shanghai Incident seems to have passed upon the arrival of Japanese troops sweeping before them the stubborn resistance of the Chinese forces with a hundred percent efficiency and almost superhuman courage. . . ." So wrote "A Japanese Woman Refugee" in the *Japan Times,* predicting that the time would come when the world would thank Japan. At least she spoke of the incident as "the undeclared war, warfare all but in name."[11]

As the days went on, the Japanese at home became ever more bloodthirsty.

"In hand-to-hand fighting," wrote one reporter, "Japanese officers are killing many Chinese soldiers with their swords. One officer killed so many he does not remember after counting forty. . . ."[12]

Faced with crisis, the Japanese people at home were becoming more governable, said *Asahi Shimbun.* Detention rooms of the police stations were virtually empty. "The authorities attribute this condition to the China Incident which has awakened the people to their duty and responsibility." The duty and responsibility, of course, were to the emperor.

The Japanese government was aware of the growing sentiment against its policies in the Western world, and the Ministry of Foreign Affairs was trying hard to counteract the military. Thus the West was treated to the confusing spectacle of incident and apology, incident and apology. The incidents were created by the military, the apologies by the foreign office. For example, one day an American consular official in Shanghai, John Allison, was slapped by a Japanese officer.[13] The foreign office apologized. One day the British ambassador to China was seriously wounded by a Japanese army plane strafing on the outskirts of Shanghai. Navy Undersecretary Yamamoto and Foreign Undersecretary Horinouchi both apologized personally to the British ambassador to Japan. Horinouchi went on the radio to "explain" Japanese policy for Americans, and the Columbia Broadcasting System played the tape when it was flown to America.

"Why have we had to resort to arms?" Horinouchi asked. "We must emphasize first, that the expeditionary forces of Japan now in China have been sent there for no aggressive purposes and secondly that we have no territorial designs. Our forces are in China to safeguard our legitimate interests and protect our rights, and to secure the safety of our nationals. These forces will be withdrawn the very moment that their presence is no longer required. . . ."[14]

Yamamoto was sincere in his apology. Privately he was telling his friends that the army was run by a gang of fools. Was Horinouchi sincere when he apologized and went on the radio? Probably not. Certainly he knew when he said that the China incident stemmed from Chinese attacks on Japanese nationals that it was a lie. He also knew that when he said Japan had sought a peaceful settlement, it was a lie, for his superior, Koki Hirota, had not been allowed to seek a peaceful solution. These days in Tokyo the generals were calling Foreign Minister Hirota "Minister of Harm," a pun based on the characters gai 害, meaning foreign and gai 外, meaning harm.[15] Every one of Hirota's initiatives for peace was shot down by the generals. Yet the foreign office had to put the best face it could on Japanese activity. So a lot of lying was done by foreign office spokesmen.

Meanwhile, to support the military intervention, the cabinet had to raise more money. A two billion yen supplementary military appropriation was rushed through the Diet in September, doubling the budget.

"National unity" was the cry of the government and the press. *Asahi Shimbun* no longer spoke of achieving rapprochement with China, although Foreign Minister Hirota did. *Asahi* was more closely attuned to the policies of the generals. The new policy was to "strike a fatal blow at the Nanking government." The author of that policy was General Sugiyama.[16]

The whole country was mobilized now for the non-war. A Patriotic Radio Corps of amateur radio operators was organized to "cooperate with the military." The navy sent artists Tomokata Iwakura, Tokushiro Kobayakawa, and Yoshihiko Yoshiwara to Shanghai to paint the non-war for posterity. Mayor Itta Kobashi of Tokyo called on school children to "conquer the emergency" by application, as schools prepared to start for the fall. A display of war photographs and Chinese army weapons was held at the Kabukiza Theater. Boy Scouts began visiting the military hospitals to bring cheer to the wounded back from the front.

With the prolongation of the "incident" the Tokyo stock market began to slide. Textile shares dropped, for China had been a major Japanese textile market.

The propaganda speeded up as the war ground on. No territorial ambitions—the phrase was repeated over and over again. But it found its place in the newspaper pages next to articles describing "the beginning of autonomous rule" in Chahar Province, a puppet government established in Kalgan to do the Japanese bidding. Japanese patriots at home might be fooled, but the Chinese were not.

The worsening military situation caused the United States to prepare three cruisers for movement to Shanghai. The story made the Japanese newspapers. But so, too, did an article about the increase in American scrap iron sales to Japan that fall.

Now came the new hard line. "China must be defeated wholly," said Prime Minister Konoye, and Foreign Minister Hirota had to agree, although his agreement was notably unenthusiastic.[17]

The people cheered, the non-war war seemed to have been just what the country wanted:

Sublieutenant Tatsuo Yamanouchi of the Imperial Navy air arm was lost on a bombing mission over Nanking. When his mother received the word she wrote a grateful letter to the navy:

> Look up and see the aeroplane in the sky. In that plane Tatsuo lives forever. I have three more sons whom I love dearly; I am educating and encouraging them so that they might one day offer their humble service to The State. . . .
>
> Your obedient servant
> Yasu Yamanouchi[18]

Yes, Yasu's sons, too, would go to die for the emperor, as had Major Horigane, mortally wounded by bomb fragments at Shanghai. His captain came to him as he lay dying and asked if he had any last wishes to relate. Major Horigane could no longer speak, but he smiled and traced the characters with his finger:
Tenno Heika banzai!
Hurray for His Majesty The Emperor!
And then Horigane died.[19]

Army Captain Kasahara was ordered to assault an apparently impregnable Chinese position at Shanghai. When he received the order, he organized a "death band" of men wearing white sashes as they charged the enemy. "Captain Kasahara drew his samurai sword and dashed into the crowds of resisting enemy . . . mines exploded in the dark . . . they slipped and fell in the trenches . . . Captain Kasahara charged on and on, stepping over the corpses of his comrades, not caring for his safety. His face looked terrible, and his eyes and sabre sparkled as he advanced through gunfire, commanding his force. But Alas, an enemy's bullet pierced his heart and he fell."

With the brave captain was First Class Soldier Masamune Tani.

"He received a piercing bullet in his left femoral region. He was smeared with blood. He had to repress his anger when he was taken to a hospital. But it was too late, the doctor's operation was of no use. He stared at the battlefield from the bloodstained bed, and all of a sudden he began to sing the national song ["Kimigayo"]. When he reached the words Chi of Kimigayoowa chi . . . he breathed his last. The doctors and nurses who were present solemnly prayed for the soul of the brave soldier Tani . . ."

This sort of reading was normal fare in the daily newspapers. The magazines had more of the same. The radio broadcast battlefront dramas. The motion picture industry was enlisted to make patriotic films. And all of this was done with great zest; a handful of generals and diplomats might oppose the war, but the people of Japan were behind it.

The 12th Olympic Games were scheduled to be held in Tokyo in 1940. They were canceled because of the wars in China and Spain and the tense international situation in Western Europe. (They would not be held again until the 1948 Olympic games in London.) The Japanese government was not upset, there had been talk in Japan of canceling unilaterally anyhow, because the full national effort, said the generals, should be turned toward ending the "China Incident" in victory.

In mid-September Prime Minister Konoye opened a drive for "National Unity" at a rally in Tokyo's Hibiya Park.

"Furtherance of the Japanese Spirit," "National Unity," "Perseverance and Endurance" were the mottoes. The reality was the mobilization of the country for war: farm families to give joint labor service to farm the lands of men called to war; the people to labor on public works; children throughout the country to be mobilized during Iron Week to collect scrap iron for the government. And all this would be managed by The Central League for National Spiritual Mobilization.[20]

Another sort of mobilization was taking place in industry with the enactment of the War Industries Mobilization Law, which, in effect, put every factory at the government's disposal, even if it meant changing completely the line of products.

Incident at Shanghai? Or war with China?

Japan was branded "aggressor" by President Franklin Roosevelt in a speech in Chicago in October, but the scrap iron kept coming from Baltimore.

Former Secretary of State Henry L. Stimson suggested that the United States and Britain agree not to ship any more arms to Japan. The arms kept coming.

Winston Churchill praised Roosevelt's speech, but British interests in Tokyo did not move out.

A new supreme war council was organized in Tokyo: its membership read like a roster of the war party: General Araki, General Ugaki, Admiral Suyetsugu, Yosuke Matsuoka, General Noboyuke Abe.[21]

In north China the Japanese advanced steadily, but the Chinese, Communists and Nationalists, fought and lost, fought again, retreated, and fought.

The Japanese did not seem to be aware of the Chinese strategy of attrition, enunciated by Chiang, and also by Mao Tse-tung from Yenan:

> Enemy advances, we retreat
> Enemy stops, we harass
> Enemy withdraws, we attack.[22]

This strategy was intended for a long, long war, one in which newspaper headlines about battle after battle had no validity.

The fighting dragged on. Every day the Tokyo newspapers reported new victories. The Chapei district of Shanghai was reduced to a mass of rubble. Still the Chinese soldiers fought there. Nanking was bombed day after day. The Japanese captured the rail towns of the north. And finally Shanghai fell. Japan had achieved the "great victory" that General Sugiyama had promised the emperor. What if it had taken four months instead of one? It was still a major defeat, the defeat that military strategists had said would mean the end of the "incident." The loss of China's greatest port should have been fatal. If not that, then the undoubted success of Japan's blockade of all China's ports should have brought Chiang Kai-shek down.

But Chiang Kai-shek did not sue for peace. Japan, working through the German ambassador to China, Oskar Trautmann, offered a treaty,[23] which is an indication of who wanted peace. But the treaty appeared to have been written in the Ministry of War: arrogant, demanding, insulting, demeaning, it insisted that north China become a Japanese colony and that China become virtually a Japanese dependency. When Ambassador Trautmann read it before passing it along to the Chinese he knew it would be unacceptable. So why was it submitted at all? The only reason could be the recognition by the Japanese war party that they had to make some concession to their words of peace to keep the emperor from acting.

General Ishihara lashed out at his fellows. Did they not understand that "as long as China holds sovereignty over a single acre, Chiang's government will find popular support for protracted resistance"?[24]

These were not the words the militarists wanted to hear, and in the past four months the militarists had strengthened their grip on the nation and the government. General Ishihara was quietly transferred out of his important job as operations officer of the Imperial General Staff to a field command outside Tokyo.

In the fall the army prepared for that great battle that would bring Chiang Kai-shek to his knees. It was going to be fought at Nanking. After the army had captured Nanking, the Chinese capital, everything would be all right. Chiang would sue for peace. The generals knew it.

困厄は ねずみ算で増える

16. "Troubles increase geometrically"

*I*nstead of acting—which the Japanese generals would have understood—with the continuing escalation of the China incident the Western powers chose to talk. The talk was to be held in Brussels in October. The talkers were the members of the nine-power Washington treaty, signed in 1922. Given the course of events since September 1931, there was no chance of the meetings succeeding. For, as the New York *Herald Tribune* pointed out editorially on the eve of the conference, "Japan seems to think that her vested interests in China are larger than those of all the occidental powers combined." Then the conference was postponed until November.[1]

But it made no difference. Japan said no. She would not attend. She was not interested in talking. She was not interested in mediation, arbitration, or any other outside interference with her ambitions in China. The generals were digging their hole deeper and wider every day.

Even at this late date, given the will to act, the United States and Britain could have forced a Japanese withdrawal from China. The Japanese navy was building but it was not built. Navy Minister Mitsumasa Yonai had stated the truth in the winter when he said "The Imperial Navy has no force to match the combined strength of Great Britain and the United States. . . ."[2] He did not go on to say that Japan was building the two mighty battleships *Yamato* and *Musashi* and would soon have more aircraft carriers than any other navy. But what he said in 1937 was true enough.

The Americans, however, were preoccupied with themselves. The British were preoccupied with problems of empire and Europe. The Spanish civil war was far more important to London than the China incident. Germany, which had formed the Japan-German Anti-Comintern alliance in 1936, was a more formidable problem to London than Tokyo by far. The USSR had a treaty with China but was in no economic position to take on any foreign adventures. So no strong action was expected by the Japanese generals. China was there to do with what they wished as far as the outside world was concerned.

The Japanese played very cleverly on American anticommunism: Ambassador Saito told a U.S. nationwide radio audience that the only reason Japan was fighting in China was to "end the organized campaign to stir up hatred of Japan" and to force "the Central Government to renounce its union with Communism, which was announced at Hsian a year ago." He referred there to the agreement between the Chinese Communists and Nationalists to fight until the Japanese were driven from China. But as for having territorial ambitions in China, absolutely not, said Ambassador Saito.[3]

As he said those words the government announced formation of a vast new holding company to exploit the resources of Manchuria, starting by taking over all the South Manchurian Railway's enterprises. Since the South Manchurian Railway already had established companies inside China, the government's statement was obviously contradictory to the ambassador's. But no one seemed to notice.

Late in October the generals of the Kwantung Army achieved one of their dreams with the formation of a puppet state in Inner Mongolia, headed by Mongol Prince Teh. The new Manchurian exploitation company would be welcome here.

On November 5 the Japanese landed three new divisions of troops at Hangchow Bay, and they outflanked the Chinese. Shanghai was gone. Nanking was to be next.

The Japanese navy was participating fully in the China campaign at this point. The training received by the warship crews was invaluable: live targets to fire at to test and improve gunnery. The airmen had a perfect opportunity; their superior Zero fighters and Mitsubishi twin-engined bombers gave them every edge over the Chinese air forces. The Japanese planes could be shot down, and some were, but the experience in bombing cities and other targets gave such good training that even Admiral Yamamoto came around to support the China war. He was, after all, the man who had developed the Mitsubishi Type O Bomber (Betty). The Japanese naval air force was in operation almost constantly from August 1937, and by the end of that year its carrier pilots were the most experienced in the world.[4]

Chiang Kai-shek moved out of Nanking and back to Hankow, up the Yangtze River. Japan brought more reinforcements. On the line under General Matsui were six reinforced Japanese divisions, about 120,000 men altogether.

From November 5 on, the incremented Japanese army forces drove the Chinese steadily back along the Yangtze River. Most of the fighting was south of the river, along the Shanghai-Nanking rail line. The Chinese gave ground slowly, but they could not match the Japanese tanks, field guns, and planes. After a five-day battle, the Chiang Yin fortress fell on December 1. The Chinese moved back to Chen Chiang, on the rail line. But the Japanese were approaching in two other columns to the south and east. The Chinese fell back from one prepared position to the next, but always fell back. Finally, the Japanese converged with four divisions and one independent column against Nanking. On December 6 they captured a line that extended from Lungfan to Tangshan to Molin Kuan, to Chiang Ning. Nanking was surrounded on three sides, with the river at the north. All this time Japanese army and navy planes were plastering Nanking with bombs daily, and the carnage among the civilians was terrible.[5]

The Chinese defenders grew ever more stubborn, and Japanese losses rose. The Chinese were defending with elements of two armies and six army corps. But the Japanese moved ahead, taking heavy casualties to capture the ground. Between December 8 and December 12 the fighting was hand to hand in the streets of the suburbs of Nanking. On December 12 the Japanese began to break through the Chinese line, and two units crossed the river at Tangtu and Chen Chiang. They threatened to surround the defenders. General Tang Sheng-chih, the garrison commander at Nanking, had no plans for withdrawal. His orders were to fight to the end. But with this envelopment Tang told his troops to break out and withdraw. Only the 66th Corps was able to do so, fighting its way out to the east. A few small units also managed to cross the river and escape, but the vast majority of the troops were caught in the Japanese vise.[6]

What happened then was the Rape of Nanking. With the surrender, the Japanese units, bloody and excited, faced perhaps a hundred thousand of their enemy, some of them still armed, most not. In the blood lust most of these Chinese soldiers were killed. One Japanese soldier wrote in his diary an account of his single platoon's actions:[7]

"The Chinese were too many for a platoon to kill with our rifles, so we borrowed two heavy machine guns and six light machine guns from the Army company. . . ." With these weapons the Japanese platoon then mowed down five hundred Chinese in front of the city wall. The reasons: they were in civilian clothes and might be soldiers.

Members of one Japanese regiment alone reported killing 13,000 prisoners in the next few days. The civilians suffered equally. Nanking had been virtually destroyed by the navy and army bombing and then by the field guns of the artillery. What remained was declared by the officers of the army units to be open game to the troops who had fought so valiantly for the emperor. So Nanking was looted, the women were raped and murdered, and children were shot or bayoneted if they annoyed the Japanese. The disciplined Japanese soldiers, who would not move without an order, became a horde reminiscent of the Mongols.

General Iwane Matsui, the commander of the central China front, had reached Nanking as he told the prime minister he would that day on the Tokyo station platform. He had achieved the great victory (although he did not know that his commanders had turned the troops loose on the city).

Once more the Japanese offered peace.

What a peace:[8]

1. China would recognize Prince Teh's Inner Mongolian Republic as a state.
2. Japan would be free to enlarge her garrison zones of troops in north China.
3. No anti-Japanese would be appointed to administrative posts in north China.
4. The demilitarized zone of Shanghai would be enlarged. (That meant more Japanese territory in Shanghai.)
5. Anti-Japanese policies would be eliminated by the Chinese government. (No one knew what that might mean. Anti-Japanese was anything the Japanese said.)

6. China would join the Anti-Comintern pact between Germany and Japan.
7. China would take steps to improve tariff relationships. (That meant China was to cut tariffs to Japanese goods.)
8. China must respect foreign countries' rights and interests in her territory. (An extended sort of extraterritoriality. Japan had already indicated her concept: Japanese rights meant everything Tokyo wanted.)

Chiang Kai-shek might have accepted a peace if it had been a real peace between equals, for his main concern was to build a united China, but what Japan offered was slavery. On December 17, Chiang issued "A Message to the People Upon Our Withdrawal from Nanking," in which he vowed to fight to the end.

And the great victory for Japan?

She now controlled the lower Yangtze River valley and had a ruined capital on her hands. The new capital had been moved far inland to Chungking in Szechuan Province, so far up the Yangtze that Japanese naval vessels could not profitably operate up there. The rail lines and the roads would be of no help to the Japanese now. China's center had moved west. Her supply line, cut off from the coast, now extended down through the Himalayan mountain range to the Irrawaddy River, over the Burma Road. For the moment, except for aerial bombardment, the Chinese government was beyond Japanese reach. The Japanese militarists were beginning to learn what Chiang meant when he had spoken of a war of attrition.

Japan, however, was determined to conquer China. The next step was to mop up along the east coast. Japanese troops moved into Shantung Province, and the naval forces prepared for an amphibious landing at Tsingtao. Down south, they captured Suchow and launched campaigns against Canton and Wuhan, Hanyang and Hankow.

The Chinese armies had now been split into regional units. They operated more as guerillas than as army units. The attrition continued. The Japanese advanced, the Chinese withdrew, the Japanese took a city, the Chinese disappeared. The Japanese moved, the Chinese retook the city. In China the Japanese military enthusiasm for the war was boundless. But in Tokyo some of the generals were beginning to remember what General Ishihara had said more than a year earlier. The trouble was that by December 1937, it was too late to turn back without a total reversal of Japanese policy, and the army could never admit that it had been wrong.

In November Prime Minister Konoye, in an attempt to bring the generals under political control, suggested the reestablishment of the Imperial General Headquarters, an organization established by Emperor Meiji in 1903 to prosecute the Russo-Japanese War. Imperial General Headquarters would run military operations of army and navy and everything pertaining to them, including procurement. It created very nearly a military dictatorship, subject to the will of the emperors. Prime Minister Konoye proposed that he be a member and chairman of the Imperial General Headquarters. The generals gladly accepted the IGHQ idea, but rejected the prime minister's demand to run it, on the basis that they reported directly to the emperor. Consequently, the emperor was head of the Imperial General Headquarters with one exception: the generals never told him when they were meeting, what they were discussing, or asked for his approval of their decisions.[9]

The Imperial General Headquarters concept had one basic weakness. It gave tactical and even strategic control of operations in a given area to the local commanders. That is why the Kwantung Army had grown so tall. That is why the Rape of Nanking occurred. Japanese regimental commanders had far more authority in their sphere of operations than did Chinese, or American, or British, or any other. If there was protest against their actions, by the time it was registered the battle had been won or lost and the matter was almost always moot.

By December 1937, Imperial General Headquarters had realized that the army was bogged down in China. But what was to be done about it? The generals in the north, central China, and the south were all moving and demanding reinforcement. The China tail was wagging the Japanese army dog.

To a greater extent than the Imperial Navy staff was prepared to recognize, the Japanese navy in China waters was infected with this army disease. Because of this state of affairs, Japan now became involved in an incident that was to warn the world of her ambitions and her ruthlessness.

It happened on December 12, the day that the victorious Japanese troops swarmed atop the Nanking city wall to have their pictures taken. The news was rushed to Tokyo, and nearly half a million jubilant Japanese citizens staged a massive lantern parade in Tokyo that night. The newspapers published extra editions, emblazoning the headlines and photographs across the front pages. Almost unnoticed in the jubilation was a small note:

> On the evening of December 11, a naval air unit that had set out to bomb steamboats of the Chinese army reportedly escaping from Nanking and sailing upstream mistakenly bombed three steamboats of the Standard Oil Company, sinking the vessels in question together with an American warship that happened to be in the vicinity. This unfortunate incident, involving as it does the American navy, is extremely regrettable, and Commander in Chief Hasegawa promptly began studying appropriate ways of making full amends.[10]

It was true. In the excitement of the final attack on Nanking the Japanese naval forces went mad, as had the army earlier. The carrier pilots went out with blanket approval to sink anything that floated on the river, and they sank the U.S. gunboat *Panay,* and three American tankers. Two U.S. Navy sailors were killed and seventy-four were wounded, many of them by the repeated strafing of pilots who came so low the Americans could see their faces. The *Panay* was flying a huge American flag, and the crewmen were certain there was no "error" involved. After the *Panay* was sunk, Japanese planes came down low over the water and strafed American sailors swimming to the shore.

The British that day suffered, too, somewhat from the antics of the Japanese dive bombers, but more from the villainy of a Japanese artillery commander, who fired from the shore on the HMS *Ladybird.* The gunboats *Bee, Cricket,* and *Scarab* were also hit by naval bombs.

At the Japanese foreign office and navy headquarters the lights burned late that night. Orders were sent to the Japanese commander at Shanghai, telling him to get a naval vessel up to Hankow to rescue survivors. Foreign Minister Hirota hurried to the American embassy to make a personal apology to Ambassador Joseph C. Grew. By that time the reports of American reaction were coming in, and they were bad, very bad. American newspapers were demanding that the United States break off relations. This incident was the first "official" problem, but for months Americans had been reading about the way their fellow citizens were treated on visits to Japan, where jingoism and contempt for white foreigners was increasing daily. Ambassador Grew was thinking about packing up, not at all sure the United States would not break diplomatic relations with Japan over this attack that the *Panay* crew claimed was unprovoked and repeated.

Hirota did not stop with talking to Grew. He ordered the Japanese ambassador to Washington to make an apology and the Japanese officials in China to be in touch with U.S. officials and express their regrets. This last was difficult, for the Japanese in China were riding high and not inclined to apologize. Deputy Navy Minister Admiral Yamamoto settled that as far as the navy was concerned. He recalled Rear Admiral Teizo Mitsunami, the commander of the Second Combined Air Force, a gesture so seldom employed in the Japanese navy that it had to be effective. He also issued a public statement in behalf of the navy, saying the Japanese navy had to hang its head in shame. And he made sure that this statement reached the naval forces in China. Even further, Yamamoto stopped a civilian interpreter, a friend of his, Shuichi Mizota, who was on his way home from London, and sent him to Shanghai to remain and interpret for the Japanese naval commanders there. Mizota had a greater role, he was to watch and be sure there were no more incidents involving the navy.

Hirota was in touch with Ambassador Saito again, and Saito made more apologies in Washington and to Americans in general.[11]

In Washington the Americans were not inclined to accept them. They had heard Japanese apologies before. The word reached Yamamoto that President Roosevelt was ordering Ambassador Grew to go directly to the emperor. The whole naval high command flinched at that. Yamamoto then made it clear that in investigating the facts there would be no attempts to evade the truth, but that blame would be admitted and proper amends made, and compensation. He could not have said mea culpa maxima more clearly. When Admiral Mitsunami appeared in Tokyo he was fired out of hand, a practice so unusual for the Japanese navy that it had to be recognized as a genuine act of contrition.[12]

Finally the Americans calmed down. Admiral Yamamoto issued a statement expressing gratitude to the American public for accepting Japan's good faith. Thus, by a very narrow margin, Foreign Minister Hirota and Admiral Yamamoto managed to quiet troubled waters and prevent the *Panay* incident from becoming something much more serious.[13]

But the army did not respond in kind, and the same must be

said of the Japanese naval contingent in China. Colonel Kingoro Hashimoto, the commander of the Japanese artillery regiment that fired on the British gunboats, had known precisely what he was doing. He was not fired or even reprimanded by the army. The Japanese in China continued to behave in a most arrogant and insulting manner to foreigners. In Tokyo the victory parades continued. Big maps of China were displayed by the nationalistic organizations, with Rising Sun flags showing that more than two hundred million Chinese were now colonial dependents of Japan. It would only be a little while, the militarists assured them, and then all China would be pacified. *Hakko ichiu!*[14]

Foreign Minister Hirota's task of calming the Americans and the British was made more difficult by press reports and photographs of the Rape of Nanking, which appeared in newspapers throughout the world, and helped convince the world that Japan was a nation of beasts gone mad.

When Foreign Minister Hirota got the word he visited War Minister Sugiyama and angrily demanded an explanation.

He got lame excuses. He asked that army discipline be tightened up. Sugiyama said of course, and did nothing. Hirota sent his representatives at Nanking to see the army commanders. Only from General Matsui did they get any sense: he admitted that his subordinates had behaved badly. The foreign office representative suggested that perhaps the soldiers had not paid attention to their superiors' orders. General Matsui frowned; the trouble, he said, was that the superiors were to blame. He had issued orders that only picked units were to enter Nanking, and that they must be subject to the strictest military discipline.

Under the Japanese army system, Matsui could issue the orders, but his commanders had to listen only to his strategic instructions. Imperial Prince Asaka, brother of the emperor, was one of the generals involved. The other was Major General Heisuke Yanagawa. General Yanagawa did not like General Matsui, and he simply refused to obey orders. Prince Asaka passed down the orders from General Matsui. Later the prince wrote in his memoirs of the shock to him when one of his regimental commanders confided that the best bayonet training in the world was to let the troops work on people.[15] Whether the Prince ever confided this horror to his imperial brother is not recorded. What it all indicated, of course, was the fury of the Japanese at the strength of the Chinese resistance and the fatal flaw in the militarist doctrine of divided authority. The Japanese forces in China, it seemed, were suffering from what was sometimes called the Kwantung Army disease. It was more than that: it was a result of the Araki-inspired policy of brutalization of the troops from the day of the enlistment that destroyed the humanity of the officers, noncommissioned officers, and the common soldiers. In the name of discipline the most violent and inhumane actions had been taken against these soldiers, and this discipline had destroyed most of the admirable tender elements of the Japanese character. The new *bushido* had made of them brutes, and they acted like brutes. The world would see more of such scenes.

Foreign Minister Hirota kept up his complaints to the army, and the continuing stream of reports abroad could not be denied; the foreign eyewitnesses had chapter and verse of rapes, murders, mass killings, arson, and looting. General Sugiyama seemed constantly to temporize. Finally Hirota went to the Military Affairs Bureau, the real control of the army. Lieutenant General Masaharu Homma was sent to Nanking, and he came back with a report that caused the recall of General Matsui, Prince Asaka, and some eighty staff members.[16] Somehow General Yanagawa managed to escape the implied censure of the recall. However, the matter went no further; the army could not afford to admit that Imperial General Headquarters, and even an expeditionary force commander, had so little control of his division and regimental officers as this scandal indicated. The Rape of Nanking was hushed up at home. The Japanese press, of course, printed none of the reports from Nanking, and the people of Japan knew absolutely nothing of the Rape of Nanking until many years after the war, when the story began to arouse controversy, for at first most Japanese simply could not believe it. Then after a documentary film was produced early in 1980 the flood gates loosed.[17]

How many people were killed in the Rape of Nanking? No one will ever know for sure. At the end of World War II the Allied war crimes prosecutors put the figure at 200,000. In the 1980s Japanese revisionist historians tried to put the figure at about 20,000, and to conclude that there really had been no Rape of Nanking at all. But other Japanese and Chinese historians more or less restored the original estimate of 200,000 killed. Tomio Hora, a professor at Waseda University, wrote a book on Nanking. His researches showed that two Chinese organizations that operated burial squads after the massacre counted 150,000 corpses. *Asahi Shimbun* assigned a reporter to spend months doing research on the Rape of Nanking, and in a twenty-five part series of articles, the reporter concluded that the war crimes tribunal's estimates were substantially correct. Nanking has to go down as one of the cruelest victories ever wreaked by any army.[18]

During the last days of December and the early days of January, the Japanese waited for the Chinese reply to their demands. They never got a direct answer, only a call from Chiang for "further clarification." By mid-January it had begun to sink in among the leaders in Tokyo that they were badly mired in China. Instead of trying to get out as gracefully as they could, however, the army leaders urged that the war be pressed, that victory must be just around the corner. Prime Minister Konoye then issued a statement on January 16. Hereafter, he said, Japan would no longer deal with the Nationalist government of China. The Japanese were now going to establish their own government in the area they controlled. "Harmonious coordination" with a new Chinese government would prevail.[19] So the Japanese government recalled its ambassador to China and broke diplomatic relations. Whatever the Japanese had called the invasion of China before, now they had to call it war.

角を矯めて 牛を殺す

17. "To straighten the horns he kills the cow"

After the fall of Nanking the true state of Japanese government affairs was to be seen in China, not in Tokyo. When Colonel Hashimoto, the gunner of the Yangtze, was recalled to Tokyo for his part in the gunboat attacks, not only was he unpunished, but he went around army headquarters saying loudly that Japan's next task was to drive the white man out of Asia. Admiral Yamamoto was quietly hoping that someone would put a bullet into Hashimoto,[1] but the fact was that Yamamoto and other moderates were in a good deal more danger than the colonel. Hashimoto's sentiments were echoed throughout the army, particularly by officers of colonel's rank and below.

In China, these sentiments led to the constant harassment of foreign nationals. In Tientsin the British were particularly beset. Coming to a Japanese checkpoint, they were questioned, abused, slapped, and sometimes stripped for the simple purpose of humiliating them. The Japanese particularly liked to strip foreign women. Certainly this was a part of a deliberate policy of the China army to humble the whites. But it was overshadowed by the brutality of the Japanese to the Chinese, who were now raped, murdered, and looted to the hearts' content of the Japanese soldiers.[2]

One officer who shared the view that Westerners were weak, after his short trip across the United States by train, was General Hideki Tojo, chief of staff of the Kwantung Army. Tojo had come to the attention of Tokyo by his ability to control the Kwantung Army after years of that army's embarrassments to Tokyo.

Shortly after Prince Konoye's drastic decision to fight Chiang Kai-shek to a finish, the army and navy recognized the problem they faced in bogging down in China and spending Japan's resources in a hopeless attempt to police the enormous territory of China they had captured. It was time for a new policy. The militarists now insisted that they have a much larger share in the formation of government policy than in the past. So, in May 1938, Prince Konoye reorganized his cabinet. General Itagaki, the executioner of the Mukden plot and more recently the fierce commander of the Japanese Fifth Division in north China, was brought home to serve as war minister. General Ugaki became foreign minister. Admiral Yonai continued as navy minister, but his was the most moderate voice in the cabinet. The education minister was General Araki, and even the finance minister was committed to the militarists—he was an official of the Mitsui *zaibatsu*, which by this time was at the heart of the Japanese military-industrial complex.[3]

After General Itagaki took over as war minister, the army brought General Tojo back from Manchuria to be his assistant. There was more than one reason for the selection of Tojo. He was an able administrator, if devoid of much imagination. He was also a believer in the theory *Sovietica delenda est*—Communist Russia must be destroyed. Indeed, under his command of the Kwantung Army forces, one incident with the Soviets had already occurred. It had come in June 1937, about two weeks before the Marco Polo Bridge affair. With the establishment of the puppet state of Manchukuo Japan had taken a proprietary interest in the borders between Manchukuo, Outer Mongolia, and the Soviet Union. As Japan was sponsor of Manchukuo, so the USSR became sponsor of the Outer Mongolian republic. Watching Japanese ambitions rise in Asia, the Soviets had also built up their Far Eastern defense forces until by 1937 they were about three times the size of the Kwantung Army. When the Japanese built railroads through Manchuria to carry troops to the northern borders, the Russians countered by building railways in Siberia and double-tracking the Trans-Siberian Railway.

Diplomatic relationships between the USSR and Japan hit a new low when the Japanese signed the Anti-Comintern pact. The most telling clauses of the pact were "secret," or so the Japanese believed. They did not know that the Japanese foreign office was infiltrated by spies of the Richard Sorge ring, which was believed by the Germans to be a German espionage organization but was actually reporting all to the Soviets.

After the Anti-Comintern pact was signed, the Russians showed their displeasure with Tokyo by refusing to renew a fisheries agreement which was very important to the Japanese economy.

In this atmosphere of tension, a border dispute suddenly loomed very large. It concerned the Amur River, the traditional border between Siberia and Manchuria. The exact delineation had never been clear nor very important during the days of China's empire. But with Manchukuo a Japanese dependency, the situation changed. The Japanese claimed that the boundary lay on the north side of the sandbar island of Kanchas. The Soviets claimed that it lay on the south bank.

On June 19, 1936, a Soviet army unit landed on the island. General Tojo rushed a Japanese mechanized unit to the Amur River. The Soviets sent reinforcements down.

The incident was settled with no more than a minor clash by negotiation between the Soviet foreign office and the Japanese ambassador, and the Soviets withdrew their troops. But the issue was not really resolved, it was just that the Soviets had other matters in mind just then. In response to the Anti-Comintern pact, the Soviets signed a nonaggression pact with China and began sending military aid.

This action infuriated the Japanese, but General Tojo was occupied with his foray into Inner Mongolia, and then Japan became so entangled in the China war that the Soviet question was put aside.

Put aside, but not forgotten, had to be the reality. For General Tojo was a man of whom it was said "he never learns and he never forgets." General Itagaki also belonged to the group that expected war with the USSR. That concept was a part of the Kwantung Army's philosophy.[4]

In the winter of 1938 the Japanese leaders proposed a National General Mobilization Bill, which would mobilize the entire resources and people of Japan under government orders, any time the prime minister declared a national emergency. This meant tighter press controls, price controls, wage controls, curtailment of the right to strike. It meant the tightening of the laws against sedition, which could be invoked on almost any pretext. Anyone who criticized the Japanese army in print might expect to be arrested. It also meant national registration of all citizens, higher taxes, and compulsory savings programs. Some members of the Diet protested that this bill would completely destroy the last of Japanese freedoms. Nevertheless, it was passed in March. At the same time, the government became more active in enforcing the laws governing expression of ideas and associations of citizens. The Japanese were now under central government control in nearly every aspect of their lives.[5]

Having tried various committees over the past year or so, Prince Konoye now reverted to the Five Minister Committee: prime minister, war, navy, foreign affairs and finance. Since two of the ministers were generals, and Konoye and the minister of finance sided with them, only the navy's Yonai remained as a force for moderation in international policy. Even Yonai was having his difficulties, because by the end of 1938 the Japanese navy's building program had produced a fleet that was superior in force to the United States Pacific Fleet. The "fleet faction," bolstered by the succession of naval "victories" in China, was becoming nearly as outspoken for war against the whites in Asia as the army was for the China war.

Later it was the recollection of Admiral Yonai that he and Admiral Yamamoto spent the years 1937–39 fending off the "young turks" of the navy who shared the young army officers' rebellious spirit. Yonai, Yamamoto, and the other conservatives held the top positions in the navy. Yonai managed to get Admiral Suetsugu appointed to be a cabinet councillor, a post that demanded he be put on the navy reserve list, which made Suetsugu ineligible to become navy minister.

"Admiral Suetsugu has been driven up on to the roof—and the ladder has been taken away," said Vice Minister Yamamoto.

But just below the ranks of the seniors were the young commanders, who were growing more important each year. Commander Takazumi Nagaoka, an avowed pro-Axis man, became chief of the Naval Affairs Bureau's First Section. Commander Shigenori Kami headed another bureau. The events of 1938 began to raise the prestige of the "fleet faction" of the navy, and the agitation of the young commanders.[6]

In April 1938 the Japanese army mounted two new offensives against China in north and south. Fourteen Japanese divisions were now occupied in China. The army had been increased by the doubling of the budget to thirty-four divisions, but twenty of these were held in reserve because of War Minister Itagaki's plans to attack the Soviet Union.

The plan had to be delayed. The Wuhan offensive in central China seemed to be on the verge of producing a debacle that would force China out of the war. A large Chinese force was surrounded but managed at the end to break out and fight its way west. The Japanese had won another "great victory" and had occupied more territory and were worse off than ever.

The army pressed the foreign office to obtain the disputed territories along the Soviet-Manchukuo border. In Moscow in July, Ambassador Mamoru Shigemitsu presented Soviet Foreign Minister Maxim Litvinov with a demand for transfer of disputed territories to Manchukuo and Japan (in the case of territory next to Korea). On receipt of this demand the Red Army instructed the forces in Siberia to occupy the lands to which the USSR laid claim. On July 13 Russian border troops took positions on Changkufeng Hill. The Japanese troops of the Korea army sped to the scene but did not attack. The Soviets, unopposed, withdrew from the hill. At the same time, War Minister Itagaki asked the emperor to approve an offensive against the Soviets in the region of Lake Khasan, which Itagaki declared was poorly defended. The idea was to push in with the military and then force the Soviets to give up the territory at the bargaining table.[7]

The supercabinet, now dominated by the army, met to discuss this subject and on July 22 agreed to reinforce the northern border. Imperial General Headquarters, however, suggested that they go slowly. The offensive against Hankow on the central China front was at its height and commanded a growing percentage of the Japanese resources. The Japanese Nineteenth and Twentieth divisions were sent north, with an infantry brigade, three machine gun battalions, a cavalry brigade, tanks, and seventy aircraft. On July 27 these forces were in place along the disputed border. The Soviets occupied another hill north of Changkufeng. (These hills were called Zaozernaya and Bezymyanaya hills by the Russians.)

On July 29, while Ambassador Shigemitsu was talking to Foreign Minister Litvinov in Moscow about the disputed territory, the Japanese attacked. It was reminiscent of the opening of the Russo-Japanese War, except that this time the results were quite different. The Japanese captured their hills and inflicted casualties on the Soviet border forces.[8]

The Japanese troops had orders from Imperial General Headquarters to halt on the border and go no farther. But the Japanese commanders were heady with victory. Also they had before them the illustrations of the Kwantung Army's success in defying Tokyo's authority and also the success of the China armies, and the knowledge that War Minister Itagaki and Vice Minister Tojo fully supported their aims. So the Japanese began to move again, their next objective was the Posyet area, which would put them in a position to threaten the naval base and port of Vladivostok. The Soviets called up the 32nd Division, the 40th Division, and the 2nd Motorized Brigade. These were supported by armored units and artillery and aircraft.

On August 6 the Soviets launched an offensive that drove the Japanese completely out of Soviet territory in three days. Five hundred Japanese soldiers were killed and nearly a thousand wounded. Ambassador Shigemitsu asked for a cease-fire and mutual withdrawal, and the Soviets, concerned with their own troubles in European Russia, were eager to agree. What the Korea and Kwantung armies had hoped would be a major Japanese military action fizzled out completely.[9] What nobody seemed to see at that point was the pattern of Japanese aggression:

Make the attack; if it succeeds, proceed; if it fails, withdraw and pretend it was all a mistake of overenthusiastic subordinates. This policy had worked at Port Arthur, failed in the 1928 assassination of Chang Tso-lin, worked in the Manchuria incident and the two 1937 invasions of China, and failed in southern Siberia.

When the emperor was advised of the ill-fated expedition, he grew furious with War Minister Itagaki and reprimanded him personally for misleading the throne.

"Abominable," he called the army's recent conduct. "Not one soldier is to be moved again without the express permission of the throne," he told the war minister.[10] If only he had been able to sustain his anger, the army still might have been brought under control. But by nature Hirohito was a mild-mannered man, and he soon cooled down. He was now almost entirely surrounded by sympathizers with the army, and so the words he was getting tended to play down the excesses of the militarists.

General Tojo now overreached himself. Holding a procurement meeting with representatives of Japan's industrial council, the deputy war minister spoke to these millionaire industrialists as though they were junior officers. He laid down the law to them about what they were going to have to produce. He also warned them that Japan's enemies were the European nations and the United States, and particularly the Soviet Union. Japan must be prepared to go to war with the Soviet Union. If the industrialists were not prepared to support the army's view, the army would make sure they did so in the future.[11]

General Tojo and General Itagaki were prepared to go to war with the USSR just then, but the emperor, Premier Konoye, the Supreme Military Council, and the industrial powers of the nation were not so prepared. Tojo's remarks made the newspapers in Japan and abroad and the uproar was immediate. "Japanese General Predicts War with Russia" was a London headline.

The American ambassador called at the foreign ministry to ask questions. General Ugaki, the foreign minister, spent the next week trying to explain these hostile remarks. General Itagaki, the minister of war, had to field questions in the Diet about the Tojo belligerence to the industrialists and his threats to the USSR.

Tojo had to go.

Quietly he was removed from the war ministry in December 1938 and assigned as inspector general of the army air forces, a job in which his technical military skill would be paramount and his political opinions submerged. There is no doubt that he took the blame for opinions that were shared by his superior, General Itagaki.

The China war dragged on. Japan now had committed 1.6 million men to the China fronts, and they were winning victories, although the casualties in these famous Japanese *banzai* charges were very heavy. They captured Hankow on the Yangtze front and Canton in the south, but the Chinese simply melted behind the victorious Japanese armies, formed up again, and attacked somewhere else.

Having burned the diplomatic bridge that had connected Japan to the Chiang Kai-shek Nationalist government, the Japanese began to work in the fall of 1938 to organize a new Chinese government, with its capital at Nanking. They negotiated secretly with Wang Ching-wei, one of the original leaders of President Sun Yat-sen's Republic of China. Wang had grown restless recently, in the cooperation between Chiang Kai-shek and the Chinese Communists who controlled most of the countryside of north China, even as the Japanese held the cities and the railroads. In December 1938, Wang and his wife left Chungking and traveled down to Hanoi in Indochina. From there Wang sent a cable to Chiang Kai-shek asking him to end the war against Japan immediately and fight the Communists instead.

Chiang rejected the proposition instantly, the Kuomintang branded Wang "traitor" and put a price on his head. Wang then went up to Shanghai, met the Japanese there, and went to Tokyo for talks. There the Japanese government leaders explained their plans: they proposed to build a new Asia, around the combination of Japan, Manchuria, and a New China. It would be the New Order of East Asia.

In January 1939, Prince Konoye was so discouraged with the prospects of finding a route to peace in China, and so tired of fending off the army's constant demands for money and power, that he resigned, as he had been threatening to do for months. He was replaced by Baron Kiichiro Hiranuma, an ultranationalist, who lasted until August 30, 1939. He was replaced by General Noboyuki Abe, who lasted until January 16, 1940. He was replaced by Admiral Mitsumasa Yonai, a moderate, who lasted until July 22, 1940. All these cabinets faced the same problem: the growing power of the militarists in army and navy.

There were differences in degree and approach in all these cabinets, but the one fact stood out: no matter the cabinet, from 1937 on, the march of militarism was steady and speedy. In February 1939, the Japanese navy occupied Hainan Island, off the south coast of Kwangtung Province of China. The French, whose Indochina colony was directly threatened by the move, were unable to do a thing about it: their fleet, had they chosen to send it to the Pacific in its entirety, would have been chopped up by the Japanese.

In China, the war continued. The General Headquarters of the China Expeditionary Army was established at Nanking under General Juzo Nishio, a former commander of the Kwantung Army. But the China army now faced a new problem—the policing of this enormous area of China that they had seized, in the absence of a civil government. General Nishio had to ask for more troops and still more troops. The result was that the Tokyo authorities had to dip into their reserves which had been saved to prosecute a war against the USSR. The Itagaki policy of fighting the Soviet Union had to be abandoned.

In the spring of 1939, the Kwantung Army was still secretly committed to an attack on the Soviets. In April, new regulations to govern the Kwantung Army's conduct vis-à-vis the Russians were forced on the army. They called for an evenhanded approach, "never to invade and never to be invaded." That high-sounding statement obviously came down from Tokyo. But the rest of the policy was much less placid. If the Soviets crossed the border they were to be "annihilated" (a common Japanese military term of excess). Where the borders were not precisely known, the area defense commander had the final decision as to what action would be taken.[12]

This time, in 1939, the Kwantung Army decided it would launch a probe into Outer Mongolia to see what would happen. Under the Kwantung Army's "Principles for the Settlement of Soviet-Manchurian Border Disputes," if the assault failed, then it could be regarded as a local mistake. The policy had worked before, if the results had not always been to the army's liking.

The place chosen was the Kalkha River area, which separated Outer Mongolia from Manchukuo in the Homonhon region. The Japanese said that the line ran along the Kalkha, which flows into Lake Buir Nor. The Soviets and Outer Mongolians said that the border lay thirty kilometers to the east of Homonhon.

The Japanese saw their chance when a small Mongolian cavalry unit crossed the river. The Manchukuo border guards immediately attacked and drove them back. The Mongols then built a bridge across the river to establish their rights. The Kwantung Army appeared on the scene and crossed over into Mongolia. A large Mongol force attacked the Japanese in Mongolia and very nearly wiped out the Kwantung Army regiment involved, because the Mongols were supported by Soviet tanks and planes.

The Kwantung Army decided to launch a major blow at the Mongols and to go into Siberia to punish the Soviets. Forgotten were the "Principles for the Settlement of Soviet-Manchurian Border Disputes." The Russians would be taught a lesson and, if all went well . . .[13]

The Kwantung Army set up a plan to send 15,000 troops up to the border and across. They would be supported by antitank guns, artillery, planes, and tanks. The plan was approved by War Minister Itagaki, and the Kwantung Army marched.

The battle began with Inner Mongolian troops riding camels to fight for the Japanese against Outer Mongolian troops on their bandy-legged ponies. But very shortly it became a battle of modern armies. The Kwantung Army at first had all the best of it with its fast new aircraft bombing and strafing in support of the troops. But on June 22 the Soviets brought up a force of 150 planes and attacked the Japanese. About a third of the planes were shot down, but the Japanese ground forces were hard hit. In retaliation, the Kwantung Army sent up more planes and on June 27 the Japanese attacked with 130 aircraft and destroyed 100 Soviet planes, mostly on the ground at air bases. This was real escalation of the war, into Siberia, and it was done without the knowledge of Imperial General Headquarters. When the IGHQ learned of the assault, the emperor was informed and the Kwantung Army was accused of usurping the imperial prerogatives. The emperor issued a personal reprimand to the Kwantung Army. The army did not reply but its anger was enormous against Imperial General Headquarters for not backing up the troops in the field.[14]

On July 1 the Kwantung Army launched a major attack by the Komabatsura force, which consisted of a greatly reinforced division. Across the river and into the Soviet-Mongol positions charged the troops, the company officers out front, leading with their unsheathed samurai swords. The Soviets by this time had prepared for war and had brought in their most modern weapons, including heavily armored tanks and fast planes. The samurai swords were no match for armored vehicles with heavy machine guns. The Japanese found their antitank weapons too small and were soon launching suicide squads with satchel charges to throw themselves under the enemy tanks and blow them up. The Soviets had produced far more armor than the Japanese could assemble, and the armor did the job. The Japanese took enormous casualties and failed to penetrate farther than the first few miles into Mongol territory. Their plan had been to move to the Trans-Siberian Railway, and, according to the Russians, to seize the territory from Irkutsk to Vladivostok.

The weather was extremely hot, temperatures went up to 130 degrees Fahrenheit on the Mongol plain.

"Our men were having a hard time getting even a trickle of water," said one artillery officer. "I, myself had to spend three days without any supply of water. And when the night comes the thermometer plummets. Our men sleep on the grass and sand, trembling with cold."[15]

By August the battle had been reduced to stalemate. The Kwantung Army asked Tokyo for a great air armada to decimate the Russian troops, but Imperial Headquarters called their attention to the regulations about border disputes, pointed out that the Kwantung Army was on the wrong side of the border, and said no.

On August 20 the Soviet forces launched their great counteroffensive. They had amassed armor and artillery far stronger than the Japanese. They attacked frontally and then brought equally large forces of armor around on both sides to outflank the Japanese. The Japanese 23rd Division was virtually destroyed. Two regimental commanders burned their flags. One committed *seppuku* with his samurai sword. The other charged into the face of enemy fire and was killed.

The Japanese retreated and then prepared to launch a new offensive, utilizing the major elements of the Kwantung Army. The generals on the field were prepared to use every man in Manchuria if necessary. Imperial Headquarters stepped in to save the Kwantung Army from itself, for the Soviets were bringing in even more troops, big guns, and armor and planes. Tokyo was not prepared to try to wage a major war against such strength. This was particularly true when the generals in Tokyo had a report on the Japanese casualties. Japanese casualties had been an astounding 73 percent! This compared to less than 20 percent casualties in the land fighting of the Russo-Japanese War. Something certainly had changed. The Imperial General Headquarters ordered the Kwantung Army to break off contact and retreat back into Manchukuo territory. In Moscow, Ambassador Shigemitsu approached the Soviet foreign office for a cease-fire and was treated very gently, all things considered. Both sides retreated behind their borders and gave guarantees not to come out again.[16]

The Kwantung Army was humiliated by the emperor's rebuff, and now by IGHQ: General Ueda, the commanding officer of the army, was sent back to Japan and that was the end of his career. General Rensuke Isogai was also retired from active duty. General Yoshijiru Umezu, commander of the First Army, came from Japan to bring order to the Kwantung Army. He came with a new order for the army. In the future no troops would counterattack or attack without the specific order of the commanding general of the army. Disobedience was a court-martial offense. General Tojo had controlled the Kwantung Army as he wanted to, by force of his personality. For the first time, now, the army was controlled by rules.

The opinion the Japanese generals offered the rest of the government was that the Soviets had maneuvered to prevent the Japanese from disposing of the China incident. Perhaps that tortured reasoning made it easier for the generals to live with the monster they had created. In the summer of 1939, two years after General Sugiyama had promised the emperor that he could end the China incident in a month, the involvement had tied up more than half Japan's military resources and there was no end in sight.

As for Siberia, the generals had another great shock on the heels of the border cease-fire. The USSR and Germany signed a nonaggression pact, thus nullifying the effects of the Anti-Comintern alliance between Japan and Germany, which the generals had hoped would assist their designs on the Soviet maritime provinces. Two years earlier it had all seemed so easy; first China to be brought to heel, and then Russia to be defeated once again. But at the end of August 1939, the world of the militarists had turned upside down.

月に叢雲 花に風

18. "In the month of storms, flowers appear"

*T*he summer of 1939 changed the world.

In July the United States slashed Japan's oil futures. The official announcement was that the United States intended to terminate its Treaty of Commerce with Japan at the end of the six months' notification period. That meant no more American oil. Without oil, neither the army nor the navy could move.

In September Germany marched into Poland, and the European war began. The implications to Japan were enormous: those who wanted to expand the empire to Southeast Asia saw their chance coming, particularly after Britain withdrew her gunboats from the Yangtze River and her troops from Peking and Tientsin. The Japanese militarists saw more weakness here, something on which they could capitalize. But they were held back by the last of the moderates. General Abe's government, which came to office just before the European war broke out, declared that Japan would not become involved in that conflict.

The words sounded good, as though Japan was going to settle down, but the crosscurrents in Tokyo told an entirely different story. As noted, for two years Admiral Yonai and his assistant, Admiral Yamamoto, had been fighting a running battle against army excesses and against turning the navy into a jingoist organization. They had warned so many times that Japan would ultimately lose a war against the United States that their warnings were no longer heard. When General Abe took over the government Admiral Yonai's service as

navy minister ended. Personally, Yonai was relieved because in recent months he and Yamamoto had been receiving an increasing
number of death threats, obviously from young naval officers and
other supernationalists.[1]

Here is an indication of the tenor, a note sent to Yamamoto:

> The next war will be a holy war . . . between Japan
> and England. . . . You, as a leader of the pro-British forces,
> and in league with Navy Minister Yonai, constantly ob-
> struct the carrying through of policies based on the national
> polity headed by the emperor, and are putting the glorious
> imperial navy in danger of becoming a private force of the
> senior statesmen and big business.[2]

These threats increased weekly. As Yonai went out of office,
he urged Yamamoto to go to sea as commander of the Combined
Fleet. Only thus could he be assured of safety from assassination.

The Abe government lasted four months, long enough to get
Yamamoto safely into the fleet and away from Tokyo, but that was
one of its few accomplishments.

Admiral Yonai was then persuaded to form a government—
this was a direct result of the emperor's attempt to avoid signing of
a treaty with the Nazis, a course the militarists were urging. The
antimilitarists, and this included the handful of navy leaders of the
"treaty faction," were trying to stop it.

Yonai was the emperor's last gasp, so to speak. Hirohito insisted
that he lead the new government, in the hope that as a military man
he could control the military and prevent the signing of the pact with
Nazi Germany and Fascist Italy. Lord Privy Seal Yuasa said privately
at the time that Hirohito felt the Yonai government had to be the
last effort, "a final attempt to check the rise of fascism."[3]

The radical element of the army charged that the selection of
Yonai was the work of the "pro-British senior statesmen." They were
right in one sense: Hirohito was the biggest Anglophile in Japan.

During the Yonai tenure the matter of China came up with the
inauguration of the puppet Wang Ching-wei government in Nanking
in March 1940. But even as Wang took office, he was a badly dis-
illusioned man; he had been promised that his government would
have support to become a government of national Chinese unity.
But the Japanese army had already increased control, now insisted

on Wang's immediate recognition of the "independence" of Manchukuo, a sure tip-off to the world that Japan was pulling the strings.

At this time, as if looking into the future, Former Prime Minister
Konoye put together the machinery for Japanese totalitarianism: the
Imperial Rule Assistance Association. It was supposed to be a party
above parties, a nonpartisan group of leaders whose one aim was to
further the ends of the empire. Actually, the Imperial Rule Assistance
Association was composed of the most violently jingoistic men in
public life. It was the twin of General Araki's *kodo ha*—Imperial
Way—group of the army.

Far more important, the machinery of totalitarian control was
built into the Imperial Rule Assistance Association's organizational
structure. Its tentacles reached down to the village level and to the
neighborhood level of the cities. The *koban,* police box, was a sort
of miniature city hall to the Japanese; they went to the *koban* for
licenses, to pay fines, and to secure all sorts of information. Traditionally the police of the *koban* kept track of all the people who lived
in their neighborhoods. Now the *koban* was to have a new, more
sinister significance. It would soon become the watchtower from
which the police and the district associations spied on the people
and kept them in line.

Japan's democracy had always been limited; the nobility and
rich had always run the country, and their main opponents in the
Taisho and Showa periods had been the army. Now, the Meiji Constitution had been shorn of all the slender protections offered the
people, and the machinery was ready to establish totalitarian control
by the government.

The promotion campaign for the Imperial Rule Assistance Association was begun that summer of 1939. Prince Konoye called on
the people to join up, "to restore the spirit and virtues of the old
Japan." Read that: the spirit of the old Japan, as modified by the
believers in the Imperial Way.[4]

From the beginning the Yonai government was in trouble over
the burning issue of the Rome-Berlin pact. To sign meant to cast
Japan's lot with the totalitarian countries of Europe, seen, perhaps
more clearly in Tokyo that summer than in Washington, as the enemies of Britain and the United States. Yonai said no; Japan did not
want to be part of that group. The army said yes. So did Admiral
Suetsugu, General Iwane Matsui, and former Ambassador Yosuke
Matsuoka, all members of the cabinet council. They resigned in

protest. The resignations shook Tokyo. Admiral Yamamoto stopped laughing.

Late in the spring of 1940 "the phoney war" came to an end, with the battle for Norway, the German blitzkrieg through Belgium, the fall of France, the near disaster of Dunkirk, and what appeared to be the imminence of the German invasion of England. Mussolini— "that jackal," Winston Churchill called him—hastened to join the war on Germany's side. The pressure from the Japanese militarists to join the "winner" became almost unbearable.

In June 1940, the Japanese army forced the Japanese government to demand that Britain close the Burma Road, over which China was receiving its slender supply of war materials. Facing possible invasion, the British could not spare an iota of energy in Asia, so they acceded for three months. Once again, this agreement to an outrageous demand only whetted the appetite of the Japanese militarists, who could now see themselves as the inheritors of the British empire in Asia.

Two days after the British agreed to close the Burma Road the Japanese army in China closed in around Hongkong, ready. The army agitated: Japan must join Germany and Italy before their world victory. Only thus could the Japanese expect to share in the spoils.[5]

The end of June found Admiral Yonai's government in shambles. Colonel Hashimoto, whose attempted coups and murderous plots were by now legendary in Japan, tried another: the police learned of it just in time and seized thirty-eight young men who were planning to kill the prime minister and a number of the elder councillors to the emperor as "hindrances to Japan's fulfilment of her destiny." Once again, Colonel Hashimoto, the gunner of the Yangtze, got off scot-free.[6]

By mid-July 1940, the Japanese army was prepared to seize power. War Minister General Hata told Prime Minister Yonai that the army now insisted on an end to political government, and that he was resigning to force the issue. On this rock the Yonai cabinet capsized. This time the emperor's senior councillors had virtually no choice: they could have Prince Konoye, who was acceptable to the army, or they could have an army prime minister. Period.

The emperor chose the least dangerous: Konoye. But even then, he lost.

Prince Konoye came to power this time with several understandings with the army: Japan would ally herself with Germany and Italy; a planned economy would be established; Japan, Manchukuo, and the New China would form an economic bloc; and all aspects of Japanese life would be subordinated to the military.

The makeup of the new cabinet gave the clues as to what was coming. The foreign minister would be Yosuke Matsuoka, negotiator of the Anti-Comintern pact with Germany, a prime mover in the plot against Manchuria, and perhaps Japan's number one America-hater. Matsuoka had grown up on the West Coast of the United States and had been subjected to some of the American racism against Orientals. He had also gone to college at the University of Oregon, where he apparently fine-tuned his hatred of things American.[7]

The war minister would be General Hideki Tojo, one of the prime advocates of war with the Soviet Union, and Matsuoka's long-time associate in the manipulation of Manchukuo. Prime Minister Konoye had not even made the gesture of asking the army to submit a list of names, as had been the custom in the old days. He told General Hata to pick his own successor, which meant that the board of generals who controlled the army would pick the man. It had to be someone who could control the army, said the prime minister. Tojo had controlled the Kwantung Army, and as assistant war minister he had gained the confidence of his fellow generals. Tojo was just then busily building up the army's air force installations in Manchuria, with an eye to developing a strength that would overcome the Soviet air forces the next time they met the Japanese.

The navy minister would be Admiral Kashiro Oikawa, a mild, scholarly admiral, whose major claim to fame was his attempt to constantly please everyone. Consequently, everyone, inside the navy and out, knew that he would blow with the wind.

In June, Prince Konoye came down to Tokyo from his summer villa at Karuizawa to resign as president of the Privy Council and once again take on the responsibilities of prime minister.

Japan was ready for new military adventures. In the Imperial Rule Assistance Association, she had created the mechanism to bring "The New Order" to Asia. The Imperial Rule Assistance Association was now going to replace all the political parties and help the cabinet rule the country. One by one all the political parties would disband.[8]

This new Konoye cabinet brought totalitarian control to Japan.

With France and the Netherlands now German colonies, the glitter of Indochina and the Dutch East Indies attracted the Japanese.

Here were European colonies ready for the taking. Now, to take them.

The first step began in August, as Britain staggered under the blows of the Nazi attempt to knock out the Royal Air Force, then invade England by sea. Japanese representatives at Vichy, France, announced that Chiang Kai-shek's armies had established a new war zone in southern China, and that the French must grant the Japanese the use of Indochina airfields from which they could attack the recalcitrant Chinese. Also, the presence of Imperial Japanese Army forces in northern Indochina was essential to prevent supplies from reaching Chiang Kai-shek through the Japanese blockade. There was virtually nothing the Petain government could do. Germans badgered them at Vichy, and in Hanoi the Japanese threatened the colonial governor that if he did not agree they would come in anyhow, and with far less courtesy to the French inhabitants. So, in September 1940, the Japanese army prepared to move into northern Indochina. It was to be the first overt act in the establishment of "The New Order" in Asia.[9]

As soon as the cabinet took office that summer of 1940, Foreign Minister Matsuoka had begun negotiation of a Tripartite Pact with Germany and Italy. The one stumbling block could be the navy, where there was known to be much opposition. Navy Minister Admiral Oikawa called a conference of admirals in Tokyo. From the Combined Fleet flagship *Nagato* at anchor at Hashirajima in the Inland Sea, up came Admiral Yamamoto, former vice minister of the navy, bearing an armload of reference materials from which he prepared to argue that Japan was in no position to antagonize Britain and the United States.[10]

When the meeting opened around a large table, Minister Okawa began by announcing that Prime Minister Konoye and the rest of the cabinet were bent on this treaty, and that if it was not signed, Konoye would quit, and the cabinet would resign. All the admirals knew the probable outcome of such an eventuality: a coup and dictatorship by the army.

Having said that much, Minister Okawa then asked the assembled admirals to give their consent. Around the table not one admiral moved. Finally, Admiral Yamamoto stood up. He had no objection to any steps on which the minister had decided, he said. But one point did worry him. When he was vice minister—August 1939—

the cabinet planning board had produced a plan for mobilization of material resources. Eighty percent of the materials needed by the navy were controlled by sources in the United States and British empires. When Japan allied herself with Germany and Italy, she could expect to lose these sources. What new arrangements had been made to replace the materials?[11]

Navy Minister Oikawa did not even try to answer the question. He repeated his request that the admirals approve the Tripartite Pact. One after another, they did. Later on that visit to Tokyo, Prime Minister Konoye insisted that Admiral Yamamoto come to see him, and the admiral spent two hours with the premier. Yamamoto then advised Konoye against seeking trouble with the United States at least, because of the materials shortage. Konoye pretended to know nothing about this and complained that Yamamoto should have stood up and refused at the meeting.[12] Yamamoto was furious; this, he said, was typically Konoye, always attempting to put the responsibility for what he did on other shoulders. Among Yamamoto's friends it was small wonder that the admiral was kept at sea; even the reporters found him the most open and unpolitical military man in Japan in his comments. When Admiral Yonai, then retired and living in the country, heard about the Tripartite Pact, he told a friend that looking back, his and Yamamoto's opposition had been like rowing a boat against the current above Niagara Falls. What if Yonai and Yamamoto had been kept on as minister and vice minister of the navy? Would they have continued to oppose the treaty?

"Of course," said the admiral. "But I imagine we would both have been killed . . ."[13]

Indeed, such an attempt would have been made, for the government was already deeply involved in its preparations to expand the Japanese empire southward.

The program was outlined at a conference held at the Imperial Palace (and thus called an Imperial Conference) on September 19, 1940. The conference was called to discuss the Tripartite Pact. In the course of the discussion, Naoki Hoshino, director of the planning board, spoke of the difficulties the navy would have in securing an oil supply if the United States cut off exports to Japan, which might come about, since the pact was so clearly aimed at the United States. Foreign Minister Matsuoka tended to discount that possibility.

"To be sure," he said, "the United States may adopt a stern attitude for a while; but I think that she will dispassionately take her interests into consideration and arrive at a reasonable attitude. As to whether she will stiffen her attitude and bring about a critical situation, or will levelheadedly reconsider, I would say that the odds are fifty-fifty."[14]

War Minister Tojo set out the army's plan for the future then:

> The army, like the navy, considers oil important. I think this question, in the end, comes down to the matter of the Netherlands East Indies. The matter was decided by the Liaison Conference between the Government and Imperial Headquarters held shortly after the formation of the present Cabinet, when the policy statement "Outline of Policy on the Settlement of the Situation" was adopted. It was agreed that we should settle the China incident quickly and at the same time cope with the Southern Question, taking advantage of favorable opportunities. As for the Netherlands East Indies, it was decided that we would try to obtain vital materials by diplomatic means, and that we might use force, depending on the circumstances. We are most certainly not moving forward without a policy.[15]

On September 22, 1940, Japanese troops crossed the border from China into Indochina.

The reaction from London and Washington was swift. Britain immediately announced the reopening of the Burma Road to China, giving Chiang Kai-shek back his lifeline to the West. The United States announced an embargo on iron and steel scrap exports except to nations of the Western Hemisphere and Britain. Japan, the largest importer of American steel, would get no more.

On September 27, 1940, Japan, Germany, and Italy signed the Tripartite Pact and the pictures of the event circled a world that was now firmly divided into three major camps: the totalitarians of Germany, Italy, and Japan, with their peace pacts to keep the Soviet Union from interfering while they dismembered the rest of the world; that world, the new German colonies of Europe, the old colonies of Africa and Asia, and the undeveloped republics of Latin America; and, third, the disorganized English-speaking peoples, with the most powerful military element, the British empire, already under siege.

Mainichi Shimbun's editorial showed how the Japanese public felt about the turn of events:

> The time has at last arrived when Nippon's aspiration and efforts to establish East Asia for East Asiatics, free from the Anglo-Saxon yoke, coincides exactly with the German-Italian aspiration to build a New Order in Europe and to seek a future appropriate to their strength by liberating themselves from the Anglo-Saxon clutches.[16]

There was, however, something to be learned before the Imperial Japanese Army was prepared to conquer its half of the world. Imperial General Headquarters had studied those casualty figures from the Homonhon incident of 1939 carefully and concluded that it was time to make a serious survey of the most modern methods of land warfare. The Germans and the Russians had been steadily improving their weapons and testing them in the Spanish civil war. Under the anti-Comintern pact, the Japanese had a special access to the Germans, and they decided to use it.

An obscure general named Tomoyuki Yamashita was chosen for the task. He had been one of the supporters of the 2-26 Incident plotters, who had finally arranged for their surrender and thus restored himself to the imperial favor just as he was preparing to resign from the army in disgrace. He had kept a low profile since that time, as commander of the North China Mixed Brigade garrison in 1937 and chief of staff of the North China Area Army in 1938, and as 4th Division commander in September 1939. His "progressive" ideas were well known to his fellow generals as was his military expertise. He could be trusted. So General Yamashita was selected by the senior generals of the army to be sent to Germany to learn from the Wehrmacht how to make war in the most modern manner. War Minister Tojo was not enthusiastic; Yamashita was a man of his own generation and Tojo was jealous of the power he had just attained. But the senior generals insisted, and Tojo's power was not then great enough for him to resist. General Yamashita was appointed inspector general of the air force—Tojo's own vehicle to prominence. He and a party of generals, admirals, and technicians set out on the Trans-Siberian Railway for Moscow, and then Berlin.[17] Japan was not losing a moment in taking advantage of the new commitment to conquest.

我田引水

19. "Every man draws water for his own field"

1940. The New Order demanded a special celebration, and some enterprising historian came up with an excuse: this year marked the 2,600th anniversary of the founding of Japan, he said, and so a series of nationwide holidays were declared. In October the emperor went to sea to review the Combined Fleet, and Admiral Yamamoto greeted him aboard the battleship *Hiei*. It was a most impressive display clearly visible from the parks in Yokohama, 600,000 tons of ships and 525 aircraft flying over; the Combined Fleet, the third largest in the world, and the largest to be massed in one ocean.[1] In November an imperial celebration was held in Hibiya Park. The park was a sea of lantern lights on the night of the affair. Their Imperial Majesties, the emperor and the empress came out of the Imperial Palace to attend a celebration in the outer garden. Fifty thousand notable persons were invited inside the sacred enclosure, and army and navy bands played stirring music. The common people outside shouted *banzai* as they looked in. Their Majesties sat down to *bento* (lunchbox) lunches. The emperor read an Imperial Rescript.

"It is Our earnest hope that peace will be restored soon and that We may share with all countries happiness and prosperity, albeit the world is now in the midst of great turmoil."[2]

No one paid any attention. That was what an emperor was supposed to say on such an occasion. Everybody in Japan knew that a great day was dawning for the nation. Japan was on the road. *Hakko ichiu!*

At the end of the year, in Tokyo, Isoroku Yamamoto became a full admiral, along with Zengo Yoshida and Shigetaro Shimada, all classmates at the naval academy at Eta Jima. Yamamoto, certain that "those idiots" of the army, who were clearly running Japan, were now embarked on a course that must take Japan to war with the United States, was beginning to consider a war plan that would violate all the rules of the Imperial Navy's traditional plans for a Pacific war. It would involve a preemptive strike, of the sort that Admiral Togo had launched against the Russians at Port Arthur. One difference was that in 1941 the distance to be traveled was two-thirds of the width of the Pacific, to Pearl Harbor, where the American Pacific Fleet would be found. Another major difference was that the strike would be carried out entirely by aircraft and submarines, with the battleships and cruisers of the striking force offering protection to the carriers. The striking force's destroyers would have the task of rescuing crew members from any carriers that might be sunk. It would mean the use of half a dozen aircraft carriers in a fashion never before considered in naval warfare. It was, said Admiral Yamamoto, a do-or-die operation. The outcome would be decided on the first day.[3]

When Admiral Yamamoto showed this plan to Admiral Takajiro Ohnishi, the chief of staff of the Eleventh Air Fleet, Ohnishi thought he was mad. So did others, and they obviously talked among themselves, because in January Ambassador Grew had the rumor and reported it to Washington. Admiral Stark, the American chief of naval operations, reported it to Admiral Husband Kimmel at Pearl Harbor, but appended the remark that he believed the report to be incredible. Why? Because naval battles were simply not fought that way. In the U.S. and British navies, the battleship was king. Some admirals still doubted the viability of aircraft carriers for naval warfare. So why should they believe so ridiculous a story?[4]

As the year 1941 opened, from Berlin, where General Yamashita's military mission had just arrived, came a report to gladden the hearts of the militarists:

"It is now absolutely impossible for Britain to defeat the Reich. Not only that, but the end of British resistance is merely a question of time. The United States at present is not prepared militarily enough to fight Japan, Germany, and Italy simultaneously, and the United States' preparedness will not be completed before 1944."[5]

And in Tokyo War Minister Tojo completed a new *senjinkun,* moral code for the fighting men, and presented it for imperial approval. The booklet reiterated the Araki theme, now dinned into two generations of Japanese soldiers: the warrior's duty was to die for the emperor:

"A sublime sense of self-sacrifice must guide you throughout life and death. Think not of death, as you push through, with every ounce of your effort, in fulfilling your duties. Make it your joy to do everything with all your spiritual and physical strength. Fear not to die for the cause of everlasting justice."[6]

Here was the glorification of the *banzai* charge. Here was the warning that to become a prisoner of war was to dishonor the soldier, his family, the army, and the emperor. Death was mandatory.

General Yamashita's commission had indicated that the Japanese tactic of sending company officers out in front with their samurai swords to strike terror into the hearts of the enemy might work well with the ill-armed Chinese, but had worked so badly with the Soviets that the Kwantung Army on the Mongolian border had been decimated. While Yamashita was trying to find a better way, Tojo was glorifying the system of the Imperial Way, which would cause so many young men to lose their lives so needlessly, on the erroneous premise that the *bushido* spirit was more powerful than .50 caliber machine gun slugs.[7]

The Japanese military mission arrived in Berlin at the end of December 1940, to be greeted with full ceremonial honors. General Yamashita was received by Adolf Hitler, and he reported after the audience that Hitler had pledged that the Germans would bind themselves eternally to the Japanese spirit, which made good reading back in Japan. Privately, Yamashita thought Hitler looked and behaved like a clerk.

The meetings with Nazi officials were full of hearty cordiality. "All our secrets are open to you," said Hitler. "His promise to show all his equipment was meaningless," Yamashita said. He asked specifically about radar, but the Germans turned the questions aside.[8]

What Hitler wanted from Japan was an immediate declaration of war against Britain, and especially against the United States. But Yamashita offered him little hope. Japan, he said, was so deeply involved in China and so fearful of attack by Russia that she was not going to attack anyone. The Japanese were in Berlin to learn how to improve their defenses, not their offensive capability.[9]

Actually, General Yamashita avoided the political questions, and quite properly, because that March 1941 Foreign Minister Yo-suke Matsuoka was in Berlin, cementing relations with Hitler and putting his official signature on the Rome-Berlin-Tokyo pact. Mat-suoka then stopped in Moscow on his way home and secured a neutrality treaty with the USSR which would run for the next five years. When the treaty was signed and Matsuoka was ready to go home to Tokyo, Stalin entertained him and they stoked up on vodka for so long that Matsuoka's train had to be held for him. Stalin took the blowsy Japanese foreign minister to the station, gave him an immense bear hug, and announced his blessing:

"We are both Asiatics," he said. "Japan can now move south."[10]

South, he meant, and not north into Siberia. For that he had guaranteed the USSR's nonintervention in Asia.

The way for Japan to move now in Asia certainly had become clear. The Tripartite Treaty with Germany was specifically aimed at the United States in Article 3:

> The . . . signatories . . . are bound . . . to assist one
> another with all political, economic and military means
> when one of the three Contracting Parties is attacked by
> a power at present not involved in the European War or
> in the Sino-Nipponese Conflict.[11]

There was only one such power in the world: The United States of America. Thus, in nine months the new Konoye cabinet had set the stage for conquest of Southeast Asia.

That is precisely how it looked in Washington. When the news of the pact came out on April 13, President Roosevelt had been considering aggressive action by American warships in the Atlantic against the U-boats. He dropped the idea for the time being, considering that the new development in Moscow had created too much danger in the Pacific.

As far as the Japanese military mission to Germany was concerned, Reichsmarschal Hermann Goering renewed the persuasion when he took the Japanese mission to see the Maginot line, which Germany had simply ignored in rushing through Belgium, and Marshal Kesselring's air force headquarters in northern France from which the blitz on London was being directed. Goering boasted that he would defeat England by bombing alone. The Japanese ought to enter the war quickly, he advised, before it was all over. Only thus could they hope to have their share when Germany and Italy divided up the world.[12] Goering's argument might have been more persuasive did not Yamashita observe that the German planes were not crossing the channel by daylight any more and that pilot morale seemed low. He gathered that the British had already won the air Battle of Britain. But seeing both British and German planes in action, Yamashita concluded that air power was far more important than the Japanese army had hitherto believed. He made a rough estimate that it would take Japan, using all her resources, two years to bring her army air forces up to the proper level for attack. What impressed Yamashita was the skill of the German engineers and the competence of the production lines, employing unskilled female labor. Japan had lots of unskilled female labor. He was also impressed by the unification of the German armed services; the bad feeling between Japanese army and navy was something he saw that Imperial General Headquarters would have to address.[13]

The Yamashita mission spent five months in Germany. The generals and admirals toured scores of factories, watched war games, and conferred with most of the important figures in Germany's defense industry. Still no one would show them radar. One day Yamashita told his air advisor to "get lost." The Japanese had discovered the whereabouts of a secret radar factory near the installations they were being shown in the Baltic area. The air advisor with his staff set out for a drive the next day and "got lost." He went directly to the factory. The Germans assumed it was an official visit, sanctioned by the high command, and showed them everything. The Japanese, who knew virtually nothing about radar, learned there of its enormous importance, and they also captured the basic technological idea.[14]

Following the German visit, the Japanese flew to Italy to meet Mussolini. The Italian trip was cut short by a demand from Adolf Hitler that they return immediately. When Yamashita arrived in Berlin, Hitler told him he was expecting "to be attacked by Russia" in a few days and that the Japanese had best get on the Trans-Siberian Railway and get home. Yamashita listened and obeyed. The independent-minded navy contingent scoffed and said there was more to be learned. They stayed behind.

When Yamashita and his party were traveling up near the

Polish-Russian frontier they could see the ammunition dumps, fields filled with tanks and trucks, and all the temporary military camps in the area. It was apparent that Hitler was getting ready to attack Russia. Across the Soviet border there was little to be seen of Soviet defense efforts except the building of antitank ditches. When Yamashita reached Moscow, the party was met by General Zhukov. They lunched at the Kremlin but did not see Stalin. Then they left that night for Siberia. They did not talk to the Russians about the German war plans, and the Russians asked them no questions.[15]

Three days later, when the Yamashita party reached Irkutsk, they learned that Hitler had invaded Russia. The naval contingent, stuck in Germany, was put aboard a submarine and sent to Argentina, minus their baggage. They were months in getting back to Japan.

As General Yamashita and his party neared Japan he held a meeting and warned all that they must be very careful. He had noted that the Germans were not doing well. The members of the mission should not give anyone ammunition if they wanted Japan to declare war on Britain or the United States. They had all seen how modern war machines were built, and they must know that it would take Japan years to rebuild her defenses properly.

When the Yamashita commission submitted its report, it suggested unification of the armed services and preparations for war against Russia. Yamashita warned officially and personally that the Japanese army's air force was inferior in equipment and training and organization to those of the Germans and the Western powers. The commission recommended concentration on the building of medium tanks, the mechanization of the divisions, the development of firepower, the establishment of a large parachute infantry force, and the modernization of command.[16]

The Yamashita report created a sensation in army circles. In a sense that was unfortunate, because General Tojo's ambitions had been stirred, and he was extremely jealous of Yamashita, who was four years younger. Tojo believed that Yamashita was scheming to get his job. So a few days later, General Yamashita suddenly was shipped off to Manchuria on the pretext of setting up a new Kwantung Army Defense Headquarters, to prepare for war against the USSR.

In the months that Yamashita had been away in Germany, Tojo had not been idle. One of his tactics had been to purge the army command of Anglophiles and Americanophiles and replace them with officers who, like himself, had been trained in Germany or in Russia. The others were assigned to field positions as far from Tokyo as possible. Their influence in the coming vital months was virtually nil.

The Yamashita report was pigeonholed. War Minister General Tojo and his fellow generals were too far along with their plans for Southeast Asia to accept critical appraisal that would involve two years of rebuilding.

In the summer of 1941 the decision to extend the war was inherent in everything being discussed by the military authorities in Tokyo. The only question was: which way to go?

The first thought of Imperial General Headquarters, developed while Foreign Minister Matsuoka was in Europe, was to end the "China incident" by sending one army up the Yangtze River to Chungking, and another across from north China and Manchukuo to Sian and down, thus pinching out Chungking and surrounding Chiang Kai-shek.

But the Berlin-Rome-Tokyo pact now came home to haunt the Japanese. Once Hitler invaded Russia, they were afraid to ignore the pact. What if Hitler won without their assistance? Then they would have the Germans on their northern border. What if Hitler also occupied England? Then they would have to deal with Hitler over the British colonies in Asia.

The Germans, having failed to "blitz" the Soviets, now demanded with increasing shrillness that Japan attack Siberia. Foreign Minister Matsuoka favored this course. But the army wanted to occupy Indochina. When Prime Minister Konoye sided with the army high command, Foreign Minister Matsuoka knew he was defeated. The next step was to secure the approval of the War Council, which consisted of the field marshals, fleet admirals, war and navy ministers, and army and navy chiefs of staffs, plus some other admirals and generals appointed to the council by the emperor. This council was then to approach the emperor and persuade him to its point of view. Matsuoka played his last cards: he warned that to get involved in the south would lead to serious consequences with the United States, while to attack the USSR might not mean anything to the United States, which was anti-Communist. He so argued at a conference of the government military liaison forces. General Muto, chief of the army Bureau of Military Affairs, said they must go south, to guarantee a supply of rubber and tin. Navy Chief of Staff Osumi Nagano said all the preparations had been made to invade Indochina. To go north would delay action for fifty days. The plan now was to move first into Indochina, and then farther, into Malaya and the Netherlands East Indies, step by step, hoping, of course, that Japan could swallow these chunks of territory without arousing the sleeping eagle—the United States, which was the only power uncommitted to the European war and thus free to take on Japan if it would.[17]

On July 2, 1941, another Imperial Conference was called, and this one was so important that the emperor appeared, to hear the discussion of the document "Outline of National Policies in View of the Changing Situation." The policy was the establishment of the Greater East Asia Co-Prosperity Sphere. The method: preparation for war against the United States and Britain. The immediate new move: investment of all of French Indochina.

Privy Council President Yoshimichi Hara said he was worried about war with the United States. Foreign Minister Matsuoka said that a war with the United States and Britain was unlikely if the Japanese military proceeded with great caution. "The trouble is that the officers in the front line are aggressive, convinced that we will use force. . . . Of course I have sanctioned the aggressive behavior of the officers, trusting in the wisdom of the Supreme Command."[18]

But Hara was not satisfied:

"What I want to make clear is whether the United States would go to war if Japan took action against Indochina."

Matsuoka: "I cannot exclude the possibility."

At this point General Sugiyama, the army chief of staff, interrupted. Sugiyama had favored war with the United States for a year.

> Our occupation of Indochina will certainly provoke Britain and the United States. . . . At this juncture, Japan must resolutely carry out the policy she now has in mind: this policy is absolutely necessary in order to stamp out the intrigues of Great Britain and the United States. . . . I do not believe that the United States will go to war if Japan moves into French Indochina. Of course, we wish to do this peacefully. We also wish to take action in Thailand but that might have serious consequences since Thailand is near Malaya. This time we will go only as far as Indo-

china. We will be careful in sending our troops into Indochina, since this will greatly influence our policy with
regard to the South.[19]

Hara, speaking for the Imperial Throne, said he now understood
and agreed. But he did want the Supreme Command to attack Soviet
Russia as soon as possible and to refrain for the moment at least
from going to war with the United States.

Everyone was agreed, save one. War Minister General Tojo felt
he had to respond belligerently to Matsuoka's complaint that the
front-line troops misbehaved themselves, as everyone in the meeting
knew they did.

Foreign Minister Matsuoka implied that some members of the army in the front lines are intemperate; but I
wish to say that the army gets its orders from the emperor.
What the foreign minister has implied has never happened.
We took severe disciplinary measures when we sent troops
to French Indochina. Coordination between military and
diplomatic action is very difficult. I will try to avoid problems in this respect by cooperating with the Supreme Command.[20]

That peculiarly Japanese statement was to warn Matsuoka that
he had gone almost too far in provoking the army by telling the truth
about it, that everything the army did was in the name of (and the
responsibility of) the emperor, and that Matsuoka had best remember the army was now in charge.

This was so apparent to navy Chief of Staff Nagano that he
made only one attempt to speak during the conference and when he
was ignored, he sat down and did not try again.[21]

And so that vital Imperial Conference became history with the
final assent of the emperor to a policy he knew very well was going
to lead to war with the United States and Britain. Whatever the
emperor's feelings before this time, the stark replies of the army to
all questions on July 2 showed that there was no turning back short
of an imperial demand that they do so. And by this time, such an
imperial demand could very easily have been met with army insur-
rection. The army was talking about proceeding slowly, but with no
indication that anything could occur to make them stop their expansion of Japan's empire. What had happened was the abandonment

of the pincers movement against Chiang Kai-shek at Chungking, which at that point might very well have succeeded had Japan been willing to devote most of her fifty-one divisions to the task.

Tojo had reminded everyone that the China incident was still very much with them, but the rapid change in the fortunes of war in Europe had brought a feeling to Tokyo that if the Japanese did not move now to secure more empire, it might be lost to them. The generals were overwhelmed by the speed of German victories in the European war, and, as Saburo Hayashi put it in his study of the Japanese army, "afraid of missing the bus."[22]

While Foreign Minister Matsuoka had failed in his bid to secure commitment for an immediate attack on the Soviet Union, the throne had indicated its support of a strong and watchful presence on the Manchurian border. Tojo took this to be an invitation to attack the USSR as soon as the military situation in western Russia would justify it. Forsaking the chance to defeat China once and for all, the Imperial General Staff began moving north and south.

The decision was not clearly recognized at the time for what it was: an overextension of Japan's military resources. Tojo was committing Japan to fight on three fronts, Siberia, China, and the south.

The orders were prepared to double the size of the Kwantung Army and increase its armaments commensurately. The army had 400,000 troops; it was to have nearly 800,000. Manpower was not the basic problem: The Imperial Way philosophy that had permeated the nation from top to bottom made the creation of cannon fodder easy. It was the trucks and tanks and guns, and, above all, the gasoline to run them that was the never-ending problem.[23] Under war conditions the only petroleum available to Japan would be that of the Dutch East Indies, which they must capture.

The quarrel between Matsuoka and the army led to a typically Japanese contretemps. Prime Minister Konoye had so many complaints about Matsuoka that he wanted to get rid of him, so he dissolved the cabinet, and formed a new one with a new foreign minister, Admiral Teijiro Toyoda.

The new cabinet met to reaffirm the old policy on July 24. At this meeting, Navy Minister Nagano made a remarkable speech:

> As for war with the United States, although there is now a chance of achieving victory, the chances will diminish as time goes on. By the later half of next year it will

already be difficult for us to cope with the United States; after that, the situation will become increasingly worse. The United States will probably prolong the matter until her defenses have been built up and then try to settle it. Accordingly as time goes by, the Empire will be put at a disadvantage. If we could settle things without war, there would be nothing better. But if we conclude that conflict can not ultimately be avoided, then I would like you to understand that as time goes by we will be in a disadvantageous position. Moreover, if we occupy the Philippines, it will be easier, from the navy's point of view, to carry on the war.[24]

Admiral Nagano was at this point making one last appeal to reason. The sentiments were not his alone, but Admiral Yamamoto's, in particular. Yamamoto had been telling his naval friends for years that Japan could not win a war against the United States. But for the past year, as a loyal Japanese, Yamamato had occupied himself with seeking the outside chance; this was to strike so hard a blow against America before she could prepare herself, that the Pacific Fleet would be destroyed. Japan could then make a benevolent offer for peace, and there was a chance it might be worked out. A chance, a very small chance, Yamamoto believed, but it was the only chance. Here at the conference, in the guise of discussion, Nagano offered another huge difficulty: the army would have to throw in several more divisions of troops to occupy the Philippines. So the move south, which the army had suggested as an extension of the China war, now began to have all sorts of complications. But the juggernaut was moving, and no one at this point had the temerity to try to stop it.

Admiral Yamamoto was summoned to Tokyo so he could be told what had been decided in the conferences. When he learned of the move to be made into Indochina, he quit hoping for peace. "There's nothing we can do now," he said.[25]

The Japanese were unaware that the United States code breakers had been reading the messages of the foreign office to the Japanese embassy in Washington, and thus had the information that Japan would move into Indochina. On July 18 President Roosevelt's cabinet discussed the Far East situation and concluded that the time had now come to take some strong action against Japan. The State

Department began to prepare for the actions: freezing of Japanese funds in the United States and cutting off the supply of petroleum to Japan. Ambassador Kichisaburo Nomura, in Washington, had wind of the American feeling, and so reported to Tokyo. It was too late. Japanese troops set sail for Nha Trang and Cape St. Jacques. On July 25, the United States acted. There would be no more trade, there would be no more oil for Japan from American refineries.

In view of what Yamamoto knew of reserves, production, and consumption of oil, if it stopped coming from America, Japan would either have to move within four months to secure new supplies, or withdraw from the China war.[26]

As it turned out, it was worse than even Yamamoto had feared. The next day Britain also cut off Japanese supplies, and on the second day so did the Dutch. Those actions meant the American cut-off was immediately effective. Further, those actions also warned the Japanese that in the future they could expect the ABD (America-British-Dutch) powers to act as one. The trilateral action convinced even the most antiwar generals and admirals that the die had been cast, and that Japan now had no recourse but to prepare for war. In a meeting of the chiefs of the navy, Admiral Koga protested that the government had no right to take so important a decision as to provoke the United States without consulting the men who had to do the fighting, especially Yamamoto, chief of the Combined Fleet. The navy chief of staff, Admiral Nagano, spoke vaguely of the government's decision. "I suppose we'll have to go along with it," he said.

Admiral Yamamoto snorted. "Nagano's a dead loss," he said. But he also said something else at that meeting that indicated what the decision meant to Japan's loyal fighting men, especially those who had opposed the generals all the way till now.[27]

"There's nothing we can do now," said Admiral Yamamoto, and he went back to the fleet to consider the best method of crippling the American fleet before it could get started in the war that was most certainly going to begin in a few months.

虻蜂取らず

20. "Who's to choose between horsefly and hornet?"

O rientals have a greater problem in the making of policy decisions than Occidentals: if they reverse the policies, the matter
of "face" intervenes.

This problem was inherent in the difficulties Japan faced in the
summer of 1941. From Berlin came a stream of insistent demands
that Japan attack the Soviet Union in Siberia. The fact was, however,
that by midsummer 1941, Hitler's rosy predictions of the swift defeat
of England and Russia had already proved illusory, and the Japanese
were not willing to take the risk. Also, even General Tojo, who
seemed to want to attack everybody, recognized that Japan had some
limitations, and he was committed to moving south as an adjunct to
the China war.

By August 1, U.S. policy had hardened, and President Roosevelt was demanding that the Japanese guarantee the neutrality of
Indochina and Thailand. The Japanese replied obliquely, saying they
would not move farther south than Indochina, and that they would
remove their troops from Indochina when the China war was settled.
They asked the United States to refrain from fortifying Guam or
Samoa, to help Japan secure materials from the Netherlands East
Indies, to persuade China to negotiate a peace with Japan, to restore
normal trade with Japan, and to recognize a special Japanese position
in Indochina in the future.

Meeting these demands would give Japan all she had now conquered plus China, which she had not. The Americans refused.

Since 1937 the Americans had been trying to persuade the Japanese to cease their conquest of China, without success. The movement into Indochina had indicated the expansion of Japan's ambitions in Asia.

The question has been raised, since the end of World War II: was not the United States concerned about forcing Japan into an expansionist policy to seek raw materials by this refusal?

The answer, as seen in 1941, was that Japan had been embarked on an expansionist policy since 1931 and that there was a point beyond which the United States could not permit itself to be party to that expansionism. The Japanese showed no signs of giving up that policy. It is true that Americans in and out of government did not fully understand the symbolism of the oil cut-off, for they knew that Japan had reserves (she did indeed). But to the Japanese military, oil had become the symbol of power and continuity. Without oil the military machinery must come to a grinding halt. And so, when the United States made that decision to cut off oil and it was immediately followed by like actions from the other two nations who controlled most of the world's oil resources outside the Soviet Union, the emotional impact in Japan was like an earthquake.

The Japanese were thus faced with the coming inevitability of war unless they changed their policy. Within the cabinet and other government bodies there were men who were willing to change, but the man who was already in charge in fact was not. This man was War Minister Tojo.

He remained obdurate all summer. Japan was going to follow her course, and if that meant war with the United States, it was just too bad.[1]

The problem in the summer of 1941 was that there was no person in the Japanese government leadership who asked the question: if we go to war with the United States can we possibly win? The only person in high authority who seriously addressed that question was Admiral Yamamoto, and he was at sea, not in Tokyo, and his relations with Admiral Oikawa, the navy minister, were not such that he could press the issue. Oikawa knew Yamamoto's views, and actually the navy minister agreed that the chances of winning a war with the United States were extremely slender, but he never pressed that view in the cabinet and special meetings. Prime Minister Konoye had the most serious doubts about war with the United States, but he counted on some miracle to save the world from that development. Specifically, he was proposing to go to Washington to meet personally with President Roosevelt. That act, he believed, would prevent war.[2] Actually, by this time, there was virtually no one in Japan in authority who knew the United States and its industrial power. Only the navy seemed to be addressing itself to the question of Japan's war resources, too.

Another question asked in America at the end of World War II was: why had not the Americans known by the summer of 1941 that Japan was stockpiling resources and preparing for war with the West?

The reasons are not very complicated.

First of all, since 1931, Japan had been engaged in military adventures on the Asian continent, which meant the world was used to seeing Japanese military buildup.

Since 1937, and certainly effectively since 1938, the Japanese military had forced the establishment of a police state in Japan, which meant constant counterespionage, particularly against foreigners. Foreign tourists who appeared around ports or airfields or military camps with cameras were very likely to be taken into custody. They would be questioned, they might be manhandled, they would be treated most unpleasantly at least, their cameras might be confiscated, the film would certainly be destroyed. Even the photographing of such public buildings as the Diet and government offices was regarded as espionage. Foreign military and naval attachés, whose jobs were to keep track of Japanese military preparedness, found themselves cut off from all the usual sources and subjected to constant watch of their activities. Japan had been granted a "mandate" over the old German colonies in the Pacific and had promised not to fortify them. Had she or had she not? When war came the Americans recognized Truk, in the Bismarck Archipelago, as the most highly developed naval base in the Pacific outside Pearl Harbor and the Japanese home bases. Each year travel to Japan became more restricted. Each month foreign journalists in Japan found themselves under closer watch. In 1937 the internationally famous American aviatrix Amelia Earhart set out on a round-the-world air trip. After leaving Honolulu, her plane was unreported in the Central Pacific, and among all nations, the Japanese alone refused searchers the right to enter their mandated areas to try to find the plane. That was a typical Japanese response of the period. Anything that smacked of the military was top secret. After 1938 everyone knew that Japan was arming, but how much and for what remained a mystery.

By the summer of 1941, courtesy of the American breach of Japanese codes and the breach of the German codes by the British, the Americans expected further Japanese adventures. The Pacific Fleet was on the alert that summer, awaiting an attack on Pearl Harbor.

Even so, so great was the well of isolationism in the United States that millions of Americans truly believed the winds of fire that coursed Asia and Europe would somehow stop at the American shores and leave the United States unbothered. The simple matter of not wanting to believe was the greatest single element in American unpreparedness for war. The military, observers in Asia and Europe, and the journalists knew what was coming, and so reported it. But somehow when all this was strained through the American dream it became unreal and otherworldly. Americans knew intellectually that terrible things were happening in the rest of the world, but emotionally they turned it all off. Even when the draft came, and the American naval involvement in the Atlantic war against Hitler's U-boats became more or less common knowledge, the U.S. newspapers still reflected a national attitude of fence-sitting. Somehow, all those millions of Americans believed, this unpleasantness would pass America by.

On September 3, 1941, the Japanese leaders of government and the army and navy met again to make the most momentous decision of the year. Their conference lasted seven hours:

Admiral Nagano, the navy chief of staff, made an "on-the-one-hand-and-then-on-the-other-hand" statement that would have warned any disinterested party against war:

> In various respects the empire is losing materials: that is, we are getting weaker. By contrast the enemy is getting stronger. With the passage of time, we will get increasingly weaker, and we won't be able to survive. Moreover, we will endure what can be endured in carrying on diplomacy, but at the opportune moment we must make some estimates. Ultimately, when there is no hope for diplomacy, and when war cannot be avoided, it is essential that we make up our minds quickly. Although I am confident that at the present time *we have a chance to win the war, I fear that this opportunity will disappear with the passage of time.*

Regarding war, the navy thinks both in terms of a short war and a long one. *I think it will probably be a long war.* We hope that the enemy will come out for a quick showdown [Yamamoto's plan]; in that event there will be a decisive battle in waters near us, and I anticipate that our chances of victory would be quite good. *But I do not believe that the war would end with that. It would be a long war.* In this connection I think it would be good to take advantage of (the fruits of) an initial victory in order to cope with a long war. If, on the contrary, we get into a long war without a decisive battle, we will be in difficulty especially since our supply of resources will become depleted. If we cannot obtain these resources, it will not be possible to carry on a long war. It is important to make preparations so that we will not be defeated, by getting essential resources and by making the best of our strategy. There is no set series of steps that will guarantee our checkmating the enemy. But even so there will probably be measures we can adopt, depending on changes in the international situation.

In short, our armed force have no alternative but to try to avoid being pushed into a corner, to keep in our hands the power to decide when to begin hostilities and thus seize the initiative. There is no alternative but to push forward in this way. (Italics added.)[3]

The Nagano statement was an extremely intelligent prognostication of what was going to happen to Japan in the next four years.

It was followed by the statement of army Chief of Staff General Sugiyama, who wanted and expected to seize all the territory designated in the south and then be prepared by spring 1942 to attack the Soviet Union. His theme was: get on with the wars.

The decision was made by the government leaders at this conference to continue negotiating with the United States until October 10. If, by that time, negotiation had not gotten Japan her way, then the decision would be made to begin war with the United States, Britain, and the Netherlands.[4]

So important a decision could only be made final through an Imperial Conference. One was called. The emperor insisted first on seeing the army and navy chiefs of staff about military matters.

Navy Chief of Staff Nagano repeated his little speech. Emperor Hirohito turned to General Sugiyama:[5]

In case of war with the United States how long would it take Japan to win?

The operations in the South Pacific would be finished in three months, said the general confidently.

"Oh?" asked the emperor. He then recalled 1937, when he had asked General Sugiyama, the war minister, how long it would take to end the China incident. "One month," had said War Minister Sugiyama. That was 1937. This was 1941 and the "incident" was not yet ended.

"The interior of China is huge, Your Majesty."

"If the interior of China is huge, isn't the Pacific Ocean bigger? How can you be sure that war will end in three months?"

After this outburst of anger, the emperor then asked what emphasis was being put on diplomacy to resolve the problems. That was the way out for the military men: they soothed the emperor with soft words about diplomacy, and the meeting ended with their promises and assurances that diplomacy probably would work—statements neither men could possibly have believed, given their own previous arguments in the government meetings.

Then came the Imperial Conference. Hirohito listened and said nothing until the very end, when he read a little poem, which had been written by his grandfather, the Emperor Meiji.

> All the seas in every quarter
> Are as brothers to one another.
> Why, then, do the winds and waves of strife
> Rage so turbulently throughout the world?[6]

This poem was an Imperial Censure of this war council, and they all knew it. For the emperor knew, too, that by putting a time limit on negotiations, and stating demands that all knew the United States would never meet, the government had already decided to go to war. Indeed, in one previous meeting Tojo and Sugiyama had discussed the stockpiling of war materials in Indochina, and Tojo had observed that this would tip off the world about the war preparations. Sugiyama said it could not be helped. From the standpoint of the militarists, the decisions had all been made. From now until October would come the window dressing that was supposed to quiet the small group of Japanese leaders who did not want war, and prevent the emperor from being troublesome. The key lay in one of the policy papers in support of the decisions, a paper that represented the combined views of cabinet and Supreme Military Command.[7]

"Is war with Great Britain and the United States inevitable?"

"Our Empire's plan to build a New Order in East Asia—the central problem of which is the settlement of the China Incident— is a firm policy based on the national principle of *hakko ichiu*. The building of the New Order will go on forever, much as the life of our State does."

There it was again. *Hakko ichiu,* all the corners of the world under one roof: a Japanese roof.

All that was said about the decision being deferred until October was again window dressing. Here was the militarists' justification:

> We need not repeat that at present oil is the weak point of our Empire's national strength and fighting power. We are now gradually consuming oil that has been stockpiled. If things continue as at present, we will be self-sufficient for a two year period, at the most. This period will be further shortened if we undertake a large-scale military operation. As time passes, our capacity to carry the war will decline and our Empire will become powerless militarily.
>
> Meanwhile the naval and air forces of the United States will improve remarkably as time goes on; and defensively, the United States, Great Britain, and the Netherlands will gradually grow stronger in the south. Hence the passing of time means not only that we will face more difficulties in military operations, but also means that the increasing military preparedness of the United States Navy will surpass the naval power of our Empire after next autumn, and that we will finally be forced to surrender to the United States and Britain without a fight.
>
> In view of the meteorological conditions in winter, it is very difficult for both Japan and her enemies to undertake large-scale winter operations in the north. Accordingly it is necessary to fully prepare for war in the

south quickly during this season and preserve our freedom of military action in the north after the spring of next year.

If we begin preparations for war immediately, it will be about the last ten days of October before we complete mobilization, the requisitioning and equipping of ships, and the deployment of forces in the main strategic areas by means of long-distance sea transportation.[8]

And so the preparations for war began early in September. Only a miracle could now prevent the war, for the prime demand of Japan was freedom to act in China, and that is the one demand the Americans would never accept.

The people of Japan were now prepared for war against the United States, Britain, and the Netherlands. ABCD was the way the Japanese expressed it, so that every school child could understand. Japan was being "strangled" by ABCD: America, Britain, China, and the Dutch East Indies.[9] For had not the United States, Britain, and the Netherlands imposed trade embargoes on Japan, and did not the Chinese in the interior of China still boycott Japanese goods? To the Japanese people all that the militarists did was now a part of the "struggle for survival." It was Japan against the great powers, with Japan's friends, Germany and Italy, unable to help since they had no presence in the Far East. So the aggressors managed to paint themselves at home as the injured parties, and the enthusiasm for war continued unabated in Japan.

Admiral Yamamoto's plans for the preemptive strike on the American fleet were already well along. In August the carrier *Akagi* was sent to Kagoshima for training exercises. The topography of Kagoshima Bay is similar to that of Pearl Harbor. Lieutenant Commander Mitsuno Fuchida, a young man highly regarded by Admiral Yamamoto, was chosen to lead the strike. Soon the other carriers of the First Air Fleet arrived, also to begin training for a strike against ships at anchor.[10]

Admiral Yamamoto had presented his plan for the preemptive strike to naval headquarters in April and had gotten a very cool reception. Admiral Nagumo was opposed. So was Admiral Ohnishi, and so were a number of other officers. Yamamoto remained firm; as long as he was commander in chief of the Combined Fleet, that was the way they were going to do it. It was, as Yamamoto said, "an article of faith" with him: only if Japan managed to strike the miraculous blow could America be forced to the peace table. If the war dragged on, Japan would lose.[11]

From this rationale, one would believe that Yamamoto had come to favor the militarists' position for the war, but the opposite was true. He still referred to the army as "a gang of idiots," but he also knew that they were firmly in control of Japanese policy. "The only possibility left is that the emperor should make a personal decision, but even then I'm sure that things would be difficult at home." For the militarists were so determined for empire and they had gained so much power, that if the emperor now intervened, there was a good chance that the army would try to overthrow him and put someone more pliable, one of the imperial princes, onto the throne. Yamamoto found himself trapped by his own loyalties— "obliged to make up my mind to and pursue unswervingly a course that is precisely the opposite of my personal views."[12]

On September 12, Yamamoto had a secret meeting with Prince Konoye to discuss the possibility of a Konoye-Roosevelt meeting in Hawaii.[13] Nothing came of it. A month later, Yamamoto was finishing up the operational orders for the Pearl Harbor attack. The army, which had never believed in the negotiations, was pressing the government to break them off and get the war going. Only the navy kept pushing the foreign office to keep negotiating to the last. Given the American position that the Japanese could not have China there was never any real hope of the negotiations succeeding. The China incident had become a symbol to the army; it must win in China.

On October 12, Prince Konoye suddenly awakened to the fact that the course on which he was taking the nation led inevitably to war. In three more days he would have to say: war or peace. He called a conference of the war, navy and foreign ministers at his house in Tokyo. Konoye tried to persuade War Minister Tojo that there was hope of achieving what Japan wanted through negotiation. Could he guarantee it? asked Tojo. No, said the prime minister. Then the army was ready for war.[14]

The cabinet met on October 13. War Minister Tojo suggested that if the prime minister did not wish to stick with the decision for war if negotiations had not succeeded by October 15, the cabinet ought to quit. Konoye agreed and he resigned.[15]

Then came the problem of putting together a new government. The advisors to the emperor made the final error: they chose General

Tojo to run the government since he could "control" the army. Indeed, he could, and he controlled them on the road to war. By this time it would have taken a man much stronger than Prince Higashikuni, the other candidate for prime minister, to stop the drift to war. Only the emperor . . . but he did not show the courage to say no. Even Yamamoto had given up on that.[16]

The emperor then had his bitter tea: he had to appoint Tojo to head the government, knowing quite well what Tojo would do. He did ask the war minister and navy minister to "study the situation at home and abroad without being bound by the Imperial Conference decision of September 6."[17] Everyone knew what that meant: it was one last cry from the emperor against war. But it was made in such a way as not to be binding on the prime minister. And so General Tojo came to power in Japan, prepared to take his country down the road to war.

There continued to be reflex actions by the civilians in the government. But they were no more than that; each time the civilians asked for figures to back up the militarists' positions, they were denied the figures. Half a dozen more conferences were held between the day Tojo became prime minister—October 17—and November 1. Tojo made a number of speeches and appeared at the various shrines to pray for peace, all the while planning his war.[18]

The war did not mean just an attack to immobilize the forces of the United States, Britain, and the Netherlands. It was to be the first step in *hakko ichiu,* and a major instrument to bring the world under Japanese control was to be the Greater East Asia Co-Prosperity Sphere, which could certainly be extended beyond Asia. There was already such thought in the various ministries. Very early in the planning for the attack on Pearl Harbor, Admiral Yamamoto had suggested that the army might want to send an expeditionary force along to occupy Hawaii, which he said could be done with little difficulty. The result would be to capture a large number of highly trained American naval officers, and thus cripple the American navy even more fully than could be done by attack. Besides, the crushing blow to the United States of having this important possession seized by Japan should have a positive effect on helping bring Washington to the conference table in a hurry, which Yamamoto knew was essential to Japan.[19]

But the idea of capturing Hawaii was completely foreign to the army, which could respond positively to talk about Siberia, or even the Caucasus, but not Hawaii. The army, planning its complex operations against Indochina, Hongkong, Singapore, Malaya, the Dutch East Indies, the Philippines, the British and American Central and South Pacific island bases, and British New Guinea, had not responded. But inside the naval organization, a few staff officers had continued to think about the possibilities. The question that had to be resolved was: who was to take the responsibility for management of an invasion? Small Pacific areas automatically became a purely naval responsibility. Large ones were administered by the army. In the summer and fall of 1941 there was no inclination by the army to make time for a study of the possibilities of Hawaii under the Greater East Asia Co-Prosperity Sphere.

The army and the government, however, were already at work establishing the machinery for the Prosperity Sphere, and Indochina was to be the primary experiment in the seizure of a hostile territory. On October 31 Ambassador Kenkichi Yoshizawa sailed from Kobe for Haiphong to take over the Japanese embassy. He took with him a whole new crew of eager young foreign officers. Their task, announced the ambassador, was to promote economic growth of Indochina. The correspondent for *Asahi Shimbun* put it more bluntly: the ambassador would reorganize the Indochina economy for the Greater East Asia Co-Prosperity Sphere.

> The economic affairs of the colony have to be adjusted. By placing the colony on a wartime economic basis it will be possible to control it as a component part of the co-prosperity sphere. No useful purpose will be served by the colonial authorities continuing to dream of the conditions which prevailed in the days of economic liberalism. The colony's economy will be in danger if the authorities look with folded arms while inflation is starting. The future of the colony lies only in cooperation with Japan in all fields of endeavor.[20]

Reduced to essentials, all this meant rice for Japan. There would be a little tin, a little rubber, a little sugar. But Indochina was the major rice-exporting area of Southeast Asia, and as such invaluable to a hungry Japan. The war, then, had already been extended.

On November 1 the government leaders held the sixty-sixth conference since the liaison organization between government and military was established and hashed out one more time the arguments for and against immediate war. The civilians still dragged their feet:[21]

Navy Chief of Staff Nagano said they might avoid war now and then go to war in three years.

Finance Minister Kaya suggested that the chances of the United States making war on Japan were very slight and for that reason Japan should not go to war.

Foreign Minister Togo: "I, too, cannot believe that the American fleet would come and attack us. I don't believe there is any need to go to war now."

Navy Chief of Staff Nagano: "There is a saying, Don't rely on what won't come. The future is uncertain. We can't take anything for granted. In three years enemy defense in the south will be strong, and the number of enemy warships will also increase."

Kaya: "Well, then, when can we go to war and win?"

Nagano: "Now!! The time for war will not come later!"

So the decision was made for war.

The newspapers of Japan were prepared for war and they were preparing the Japanese public.

"The Japanese spokesman in Washington is reported to have warned the United States that if there should not be any development in the Japanese-American negotiations it will lead to Japan's applications of self-defense measures," said Tokyo's *Nichi Nichi*, one of the more bombastic journals, on November 1.[22]

General Tojo was carefully leaking aspects of the cabinet and liaison meetings to the press, which quoted "well-informed observers," who were, indeed, so well informed that they had to have access to the secret government meetings.

Nichi Nichi's "well-informed" source revealed that on the cabinet level the war now seemed almost inevitable. The only solution was for the United States to give in to Japan's demands, said the newspaper.

On November 5 another conference was held, at which the various officials made their public faces for posterity: long speeches marked by pious hopes that the final negotiations with the United States, then in progress, would succeed.[23]

By November 17, nothing concrete had been accomplished. On that evening Admiral Yamamoto held a send-off sake party aboard the flagship for Admiral Chuichi Nagumo, the commander of the

Pearl Harbor striking force. Next morning the force sailed for Hitokappu Bay off Etarofu Island in the Kuriles. This point was the assembly station for the striking force. The ships came in secretly and silently until they had all arrived, six aircraft carriers, two battleships, and enough cruisers and destroyers to protect them on the voyage. Separately, a number of submarines were moving, to scout out the track, and also to help in the attack.

On the morning of November 26 the task force sailed from the Kuriles, bound for Hawaii. On December 1 the task force crossed the international date line. That afternoon at the Imperial Palace, the final conference was held. Tojo outlined the final plans for war.[24]

Here was the last chance for anyone to make an objection to the decision. No one did. Finally, Tojo summed up:

> I would like to make one final comment. At the moment our Emperor stands at the threshold of glory or oblivion. We tremble with fear in the presence of His Majesty. We subjects are keenly aware of the great responsibility we must assume from this point on. Once His Majesty reaches a decision to commence hostilities, we will all strive to repay our obligations to him, bring the government and the military ever closer together, resolve that the nation united will go on to victory, make an all-out effort to achieve our war aims, and set His Majesty's mind at ease.

There was no comment.
Tojo: "I now adjourn the meeting."
The emperor said nothing.
The war was on.

On December 2, Admiral Yamamoto was summoned to the navy ministry at Tokyo and came up by train from the fleet anchorage at Hashirajima via Iwakunijun to Tokyo. At 5:30 P.M. off went the prearranged signal:

"Climb Mount Niitake."[25]

Earlier, when giving instructions for the Hawaii operation to Admiral Nagumo and his staff, Yamamoto had made one caveat.

"Should the negotiations with the United States now in progress in Washington be successful, we shall order our forces to withdraw.

If such an order is received, you are to turn about and come back to base, even if the attack force has already taken off from the carriers."

There had been a chorus of objections to the commander in chief's words. Admiral Nagumo said it couldn't be done once the planes had taken off.

Yamamoto, who did not like Nagumo anyhow, frowned at him.

"Just why do you think we spend so much time training military men?" he asked. "If there's any commander here who doesn't think he could come back if he got the order, I forbid him to go . . . he can hand in his resignation. . . ."

There had been no more complaints. But there was no withdrawal order issued, either.[26]

On December 3 Admiral Yamamoto called at the Imperial Palace for a formal audience as required by imperial protocol, to receive the command of the Combined Fleet and take it into battle.[27] The emperor made his little set speech, and the admiral made the reply prepared for him. Each man knew that the other hated what was about to happen, but they were captives of the Imperial Way, and they went through the little charade so the two messages could be broadcast to thrill the officers and men of the Combined Fleet.

Japan's war was entering another phase.

人は身かけによらぬもの

21. "Appearances are deceitful"

The Japanese carrier striking force steamed across the North Pacific from the Kuriles in weather that was perfect for the operation. It was cold and misty, which meant the chances of discovery were minimal. The big worry had been storms; the North Pacific in winter usually presents four stormy days to one fine one. But not in late November 1941. The ships were traveling with a high pressure front—"a front from Heaven," Admiral Yamamoto called it. They were able to fuel halfway across from their three oilers. On December 3 the weather roughed up, but by then it did not matter. On December 5 the striking force moved into warmer water and the weather brightened.

The striking force was moving down on Hawaii from the north. From Japanese agents in the Hawaii consular force and from special agents sent to Hawaii aboard merchant vessels, the Imperial Japanese Navy had learned several vital facts: that there was little ship traffic north of Oahu in the winter months; that the Americans had for months been flying air patrols out of Oahu to discover any attack force but that for some reason they had recently ceased flying to the north. This latter bit of information, so vital to the attack, was discovered by the observations of Japanese Naval Intelligence Agent Takeo Yoshikawa, who had been sent to Hawaii after four years of training in English and espionage techniques. He was already a naval expert, having graduated from the Eta Jima naval academy, but had been invalided out of the service for stomach ailment. His discovery of the lack of air patrols off northern Oahu was a key factor in the planning of the Pearl Harbor attack.[1]

Still, there was a great deal of tension within the Japanese force as it steamed almost due south on December 6, for not all these men, by far, agreed with the Yamamoto strategy that had brought them here. On December 6 a merchant ship was sighted. The radio operators of the flagship were alert for any indications of a report made by this vessel, but the radio was silent, and the vessel soon drew away and was lost to sight. If her captain wondered what a fleet was doing here in these virtually unused waters, he was either confused as to their identity or afraid, and no report was ever made.

Other than the worry about premature discovery, the principal concern of Admiral Nagumo and his attack pilot leaders was whether or not the U.S. fleet would actually be at anchorage at Pearl Harbor on this Sunday morning, December 7, U.S. time, December 8, Tokyo time. All the espionage agents from the consulate could tell them was that it was the habit of the fleet to be in port so that the men could enjoy the American "Saturday night" ashore, whether in the cheap bars of Hotel Street, the expensive restaurants of Waikiki, or the houses of the family men.

On the night of December 6 (Hawaii time) the messages continued to pour in from Tokyo, although, of course, the fleet was only listening, not sending, to maintain radio silence. The messages told of ship movements: the battleships *Nevada* and *Oklahoma* had entered Pearl Harbor on December 5, to join the *Arizona, California, Tennessee, Pennsylvania, Maryland,* and *West Virginia.* All the battleships of the U.S. Pacific Fleet were there. *Banzai!* So were the cruisers *Raleigh, Honolulu,* and *Helena.* But where were the carriers? There might be four of them, but there were none, the reports from Tokyo said. That was a disappointment coupled with a worry: what if the carriers showed up to challenge the Japanese fleet at sea? Admiral Yamamoto had taken this possibility into consideration, he was ready to lose two carriers if necessary, two of the six. As Yamamoto had said himself, and as everyone knew, this shot at Pearl Harbor was a gamble, the gamble that by knocking out the U.S. fleet in the first minutes of the war, Japan would demoralize the United States and give Japan the time to consolidate her new empire, and then be in position to come to the peace table with all in place. Let the Americans then simply accept the status quo and the Japanese settlement of the China incident.[2]

When Admiral Yamamoto had gone to the Imperial Palace for the ceremonial passing of command of the fleet from emperor to admiral, Hirohito had said the words written for him:

"In commanding our forces in action we entrust to you the command of the Combined Fleet. The task facing the Combined Fleet is of the utmost importance, and the whole fate of our nation will depend on the outcome."[3]

Yamamoto had replied with the more or less prescribed formula, this written for him in advance by his chief of staff, Vice Admiral Matome Ugaki, a man with a strong sense of destiny, who reached back to the Russo-Japanese War and Admiral Togo's words for inspiration.

Yamamoto said, "I reverently accept the Imperial Command and assure Your Majesty that all the officers and men of the Combined Fleet will devote themselves unsparingly to their mission. . . ."[4]

And now, on the eve of battle, all this inspirational material was transmitted to the fleet at sea, with Yamamoto's final injunction: "The fate of the Empire rests on this enterprise. Every man must devote himself totally to the task at hand."[5]

Staff officers tended to make jokes of messages such as these. The story aboard the flagship was that Admiral Ugaki had thought of that last message while in the ship's "head" one morning. But it really was not a joking matter, and Yamamoto really did believe that the fate of the empire depended on his ability to strike so crippling a blow at the Americans at the outset that they would not recover for many months. The army, then, would be able to consolidate its first gains and encircle the new empire protectively.

That night, as the Japanese striking force lurched down the alley toward Oahu through the freshening seas, the armorers loaded the dive bombers and torpedo bombers, and the plane handlers brought them up the elevators to the decks of the six carriers. In the way of soldiers and sailors everywhere, messages were scrawled on torpedoes and the bombs. The men who would stay behind and wait wanted to feel their part in this historic hour to come.

That night came one more welcome message: the battleship *Utah* had also entered Pearl Harbor with a seaplane tender. The battleships now numbered nine. So even if the carriers were not present, the pickings would be very good indeed.

The first plane aloft this morning was not from a carrier, but a seaplane catapulted from the cruiser *Chikuma,* which had been sent ahead to scout out Oahu and make sure the air attack force did not run into any unexpected trouble.

Long before dawn, aboard the carriers, the Japanese air crews were up, washed, dressed, and at their breakfast of sea bream and red rice and chestnuts. Dawn was not yet breaking when the propellers of the bombers and fighters began to turn, and very shortly 183 aircraft, the first wave of the attack, were in the air. The first plane off the deck of the flagship *Akagi* was a Zero fighter. Less than fifteen minutes later all planes were airborne. Commander Mitsuno Fuchida, the man selected by Admiral Yamamoto to lead the air strike force, was aboard his plane with its distinctive markings, heading toward Pearl Harbor, two hundred miles to the south.

Months of research and backtiming had gone into the planning of this attack. Admiral Yamamoto's staff had instructed Commander Fuchida that the first bomb was to drop on Pearl Harbor just as close to 3:30, Tokyo time, as possible. That meant it would be falling one-half hour after the Japanese representatives had handed to the American government their final words of peace. Much has been made of the question of the surprise attack: was it the dastardly blow of a treacherous enemy, given without warning? Many accounts have tried to absolve the Japanese, with excuses about the failure of communications in Washington. But the fact was that the surprise attack was entirely within the Japanese tradition; the samurai used it constantly. Anyone who did not take advantage of the first blow in the days of the shoguns was regarded as a fool. The man who undertook the preemptive strike was regarded as intelligent. Admiral Togo had opened the Sino-Japanese War with a surprise attack on a Chinese troop carrier. He had repeated the performance with a surprise attack on the Russian fleet at Port Arthur when the diplomats were still talking in St. Petersburg. What was important about the Pearl Harbor attack was not whether or not President Roosevelt had been apprised of the Japanese ultimatum when the bombs fell, but that the bombs succeeded in immobilizing the U.S. forces in the Pacific.

About an hour and a half before the air strike force reached the north shore of Oahu, the first report from the *Chikuma*'s float plane was received by Commander Fuchida's radio operator. The words were informative and comforting: wind speed and visibility were satisfactory. There was no sign of enemy activity. The American warships were lying quietly at anchor in the sun on this Sunday morning.

Commander Fuchida's task was to decide what sort of attack to make. If there was no sign of activity, then a surprise attack was in order, and this would mean the torpedo bombers would go in first, at a few feet above the water, and torpedo the warships with their special shallow-depth torpedoes. That was what Fuchida wanted. But in their eagerness some of his flight commanders became confused and began rushing toward Pearl Harbor. To prevent even worse confusion Commander Fuchida signaled the general attack and all the planes began their approaches. Thus they were five minutes too early even for Yamamoto's tight schedule, and at 3:25 A.M., Tokyo time, the first weapon exploded, a 550-pound bomb dropped by one of the dive bombers on Wheeler field, up on the cane plateau above Pearl Harbor.[6]

When the word reached the *Nagato* in Hashirajima Bay, Admiral Yamamoto was playing *shogi* with a staff officer to while away the time. The signal that the attack had begun was to be "to-to-to-to," and a young radio operator came rushing up to announce that it had been sent at 3:19. Too early, of course, by any standards, but who cared? A few minutes later the airwaves were filled with reports from the planes, picked up directly and remarkably clearly in Japan. They told of the successes of the dive bombers in plastering the bombers and fighters on Wheeler and Hickam airfields and the success of the torpedo bombers in hitting the ships. As telling was the excited radio traffic in plain English from Pearl Harbor, reporting on the surprise attack.

The planes returned to report formidable damage—four battleships sunk they told Admiral Nagumo—and the loss of only five torpedo bombers, one dive bomber, and three Zero fighters. As the planes left no American aircraft were observed in the sky.[7]

An hour after the first attack came the second wave of 170 planes. The Americans had made some recovery from their surprise by this time, and the pilots of the second wave reported that antiaircraft fire, almost negligible in the first attack, had now become formidable at various installations around the island. The second wave lost fourteen dive bombers and six Zeros, a tribute to the reorganizing power of the Americans.

In fact, the worst losses were to the submarine service, which had played a peripheral role in the attack. The five midget submarines launched from parent submersibles off the Oahu coast had all been lost. Some of them had given the Americans bad moments, but, in the end, all had sunk or gone aground, without doing any damage.

This was nothing. Yamamoto and the other senior officers of the navy had been prepared to lose two or even three carriers; the operation was deemed that important. Of course, it was not yet over; no one had expected Admiral Nagumo to do it all at once. Commander Fuchida had remained in the attack area after the two attacks ended, circling among the clouds, trying to take stock of the damage. He returned to the *Akagi* to report on the sinking of at least four battleships and damage to four others. The Japanese had wrecked the seaplane base at Kaneohe, wrecked aircraft and burned hangars at Wheeler and Hickam fields, and damaged buildings in the military zones. The report was very satisfactory. Fuchida recommended that the next strike be aimed at the oil tanks, repair facilities, and the arsenals. Commander Minoru Genda, one of the chief operational planners of the mission, also favored repeated attacks, hoping to destroy the naval facilities so completely that an amphibious landing force could then take the Hawaiian islands.[8]

Once the aircraft had landed aboard the carriers, Rear Admiral Tamon Yamaguchi, commander of the Second Carrier Division, sent a message from his flagship, the *Hiryu,* to Admiral Nagumo. He was ready, he said, to make the second attack. And aboard the other carriers so were all the pilots. They gathered excitedly on the flight decks.

Admiral Nagumo was interviewing Commander Fuchida. Did Fuchida believe the American Pacific Fleet was now immobilized for the next six months?

Fuchida hesitated. He did not know what to say, but he knew what his admiral wanted to hear. The main force of the American fleet—the battleship force—certainly could not come out for six months, he said.

Nagumo seemed pleased. The talk then turned to the next step. Fuchida favored more attacks quickly. The weather was getting choppy, however, and even Commander Genda, who favored further attacks, felt they should be put off until the next day. The attack force should remain about two hundred miles out from Hawaii and continue the attack.[9]

But now, from the admiral's bridge came the order to stow all bombers below and keep only fighters on deck. Nagumo was worried. So far he had succeeded in an operation he had never liked. Now he worried about the missing American aircraft carriers. None of them had been in port; he did not even know how many there were in Hawaiian waters. He thought there might be four. Actually there were only three carrier task groups in the Pacific just then, the group built around the *Enterprise,* another built around the *Lexington,* and the third around the *Saratoga.* They were called task forces, but the name was a misnomer. The last was at Puget Sound on the American mainland for repairs, but Nagumo did not know that. The other two were, indeed, out on patrol to the west and south of Hawaii. What if the American carriers suddenly descended on the Japanese carriers when they were launching planes? His chief of staff, Rear Admiral Ryunosake Kusaka, quite agreed. Like Nagumo, he had never liked the Pearl Harbor attack plan from the outset. Now he, too, could see all sorts of reasons why the attack should be broken off and the attack force should head home to Japan.[10]

Nagumo and Kusaka agreed: the purpose of the attack had been to protect the flank and rear of the amphibious forces that were now moving against Malaya and the Philippines. Now they could go home with their six carriers and the knowledge that they had saved the carriers and struck the blow that would keep the American battleship fleet out of the Pacific War for months to come. Within an hour came the word from the flagship to turn around and retire to the northwest, home to Japan.

Commander Fuchida was aghast at what he had done, for he blamed himself for overstating the case for destruction at Pearl Harbor to Admiral Nomura, not then realizing that he was playing into Nomura's timid hands. He had expected, and so had most of the carrier admirals and captains, that the striking force would finish the job. Now, they were leaving it half done.[11]

The ships' radios, tuned to Tokyo, could not help but pick up the excitement of the Japanese capital, where the news of war had burst so suddenly. It was almost too much for anyone to assimilate in a single day. On the morning of Monday, December 8, the newspaper headlines in Tokyo screamed:

WAR IS ON
JAPAN'S NAVY PLANES ATTACK HAWAII

SINGAPORE, DAVAO, WAKE, GUAM.

JAPANESE TROOP TRANSPORT OFF HAWAII.
GREAT SUCCESSES REPORTED IN ALL AREAS
RAIDED IN NAVAL ANNOUNCEMENT.
BRITISH TROOPS IN THAILAND BEING WIPED OUT.
HONGKONG HEAVILY BOMBED BY NAVY.
—LANDING IN MALAYA ANNOUNCED.
—CABINET MEETING IN EMERGENCY SESSION.[12]

How well it had all been planned. All these attacks were carried out before the Americans had received the message breaking off negotiations. The British were given no warnings at all, nor any belated explanations.

How thorough the plan! That morning of December 8, the newspapers carried the emperor's words about the war, words obviously written for him days before the fact. Radio Tokyo also broadcast these words, and they were flung to the far corners of the world, to announce, to the striking force and its victims, to the Southern Attack force and its victims, the course that Japan had set upon.

Hakko ichiu!

IMPERIAL RESCRIPT

We, by grace of Heaven, Emperor of Japan, seated on the Throne of a line unbroken for ages eternal, enjoin upon ye, Our loyal and brave subjects:

We hereby declare war on the United States of America and the British Empire. The men and officers of Our army and navy shall do their utmost in prosecuting the war. Our public servants of various departments shall perform faithfully and diligently their appointed tasks, and all other subjects of Ours shall pursue their respective duties; the entire nation with a united will shall mobilize their total strength so that nothing will miscarry in the attainment of Our war aims.

To insure the stability of East Asia and to contribute to world peace is the far-sighted policy which was formulated by our Great Illustrious Imperial Grandfather and

Our Great Imperial Sire succeeding him, and which We lay constantly to heart. To cultivate friendship among nations and to enjoy prosperity in common with all nations has always been the guiding principle of Our Empire's foreign policy. It has been truly unavoidable and far from Our wishes that Our Empire has now been brought to cross swords with America and Britain. More than four years have passed since China, failing to comprehend the true intentions of Our Empire and recklessly courting trouble, disturbed the peace of East Asia and compelled Our Empire to take up arms. Although there has been reestablished the National Government of China, with which Japan has effected neighborly intercourse and cooperation, the regime which has survived at Chungking, relying on American and British protection, still continues its fratricidal opposition. Eager for the realization of their inordinate ambition to dominate the Orient, both America and Britain, giving support to the Chungking regime, have aggravated the disturbances in East Asia. Moreover, these two powers, inducing other countries to follow suit, increased military preparations on all sides of Our Empire to challenge Us. They have obstructed by every means Our peaceful commerce, and finally resorted to a direct severance of economic relations, menacing gravely the existence of Our Empire. Patiently have We waited and long have We endured, in hope that Our Government might retrieve the situation in peace. But our adversaries, showing not the least spirit of conciliation, have unduly delayed a settlement and in the meantime they have intensified the economic and political pressure to compel thereby Our Empire to submission. This trend of affairs, would, if left unchecked, not only nullify Our Empire's efforts of many years for the sake of the stabilization of East Asia, but also endanger the very existence of Our nation. The situation being such as it is, Our Empire for its existence and self defense has no other recourse but to appeal to arms and to crush every obstacle in its path.

The hallowed spirits of Our Imperial Ancestors guarding Us from above, We rely upon the loyalty and courage of Our subjects in Our confident expectation that the task bequeathed by Our forefathers will be carried

forward, and that the sources of evil will be speedily eradicated and an enduring peace immutably established in East
Asia, preserving thereby the glory of Our Empire.[13]

Prime Minister Tojo declared that day that he was "filled with
awe and trepidation. Powerless as I am, I am resolved to dedicate
myself, body and soul, to the country and to set at ease the mind of
our Sovereign. . . ."[14]

He reminded the people that "The key to victory lies in a faith
in victory. . . . as long as there remains under the policy of *Hakko
ichiu* this great spirit of loyalty and patriotism, we have nothing to
fear. . . ."

From the point of view of Admiral Yamamoto, it was too bad
General Tojo had not personally reminded Admiral Nagumo.

When the word of the retirement of the Hawaii attack force
reached the Yamamoto flagship, many of the staff officers urged the
admiral to order Nagumo to return to Pearl Harbor and finish the
job. Admiral Ugaki, Yamamoto's chief of staff, argued that Nagumo
should be made to stay and exploit his remarkable victory. Even the
Americans had expected Nagumo to do that, it was a basic tenet of
naval warfare.

Admiral Yamamoto said no. There was no point in ordering a
commander to do something he did not want to do. He would do
it badly, almost every time. And Yamamoto knew now that to leave
Nagumo in charge of the Hawaii operation, with a chief of staff who
aped his conservative views and timid manner, had been a major
error in the judgment of the Japanese naval authorities, including
himself. As he later confided to Admiral Ugaki, what Nagumo had
done had brought that officer to the end of his imagination and ability.
To ask him to do more would have been useless, and would only
have annoyed the striking force commander. To Nagumo, Yamamoto noted only that on the way home the striking force should stop
by and raid Midway and if possible put it out of action once and for
all.[15]

So Admiral Nagumo and the task force returned to Japan, as
proud as they could be.

On December 9 Tokyo said two battleships had been sunk at
Pearl Harbor, and four battleships and four large cruisers damaged.

Each day the casualty list was raised. Each day it was victory on victory.[16]

But beneath the tone of victory there was another, readily discernible to Admiral Yamamoto and others who had more than surface knowledge of the Americans. The smashing blow at Pearl Harbor was to destroy the American Pacific Fleet's capacity to fight, and to destroy American morale and will to fight. The fleet was not destroyed, and the American will to fight seemed to have been kindled. With a sinking heart Admiral Yamamoto had learned that through confusions he never understood, there was nothing like even a twenty-five minute lapse of time between the Japanese ultimatum to the Americans and the attack; the attack had come hours before, and the result had been to infuriate the Americans and cause them to vow the destruction of Japan. This was not at all how Admiral Yamamoto had expected the end of negotiations to work out. Already, in the first words from America—the reports of "sneak attack" and "infamous behavior"—Yamamoto was sensing that the effect on the Americans had been the opposite of what the Imperial General Staff had hoped. What he did not then know was that the fury of the Americans would remain, and that Nagumo's failure to strike the crushing blow would also seal Yamamoto's personal fate on a little South Pacific islet in less than two years, for as the architect of the sneak attack on Pearl Harbor, he would be condemned to death by assassination by his enemies, the Americans.[17]

By the time that Admiral Nagumo and his ships returned to Japan near the end of the month, Yamamoto had a very good picture of what had happened at Pearl Harbor. He had always said Japan must strike a deadly blow at the beginning, win a great battle, and could then negotiate a peace with the Americans from a strength that could not last more than a year and a half. Nagumo had held just this victory within his grasp and had turned away to lose it.

Now to see Nagumo come triumphantly home, not even understanding what he had done, was an enormous trial for Yamamoto. Privately he told Ugaki and others of his staff just how he felt, that Nagumo had failed.

Nagumo immediately proved out the Yamamoto contention about his abilities and attitudes; he let it be known that he had felt it an insult after his triumph to be asked to do so lowly a task as raid

Midway, and so he had not done it. His excuse at the time had been bad weather. Back in Japan he felt he was too powerful to offer excuses.

It was December 24 before Commander Fuchida, flying ahead, reported to Admiral Yamamoto, who spoke to him in a kindly way and said he had done a good job. But when Nagumo and the others arrived, expecting nothing but praise and smiles from Admiral Yamamoto, they got frowns, and an address that was more a scolding. Yamamoto did not directly berate them for their failure to exploit opportunity, but he did tell them that they had conquered nothing, and that they had come home only temporarily to prepare for the next battle.

Yamamoto was starting all over again. One of his eighteen months had gone by and the chance to win the decisive battle had been lost through timidity. Within a week it was apparent that there was no use talking to the army about constraint and the dangers. The headiness of victory achieved almost without effort had lifted the army's spirits above reason. Yamamoto could only hope there would be another chance for him to achieve the necessary victory while there was time.

思いたった 吉日

22. "Strike while the iron is hot"

*I*n the euphoria of the enormous success that had met Japan's initial attacks in the new war it would have been impossible for Admiral Yamamoto to convince any but his closest associates that the Pearl Harbor attack had failed.

For one reason, Japan had its "battleship men" just as did the Western navies. In fact, Admiral Nagumo was a battleship man, not a pilot and not very confident of the use of carriers. That, of course, was one of the reasons he was so timid about subjecting his six carriers to attack by a possible American four carriers, even when he knew that the American air potential of Pearl Harbor had been virtually destroyed.

Nagumo's timidity puzzled even U.S. Admiral Chester W. Nimitz, who was on his way to Pearl Harbor to pick up the pieces from the raid. On arrival he would look around and wonder why the Japanese had failed to finish the job. For with the repair facilities in good shape, the submarine base virtually untouched, and the carriers and most of the cruisers and destroyers available, the American Pacific Fleet was far from knocked out. As for the battleships, there was still something to be learned. Admiral King, the newly appointed commander of the U.S. naval forces, was one who believed in the American battleship force, but the fact was that even before the strike at Pearl Harbor the battleship fleet had proved to be obsolete. The battleships could not keep up with the carriers and cruisers, so they could not be used with the carrier task forces. It took a while for some officers to see this; even after Pearl Harbor Admiral King spoke urgently of the need to repair the battleships as quickly as possible. He still considered them to be the navy's first line of defense in the Pacific.[1]

Actually, because of the failure of Admiral Nagumo to destroy the base at Pearl Harbor and the American aircraft carriers, the strike might better have not been made at all. The announced purpose of knocking out the American Pacific Fleet had not been achieved. The basic American plan for the conduct of the Pacific War (Plan Orange) called for the United States to abandon the Philippines in case of war and then to strike back at Japan across the Central Pacific. So if the Japanese had simply gone ahead with their southern move into Malaya, Thailand, and the Philippines, Admiral Yamamoto might have had a better chance of drawing the U.S. Pacific Fleet to the Western Pacific early in the war. There, given the American belief in the strength of the U.S. battleship fleet, and the Japanese superiority in the strategy and tactics of carrier warfare, Admiral Yamamoto's ten modern aircraft carriers might have given him the victory he wanted, crippling the American naval effort for many months. The Pearl Harbor attack could have done the same, if it had been relentlessly executed to achieve utmost destruction. Yamamoto, however, had not been free to choose his own commander for the Pearl Harbor striking force. The Japanese navy had counted on an imperfect instrument in Nagumo, when what was needed was a man like Yamamoto or Togo.

There was yet another reason that it would have been useless for Admiral Yamamoto to complain about the Pearl Harbor raid immediately afterward: everything the Japanese were doing seemed to bear the imprint of success. The Southern Assault, conducted by the army with the cooperation and protection of the navy, was far more than a regional push. All at once the Japanese were moving to destroy the white man's influence in East Asia. Much has been said about the timing of the Japanese attacks relative to the note handed Secretary of State Hull by the Japanese negotiators in Washington nearly half a day after the fact. Actually, the army attacks were already in motion and it is doubtful if under any conditions all of them could have been recalled. At the end of November 1941, the Japanese militarists were bent on war, and it would have taken an American surrender to have stopped the whole series of surprise attacks on which Japanese strategy was based, just as it had been in 1904.

Starting in the north:

Tientsin: the Japanese moved early that morning of December 8 into the International Compound, where they disarmed sixty-three American marines. They also disarmed British troops and took over British and American establishments at Tangku, Taku, and Chinwangtao.[2]

Shanghai: the Japanese ordered the British gunboat *Peterel* and the U.S. gunboat *Wake* to surrender. The British chose to fight, and their gunboat was sunk. The commander of the *Wake* was ashore, and the Japanese, who knew it, boarded the ship in the darkness, seized the ship from the crew and announced that the ship was now His Imperial Japanese Majesty's vessel *Tatara*.[3]

The Japanese moved into the International Settlement. Firing was heard along the Bund and in the area of the Garden Bridge near Broadway. The Japanese had seized Shanghai.

Hongkong: On December 8, Vice Admiral Mineichi Koga announced the complete blockade of Hongkong and moved ships round the island. Japanese planes from south China bases bombed Hongkong several times.

Singapore: The Japanese air forces bombed the naval base and the city on December 8.

Japanese navy planes bombed Davao and Japanese warships bombarded Wake and Guam islands.

From Indochina the Japanese moved swiftly by rail and by truck to the Thai border and crossed over. Within twenty-four hours they had taken over Thailand and achieved a "diplomatic" accommodation that made Thailand a member of the Greater East Asia Co-Prosperity Sphere and gave Japan freedom to move troops in and out of Thailand.

Hakko ichiu!

On December 4, Lieutenant General Tomoyuki Yamashita, the officer who had pleaded for the modernization of the Japanese army after his mission to Nazi Germany, embarked the Twenty-fifth Army for assault against British Malaya. The place was chosen, the Kra Isthmus. The twenty transports were escorted only by submarines. The cruisers and destroyers of Vice Admiral Jisaburo Ozawa's First Fleet stood a hundred miles offshore, ready, but trying to confuse any enemies and retain the element of surprise to the last. The Japanese force was sighted by British reconnaissance planes and turned north, as if moving into the Bay of Thailand. The British relaxed. The Japanese turned back, and on the night of December 7, they began their landings. So much for "warnings." In fact, at Singora most of the members of the Japanese consulate staff were drunk, celebrating the outbreak of war.[4]

The Singora landings were fantastically easy. Nine men, including three officers, were killed. The high ratio of officers to men was caused by the *bushido* spirit, which General Yamashita had wanted to replace with modern weapons. Officers who insisted on jumping out in front of the troops waving samurai swords were bound to get killed in large numbers. But with these easy victories, who was to listen to such talk?

On December 9 the news from the fronts was just as good. Japanese planes again attacked Davao. Again they were Japanese navy planes from the carrier *Ryujo*. The Japanese also bombed northern Luzon Island that day, operating from bases on Taiwan. In mid-morning they sent down about two hundred planes to attack the Clark Field complex near Manila. Here they found most of the American Far East Air Force, lined up neatly on the runways and aprons. The Americans were worried about sabotage and had tight ground defenses protecting the airfields. The Japanese attackers destroyed most of the B-17 bombers and P-40 fighters, at a cost of seven Japanese planes.[5]

Back in Malaya, in the second landing on the coast at Khota Baru, the going was a little harder for the Japanese. They lost one transport to a British bomber, but that day the Japanese army captured the Khota Baru airfield. They now had a field within easy striking distance of Singapore.

On December 8, Admiral Sir Tom Phillips of the British Navy had set off from Singapore northward with the new prides of the British Asiatic Fleet, the new battleship *Prince of Wales* and the old but war-worthy battlecruiser *Repulse*. In November Prime Minister Churchill had consigned these major ships to the Far East in the belief that such naval strength would give the Japanese second thoughts about launching attacks on British territory.

The two big ships, with an escort of three destroyers, moved northward, toward the southern tip of Indochina. On the afternoon of December 9 they were sighted by the Japanese submarine *I-6*, which radioed its headquarters. The report went to Admiral Yamamoto aboard his flagship, the battleship *Nagato,* which was at sea, but so far north, off Sapporo in Japanese waters, that Yamamoto could not expect to enter the action. The Japanese problem at the moment was a shortage of capital ships in this area, since so many were detailed elsewhere to cover the simultaneous naval actions in Hawaii, the Philippines, China, and Malaya. Vice Admiral Ozawa's First Fleet had been denuded of its carrier division for the Hawaii adventure, Yamamoto deciding that land-based naval forces on Taiwan and in Indochina could meet any needs that came up. Had the new battleships *Yamato* and *Musashi* with their eighteen-inch guns been readily available, they would have solved the problem quickly enough, and the world might have seen a mighty sea battle between behemoths, but the *Yamato* and *Musashi* were just commissioning in Japan. Ozawa's five cruisers were hardly adequate with their eight- and ten-inch guns to meet the *Prince of Wales'* fifteen-inch weapons.[6]

What to do was the problem that coursed the *Nagato's* operations center that afternoon. Japan, as noted, had its share of battleship men, and they were mightily impressed by the *Prince of Wales.*

But not Admiral Yamamoto. He was the world's foremost naval advocate of air power. He had built the naval air force of Japan to be the strongest in the world. He had noted the British victory at Taranto, when a flock of fluttering biplanes from a British carrier had laid low the Italian fleet at anchor. Before him in his cabin he had the reports on the Pearl Harbor raid, which had again shown that the day of the battleship was done, no matter what others insisted. What these others still believed, and they had plenty of company, was that even Pearl Harbor had been a "fluke" because the ships were closely anchored and in shallow water. Now if those Italian and American battleships had been steaming at speed on the high sea . . .[7]

So while others aboard the *Nagato* fidgeted and worried about the danger posed by the two great British ships, and Admiral Ozawa sent the transports off Malaya scuttling for the Bay of Thailand, Admiral Yamamoto ordered up a force of thirty dive bombers and level bombers from one of his Indochina air bases. The planes, loaded with 1000-pound bombs, were sent out to find the British battle force.

The Japanese airmen did not find the two big ships that day. Darkness closed in and they returned to their base.[8]

Next morning Yamamoto increased the order to eighty-four

planes. This time he sent bombers and torpedo planes. They flew all morning and in the afternoon had come within a half hour of their point of no return when the battle force was located. In less than an hour the torpedo planes and bombers sank the *Repulse* and the *Prince of Wales*.[9]

The argument about whether aircraft could sink battleships had finally come to an end. Yamamoto had laid a ghost. Satisfactory as it was to sink these two big ships and put an end to British sea power in the Western Pacific, Yamamoto knew that he had not yet given Japan the turnaround time she needed to consolidate victories not yet won. It was still too early to begin planning for the second phase. He could not even be sure that the Americans would not immediately come forth to do battle, with the two to four carrier task forces the Japanese naval estimates gave them.

In fact, the Americans *could* have come forth to do battle, at least for the valuable U.S. base at Wake Island, and Wake Island, at least, could have been saved from Japanese invasion if the Pearl Harbor attack had not almost completely paralyzed the American military establishment in the Pacific. So enormous was the outcry in Washington on December 7 (U.S. time) over the "surprise" at Pearl Harbor that the politicians in Washington called for heads to roll immediately. The heads that rolled were those of Admiral Husband E. Kimmel, a first-class fighting admiral, and Lieutenant General Walter C. Short. They were relieved of command *immediately*, even as Kimmel was mustering his forces to do battle. In doing so, the military establishment left a vacuum at Pearl Harbor in this vital period when the Japanese were moving and their naval forces were scattered. Two carrier task forces were available to strike back at the Japanese, and the commander of one of them, Vice Admiral William F. Halsey, was eager for battle. Within days a third force, the *Saratoga* task force, was also available, until she was damaged by a Japanese torpedo.[10]

The Japanese Third Fleet, under Vice Admiral Takahashi, was escorting sixty transports filled with troops toward Luzon in the Philippines. The Second Fleet, under Admiral Kondo, was standing off the Pescadores Islands in support of the Malaya landings.

In the south, Vice Admiral Inouye with the Fourth Fleet at Truk was entrusted with the capture of Guam and Wake islands. The capture of Guam was almost certain, for the island was defended by thirty American naval officers and a combined force of Chamoros and Americans of fewer than five hundred men. The Japanese had only to send Rear Admiral Goto in the cruiser *Aoba,* escorting transports carrying five thousand troops.

Wake Island, however, was a different matter. That American base was located a thousand miles west of Midway Island, and the Americans considered it valuable enough that early in 1941 they had begun strengthening the facilities and defenses there. In the spring, waiting for the Japanese attack he knew was coming, Admiral Kimmel had written Admiral Stark, the U.S. chief of naval operations, that he intended to hold Wake Island, because from that point he could launch a swift counterattack on Japanese naval forces within their empire.[11]

On December 8 (Tokyo time), Admiral Inouye's bombers arrived over Wake Island just a few minutes after the bombers hit Pearl Harbor. They came from Kwajalein Atoll in the Marshall Islands, part of that Pacific territory mandated to the Japanese by the League of Nations. For two days the Japanese bombed Wake Island. The defenders fought back, although most of their fighter planes were knocked out in the first raid. They did shoot down some Japanese bombers.[12]

On December 7 (U.S. time), Admiral Kimmel had set up a plan of defense for Wake Island. Admiral Aubrey W. Fitch's *Saratoga* task force had been at Puget Sound for repairs, but had then gone down to San Diego and there picked up the officers and men of Marine Corps Fighter Squadron 221. The squadron and eighteen fighters were aboard the carrier, heading out to reinforce Wake Island. Also heading that way and scheduled to join up was Vice Admiral Frank Jack Fletcher's *Yorktown* task force. Vice Admiral William F. Halsey's *Enterprise* task force was heading toward Johnson Island, to stay there to await the arrival of Fitch, then to support Fitch if necessary. After the attack on Pearl Harbor, however, Admiral Kimmel changed the orders: Vice Admiral Fletcher, in command of the *Yorktown* carrier group, would be in charge of the Wake relief. This change was made because Fletcher was senior officer of the force heading toward Wake, and by U.S. naval protocol, senior officers always commanded, even if they were inferior in training and aptitude. That was the case with Fletcher and Fitch; the former was a battleship man who had come to command a carrier task force by seniority, the latter, Fitch, was a full-fledged naval aviator.[13]

Meanwhile, Vice Admiral Wilson Brown, with the *Lexington*

task force, was to make a diversionary attack on the Marshalls, hitting the Japanese air base at Jaluit.

But the Kimmel plan to fight back was canceled in midpassage. Kimmel was relieved temporarily by Vice Admiral W. S. Pye, commander of the now immobilized battleship fleet. Pye, who knew nothing about carrier operations, was intimidated by the fate of Admiral Kimmel. Not wishing to join Kimmel in ignominy, he decided not to risk the carriers. Brown was told to abandon the Marshalls strike and move toward Wake "to support" Fletcher and Fitch, who were already being supported by Halsey.

The Americans moved with tantalizing slowness toward Wake. The Japanese invasion force arrived off Wake on December 11. It consisted of two cruisers and six destroyers, covered by aircraft flying out of the Marshalls, and escorting two transports filled with Japanese troops to make the landings.[14]

The American defenses at Wake consisted of five-inch shore guns, antiaircraft guns, and three fighter planes. They drove off the Japanese invasion fleet, damaging the Japanese flagship *Yubari* and the other cruiser, sinking the destroyers *Hayate* and *Kisaragi,* damaging three more destroyers and one of the transports. This Japanese invasion fleet was the only one to fail. It turned around and headed back to the Marshalls. Only two ships of the invasion fleet were undamaged.[15]

Had the Americans hurried, they might have caught this mauled force on its way back to Kwajalein, but there were no orders. From Truk, Admiral Inouye now sent Admiral Goto with four heavy cruisers and half a dozen destroyers. Admiral Nagumo was ordered to detach the carriers *Soryu* and *Hiryu* from his returning Pearl Harbor strike force to join the attack on Wake.

With four carriers and assorted cruisers and destroyers the Americans had a formidable force at sea, one capable of destroying the reinforced Japanese attack group. But Kimmel was out, and Pye was governing the fleet by committee. The committee got cold feet and ordered Admiral Halsey back to "protect" Hawaii against the retreating Japanese strike force. The three other carrier task forces, instead of being flung into a battle in which they would have had superior force, were withdrawn, ordered to return to Pearl Harbor. So Admiral Kajioka returned to Wake with his reinforcements, and the American five-inch shore guns and fighter planes, now down to two, gave them relatively little trouble. On December 22, the Japanese landed on Wake Island. The last radio message indicated the issue was in doubt, but it really was not. The silence that followed told the story of an American defeat snatched from the jaws of victory.[16]

The American failure in the first three months of the war was more a human failure than a matter of ships. The actual coming of war was an enormous wrench to the American military forces, so long trained to spit and polish as a substitute for fighting spirit. There was American fighting spirit, the heroic defense of some men at Pearl Harbor and at Wake certainly indicated that much. But the Japanese surprise attack had achieved the psychological aim of putting the Americans and the British on the defensive. The Japanese navy, after all, had been fighting since the summer of 1937 and the Japanese navy was continually on a wartime footing. War was all new to the Americans. It would take them a little time to get going. Meanwhile, the constant stream of victories for the Japanese continued and the euphoria and sense of superiority continued to grow within the Japanese military establishment.

Defeat in the Philippines, 1942. Remnants of the Philippine Constabulary surrender to the Japanese on the Bataan Peninsula.

(Imperial War Museum.)

A Japanese navy battle line. Note the curious "pagoda" superstructure of the Japanese battleship in the lead, typical of the Japanese.

(Imperial War Museum.)

The Imperial Family also went to war.
Here is Prince Chichibu, an infantry
major with the army in China.

(Japanese Defense Agency.)

Japanese recruiting poster for the war.

(Japanese Defense Agency.)

A Japanese field hospital in China.
Probably this was a converted school.

(Japanese Defense Agency.)

Prince Higashikuni emerges from his plane at Tokyo. The prince served during the war, and also was the first postwar prime minister of Japan.
(Japanese Defense Agency.)

A Japanese ambulance unit in north China. So fierce were the attacks of the Chinese Communist forces on small units that ambulances were protected by machine gun squads.
(Japanese Defense Agency.)

Admiral Yamamoto, Japan's greatest war hero of the Pacific War, on the deck of his flagship. He was assassinated by the orders of President Roosevelt in 1943.

(Japanese Defense Agency.)

Emperor Hirohito astride his favorite horse, White Snow. Once each year the emperor posed on the lucky white stallion for an official picture—until 1946.

(Japanese Defense Agency.)

General Sugiyama. He was the war minister who in 1937 told the emperor he would defeat China in thirty days. That sort of wild promise was his specialty.

(Japanese Defense Agency.)

General Tojo speaking to the Japanese Diet (parliament). He started as a constitutional prime minister, but before his disgrace with the fall of Saipan he had become absolute dictator of Japan.

(Japanese Defense Agency.)

U.S. Marines prepare to go ashore from an American transport. The marine landing on Guadalcanal in August 1942 began the first stage of the U.S. counteroffensive against Japan.

(National Archives 208-N-22498.)

Admiral William F. Halsey, the most successful and flamboyant fleet commander of World War II.

(National Archives 80-G-470887.)

Two of the most successful American submarine skippers of World War II: L. Mush Morton and, right, Dick O'Kane. The principal accomplishment of the American submarines in the Pacific War was to bottle up Japan and stop her import of oil.

(National Archives.)

A typical American fleet-class submarine of World War II.
(National Archives.)

The shark nose of the P-40 aircraft on Guadalcanal's Henderson
Field was devised by a German Luftwaffe fighter pilot, and copied
by the Flying Tigers of General Chennault's American Volunteer
Air Group in China. Later, American army pilots decorated their
planes in this way.

(National Archives 208-N-4932.)

A Zero fighter at Buna
amid the debris of
wrecked planes. This one,
missing its canopy, still
might have been salvaged
to fly again.

(Japanese Defense Agency.)

Part of the plan to encircle Rabaul was to capture the nearby Green
Islands. Here, after the capture, Admiral William F. Halsey, commander of the South Pacific, talks with Vice Admiral Aubrey W.
Fitch, Jr., commander of air forces. In the back seat of the jeep,
wearing helmet and pistol, is Rear Admiral Robert B. Carney, Halsey's chief of staff. The driver and the man behind Halsey are un-
identified.

(National Archives 208-N-23845.)

The Allied strategy called for the encirclement of Rabaul, New
Britain Island, the main Japanese base in the South Pacific. Here
white phosphorus incendiary bombs dropped by American aircraft
burst over Japanese planes on the airfield.

(National Archives 208-N-23831.)

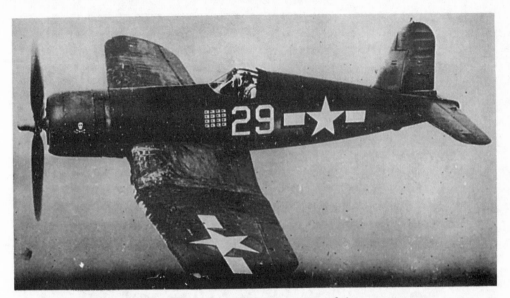

When the Pacific War began the Japanese Zero fighter was unquestionably the finest in the battle zone. But as the war continued, the Americans caught up. By the spring of 1944 carrier pilots were flying Corsair fighters like Lt. (j.g.) Ira C. Kepford's, shown here. The skull and crossbones plaque painted on the engine cowling is Kepford's squadron insignia. The 16 "meatball" flags in front of the "29" represent 16 planes shot down by Lt. Kepford.

(National Archives 208-N-27044.)

Gunsmoke hangs over the American bombardment force during the landings on Saipan in the Marianas on June 14, 1944.

(National Archives 208-N-30240.)

来年のことを言えば 魁が笑う

23. "Brag about next year and the devil laughs"

*I*t had all seemed so easy.

At the end of the first week of war, Domei, the Japanese news agency, began referring to the "marvel" of Japan's successes. Compared to them, "the famous naval engagements such as Trafalgar and Jutland are as sailing exercises on a lake," said the official government news service.[1]

A neutral would have to forgive Domei for this boasting. The American base at Pearl Harbor was still burning and the Japanese crowed as Washington announced the sinking of four battleships (350,000 tons of ships sunk or damaged, said Tokyo, adding up British and American figures).[2]

As Washington gave details, they were transmitted by the wire services to Buenos Aires, and there the Domei correspondent had them to send home. The Japanese newspapers ran pictures of the sunk American battleships. Artist Ken Matsuzoe painted for the government a stirring scene of a sky filled with Japanese planes and American ships burning and sinking below.[3]

All Japan was agog in these first days of the war, and the newspapers led the pack. The eight major Toyko newspapers sponsored a national "Rally to Crush the United States and Britain" at Korakuen Stadium. The editors made speeches, promising to do everything possible to bring all the world under one roof.

Hakko ichiu!

Banzai!

The *banzai* were so loud and so repeated that the speakers could hardly be heard. From that meeting came organizations at the neighborhood level. Each neighborhood organization would meet at 6:30 on the morning of December 10, ordained the organizers. And from there the whole of Japan would plunge on to certain victory.[4]

Here is the report of one such meeting carried by *Mainichi Shimbun*:

It was held in the one tiny *cho* (precinct) of the Kojimachi district of central Tokyo. The object, as the organizers said, was to "turn Japan into a giant fireball."

Radio Tokyo cooperated, by presenting at 6:30 that morning an up-to-the-minute war report from all fronts which, of course, spoke of nothing but Japanese victories.

The citizens of Kojimachi *ichi ban cho* (Kojimachi No. 1 precinct) gathered on the second floor of the Nakazawa Confectionery, which at the rear overlooked the British embassy grounds. Nakazawa-san, the owner of the confectionery, presided.

Up came the news report on NHK, the national radio network. It was followed by an inspirational message from the government broadcast nationwide:

"Every home is a battleground now! We are all comrades in arms! We must fight through to the end! Neighborhood love is burning like a flame. Let us sacrifice every bit of our lives for the Emperor!"

Nakazawa-san then spoke.

"I presume that every one of you fully understands what the radio announcement means. Now, every one of my neighbors, let us join hands and march on."[5]

And what was the public to do?

Let the people assume the proper attitude toward the war, first of all. Newspaper photographers began taking pictures of Japanese women in the Ginza dressed in European fashions. "Unpatriotic," declared *Asahi Shimbun*'s editorialists. "Western costume that should belong to sexy Hollywood actresses." Even foreign perfumes were assailed: "Down with American Odor" said a headline.[6]

"Chop Up Anglo-Saxon Devils," said another.

The inherent chauvinism of the nation was stirred as mightily as the pen could do. The barrage of antiforeign propaganda covered Japan within the week and did not let up.

It was easy enough for the Japanese to tell the truth about the war just then, for everywhere they were winning.

The war "is to emancipate the East Asian Nations from Anglo-Saxon domination and to construct a new order."[7] That was the new Japanese government line. A correspondent of *Asahi Shimbun* who boarded the captured U.S. gunboat *Wake* in Shanghai reported "it seems to have been a pleasure boat to its crew of twenty-five members. They all had their own private servants. They had provisions and whiskey enough to last for a year, at least."[8] As anyone along the Yangtze River knew, the charge was essentially true; the Western warriors in Asia did themselves very well in those years before the war.

Many people in Asia were more pleased with this Japanese promise to eradicate colonialism than the Anglo-Saxons have ever known. They cheered as the Japanese rolled up their victories. The Japanese troops marched into Bangkok on Thai Constitution Day. The Thai government pledged its unwavering support to The Greater East Asia Co-Prosperity Sphere. Wang I-hung, chairman of the North China Political Council, pledged Chinese support for "the emancipation of the Asian peoples by driving out the Anglo-Saxons." A Taiwanese banana dealer named Sei Suigen sent the Japanese Ministry of War Y 2000 to further the cause. Manchukuo Prime Minister Chang Ching-hui praised Japan for "establishing the new order." Prince Teh, chairman of the Federated Autonomous Government of Mongolia, pledged "the full support of six million people." The natives of Guam "greeted the Japanese with joy." Wang Ching-wei, the president of the Nanking China government, congratulated Japan on her initial victories. In Indochina, Governor Vice Admiral Jean Decoux pledged cooperation with the Japanese against the Anglo-Saxons. To be sure, many of these leaders were de facto captives of the Japanese, but the sentiments were often real. From Timor and other South Pacific islands came indications that the Japanese were being welcomed. From Argentina, which ostentatiously declared its "neutralism," came report after report of pleasure in the victories of the Japanese.

The world seemed turned upside down with the sudden victories of the little brown men over the Europeans and Americans. So quickly were the victories coming that the Japanese propaganda machinery was unable to keep up. In future months Tokyo would begin to capitalize on the reservoirs of anticolonial feeling, particularly in the Dutch East Indies, where Holland's rule had been among the most unenlightened in the world.

In Tokyo, the Diet met in special session on December 15, to promise renewed efforts to win the war quickly. That same day a drive to sell war bonds was begun in the Japanese capital in spite of the cold; that day marked the first snowfall of the winter.[9]

All sorts of changes accompanied the outbreak of war, including changes in terminology. The government declared the word *Kyokuto* (Far East) to be obnoxious. Hereafter, said a government announcement, that word would not be used, but the phrase *Dai-Toa* (Greater East Asia) would describe the area.[10]

At the end of that first week, Kowloon had fallen, and Hongkong, across the bay, was under attack. The Japanese army was marching down the Malay peninsula toward Singapore. Guam was in hand, and American and Chamorro soldiers were being hunted down in the far reaches of the island. Japanese troops in Thailand joined Thai troops to fight off British forces on the border. Japanese tanks clanked through the streets of Shanghai.

That day Imperial General Headquarters announced the landing of Japanese troops on Luzon Island in the Philippines.

In the second week, the Japanese invaded Borneo. On Christmas Eve Tokyo learned of the occupation of Wake Island. Hongkong surrendered. Admiral Thomas C. Hart moved the U.S. Asiatic Fleet down to the Dutch East Indies to make a stand with the Dutch and British, the ground troops fighting under Field Marshal Sir Archibald Wavell. General Douglas MacArthur evacuated Manila and moved onto the Bataan Peninsula, declaring that Manila was a "defenseless city." Nonsense, declared Japan's international lawyers, and they urged the Japanese airmen to continue to bomb the Philippine capital.

In China, the Japanese armies launched a new Christmas offensive in Kiangsi and Hunan provinces, "crushing" the Chinese, and "advancing swiftly." Cheers came from Wang Ching-wei's puppet government in Nanking.

The Japanese began accusing the Western Allies of all sorts of war crimes. The British, they charged, had sent the Indian troops to the front at Hongkong to be massacred. In the battle for the Philippines, General Tojo charged, in a speech to the Diet, that in Davao on Mindanao Island, just captured, the Americans had tortured to death ten Japanese civilians, and machine-gunned thirty-eight to death. These details were part of Tojo's report to the Diet as war minister. "The army is taking appropriate measures in dealing with the cruelty with which the enemy has willfully treated Japanese subjects."[11]

ARMY CHIEF REVEALS
MASSACRE AT DAVAO

said the Japanese newspaper headlines.

The really big news of Tojo's speech to the Diet, however, went unremarked by any heroics or emphasis.

At daybreak on December 17, Imperial forces effected a surprise landing in the northern part of the island [Borneo]. . . . The Japanese units report that the enemy had destroyed the oil refineries and taken out machinery as early as three months ago. However out of the total of 150 oil wells it will be possible to extract oil from 70 wells in a month's time, enabling a daily production of about 1700 tons. It is further reported that during the next year there is a possibility of extracting 500,000 barrels of oil.[12]

The war had been going on for just over two weeks. Japan had already accomplished her major aim. For the first time in her history, she controlled her own source of petroleum. "Japan is no longer a have-not nation," boasted the Japanese planning agency.[13]

On December 29, Imperial General Headquarters announced the fall of Ipoh, the tin and rubber center of Malaya. Japan had achieved another first, Kuching on the northern coast of Sarawak. "The occupation of Kuching means Japan will secure all important natural resources, including a large amount of petroleum."[14]

The army drove on.

The navy and the Japanese media were crowing ever more loudly about the enormous successes achieved. Domei news service sent a long article from Buenos Aires, quoting the highly regarded newspaper *La Prensa* as saying Japan had seized control of the Pacific from Britain and America. Building on this neutral report, the *Asahi Shimbun*'s naval reporter, Masanori Ito, said that the old naval ratio of 5-5-3 had been changed by Japanese victories to 2-2-3 in favor of Japan, and that it would take the Americans and British at least three years to recover.[15]

"The U.S. Pacific Fleet and U.S. Air Forces in Hawaii have been totally destroyed," announced the navy department of Imperial General Headquarters on December 19, after the American revelation of the extent of damage at Pearl Harbor.[16]

The navy's statement was remarkably accurate about Japan's losses (twenty-nine planes and five "special" submarines) but far less so about America's losses. The implication was picked up by the newspapers:

"U.S. Pacific Fleet is Wiped Out!" said the headlines in the Tokyo press.

But further the Japanese could not go, for the Americans had revealed the extent of the damage done by the Japanese carriers. This announcement marked a change in American publicity policy. At the outset of the war, Admiral Thomas C. Hart's Asiatic Fleet command at Manila had erred badly in claiming to have sunk several Japanese warships, when actually only one small minesweeper had gone down. The Japanese had leaped on the false Asiatic Fleet claims with contempt. The Japanese had been much more honest in their claims: at Wake, for example, they announced the shelling of early December but admitted that Japan, too, had suffered losses at Wake. Publicity policy was going to become an important factor in the war.[17]

Admiral Yamamoto was annoyed at the new braggartry of the Imperial General Headquarters publicity machine.

"The mindless rejoicing," he called it. Imperial Headquarters adopted the practice of accompanying their naval boasting with a rendition of "The Battleship March," and Yamamoto came to flinch every time he heard the piece on the radio. He agreed with the Americans: "Official reports should stick to the absolute truth. . . . All this talk of guiding public opinion and maintaining the national morale is so much empty puff." When the press began to laud Yamamoto as the hero of the day, this inveterate gambler and card player analyzed his "success" in a *waka,* a thirty-one-line *tanka* (poem):

> Gurasura ni hodo tokeredo
> Ridaburu nite "just make" no
> Kokochi koso sure

Hardly a grand slam have I played,
Modestly I have to say,
It's more like a redoubled bid barely made[18]

Admiral Yamamoto knew that the war was not going to continue so easily, and that difficulty would come when the easy victories stopped. Then what of the shouting?

But the puff grew every day. Yamamoto could not escape it himself, even though he spent most of his time at sea and none of his time seeking publicity. *Yomiuri Shimbun* compared his exploits to those of the Great Admiral Togo. He was called "the father of the Japanese Naval Air Force," which was more or less true; credit was given him as developer of Japan's enormously successful carrier tactics, which was true. When the emperor issued a special Imperial Rescript honoring Yamamoto, that was enough for press and public. Overnight, Yamamoto became Japan's greatest war hero.[19]

The hoopla, almost unbearable to Yamamoto, kept building in volume. Three weeks after Pearl Harbor, Imperial General Headquarters announced "Hawaii is now entirely isolated from the mainland and in danger of starvation" because of the activity of Japanese submarines.[20]

That claim *might* have been true. Japan had the weapons, the finest fleet of long-distance submarines in the Pacific. The claim was not true, however. Japan was not using them as commerce raiders, and the submarine men at Imperial Headquarters knew it very well.

Still the information section of Imperial General Headquarters refused to be quiet.

"The comparatively small number of ships [about half a dozen] that have been sunk or damaged by Japanese submarines in those waters proves how commercial navigation in those sea areas is now restricted due to the fear and danger of submarine attack."[21]

Nothing could have been further from the truth. The Americans were not even running convoys; individual ships were sailing from West Coast ports to Hawaii nearly every day and encountering no difficulty. The Japanese submarine service strategy was to utilize the submarine force to attack warships, and in this they were, and would be, very successful. An I-boat would make an attack on the carrier *Saratoga* early in January and put a torpedo into her. She had to go back to the West Coast for repairs once more, leaving only three

American carriers in the Pacific—four, if one counted the super-annuated *Langley* with the Asiatic Fleet. The Japanese submarines were on the lookout for those carriers and for all American capital ships in the Western Pacific, but they were paying no attention to the destruction of commerce.

The day was not far off when the Anglo-Saxons would cease to dominate Asia, said Professor Toshiyoshi Miyazawa of Imperial University, in an article widely reprinted in the Japanese press.

"The Anglo-Saxon influence is rapidly waning and in its place a rapid rise is being witnessed in the Asiatic countries. The war of Greater East Asia will create a new and glorious page in the history of the world."[22]

"The war of Greater East Asia," said General Tojo, "is only in its primary stage and the major battles are yet to be fought. The officers and men of the Imperial Forces are fully aware of this fact and are resolved to exercise their utmost efforts in attaining the objects of the holy war, thus serving the cause of the Japanese Empire."[23]

The end of 1941, then, saw Japan beginning to implement its Greater East Asia Co-Prosperity Sphere as a diplomatic and propaganda weapon against the Western powers. The victories continued, with startling rapidity.

Early in January 1942, the Japanese seized Tarakan, the Balikpapan. Makassar in the Celebes fell. Japanese paratroops landed in southern Sumatra and began to attack Palembang.

Victory brought a pattern reminiscent of the Rape of Nanking:

The Japanese took Hongkong on Christmas Day. Troops entered the St. Stephen's College and systematically bayoneted to death all the wounded prisoners in the beds. Any officers or nurses who tried to stop them were also bayoneted. Corpses were carried outside, and fires built of broken furniture became their funeral pyres. The nurses were taken into a small room, held there, and taken out one by one by Japanese soldiers, raped, and then returned to the room. The raping went on all Christmas Day and all Christmas night. The nurses could not remember how many times they had been raped.[24]

The tragedy at St. Stephen's College was the fault of the regimental commander of the Japanese. But the aftermath, the systematic cruelties heaped on the Chinese residents of Hongkong, and the systematic humiliation of the Europeans, was something else, a part of the Japanese pattern, which called for the bringing down of the Anglo-Saxons in the eyes of Asians.

The Japanese moved down the Malay Peninsula in January and February and besieged Singapore. They captured the British military hospital at Alexandra, and repeated the St. Stephen's performance. One patient was bayoneted to death on the operating table.[25] Singapore fell. A hundred thousand prisoners of war had to be dealt with. It was not an easy task for General Yamashita, and the task was made more difficult by the brutality of some of his subordinates. Worst of these was Major General Takuro Nishimura of the Imperial Guards Division. He encouraged rape and murder and pillage among his troops. After the fierce battle of the Muar River, Japanese troops were sent onto the battlefield to bayonet to death enemy wounded. Yamashita gave orders; the orders were disobeyed. Finally Nishimura went too far and defied a direct order. Yamashita took the matter to Marshal Terauchi, the commander of the whole southern army region, and Nishimura was sent home to Japan in disgrace. He sat out the rest of the war on the retired list. Worse, for the Imperial Guards Division, the Guards alone, among the three divisions assaulting Malaya, did not receive an Imperial Rescript after the victory. The Imperial Guards Division had dishonored itself.[26]

But the problem remained; the fact was that the Japanese army was never under the proper control of the authorities in the matter of treatment of prisoners and civilian populations. General Yamashita was painfully aware of the limits of his own control of his troops.

"I want my troops to behave with dignity," he wrote in his diary, "but most of them do not seem to have the ability to do so."[27]

The reason was largely that the militarists had been encouraging a hatred for foreigners, and particularly for white foreigners, for a long time. It did not take much encouragement. Foreigners had been maligned and mistreated in Japan from time immemorial. The natural attitude of the Japanese toward outsiders had always been jingoistic and hostile. Only when the government insisted were foreigners accepted to a point, never totally. The murders by the Satsumas and other clans during the treaty years showed the deep Japanese anti-foreign sentiment that persists to this day, ever quick to rise in any time of international crisis. During the Russo-Japanese War, many foreigners were killed or mistreated in Japan, even if they had nothing to do with the Russians. The best-known foreigner ever to take up residence in Japan, Lafcadio Hearn, was a victim of Japanese hatred of foreigners, not once but several times, although he married a samurai lady and took a Japanese name (Koizumi Yagumo) and Japanese citizenship.[28] During the Russo-Japanese War Hearn lost a teaching post for no other reason. At the end of his life he was preparing to leave Japan forever, convinced that his children would not be accepted either. In fact, however, at least that much resilience has developed in the Japanese character in a century: Koizumi's son grew up Japanese, and in the 1980s was working as a translator for the American military; his Japanese contemporaries completely accepted him as one of them. So much for partial success; that attitude did not exist in 1941. What did exist was the result of a lack of discipline and of a considered policy.

The first factor was responsible for at least half the early atrocities; the second factor, the considered policy of humiliation of whites, was responsible for the rest. It was a measured change, planned by the militarists, and the proof of it is in the enormous difference between the behavior of the modern Japanese soldiers (1931–45) as opposed to those of the Russo-Japanese War and World War I. In those wars the Japanese soldiers and sailors had been completely under control, and there were virtually no atrocities or cases of mistreatment.[29] But the policies inaugurated by General Araki and the other supernationalist officers called for brutality. Anyone who allowed himself or herself to be conquered was an inferior, and thus subject to any treatment the conquerors wished to give them. Here was the reverse side of *bushido,* the warrior's way, developed by the Japanese militarists. Generals Araki, Tojo, Sugiyama, and their close associates were to blame for this perversion of the samurai spirit to fit their perceived needs.

Tojo stated the case that winter when, as war minister, he informed the commandants of the newly established POW camps that they were not to be bound by the Geneva Convention of 1909, which had set down the rules of war. The militarists knew precisely what they were doing, and they were not going to be swayed by any outside arguments.[30]

Tojo was very careful to bring his sycophants into power and to keep out of the road to power any he considered to be rivals. Admiral Toshio Shimada had become Tojo's navy minister. He was complete toady to the general; there was no point in a Yamamoto protesting against government policy with a Shimada in office. The only thing protecting Yamamoto against the wrath of the militarists was his status as national hero. The same became true of General Yamashita after the fall of Singapore. Yamashita's victory was the result of a brilliant military coup: with 30,000 troops he had bluffed the British General Percival into surrendering a force four times as large. It must be said that the Japanese force was better trained, better armed, and much better led. The victory brought Yamashita the sobriquet "Tiger of Malaya," and the status of national hero compared only to that enjoyed by Admiral Yamamoto in the spring of 1942. But unlike Yamamoto, General Yamashita had to enjoy his fame in the wastes of Manchuria. Immediately after the victory, Tojo ordered his potential rival to command the Japanese First Army Group at Botanko on the Siberian border. Up there on the lonely steppe, Yamashita would be out of touch with Tokyo. Tojo could claim, as he did, that in case of trouble with Soviet Russia, he wanted his best general on the Siberian border. The catch, of course, was that until the West was defeated and China subdued, Tojo had no intention of moving against Soviet Russia.[31]

The Tojo government's plan in the early months of 1942 called for the rapid expulsion of the Anglo-American-Dutch powers from Asia. Next would come the manning of the defenses and the strengthening of the Greater East Asia Co-Prosperity Sphere, which would encompass all the conquered territory. Once the territory was occupied, then the economic strength of the Greater East Asia Co-Prosperity Sphere was to be increased by sending the *zaibatsu* into the new territories to start industries that would bring profit back to Japan and supply all her needs. As speedily as possible, the conquered territories would be turned into allied nations, with friendly governments that would contribute to Japan's defense and power rather than draw on it. Then all of Japan's efforts could be turned to the successful ending of the war with China. Once that was accomplished, the United States could be dealt with, according to circumstances. At the very least, the United States would have to remain outside the Western Pacific. Perhaps Hawaii and even more American territory might fall under the great Japanese roof. Then Soviet Russia could be dealt with, and ultimately *hakko ichiu* would be secured. How Japan would deal with her allies remained to be seen. Perhaps *hakko ichiu* would have to be adjusted, but at least the Pacific basin, from pole to pole, would belong to Japan.

Just now, in February 1942, the war had moved into what the Japanese army termed "the second phase." The Java and south Burma operations would be next. No one had expected the war to proceed so rapidly, and the army was planning to move that way in March or April. But with the Anglo-Saxons falling like gingerbread men, at the end of December Marshal Terauchi had recommended that the second phase be advanced by a month.

So it was done. The center of Japanese attention moved to the Philippines, where the Americans and Filipino troops were fighting a grudging battle down the Bataan Peninsula, to the Java Sea, where the next naval battles would be fought, and to Burma, where that lifeline, the Burma Road, connected Chiang Kai-shek's Nationalist China with the outside world. Japan's most serious problem at the moment was the assimilation of all these victories.

勝って兜の緒を締めよ

24. "After a victory, tighten your helmet strap"

*T*he fall of Singapore, coming so much more quickly than anyone had expected, and with so little difficulty, brought a whole series of complications to the victorious Japanese army.

Primary among these was the question: what was to be done with the enormous number of prisoners of war? At Hongkong about 10,000 had been captured, but in Malaya more than ten times that number were taken. In February and March 1942, fighting in the Dutch East Indies brought the capture of thousands more British and Dutch troops. The Japanese army was in no way equipped to handle this new difficulty. In Tokyo, General Tojo devised a policy to meet the occasion, a policy that would control Japanese attitudes during the whole war. Everyone in the Greater East Asia Co-Prosperity Sphere, said General Tojo, must earn his keep by working for the war effort. This included prisoners of war. They would be put to work.[1]

Some prisoners were sent up to Korea, where General Itagaki was now in command. He made a point of parading these ragged men, many of them sick, through the streets of Seoul and Panmunjom. "Lo, how the mighty are fallen" was the message for the Koreans. The great Japanese army conquered all.[2]

Hakko ichiu!

In the south, Field Marshal Terauchi was given the gigantic task of building a railroad through Thailand into Burma to connect the farthest westward reaches of the new empire, so that supplies and men could be moved overland, instead of down around the long Arakan Peninsula by sea. The distance was two hundred and fifty miles, through deep jungle, across mountains, over raging rivers.

It would take five years, said Field Marshal Terauchi's engineers.

The railroad must be completed in eighteen months, said Imperial General Headquarters. At that time Japan would be prepared to move against India, and the transportation system must be ready.[3]

It could only be done with forced labor, said General Terauchi.

Then get the forced labor, said Tokyo. Use the prisoners of war; that would be useful employment for them.

It was done. Before the Japanese were finished with their railroad, 16,000 Allied prisoners of war and 60,000 Asian forced laborers died in its building. The scandal was so enormous that before war's end it had spread halfway around the world, despite Japanese security precautions, and even the Japanese government was trying to hush it up. Even in this flush of victory the Japanese were trying to convince the world that their policies were humane.

Three British POWs escaped from the Japanese concentration camp at Hongkong and made their way to Chungking, where they told of the long nightmare that followed the Japanese capture of Hongkong, of the murders and rapes, and maltreatment of prisoners of war.[4]

Next day Colonel Nakao Yahagi, the army press spokesman at Imperial Headquarters, denied the charge.

"More than 200,000 enemy war prisoners are being accorded the best possible treatment," he said, "by virtue of *bushido* generosity. They are unanimous in expressing their appreciation for the magnanimity of the Japanese."[5]

But more was needed, Imperial Headquarters knew. So interviews were arranged. Commander Smith of the U.S. gunboat *Wake* and Major Smith of the U.S. Marine Corps detachment in Shanghai were brought before microphones, to tell the world just how wonderfully the Japanese were treating them. They were photographed at the microphones, appearing unbeaten, but also somber. The result was not quite what had been hoped for.[6]

Also interviewed were about a thousand other captives.

"Almost without a single exception," said an article in the *Asahi Shimbun,* "these prisoners are highly appreciative of the treatment extended by the Japanese authorities.

"They are also beginning to gasp in amazement at the great

might of Japan and the solidarity of the Japanese people behind the guns.

"The Japanese authorities are not using them for propaganda but are permitting them to broadcast out of sympathy for the enemy . . . such sympathy as only the *bushido* spirit knows."[7]

To prove it, the Japanese quoted some of the lucky prisoners:

> First lieutenant, captured at Guam: "I lost my valued bicycle at Guam. And I miss it greatly. I am in the best of health."
>
> A trained nurse said, "My dear mother, I sincerely hope you are not depressed. We are in high spirits and are enjoying life immensely. I will be with you after the war. Please look forward to our reunion."
>
> A surgeon first lieutenant said: "I wish to take the opportunity to my coming to Japan to enjoy Japanese scenery. . . ."
>
> A telegraph operator said: "Be sure that I will be back. Keep the home fires burning. And be careful not to break dishes. . . ."
>
> A commander said: "I was taken prisoner at the time Wake Island fell into Japanese hands. We are allowed to use the clothes that we had on at the time we were taken prisoner. . . ."
>
> A foreman said: "The Japanese army is kind and is allowing us freedom. Our food is o.k. We are allowed to use the clothes which we had left in the trenches. . . ."

Anyone in Allied territory who heard or read these messages had to be impressed, but not the way the Japanese had hoped. A naval commander—the equivalent of a lieutenant colonel—was to the Japanese a senior officer, and not a person to be kept in the same clothes he was captured in. So the commander got the word through. And so did the lieutenant who spoke so blithely of enjoying the "Japanese scenery," and the nurse who spoke of her "high spirits" and enormous enjoyment of life.

A few days later, an *Asahi* correspondent in Java interviewed Tomojo Abe, a propaganda writer for the Japanese army, who had been touring the island since its capture. Abe came into the *Asahi* bureau at Batavia to report on his adventures:[8]

I have seen something wonderful! It is my desire that it should be known to all the people in Japan and all the people in the world. Oh! My heart is full with this desire!

I was in the town of Galu which is 70 kilometers from Bandoeng. There were 5000 prisoners in the town, including, British, American, and Australian soldiers. I wanted to find out their daily mode of living and the psychological state of their minds.

The prisoners were put into separate departments according to their nationalities. I visited the Americans first and was astonished.

As soon as they saw me the American officers sprang forward and began bowing and scraping before me. Although I did not ask them any questions they vied with one another in telling all about their past records and life histories. I was disgusted with them.

I picked out a young officer and asked him, "Are you a bachelor?" The officer at once pulled out a picture of a woman, his sweetheart, from his pocket, and jabbering something excitedly, he began to weep copiously. Not to be beaten by this, the other officers also pulled similar pictures from their pockets and began to weep, too.

The British were made of much sterner stuff. . . . Even when I asked them questions, they did not answer.

"What was the name of your regiment?" I asked one of them.

"I can't tell you without the permission of my superior officers," he replied in a surly manner.

"If you don't tell me I'll shoot you," I said, to find out the psychological effect, to test the reaction of the prisoners.

I pointed the muzzle of my gun at him, but of course had no intention of hurting him. I only intimidated him.

The prisoner glared at the gun, his face gradually growing paler, until something seemed to snap in his brain and he fell down unconscious. We got him first aid treatment and he soon revived.

"All right," I told him. "We pity you and will spare your life. Be thankful."

"I don't know," muttered the prisoner.

After this generous gesture, Propagandist Abe went on to visit a colony of Germans who were now being protected by the Japanese army. One of the nice German ladies told him, "The Japanese Army seems to consist of Gods." She was that grateful for being released from captivity under the Dutch.

"Ah," said the *Asahi* reporter, adding his own comments to the story, "The likening of the Japanese army to an army of Gods is not without foundation. Viewed from any angle, is not the Japanese army a veritable army of Gods?"

Yes, the world got the message, and there were more such messages to come, unfortunately. The faster and greater the Japanese push became, the less time the Japanese military had for the prisoners. There would come a time. . . .

But, of course, no thoughts of future retribution now entered the minds of the men who were conquering Asia. They were the forces of vengeance, repaying the Westerners for all the indignities heaped upon Asians for three centuries.

And what about China? How did the Japanese treat the Chinese? In the Rape of Nanking lay the answer. The scandal that had resulted from that action, causing the withdrawal of at least four major commanders from the China war and the embarrassment of the army before the disapproving emperor, prevented any repetitions of that horror. But the Japanese continued to murder prisoners of war, and kill the wounded on the battlefields. Their treatment of the Chinese civilians and military depended almost entirely on the temper of the senior officer in the area at the time. Individual Japanese could be as kind as they were at home, but that was not the norm, or the impression they left in China. China was different. Chiang Kai-shek had had his chance; he was a "traitor to Asia," and his forces would pay the price. So, unfortunately, did the common people of the towns and villages through which the Japanese passed. Particularly after a hard fight, the Japanese soldiers became wild and vicious in their treatment of prisoners and civilians, and usually their officers did nothing to stop them.

On March 7, 1942, at a liaison conference between government and Imperial General Headquarters, a new policy was settled. The communications routes and the major cities of the Southeastern Asian mainland were now in Japanese hands, with the exception of a handful of straggling forces in Burma. On that very day the Japanese Fifteenth

Army had defeated the British-Indian forces in a battle near Rangoon. The city would be occupied the next day. The British were retreating through central Burma toward the Chindwin River. Following the occupation of Burma, no further offensive actions were contemplated toward India until the completion of the Thai-Burma railroad.[9]

The war in the Dutch East Indies was proceeding satisfactorily. The Americans had written off Java and Sumatra and their own Asiatic Fleet, and the sea command of the Allied naval forces had been given to Dutch Admiral C. E. Helfrich. Admiral Ozawa had fought the Battle of the Java Sea and won; the Allied naval forces in the Pacific were reduced to a handful of scattered ships. The Japanese naval forces were tracking them down, one by one. Admiral Nagumo's carrier force had come south and raided Darwin on February 19, sinking eight ships and damaging nine. The only conceivable naval threat the Japanese could see was from the British base at Trincomalee on Ceylon, where the British Eastern Fleet lay. But that fleet's main object was to protect India and Ceylon, and its principal weapon was the light aircraft carrier *Hermes*. A plan was in the offing for a raid by Admiral Nagumo's carrier striking force on Trincomalee, which was expected to accomplish the same sort of damage that had been inflicted on Pearl Harbor. It would be executed as soon as Admiral Yamamoto released the striking force after the southern waters were cleared. Already it was certain that the Allies had nothing with which to stop the march of the Imperial Japanese forces through Sumatra and Java. The oil fields now belonged to Japan.

The Philippines had been captured, for all practical purposes. The Americans and Filipino Scouts who still resisted had been driven onto Bataan Peninsula, and there was no escape for them. It was simply a matter of time. All the major American bases in the islands had fallen. All that was left was the force on Bataan and the guerillas in the south, mostly in the Visayas and on Mindanao.

What now were to be Japan's military aims?

At this point in the war, the army and navy thinking diverged. The navy wanted to capture Hawaii and Australia.[10] The plans had been drawn, even to the preparation of occupation currency and outline of occupation governments. The army operations and planning sections had looked into these ideas but rejected them. It would take too many troops to garrison Hawaii, and the line of supply was too long. As for Australia, it was patently impossible; a whole continent to be occupied! Under the best of conditions it would take at least ten divisions. The army did not have the resources. Let it not be forgotten that the principal reason for everything else was the settlement of the China incident. More than two million Japanese soldiers were tied up in China. Nearly a million were waiting along the northern border for possible conflict with the USSR. Having now added Southeast Asia to the occupation areas, the army was coming to the limit of its powers of expansion. The principal war aim had to be to defeat Chiang Kai-shek, to help Germany defeat England, and to destroy the American will to carry on the war. Other problems would have to be resolved before Hawaii and Australia could be occupied.[11]

All at the liaison meeting agreed, however, that the pressure must be kept on the Allies and that to do so the war gains achieved must be supplemented, although in a fashion that would not draw heavily on the army's resources. At the same time the defenses of the territories just conquered must be strengthened and the resources exploited to prepare for a protracted war.

What must be agreed upon at this meeting, said General Tojo, was the outer perimeter of the new Japanese empire, which was to be strengthened and protected.

What, asked General Tojo, was the navy's estimate of the date when the United States Navy would be restored enough to counterattack?[12]

Not until December 1943, said the navy high command. The destruction of the Pacific and Asiatic fleets had made that quite sure. It might be possible, however, for the Americans to launch air attacks against Japan from the Aleutian Islands before that date.

On that basis, then, the liaison conference agreed that the army and navy would operate together to take New Caledonia, Fiji, Samoa, British New Guinea (Papua), and the Aleutian Islands. The navy would capture Midway Island. Navy and army would operate from the main southern air and army base at Rabaul in the Bismarck Islands, against the southern areas. The main naval base for these operations would be Truk, and elements of the Combined Fleet would be stationed there.

This movement, army and navy officials agreed, should be ridiculously easy. In fact, said the army, they could look forward in a few months to withdrawing most of the troops from the southern area, because the Allies had shown so little disposition to fight. To be left in the south would be only enough troops to establish the new perimeters. These were measured in battalions, not divisions. Five divisions now in the south would be brought back to Japan, Manchuria, and China.[13]

Why tie up more troops? The victory was almost complete now, all the major war aims of November had been realized. The weakness and lack of stamina of the Westerners had been proved in Malaya. There was no indication in Tokyo that the Westerners were ever going to fight. Well, there was *almost* no indication. On March 1 Imperial Headquarters had reported belatedly on an air attack on Otori Island (formerly called Wake Island) by one aircraft carrier, two cruisers, and six destroyers. The Japanese claimed to have set one cruiser afire, damaged one destroyer, and shot down five enemy planes. The enemy, said IGHQ, had sunk one patrol craft and damaged some installations.

"With a view to annihilating the enemy, Navy Air Units in that region pursued him in full force, but the enemy made good his escape."[14]

Thus Imperial General Headquarters passed off Admiral Halsey's raid on Wake Island, the first American offensive action of the Pacific War, and turned its attention to the knotty problem that had created so much difficulty and so much error in the past four and a half years: China.

General Tojo never lost sight of the main problem—resolution of the China incident at the earliest opportunity. That victory would free millions of troops from China, and the establishment of a national Chinese government friendly to Japan would bring immense strength to the Greater East Asia Co-Prosperity Sphere. China settled, the Philippines gone, the Americans would have no further physical interests in Asia, and it should be easy to persuade them to come to the peace table and ratify the Japanese victories.

The Japanese four-man supercabinet could agree on all these matters in March 1942, so to China they addressed their attention.[15]

Analysis of the Chinese military situation was a task for a real expert. The Chinese had an army of some three million men. But of these only 40 percent were under control of the Kuomintang's central government. The others were warlord troops and Communist troops.

Of the 1,200,000 troops under Chiang's control, only 650,000 were directly controlled by his generals, and another 550,000 were controlled by warlords who claimed loyalty to his government; the strongest force was the Szechuan army of 320,000 men. The defeat of this army would do much to end Chiang's power.

The next move, said the army planners, should be to push toward Chungking, from the south, with new divisions brought in from Malaya and the Dutch East Indies and the Philippines as soon as the victories were consolidated. In a few weeks, the whole of Burma would be occupied, from Rangoon to Mandalay and north, and the Burma Road would be totally sealed off. Thereafter China would have no contact with the outside world except by air. Already the pinch was being felt, virtually no supplies of any kind were coming into China, and the Nationalist government's currency had fallen to 2.5 percent of its prewar value. Still, Chinese morale was very high; for some reason the Chinese really believed the British and Americans would win the war. That problem, too, had to be addressed by a firm policy. The Chinese had to be shown that the white foreigners were paper tigers.

Preparations would begin now, in the spring, for the great offensive in China, to be carried out against Chiang's Szechuan Province in the fall. As the generals looked at the map of China, the future appeared bright. The little Rising Sun flags stuck in the map, from the Siberian border all the way south to Hongkong, and beyond, and inland past Peking and down on a line to Hankow, showed the enormous amount of Chinese territory under Japanese army control. But the little flags were misleading, as General Shunroku Hata, commander of the China Expeditionary Force, knew very well. In the north the Chinese Communist armies slipped in and around the Japanese installations, burning, shooting, killing by night. By day the Japanese controlled the countryside, by night it was Chinese territory. And in the south the same was true. Guerillas operated in every province. Every truck, every train had to be escorted by troops; if not, they were prime targets for the guerillas. The Japanese claimed they had China in their grip; the reverse was true; they were still bogged down in a war that demanded more men and more guns and more equipment every month. By the winter of 1942 the need to "settle" the China incident—which meant complete the conquest of all China—had become so ingrained an article of faith with the militarists who controlled the army that there was no way of turning back. Once the China incident was settled, the militarists promised themselves, all else would be simple.[16]

目 の 上 の 瘤

25. "A thorn in one's flesh"

*I*n the spring of 1942 the Imperial Japanese Navy's basic task was to prevent enemy attacks inside the defense perimeter established by Imperial General Headquarters at the March meeting.

On March 1, Rear Admiral Tanetsuga Sosa gave an interview to the *Japan Times* in which he revealed the basic navy strategy of the period:[1]

The only possible American attack on Japan could come from bases in Alaska and the Aleutian Islands. Such attacks could hardly be staged until the end of May when the weather became favorable. The Americans were hurriedly trying to improve their facilities in the Aleutians for this purpose, said the admiral. "But the American plan can be smashed beyond recovery," he added, "because America lacks a navy strong enough to block the Japanese attempt to reduce the possibility of attack from the north to a myth."

Attacks elsewhere from the Americans could come only by using bases in Australia, through the several seas that join the Pacific and the Indian oceans, seas now lumped together by Japan under the name the "Sea of Greater East Asia." Admiral Sosa noted that the Americans had already begun trying to launch a submarine campaign from Australia. "But that attempt is hardly worth apprehension, since it will mean total destruction of the remaining submarines and aircraft carriers . . . since the Japanese forces now have under their domination the Bismarcks and Timor Island. It will be a simple matter for the Japanese forces to pound the Australia coastal cities from bases lying within hailing distance."

Britain, said the admiral, might try to hamper Japanese movements in Burma by dispatching her Eastern Fleet from Ceylon.

"The Japanese forces," he said, "by using the newly acquired bases at Shonanto (Singapore) can chase the British armada into the Mediterranean."

There, laid out in public print was the Japanese naval plan for the next six months. Admiral Yamamoto was already working out the details of an attack on Midway Island, which would then become the advance Japanese naval base in the Pacific for an invasion of Hawaii. At the same time, the Combined Fleet would escort an army amphibious force to the Aleutian Islands, to seize the advanced American bases there, and thus safeguard the northern approaches to the empire. This attack would come in June.

Meanwhile, the Combined Fleet had some other tasks. The clean-up of the Sea of Greater East Asia would continue, and Allied vessels would be sunk or driven away. Admiral Nagumo's carrier striking force was operating in these waters, paving the way for further attacks and protecting landing operations. Nagumo would move west in a few weeks to strike the British naval base at Trincomalee, then return to Japan for rest and resupply before heading east toward Midway. Not all the carriers were needed, so three would be employed in protecting an army landing at Port Moresby in British New Guinea (Papua). The capture of Papua would be followed by the move into French Oceania and Samoa. Those captures would complete the establishment of the southern perimeter of the empire. They would be accompanied by the building of seaplane and land air bases in the southern Solomon Islands. Then Australia would be within easy bombing distance of the southern perimeter.[2]

The activity began on March 8, with the bombing of Port Moresby. Japanese army forces from Rabaul landed at Salamaua and Lae on the coast of Papua and began moving overland. At sea this operation was supported by Admiral Nagumo's carrier striking force with a number of bombing raids on Port Moresby, Darwin, Derby, Broome, and Tulagi in the Solomon Islands, all this part of the softening-up process.

At this point, the Japanese army began to believe its own propaganda, and it is hard to blame them. For as in Malaya, the Dutch in the East Indies—an army 100,000 strong—had allowed themselves to be so disorganized that they ended up surrendering en masse to a Japanese force of 25,000 men. In due respect to the Dutch, they had an enormous problem, brought about by their own colonial policy. The Indonesian troops of the army had little desire to fight for the Dutch, and the Japanese propaganda line—Asia for Asians—was very effective. It was no great wonder, then, that the Japanese military men in Southeast Asia had slight respect for the Europeans and this attitude was carried home where it proliferated.

There was one fly in the ointment. The Japanese high command was not happy to learn that General Douglas MacArthur had escaped the Philippines and arrived in Australia on March 21. The news was conveyed to the Japanese public three days later in a news story reporting that MacArthur was meeting with Australian leaders. The army leaders of Imperial Headquarters had scoffed at the navy's talk about the need to bring Australia under control. But the Japanese army respected General Douglas MacArthur, possibly more than any other Allied military leader, for he had been a World War I hero, and chief of staff of the United States Army, and, finally, commander in chief of the Philippine defense forces. Although he had no American troops to command and virtually no American navy in the area to support him, his arrival gave the Japanese pause. At some point, the generals knew very well, they would have to expect an attempt at a counterblow from the Americans.

Only hints, such as the statements by Admiral Sosa, gave any indication to the public that the war was not already won and the peace assured. At the end of March, with fanfare the Economic Federation of Japan (a *zaibatsu* creation) established a special committee to study the ways in which the Greater East Asia Co-Prosperity Sphere could begin bringing greater co-prosperity. At a meeting attended by high-ranking officers from army, navy, foreign ministry, and many *zaibatsu* officials, at the Tokyo *kaikan* (assembly hall) in Marunouchi on March 25 the program was laid out: Malayan tin and rubber, Philippine sugar, Borneo mercury, rice from Burma and Indochina were now all Japanese. All that was required was that the best methods of extracting and organizing the distribution of these raw materials be established. This was to be the task of the new committee. It went without saying that the newly secured resources existed for the greater glory of Nippon.[3]

Aichiro Fujiyama, president of the Japan and Tokyo chambers of commerce, suggested that a *Dai-Toa* club be established in Tokyo. Capital idea! It would be done. It would give the visitors from the co-prosperity sphere a place of their own in busy Tokyo.

Day upon day the *zaibatsu* gloated in the press about the bright new future: the bauxite deposits of the Indies would create a new aluminum industry for Japan, just one of scores of new enterprises. Before the end of March, the military government at Batavia had laid down a whole set of regulations forcing the immediate revival of the various industries established by the Dutch. In Tokyo the Ministry of Commerce and Industry was working on legislation to bring all these new affairs within the structure of the ministry. Nobosuke Kishi, the minister, held a meeting at the Industrial Club with the Key Industrial Council (read *zaibatsu*) to guide the organization in the right direction. At the meeting he also announced creation of a Machinery Manufacturing Industrial Council. Dr. Mazatoshi Ohkochi, one of the leaders of the *zaibatsu,* would be chairman. Chief operating officer would be Vice Admiral Tomisaburo Ohtagaki. It was a symbol of the cementing of relations between militarists and *zaibatsu* for a greater Japan.[4]

The next problem was to eliminate military government of the "liberated" territories just as soon as possible. The procedure everywhere, directed by the foreign ministry, war ministry, the new Greater East Asia Co-Prosperity Ministry was to find local leaders and make governors of them. At Batavia, General Hitoshi Imamura freed Achmed Sukarno from a Dutch prison in Sumatra, where he was being held on political charges, and had Sukarno brought in to headquarters. The general suggested that Sukarno might want to cooperate with the Japanese and that if he did Imamura would consult with him during the period of military government. That course would certainly be in the interest of the Indonesians. Sukarno thought it over and decided to cooperate. He held one reservation: at the end of the war, he said, he would maintain his freedom of action to choose his own course.[5]

So a Japanese general and an Indonesian patriot came to terms. The result was the rapid appointment of Sukarno's followers to a large number of important government positions that had previously been held by Dutchmen only.

Imamura chose a supreme military advisory council on which served five Japanese officials and ten Indonesians. Sukarno was one of them. Within weeks after the conquest of Indonesia by Japan, the Indonesians were telling one another that they had, indeed, been liberated from colonialism.

From Tokyo came complaint that the Imamura military government was much too easy on the Indonesians. A military commission was sent down to investigate, and when the generals discovered how little difficulty Imamura was having in restoring order and productivity to the islands, the commission went back to Tokyo and endorsed his policies.[6] In every way the Indonesian adventure was one of the most successful of Japan's colonial excursions.

In Japan at the end of March, the excitement of constant victory began to slow down. In the Southern Operations, all military advances had been successful; the single thorn in the side of the Japanese high command at the moment was the pitiful remnant of the American forces in the Philippines, abandoned by their government, as they knew they would have to be, but fighting on from the old fortress rock at Corregidor on Manila Bay, in defiance of the imperial forces.

In mid-March Imperial Headquarters indicated that the Americans could not last much longer, capture of the old Corregidor fortress was imminent. Then, for two weeks, no more was said. On April 12 readers between the lines of the Japanese newspapers learned that Corregidor was still holding out. Imperial Headquarters reported that the fortress had been bombed repeatedly for eight days; "havoc was wreaked on the high-angle gun batteries." That was all. Nothing more was said about the "havoc" wreaked on Corregidor.[7]

The Americans were, in fact, in rough shape. Short of medical supplies, very short of food and ammunition, they fought on with no real hope of rescue.

On April 5 the Japanese carrier striking force raided Colombo, with little result. Imperial Headquarters announced the usual resounding victory but had no facts. The press was hard put to keep up the drumbeat of victory, and the government obliged by commemorating the Imperial Rescript of December declaring war on the West, and by posing cabinet members for war pictures. The Americans had announced the destruction of five midget submarines in the Pearl Harbor attack, and the Japanese held a memorial service at Hibiya Park, Tokyo, in honor of the nine "living war-gods" who had passed on to other climes. The newspapers were now full of photographs of the capture of Singapore and Batavia and other victories. The government's announced program was to keep the Japanese war fever at the highest level.[8]

But retreads are retreads. What Japan needed was the clean sweep of victory, and the Americans on Corregidor were keeping them from it. On April 10 Imperial Headquarters announced the sinking of the British carrier *Hermes* in Admiral Nagumo's strike against Trincomalee. Also sunk were three British cruisers and a destroyer. Captain Hideo Hiraide, the navy spokesman at Imperial General Headquarters, made a thirty-minute radio broadcast. Japanese naval superiority, he said, now extended from the U.S. West Coast to Africa, and from the Aleutians to Australia. The Pacific Ocean was a Japanese lake.[9]

The last U.S. stronghold on Bataan, Mariveles, fell on April 9. The Japanese reported excellent results in mopping up on Cebu and Mindanao, results they had reported a month earlier. What they were saying was that the guerillas were getting organized.[10]

On April 14 the news Tokyo was waiting for happened—almost.

"Bataan Falls" screamed the four-inch headlines in the newspapers. "Corregidor Collapse Imminent."[11]

Lieutenant General Masaharu Homma, who evidently had been sitting in his lounge in Manila, was now reported to have taken personal charge of the fighting. What that meant was that Homma had been told by Imperial General Headquarters that the continued holdout of the effete, cowardly Americans was becoming embarrassing, and to get it over with, no matter the cost. A few days earlier the Japanese had been bragging that a handful of troops had tied the Americans down at Bataan. Now they indicated that "every sort of modern arms" was being used by the Japanese on Bataan. As for the Americans, they were suffering from vitamin deficiencies and starvation, and the Americans were tying Filipinos to trees so they would stay and fight while the Americans fled. That is the Japanese story.[12]

Finally, driven to the tip of the peninsula, out of ammunition, out of food, the Americans had no recourse but to surrender. From Tokyo, to exhort the troops in the name of the Imperial General Staff, had come one of those young staff officers who knew all the answers, Lieutenant Colonel Tsuji. He set the style for Japanese treatment of the prisoners, by pulling out his pistol and shooting a prisoner dead.

"This is the way to treat bastards like this," he said.[13]

All too many of the young Japanese officers and noncommissioned officers felt the same. So the sick prisoners were forced along at a fast pace. If they fell, a Japanese soldier might bayonet them as they lay, or shoot them, or if of less choleric disposition leave them behind to die.

"Bataan defenders deserve no praise," said the Japanese retired

General Takaaki Kuwaki. "It was the terrain that protected them. Any army corps under such circumstances could have prolonged its resistance as long as provisions and ammunition held out. It is no credit to the United States soldiers that they resisted for some time in such a naturally protected place."[14]

The Japanese had expected to find about 25,000 American and Filipino troops on Bataan. But when the surrender came, of those who could not escape to Corregidor, the total was found to be nearly 76,000. Following their surrender, the prisoners were told that they would now march to San Fernando, sixty kilometers away. It was, said the Japanese, a mere two-day hike for a Japanese soldier. But the Japanese were not half starved and sick with malaria, dengue, and dysentery. The Americans and Filipinos were.

Such was the Japanese fury at these Americans and Filipinos who had thrown a monkey wrench into their timetable, that they marched them mercilessly back up the Bataan Peninsula toward Manila and prison. Any man who fell and could not get up died on the end of a bayonet or a bullet, or was left to die in the heat. What of the Filipino Constabulary troops? They had cast their lot with the Americans, said the Japanese, and were to be treated just as badly. They were. More than 7000 prisoners died on the Bataan Death March, one-third American, two-thirds Filipino.[15]

With the Bataan Peninsula fallen, the collapse of Corregidor could only be hours away, said the experts in Tokyo. And a Japan made breathless by the media waited for the other shoe to drop.

But how many hours!

The Americans who had managed to escape continued to hold out against constant bombing and shelling. The embarrassment of the Imperial General Staff continued. It was eased perhaps by photos on the front pages of the newspapers, such as the one on April 15 in the *Japan Times* showing a sign

U.S. NAVY BASE
MARIVELES

And above it, waved a Japanese army flag—the "meatball with spokes."

APRIL 16—BOMBING OF CORREGIDOR INTENSIFIED
JAPANESE ARTILLERY SMASHING ENEMY

APRIL 17—BATTERED CORREGIDOR ISLAND AT DEATH'S DOOR
UNDER FURIOUS ONSLAUGHTS FROM LAND AND
AIR
APRIL 18—GUNS SMASH CORREGIDOR[16]

Smash, yes. Destroy, no. Corregidor fought on.

On April 18, Tokyo suddenly had something else to consider.

Shortly before noon the air raid sirens began to sound through-out Japan, and it was not long before American bombers appeared over Kobe, Nagoya, Yokohama, Yokosuka, and Tokyo. In all, there were sixteen B-25 army medium bombers, carrying high explosives and incendiaries. They aimed at dock areas, steel mills, factories. They hit some, damaged ships and a steel factory. They also hit houses and killed civilians, as might have been expected.

But the fact was that it was not expected in Japan. The Japanese had been at war really since 1931, and their homeland had never been touched by war, except for some bombing raids on Taiwan by the Chinese, and Taiwan, despite its large Japanese population, was not homeland.

Privately, the militarists of the Japanese army and navy knew that they were going to have to expect some Allied counterattacks. The Midway-Aleutians amphibious invasions scheduled by the navy and army for June were expected to forestall any such activity for a while at least, and if Admiral Yamamoto could realize his original dream, lure the American fleet out to battle at Midway as he planned, and wipe out the American carriers, then Japan might get to the peace table yet unscathed.

In Japan the government recognized the pressures that were building in the West for counterattack. From Stockholm and Lisbon came reports that the fall of Bataan had brought American morale to a new low, and there was much truth in those reports. President Roosevelt was well aware of the morale problem that had dogged the nation: unrelieved bad news coming nearly every day after December 7. The President had recognized the problem in December and had then asked his military leaders to give him some sort of bombing raid on Japan as soon as possible, if only to boost American morale. Roosevelt had repeated the request in January.[17] By the end of the month a plan was made: a carrier would be used to take as many medium bombers as possible as close to Japan as possible, and the bombers would strike, and then head west to land in free China territory. It was all plotted out logistically, and it could be done.

The man chosen for the job was a fiesty little flying lieutenant colonel of the U.S. Army Air Corps named James Doolittle. In a month he had a squadron put together, and the pilots were training in takeoffs from a carrier. As the Americans fought their hopeless delaying action down the Bataan Peninsula, the Doolittle squadron headed west. Early in March, Admiral William F. Halsey made his raid on Wake Island and then moved on to raid Marcus Island, much closer to Tokyo, in the hope that this action would upset the Japanese sufficiently to make them pull away from the Philippines. It was a forlorn hope, the Halsey raids were recognized for what they were at Imperial Headquarters and caused no change at all in military policy. The real effect was to stimulate Admiral Yamamoto's feeling that he ought to come to grips with the American fleet as soon as possible, now that Nagumo had failed him. He still held the hope that by such action he could force the Americans to the conference table in a matter of weeks.[18]

On April 1, 1942, the carrier *Hornet,* deck-loaded with the sixteen B-25 bombers, sailed from Alameda, California. A week later, Admiral Halsey in the carrier *Enterprise* set out with a task force from Pearl Harbor.

Early on the morning of April 10, the Japanese radio intelligence unit with the Combined Fleet at Hagashishima was aware of the approach of an American task force built around two or three carriers. Admiral Yamamoto was not particularly worried, nor was there a great deal he could do at the moment. The carrier strike force had just attacked the British at Trincomalee and was coming home after a long multiple-mission voyage of 50,000 miles. The Japanese sea defense network of picket ships extended out 700 miles from the home islands, which would give a warning time of at least fifteen hours; the Americans would have to move up to within 300 miles offshore to launch planes.

Early on the morning of April 18 (Tokyo time) the American task force began running in through the Japanese picket line. Admiral Halsey assumed they had been seen and gave the order to launch the B-25s. Not only had they been seen, they had been tracked by the Japanese for a week, since those radio interceptions so carelessly made on April 10 to set the point of rendezvous of the *Enterprise* and *Hornet* task forces. The radio silence observed since that time had prevented the Japanese from knowing precisely where the Americans were, but plans were made to launch the Twenty-Sixth Air Flotilla's sixty-nine bombers when the American ships were picked up by the picket line.[19]

A carrier force would have been sent out to meet them, except that there was no such force available. Admiral Nagumo's striking force could not make contact. Three other carriers, the *Zuikaku, Shokaku,* and *Shoho,* had been sent down to Truk, to support the Port Moresby invasion that was next on the schedule. The only carrier in Japan at the moment was the *Kaga,* and she was not fit for operations.[20]

Halsey's prudent decision to launch and move out may well have saved the two carriers for if the scouting planes had found them, and attacked, the next day Nagumo's six carriers would have been in position to attack, and then half the American carrier strength in the Pacific might have been sacrificed for what after all was only a gesture.

The carriers were 550 miles out from Japan when the B-25s were launched. The ships moved out and in a few hours were safe.

The sixteen bombers winged toward Japan. One was sighted by a Japanese patrol plane, but when the pilot reported seeing a two-engined land plane, the report was rejected, for it was well known that the Americans did not have any twin-engined carrier planes.

So the Doolittle squadron penetrated Japan's air defenses and made a successful attack—successful in the sense that although some planes were shot up none was shot down over Japan (despite the Japanese claim to have destroyed nine planes).[21]

Having bombed, the planes turned toward China, except one, which landed near Vladivostok. Four planes crash-landed in Chinese territory. The crews of eleven others bailed out over China or China waters. The crew survivors of two of the planes were captured by the Japanese. The others all encountered Chinese civilians or troops, and all who survived landing were rescued.

Imperial General Headquarters' first report of the bombing made certain that the people of Japan knew that the imperial family had not been hurt. In fact, said IGHQ, the emperor had carried out his normal routine during the attack. That evening Prime Minister Tojo visited the Imperial Palace to pay his respects. Home Minister Yuzawa reported to the emperor on damage, which was slight. The newspapers speculated on the American reasoning behind the attack, and most of them came to the conclusion of the newspaper *Miyako:*

"A possible explanation is that the enemy hoped to achieve results which he could show to the people in his country in an attempt to placate the people who are getting restless after the serious reverses have been suffered by the Allied Forces in the War of Greater East Asia."[22]

How right they were. The announcement of the bombing was made by President Roosevelt, and the results were all he could have asked; electric would be a fair statement. The euphoria was doubled by President Roosevelt's mysterious reference when asked from where the planes had come to bomb Japan. "Shangri-la," he said impishly, referring to a mythical monastery in Tibet that had been the site of a popular novel *Lost Horizon.* The American people were satisfied, mystified, and asked no more. The Japanese, of course, were not at all fooled.

"Although this was Japan's first experience of a hostile air raid, the nation must be prepared for a frequent recurrence of similar incidents hereafter," said the newspaper *Nichi Nichi.* "Saturday's experience has shown that despite the series of crushing defeats which he has suffered so far, the enemy still has the spirit left to make air raids on this country."[23]

At this point, General Tojo stopped for a moment to reassess Japan's position and strengthen his own. The first change was to get rid of Lieutenant General Akira Muto, director of the powerful Military Affairs Bureau of the army. He was sent down to Malaya to take over the dispirited and disgraced Imperial Guards Division from General Nishimura. In his place was appointed Major General Kenryo Sato. "He enjoys the deep trust of General Hideki Tojo," said *Asahi Shimbun,* "and is regarded as one of Tojo's brain trusts."[24]

The wheels were set in motion by enactment of ex post facto military law, for the execution of the Doolittle fliers who had been captured, and the future execution of any other Allied fliers who attacked Japan. Three of the American fliers were killed by a firing squad, and five other captives from this mission were imprisoned. General Tojo, General Sugiyama, who approved the death sentences, and the other militarists were still confident of ultimate victory in this war. Tojo was the final authority for everything.[25]

General Yamashita had been banished to the border of Siberia. General Homma, the conqueror of the Philippines, was soon to be disgraced. Homma's trouble was that he was a gentleman, and he proposed decent treatment for the Filipinos, even those who retained tender memories of the Americans. When he heard the truth of the Bataan Death March, he erupted in anger. Colonel Tsuji stuck the knife into Homma; moving with the ease of a born conspirator he arranged for the execution of many of the former Filipino officials who had served under the Americans. Homma was declared soft on the Filipinos and given the blame for the difficulties the Japanese encountered immediately in establishing a friendly regime. The real reason was that the conquest of Bataan had taken too long; and Corregidor held out until May. This was too much for the militarists in Tokyo and there had to be a goat, particularly after the Bataan Death March gave Japan a whole new blanket of ruinous publicity abroad. The insidious Colonel Tsuji continued to function. General Homma was sent home and retired.[26]

嘘は 泥棒の始まり

26. "The lie is the first step to disaster"

*T*he Big Lie in Japan began with the stories the military told about treatment of prisoners of war and civilians who fell under the power of the military. Had the Japanese believed that the way they were treating foreigners was correct, they would not have lied, but lie they did, and from that beginning the tissue of lies began to enfold all Japan.

The army had begun lying about China, the Nanking massacre and a hundred lesser ones. The generals lied about Hongkong, and lied about Malaya, and about Indonesia, and the Bataan Death March. It was no great strain then to begin lying about other matters. The stories told about the Doolittle Tokyo raid—how nine American planes were shot down—were pure fabrications. In fact, having told the lie, the army had to send couriers to China to try to find the pieces of aircraft and American parachutes which they could put on display at a huge rally in Hibiya Park ten days after the bombing. They managed to bring back a parachute and a few bits of wreckage that, the authorities claimed, had fallen in Japan.[1]

Such little lies, so useless, and so senseless. They begot other lies, even greater ones. Before the war was half finished the militarists were lying to one another, and when that happened disaster became inevitable.

General Tojo, no matter his military skills, was essentially stupid, very badly educated, and worse read. He was the prime example of what had happened to Japan since 1853. His family were *ronin*, masterless samurai of a very low rank. He came up through the army, had he not he would have ended up as a shopkeeper or a clerk. All his life he had a clerk's mind, that was his road to power in the army; he knew all the regulations and how to use the system. But once Tojo rose to power he made the great mistake of surrounding himself with sycophants who would tell him what he wanted to hear, not what he should know. He also made it a policy to get rid of any officer or official who had the temerity to disagree with him.[2]

The Doolittle raid on Japan was a remarkably effective political gesture inside the United States, but it also cost thousands of Allied lives. When the Americans informed Generalissimo Chiang Kai-shek of their plan to use the central China airfields as landing places for the Doolittle planes, the Chinese leader had objected to the whole plan. If Doolittle carried out the raid and headed to China, the result would be a violent Japanese reaction.[3] The victims would be the Chinese. President Roosevelt was in no mood to listen, and Chiang Kai-shek was almost totally dependent on the Americans for the slender stream of supplies that were coming in, flown "over the Hump" of the Himalayas. He could not object further.

But how right the Generalissimo was in his estimate of the Japanese reaction. General Sugiyama, the man who had promised the emperor that the China incident would be over in a month and that the Americans and British would be defeated in six months, had also told the emperor that he need not worry, no bomber would ever break through Japanese air defenses. When the Doolittle planes *all* broke through and *all* escaped from Japan General Sugiyama was virtually beside himself. He threatened every single air defense commander with court-martial. He demanded from General Tojo that all the captured Doolittle fliers be executed as murderers of Japanese school children and bombers of hospitals. (As noted, three of them were.) Equally important, the Allied, and particularly American prisoners who were taken in the spring of 1942, and even afterwards, were mistreated because of the propaganda campaign that began with this incident. The Japanese media reminded Japan that Americans had mistreated Japanese in the Philippines, that thousands of Japanese had been imprisoned (and they said killed and tortured) in America. Magazines and newspapers ran pictures showing American children playing with toys made, they said, of the bones of Japanese.[4]

Militarily the Doolittle raid also brought a change that was immensely costly to the Chinese in terms of life.

When Imperial General Headquarters considered the Doolittle

attack, these facts were clear: The planes had taken off from an American carrier, but they had planned to land at China air bases. Therefore, the China air bases must be destroyed so that the Doolittle raid could not be repeated.

On April 21 the China Expeditionary Army was ordered to advance the schedule of its 1942 offensive from fall and carry it out immediately against the central China air bases. Operation Che-Kiang was launched, to clean out Chekiang and Kiangsi provinces. From Shanghai the Japanese 13th Division would move and from Hankow the 11th Division would join. They would push along the railroad from east and west, to capture thirteen airfields in three provinces. "Annihilate the enemy forces and destroy the air bases"—that was the order. The assault began immediately with a continual round of air raids. "Japanese troops attacked the coastal areas of China where many of the American fliers had landed," Chiang told the American government. "These Japanese troops slaughtered every man, woman, and child in those areas—let me repeat—these Japanese troops slaughtered every man, woman, and child in those areas."[5]

One of the American planes, piloted by Lieutenant Dean Hallmark, had landed in the sea off Chiachsi. Two members of the air crew had died in the sea, but three survived. When the Chinese heard about them, they went out to rescue them, but puppet troops in the area reported to the Japanese, and in the middle of the rescue trip the Chinese were surprised by two platoons of Japanese soldiers. The Americans were sent to the town of Macyang, but all the Chinese captured were stood up and machine-gunned. Chiachsi village was pillaged and burned and many inhabitants murdered.[6]

The Japanese Thirteenth Army, which consisted of thirty-four battalions from four divisions, launched an attack against the Chinese in the east Chekiang area, defeated the Chinese, and took Chinhua on May 29. The Chinese moved back along the Toyo River. Twenty-six battalions of the Eleventh Army launched another attack southeast of Nanchang. The idea was to develop a pincers that would move all the way west, and crush Chiang Kai-shek's armies.[7]

But the other object was to punish the Chinese, and punish the Japanese did. In three months they killed a quarter of a million soldiers and civilians.[8]

For example, they discovered a man who had given shelter to one of the American pilots near Ihwang in Kiangsi Province. Here is the statement of Bishop Paul Yu Pin of what happened:

They wrapped him in some blankets, poured the oil of the lamp on him and obliged his wife to set fire to the human torch. They threw hundreds of people to the bottom of their wells to drown there. They destroyed all the American missions in the vicinity (twenty-nine), they desecrated the graves of these missionaries, they destroyed the ancestor tablets in the various villages they went through.[9]

They searched twenty thousand square miles of territory, killing everyone they could find who had helped the Americans in any way. Chiang Kai-shek, who knew his Japanese, was sure of what would happen, and had tried to dissuade the Americans from the gesture. But the Americans apparently were so naive they had not believed. Much as President Roosevelt valued the psychological effect of his gesture, would he have carried it out had he been told it would cost a quarter of a million lives?

Equally important, the Doolittle raid triggered the Japanese into new attention to putting an end to the "China incident." The first phase had been the attack on the colonial bases of the Western powers. The second phase had been the establishment of a perimeter of empire that extended to the shores of Australia on the south, to the Soviet border on the north, and eastward into the Pacific as far as Wake Island. The third phase was to be expansion of the war in the east, followed by expansion in the south, and, concurrently, the settlement of the "China incident."

The Thirteenth Army sent most of three divisions along the route toward Yushan. The Chinese had moved back and escaped the trap, but the Japanese prepared to undertake Operation 5, which was planned to take Chungking, move south and either capture or dissipate the Chinese armies once and for all.[10]

In the midst of this campaign came two other incidents. One was the surrender of General Wainwright on Corregidor early in May, which put an end to the Imperial Japanese Army's worst embarrassment of the war. A handful of other Americans held out in the mountains for a month, but that was unimportant. The Philippines were now safely inside the Greater East Asia Co-Prosperity Sphere.

The second incident began with the planned drive to take Port Moresby and sew up Japanese control of Papua (British New Guinea).

In April, the Fifth Carrier Division of the Combined Fleet moved down to Rabaul, the center for Japanese army operations in the South Pacific. Vice Admiral Shigeyoshi Inouye brought the Fourth Fleet from Truk, and this included a light carrier. From this time until early May the carriers moved back and forth to Truk, bringing down to Rabaul Japanese naval fighter planes and bombers. Lakunai airfield was extended and a new airfield was built at West Foresdore. Another airfield lay at the foot of the mountains at Vanakanau. The Japanese were building a major air installation at Rabaul. It was an adage in the Japanese navy that an island was an unsinkable aircraft carrier, and thus the Japanese navy maintained several "air fleets." In this operation coming up, the army would be landed at Port Moresby, to complete the occupation of Papua. Already the two landings had been made at Lae and Salamaua.

The new operation would have one other aspect: the navy was to land forces at Tulagi in the southern Solomon Islands, to establish a seaplane base, and, across the sound there, construction troops would also be landed on virtually deserted Guadalcanal Island, where they would build an airfield. That airfield would give the Japanese naval air forces control of northern Australia's space, and from there long-distance planes could be sent down as far as Sydney. Thus any attempt of the United States to build up Australia as a base for operations against the Japanese would be frustrated at the start.[11]

On April 30 Japanese intelligence indicated that the Allies had about two hundred fighter planes in Australia, and that somewhere in these southern waters one American carrier task force was operating. That was Rear Admiral Frank Jack Fletcher's command, built around the carrier *Yorktown*. Its operational base was Noumea in New Caledonia, a French possession taken over by the Americans.

The first step in Japan's Operation MO was the landing of naval forces at Tulagi. They came on May 3 and found the sandy coral beach deserted. The Australian civil authorities had moved out two days earlier, aware that something was coming. The transports and a seaplane tender were accompanied by a light cruiser and two destroyers. But there was no need for all that protection; the landing was completely unopposed and by nightfall the first work had been done to complete the seaplane base. Six seaplane scout bombers rode at buoys in the harbor.[12]

Vice Admiral Shigeyoshi Inouye, commander of the Fourth Fleet, was in charge of the overall Operation MO. From the intelligence reports he expected he might have a fight on his hands before landing the troops at Port Moresby. His plan was to entice the American carrier task force into the Coral Sea, bounded roughly on the north by New Guinea and the Solomons, on the west by Australia, and on the east by New Caledonia. Pulling the Americans into the Coral Sea, Admiral Inouye would catch them in a vise between his carriers and the naval air base at Rabaul.

At Pearl Harbor, Admiral Chester Nimitz was willing to oblige. Sensing—from all the activity around Rabaul and the landings in March at Lae and Salamaua—that a new Japanese operation was afoot, Nimitz sent down to the South Pacific another carrier task force built around the *Lexington*. This force was under the command of Rear Admiral Aubrey Fitch. Also, Nimitz found the cruiser *Chicago* and the destroyer *Perkins* to add to this force. Australian Rear Admiral J. G. Crace was in command of a cruiser force, and these, too, were assigned to the augmented Allied navy. The whole was put under the control of Admiral Fletcher, and he was told that as of May 1 he was to be operating in the Coral Sea. Admiral Nimitz thought he would find a battle there.

The first indication of action came on the evening of May 3, when Australian scout planes reported on the Japanese landings at Tulagi. By dark Admiral Fletcher had the word and was preparing to attack Tulagi the next morning with a carrier strike force.

Forty American planes hit the Japanese seaplane base the next morning. Some of the invasion fleet had already moved out, but the Americans caught the transports, two small minesweepers, and a destroyer off Tulagi. They sank the minesweepers *Toshiu Maru* and *Tama Maru* and put a torpedo into the destroyer *Kikuzuki*. They shot up the anchored seaplanes and wrecked them. Three strike waves hit the island and at the end of the day the Japanese were gone from Tulagi. For the first time since the war began the Imperial forces had been frustrated in an attempt to seize territory.[13]

In the meantime, Admiral Inouye's Port Moresby invasion force was at sea, protected by three carriers and the land-based air force at Rabaul. They were ready to land, but Admiral Inouye now knew of the American threat and held them back in the vicinity of the Louisiade Islands, until that threat could be eliminated and the landings could proceed properly.

In the Coral Sea the Japanese and American naval forces were trying to search one another out, to make the first strike. Admiral Fletcher, in particular, felt that unless a carrier could make a surprise attack, the carrier was in mortal danger. In this case the first strike was made by Admiral Fitch's *Lexington* aircraft, which found the light carrier *Shoho* and attacked. *Yorktown* planes joined up and also attacked, and they sank the *Shoho*.

This was the first encounter of Japanese and American naval airmen, and there were lessons to be learned. The Japanese Mitsubishi Type Zero fighter was faster and more maneuverable than the American F4F Grumman fighter. The Zero was also unarmored and extremely vulnerable to fire. The armored F4F was much safer, particularly with that armor plate immediately behind the pilot; its self-sealing gas tanks were less apt to burn, and because of its greater weight it could outdive the Zero, though not turn with it. The American torpedo planes, the TBDs, were very slow and vulnerable. The Japanese pilots were very skillful and more experienced (after at least four years of war) than the Americans. One American bomber pilot, for example, was foolish enough to try to engage in a dogfight with a Zero. It lasted about two passes, and the American plane was shot down. Safety for bombers lay in tight formation.

The two-carrier Japanese force that was left sought the two-carrier American force, that night of May 7, but did not find it. On the morning of May 8 the enemies found one another. The Japanese had the advantage: their carriers were under scattered cloud cover; the Americans were out in the bright sun. In the battle that followed that day, the Americans lost the carrier *Lexington*, which was so badly damaged that she was sunk by American torpedoes. The Japanese did not lose any more carriers, although the *Shokaku* was damaged. But the Japanese still had the *Zuikaku* and all that land-based air force at Rabaul, the "unsinkable carrier." The Americans had only the *Yorktown,* which had been damaged by a bomb hit amidships, although not seriously enough to stop her. At the end of the day, Admiral Fletcher was trying to decide whether to launch a night attack against the Japanese or to retire. The issue was settled at Pearl Harbor by Admiral Nimitz who ordered Fletcher to return there, a decision that would mean a good deal to the Americans a few weeks later.

Admiral Inouye at Rabaul considered the Japanese position. He had lost a light carrier, and a big carrier had been so badly damaged that it had headed home for Japan. The Americans still had a carrier out there somewhere. Inouye was also worried about the increased American and Australian air activity of the past few days, which indicated to him that the Americans had what he had: a large land-based air force. (He was wrong.) On the basis of fact and supposition, the admiral postponed the Port Moresby invasion indefinitely and ordered the *Zuikaku* back to Truk, to take on more planes and fuel. The next operation, he announced, would be the capture of Ocean Island and Nauru Island.[14]

When Admiral Yamamoto learned that Admiral Inouye had left a damaged American carrier down there, while he had an undamaged carrier, he ordered Admiral Takagi, the carrier commander, back into the battle. But it was not quite that easy; the Japanese had lost most of their aircraft, either forced into the sea or crash-landed, and only nine were operational aboard the *Zuikaku*. So the pursuit was left off, and the enemies moved apart.[15]

On May 10, Admiral Inouye dispatched an invasion fleet toward Nauru and Ocean islands, a fleet augmented by several units from the now-abandoned Port Moresby invasion force. But the fleet flag-ship, *Okinoshima,* was sunk by the American submarine *S-42.* On the heels of that disaster came a report to Rabaul that two more American carriers had been sighted 450 miles east of Tulagi. (This might have been Admiral Fletcher limping eastward in the damaged *Yorktown.*) Admiral Inouye, who was not noted for his aggressive instincts, immediately canceled the Nauru invasion and ordered his force back to Truk.

As for the Battle of the Coral Sea, both sides claimed victory; the Americans, because they had destroyed the Japanese seaplane base, a light carrier, and damaged a large carrier; the Japanese, because they had sunk the carrier *Lexington.* In fact, it was a draw, with the immediate results favoring the Japanese because they still had eight carriers in the Pacific to the American three.

An Imperial Headquarters' naval spokesman played the Battle-ship March on Radio Tokyo and announced an absolute victory in this battle:[16]

The Japanese fleet succeeded in sinking the American *Saratoga* and the *Yorktown*-class carriers and a capital ship of the *California* class, British warship of the *Warspite* class. An Australian cruiser of the *Canberra* class was severely damaged, and another cruiser sunk. A 20,000-ton oil tanker was sunk, and a destroyer was sunk. Ninety-eight American planes were destroyed. Japanese losses were negligible . . .

That sort of reporting, with only a few grains of truth about the enemy (one carrier, one oiler, one destroyer) and virtually none about the Japanese losses, was the sort of information the navy was giving out these days. Admiral Yamamoto was nearly beside himself. He knew these chickens were going to come home to roost one day, for the navy could not indefinitely conceal its losses and exaggerate the enemy's.[17]

In Tokyo, a number of people were now beginning to take stock of the real situation that was developing in the Pacific. Those who knew much about the United States and its industrial potential became aware after the Tokyo raid that something also had happened to the American will to fight. Instead of collapsing in the face of disaster, as the most ardent jingoists had predicted, the American will had somehow strengthened. What the Japanese did not then realize, with the exception of a handful like Admiral Yamamoto, was the American relationship to the British, and the spirit of "fair play" that had passed across the Atlantic generations earlier. The Pearl Harbor attack, so natural for the Japanese, had been seen by the Americans as a dastardly stroke of infamy. Every story of rape, murder, torture, and maltreatment of civilians and prisoners of war brought a new fuel to the fire of American indignation. Oddly enough, the racially prejudiced Americans found themselves allied to the Chinese, who looked very much like the Japanese. For the average American soldier the equation was just too difficult to manage: they spent the war calling the Chinese "gooks" and "Chinks" but that was no more than the usual racism. When they referred to the "Goddam Japs" it was something else again, a real hatred piled atop the racism, an enmity fed by real wrongs, which would exist with some of these people forty years after the fact.

This strong American feeling about the Pacific War (much stronger at this time than any feeling about the war in Europe) lent those in Japan who knew their Americans a sense of urgency about bringing the war to an end *before* the American industrial production machinery could become fully operative.

Admiral Yamamoto's plan for the invasion of Midway Island

and the capture of the Aleutian bases which would prevent the United States from attacking Japan by air from that direction had been given only reluctant consent by the Imperial General Staff, but after the Doolittle Tokyo raid and the unsatisfactory end to the proposed capture of Port Moresby, the generals took another look and approved. They also made several changes in their plans. With the Port Moresby operation put into mothballs until after the Midway operation because of the shortage of carriers in the Japanese fleet for so many missions, Imperial General Headquarters on May 18 reshuffled the South Pacific forces. They were not going to give up the capture of New Guinea because the Port Moresby operation was now stalled. A different approach would be necessary.[18]

Lieutenant General Haruyoshi Hyukatake was assigned command of the Seventeenth Army. At the moment the army consisted of about four infantry regiments. It was to prepare at Rabaul to take New Caledonia, Fiji, Samoa, and to occupy Port Moresby. The new operations would begin in July, just as soon as the aircraft carriers could be brought back from the Midway-Aleutians operation. That move was using six of the remaining eight carriers. The other two were in or on their way to drydock for repairs, the *Shokaku* for repair of serious damage caused by the American bombers.

That carrier problem was one of the points that nagged Admiral Yamamoto. Other carriers were being built, but it would be a year or more before new carriers and converted carriers could begin coming off the ways. Knowing his American navy, the admiral now sensed that it would be nothing like a year before the Americans began bringing new ships into the battle for the Pacific. Nagumo's failure at Pearl Harbor loomed larger and larger. This time, Yamamoto's staff officers were saying, the job was going to be done right. In the navy ministry ardent young officers were working out plans for the occupation of the Hawaiian Islands shortly after the capture of Midway. It seemed only natural that the Japanese could expect the cooperation of their Hawaiian cousins, the Japanese who had gone to Hawaii to work in the cane fields, and their children. These people represented more than a third of all the population of Hawaii; theirs was the largest single racial group. With the defeat of the American fleet at Midway, which was a major part of the Yamamoto plan, and the capture of Hawaii, the Americans would be thrown back to San Diego and Seattle, which was a comfortable distance from the Western Pacific. The American fleet finally destroyed, as it should have been months earlier, overtures for a reasonable peace certainly ought to find welcome reaction in Washington.

That was the view of Admiral Yamamoto and other naval officers who understood the potential of the Americans. Unfortunately, the militarists in command of Imperial General Headquarters, and this included Admiral Shimada, General Tojo's toady navy minister, believed the propaganda they had created: that the Japanese were a master race, and that it was their destiny to rule Asia, the Pacific, and perhaps the world.[19]

This attitude was going to be a problem once the American fleet was dealt with at Midway, but Admiral Yamamoto could only hope that reason would prevail. His task here in the spring of 1942 was to make sure that Admiral Nagumo made no more mistakes. Thus, while Nagumo's carrier striking force would be the key unit assigned to draw the Americans into the battle of Midway and destroy the American fleet as the Aleutians unit was moving to land the army troops on Kiska and Attu islands, Admiral Yamamoto was not leaving the issue to chance. This time the Combined Fleet's flagship would not remain behind at Hashirajima, dependent on wireless communications to influence the course of the battle. This time Admiral Yamamoto would be in personal command of the Combined Fleet as it went out to destroy the Americans.

盃つれば かくある世の習い

27. "Every tide has its ebb"

*T*heoretically, the plans for all Japanese naval operations came out of the office of Admiral Osani Nagano, the chief of the Naval General Staff. Admiral Nagano, however, was not the aggressive sort of officer who would order his subordinates to come up with plans. He allowed the staff to make plans and then exercised his veto power. The actual Naval General Staff plans came out of the office of Rear Admiral Shigeru Fukudome, chief of the Operations Section.

With the surprisingly easy attainment of the aims of the initial southern movement, months ahead of schedule, Admiral Fukudome's plans officers began looking ahead. Their thought was that Australia would have to be the point of departure for any American and British moves to counter the Japanese conquest of the East Indies, the Philippines, and Malaya. Thus, in January 1942, the naval planners in Tokyo turned their eyes south. At first they had hoped to secure army participation in an invasion of Australia. The army refused. Navy men said the refusal was because Tojo was still hoping that the Germans would run up a string of victories in the spring and summer of 1942, and he could then safely attack Soviet Russia. The problem was that the admirals did not really know what was on the minds of the generals. The two services had always remained separate, and Tojo's bullying personality did not make for confidence on the part of the naval officers.

After the army's refusal to consider an attack on Australia, the Naval General Staff planners considered the means by which they could cut Australia off from the United States. The naval planners then suggested the army and navy cooperate to control Papua, the Solomon Islands, the New Caledonia-Fiji area, and Samoa. The capture of these territories would give the Japanese a ring of air bases that could cover all of Australia and interdict American war materials.

The first step in this plan had been the invasion of the villages Lae and Salamaua on March 8, accomplished by the army. The Naval General Staff and the army agreed on the next move of their new southern drive: the capture of Port Moresby by the army's South Seas Detachment, at the same time that the navy captured Tulagi. Those operations would give the Japanese a big air base at Port Moresby and a seaplane base in the southern Solomons, as noted. The arrival of General Douglas MacArthur in Australia late in March and his almost immediate appointment as commander of Australian and American forces indicated to the Naval General Staff just how right their plans had been. The army now agreed to the extension of the plan to New Caledonia and all the rest of the fringe islands.[1]

Meanwhile, at the Combined Fleet anchorage at Hashirajima, a plan for the capture of Midway Island in the Pacific was drawn up by Admiral Yamamoto's Combined Fleet staff officers. They, too, had been considering new possibilities since January. Two other offensive operations had been laid aside for the moment, the invasion of Hawaii and the capture of Ceylon. The Hawaii invasion was abandoned because it was not believed surprise could again be attained and because the Americans were known to have air bases on several of the islands. The Japanese airmen feared that they could not achieve air superiority. The Ceylon invasion was dropped at this time because the army would not participate, and Ceylon was too large an island to be taken by the navy alone.[2]

Elements of the Hawaii plan were retained in the Midway plan, however. Midway Island, 1130 miles from Hawaii, would be valuable to the Japanese as an advance air base for scouting. There was also the thought that Midway would become a staging base for a future invasion of Hawaii. Most important to Admiral Yamamoto was the calculation by his staff that by attacking Midway the Japanese would force the Americans to oppose them with their Pacific fleet, which was greatly inferior to the Japanese Combined Fleet. The American fleet would be destroyed, which would give Japan another year or so to consolidate its victories, and perhaps to capture Hawaii and Australia. At the end of March 1942, Admiral Yamamoto approved the Midway operation plan.[3]

Despite the fact that the new Combined Fleet flagship *Yamato* was connected to Tokyo by telephone lines that hooked up to its buoy at Hashirajima, Yamamoto and the Tokyo admirals were not in close communication. Yamamoto had bulled his way against the Navy General Staff in the 1941 Hawaii operation. The Pearl Harbor attack had been apparently so successful that the Naval General Staff was not eager to oppose Yamamoto's ideas.

For that reason, when Admiral Yamamoto's plan for an Eastern Pacific operation was sent on to Tokyo for the necessary Naval General Staff approval, its arrival created a stir. Admiral Fukudome's officers argued that their plan was already in the works and should be carried out before anything else was begun. They raised all sorts of difficulties about logistics and timing.[4] Even on the question of drawing out the American fleet, the general staff officers held that it was more probable that operations against New Caledonia, Fiji, and Samoa, where the Americans already had bases, would bring the U.S. fleet forth more quickly. The general staff tried to counter every Combined Fleet argument, even the claim that the capture of Midway and the threat to Hawaii would hurt American morale. The capture of the southern areas would hurt American morale worse, they said.

The Combined Fleet men then played their hole card, Admiral Yamamoto's prime argument:

In the final analysis, the success or failure of our entire strategy in the Pacific will be determined by whether or not we succeed in destroying the United States fleet, more particularly its carrier task forces. . . . We believe that by launching the proposed operations against Midway, we can succeed in drawing out the enemy's carrier strength and destroying it in decisive battle.[5]

The argument continued within Imperial General Headquarters. Here, the Combined Fleet plan got unexpected support from the army, because the plan called for very little use of army forces. The Naval General Staff, defeated on the plan, then tried to postpone the execution for a month on the basis of shortage of supplies. But the Combined Fleet insisted that even a month's delay could allow the Americans to build up their forces in the Pacific and wreck the operation. The argument was still going on April 18, when the Doolittle B-25s came storming in over Japan and out again without suffering a single loss. That attack settled the matter. The Midway strike, Operation MI, was on.

If the Japanese had the advantage of surprise at the beginning of the Pacific War and the initiative in the first six months, the Americans had a weapon which ultimately proved more valuable: they had broken one of the major Japanese naval codes to the degree that radio intelligence experts had a good chance of figuring out Japanese plans and operations. In the Midway operation the American possession of information about the Japanese plan certainly meant the difference between a chance of victory and defeat. For example, in March, the Japanese had reconnoitered Pearl Harbor again, using an enormous new Kawanishi flying boat with four engines, which had a range of four thousand miles. One Kawanishi flying boat came to Pearl Harbor from Wotje Atoll by way of French Frigate Shoals, where it put down and refueled from a submarine. It then flew on to Pearl Harbor, made the reconnaissance and dropped some bombs, then headed back to Wotje. On March 10 the Japanese sent a Kawanishi to Midway, but the Americans intercepted and decoded the message, and shot it down. The affair gave Admiral Nimitz an indication that the Japanese were interested in Midway.

In April, a marked increase in radio traffic between various units of the Combined Fleet indicated to the Americans that some sort of naval action was being planned. What, when, and where were not readily ascertainable then. The geographical designation AF began to appear in Japanese naval messages. So did the names Attu, Kiska, and Dutch Harbor. They appeared so frequently that in May Admiral Nimitz set up a special force of five cruisers and ten destroyers to defend the Aleutian Islands.

The AF designation puzzled the Americans more because the Pacific was a very wide ocean. On May 20 U.S. naval radio intelligence intercepted Admiral Yamamoto's order of battle message for an attack on AF. The Americans still did not know where AF was, except that it was not the Aleutians, for the Aleutians and AF were mentioned in the same message. Back in Washington the American naval authorities were inclined to believe that AF meant Hawaii. Admiral Nimitz thought it was going to be Midway, but he had to know because his forces were so much smaller than the Japanese that every ship and every plane counted.

The Americans then had a stroke of luck. Lieutenant Commander W. J. Holmes, Lieutenant Joseph Finnegan, and Commander Richard Rochefort were sitting in the intelligence office, talking about AF, Midway, and the difficulty Nimitz was having in deciding where to place his defenses.

Holmes had been an engineering professor at the University of Hawaii before the war, and he knew a good deal about Midway Island, including the fact that it often had fresh water problems, since all its water had to come from rain or distillation. He mentioned this. Finnegan said if the Japanese discovered that Midway was short of fresh water, they would report it to Tokyo. An idea was born: The word was given secretly (by underwater cable) to Midway to send a plain language radio message that the distilling plant had broken down. Pearl Harbor replied in a plain language message that water would be sent. Sure enough, in the Japanese radio traffic a few hours later came a message reporting that AF's distilling plant had broken down. Admiral Nimitz had already staked his future on the fact that the Japanese target would be Midway, but this was welcome confirmation. The Americans had made optimum use of their one great advantage in this coming confrontation.[6]

Vice Admiral Nobutake Kondo named another American advantage, when he was informed of his part as commander of the Japanese Second Fleet. He objected, saying that the Japanese would have to land their forces at Midway without the support of land-based aircraft and carriers as well. Admiral Yamamoto disagreed. Besides, he said, it was all settled and there was no point in discussing it. There was no need to worry, he said, as long as the Japanese retained the element of surprise.[7]

Kondo then spoke to Vice Admiral Matome Ugaki, Yamamoto's chief of staff, and asked him flatly how prepared were they to *supply* Midway after the capture; it would be sticking out into the Eastern Pacific like a thumb. Ugaki's reply was far from satisfactory to Admiral Kondo, but there was nothing to be done; Admiral Yamamoto was going to have his way.[8]

The Midway plan encompassed only the occupation of Midway and the Aleutian Islands. But Admiral Yamamoto's plans were far more grandiose. Midway would be taken in June. Afterwards the battleships of the Combined Fleet would return to Japan, but the cruisers and carriers and destroyers would go to Truk, to prepare for the July capture of New Caledonia and the Fiji Islands. Admiral Nagumo's carrier striking force, no longer inhibited by the sunk

American fleet, would strike Sydney, Melbourne, and other south-east coast Australian cities. Then the naval forces would reassemble at Truk and prepare for the invasion of Johnston Island and the Hawaiian Islands in August.[9]

To show how easy it was going to be, Combined Fleet set up a series of war games. Admiral Ugaki then interfered with the judges' decisions about the outcome of attacks, thus making it possible for the Combined Fleet to carry all its objectives without difficulty.[10]

After that, the Combined Fleet staff was impossible to move. Admiral Kondo said they needed time to get ready, and he was refused. Admiral Nagumo's staff said the carrier flagship *Akagi*'s radio setup was inadequate for command purposes. They suggested that the Yamamoto flagship *Yamato* operate independently of the battleship fleet and relay all important messages to the Nagumo striking force. Either that or Admiral Yamamoto should operate with the Nagumo carriers, taking command of the whole operation. All of these recommendations were overridden without real consideration.[11]

On the last night of the war games, Admiral Yamamoto sent a message to all Combined Fleet forces telling them that they were going into battle with "an invincible" position. "This position, however, cannot be maintained if we go on the defensive. To secure it we must keep striking at the enemy's weak points one after another."[12]

On the eve of sailing into battle, the Japanese were still not quite sure how strong the Americans were. They did know that with the six carriers they were taking into operation they had by far a stronger carrier force than anything the Americans could muster. Their battleship force, too, was far superior in case it came to surface action. All they had to do was be aggressive enough to take advantage of their numbers.

Rear Admiral Kakuji Kakuta's Second Carrier Striking Force sailed first, bound for the Aleutians. Admiral Yamamoto's main force sailed last.

On May 30 the weather began to turn rough, and the main force cut its speed to fourteen knots. Yamamoto had one bad break: he had intended to use Kawanishi flying boats operating out of French Frigate Shoals to keep an eye on Hawaii and let him know about the movement of ships in and out of Pearl Harbor. But when the

Kawanishis got to French Frigate Shoals, they found that Nimitz had outsmarted them. The shoals were no longer empty. Nimitz had sent a pair of American seaplane tenders with several seaplanes up there. Yamamoto would have to operate without his "eyes."

On June 1 the weather was still forbidding. The light carrier *Hosho* sent out search planes to find the oilers so the main force could fuel. But the weather was too bad, and the main force had to break radio silence to all the oilers. For the next two days fueling was a problem in the heavy weather.

On June 2 submarine *I-168* reported the good news that no ships had been seen around Midway except a picket ship south of Sand Island. The submarine did report air patrols flying to the southwest and much construction activity on Midway. Increased radio activity between Pearl Harbor and Midway indicated that the approach of the Japanese might have been discovered by that transmission calling up the oilers. This was the big worry of Admiral Nagumo, who was not very confident of this operation. Yamamoto did not inform him of his own concerns, but let it be still believed that there was no chance they had lost the element of surprise.[13]

Indeed they had.

On May 28 the Americans sailed from Pearl Harbor with the carriers *Enterprise, Hornet,* and *Yorktown,* six cruisers, and ten destroyers. On June 2 they met northeast of Midway. By this time, through code breaking, the Americans knew that Admiral Nagumo was bringing four carriers from the northwest, when they would launch their first attack on Midway, and the strength of Midway occupation force.

On June 3 Admiral Yamamoto learned from Tokyo that an American carrier force had been sighted at sea near Midway. He did not pass that information to Admiral Nagumo because he did not want to break radio silence. He hoped that Nagumo's flagship, the *Akagi*, had also picked up the message. But the *Akagi*'s radio system was not powerful enough and so Nagumo knew nothing of the position of the Americans and had to assume that they were still at Pearl Harbor.

On June 3 the Japanese fleet was still operating in heavy fog. Back in Tokyo naval headquarters sent a reassuring message indicating that American fleet forces were still operating in the Solomons area—and this seemed to indicate carriers. Admiral Nagumo did not get this message, either, but Yamamoto did, and he was relieved.

Since the Americans could not be in two places at once, it appeared that he still had the element of surprise.

At Dutch Harbor in the Aleutian area, sunrise came at 2:58 on the morning of June 3. The Japanese fliers were launched from the carriers *Junyo* and *Ryujo* to attack. They hit the radio station tower and oil tanks and attacked a few flying boats in the harbor. There really was not much to find, except five destroyers, which the pilots saw at anchor on the north coast of Unalaska Island on their way back to the carrier. When Admiral Kakuji Kakuta learned of the presence of the American ships he ordered an attack. But the weather closed in, and American planes attacked the Japanese bombers, shooting down several of them. The day ended without any further successes for the Japanese. They now knew that the Americans had several bases nearby, but they did not know where the bases were.

From the standpoint of the Japanese plan, the day's work was a complete success. The idea had been to attack Dutch Harbor and thus fool the Americans into believing this was the major Japanese thrust. But, of course, what no one on the Japanese side knew was that the Americans were well aware through intelligence that the main attack was going to be on Midway.

In fact, the Americans were standing north of Midway, searching for the Japanese. On June 3 (Western time) the rain stopped and the skies grew a little clearer in the Midway area. At nine o'clock that morning an American PBY search plane discovered the Japanese assault transports about 600 miles west of Midway. That afternoon the transports were attacked by a flight of B-17s which bombed but secured no hits.

On the morning of June 4, the transport column was hit by the enemy torpedo bombers, and one American plane put a torpedo into the tanker *Akebono Maru*. It was only damaged, not sunk.

On the afternoon of June 3 the Nagumo force had moved toward Midway, traveling southeast at twenty-four knots. The ships were in the Japanese ring defense, four carriers in the middle, surrounded by two battleships, three cruisers, and a dozen destroyers. Except for a false start or two, there was no excitement. At 2:30 on the morning of June 3 someone aboard the flagship *Akagi* claimed to have seen a light of a plane overhead. But it could not be found. Fifteen minutes later the carriers began to launch planes for the first attack on Midway.[14]

Admiral Nagumo felt that everything was just fine. He expected the American fleet to come out to engage the Japanese, but felt that the enemy had not yet detected the Japanese force. There was no evidence of an enemy carrier in the vicinity, so he should have plenty of time to attack Midway, destroy the land-based planes there, and support the amphibious landing of the troops. Once that was completed, he could head out, find the Americans coming in from Hawaii, and destroy the American fleet. It was really going to be simple, so simple, that the admiral was not very careful about ordering general search operations just in case some American forces were hiding near. Two of the cruisers launched seaplanes to help with the search. They had trouble with catapult and engines, and the searches were late. One plane from the cruiser *Chikuma* developed a sputtering engine about halfway out and had to turn back to its ship. If it had gone on into its search area, it would have discovered the American carrier force. As it was, no one discovered the Americans. Also no one told Admiral Nagumo that the American land-based aircraft had already attacked the transport force. Nagumo steamed blissfully on, still believing that the enemy was going to be surprised.

The carrier *Akagi* launched its planes, first Zero fighters, then dive bombers carrying 250-kilogram bombs. In fifteen minutes the four carriers, *Soryu, Hiryu, Kaga,* and *Akagi* launched 108 planes. They formed up and headed off to the southeast, while on the carriers the second strike force was called up. This wave also consisted of 108 planes, dive bombers, torpedo bombers, and fighters. That left eighteen fighters on the four carriers to provide combat air patrol.[15]

When the first strike was about 150 miles from Midway, a PBY saw them and reported, then trailed them unseen. The PBY dropped a flare, and American fighters attacked. But the Japanese fighters drove them off, without the loss of a single bomber. The bombers attacked, but found no planes on the fields. The Americans had known they were coming and all planes were in the air. The Japanese bombers burned hangars, fuel tanks, and buildings, but did not destroy any aircraft. That had been the purpose of the mission. The strike leader radioed back to the carrier that it had failed and a second strike was needed.

At 5:40 that morning an American patrol bomber found the Japanese carriers. A number of medium bombers attacked, but were shot down or driven off by the Zero fighters of the air patrol. Several torpedo bombers managed to launch their torpedoes at the carriers before being shot down, but the carriers evaded all torpedoes. Of ten American bombers, only three returned to base.

Admiral Nagumo had still not been told of the existence of an American carrier force nearby. Believing that he faced only land-based air defenses, he ordered the second strike, loaded with torpedoes to fight a fleet, to unload and load up with bombs to complete the destruction of the Midway air facilities.[16]

The planes were taken below to the hangar deck and the armament changed from torpedoes to bombs. While the armorers were making the changes, a group of fourteen B-17s came over to bomb the carriers. They bombed, but they scored no hits with fifty-six tons of bombs. But neither did the fleet's antiaircraft knock down any bombers, and the Zero fighters wisely left the "flying fortresses" alone.

After this attack came another, by sixteen American dive bombers. But they did not dive bomb, they came in to glide bomb (because the American commander knew his pilots were inexperienced). They hit nothing and only half the planes survived to get back to base.

By this time the Japanese had become more than a little contemptuous of the ability of the Americans. For months Tokyo's propagandists had been telling the Japanese people that the Europeans and Americans were cowardly and soft—certainly no match for the Imperial forces and the Imperial spirit of *bushido*. On this day in mid-Pacific the men of the Japanese carriers were finding the Americans brave enough, but not skillful. Brave enough—the Japanese had seen several of the American pilots die trying to score hits—but they scored no hits. The inherent Japanese feelings of superiority were enhanced, and the men aboard the carriers became a little less worried about counterattack than they had been before.

At 8:30 in the morning the first attack wave returned from Midway, and the carriers moved to recover their planes.

On the admiral's bridge of the carrier *Akagi,* Admiral Nagumo was fretting over a report received before 8:00 A.M. from a search plane sent out to the east by the cruiser *Tone.* The pilot had sent a snapshot report on sighting ten ships at the end of the outer leg of his search. They were about two hundred miles away, northeast of Midway atoll.[17]

But what sort of ships were they? If there were no carriers, the sighting meant opportunity. If there were carriers, the sighting meant danger. Nagumo ordered suspension of the rearming of the planes for another strike on Midway, and he demanded more information. Twenty minutes before the returning planes began to arrive he had it: five cruisers and five destroyers. On the admiral's bridge the admiral's staff relaxed. No carriers.

But ten minutes later the tension began again. Another report said the enemy force was accompanied by what seemed to be a carrier. What seemed to be? Another report in another few minutes mentioned more ships, apparently cruisers. Admiral Nagumo decided he must turn his attention to the ships in case there was a carrier out there. The only planes ready for action were thirty-six dive bombers aboard the *Hiryu* and *Soryu*. The torpedo bombers on the decks of the *Akagi* and *Kaga* were now armed with 800-kilogram bombs, which could be effective against ships as well as land installations. The problem was that the torpedo bombers had to drop horizontally, which meant maintaining course and speed over the target, and without fighter protection they were sitting ducks. All available fighters were in the air, launched to fight the American land-based attackers. If the bombers went out alone their losses might be very heavy.

As the first strike moved in, the admiral was forced to a decision. The planes on the decks either had to be flown off or moved below to accommodate the returning aircraft. Rear Admiral Yamaguchi just then sent a message asking permission to launch his planes. But Admiral Nagumo was a cautious man who did not like taking risks. He decided to recover the first strike before doing anything else, and so the planes on the decks of the four carriers were taken down in the elevator and the decks were cleared for the returning aircraft.[18]

The planehandlers and armorers on the hangar deck were in an enormous hurry. Instead of stowing the bombs back in the magazines as regulations provided, they piled them on the deck. Less than half an hour passed, all the bombers were down, and all the first strike aircraft were recovered. Admiral Nagumo now knew he faced at least one carrier, and he headed the force north to go after it. But he would not launch the planes now, there was plenty of time. He would reorganize his force and then attack.

Down below, on the carriers, the armorers again worked at feverish speed, loading torpedoes and bombs for attacks against ships. The strike was scheduled to take off at 10:30.

The Americans had also sighted the Japanese force, and, without concern for fighter protection, had launched 131 dive bombers and torpedo bombers. They came in on the Japanese force around 9:30. First to arrive were fifteen torpedo bombers from the *Hornet*. They were ordered to attack, and they did attack. In the air around the Japanese defense circle were fifty Zeros. One by one they zoomed in on the slow torpedo planes, holding their course and speed to attack, and the Zeros shot down all fifteen torpedo bombers.

Next came the torpedo bombers of the *Yorktown* and the *Enterprise,* and these, too, were decimated by the Zeros. Finally, seven planes managed to launch their torpedoes, but not one hit was made. Some forty American torpedo planes had attacked. All but a few of those planes and pilots were lost, and the Japanese force was untouched.

By this time some Japanese fighters were out of ammunition. They landed, rearmed, and took off again. The others kept working their way down toward the water, attacking the torpedo planes. At 10:20 Admiral Nagumo gave the order to launch the strike against the Americans. Four minutes later, as the ship was still turning to launch position, American dive bombers attacked. The Japanese fighters were no help at all now, for they were down low, drawn by the torpedo attackers. The dive bombers came in and bombed. Admiral Nagumo was caught with decks full of planes, and no fighter cover.

The *Akagi* took one bomb on the flight deck amidships, and one on the port side aft. The first bomb set off the bombs in the hangar deck, and they began to blow up. The second bomb set fire to the planes loaded with torpedoes, and they began exploding. In a few minutes the fires were so bad that Admiral Nagumo could escape to another ship only by going down a rope from bridge to deck, and then over to be picked up by a cruiser's boat.

The story was almost the same on the carrier *Kaga*.[19] She was hit by three bombs and in a few minutes, that ship, too, was floating wreckage.

In fifteen minutes that morning, the Japanese advantage, four carriers to the enemy's three, had been reduced to one to three. The only Japanese carrier left was Admiral Yamaguchi's *Hiryu*. The admiral got his air strike away at 10:40, eighteen dive bombers and six Zeros. Eight bombers got through to attack the *Yorktown* and she was hit. However, in two hours the fires were put out and she was under way again.

The *Hiryu* launched another strike at noon and put two more bombs into the *Yorktown*. She was abandoned that day. The ratio was now one Japanese carrier to two enemy carriers. That was changed late in the afternoon, when *Hiryu* was attacked again by dive bombers, which scored four hits. She was abandoned in the middle of the night. Admiral Yamaguchi and Captain Kaku went down with their ship, which was torpedoed by a Japanese destroyer.[20]

The ratio was now zero Japanese carriers to two American. Aboard the cruiser *Nagara*, Admiral Nagumo was urged by staff officers to make a night surface attack on the enemy with his two fast battleships, two heavy cruisers, and one light cruiser, and twelve destroyers. He so ordered, but then learned that the Americans were drawing out of surface ship battle range. Admiral Yamamoto wanted to fight on. He planned for a surface battle, and called for Admiral Kakuta to come down from the Aleutians with the carriers *Ryujo* and *Junyo*. But an exchange of messages indicated that it would be June 8 before Kakuta could arrive. And then Admiral Nagumo chimed in to announce that the Americans had five carriers, six heavy cruisers, and fifteen destroyers, and that he was retiring to the northwest.

There was no way that Admiral Yamamoto could carry the fight to the enemy. On June 6 the retreat began, an ignominious retreat, pursued by the American carriers, which bombed the cruisers *Mikuma* and *Mogami*. The *Mikuma* was sunk and the *Mogami* was hit six times. As the force neared Wake Island, Admiral Yamamoto thought he might try again. The light carriers *Hosho* and *Zuiho* and the cruisers and battleships carried about a hundred planes. If he could lure the American carriers near Wake Island's air base, another fifty bombers could attack. But on June 7 the enemy had disappeared, and there was no prospect for a fight. Admiral Yamamoto turned toward Japan, having suffered the first defeat in Japan's naval history.

糠に 釘

28. "Paper spikes"

D espite the knowledge in the upper echelons of the Combined
Fleet and at naval headquarters that Japan had suffered a
disastrous defeat at Midway, no indication of the truth was permitted
outside the fleet.

As the Japanese steamed home, Radio Tokyo was blaring out
its braggartry about the "great victory" won by the Imperial forces
in this battle. They had sunk two American carriers, one destroyer,
and damaged a cruiser. (The fact was they had sunk one aircraft
carrier and one destroyer.) They had shot down 179 American planes.
(Actually the Americans had lost 147 planes, but not nearly that
many pilots. Many pilots were rescued and the planes included those
lost with the carrier *Yorktown* when she sank.)[1]

Japanese losses, on the other hand, said Radio Tokyo, had been
one carrier sunk and one carrier damaged. The fact was quite different. Japan had lost four carriers and one cruiser, with one cruiser
badly damaged, two destroyers damaged, and one oiler, one destroyer, one battleship slightly damaged.

Worse, Japan had lost 322 planes and a large number of highly
skilled aircrews. Some pilots and crewmen had gone down with their
planes. Others had been lost in the sinking of the carriers.[2]

So it was a dispirited Combined Fleet staff that came ashore at
Japan. As for the Combined Fleet, drastic action had to be taken to
prevent the truth from becoming common knowledge in Japan. The
survivors of the *Akagi, Kaga, Soryu, Hiryu,* and *Mikuma* had to be

Twenty-five days after the Americans landed on Saipan, all Japanese resistance ended. Here American marines try to soothe a Japanese child by offering him a shiny C-ration tin. In the background are more of the few civilians who were captured. Most of the 20,000 civilians chose to commit suicide by casting themselves off the high cliffs at the northern point of the island, in the belief that they would be enslaved by the Americans.

(National Archives 208-N-30075.)

A rocket-firing landing craft heads in to Morotai Beach. This was part of the landing of September 14, 1944, of U.S. forces in the Molucca Islands, preparing for the attack on the Philippines.

(National Archives 208-N-34194.)

On October 18, 1944, the navy assault on Leyte Island in the Philippines began. A few days later American troops were on the ground. These men of the First Cavalry Division cross a tank trap on their move inland.

(National Archives 208-N-34914.)

One of the first of the army's helicopters lands in a town on Leyte. Towards the end of World War II, helicopters came into use, mostly for evacuation of wounded and for courier service to the front lines.

(National Archives 208-N-38541.)

Iwo Jima. March 1945. This rocky island was needed by the Allies as a base for fighter planes to protect the B-29s on their long run to fire-bomb Tokyo. Here officers of the Fifth Marine Division direct operations from a sandbagged command post. With the field telephone is Major General Keller E. Rockey, Fifth Division Commander.

(National Archives 208-N-38601.)

March 1945. One of Tokyo's industrial districts after firebombing by American B-29s. The firebombing of Japanese cities killed more than 500,000 Japanese civilians and was regarded by the Japanese as the principal American atrocity of the war.

(National Archives 80-G-490424.)

The high command of the American assault on Iwo Jima. Vice Admiral Richmond Kelly Turner, commander of the amphibious forces, Marine Major General Harry Schmidt, and Marine Lieutenant General Holland M. Smith. The smiles are illusory. "Howling Mad" Smith's star had fallen and his command of the Iwo Jima operation was largely illusory. Following the assault on Saipan, in which army forces had not at first performed very well, Smith's tough actions ultimately cost him command of the ground forces.

(National Archives 208-N-39097.)

Here's what General Rockey's Fifth Marines faced: Two army soldiers and a marine advance into a cave on Iwo Jima. Resistance ended March 15, theoretically, but weeks later, pockets of Japanese troops were still holding out. Very few of them surrendered.

(National Archives 208-N-41275.)

Here's what it was all about. A B-29 flies over Mt. Suribachi, famous for the "flag-raising" photograph taken by Associated Press photographer Joe Rosenthal. B-29s from the Marianas, damaged in raids on Japan, now had a halfway base for safety, as well as fighter cover from Iwo Jima airfields.

(National Archives 208-N-41885.)

The Americans landed on Okinawa on March 31, 1945. An American marine charges forward through Japanese machine gun fire. Capture of Okinawa gave Americans an air base close enough for tactical operations against Japan. From here they expected to support the landings on Kyushu and Honshu in the coming months.

(National Archives 208-N-41607.)

Smoke pours from the flight deck of HMS *Formidable* of the British
Pacific Fleet after she was hit by a kamikaze suicide plane in operations off Okinawa. The toll of kamikazes was very high and a constant concern to the Allied naval command.

(Imperial War Museum.)

The Japanese were prepared to fight to the last man,
woman, and child. Above, Japanese women learn to use gas
masks to protect them from the poisonous gas they expected the Allies to spray over Japan. Center, Japanese
women learn sharpshooting so they can harass Allied troops
from the mountains. Below, Japanese schoolgirls learn to
use rifles. But for the most, women, children, and the old, it
would be a satchel charge or a grenade, with instructions to
hurl themselves under a vehicle and blow it up.

(Japanese Defense Agency.)

August 1945. Hiroshima, or what was left of it, after the atomic
bomb was dropped on August 6, 1945. An estimated 79,000 people
were killed or died here. But the Japanese militarists, who knew
that half a million civilians had died in the B-29 raids on Japanese
cities, said of the A-bomb: "We can live with it," and prepared to
go on fighting.

(National Archives 80-G-373269.)

On August 15, the war ended
when Emperor Hirohito defied
the militarists, who had been in
control of the Japanese government, and insisted on the surrender because he feared that the
enemy would destroy all the
people of Japan. It took a long
time for the emperor of Japan's
loyal soldiers to get the word
that the war had ended. Here
balloons bear a streamer announcing war's end in Japanese
to Japanese troops holding out in
the Sierra Madre Mountains of
northern Luzon. The message
said simply "Great Emperor Accepts Peace." The troops in the
field would never have believed
that their government had violated all the rules of *bushido* and
surrendered. They would learn
the stunning details later.

(UPI/Bettmann Newsphotos.)

dealt with. Had it been the American navy they all would have been sent home on leave and then assigned to new construction, as replacements, or as instructors in various schools. But the Japanese system and the Japanese arrogance (which they came to call the "Victory Disease") prevented such pragmatic approach. It was deemed vital by the naval authorities that the news of the dreadful defeat be concealed. Therefore, all the enlisted men of the sunken carriers were sent to naval bases, confined to the bases, and shipped out as quickly as possible to the far reaches of empire, such as Truk. So were many of the junior officers, and the others were sworn to secrecy.

By American standards this use of trained manpower would have seemed a great waste, but the Japanese had no sense of urgency yet about their carrier situation. They did not even amplify their pilot training program, unchanged since the 1930s, to make up for the hundreds of trained airmen lost at Midway.

The Japanese navy then was working on much construction and even more after Midway. But as of that point in the war, the Japanese carrier situation was still superior to the American situation in the Pacific. The Japanese had no particular sense of urgency.

The Americans had the fleet carriers *Hornet, Wasp, Enterprise*, and *Saratoga* in the Pacific. That was all; the Japanese still very definitely had the edge. The fleet carrier *Shokaku* was under repairs in Japan. Her damage suffered in the Battle of the Coral Sea was approximately the same as that suffered by the American carrier *Yorktown* in that battle. The Americans repaired their ship in three days, in time for it to go to Midway. The Japanese were months at the job.

Zuikaku, another fleet carrier, had not been able to participate in the Midway battle because of a shortage of trained carrier pilots. The Japanese had never thought of bringing combat veterans back to teach, and so they suffered also from a shortage of instructors.

The Japanese also had available at the moment the light carriers *Ryujo, Hiyo, Zuiho, Hosho*, and *Junyo*. A giant carrier, the *Taiho*, would be in service in a year. A supercarrier, the *Shinano*, was under construction, too. The Japanese naval leaders had access to a great deal of information about American naval construction through the newspapers, which reported the acts of Congress in authorizing building and the general tenor of construction. This information was picked up by Domei, the Japanese news agency, from such spots as Buenos

Aires and Lisbon, and duly reported in the Japanese press.[3] But the militarists in Japan had so conditioned themselves to believe in Japanese superiority and Western inferiority that they did not believe the reports, even in the summer of 1942. For example: Commander Yuzuru Sanematsu had been stationed in Washington at the time of the Pearl Harbor attack, and he was repatriated that summer in the exchange of diplomats. He was assigned to the Naval General Staff and appointed to give lectures on American military affairs to the Navy Staff College. He told his listeners of the enormous productive capacity of the Americans, of the shipbuilding he had seen in progress even before the war, and of what he had learned through the media as an internee of the expanded naval building program in America. His students did not believe him, and privately they called his "praise of America" nonsense and accused him of being smitten by love for the materialism of the West. That same attitude was shown by Minister Shimada and Admiral Nagano.

So the Japanese laughed while the Americans built carriers. They were told the truth, but remained unaware of the new American emphasis on carrier building that had caused the U.S. Navy to convert nine cruiser hulls to become light carriers and to undertake a desperate program of building fleet carriers and auxiliary carriers. In June, shipbuilder Henry Kaiser signed a contract with the U.S. government to build escort carriers and would soon be building them in a matter of weeks, and finally in days.

After Midway, however, the Japanese navy had to do its best to build more carriers. Yamamoto and a few others were aware of the serious need and the limitations of Japanese shipbuilding. Even the supreme jingoists, Navy Secretary Shimada and Naval General Staff Chief Nagano could see the need at least to replace the four sunken carriers. Conversion of existing hulls, never very satisfactory in terms of producing an efficient carrier, had to be most of the answer to the carrier problem. Several seaplane carriers were sent to the yards for conversion to aircraft carriers. Conversion of two battleships to short-deck carriers, retaining some of the big guns, was also begun. The trouble was ahead, however, for as Admiral Yamamoto had observed, the danger to Japan was that America would be able to bring its enormous industrial skill and resources to play before a "decisive battle" could be fought that would destroy the American fleet.

The danger grew greater each day. The Naval General Staff was so upset by the setback at Midway that a pall of secrecy was put over the affair. Not even Prime Minister Tojo was told what had happened.[4] The secret was kept from him—*the Prime Minister of the Empire*—for a whole month. The Japanese public was bombarded with propaganda about the "victory" and the people never were told the truth of Midway until after the war had ended.[5]

But the navy leaders knew. Admiral Yamamoto told his staff not to criticize Nagumo and his staff for the fatal errors that led to the defeat. The responsibility was all his as commander in chief, he said. Nagumo and his chief of staff, Admiral Kusaka, decided that their only recourse was to commit suicide, but they were restrained by friends. For his reputation, Nagumo might better have committed *seppuku* right then, for Yamamoto never trusted him again and eased him out as commander of the carrier striking force. Ultimately, Nagumo was assigned to command the land-based air force at Saipan for the Battle of the Marianas, and he died there by his own hand in the midst of the disaster.

After the Midway battle, the Imperial General Staff sensed that there had been a change in the course of the war. Little by little the media began to understand that the Midway "victory" had been a defeat, and in a left-handed editorial, *Asahi Shimbun* warned that Japan had to expect to suffer some losses before achieving final victory in this war.[6]

The surrender of Corregidor had come during the Battle of the Coral Sea and that helped perpetuate the song of victory that was being sung at home. Actually the Allies were gearing up for a war that would never let the Japanese rest again.

The primary result of the Battle of the Coral Sea was failure to take Port Moresby. Japan still had two enclaves at Lae and Salamaua on the New Guinea coast, and the Imperial General Headquarters plan to capture all of New Guinea remained. The plan also still called for the capture of New Caledonia, Fiji, and Samoa. The new attempt was to begin on July 11, built around nine infantry battalions of the Seventeenth Army, with navy assistance from the Second Fleet and the air arm of the First Fleet. But as the time drew near, the navy had to admit the loss of the carriers at Midway. The army was also having some second thoughts about the southern push. Many generals preferred to move west, through the Indian Ocean, to the Suez Canal, to link up with the Germans. The army was as myopic about the course of the war in Europe as the navy was about America.

So the southern plan was scaled down to fit the new army

yearnings. Port Moresby was to be taken, by troops moving overland from Lae and Salamaua. The navy was to defeat the Allied air effort and destroy the Australian fleet, which was the only Allied naval body apparent in the South Pacific in July.

An army unit was reconnoitering the road across the Owen Stanley Mountains that showed on the maps. What the Japanese learned was what the Australians already knew: the "road" was nothing more than a mountain trail, moving across some of the steepest and muddiest terrain in the world in the Owen Stanley Mountains.[7]

All spring, General MacArthur had been trying to make the best use of his minimal resources. What was needed to fend the Japanese off in their attempt to take New Guinea, and thus threaten all Australia, was an airfield on the southwestern coast of New Guinea, and a supply of aircraft, which might come in the beginning from the Australians but would have to be augmented swiftly with a steady flow from the United States.

The place chosen for the airfield was Milne Bay, at the tip of the island, where Lever Brothers (soap) had a plantation and an airstrip that would do for starters. After the Midway battle the Americans were cocky, too, and MacArthur began to believe the Japanese navy was finished. A naval command was set up by Admiral Nimitz to provide naval support. The Americans suffered to a lesser degree from the bristling independence of army and navy from each other, and the U.S. Navy was not willing to serve under MacArthur. That attitude was responsible for what might have been about a year's delay in the American prosecution of the war. Just after the Midway battle, General MacArthur suggested that the Allies capture the Japanese stronghold at Rabaul. The army in Washington approved a plan that would use three carriers, a thousand planes, one marine division, and three army divisions to force the Japanese to retreat to Truk, whereupon the whole South Pacific would be safe.

Admiral King refused. He gave reasons, but the real reason was that the navy did not want to be subordinate to the army. The feeling was mutual. Finally the Joint Chiefs of Staff, the American equivalent to the Supreme War Council, settled the matter by setting up a navy command in the South Pacific, separate, strategically responsible to MacArthur, but tactically independent, which meant the navy had to go along with MacArthur's basic plans, but would carry them out in its own way.[8]

August 1 was set as the date that the American navy would take over Tulagi, that aborted Japanese seaplane base. In the meantime, MacArthur moved with Australian troops to take Buna, across the Owen Stanley Mountains from Port Moresby. The 39th battalion of Australian militia and a battalion of New Guinea constabulary troops were ordered to move. On July 7 they started across the Owen Stanley range on the road called the Kokoda Track. They had a force of 600 native porters and ahead of them their Australian guides had built bivouac camps. Even so, it took this force eight days to climb up and down the 100 miles of the Owen Stanley range to Kokoda. Next, two weeks later, would come four Australian army companies and a party of U.S. Army engineers. At the same time, anticipating operations, General MacArthur prepared to move his headquarters up from Melbourne to Brisbane.

General Hyukatake had the word of the Australian crossing of the Owen Stanley range within hours after the arrival at Kokoda. Behaving in a manner especially Japanese, without waiting for the reconnaissance reports from the Salamaua detachment, or a proper assessment of the possibilities open to the enemy, he hurriedly organized a sea lift and landed 2000 troops of the South Seas Detachment near Buna, with orders to cross the Owen Stanley Mountains and capture Port Moresby.

When General MacArthur reached Brisbane on July 21, he was informed that the Japanese were landing at Buna. They were to go to Kokoda, cross the Kokoda Track, and then take Port Moresby. They would soon be reinforced by the remainder of Major General Tomitaro Horii's South Seas Detachment. The initial force was to "put the road in order" to handle tanks and trucks. Outnumbered, the Australians began to fall back across the Kokoda Track. The battle for New Guinea began.

After the Battle of the Coral Sea, unnoticed by the Allies, the Japanese began building an airstrip in the Lunga district of Guadalcanal Island, across Lunga Strait from Tulagi. Australian coastwatchers, who had been recruited from the corps of planters and missionaries who had worked in these islands before the Japanese came, watched the Japanese and reported by radio to Australia.

As the importance of the Japanese activity on Guadalcanal sank in, Admiral King decided a stroke must be made to prevent Japanese use of that airfield. The Americans must seize Guadalcanal. General

MacArthur was opposed and so was Admiral Robert Ghormley, the navy's new commander of the South Pacific. But on August 7 the Americans landed a force on Tulagi and another on Guadalcanal and in a few days 17,000 Americans were ashore there, building the airstrip, building roads, and digging in.[9]

The Japanese had a convoy at sea on its way to New Guinea when the word came of the American landings. The convoy stopped, turned around and went back to Rabaul to await developments. Admiral Yamamoto sensed that something important was going on when the Americans invaded Guadalcanal just one week before he was to begin using the airstrip to fly off planes that would attack Australia. He ordered Admiral Mikawa, commander of the Eighth Fleet at Rabaul, to attack immediately and destroy the enemy transports so the troops could not be supplied and could not escape. Mikawa took a cruiser force down to Guadalcanal, and in a night battle on August 9 he sank four Allied cruisers, and damaged another cruiser and two destroyers. But when he got back to Rabaul he was greeted by faint praise from Admiral Yamamoto, who was privately angry that Mikawa had not followed his orders and destroyed the transports. He issued those orders again.[10]

At Rabaul General Hyukatake paid but scant attention to the Americans on Guadalcanal. It was the navy's province, not his. He was concerned with New Guinea, and after the naval victory of Mikawa he felt all was well and dispatched the convoy back toward Buna. It arrived on August 13. The Japanese began sending more reinforcements and soon the number of troops reached 12,000.

Soon Rabaul learned that the Japanese contingent on Guadalcanal was threatened with total defeat. A report came that thousands of Americans were on the island, but the army did not believe it. Admiral Yamamoto believed there was reason for concern at least, and he created the Guadalcanal Reinforcement Force, which consisted of a number of destroyers of Rear Admiral Raizo Tanaka's Destroyer Squadron Two. At the time Tanaka was at Truk loading supplies. He was told to pick up 900 men of the Ichiki Detachment and take them to Guadalcanal. The Ichiki Detachment consisted of about 5000 men, built around a regiment commanded by Colonel Kiyonao Ichiki. Originally they had been scheduled as the attack force for Midway. Now they had nothing to do. Yamamoto's designation of only 900 men showed what he thought of the American activity on Guadalcanal. Admiral Tanaka was indignant but orders were orders. The Americans were to be driven off Guadalcanal by a battalion. It was odd that neither Admiral Yamamoto nor General Hyukatake had any real conception in the middle of July that they faced a major American landing. General Hyukatake could be more easily forgiven because the Solomons were not his worry. But the navy's ignorance was another matter, and indicated a real breakdown in intelligence.

Admiral Yamamoto did send the Second Fleet and part of the Third Fleet to Rabaul and also moved the Eleventh Air Fleet from Tinian Island in the Marianas group to Rabaul. He decided to shift the command of the Combined Fleet to Truk, where he would be closer to the scene of what might become the "decisive battle" he sought.

August came. The marines were dug in but their supply line was tenuous. The Eleventh Air Fleet began attacks on the airfield area. On August 7, Warrant Officer Saburo Sakai, who was to become one of Japan's greatest air heroes, noted an "almost unbelievable" armada of American warships and supply ships in the waters off the island.[11] But naval air force intelligence did not get in touch with army intelligence or naval fleet intelligence. The army remained unaware of the strength of the enemy, and so did Admiral Yamamoto.

On Guadalcanal on August 12, the Japanese began attacking in small groups. Planes flew over the Japanese area, dropping food packages and leaflets telling the soldiers to hold on, help was coming. On August 5 Admiral Tanaka delivered a thousand troops of the Ichiki Detachment at Taivu Point. They thought there were only 2000 Americans on the islands and that with the help of the Sasebo Special Landing Force troops who were already on Guadalcanal, they would be able to put an end to the American threat in short order. The Japanese destroyers began what became an almost nightly event: they shelled the airstrip which the Americans now called Henderson Field.[12]

Thus, slowly, a giant naval, air, and land battle was joined.

Beginning on August 20 the Japanese attacked. Most of Colonel Ichiki's men were killed in one night battle in the early hours of August 21. Colonel Ichiki committed suicide. The Americans did not know it, but this was a historic moment, pregnant with meaning for the war: Colonel Ichiki had been the man in command of Japanese troops on Marco Polo Bridge that night in 1937 at the beginning of the China incident, the China incident that had triggered this Pacific War. His force had lasted less than a week on Guadalcanal. The manner in which it was sent to Guadalcanal, without adequate knowledge of what was to be found there, the idea that a thousand men could do the job of a regiment, and the tightly disciplined behavior that caused most of the men of the Ichiki unit to charge into guns and be mowed down were all typical of the Japanese approach to the war. Admiral Yamamoto spelled it out:

"The real battle now is a competition between Japanese discipline and American scientific technology."[13]

The Imperial army and navy, unfortunately, were wedded to the idea that fighting spirit was everything, and material resources were nothing.

During August and September the army continued to feed troops into Guadalcanal in battalion and regimental strength. They did not recognize the nature of the problem even yet. General Hyukatake had little time to worry about Guadalcanal. He was just launching the attack over the Owen Stanley Mountains against the Australians. The Japanese landed troops to attack the airfields at Milne Bay. They did not capture them.

The Japanese controlled the air over Guadalcanal. They basically controlled the sea, or could have with their resources. Imperial General Headquarters gave the army the task of restoring Guadalcanal to Japanese control, almost offhandedly. If General Hyukatake had understood the nature of the American invasion, and had been able to put two divisions on the island, it could have been all over in a week or two. The American supply situation in August was very serious.

But Imperial Headquarters did not pay much attention to the Guadalcanal problem, and instead of sending divisions, the army sent battalions.

The opportunity for the "decisive" sea battle seemed to arrive off the Eastern Solomons on August 23. Two of the five American carriers in the Pacific were in the area. The sea battle became a trade-off: the Americans sank the carrier *Ryujo*, and the Japanese damaged the *Enterprise* severely.

Unfortunately for the Japanese and fortunately for the Americans, Admiral Nagumo was still in charge of the carrier striking force, although Admiral Yamamoto had the gravest of misgivings about keeping him in that position. The *Shokaku* was damaged and so was the *Zuikaku*, but they were still operational at the end, on the night of August 24. In this battle Nagumo had six carriers, and Yamamoto was furious that Nagumo had by indecision and confusion once more lost a chance to wipe out the American carriers. The Americans had a chance to do the same, but they had Admiral Frank Jack Fletcher, who surpassed Admiral Nagumo in timidity. Between the pair, they avoided the grand confrontation.[14]

Guadalcanal and New Guinea became a two-ring circus. The Americans were fighting with two forces, the marines on Guadalcanal and the army, with its air forces and Australians, in New Guinea. The Japanese were fighting with one land force sent in two directions by General Hyukatake. He was supported by both naval and army air forces, but the navy was far more effective than the army. At sea, the navy won engagement after engagement with the Americans, and Admiral Tanaka's destroyer force became the night terror of the island, moving almost at will. But in time the Americans wore the Japanese down; the same Japanese ships had to fight one engagement after another and ships and crews tended to become battle-weary.

On the land, Major General Seiken Kawaguchi's brigade, intended for New Guinea, finally had to be diverted to Guadalcanal, but the ships bringing it were hit by American planes; two-thirds of the ships were destroyed, and most of the equipment was lost as well as many of the men. About 4000 Japanese soldiers arrived on the island. Even in September, Kawaguchi did not know how many Americans were on the island, and there were about 20,000 by that time.[15]

General Hyukatake offered to send a whole division, but Kawaguchi said he would not need it. As the Japanese force grew greater, battles were fought around Henderson Field. The Japanese lost all the battles. They never did have enough force to do the job in the period that they held air superiority. On the sea, the navies traded ships, the Japanese proving themselves far superior as night fighters (partly because their night binoculars were far superior to the American), but the American radar changed the ratio. Even then the Japanese torpedoes were much more effective than the American. The fighting spirit of destroyer men like Admiral Tanaka was matched by that of men like Captain Arleigh Burke. In these desperate months of the summer and fall of 1942, the war seemed to hang in the balance, although this was hardly true in the long view. The Americans, fighting on the European front and devoting most of their resources to that area, were still beginning to bring new warships into action, cruisers and destroyer escorts and carriers. The Japanese had to work mostly with the ships at hand. There was no question for them of a change in naval strategy to match a different sort of force, as there was for the Americans.

American leadership faltered, and finally Admiral William F. Halsey took over the South Pacific command and brought to it his fighting spirit, which matched that of any Japanese general or admiral. Just before Halsey entered in October, the Japanese decided on a great push to defeat the Americans, a combined air, sea, and land assault. They had waited too long. They still had air superiority but by sheer courage the American fliers held off the Japanese attackers. X-Day was the date set for the Japanese attack. It was delayed, and Y-Day was set for October 2. That was the day the Japanese would take Henderson Field, and the day that Admiral Nagumo would find and defeat the American fleet. But Y-Day failed, and at the end of it the Americans still had Henderson Field, Guadalcanal, and the air superiority over the island was split. When the Japanese came down in force from Rabaul, they controlled. When they left, the Americans controlled. And the Americans were bringing in ever more aircraft, while the Japanese at Rabaul were scraping the bottom of the barrel to keep the old battered planes flying.

By October the Imperial Army had begun to regard the recapture of Guadalcanal as a matter of national pride. The Naval General Staff suggested that the island was not that important, and that they ought to let it go without further effort. The army said, no, the island would be retaken. The navy must supply the troops with food, clothing, and ammunition.[16] This was the rub, for the Americans were growing stronger all the while. The new battleship *Washington* now came to the Pacific. She was a bigger, more powerful battleship than those trapped by the Japanese at anchor in Pearl Harbor. She could make thirty knots and keep up with the new fast carriers. The new carriers were also beginning to make their appearance. Together the new fleet-carriers, the fast battleships, and the new cruisers that were also coming would make up new multi-carrier task groups, and, ultimately, the greatest carrier task force in the world.

The American air forces on Guadalcanal had survived the desperate period and were growing stronger, with reinforcements of planes and men. By November the United States controlled Guadalcanal's skies.

Even so, the Japanese managed to land the Second Army Division on Guadalcanal and the fighting continued. Steadily, however, the Japanese were being worn down, their supplies intercepted until many troops were thin as scarecrows, moving barefoot through the forest, trying desperately to stay alive.

Naval battle after battle created an immense demand for fuel, and the fuel supplies of the East Indies were not great enough to accommodate all the demands of army and navy, from Manchuria to Rabaul. By mid-November, the sea battles more or less ended, as the Japanese quit dispatching ships into the waters around Guadalcanal to save fuel. Given his carrier commander, Admiral Yamamoto seemed to have given up the hope of staging the great naval battle that would bring victory.

The Japanese brought still another division to Guadalcanal, the 38th Division. But once again it was a story of American air attacks that sank so many ships the division arrived without most of its equipment and without adequate food supply. By the end of the month there were 28,000 Japanese on the island and most of them were starving. The attempts to resupply the troops by destroyer did not work because too many times the destroyers had to fight. Even such desperate measures as packing rice in drums and throwing them overboard to float in to land did not work. Too many drums went out to sea. Attempts were made to supply the garrison by submarine. It was too little and too late.[17]

Early in November 1942, General Hitoshi Imamura was sent down to Rabaul to take a new job, commander of the Rabaul area army. He flew down by way of Truk and stopped off for a meeting with Admiral Yamamoto. The admiral spoke frankly to this old bridge partner from London days when he had been a delegate to the naval disarmament conferences and Imamura had been a military attaché. They talked as did few admirals and generals. Yamamoto said that the Zero, a few months earlier the best fighter plane in the Pacific, had now been challenged by the U.S. Army P-38 and the improved navy and marine Grumman fighters.

The worst of it was that American production was now beginning to tell in the whole of the South Pacific and Southwest Pacific. In the air the Americans had a margin of three to one in aircraft numbers. As for training, the Americans were growing steadily more skillful, while the level of Japanese pilot skill was dropping. Too many pilots had been lost in the Coral Sea and Midway battles and in the air fights over New Guinea and Guadalcanal. In the past six months the navy had lost 893 planes and 2362 airmen. Under the naval system it took two or three years to train a flier. No acceleration program had been pushed through with the coming of the Pacific War; now times were being shortened. That meant the replacements coming in were neophytes, coming direct from school to battle. Too many did not survive their first mission. As Admiral Yamamoto said:

"Our emphasis on intensive training and discipline isn't wrong, but we should have made sure it was accompanied by scientific and technological improvements as well. I have a strong sense of responsibility for our failure in that regard."[18]

General Imamura could see that his old friend was depressed and he tried to raise his spirits by telling him of his orders. He was to establish the Eighth Area Army and utilize the Seventeenth and Eighteenth armies to capture Guadalcanal and the Solomons in connection with the navy. He was also to secure the strategic points necessary to prepare for a major action the next year in New Guinea, to capture that territory. Imperial General Headquarters was prepared to employ virtually all of the strength of the Combined Fleet for that purpose. Four new divisions would be brought down.

What Admiral Yamamoto knew but did not tell General Imamura, was that every day the planes and pilots of his beloved carriers were being sucked away to Rabaul and battle. If the "decisive battle" had been laid out for him for the next day, and there was no timidity, no failure to meet the enemy, it was now questionable if the Japanese would have any advantage at all.

November became December and still the Japanese were trying to capture Guadalcanal. In New Guinea the Americans committed thousands more troops, and at the end of November the Americans broke through the perimeter of the Japanese Buna beachhead for the first time. Early in December the Australians took the embattled town of Gona. With the army's view that the capture of New Guinea was much more important than Guadalcanal, matters began to change at Imperial Headquarters in Tokyo. Lieutenant Colonel Tsuji, who had behaved so badly in the Philippines, came down full of venom to see for himself what was happening on Guadalcanal, and returned to Rabaul a much chastened officer. He went on to Tokyo, and there shocked his friends of the Imperial General Staff by telling them the true situation in the south: that the Americans were in control of air and land and sea around Guadalcanal, and that Japanese soldiers were starving to death. At the same time, Admiral Yamamoto had come to the conclusion that Guadalcanal was draining far too many of the navy's resources, and must be evacuated. Imperial Headquarters remained adamant: Guadalcanal must be held as a matter of pride.

The final decision was forced by the war ministry, when the army asked for 300,000 tons of ships to deliver supplies to Guadalcanal. General Shinichi Tanaka, chief of the Operations Bureau of the army, insisted flatly. He was supported by Colonel Takushiro Hattori. On the other side stood General Tojo, as minister of war, as well as premier. Tojo said Guadalcanal must be evacuated. Tanaka said no. They almost came to blows. Some of their subordinates did actually come to blows. A few days later General Tanaka was transferred to a minor operational post and so was Hattori. It was the first breakdown of army unity since the beginning of the war and was followed by the seizure of operational control of the army by General Tojo through his new appointee, Major General Kitsuju Ayabe. Guadalcanal was lost. And, as Admiral Yamamoto now knew, so was the war.

進退 これ きわまる

29. "Here the progress stops"

*T*he invasion of Guadalcanal had brought a subtle, unannounced change to the Japanese war that was felt by the people long before official announcements gave any indications. All autumn it had become growingly apparent that the euphoric days of constant victory had ended.

Six months earlier, the newspapers were so bursting with reports of Japanese victories throughout Asia and the Pacific that the news editors of the newspapers found it hard to decide which stories to report in the most prominent columns. By September 1942, fully half the front pages were devoted to stories of the world war on the Western and Soviet fronts, and to articles about life inside the Greater East Asia Co-Prosperity Sphere. It was mandatory (to keep up civilian morale) to have reports of victories. This took a bit of sleight of hand. On September 1 several newspapers published a report released by naval censorship by novelist Fumio Niwa, who had been aboard Admiral Mikawa's flagship *Chokai* as a war correspondent during the first battle of the Solomon Islands (Savo Island) when Admiral Mikawa had sunk four Allied cruisers. The battle had been fought on August 9. The report appeared on September 1.

VIVID STORY OF VICTORY
BY JAPAN OFF SOLOMONS
GIVEN BY WAR REPORTER

IMPERIAL UNITS WADED
INTO ENEMY FLEET IN
PITCH DARKNESS

FLIERS BRAVED SQUALL

ALLIED WARSHIPS GO DOWN IN
RAPID SUCCESSION BEFORE
BLAZING NIPPON GUNS[1]

Correspondent Niwa's eyewitness account began with homage and historical comparisons to the glorious Japanese past, but he also described some thrilling moments:

> We all held our breaths when a San Francisco type cruiser suddenly re-pointed its prow and plowed its way toward us. With its aft enveloped in flames, the ship was plunging toward us. What a magnificent sight! For the first time I realized the imminent danger that threatened me. Half paralyzed, the San Francisco type was spitting fire from its fore embrasure in the last desperate resistance.
>
> Because of that A-type cruiser I was wounded. My left arm was hit by one of the fragments from the three shots that struck the bridge. My body was covered with countless wounds and my face and my heatproof suit stained in a bright yellow. Many of the men had fallen. The collar of my heat suit was stained with blood and my hat was spotted too.
>
> "Damn the shot." This was my feeling. The note in my right hand was smeared with blood. However, that was the enemy's last struggle. The bridge was right in front. It was blown off and the San Francisco type cruiser reared up its prow, stood upright, and then slipped into the sea. The detestable enemy had been sunk.
>
> A tumult of excitement rose within our ship, but the sunken cruiser was soon forgotten as we turned about in search of another prey.

Correspondent Niwa went below to the wardroom, and found a surgeon there who dressed his wounds.

The sound of firing ceased after I came down to the officers' quarters. Our fleet was making a striking withdrawal. Not one enemy ship was following us. Eight A-type cruisers and six destroyers instantly sunk, two destroyers damaged beyond repair. All this achieved with our ship in the condition of "At Your Posts." No disorder with the ship from the ordinary except for taking care of the wounded.

Satisfaction and joy lighted the faces of the chief gunner and the chief engineer. The chief torpedo officer modestly showed his joy in being the first to put the coup de grace to an enemy cruiser. . . .

Two staff members of Headquarters also joined the group and started to make out reports of the battle for Imperial Headquarters.

Leaning against the long sofa, I withstood my pains. I watched the results of tonight's battle being written on the blackboard in the officers' quarters. I thought of how the chief gunner must be feeling after he had struck to his heart's content.

The Niwa report was not much different from the sort of eyewitness accounts that American correspondents were writing from shipboard. It was, however, a "feature story" and not the sort of material that would have appeared on the front pages a few months earlier. Less than a year after the beginning of the war, editors were searching for victory stories. This account and a story from Nanking about the Imperial forces "adjusting their lines" after the end of the Chekiang-Kiangsi campaign, were all that *Asahi Shimbun* could find to raise civilian morale that September 1.[2]

Next day the front page was dominated by a war ministry article describing citations for valor presented to two army tank companies for especial heroism in the Malaya campaign which had ended in February. The only "news" from the front concerned Shantung Province of China, where the Japanese "annihilated" eleven hundred more Chinese troops. The Japanese had been annihilating the Chinese now for five years, and yet they were still encountering the Nationalist forces in the coastal provinces.[3] No wonder the Japanese people were beginning to have some doubts about the progress of the war.

In September Prime Minister Tojo announced the creation of the Greater Asia Ministry, to bring the economies of all the captured territories under control. That is not how it was put, but concurrently the China Affairs Board, Manchurian Affairs Bureau, Ministry of Overseas Affairs, and the East Asiatic Affairs Bureau of the foreign ministry were all abolished.[4]

Without victories, the government must have heroism to laud. On September 21, 1942, a splendid military funeral was held for Major General Takeo Kato of the Imperial Japanese Army Air Forces, who had been killed in Burma. General Tojo made a funeral oration. So did General Sugiyama, chief of the Army General Staff, and General Doihara, who was now chief of army aviation; General Terauchi, commander of Southeast Asia, sent a telegram. So did the German general staff. Students at the various military academies and military units were called up to parade. The public was invited to burn incense, all in honor of this "hero God."[5]

A week later another "hero God" was laid to rest with the same sort of ceremony: Lieutenant General Naotsugu Sakai, commander of the Chekiang-Kiangsi front, who had been killed by a land mine laid by a Chinese guerilla.[6]

On October 9 the Japanese minister to Australia was repatriated and he brought home with him the ashes of four more God heroes, the crews of the two-man submarines which had penetrated Sydney harbor on May 21 in an abortive attack. Huge picture spreads and long articles appeared in the press in connection with the funeral ceremonies. Four months had gone by and there had been no previous mention of any attack on Sydney. This occasion of the funeral and memorials defied censorship; it was the method by which the Japanese received much of their information about the conduct of the war.[7]

Occasionally a glimpse of reality pushed through the censorship. On October 19, 1942, Tomokazu Hori, spokesman for the Japanese Board of Information (the cabinet's mouthpiece), warned of a "second front" in the war.

"The creation of a second front in the Pacific means America's plan to launch a general offensive against Japan and Chungking's attempt to recapture Burma and other Japanese-occupied areas.

"The war situation has now entered a new stage," Hori said,

"indicating every sign of a protracted strife. . . . We are facing a stage of real war, a stage which demands the nation's totalitarian strength."[8]

Three days later the *Asahi Shimbun* announced that China's "jugular vein has been slashed" with the capture of the Burma Road. But. . . . Even with a slashed jugular vein, the Japanese noted, China fought on.[9]

The confused battle off the Santa Cruz Islands, in which the Americans and Japanese exchanged carrier strikes like chess players exchanging knights, was greeted in Japan as an enormous victory. In fact, it was a Japanese victory in the sinking of the carrier *Hornet,* and other damage to Allied ships. But three Japanese carriers had been damaged, two of them badly, and at this stage of the war the Americans were nearly in a position where an American carrier sunk could be regarded even up for a Japanese carrier seriously damaged, so great was American ship production by the fall of 1942.

At the moment, the sinking of the *Hornet* posed serious problems for the Americans, reducing their South Pacific carrier force to one. Admiral Halsey would have to avoid "the decisive battle" for a while.

Japan literally went wild with the news of the battle victory. It had been so long since there had been anything to crow about that Imperial Headquarters pulled out all the stops:

The Invincible Japanese Naval Forces, said headquarters, had scored an enormous victory, sinking four American aircraft carriers, one battleship, many other ships, damaging more ships and shooting down two hundred American planes. Japan's navy, in turn, had lost no ships, but suffered slight damage to two carriers.

"Note:" said Imperial Headquarters. "This battle shall be called the Battle of the South Pacific." The statement read as though the spokesman was describing a victory as important as the Battle of Trafalgar.[10]

The victory, said Imperial Headquarters, had completely foiled the American attempt to launch a counteroffensive against Japan.

"The results," said the editor of *Asahi Shimbun,* "were enough to make us all dance with joy."[11]

But once again, although "annihilated," the enemy refused to stop fighting.

The Imperial Navy's problem, not at all helped by the damage to the carrier fleet, was to keep Henderson Field under bombardment at every opportunity, and to supply the Japanese forces in the Taivu

Point area. The navy failed. The Japanese "won" one naval engagement after another, but they could not reach Guadalcanal with enough supply ships or keep those that did get through on the shore long enough to empty them. The Japanese troops continued to starve, so weak that simply going out to forage for food became a day's major occupation. The rice had given out. The Japanese lived on rats and insects and on the roots of jungle plants.

By December, the South Pacific situation had become so serious that drastic measures were demanded. A new China offensive, against Chungking, was scheduled for September. But all available resources were being pushed south, and before the end of the year General Tojo put the China assault aside. Divisions from Korea and China were ordered to the South Pacific. The war was changing. General Tojo hoped to regain the initiative with the capture of Port Moresby, but Admiral Yamamoto had no such hopes. Better than Tojo or the Imperial General Staff, he knew the enemy, and the enemy's rising capability. More important, he was only too well aware of his own falling capability to carry the battle.

On December 31, 1942, for the first time the Japanese held an Imperial Conference, the subject of which—no matter how it was masked—was defensive. Guadalcanal would be evacuated by the first week in February. The defense line would then run north of New Georgia and Isabella islands. The offense would turn to New Guinea, where reinforcements were to help capture Port Moresby.[12]

In the first week of February 1943 the Japanese navy carried out one of the most successful retreats in history, moving nearly all of the 17,000 remaining troops on Guadalcanal. One unit, the Oka Regiment on Mount Austen, was surrounded and wiped out, except for one lieutenant who wrapped the regimental flag around his body, broke through the lines and found his way to one of the evacuation points. Another unit, the Yano Battalion, fought a rearguard action to assist the evacuation with such vigor that the Americans believed reinforcements had come in and that they could expect a new Japanese attack. The Americans were planning an attack of their own to crush the Japanese in pincers coming from east and south. The two U.S. forces met at Cape Esperance on February 9, but there was nothing to pinch. Every living Japanese had left Guadalcanal.[13]

The battle was over. It had cost the Americans two dozen warships, about two thousand killed and five thousand men wounded. Japan had also lost twenty-four ships, plus nine hundred aircraft and more than two thousand air crewmen. On land eight thousand Japanese soldiers and sailors had fallen in battle, and eleven thousand had died of starvation and disease. Guadalcanal was the saddest page yet written in Japanese military history.

As the war situation deteriorated the demands on the Japanese people for more patriotic efforts grew steadily. "Down with the American and English Devils" was one theme, hammered week after week by radio and press.[14]

"*Ichioku Ichigan*" was another—One hundred million as one bullet. Such slogans were presented in all seriousness, and in all seriousness they were accepted by the vast majority of Japanese. The almost total acceptance of every measure, every slogan, led some on the staff of *Mainichi Shimbun* (then called *Nichi Nichi*) to suggest (long after the war) that a look back into the files indicated that "the Japanese have had an incurable liking all along for totalitarianism. . . . The Japanese once liked, and may in the future like, to bask in a blissful sense of national one-ness."[15]

When 1943 came in, the supernationalism grew. Take *besu-boru*, that fine old sport of Abner Doubleday's derived from the Americans. It became *yakyu*. A *sutoraiku* became a *yoshi*. *Boru* became *tama*, "you're out" became *hike* (heekay).

The teaching of English ended in the public schools and in the universities; finally, only the naval academy continued to teach the English language. Crowds would descend on the English-language newspapers to demand that they close down. The argument used to prevent violence was that the editors were representing the Japanese people, keeping track of the English language so they would know their enemies after they had defeated them.

Many of the media people of Japan were up front with the jingoists, but a few were dedicated to trying to tell the truth about the war. Here is a recollection from the *Nichi Nichi* offices:

A part of the *Mainichi Daily News* staff stealthily vanished into the women's toilet converted into a "black chamber." They set up a monitoring apparatus inside the toilet converted into a sanctuary free from military inspection and listened to shortwave radio (forbidden to civilians at the time) to the BBC, Voice of America, Treasure Island, Ankara, and other foreign broadcasts. The news obtained was circulated among the editors of both the vernacular and the English newspapers. Some of it was printed under the datelines of neutral countries—Stockholm, Zurich, Lisbon, Buenos Aires, where there actually were *Mainichi* correspondents, isolated by the outbreak of the war. This valuable but highly secret newsgathering activity was given an inglorious name, Benjo Press (Toilet Press).[16]

In February 1943, Rabaul and New Ireland really represented the reality of the Japanese defense line. Everything south, in the Solomons, was expendable, but it was expected that the fight would be island by island. Perhaps by the time the Americans moved up the string of the Solomons, the army would have defeated MacArthur's forces in New Guinea, and the South Pacific effort would be deemed by the Americans to be useless. Perhaps, even more desirable, a new drive into China would bring an end to the China incident and thus eliminate the whole United States reason for fighting the war. If the China war could only be settled, Tojo was certain, the war against the Americans and the British could be brought to a successful climax at the peace table. By this time, Tojo would have been willing to withdraw from the South Pacific.

In January 1943, at the Casablanca conference the United States and Britain promised to give more help to Nationalist China. A new road was to be built through the Himalaya Mountains from Assam Province, India, to pick up the old Burma Road in Northern Burma.

The American air force also began launching air raids on Indochina, to destroy the Japanese potential to strengthen forces in Burma.

The Japanese response was to prepare new troop units for dispatch to Indochina and to send three battalions to Hainan Island.

At the same time, Tojo wanted to attack India. Since the beginning of the war, the Japanese had gained the adherence of the Provisional Indian Government of Subhas Chandra Bose, a nationalist leader who had abandoned Nehru and the Congress party to embrace Japan's Greater East Asia Co-Prosperity Sphere and the concept of Asia for the Asiatics. For months Bose had been pleading for an advance against India, to seize a corner of that country where he could set up his government "on India's soil." He promised the Japanese that if they would do that much, he would bring millions of Indians flocking to his banner.

In the Solomons the Americans were planning to move up the chain of islands toward Rabaul. The strategy called for movement, island by island.

Just after the Japanese evacuation of Guadalcanal the Americans seized the little Russell island chain to the north. The Japanese, meanwhile, were building up their forces at Kolombangara Island and on New Georgia, across the Kula Gulf. Admiral Yamamoto had ordered the building of new air bases on Buka and Buin and Munda on Georgia Island. From these advance bases, the Japanese proposed to harry the Americans on Guadalcanal and pin them down so they could go nowhere.

The catch, however, was that the major Japanese bases in the south had to be supplied. And what was going to happen about supply was indicated on the night of March 5, 1943, when the Japanese destroyers *Minegumo* and *Murasame* came south to Kolombangara to supply the garrison there with food and ammunition. An American squadron caught them and destroyed them in short order. They had delivered their cargoes but they would deliver no more.

The sinking of the *Murasame* and the *Minegumo* marked another turning point in the naval war. The Americans had tracked the Japanese ships with radar and had fired on them with radar-controlled guns, before torpedoing. The enormous advances in American radar at this point more than balanced the superiority of Japanese torpedoes and Japanese skill at night fighting. For the rest of the war the Japanese would labor under a distinct technological disadvantage, just as Admiral Yamamoto predicted.[17]

Following the initial landings on the Aleutian islands of Kiska and Attu at the time of the Midway assault, the Japanese had planned to make another landing at Adak. Where they would go from there no one at Imperial Headquarters quite knew. There were dreamers who talked about using the Aleutians base as a jump-off point for invasion of Alaska. But after the failure of the Midway operation and the call of Admiral Yamamoto for the return of the northern carriers to the Combined Fleet, the landing on Adak was cancelled. The three battalions of Major General Juichiro Mineki's Hokkai Detachment remained on Kiska and Attu with no orders. The name was changed to Hokkai *garrison*, which meant there were unlikely to be any orders for attack. The garrison was soon under threat: the Americans built air bases on Adak and Amchitka. They also increased the U.S. naval force in the Aleutians area. On October 24, 1942, the Hokkai garrison was resupplied, but it was an enormous effort, involving the use of carriers and a number of destroyers to escort the transports. It was a most unsatisfactory bit of territory for Japan to hold.

Admiral Yamamoto and General Imamura were now under orders to cooperate in the capture of New Guinea and the defense of the central Solomons. The first effort to speed up the capture of Port Moresby came late in February 1943. Between July and December of 1942 the Japanese had sent 18,000 men onto the Buna coast for the assault on Port Moresby. In the assault on the Owen Stanley Mountains they lost six thousand men. Between November 1942 and January 1943, disease and hunger and battle had killed another eight thousand.

In February a convoy of troops and supplies was sent from Rabaul, protected by ships and planes of the Eighth Fleet: eight transports, eight destroyers, and the resources of the land-based air force at Rabaul. The convoy was completely decimated by American air attack. Of the seven thousand men aboard the transports, only twelve hundred had reached New Guinea and three thousand men were lost. Four destroyers were lost. Scores of Japanese aircraft were shot down. When the damage was assessed at Rabaul the decision was made in the middle of March that no further effort would be taken to resupply New Guinea by ship. All supply would be done in stages, by barges that could duck in and out of the little bays and travel by night. Virtually no supplies made it across to the Buna coast. At this stage of the battle for New Guinea it was known that the initiative was lost. But the Rabaul command could not admit defeat in view of the attitude of Imperial Headquarters, so the growingly unequal struggle continued. The mysticism of *bushido* was invoked: rather than with food and weapons, the troops on New Guinea were ordered to fight with courage, and in the end to sacrifice their lives for the emperor. Of courage there was no shortage among the Japanese troops, and ultimately nearly all of them died fighting. They did not know it, but back in Tokyo they had already been written off.[18]

As for the Solomons, Admiral Yamamoto's task was to build up the Eleventh Air Fleet at Rabaul, which had been badly decimated in the Guadalcanal battle, and send down such a hail of bombs on the Americans that Guadalcanal would be useless to them. It was a hard task for Guadalcanal was a long, long way from Rabaul. But by staging fighters and bombers from Rabaul to Buin and Buka, it could be done.

By robbing the five carriers at Truk, Admiral Yamamoto managed to reequip the air forces at Rabaul for this new struggle, called Operation I, which was supposed to knock out American air and sea power around Guadalcanal. A hundred and sixty carrier planes, with those precious pilots who could operate from ships, were sent down to Rabaul to join a hundred and ninety planes of the Eleventh Air Fleet. On April 7 they began the assault on Guadalcanal with a 170-plane attack. For six days they attacked, day after day with such force, alternating between New Guinea and Guadalcanal. The pilots came home with stories of their successes, most of them creations of overactive imaginations. At the end of the week, the operation was ended and declared to be a success. The real reason for abandoning it was the shortage of aircraft. Hundreds of planes were needed to replace those worn out and those lost. But from Tokyo came the message: there were no more planes.

The grim knowledge that the war was no longer going Japan's way was not easy on morale, and Admiral Yamamoto decided to make a tour of his advanced bases to put spirit into the men. On April 18 he set out on a long day's air journey from Rabaul. His trip had been given advance notice by radio, and the radio messages had been intercepted by the Americans, who, as noted, had cracked the Japanese naval codes. A decision was made by the highest American authority (President Roosevelt) to assassinate Admiral Yamamoto. A special group of P-38 fighter planes was given the task and performed it admirably, shooting down Yamamoto's twin-engined bomber and also that of Admiral Ugaki, his chief of staff. Ugaki survived, but Yamamoto was killed.

In a sense, it was fitting that Admiral Yamamoto should die just then: his strategy had failed, as he knew so well himself. Four times the Combined Fleet had been given the chance for the major naval victory that Yamamoto wanted. At Pearl Harbor, at Trincomalee, at Midway, and at Santa Cruz Admiral Nagumo's carriers had been within reach of victory only to be diverted by the admiral's timidity. Only at Midway was there even the excuse of superior enemy intelligence, at no point was there greater American strength. Nagumo had failed, and Yamamoto had to bear the responsibility.

As of the spring of 1943 the days of the superiority of the Combined Fleet had ended. Two weeks before the ambush of Admiral Yamamoto, Mrs. Franklin D. Roosevelt traveled to the Henry Kaiser Swan Island shipyard in Portland, Oregon, to christen the first of a new class of aircraft carrier, the USS *Casablanca*. She and her sisters would carry thirty planes each—as many as a Japanese light carrier. The *Casablanca* had been built in nine months, but by autumn the time for construction had been cut by a third. The plans called for five hundred of these carriers if necessary; midsummer saw the laying down of Hull No. 319.[19]

Besides the escort carriers, the light carriers begun in 1941 were being completed and outfitted. And so were the new *Essex*-class fleet carriers of 20,000 tons and more. The Americans were preparing to carry the war to Japan.

A week after Admiral Yamamoto's death the Japanese and Americans in the Aleutians fought the Battle of the Komandorski Islands. The battle was indecisive, but, once again, it emphasized the enormous difficulty of maintaining an outpost in the Aleutians in view of the worsening military situation. A month and a half later the Americans landed in force on Attu Island, and the Japanese garrison there fought on to the death of the last man.

General Tojo called an Imperial Conference to discuss the need for a changed strategy.[20] Tojo, the army, navy, and the emperor's representative agreed that the army must be withdrawn from the Aleutians, and in a few weeks, naval forces saved the Japanese troops in Kiska from the fate of their friends on Attu. It was the second retreat and the end of the last vestige of Admiral Yamamoto's strategy for the Pacific War. The admiral had told Prime Minister Konoye that he could hold the Americans at bay for perhaps a year, but after that. . . . His silence was pregnant. Fate upheld the admiral's prophecy; he had held off the Americans for just over a year until the evacuation of Guadalcanal. Despite the timidity of his major operating subordinate, the Combined Fleet had scored victory after victory at sea. But in the spring of 1943 all this glory had gone down with Admiral Yamamoto. His fall, like a cherry blossom in the wind, was in its way a prophecy.

詀半分　嘘半分

30. "Half the tale is lies"

September 1943. The desperate days had begun. The death of Admiral Yamamoto had been followed by steady Allied advances up the Solomons chain; Vella Lavella Island, then New Georgia, had fallen. On New Guinea, General MacArthur was moving north.

In the summer of 1943 General Tojo had made a tour of the battle zones and occupied territories. He had learned a few grim facts: that the armies in the fields were not responsive to Tokyo's direction and did as they pleased. In Manchuria and China this state of affairs had resulted in massive corruption. It was nearly as bad in the Philippines, Burma, and Indonesia. Thailand, theoretically a willing partner in the war from the day of Pearl Harbor, had escaped much of the bullying, but the failure of the highly touted economic policies of the Japanese government was apparent in a lonely street built to commemorate the Greater East Asia Co-Prosperity Sphere, a wide boulevard that was supposed to be filled with the most modern shops, department stores, and buildings and was photographed to show the glories of the Co-Prosperity Sphere. But the fact was that nine-tenths of the "buildings" were false fronts. The only impressive structure was the new Hotel Ratanakosindh. In that structure almost immediately the plumbing ceased to work. Soon the fine concrete work was crumbling. The Great Bangkok Boulevard was symbolic of Greater East Asia, all show and very little substance, a dingy reminder of broken promises.[1]

After the fall of New Georgia, General Imamura at Rabaul expected the Allied invasion of Choiseul, the next stepping stone in the chain. But General MacArthur then unleashed a master stroke of strategy: the Americans would not go up the chain, they would "island-hop," skirting Choiseul, surrounding the troops on the island but leaving them alone to wait, and to starve, and they would attack Bougainville, which was very close to Rabaul.

The same policy was followed in New Guinea. Allied forces landed at Finschhafen on the western shore of Dampier Strait in September. Japanese counterattacks failed utterly, and the area was captured in October. "Leapfrogging" would be the Allied tactic here as well. The Japanese people learned about what happened at Finschhafen two months later when Imperial Headquarters released a boasting story of how many Allied troops they had killed before they abandoned the territory.[2]

The shock of Allied "leapfrogging" threw the Japanese defense plans into complete disarray. Prime Minister Tojo and Imperial Headquarters had agreed that the troops in the south would be abandoned, to hold out to the last and thus delay the Allied advance, but now that would do little good. Public opinion—even under dictatorship there was such a thing—insisted that some effort be made to supply the abandoned garrisons. Submarines came into use for this purpose. Among other materials they brought seeds so the starving soldiers could plant "victory gardens."

This island-hopping of the Allies in the fall of 1943 caused a frantic reaction of replanning the defenses of Japan. In September the Solomons and New Guinea were written off by the high command. The defense line would be drawn back to the Carolina Islands.

An Imperial Headquarters order called on the outposts to hold out as long as possible. This meant to the death. The outposts were the Solomon, the Gilbert, and the Marshall island groups. The garrisons would not be removed or reinforced. The order used the words "destroy U.S. forces," and demanded that the defenders deal "crippling blows" to the enemy, but that was so much of the usual Japanese official verbiage. The fact was that the Japanese perimeter was contracted in the Central and South Pacific areas. In the Southwest Pacific the new line was Burma, the Andaman and Nicobar Islands, the Malay Peninsula, and Indonesia. For all practical purposes New Guinea and the surrounding territory were written off. Imperial Headquarters still hoped to separate China from the Western Allies, secure

Chiang's surrender, and thus end the "cause" of the war for the West. This belief was an article of faith with the militarists; "conquer China and the war will go away." Thus, new attention was to be paid in the coming year to the China theater and to India. At all costs war with the USSR was to be avoided.

There was a special reason for this new care about the USSR. The German and Italian war efforts, so successful initially, had begun to collapse. Hitler had placed his hopes on Stalingrad, and an enormous German army had surrendered there. The Allies had captured North Africa and Sicily, and Mussolini had fled Rome and the Italian government had surrendered to the Allies.

A year earlier, as noted, Prime Minister Tojo had established the Greater East Asia Ministry, to try to pull together the various conquered territories and instill in them a will to fight what Japan called their common war.

The idea was brilliant, for millions of Asians did, indeed, feel that Japan had driven the colonialists out of Asia. Idealists in Japan hoped to create almost a United States of Asia, certainly something more sturdy than the League of Nations. Feeling the way, the Greater East Asia Ministry began to select a number of young Asians from other lands who would be brought to Japan for acculturization, and then looked after when they went home, in the hope that they would be the leaders of the new generation of friends of Japan.

A prime example was Leocadia de Asis, a young Filipino, whose story is followed here for what it shows about the Japanese empire at the height of the war.

De Asis was born in 1919. He had graduated from Santa Beda College and from the College of Law of the University of Santo Tomas. He was called up for the defense of the Philippines as a soldier and was captured at Bataan. He survived several prison camps.[3]

Following the establishment of Japanese control in the Philippines, an attempt was made to bring the Filipinos around to the Japanese point of view. De Asis, for one, was released from prison camp, and sent to the Japanese Philippine Constabulary Academy for reeducation. He finished second in his class and was thus called to Japanese attention. He was chosen to stay on at the academy and teach criminal law and government regulation under the new regime.

Meanwhile, the Japanese government was busily forming an "independent" government for the Philippines. It was all very well to deal with the anti-American Jose Laurel and his associates, but for the future younger men should be trained in the Japanese mold if the Greater East Asia Co-Prosperity Sphere was to prosper.

In the spring of 1943, then, about thirty potential leaders were chosen to go to Japan for study. They included two sons of Jorge B. Vargas, and one son of President Laurel, and other scions of prominent Filipino families. In other words, these were the young elite. They would go to Japan to join similar groups from the other countries of Southeast Asia.

Early in July the trip began, aboard a fast transport. The young men were treated nobly, four to a cabin, but immediately thrown into Japanese ways; they had their first meal with chopsticks, which most of them found hard to handle. De Asis and his friends were instructed about the total blackout of cabins that would be observed on the voyage.

The voyage, via Taiwan, aboard the *Miike Maru*, was an indication of the state of transportation in the Pacific waters controlled by Japan.

"Don't worry about the submarines as this liner travels very fast," their instructor told the young Filipinos the day before they departed from Manila.[4] There was plenty of reason to worry about submarines, for although the Japanese in the beginning of the war had been contemptuous of the American submarine efforts, the attitude had changed in a year and a half. Major American submarine bases were established at Darwin and Perth, to augment the great Pearl Harbor base. The old S-boats were replaced by faster, bigger "fleet submarines," whose radar and other electronic equipment improved virtually with each vessel launched. The new fleet submarines could travel to Japan and stay on station for several weeks. The Americans had a great deal of difficulty with their inferior torpedoes, but by December 1942, they were able to begin the blockade of Japan. By the summer of 1943 sinkings were taking a grave toll on Japanese shipping.

They patrolled along the Indochina coast, sinking ships that headed up from Saigon and Sumatra, carrying rice and oil, tin and rubber. They moved around north of the Philippines and along the coasts of Taiwan. Some American submarines patrolled in Japanese waters, but the problem of distance was compounded by the increased antisubmarine activity the Americans faced in Japanese waters.

In the first year of the war the Americans sank 142 Japanese merchant ships. But that number began to rise almost month by month as the Americans launched more submarines. By summer 1943 the toll was almost a ship a day.[5]

The first day out the *Miike Maru* held a submarine drill and everyone turned out. That night came a real submarine alert off the Taiwan coast, but no submarine was seen.

The *Miike Maru* stopped at Takao (Kaohsiung). Some Japanese got off there, some Taiwanese debarked as well, and the ashes of many Taiwan soldiers killed in battle in the South Pacific were taken ashore, all aboard assembling on deck to honor them as they went.

From this point on the waters were dangerous, de Asis was told. Next step was the Japanese naval base in the Mako Islands, where they joined a convoy of eight ships escorted by a destroyer and a succession of aircraft.

They passed a southbound convoy even larger than their own, also under escort. Then they reached Japan.

As they came near the shore, all the passengers, including the army officers aboard, were sent below decks so they could not see the shore defenses. Japan at home had become very conscious of the war. And yet there was little visible sign of it at Moji, the town where they landed. They stayed in a Japanese hotel with straw mat floors, steaming baths, and sliding paper doors. They were interviewed by newspaper men, and their pictures were taken endlessly by photographers. They went by ferry to Shimonoseki, then by train to Tokyo, without incident. The dining car served excellent food, European style, as well as Japanese style. There seemed to be no shortages, whereas in Manila there had been nothing but shortages. For breakfast, de Asis had bread and butter, chicken, steak, fried potatoes, mayonnaise, ham and eggs, and coffee.[6]

De Asis's party arrived at Tokyo central station at 9:30 A.M.

> Here I was touched by a very pathetic scene. Our instructor, Lieutenant Hirose, who has been away from home for nearly two years, was met at the station by his pretty wife, whom he married just a few weeks before he left for the war. I could see how she tried to control her emotions, but her tears welled down her cheeks. She half smiled and half cried at the same time. She was so happy to see her husband. But all this time she could not approach

her husband who was busy attending to reporters. Lieutenant Hirose himself just gave her a salute and was apparently unmoved, but I could feel he too was controlling his emotions. He parted from his wife at the station. We proceeded to the station hotel and it was only after lunch at 2:00 P.M. that he went home to his wife after nearly two years' absence.[7]

The lieutenant was a very lucky man. Most of those who went south in General Terauchi's command of Southeast Asia never did come home, except in one of those little urns consigned to the family or to the Yasukuni Shrine.

On the surface, life in Tokyo in the fall of 1943 was not so much different from life before the war. The island kingdom had been bombed only once, by that handful of B-25s led by Lieutenant Colonel Doolittle. The trains ran regularly, although they were sometimes delayed for troops and military trains. The streets were filled with soldiers and sailors in uniform mingling with civilians in kimono and Western dress.

These young Filipinos were highly privileged, of course, and only the best was shown to them, as part of the program to educate them in Japanese language and Japanese ways. But they saw a healthy, hardworking Japan, with plenty of goods in the department stores in the Ginza, plenty of fresh and prepared foods of all sorts in the restaurants of Tokyo.

The young cadets visited the Greater East Asia Ministry and the Ministry of War, where they were given fountain pens, "A Gift from Premier and War Minister Hideki Tojo." They met the Javan, Sumatran, Burmese, and Malay cadets, and soon they were deep in their studies of Japanese language and customs at special schools set up for them.

They lived in a dormitory and ate rationed food. But they could always leave for an evening and go to a restaurant where food was not rationed. Despite the censorship of the newspapers, de Asis felt the English-language press did much more candid news reporting than he was used to in Manila. Early in his stay he was surprised to see an editorial in the *Japan Times* predicting the imminence of air raids on Japan, in view of the increase in enemy activity on all fronts. The enormous difference between the Japanese at home—friendly, kindly and generous—and the Japanese in the Philippines—overbearing, heartless and arrogant—never ceased to amaze these Filipino visitors.

But over all, they soon learned, people in Japan expected that attack on the homeland was imminent. That summer and autumn, General Tojo was preparing them for the worst. The first attacks, the people were told, would be coming any day. Japan's air defense system was reorganized, with the Ministry of Home Affairs given major responsibility for civilian air defense. It was too great a task for the military, who were being spread thinner and thinner.

"No slackening of effort can be tolerated," Tojo announced. "Heavy battles are in progress and others must be expected. The time has come for the Japanese people to adapt themselves to the present war situation and a determined battle front will be established at home and measures taken to ensure an epoch-making increase in war output."[8]

The great increase had to be in war material, especially aircraft, which were falling by the hundreds in China and the South Pacific. A munitions ministry was established to speed production. Aircraft were allocated between navy and army, and quarreling over allocations became commonplace, for although the navy's plane losses in the south were far higher, the army would not relinquish any of its quota of aircraft.

The army was represented in the new agency by Lieutenant General Saburo Endo. The navy was represented by Vice Admiral Takejiro Ohnishi, a seasoned carrier officer. Production of planes began to rise quite satisfactorily until it would hit 2500 airplanes per month. But the production of competent pilots was quite another matter.[9]

By autumn 1943, the pilot shortage was far worse than it had appeared to Admiral Yamamoto just a few months earlier. Mastery of the air was a major consideration everywhere.

A reporter from *Fuji* magazine was allowed to interview a number of Japanese army air force officers, most of them from Imperial Headquarters, and to publish his article. The officers were Major Jiro Tsukushi, Major Taieishi Ashihara, and Lieutenant Bunyo Hara of the Imperial General Staff, and Captain Noboru Hiraoka of the Kumagai Army aeronautical school.

Reporter: "What about the tremendous air battles that occur nearly daily in the South Pacific?"

Tsukushi: "The most important issue at stake today is mastery of the air. . . . The *Prince of Wales* and the *Repulse* ventured into waters controlled by the Japanese air force without a fighter escort because in those days both Britain and the United States believed that battleships could not be sunk by airplanes. You know the fate that befell these two ships.

"[As to island warfare] If the mastery of the air is in enemy hands it will be impossible to ship the necessary materials to the island and after about a week the soldiers on the island will find it impossible to keep themselves alive from lack of foodstuffs. Then, when that island falls, the enemy immediately builds an air base there. The next island also meets the same fate . . . and the next . . . that is how the so-called 'stepping stone' tactics were born."

Reporter: "Please tell us about the actual strength of the American air force in the South Pacific."

Tsukushi: "The American air force is more powerful than it has ever been. When I went to New Guinea, I thought I had experienced hard fighting, but I met with what I consider real aerial battles. I fought from early morning, slept on a rush mat and ate only rice balls. Such is the warfare in the south."

The discussion turned to fighter planes, and the army officer claimed that their Hayabusa fighter was superior to the American fighters—but he was talking about the P-40 fighters, which had virtually been phased out by the enemy in favor of P-51s, P-38s, and the navy's Grummans.

As to pilots:

Tsukushi: "Compared with Japanese pilots the Americans are sadly lacking in training and in their technical skill. In the United States unfavorable war results are never published as this might deter students from going to the front. In fact those who have experienced the fire of battle in the South Pacific are all confined in Australia so they will not be able to disclose the true state of affairs to those in the United States."

Amid this propaganda, however, facts did emerge for the careful reader.

Reporter: "Now could you tell me something about the enemy's heavy bombers?"

Tsukushi: "Say what you will, the biggest problem is the enemy four-motored Boeing B-17 bombers. When they made their first appearance in Burma, our men, including Major Ashihara here, shot them down quite easily. However after a while they were equipped with various contraptions and those which fought us at the time of the fierce struggle for Guadalcanal Island were quite difficult to bring down. We were forced to resort to collision tactics. . . ."[10]

Collision tactics? That meant suicide for the attacking pilot. But as Allied records showed, it was true. Towards the end of the Guadalcanal campaign, the Americans and Australians noted that the desperate Japanese pilots, outnumbered and shot up, had no hesitancy in trying to collide with an enemy plane before going down. It was the sort of problem the Eleventh Air Fleet pilots discussed back at Rabaul in the evenings after rice. And from time to time a Japanese fighter would seem to head directly for a bomber, taking no evasive action in its attack. American pilots noted a certain suicidal attitude.

Paying homage to the "superiority" of the Japanese, the reporter managed to elicit from the airmen the left-handed indication that the Americans had been able to increase their production of aircraft enormously.

Hara: "However, it is the quality of the pilots that counts the most and not the quality or quantity of airplanes."

And Major Tsukushi of the general staff had the last word: "After all, everything rests on the spirit of a nation. As long as we stand firm and united, we can be sure of victory."

That was pure *bushido*. As the war situation grew worse, *bushido* became ever more important. Since before the opening of the general Pacific War the media had devoted enormous publicity to retelling the stories of the old samurai and the new samurai. *Bushido* was the answer to all the problems of the war. *Bushido*, the Imperial Way. "There can be no Japan without the Emperor to reign over it."[11]

On November 5, 1943, the Japanese Diet building in downtown Tokyo was the scene of an unforgettable meeting: representatives of five Asian nations gathered there to formalize the efforts of the Greater East Asia Co-Prosperity Sphere in prosecuting Japan's war against the Western powers and China. This meeting was the culmination of more than a year of planning by the new East Asia Ministry. The hope was to instill in the conquered areas a real loyalty to Japan and to the concept of an Asian federation. Burma had been given its independent government. So had Indonesia and the Philippines. Manchukuo was "independent" and the "independence" of China was shored up by a new treaty of alliance between Japan and the puppet government of Wang Ching-wei. Subhas Chandra Bose, the Indian patriot, turned from the Congress party, who was itching to have a foothold in his native land, came to the meeting as an observer and was treated as if he were already a head of state.[12]

This meeting was not entirely a matter of window dressing. The Japanese were hoping to make a reality of the Greater East Asia Co-Prosperity Sphere, in spite of the viselike control the Japanese army held on all this territory. This season the "reins of government" were being passed in Burma, the Philippines, and Indonesia to local governments. The Philippines, it was trumpeted in Tokyo, would have total independence in 1945. To be sure, it was illusory, but within the civil ministries and the foreign office there was real hope that out of the struggle would come a united Asia.

The government had gone far to stage this production. Twenty thousand school children had assembled outside the Imperial Palace the day before to wave to the distinguished guests as they crossed the Double Bridge across the moat. The day after the Diet meeting, the delegates attended a massive people's rally staged at Hibiya Park. "Not an inch of standing room was available," said *Mainichi*, the crowd numbered a hundred thousand. Tojo spoke. So did the German ambassador. Both talked vaguely of the coming victory. Those speeches were reported in detail. Not reported at all was another set of statements that emerged elsewhere in the world that week. Meeting at Cairo, President Roosevelt, Prime Minister Churchill, and President Chiang Kai-shek came up with a pledge to carry on the war in the Pacific until Japan surrendered unconditionally. Japan, they said, would be stripped of Manchuria, Taiwan, and all the other territories she had taken. Korea would be freed.[13]

Not long afterwards came the Tehran meeting, where Stalin promised to enter the Pacific War on the Allied side just as soon as Hitler was defeated.

The people of Japan learned nothing of these meetings and decisions, not even through the Benjo Press. Censorship clamped down tight; the people of Japan were not to have a glimpse of the possible fate of their nation, a fate that in the waning days of 1943 had begun to bring chilling forebodings to those in the military who knew how matters really stood.

The answer of the militarists was to make ever greater demands on the people of Japan:

We, of course, do not expect to return alive as we take up guns and bayonets to embark on our glorious mission of crushing the stubborn enemy. Those of you students whom we are leaving behind will, I am sure, follow in our footsteps in the not distant future and march over our dead bodies to win victory in the Greater East Asia War.[14]

That was not the statement of a wild-eyed kamikaze. Ask a Japanese what a kamikaze was in 1943 and he would tell you it was the Divine Wind that blew away the soldiers of Kublai Khan when he tried to invade Japan in the fourteenth century. For there were no kamikazes, the concept of the programmed suicide diver had not surfaced. Yet those words were much the same as the words that would be uttered by thousands of kamikazes in the months to come. The difficulty of the war was being brought home to the Japanese, and the government was demanding the ultimate effort from every citizen. The quotation above is from the speech of Shinshiro Ebashi, a senior literature student at Tokyo Imperial University, leaving his studies now, in the national crisis, to go to the colors and die. The occasion was an assembly in the Outer Garden of the Meiji Shrine. The date was October 21, 1943. Attending were thousands of students from Tokyo's seventy-seven colleges and universities called to the colors in Japan's enormous need for pilots to man the planes and officers to lead the *banzai* charges into the teeth of the enemy. The dreadful day had come when university students, the cream of the nation's intellectuals, were no more than any other cannon fodder. They marched by in the rain, school caps on their heads, but rifles on their shoulders. In the spectators' bleachers were their mothers, sisters, and girl friends, their younger brothers from the middle schools, 65,000 strong, whose tears were indistinguishable from the raindrops. On the reviewing stand were Prime Minister–War Minister Tojo, and Navy Minister Shimada. The parade and ceremony lasted three hours. The students marched at last to the plaza before the Imperial Palace, stopped, raised three *banzai* for the emperor, and dispersed. They were on their way to war, and most of them on their way to death.

That autumn of 1943, all students above the drafting age of twenty were ordered to report for enlistment by December 1. They had five weeks' notice. Always before it had been a year. The government eliminated seventeen types of jobs as male occupations and replaced men with women. The women began taking over as train conductors, bus drivers, ticket agents, cooks, waiters, and barbers. The draft age was lowered to nineteen. In a few months it would be dropped to eighteen.[15]

For the first time, conscription came to Taiwan. "Culminating the joy and jubilation of Taiwanese over the inauguration of the conscription system more than 8,000 Taiwanese residents of Hainan Island held a celebration. . . ." *Asahi Shimbun* reported. Strength through joy![16]

Autumn 1943 was the beginning of the time of Japan's sorrows. In the South Pacific Admiral Halsey's American and Australian forces were preparing to assault the Treasury Islands and Bougainville. Nearly every day the Allies raided Rabaul and the other Japanese air bases. The Japanese responded by raiding the American bases in the Solomons and New Guinea. In these raids the Japanese air force at Rabaul was ground down, down, down.

The invasion of Bougainville by the Allies was reported in Japan as:

OUR NAVY FIGHTERS BLAST
23 FOE'S PLANES AT RABAUL[17]

with lesser headlines about a large attack on Buin on Bougainville. Nothing was said about the invasion of Cape Torokina by American marines. The only mention of the army's ground operations was of those in China, where a campaign of "annihilation" was occurring in the Kaolikang Mountain area of Yunnan Province. But the annihilated Chinese just kept on fighting.

In the first week of November, the Japanese assembled a large force of cruisers and destroyers at Rabaul, intent on running down to Bougainville and annihilating the American landings at Cape Torokina. An American carrier task force hit Rabaul and virtually decimated the Japanese squadron in the harbor. The account of this battle was the first indication that the Japanese people received of the successful Allied invasion of Bougainville. The announcement from Imperial Headquarters was veiled in all the usual falsehoods about "victory" and enormous destruction of American ships and planes, but readers and listeners now knew that the Americans were not somewhere down by Vella Lavella Island, but at Bougainville, south of Rabaul. Imperial Headquarters could quote figures to show that in the past four months 245 enemy warships had been sunk. They could claim thousands of American aircraft shot down, more than the Americans had produced so far. But the fact remained: here were the Allies on Rabaul's front doorstep.

On November 8, the newspapers ran the Imperial Rescript declaring war on England and America, as they had done every month since war began. No steps were left untaken to keep Japanese war support at a fever pitch. Assembly followed assembly, with General Tojo appearing time after time in full military kit with medals. If rallies could have won the war, it would have been over in 1943. At each great public assembly, the prime minister promised victory to the people of Japan.[18]

Suddenly, on November 23, Japan learned that the focus of the war had broadened. Not only were the Japanese engaged in bitter struggle at Bougainville, but the Gilbert Islands had also been invaded.

Not Imperial Headquarters, not General Tojo, but "a military analyst" for Domei, the Japanese news agency, gave the Japanese people the word they hated to hear.

"The United States is obviously planning to thrust into waters fundamental to our Pacific strategy. The Gilbert Islands have now become a theater of decisive war between Japan and the United States."[19]

This article represented the sort of truth that Cadet de Asis found in the press. Japanese censorship was total, the names of ships, divisions, and regiments almost never appeared in the media. But there was no official category covering speculative writings by loyal journalists as long as they did not predict Japanese defeat, or in some other way show disloyalty. Thus, the Benjo Press and columnists sometimes revealed the truths of the war without violating any specific regulations. This was particularly true of the English-language publications, wherein the nuances of language often proved too subtle for the censors.

As the year ended, Sadao Iguchi, Tojo's government spokesman, summed up the accomplishments of Japan so far during the war.

"In the first year," he said, "Japan secured vast territory and inexhaustible resources by a grand military offensive.

"In the second year, she launched a great political offensive [the Greater East Asia Co-Prosperity Sphere].[20]

"In the third year Japan will launch a wholesale offensive, militarily smashing enemy counterattacks and further bolstering the unity of Asiatic peoples."

Oddly enough, however, Spokesman Iguchi did not promise that in 1944 Japan would win a military victory.

Bさん 来る

31. "The coming of the B-29s"

A s the year 1944 began, General Tojo proposed to take the
battle pressure off the Pacific area by movement on the Asian
continent. A new effort was to be made to defeat Chiang Kai-shek,
starting in central China, in order to wipe out the Chinese air bases,
particularly at Kweilin and Liuchou, from which American bombers
might attack Japan. Farther south, Tojo sanctioned a drive by the
Japanese forces in Burma against the Imphal-Kohima area of India.
If this could be captured it would put new pressure on the British
in India and provide a "homeland" for Subhas Chandra Bose's Provisional Indian Government. Bose promised, and the Japanese believed, that if he could achieve that foothold, British power would
be broken, and the Indian people would flock to the Greater East
Asian cause.[1]

There was another reason for the Imphal operation: to counter
an Allied joint attack, from the Chinese in the Hukawng and Salween
valleys, and from the British in the Akyab region. The British effort
was joined by a 5000-man force landed by glider behind the Japanese
lines near Mogaung.

The fighting in Burma had begun in January 1944, with the
Allied attack from the north. The fighting in China began in April.

In the Pacific that spring, the Americans came forth with the
strength about which Admiral Yamamoto had warned long before.
By November 1943, when the U.S. forces invaded Tarawa and Makin

islands and captured the Gilbert chain, the whole concept of American carrier warfare had undergone revolutionary change. In fact, the Americans had copied Yamamoto's tactic of bunching carriers into a huge carrier unit. Task Force 50, the new American unit was called. It was divided into four task groups, each larger than the old American task forces had been. Usually a task group consisted of three carriers, with a comfortable number of fast battleships, and/or cruisers, and always many destroyers. Task Force 50 at that time consisted of the carriers *Enterprise, Saratoga,* four new *Essex*-class fleet carriers, and five new light carriers. In this force alone the United States mounted more carrier power than Japan could now muster. On the West Coast of the United States shipbuilder Henry Kaiser was now turning out escort carriers in seventy days, and a whole new way of employing them had been developed. The escort carriers would accompany invasion fleets and convoys, leaving the task forces to strike targets in the heart of the Japanese empire. Another new factor had been added: the Grumman F6F fighter had replaced the F4F. The new fighter was faster and more powerful than the old and very much a match for the Zero. The Zero retained its superiority in turns, but that was all. Japanese pilots now found themselves outnumbered and matched by an American pilot discipline that had not always existed. The Japanese had to rely largely on their skill for survival.[2]

The first effort of the new American carrier force had been at the Gilbert Islands. It was followed early in December by an American attack on the Marshall Islands, which damaged the cruiser *Izuzu*, sank some merchant ships, and destroyed a number of precious Japanese aircraft.

The valiant Japanese defenders launched a night attack on the retreating carriers and put a torpedo into the new *Lexington*. But it did not sink, and the cost of this damage was high in Japanese planes, as it would always be from this time on. American ship radar kept getting better and better. The Japanese pilots tried a number of techniques, coming in almost at surface level to get beneath the radar, coming in very high, and then swooping down to attack low. These tactics worked better than the old, but the improvement in American antiaircraft guns and marksmanship also began to tell. Most of the pilots in these outer islands were Imperial Navy pilots, since island defense was the fleet's responsibility. The losses kept rising.

The role of the Combined Fleet had not changed with the death of Admiral Yamamoto. He was replaced in command by Admiral

Mineichi Koga, who was, in effect, a Yamamoto protégé. So the concept of seeking the "decisive naval battle" continued to be fleet doctrine. Each month, however, attrition reduced the air striking power of the carrier force. The navy was beginning to feel the fuel pinch and operations were curtailed to reduce any possible waste.

From January on, the American task force roamed the Central Pacific, striking here and there. The strike on the Marshalls, repeated in January, convinced Admiral Koga that they would be the next American target.

The January air raids on the Marshalls knocked out the last one hundred Japanese planes in the area. On January 31 the Americans landed on the outer islands around Roi-Namur. In a few days the Marshall Islands were in Allied hands. No attempt was made to reinforce the garrisons. They had been written off months before.

With the capture of the Marshalls, Admiral Koga gave an order that indicated the dreadful reverses Japan had suffered in the last few months. He abandoned the great fleet base and fortress of Truk. It was as if the British had abandoned Gibraltar. The fleet was moved to Palau far to the north, for the defense line of the Japanese empire was going back, back, back.[3]

Admiral Koga flew up to Tokyo to confer with the Imperial General Staff and had some plain words to say to them. Japan no longer had a Combined Fleet, he said. Attrition had destroyed it. The admirals argued that the Combined Fleet would rise from the ashes. Plans were afoot, they said, for fifteen new carriers. The *Shinano*, which had originally been planned as a superbattleship, was now going to be a supercarrier and ready to fight in 1945.[4]

That was all very good, said Admiral Koga, but he could fight only with the ships at hand. His losses in the Solomons battles had been so severe that the fleet had to be reorganized.

It would be called the Mobile Fleet from this point on, he said. The carrier force had been greatly diminished. The problem was pilots more than planes. Virtually the whole First Carrier Division pilot force had been lost in the Rabaul area. The Second Carrier Division pilots had mostly gone down in the defense of the Marshall Islands. The pilot force of the Third Division was almost all brand-new, with about three months training in carriers. Many of these pilots were still learning: the 22nd Air Squadron, for example, consisted of ten pilots and thirty student pilots. If seven or eight of those students survived six months it would be remarkable.[5]

Pilot training had to be improved. The islands around Japan's empire would have to serve as "unsinkable carriers." The navy must have many more aircraft than it was getting. The land-based air force must be centered in the Marianas, at Tinian or Saipan. Also, Saipan would be the new fleet headquarters; Saipan was the point, all agreed, including General Tojo, beyond which the Americans would not be allowed to pass.

Imperial Headquarters, in turn, had some bad news for Admiral Koga. The supply situation was such that the new Mobile Fleet could not be accommodated at Saipan. American depredations against tankers had grown so serious that the tanker force to keep the fleet supplied there could not be guaranteed. Therefore, much of the fleet would have to remain in Indonesian or Malayan waters, close to the source of supply. Admiral Koga, the flagship, and a handful of ships would remain at Palau.[6]

Admiral Koga prepared a new defense plan for the empire. The zone of inner defense extended on the east from the Kuril Islands on the north down past Honshu to the Nanpo Shoto, then to the Marianas, the Carolines, and the western end of New Guinea. Any enemy incursion into that line would be met with all the force the navy had to offer.

In February, the Americans seized the Green Islands, 120 miles southeast of Rabaul, which nearly completed the Allied encirclement of New Ireland Island. In mid-April the American carrier task force attacked Truk. Admiral Koga had outfoxed them. They found a few ships in the harbor and sank them. They were met by about sixty Japanese fighters and in two days of raiding shot down most of them. More valuable naval pilots lost. One cruiser was badly damaged.

The move from Truk to Palau was almost Admiral Koga's last act. His plane was lost in a storm, and he perished. In May he was replaced by Admiral Soemu Toyoda, head of the Yokosuka naval base, as chief of the fleet. Admiral Nagumo was out, pushed aside to command the land-based air forces in Saipan. Vice Admiral Jisaburo Ozawa became the new commander of the carrier forces, operating in the flagship, *Taiho*. Japan now had six operational carriers of good size: *Taiho, Zuikaku, Shokaku, Junyo, Hiyo,* and *Ryuho.* There were more carriers but all of them were converted hulls of one sort or another, mostly seaplane carriers. The fleet was now stationed mostly at Tawi-Tawi, Borneo, very close to the source of fuel supply.

The submarine menace had grown much worse in the last six months. In the spring of 1944 the United States Navy had more than a hundred submarines in operation in the Pacific Ocean. In January more than 300,000 tons of Japanese shipping were sunk. Figuring the average ship at about 5000 tons, this meant perhaps sixty ships that would no longer bring supplies to the homeland from the Greater Asia Co-Prosperity Sphere or war materials from the homeland to the fronts.

American submarines had grown so bold that they threatened the home waters unmercifully, even penetrating Tokyo Bay. Admiral Koshiro Oikawa, who was in charge of antisubmarine warfare, tried to lure American submarines with a Q-ship, the *Delhi Maru*, a merchantman that had been turned into a warship while retaining her old lines. She was manned by a crack Japanese navy crew, and her whole purpose was to sink submarines. She was sunk right off Tokyo by an American submarine during her first night at sea.[7]

Other American submarines were sinking so many tankers that the home front was feeling a fuel shortage. Two convoys sent to reinforce the Mariana Islands that spring were ambushed by American submarines (with assists from the code breakers in Pearl Harbor). The Imperial Navy was spread over so much territory that when the Imperial General Headquarters looked for trained troops to send to the Marianas they had to go to the Kwantung Army. The 29th Division was sent to Saipan by ship, the ships were sunk, and most of the soldiers were lost. A second troop convoy to the Marianas was also decimated.[8]

The spring of 1944 found Imperial Headquarters beleaguered, bogged down and retreating in northern Burma, trying desperately to move into Imphal and establish a defense line, moving back steadily in Dutch New Guinea, and winning endless meaningless victories in a China that had become a bog for Japanese armies.

Were that not enough trouble, more was on the way.

On April 26, 1944, a squadron of Japanese army fighters was flying north of the Himalaya Mountains, prepared to attack any Allied planes trying to fly supplies into China "over the Hump," when suddenly the leader saw a strange plane high above. It was huge, the largest plane the pilots had ever seen, and unlike any others, with a very long silver fuselage, four big engines, and a high tail assemblage. It wore the star of the United States Army Air Forces. Six of the red-balled fighters peeled off and began to climb. When they reached the altitude of the big bomber, for the bristling guns showed what it was, the leader drew alongside and examined the plane carefully. Finally he gave a signal, the six fighters moved into a circle and began attacking the bomber. The leader came in fast, guns spitting, and wounded the gunner on the port side. For some reason the plane did not fire back and the Japanese attacked again. Then the tail gunner caught one Japanese fighter and set it afire, it fell away smoking, and the others broke off the attack and followed their comrade down out of the high altitude.[9]

The B-29 had just arrived in China.

For many months Imperial General Headquarters had been aware of the effort in the United States to create a bomber that would bomb Japan from faraway bases. At first the Japanese airmen scoffed at the idea. That was before they talked to engineers at Mitsubishi Aircraft Company, who assured them that the theory was quite feasible. Mitsubishi engineers were working on plans for a Japanese aircraft that would be able to bomb the Panama Canal and the American West Coast from the Kuril Islands.[10]

Imperial Headquarters had many reports of the progress of the transcontinental bomber. General H. H. Arnold, chief of the U.S. Army Air Forces, told the press that it was designed for the bombing of Japan. This news was picked up by the wire services, transmitted to Buenos Aires, and there Domei picked it up and sent it to Japan.[11]

Month after month came more reports, of progress and difficulties at the Boeing plant in Seattle, of strikes at the Wright engine factory. Then, on April 26, 1944, the airplane appeared over China's skies.

Imperial Headquarters was expecting this sort of unpleasant surprise, and had been since the summer of 1943, as noted. That fall the China Expeditionary Army had been issued some new orders, which involved the capture of airfields in Kweilin and Liuchow to prevent bombing raids against Japan. Early in April Lieutenant General Eitaro Uchiyama with four divisions attacked from north China into the southern area of the Peking-Hankow railroad. The Fifth Air Army supported this force, which linked up with the southern armies the next month. The Eleventh Army began to move in the Hunan-Kwangsi region toward Changsha. They would drive on toward Kweilin and Liuchow.

The B-29s that had flown into China were hardly finished products. President Roosevelt had promised Chiang Kai-shek some evidence of real help, and the bombing of Japan was a political essential. The project had been rushed; the reason that B-29 had seemed such an easy target to the Japanese fighters in April was that the electrical system operating the guns had failed as the battle began, and the only operable gun was the tailgun worked manually. Such difficulties dogged the American airmen that spring. The Japanese army drive also upset the American plans: Lieutenant General Joseph Stilwell and Major General Claire Chennault, the two senior American officers in China, had suggested that the B-29s use the Kweilin and Liuchow bases, because from there they could reach Tokyo. But General Arnold had not trusted the Chinese ability to defend the bases and had elected to place the B-29s in the Chengtu area, far to the west in Szechuan Province. Thus, while the Japanese were successful in their drive on Kweilin and Liuchow, and captured Nanning before their campaign ended, it had absolutely no effect on the B-29 operations, except to drive them farther back into China. This victory protected Tokyo, but it did not protect Kyushu.[12]

The first use of B-29s seemed to be a vindication of all the slighting remarks the Japanese had ever made about American abilities. Nearly a hundred B-29s took off from Indian bases and raided Bangkok. Only seventy-seven planes actually bombed, and of the bombs only eighteen hit in the target area. Five bombers and seventeen crewmen (each bomber had a crew of eleven) were lost on the way back to base.[13]

In June enough B-29s had assembled in western China so that the American high command decided it was time to begin the bombing of Japan. June 13 was the day picked for the first raid. Seventy-five B-29s took off from the fields around Chengtu and headed for the Imperial Iron and Steel Works at Yawata on Kyushu. They began bombing just before midnight, coming in at 8,000 feet. The Japanese searchlights found them and Japanese antiaircraft began firing. A few fighters came up but not many. No B-29s were shot down, but as a purely military operation the raid was a failure. Only one hit was scored on a power house about three-quarters of a mile from the coke ovens, which were the real target. That was immaterial. The important matter was that Japan was now going to be bombed. No one believed this raid to be a fluke like the B-25 circus staged in 1942.[14]

The Japanese were now aware of the coming of the B-29s, and where they were coming from. In its usual fashion Imperial Headquarters released the news piecemeal, and in a manner designed to give a wrong impression. On the Kyushu raid, one B-29 had been forced to make an emergency landing at Neihsiang airfield in Honan Province, very near the front lines. The captain of the plane had called for help in an uncoded transmission to the 14th Air Force headquarters at Kunming. The Japanese had intercepted the message and sent bombers which got there before the American planes. They destroyed the B-29 on the ground. On July 3, Japanese newspapers carried photographs of the bombing. "B-29 in Flames" was the caption of the war ministry photograph, proof that the alert airmen of the emperor were on guard to prevent the hated Americans from bombing Japan. Imperial Headquarters implied that Neihsiang had been the B-29 base, not an emergency landing field.[15]

The attention of Japan was diverted that month by the American assault on Saipan. The news came to Japan in the form of dissertations on the Japanese fleet's "victory" over the American fleet in the Battle of the Philippine Sea. At this point the Imperial Headquarters propaganda machine outdid itself in misrepresentation. The battle cost Japan the carriers *Taiho, Shokaku*, and *Hiyo*, and the other three carriers involved in the action were damaged. Even worse, Admiral Ozawa had attempted to use Saipan and Tinian and Guam as "unsinkable carriers" and shuttle planes from carrier to island and back again, attacking the Americans en route. The plan miscarried dreadfully, and most of the planes were lost, which meant so many trained carrier pilots that by the end of the battle, Japan's carrier navy ceased to exist.

For days the Japanese did not learn that besides the naval battle, the Americans had landed soldiers on Saipan on June 15. This was the island that General Tojo had promised Japan to defend as the southernmost anchor of empire. Never, he had said, would the enemy pass the Marianas.

The battle raged into July. The national newspapers in Tokyo referred in sidelong fashion to the land battle with such comments as *Mainichi*'s: "The enemy still possesses some reserve power for future operations, for which we should be prepared."[16]

The Japanese reports of the battle were very sketchy. On July 4 Imperial Headquarters announced:

Units of the Imperial Japanese Forces on Saipan Island, with increased fighting spirit, are now furiously engaging a powerful enemy force in terrific battle after firmly securing the line extending from the town of Garapan to Mt. Tapochau.[17]

Any Japanese reader with access to a map of Saipan had to know from this fragmentary report how affairs were going on that island. Saipan rather resembles a brontosaurus standing on his hind legs. The widest part of the island, in about the center, runs from the town of Garapan on the northeast to Kagman Peninsula on the southwest, with Mt. Tapochau in the center of the line. If the Japanese forces had secured the Garapan–Mt. Tapochau line, that meant the Americans were halfway up the island.

The only good news was from the China front, where the Japanese drive to wipe out the air bases in central China was succeeding. But it was a pyrrhic victory, for the Americans had become established far to the west, beyond even the Japanese air force capacity to bomb them.

On July 8, fourteen B-29s raided Kyushu again. The target was once more the Yawata complex in the Sasebo area, but nothing much was hit. "All the bombs fell into the sea," said Imperial Headquarters.

"The second attack on Kyushu, too, ended completely in a brilliant victory for us," said an Imperial Headquarters spokesman. "The effect of the raid has been to increase further the determination of those in the ranks . . . and in stimulating the fighting spirit of the people in their struggle for the defense of the land." The real reason of the attack, said the spokesman, was to demonstrate the strength of Japan's air defenses.[18]

Millions of Japanese, however, could remember that the army had promised them they would never be bombed at all, and General Tojo had promised them that the Americans would be held outside the perimeter of empire. The perimeter had been changed twice in recent months. The Allied attack was to Japan like the assault of a dentist on a tooth. There was little sensation as the dentist ground into the hard enamel (Solomons) but sharp pain as he struck the dentine (Saipan). Add to that the scraping of the chisel (B-29s).

Following the communiqué of July 4, Imperial Headquarters had nothing to report about fighting on Saipan until July 12, when the communiqué announced that the Japanese were "closing in on the enemy in the neighborhood of Mt. Marpi"—located at the extreme northern end of the island. The brave Japanese were "ceaselessly battling against numerically superior enemy units, after firmly securing their strong positions as well as many cavern defenses."[19]

Then, from Imperial Headquarters, came a silence that grew daily more ominous.

The Japanese people received their first intimate view of the disaster at Saipan from an article in the July 3 issue of *Time* magazine, translated and dispatched to Tokyo by the Stockholm correspondent of *Asahi Shimbun*. The Japanese story dwelt on the furious efforts of the defenders and the heavy American losses (true), but it was an accurate account of the battle through the capture of Mt. Tapochau. The facts were well known to Imperial Headquarters from Lieutenant General Yoshitsugo Saito's final radio message: on the night of July 6, the general had sent his apologies to the emperor for failing to hold Saipan and had told Imperial Headquarters that next morning he would stage a last *banzai* attack with the pitiful remnants of his army. Then there had been silence even for Imperial Headquarters. The Saipan force had been wiped out, almost to the last man. That force included Admiral Chuichi Nagumo, the commander who had failed Admiral Yamamoto four times.[20]

The news from Burma was less spectacular but equally disastrous. General Slim's British Fourteenth Army had managed to evade the Japanese and to hold out against the march on Imphal. The Japanese had been unable to supply the Imphal operation properly, and the troops were deeply affected by hunger and disease, as well as shortage of ammunition. The Imphal campaign was in shambles. As Imperial Headquarters knew, the central China campaign was running down, and in northern Burma the Chinese and Americans and British were putting on pressure that would drive the Japanese east of the Salween River.

By July 17, General Tojo's government was still concealing the fall of Saipan from the Japanese people, but could not conceal it from the emperor and his advisors. The *Kempeitai* and the civil police were employed to root out dissent within the government, and a number of officials were entrapped into expressing doubts about the war, whereupon they were hustled off to jail.

At this point in the war there were two sources of power, Tojo's dictatorship—for that is what his rule had become since he took direct command of military operations—and the Imperial Palace, where the council of elder statesmen still could make or break a government by appeal to the emperor.

On July 16 an embattled General Tojo still tried to hold political power, by "reorganizing" his cabinet. He attempted to shift the blame for the fall of Saipan to Admiral Shimada, that naval officer who had done his bidding like a dog since the opening of the Pacific War. Admiral Naokuni Nomura was appointed to be the new navy minister.[21]

On July 18, Tojo finally issued a statement on Saipan:

> Our empire has now been confronted with a situation which in all our history is the most important. It affords us, at the same time, the rare opportunity to crush the enemy and win the victory. . . .
>
> Let us all of our one hundred million people together, renew our pledge and our determination to make the supreme sacrifice and concentrate the traditional fighting spirit of our country handed down through three thousand years to the attainment of the ultimate victory, thereby setting the Mind of His Imperial Majesty at rest.[22]

To set the imperial mind at rest, Tojo made more changes. The navy was shaken up from top to bottom. General Yoshijiro Umezu was appointed chief of the Imperial General Staff, a position Tojo had usurped in recent months. General Sugiyama was kicked over into the post of inspector general of military education, which had been reduced in function to virtually a bureaucratic department by Tojo.

But Tojo had failed. His Imperial Majesty's mind was not at rest and no amount of rearrangement of the government shrubbery or cajolery about the supreme fighting qualities of the Japanese military would now serve.

On July 20, having exhausted every resource, and having been rejected by a determined council of elder statesmen, backed privately by many of the generals of the army, General Tojo resigned as prime minister. It was a sign of the official displeasure against his behavior that he, alone, among former prime ministers was not asked to join the council of elder statesmen. General Tojo had bullied his way to absolute power, beginning with that appointment as war minister in the Konoye cabinet. Now he suffered the consequence of power abused. But Tojo's suffering was as nothing compared to what now would befall the nation.

あとは 野となれ 山となれ

32. "After him, the deluge"

*T*he fall of Saipan in July 1944 was the blow to Japanese hopes
for the Pacific War that caused the fall of the Tojo government.
One reason was the nature of Saipan as opposed to the Solomon,
the Gilbert, and the Marshall islands, which had fallen to the Allies
in recent months. The latter were all new acquisitions, bits of empire
but not part of Japan itself. Saipan, a part of the old German Marianas
colony, had been taken over as a Japanese mandate from the League
of Nations in 1920 whereupon many Japanese had settled there.
Most of the Chamorros, the native people of the Marianas, had been
pushed out, to Guam and other islands. So Saipan to the Japanese
people was quite unlike these other foreign places, and as much a
part of Japan as was Taiwan, where many Japanese had also settled.
The schools, the government, the society were all Japanese. Had
General Tojo been able to show the success of the Imphal operations
to attack India, or had the central China forces been able to move
back to Chungking, Tojo might have survived. But given those failures and the coming of the B-29s, which were, in a sense, still only
casting their shadow before them, the confidence of the people and
of the ruling class around the emperor was lost.

Once Tojo was gone, for the first time the Japanese people
were given an indication of how badly the war was going for them.
The army and navy sections of the Imperial Headquarters issued a
joint statement for public consumption which gave the basic details
of the fight for Saipan.[1]

For the first time, the Japanese people learned just how badly outnumbered and overpowered by the Americans were their forces in the Pacific. The only concealment, understandable for military reasons, related to the Battle of the Philippine Sea. And then the navy could not bring itself to admit the extent of that disaster, or to mend its mendacious ways with communiqués. But the army's almost day-by-day account of the fighting on Saipan was truthful. For the first time since Midway, Imperial Headquarters told the truth to the people. (See Appendix A.)

This statement hit Japan like a shock wave. For the first time, millions of Japanese began to understand that the war was lost. For the first time the Japanese heard of "human bullets"—men who strapped explosives to their bodies to attack the enemy. If the Japanese army had adequate antitank weapons and the like there would be no need for such tactics. For the first time Japanese people began to question the omnipotence of their forces. Three thousand wounded soldiers committed suicide in one night rather than surrender. Certainly, this gesture was a manifestation of the Imperial Way, but it was also an indication of defeat. The communiqué left no doubt that the 50,000 Japanese military men and civilians on Saipan had perished almost to a soul. No such shock had ever coursed the land before.[2]

What the people did not know, and would not be told, was that those "human bullets" of Saipan were not volunteers in the normal sense. When General Tojo had taken complete dictatorial power as chief of the Imperial General Staff, war minister, and premier, he had brought into office a favorite, General Jun Ushiroku. It had been General Ushiroku's idea to "suggest" to the field armies that they use human bullets. There had been incidents of such self-sacrifice before; but what General Ushiroku had done was make suicidal self-sacrifice a part of the military system. This was just another of the counts the army held against Tojo and his toadies. The moment Tojo went, so did Ushiroku, off to command an army in Manchuria.

On July 20 the council of elders, virtually all of them former prime ministers, met with the emperor to choose a new prime minister.

The advisors could not agree on a single figure; the animosity between navy and army was so great that neither side would trust the other. Thus a compromise was achieved, General Kuniyaki Koiso and Admiral Mitsumasa Yonai would share authority in the new government. Koiso would be prime minister, but he would consult with Yonai, the navy minister. General Sugiyama, who had been deposed by Tojo, returned to authority as war minister.[3]

The new watchword of the nation was "harmony" between army and navy. "Absolutely essential for victory," said Admiral Yonai. "In close cooperation with the navy I am firmly determined to smash the enemy," said General Sugiyama. "Still closer relations," promised Prime Minister Koiso.[4]

It was all said very sincerely. It was all a sham. So basic were the quarrels between army and navy, and so many the slights heaped on the navy over the years, that although the harmony song was sung constantly from this point on, there still was no harmony.

Despite the shock of Saipan, and the continuing shock to Japanese witnessing from afar the fall of Tinian and then of Guam, life went on in Japan with very little change. The young Filipinos at first scarcely knew there was a war. The trains continued to run on time. There had been no more bombing of Kyushu after the raid of July 8, and even that was known in Tokyo only because of the media. There had been no air raid warnings on Honshu Island.

Those cadets from the Greater East Asia Co-Prosperity Sphere continued their studies, moving around happily. The Koiso government had adopted as one of its main principles the promotion of the Greater East Asia concept, and the young visitors were welcomed everywhere. On the day that Tojo resigned, Cadet de Asis and his friends spent the afternoon at the Dai Nippon Biiru Kaisha, the Greater Japan Beer Company, which produced Asahi, Ebisu, and Sapporo beers. Everyone in the party, especially the Japanese instructors, got a little drunk. Then, they all went off for a weekend in the mountains of the Hakone National Park. Tokyo station was jammed with people that weekend. When they arrived at Hakone they found the buses to Ashinoko Lake's resorts were filled with holiday goers. Interest in the politics of war seemed slight indeed.[5]

But appearances could be deceiving. One reason trains and buses were so crowded was a realization by the new government that the bombing of Japan could not now be far away. Children from the thirteen largest cities would be evacuated to the countryside. This meant 400,000 youngsters, and they were already beginning to move out to remote villages and towns where they would be safe.

The war was closing in on Japan. Most of the fine restaurants and geisha houses were shut down and the geisha were told to find war work. As fuel became ever more scarce, travel restrictions were imposed on the average citizen. Police permits were required for anyone who wanted to make a long trip. The dining cars on trains were abolished. Rice became virtually unobtainable by the average citizen. Pumpkin became a staple of life, and almost every foot of arable land was planted in some sort of garden by somebody. City dwellers began to feel the pinch so badly they were trading off valued family possessions for black market food to augment the slender ration of bean cake and mixed unhulled grain they received each month. The shortages of everything grew by the day. Aluminum, copper, and tin were in very short supply despite the capture of Malaya with its minerals, and building firms saw all their materials going to the government. Even pots and trays were taken; the Ya-sukuni Shrine's great bronze *torii* (gates) were dismantled, taken to factories, and melted down for the war effort.[6]

The lesser nations of the Co-Prosperity Sphere were also subjected to new demands. A new Philippines Commodities Purchasing Corporation was established in Manila to ship war materials back to Japan. Philippines President Laurel urged all Filipinos to cooperate.[7]

The ignominious defeat dealt the Japanese naval air arm in the air battles of the Marianas brought firm reaction from naval airmen. Vice Admiral Takejiro Ohnishi studied the records so his naval air force might find solutions to its serious problems.[8] Aircraft production was not really a problem, but pilot production certainly was, as Admiral Yamamoto had said two years earlier. Before the war a pilot was expected to have eight hundred hours of flight time before he could be taken seriously for carrier operations. To produce a competent fighter pilot was at least an eighteen-months proposition. But as Admiral Ohnishi knew, the navy did not have eighteen months, and pilots were needed immediately. The Marianas battles had just about finished off the old hands from the China war and the days of Pearl Harbor. The liabilities of the navy now were inadequately trained pilots and aircraft that were not really competitive with the new American fighters or able to make contact with high altitude bombers. It was true that new weapons were already in production— the Shiden fighter was far superior to the Zero and in the hands of a master pilot could compete with any American plane. But where were the master pilots?

The admiral also looked back on the Marianas battle and the battles of the South Pacific for guidance.

On July 25 the Ministry of War announced that Major Katshu-shige Takada and seven other army pilots had been cited by the emperor for diving their planes into Allied ships during the landing of General MacArthur's forces at the island of Wiak at the end of May. Of course, the army communiqué indicated that they had sunk two enemy cruisers and damaged two others, facts that the Allied records did not bear out. But the principle, becoming more accept-able at every moment, was that the end justified the means, that a suicidal attack that brought damage to the enemy was an heroic effort.[9]

On July 29 the Imperial Palace released the twentieth list of honors granted posthumously to heroes of the armed forces. This concept of honoring only the dead was the Japanese way. A pilot might enlist as an army private and work his way up to corporal. The fact that he was a superior pilot had nothing to do with his advance-ment in the army service; he was expected to be a superior pilot. Unlike the American services, skill did not bring promotions and thus movement from combat to military management. Saburo Sakai, the navy's ace who survived more than two hundred aerial encounters and shot down so many Allied planes he could not count them, spent most of the war as a petty officer.[10]

Once a hero died, however, the Japanese were more than gen-erous in praise. Sometimes the awards included a medal and double promotion, posthumously.

On July 29 the emperor's aides announced that on this twentieth list of dead heroes were the names of 9,300 men, most of them from the battles for Guadalcanal and the Solomons. The medals were the Order of the Golden Kite, Order of the Rising Sun, and the Order of the Dual Rays of the Rising Sun.[11]

These awards were made for the normal sort of heroism one would expect of fighting men: Major Toshiharu Aida, killed while fighting against odds in the West Hunan operations; Major Eiji Sak-urai, killed in an air battle over Burma; Captain Tetsuo Morita, killed while leading his troops of the Kawaguchi Detachment on Guadal-canal in an assault on the U.S. marine artillery near the beach. In no case was a special mention made of suicidal action, where the hero set out to destroy the enemy and himself. This would soon change, spurred by the efforts of Admiral Ohnishi.[12]

In that summer of 1944, Admiral Ohnishi began to promote within the navy and among his friends outside the navy, the concept of a force of suicide pilots who would carry the war to the enemy, preferably by sinking all his aircraft carriers.

At first Ohnishi met a good deal of antagonism to these proposals within the naval hierarchy. *Bushido* called for the warrior to be prepared at any moment for death, but it did not say the warrior sought death as the sole end of his military action. To many Japanese military men, the concept of preplanned suicide went against all they had been taught about conservation of resources and the way to win battles.

Ohnishi broached the subject to Prince Takamatsu, a member of the royal family, an old navy comrade, and an old friend. The prince was horrified. Ohnishi mentioned it to Vice Admiral Kimpei Teraoka, a contemporary in the naval ranks. Teraoka looked at Ohnishi as though he thought he was mad. Ohnishi's answer was simple: given the straits to which the Japanese naval air force was reduced, what was the alternative?[13] Probably it was the depersonalization of the individual that upset these generals and admirals. They had no answers for him.

The Japanese army air force's senior officers had begun months earlier to think along the same lines, without any communication with Admiral Ohnishi. Since the beginning of the year, Lieutenant General Takeo Yasuda, one of the senior officers of the air force, had been working quietly on the concept of suicide operations. A Special Attack training program was under way. The young men assigned (the difference between the navy and army concept was the difference between assignment and voluntary duty) were not told what they would be expected to do, but they were enrolled in foreshortened courses. No emphasis was placed on navigation or engineering or marksmanship and weaponry. They were instructed carefully in a new technique called *tai-atari* (ramming attack), but if they asked why, they were told that it might become necessary if they got into an impossible situation. No one said the army was preparing to create the impossible situation.[14]

Army and navy were doing their best to get ready for the next blow from the enemy. The battle plan was prepared; it would be called Sho, the Victory Plan. It would force, finally, that "great decisive battle" that Admiral Yamamoto had talked about for so long. The difference between the new concept and the old was that army and navy promised that the great battle would be a joint effort. "True oneness" was the new slogan of the war and navy ministries. Army and navy would "cooperate" to destroy the enemy fleet and landing forces, whether they came on the China coast, in Formosa, in the Philippines, or in Japan itself.

Plans for all these contingencies were laid. By the end of July the odds in Tokyo were on a Philippine invasion, "the powerful deciding factor in the enemy's Pacific operations," as *Asahi Shimbun's* military expert put it.[15]

In order to achieve their aims, the war and navy ministers called on the government to raise Japanese fighting morale. This new emphasis was to be brought in various ways; one immediate instrument was a fright campaign to instill in the Japanese people a new fear and hatred of the enemy. In the field, the army had already done its job, and the witnesses to it, now dead, were the civilians of Saipan who committed mass suicide rather than be captured by the "bestial Americans."[16]

The Americans provided the ammunition for the campaign. In the fighting in the South Pacific some American marines and soldiers picked up Japanese skulls and sent them home as "souvenirs" of the war, not realizing the implications of their actions, or imbued by the hatred of the Japanese encouraged by tales of the death marches, Japanese murders, rapes, and cruelties to civilian populations and the bayoneting and other torture of live prisoners of war which was discovered on the battlefields. The Americans, too, knew that the best way to encourage ferocity against the enemy was to dehumanize him.

Some stories about such souvenirs appeared in the American press. The idea of collecting enemy bones was roundly denounced from American pulpits and by the military authorities, but, of course, the Japanese people were not told that. They were told that the practice (certainly limited to Americans of the worst possible taste) had produced a horrified comment from the Vatican.

In what had to be as vacant-minded a bit of misplaced zeal as existed during the war, Representative Francis Walter of Pennsylvania was reported by columnist Drew Pearson to have presented President Roosevelt with a letter opener made from the forearm of a Japanese soldier killed in the South Pacific, with the comment that he apologized because it was such a small portion of the Japanese soldier's body. (President Roosevelt refused the gift and suggested that the "letter opener" be given decent burial, but the Japanese did not learn this fact for some time.)[17]

That was all the Japanese government propaganda machine needed, for the Japanese revere the living symbols of the dead, the bones, hair, even fingernail clippings, in a manner quite beyond the ken of the Americans. The Japanese Shinto religion, during the war years the official religion of Japan, holds that the souls of the dead, and thus their artifacts, are always with the living and must be revered accordingly. The thought of a Japanese soldier's skull becoming an American ashtray was as horrifying in Tokyo as the thought of an American prisoner used for bayonet practice was in New York.[18]

YANKS TOYING WITH HUMAN SKULLS
WORSE THAN CANNIBALISM

That was the headline produced in the Japanese newspapers by the statement of the Board of Information. "Such sacrilege to the body of the human dead is not only a violation of international law but a violation of the highest laws of humanity. There are no adequate words in the human vocabulary with which we can speak of such sacrilege."

The new hate campaign plunged into high gear.

"That the Americans are morally inferior is common knowledge among those who know America," said *Mainichi Shimbun*. "Take, for example, American air raids on our hospital ships. Mankind must absolutely not permit such people to win the war. We shall fight to the bitter end to smash America."[19]

Yusuke Tsurumi, billed as an expert on things American, recalled that he had seen a copy of *Life* magazine containing photographs of corpses of Japanese soldiers—more insults to the dead. "Human ghouls," the *Nippon Times* called the Americans. Another writer reminded his readers of the American tank unit that used the skull of a dead Japanese soldier as a hood ornament.[20]

A few days after that revelation came a report from Berlin of atrocities committed by the U.S. 91st Division in Italy, as reported by Lance Corporal Werner Tibet of the 67th Panzer Grenadier Regiment. He and six other Germans had been surrounded near Castelliga Meritima and had surrendered. They had been taken into a

stable, lined up against a wall, and shot down by the American rifle-
men. The lance corporal had been wounded, and that night escaped
back to the German lines.[21]

True or not true? The details gave a feeling of verisimilitude.
The Japanese did not need much. The tale was just another nail in
the construction of an instrument of hate that would strengthen the
Japanese resolve to fight to the bitter end.

General Araki, the man who had done more than any other to
make of the Japanese soldier a merciless fighting machine, made a
bitter speech at a summer meeting of the Oriental Summer College,
an institution dedicated to the principles of a Greater East Asia
sphere.

The Americans could be expected to commit any brutality, he
said. "There is no such thing as mercy, or consideration or reverence," he said. "Women, children, hospital ships—everything is being
mowed down for the sake of destruction."[22]

Within two weeks after the first skull story appeared, the Japanese authorities managed to produce a photograph of an American
girl sitting pensively, pen in hand, obviously writing to her soldier,
thanking him for the skull, its empty eyesockets and grinning teeth
faced toward the letter.[23]

Desecration of the Dead
was the headline in every paper. Witnesses were called upon from
every corner of the Greater East Asia Co-Prosperity Sphere to condemn the barbarous Americans. The British did not escape, either.
From the north Burma front came a report that the British were
using Japanese and Chinese dead to fill up ruts in the roads. They
also, it was said, set mines under the Japanese dead so that when
parties came to pick them up they should be blown up. The British
also strung the Japanese prisoners of war up on trees and used them
for target practice, said the story. These were tales to match the
worst the Allies were telling among themselves about the Japanese,
and their purpose was the same: to arouse the hatred of the people
and the military men.[24]

In war there are always atrocities, although, as the cynics say,
only losers become war criminals. From the American annals are the
tales of "take no prisoners" for the first thirty-six hours after D-Day
at Normandy, or the story of the American squad that castrated one
German POW in front of another to get information, or the story
of Commander "Mush Morton," one of the most highly decorated

of American submariners, who liked to surface and machine-gun survivors of the ships he had sunk, and then brag about it in the officers' mess. There is a current in war that allows usually sane men to rationalize the worst atrocities.

There is another current in war that sweeps up the information authorized by governments. During the summer of 1944 many Japanese were considering the alternatives left open to them. As noted, army and navy officials were moving toward an acceptance of the suicide weapon as an instrument of policy. This was not officially made known to the Japanese people, but the information began to filter down through the cracks. For example, Captain Branimir Kirkoff, the Bulgarian air attaché at the Tokyo embassy, was interviewed by Kan Kikuchi, a Japanese novelist, on behalf of the government information agency. Kirkoff had been making a study of Japanese army aviation, from the Youth Flying Corps, to the active army squadrons. Kikuchi asked the Bulgarian what impressed him most about Japan.

Tai-atari (self-ramming), *jibaku* (self-destruction in the air) and *nikudan* (human bullet), said Captain Kirkoff unhesitatingly. Only in Japan could one find the spirit of *bushido* that these acts represented.

Thus, from the mouth of a foreigner, the Japanese were instructed in a new meaning of *bushido:* suicide in the common cause.

I feel that it is not the manifestation of just a single person's spiritual strength but that it signifies the spiritual force inborn in every Japanese. Only those who are lucky are given an opportunity by God to manifest it in some way. *Tai-atari* is not just the physical impact against the enemy; it is the combination of spiritual as well as physical forces which is hurled against the adversary.

The significance of the attack on Pearl Harbor by the Special Attack Flotilla can only be understood by a true realization of this awe-inspiring spiritual force which is released from time to time in the form of *tai-atari*. In the acceleration of war production this same spirit must be infused. This spirit of *tai-atari* is not a special feat of a chosen few but can be demonstrated by the united efforts of everyone engaged in productive activities. The remarkable exploits of Hero God Kato and the Special Attack

Flotillas [midget submarines] that attacked Sydney and Madagascar must not be thought of as individual expressions of this spirit but rather the result of the fervent spirit of patriotism engendered by the entire nation. Therefore, those who practice *tai-atari* cannot be compared to athletes or record holders who vie in individual competitions. . . . It is the death or victory, victory or death ideal which is embodied in the spirit of *tai-atari*.[25]

It was a remarkable statement, particularly coming from a foreigner who had just recently arrived in Japan. Is there any wonder that some Japanese believed Captain Kirkoff might have had a bit of Japanese help in working out his conception?

It was August 1944. No official suggestion had yet been made that Japan must employ suicide tactics as a weapon of the armed forces, and yet true to the Japanese way, the consensus was already being sought, and when the time would come in the near future, the people of Japan would be ready for the change.

親の因果が 子に報う

33. "The sins of the fathers are visited on the sons"

B y the end of August 1944, the Japanese government had intensified its campaign to prepare the Japanese people for new dis-
asters, and to instill in them the spirit of Saipan, so that they would
accept every privation and disaster yet to come.

When President Roosevelt and other leaders spoke of "unconditional surrender," the implications were made clear to the Japanese
that this meant occupation of Japan by foreigners, something that
had never occurred in their history.

Yasotaro Morri, writing in the *Japan Times,* compared the
American attacks on Japan with those of Kublai Khan six centuries
before.[1]

> When the Mongol expeditionary force appeared off
> the shores of Kyushu, Nippon's armament was altogether
> too inadequate. The Mongols had a fleet of formidable
> vessels while Nippon had no force to speak of, the invaders
> possessed the forerunner of a modern cannon of which
> the Japanese had never heard, until they actually faced its
> fire. . . . The Japanese fighters, then as now, were con-
> vinced of the truth of the military adage that in offense
> lies the best means of defense. What they lacked in ma-
> terial, they evened up with personal valor.

Valor, sacrifice, suffering—these were the themes of August
1944 in Japan.

All during the summer of 1944 the people of Japan waited for "B-san," the B-29s. The early raids on Kyushu had given them an idea of what to expect—they thought. The July raid on the steel facilities at Anshan, Manchuria, seemed remote and was sketchily reported in the Japanese media. Everyone was waiting.

Asahi Shimbun's military correspondent assessed the possibilities of raids from Saipan, now that the Americans had taken this island, just 2250 kilometers from Tokyo. Effective attacks were impossible, said *Asahi*. It would demand too long a runway to accommodate the B-29s, too much fuel, too many aircraft, and too many people and too many bombs and too much everything. It was beyond the ken of the *Asahi* military analyst that anyone could produce the wherewithal to carry on so large a bombing program.

"Even supposing that 300 heavies will be able to operate from these bases it can be said that raids aiming at complete destruction will be absolutely impossible. If the enemy should raid Tokyo in haste he will suffer great losses and deal only slight damage."[2]

But the manner of so writing was not meant really to convince readers that Japan would not be attacked from Saipan. What the Americans could do from western China they could do from Saipan and everyone knew it. The purpose of that article, written to avoid official displeasure, was to warn the Japanese of what was to come.

On August 20 the B-29s raided the Yawata steel works on Kyushu during the daylight hours. For the first time the Japanese air force drew blood. One Japanese fighter pilot was responsible for the destruction of two B-29s; he rammed one, and the resulting explosion of both planes sent a shower of debris onto another B-29 which caused it, too, to crash. *Tai-atari*, the ramming attack, was coming into its own.[3] A third B-29 was shot down by antiaircraft fire and most of the crew survived to become prisoners of war. Their plane was recovered by the Japanese, patched up, and brought to Tokyo for exhibition. Hundreds of thousands of Japanese rushed in to see B-san, and they were not disappointed. The government posters boasted that this was but one of a hundred planes shot down; the people smiled and looked carefully at the thick armor plate and the many machine guns, and thought about the future.[4]

The Japanese army now began the same sort of exaggeration that the navy had been guilty of for a long time. The air force claimed twenty-three bombers shot down and gave credit to three brave pilots for ramming attacks. Perhaps three pilots tried, but only one hit the target, and apparently the other two were shot down by the attackers. Once again, the damage caused by the American bombers was so slight that the Japanese military began to become contemptuous of the enemy, as they had been of the B-17s. (One Japanese ship captain claimed that whenever the B-17s flew high overhead he knew everything was going to be all right because he never saw them hit anything they aimed at.)[5]

As September came, the Japanese still waited. Imperial Headquarters reports from the fighting fronts suggested that Japanese were enjoying victories everywhere. In China they had finished up the central China campaign of 1944 by capturing Hengyang. The battle in China was the one among all where the army could claim forward movement. There was nothing very concrete in the repetitive claims that Japan's air heroes had shot down so many planes each day. The careful readers or listeners could gather, however, that the sheer number of Allied attacks on various Japanese bases in the Pacific and China had to represent very considerable forces.

And yet, nothing new really was happening.

Where was B-san?

Where was the new American invasion that the Japanese had already been braced to withstand?

On September 7, when the Diet convened in extraordinary session, Navy Minister Yonai and War Minister Sugiyama gave some hints to the people of what was to come. As always, their statements were bracketed within the proper usage ("I am filled with awe and deep emotion to have had the honor of being unexpectedly nominated minister of war. . . .").[6]

Navy Minister Yonai gave a brief resume of the war, which was notable for its usual exaggerations. ("The Imperial Navy in cooperation with the Imperial Army and other forces has succeeded in sinking 103 enemy submarines and seriously damaging 42." The fact was that the United States lost only 52 submarines during the entire war.) Minister Yonai's report brought the Allies up to the back of New Guinea. Where they would move next, he did not predict, but he spoke of Sumatra and Java in terms that indicated he believed the attack would come there. Wherever they came, he promised, they would be attacked by the full might of the Combined Fleet.

War Minister Sugiyama was more promising. He promised new adventures in Burma and China and avoided the matter of the Central

Pacific. But neither their speeches nor Prime Minister Koiso's call for even greater national effort for defense answered any questions.[7]

B-san, for that is how the Japanese universally now addressed the B-29s, came again to Anshan, Manchuria, on September 9. Four planes were destroyed; Imperial Headquarters claimed forty. The report was brief and was not followed by details, as happened when Imperial Headquarters considered a matter to be important. In Tokyo the sensation of suspended animation continued.

That sensation reflected the realities of the moment. The Japanese government was moving to shore up its defenses. Furious activity was taking place in procurement offices. Training, particularly in the air services, was speeded to the absolute minimum number of hours to put a man in the air. A new training program began, under which army pilots went to front line areas with their training half completed. They were expected to learn the fine points on the job.[8]

Attempts were now made through the China Expeditionary Army to make contact with Chiang Kai-shek and bring the China war to an end. The old hope that if the China situation could be resolved the Pacific War would vanish continued to drive Imperial Headquarters. But the negotiations with Chiang did not succeed. The Generalissimo could see as well as anyone else what was happening to Japan, and he now had reason to hope that he would get back all the China territory, plus reparations, when the war ended in an Allied victory.[9]

With the fall of the Tojo government the task of replacing his favorites had begun. One such was Lieutenant General Shigenori Kuroda, the replacement for General Homma in the Philippines. Kuroda had been corrupted by the soft life of a conqueror; he had spent most of his time on the golf course and his nights with a succession of geishas and prostitutes. The defenses of the Philippines were precisely in the state they had been left by the Americans.[10]

An investigating committee from Imperial Headquarters arrived in Manila and three weeks later Kuroda was shipped home in disgrace.

General Umezu and his staff at Imperial Headquarters fully expected the next Allied invasion to be in the Philippines. They wanted the finest fighting officer possible to take command, so they brought General Yamashita out of his exile in Manchuria and sent him to save the Philippines.[11]

When General Yamashita arrived in Manila, he found that the Japanese forces there numbered 430,000 men: 410,000 army troops, including air force, and 20,000 navy officers and men. But of the troops 60,000 were supply forces, whose use as defenders was limited.

That military force was so powerful that Yamashita should not have had much to worry about. But there was a catch: supply. He had only enough food and enough fuel for a very few weeks of operations. He predicted then that if the Americans came their victory would be achieved by starvation. He had no real hope of victory, a fact made very clear in the manner of his departure from Japan, when he indicated clearly to his wife that he did not expect to see her again.[12]

General Kuroda had cut the ground from under Yamashita in his treatment of the Filipinos; very shortly after Yamashita's arrival a bomb exploded beneath the floor of his headquarters, a bomb set by guerillas. It did no harm except to the room, but it warned Yamashita where he stood with the people of a conquered land.[13] According to the Japanese propaganda, the Philippine Republic, just established, was a firm member of the Greater East Asia Co-Prosperity Sphere. Possibly it could have been, had the Japanese in the Philippines been wise enough to treat the Filipinos as equals. But their arrogance, so much greater than the American, had turned the people against them. Too late, the generals were learning that their policy of allowing the commander in the field to dictate public policy in the conquered territories was to prove a large part of their undoing. In Japan Cadet de Asis and his friends were still being wined and dined, attending parties, eating white rice (when the average Japanese was eating a combination of unhulled rice and beans), drinking sake and beer, and visiting the Diet.[14]

Cadet de Asis was in the Diet that day when Prime Minister Koiso and the war and navy ministers reported, and he was much impressed with the ceremony. He and the other young men were preparing to go home and were now counting the days.

On September 11, however, when the cadets visited the Philippines embassy in Tokyo seeking information about their flight home, they learned that the presidential plane, *Kalayaan,* would not be available to take them back to Manila as they had expected. No one told them why. All they got were evasive looks. But if they wanted reasons, all they need do was look at the newspapers the next morning:

Mass Raid Attempted
On N.E. Mindanao Area

read the headlines in the papers. The articles, based on an Imperial Headquarters communiqué, told of raids by more than four hundred American planes on the Davao and Kagayan sectors of Mindanao that very day. Nor were these the first. Other raids for the past week had been made on southern Mindanao and Yap.[15]

"Thus the Pacific War situation is hourly becoming more intense," said Imperial Headquarters. "Of course the enemy movement against Palau, Yap, and Mindanao is only a forerunner of what is to come. The enemy actions indicate their intention to turn from a strategic, decisive war stage to that of tactical decisive war."[16]

On September 13 the young Filipinos paid a call at the South Seas Bureau of the Greater East Asia Ministry in Tokyo to find out what they could about events in the Philippines and their chances of going home. They were received with smiles and no information. They came away wondering if they would ever get home. That week they went to Toyono station in the country, near Nagano City, as guests of a wealthy farm family who owned extensive orchards. They were able to bring several boxes of apples back to Tokyo friends. Suddenly, in a matter of weeks, such things had become important. The parties for the young Filipinos continued, but it was only at parties that they saw white rice and steak and wine and beer. Nowadays when someone offered them popcorn or doughnuts, the event was worth commenting on. Japan was suffering from shortages. The rice was there in Indochina and Thailand, but getting it to Japan was another matter. All those "sunken" American submarines were taking their toll, and the slender supply of shipping was going now almost entirely for military purposes.

The Filipino contingent went by bus and train to Yudanaka Hot Springs, a popular ski and summer resort. They found it jammed up with school children from Tokyo. Across from the inn where they stayed and had stayed before, one month earlier, they saw a vacant plot of ground where had stood the biggest statue of Buddha in Japan. This brass statue had been carted away to an ammunition factory to make shell casings.[17]

Day after day Imperial Headquarters issued brief notes on the movements of American carriers around the Philippines, always, of course, leading with their figures of American planes shot down and never discussing the damage done to the installations on the islands.

The Americans, in fact, were sweeping away Japanese the way a giant would sweep away pygmies with a great broom. On September 22 Cadet de Asis was shocked to learn that Manila had been bombed, and immediately his thoughts turned to the fate of his family. The next day he had the news that the Philippine Constabulary, of which he was a member, had been rechristened Army, and that the Republic of the Philippines had declared war on the United States and Britain. All sorts of conflicting emotions now entered his mind. By this time, having been captured, mistreated, threatened, cajoled, flattered, and entertained by the Japanese, de Asis had experienced just about all that war could offer. Now he might be expected to go back to the Philippines and fight for Japan against the Americans with whom he had fought the Japanese. De Asis did not know what to do or what to expect. He consigned his future to his God. "Come what may, let it be so."[18]

One week later the Filipinos went home, enjoined to fight for Japan. General Homma and other officials saw them off at the station, bound for an airfield in Fukuoka. They flew from that place to Taiwan. The next day they flew to the Philippines, to land at Nielsen airport. The debris from the American air raid one week earlier still lay about the field, shattered hangars and burned-out aircraft.[19]

Day after day came the reports: American planes hit Palau, American planes bomb Cebu. On September 16 came an announcement of landings on Peleliu and Morotai islands by separate American units. The people were informed of the bare facts; the bare facts were grim enough.

To maintain morale, Imperial Headquarters and the government information agency prepared a series of articles about the military. The idea was to persuade the Japanese people of the superiority of the Japanese war machine even yet, and to keep up civilian morale. Navy writer C. Nakajima wrote a glorious account of the Combined Fleet from aboard a warship. "The whereabouts of the Japanese Combined Fleet is at present enveloped in deep mystery and both the enemy and the Japanese people behind the guns are watching its future with breathless interest."[20]

The fact was that the Combined Fleet was all over the map, for the simple reason that so little fuel was available that it could not be assembled in one place until Imperial Headquarters learned where the next major American assault would fall. Then the slender resources left to the navy would be put into one grand assault on the enemy.

"Aircraft forms the pivotal center of a fleet's fighting strength and all brilliant war results are traceable to the fight put up by the air arm. If the enemy presses on us with qualitative superiority," wrote Mr. Nakajima, "we are ready to meet the enemy with the self-blasting of one plane against one ship."

There! The secret was out, secret no more. The kamikazes had come to Japan, and, as usual, the people learned the facts without official announcement, through the medium of an unofficial report by an official reporter. The change in policy would not become official for another month, but the navy and the army were now both prepared for suicide tactics to try to change the course of war.

As everyone in Japan now knew, "the moment of decisive battle" was coming. It was public knowledge that the Combined Fleet was committed to do-or-die action at the first opportunity. So, for that matter, was Japan in its entirety committed by the government to the same philosophy. The Diet, which just ended its special session, had called on the government to create an organization "to respond to the needs of the decisive battle of the nation."

This meant the dissolution of the Central Headquarters of the Movement to Arouse the People to Action, and its replacement by another organization that would "give direction to various activities carried on in the proposed national movement to meet the needs of decisive battle."[21]

In terms of action, this now meant the replacement of women in industry by school children, of the military organization of men, women, and children into units that would train and prepare to fight the enemy on the beaches. It meant the stockpiling of ammunition reserves in caves and canyons in the mountains, and the preparation to fight from the beaches of Kyushu to the edge of Hokkaido.

The signs began to appear: one was a new drive to enlist young Japanese teenagers in the glider corps units that had sprung up around Japan and were now being intensified. Glider corps study gave these boys the rudimentary experience for flight. They were not told, but the progression was glider corps, then middle school, an accelerated air cadet course, and then assignment to a suicide unit. The plans were made, the problem as usual was time and equipment.[22]

September 25, 1944.

New features began appearing in the press: "Letters from Japan's Fallen Heroes" was one of them. The emphasis was on love of country, love of family, determination to give all for Japan, as one message from Lieutenant Kimio Mori, who was killed in the bitter fighting on Guadalcanal. Mori had graduated from the Law Department of Kyoto Imperial University. He worked for the Japan Board of Information for a time, then was sent to duty on the China front. When the Second Division was transferred to Timor he went there, as a squad leader. Later the unit was transferred to Guadalcanal. He was killed there in the fighting in January 1943. This card was discovered by the authorities in response to calls for such material from the public:

> Thank you for your kind letter. It brings back memories of days in Kyoto and many things you have written touch me profoundly. We are continually on the move east and west and have seen considerable action. Here on this southern isle we are now fighting day and night without a pause.
>
> I am enjoying the best of health. Until we defeat the enemy we will not stop![23]

Virtually all of the "Letters from Japan's Fallen Heroes" ended thus, with a call to all Japan for action and self-sacrifice.

The men of the "military press corps," the army and navy propaganda writers, outdid themselves to keep up the frenzied pitch. From the Philippines, Correspondent H. Onoda sent an account of Japanese airmen countering the American carrier air attacks.

After giving details of the heroic Japanese defenders and their successful assault on the American carrier force ("Every one of our fighters shot down at least two or three enemy machines. . . ."), the unit commander concluded:

> I am overpowered by the sense of regret at the thought of five of those planes under my direction which failed to return after the attack on the enemy. One of those who did not return single-handedly engaged in combat with eight Grumman planes which he met on the way from the assault on the enemy, and at the end of a very heroic fight he blasted [tai-atari] his plane and himself. The account of this fight in midair was furnished by the army unit which witnessed the struggle from the ground.

It is a profound regret that we could not deal the enemy a heavier blow than damaging and setting afire his vessels. My disappointment is all the greater as we were possessed of the spiritual and power to bravely go into the jaws of death at the first opportunity to finish the enemy completely.[24]

All it would take, the commander was saying, was a general order to finish up the attacks with suicide dives or ramming.

So the pressure on the Japanese army and navy pilots continued unremittingly at the end of September.

On September 26, seventy-three B-29s bombed Anshan again. The Japanese claimed they had shot down seven planes; actually they shot down none, but this raid so infuriated Imperial Headquarters in its growing nervousness that a long-range air raid was staged on the Chengtu bases and five B-29s were damaged.[25]

The propaganda campaign for more, more, more to the war effort addressed every aspect of Japanese life. The national income was Yen 30 billion in 1943; the forced savings of Japanese in obligatory bond purchases was Yen 17 billion, leaving Yen 13 billion for consumption, including various taxes. That meant the cash consumption of the Japanese in 1943 had been only Yen 130 per person, or less than a hundred dollars. Frugality was the watchword, as those tales indicate:

A schoolteacher was so ragged in appearance day after day that a friend finally gave him a new shirt. But the schoolteacher never wore the new shirt. "Why not?" asked the friend. "Because all my friends wear tattered clothes. It would be most unseemly for me to appear in something new."

An official went to visit an old Japanese field marshal in mid-February. He found the marshal sitting in a room, with no steam heater or stove or charcoal brazier in the house. "What do you do about the cold?" asked the visitor. "When I am cold I warm myself by sitting in the sun," said the field marshal.[26]

Ginjiro Fujihara, minister without portfolio, in the Tojo cabinet, never had even a charcoal brazier in his office, even during the coldest days of winter. Prime Minister Tojo gave him a stove. The minister thanked the prime minister politely and put the stove in a corner and did not use it.

Such tales, often repeated in the press, gave the Japanese an idea of what to expect in the winter of 1944–45. It would be privation and sacrifice far greater than anything that had gone before.

Day after day the reports of aerial attacks in the Philippines area continued. The bombing there spurred new activity in Japan, particularly in air raid precautions. Nearly 300,000 of the children of five cities had already been evacuated to the countryside, in groups of fifty, living and studying under a single teacher in some country inn or house. Industry now began to evacuate, scattering to small towns, and moving into caves and underground installations, all preparatory for the bombing of Japan that was expected any day, no matter what Imperial Headquarters said about the impossibility of it.[27]

On October 7, Admiral Toyoda, the new commander of the Japanese Combined Fleet, had flown to Manila for a personal inspection tour of the naval aerial defenses there. He was shocked at what he saw. Admiral Kimpei Teraoka, commander of the First Air Fleet, seemed to be completely under water, listless and without hope. Teraoka did not respond favorably to Toyoda's discussion of suicide attacks, and this was disturbing since the navy had already decided to employ this weapon. Admiral Toyoda hurried back to Japan and ordered Admiral Takejiro Ohnishi, the originator of the kamikaze plan, to go to Manila and take over for Admiral Teraoka, who would be sent where he belonged, with his great competence and faint heart: to a training command. Ohnishi was promised that when the expected American attack on the Philippines came he would also have the Second Air Fleet from southern Kyushu and Taiwan, the best trained and best equipped group of aviators left to Japan, as of October 10, 1944.[28]

On October 11 the danger was underlined by an Imperial Headquarters report of a new attack by the wide-ranging American carriers, this time on Okinawa and other islands of the Ryukyu chain. The enemy was now coming very close to home. The next day the Americans hit Taiwan like a thunderstorm. The battle lasted four days, and at the end of it most of the Japanese air power of the Second Air Fleet had been destroyed. But that is not the picture the Japanese people got, by far. The Taiwan air battle was claimed as a resounding victory for the Japanese. They first claimed to have sunk seven carriers and another fifteen war ships. By October 17 Imperial Headquarters claimed Japanese forces had sunk ten carriers, two battleships, three cruisers, and a destroyer, and to have damaged another nineteen ships. They also claimed the Japanese had shot down a thousand American planes. By October 19 the claim reached eleven carriers. Actually, two cruisers were badly damaged and several carriers less so.[29]

But the Japanese navy continued to make the most extravagant claims. The results of the Battle of Taiwan, said naval spokesman Captain Etsuzo Kurihara, surpassed any Japanese victory since Pearl Harbor. The pincers movement on the Philippines had been stopped; "the right arm had been wrenched off," said the captain. "When the left arm [General MacArthur's forces] tries to reach the Philippines, then Japan will wrest off this arm and crush it mercilessly. This will be done by the concerted efforts of the entire Japanese nation."[30]

If there were any doubts in Japanese minds that a great victory had been won, they were largely dispelled by an Imperial Rescript. Emperor Hirohito summoned Admiral Koshiro Oikawa, navy chief of staff, and General Umezu, army chief of staff, to the palace and read to them his rescript.

> Our army and navy forces, operating in close collaboration, counterattacked the enemy fleet and heavily blasted it in a heroic fight.
> We deeply appreciate their achievement.
> The war situation is daily growing in seriousness. We enjoin upon you to maintain ever close collaboration among you and to make greater efforts to meet thereby Our expectations.[31]

From Imperial Headquarters that day, too, came a special story about the exploit of Rear Admiral Masafumi Arima, second in command of the First Air Fleet, stationed near Manila. Arima flew out that day to oppose the American fleet, with the Japanese word *Naifu* (knife) chalked on the side of his bomber, and tried to crash into the American carrier *Franklin*. He was shot down by the carrier's antiaircraft guns, but crashed in the sea so close to the *Franklin* that a large piece of the Arima plane caromed off the surface as the plane exploded and skidded across the carrier's flight deck.[32]

Admiral Arima was the first of the kamikazes.

He had sought permission from Vice Admiral Kimpei Teraoka, commander of the First Air Fleet, to make the attack. Permission had been curtly denied; the admiral did not believe in suicide attacks. A few hours later it did not matter what Admiral Teraoka believed; Admiral Ohnishi reported with his orders, the command was transferred, and Admiral Teraoka went back to Japan.

In a matter of hours, Admiral Ohnishi was at the naval air force headquarters in Manila, counting the aircraft left operational for his use in Japan to stop the Americans, who were going to land in the Philippines at any moment. He had fewer than a hundred operational planes. He then headed for the Clark Field complex, where the pilots stayed. Admiral Ohnishi's mission was to put the last touch on the consensus for suicide as a national Japanese war weapon. He was to supervise the creation of a legend that would last for all time: the tale that the concept of suicide diving by airplane pilots came up from the ranks to be forced upon the naval high command.[33]

Admiral Ohnishi went directly to the Japanese air base at Mabalacat, the headquarters of the 201st Air Group, one of the most famous fighter units in the Japanese naval air force.

He then played out his little Noh drama. He did his job magnificently. Before he was through talking that day and that night, the battered remnants of the 201st Air Group had agreed that total self-sacrifice was the only way left for the aviators of Japan, and had convinced themselves that it was their own idea. Suicide diving on American ships would bring victory, the admiral said. And his men believed.[34]

On October 25, 1944, the Japanese people awakened to learn that the Americans had landed on Leyte Island and that the battle for the Philippines was in progress. They also learned the story of Lieutenant Nobuhiro Abe, second son of General Noboyuki Abe, governor general of Korea, who had recently joined the army's accelerated aviation program. On November 19 Lieutenant Abe had dived his fighter plane at an aircraft carrier. He sank it, of course, said Imperial Headquarters. (He did not.) His two wingmates, also diving to death, "sank" a destroyer and a battleship, said Imperial General Headquarters. The trouble was, as Allied records showed, no Allied ships were sunk by kamikaze planes on October 19.[35]

Who cared for such petty details? The Japanese airmen, army and navy, were embarked on the last great battle. The desperate days of Japan's war had now begun.

Ｂさん 到着

34. "The B-29s arrive"

*T*he nature of the fighting in the Philippines brought a new frenzy to the Japanese home front. *Mainichi Shimbun,* one of the three largest newspapers, called for "idealization of the body-crash spirit on the home front."

"From now on, up to the last moment when the final coup de grace to the enemy is given, those on the home front too will manifest in their daily life the same spirit of body crash harbored by the officers and men at the fighting fronts."[1]

But where was B-san?

A raid on October 25 on Kyushu did very little damage. When the Japanese examined the B-29 on display in Tokyo they found the discrepancies hard to understand. But the fact was that B-29s were not being used very effectively by the Americans. The haul from the Chengtu air bases was a long one, and the planes came in without fighter escort. Because of the distance, they did not maintain large formations, which also cut their effectiveness and created some dangers of B-29s crisscrossing in the bombing pattern. Thus most of the B-29s bombed more or less where they pleased, and the effects were minimal as they had been all the way through. The Japanese did not know the reasons, but they did know that B-san was so far just a paper tiger.

Shortly after one o'clock in the afternoon of November 1, 1944, a lone B-29 appeared high over Tokyo. It was the first enemy aircraft to fly over the Japanese capital since the Doolittle B-25s. The big silver plane circled for a while. Japanese fighter planes sent to attack could not even come near the B-29 for it was flying at 32,000 feet and their maximum altitude was about 25,000 feet.

Imperial Headquarters took note of the solitary plane and issued a statement for the newspapers:

> It is assumed that the Wednesday raid by the lone B-29 was largely for reconnaissance purposes as well as to divert attention from the serious enemy war situation in the Philippines and had no serious object outside of being a mere political demonstration.
>
> However the airfield for use of the B-29s is believed to have been consolidated to some extent in the Marianas area when viewed from the fact that a B-29 bomber appeared over the capital yesterday. Under the circumstances there is no need of caution against future action of the enemy air force.[2]

The days went by, and it seemed that Imperial Headquarters' predictions were correct. The news from the Philippines indicated that the glorious hero-Gods of the kamikaze corps were sinking American ships like children drowning their fleets in the bathtub. Meiji *Setsu,* the anniversary of the birthday of Emperor Meiji, was celebrated on November 3 by the emperor with worship and reports to the Gods at the Kashikodokoro, Keoreidan, and Shinden shrines. The emperor told the Gods about the great air victories over Taiwan, and the sea battle off the Philippines (the three engagements at Leyte Gulf on October 24 and 25 in which the Japanese fleet was completely decimated, and the air, sea, and land battles around Leyte, in which the Japanese were claiming victory after victory).[3] The people of Japan also celebrated, and some of them at least still must have believed that Japan was staving off the enemy advance. B-san had not appeared. Why not? Because of the "stunning air blows dealt the enemy at the Saipan and Tinian air bases," said Imperial Headquarters, which, on November 3, claimed that fifteen different places were bombed, entirely wrecking them.[4] Fifteen different places? There was something for the Japanese people to think about. A few days earlier it had been a single airfield in the Marianas, now it was fifteen different places. But still B-san did not appear. Imperial Headquarters gained a measure of belief through that.

That belief was not held by the air defense organization. They expected heavy raids on Tokyo. They began scooping out fire lanes throughout the city to prevent fires from leaping from one area to another. Whole blocks of houses were torn down and the ground leveled to provide open spaces.

Again on September 7 Imperial Headquarters announced raids on Saipan and Tinian and this time the "blasting of more than twenty B-29s" of forty encountered on one field alone.[5] Forty B-29s on one field, fifteen fields. The careful Japanese reader was beginning to get the feeling that a lot of B-san were assembling in the Marianas.

The B-29s were still raiding Kyushu from China, so that meant the Americans must have a lot of B-29s. What were they doing? Why were they waiting?

The answer to the questions came on November 24. B-san appeared in force over Tokyo for the first time.

The Japanese counted 70 planes, although the Americans had dispatched 111 planes carrying 277 tons of bombs, but not all of them made it to Japan. They flew at 27,000 to 35,000 feet to get above the weather and stay above the Japanese fighters.[6]

Major General Kiyaro Yoshita of the Tenth Air Division of the Japanese army air forces was almost beside himself. He was responsible for the air defenses of the Kanto Plain, the area west of Tokyo, the industrial center of Japan. Those B-29s, like the ones in Kyushu, were flying so high that neither the antiaircraft guns nor the fighter planes could get at them. The very highest they could go was 27,000 feet. The antiaircraft guns could reach only 23,000 feet. That latter problem would have to be remedied at the factories. For two weeks Yoshita had been considering the problem. The answer came this day. One of the B-29s suffered some mechanical difficulty and began to lose altitude. It dropped to about 25,000 feet. One of the Japanese fighters strained upward and suddenly plunged into the side of the B-29. Fighter plane and bomber erupted in a great blast of fire and smoke, and debris went tumbling to the ground. The action was seen by others, and they went back to tell the tale. General Yoshita had his answer, and his flyers helped him with the answer. The Hayabusa fighter could attain that high altitude if stripped of all extra equipment, and this meant most of the guns, ammunition, bombing equipment, and all armor. That meant it would have a few seconds' ammunition and if that did not work, the answer had to be a ramming attack.[7]

By the end of November the general and his staff had accepted the concept of the ramming attack as standard procedure. A number of suicide units were established within the Tenth Air Division.

The American raids kept coming in late November and in December. The Japanese were having some success with ramming. On the night of November 29 six B-29s were lost, several to rammers. So stout was the aircraft, however, that several B-29s survived after being rammed, one after a Japanese fighter had hit and torn out its number three engine.[8]

The American raids were not very effective; the main reason was not opposition by Japanese fighters—although they caused plenty of trouble—but the jet stream, which the pilots encountered for the first time at around 32,000 feet, and winds of 180 miles an hour up high, which made accurate bombing almost impossible. "Indiscriminate bombing," the Japanese called it, and they were right. Fortunately for the Japanese, most of the bombs fell on farmlands on the Kanto Plain.[9]

In December the Japanese air raids on Saipan and Tinian from planes coming out of Iwo Jima created much concern among the Americans. The Tokyo raids came to an abrupt halt and attention was focused on Iwo Jima. This did slow the Japanese counterattack down. Then, on December 13, the B-29s hit the Mitsubishi Aircraft Engine Works at Nagoya in a raid that blasted Nagoya very badly. The major result of this raid was the movement of more basic war facilities to underground factories.[10]

More raids, more ramming. The ramming was effective, although the Americans tried to conceal it. The toll to the Japanese was extremely high, however, as the story of the daylight mission over Nagoya on December 22 indicated. About a hundred B-29s hit Nagoya and virtually destroyed that city's industrial district. Even Nagoya Castle was bombed out in this raid. But the Americans did not have it all their own way. Major John E. Krause's B-29, called *Uncle Tom's Cabin*, was rammed by a fighter, which smashed into the right wing and tore a piece of it away. This made the plane very hard to control, but Major Krause seemed to be bringing it back, when another fighter rammed the plane on the right-hand side, ripping off both engines. Remarkably, the tough airplane continued to fly, and, although it lost altitude, was heading out to sea, when a third Japanese fighter rammed it from underneath. That was too much, and the plane headed down from 20,000 feet and crashed into Tokyo Bay.[11]

By December the Japanese had modified their fighter planes to gain more altitude and were able to take on the B-29s with machine guns as well as ramming attacks. Captain Junichi Ogata told how he had fought the B-29s one day.

> One enemy attacker flying at an altitude of 9,500 meters was downed south of Nagoya. Detecting a formation of seven aircraft I attacked the third one, which immediately opened fire. Flying to within 200 meters of the enemy I directed the first attack and it was not long before the enemy plane began to emit white smoke and then it plunged into the sea. My plane was also hit and I had to make a forced landing at a certain base.[12]

The Japanese claimed ten B-29s shot down that day. They also claimed that their raids on the Saipan and Tinian airfields and their stout air defense over Japan were discouraging the Americans.

There was a good deal of truth in the claim. At the end of the year, the American air force chiefs were discouraged and quarreling among themselves. The B-29 program was not proving anywhere nearly as successful as had been promised. They did not know that in one raid on January 19 they had virtually destroyed the Kawasaki aircraft factory and forced the movement of the salvageable machinery to another site.

The big issue in the American air force was precision bombing versus area bombing. The precision bombers held that they should concentrate on Japanese heavy industry. The area bombers wanted to burn all Japan. In the beginning of 1945 the "burners" won out, and General Curtis LeMay became chief of the 20th Air Force, the B-29 command.[13] From this time on the emphasis would be on killing Japanese civilians and destroying their homes and cities instead of on the destruction of military targets by precision bombing from high altitude. In fact, the precision bombing had not been precise at all. For example, one day in January a B-29 unloaded its bombs over Tokyo. They struck squarely on top of a subway station in Owaricho, killing a thousand men, women, and children. That day fifteen bombers flying in formation dropped their high explosive bombs on the Ginza, Tokyo's "Fifth Avenue," and on Nihonbashi, the Tokyo entertainment district. Most of the great stores were destroyed in a few minutes and so was most of the geisha quarter.[14]

The Japanese put up plenty of resistance. On one raid of about seventy American bombers, more than two hundred Japanese fighters took to the air, and several of them crashed into B-29s, others fought more conventionally, and in spite of B-san's powerful armor and many guns, the Japanese fighter pilots shot down some planes. U.S. plane losses were running about 5 percent, which was acceptable to the Americans. (At the height of the bombing of Germany losses ran 25 percent.)[15]

What the Americans wanted was a fighter base from which they could launch fighter planes to accompany the B-29s to Japan and back. The logical base was Iwo Jima. On February 19 the Americans assaulted Iwo Jima, thus beginning the most fierce land struggle yet staged between the Japanese and the Americans. The Japanese dug in and never quit. Virtually every foot of ground had to be taken with heavy toll of marines. But it was taken. Each side had about 21,000 casualties. But what a difference! The American casualties were 4500 dead and over 16,000 wounded. The Japanese casualties were 21,000 dead and 212 prisoners of war.

The fall of Iwo Jima had no immediate effect on the air war that the Japanese people could see, but from Imperial Headquarters' point of view it was a serious loss. It cut deeply into the capability of attacking Saipan and Tinian B-29 bases by air. And Imperial Headquarters knew that the Americans were lengthening and increasing the airstrips. By summer the B-29s would have an intermediate base for emergency landings and a base from which fighters could accompany the bombers on their trip to Japan.

General LeMay was an outright advocate of the firebombing of civilian populations. The war excuse was that so many Japanese people lived in the industrial districts, around the factories in which they worked, that it would be impossible to avoid civilian casualties. But some of the things the air force did seemed a little far afield from that argument. They built a "typical Japanese village" in Utah and practiced bombing it with a new incendiary made with jellied napalm. It was the perfect instrument for the destruction of Japanese-style houses. Small bombs, about six pounds, could be dropped in great numbers. They would fall on roofs and explode and burn. The napalm would stick to the surface of the roof, and it was almost impossible to extinguish. These were the bombs that were to be used to burn out the major cities of Japan.[16]

In February 1945, General LeMay was ready to begin this new sort of bombing. The B-29s would go in at low altitude, about 5,000 feet. The casualties might be high (they had been running 5 to 6 percent), but General LeMay's B-29 program was on the line. The U.S. Navy was already complaining that the B-29s never hit anything important. General Arnold, the air force commander, was not convinced that the B-29s were worth the effort it cost to supply them overseas.

On February 25 the Americans made the first fire raid on Japan. Two hundred and thirty-one B-29s set out for Tokyo, but fifty-nine of them failed to get there. The others dropped 450 tons of fire bombs on the city, destroying a square mile, and 28,000 of Tokyo's buildings.[17]

Later in February, the American carrier task force approached Japan and bombed airfields and factories between Tokyo and Yokohama. The next day they attacked Tokyo, bombing and strafing. Anyone in Japan who did not know by this time that the war was lost had to be blind and deaf.

Some attempts were made in this period to secure the intervention of the Soviets to bring the war to an end. But the Soviets were playing a different game and they refused to use their good offices. Other efforts were made in Switzerland, but again they failed. The major stumbling block that prevented an outright approach by the Japanese for peace was the "Unconditional Surrender" announcement of the Western Allies. Any time the question came up, it was put down by one argument: if Japan surrendered, the emperor system would be in jeopardy, and the Japanese military would most certainly be destroyed, because the Allies had so promised. Thus it was possible in the winter of 1945, when the war was known to be lost, for the military to force the nation to keep on fighting. The generals' justification was that if they made the cost of each victory higher, then ultimately the Allies would settle for a negotiated peace that would allow Japan to disengage from the war with honor. What that meant was not even clearly defined by the military men, but obviously it meant their personal survival.

This winter the Japanese were retreating everywhere but in central China. There they wound up the capture of the airfield chain with the seizure of Kweilin. But they had been driven out of north Burma, and the Ledo road was now a reality, which meant that trucks began carrying supplies into China. Every day Chiang's fighting power increased. The British were moving in south Burma. The South Pacific war was all but ended, with hundreds of thousands of Japanese soldiers isolated on Bougainville and New Ireland and other islands. At Rabaul, General Imamura had plenty of supplies brought in during the early period, but he had no aircraft and no naval assistance except for the occasional warship (usually a submarine) that called in at Rabaul.

In the Philippines, after a little more than two months fighting, Lieutenant General Sosaku Suzuki, the commander of the Leyte forces, left hurriedly one night with his staff in small boats, abandoning some 20,000 Japanese soldiers, many of whom were subsisting on coconuts and Filipino rice, sea salt, and jungle plants.[18]

General Yamashita, who had been told to stop the Americans, had failed to do so at Leyte and now would fight the major battle of the Philippines on Luzon. Field Marshal Terauchi moved the headquarters of the southern forces away from Manila to the much safer Singapore. In January 1945, the Americans landed on Luzon, and the battle began. General Yamashita left Manila and moved into the mountains to continue the bitter struggle. But by this time there was no chance that he could win. Supplies were very low. The Americans were very powerful, and in spite of the communiqués from Imperial Headquarters, which spoke optimistically of every engagement, the Philippine battle was a charade of death being played out in the mountain forest around Baguio. Nowhere was there good news about the war. The daily articles and broadcasts about the heroism of the kamikazes, the exploits of the suicide pilots of small, fast boats in the Philippines, the growth of the *kaiten*—suicide submarine corps— all these might solace a few who believed that national pride and honor came above all else, but to many the thought of young men dying in their first and only attack on the enemy was more than a little depressing, no matter how brave it might be.

Imperial Headquarters and Admiral Ohnishi continued to hold that the kamikaze effect would be salutary in the long run. There certainly were indications that the kamikaze weapon was the most effective the Japanese had produced during the war. The kamikazes were doing a great deal of damage to Allied shipping. A carrier hit by a kamikaze might be out of operation for weeks, or even months.

And in the operations around the Philippines a number of carriers and other warships were hit. But the problem at this point, readily apparent to anyone who read the newspapers, was that the Americans had so much power, so many ships, so many carriers, that the effect of the kamikazes did not slow the Allied drive on Japan.

And now, in the last days of winter 1945, B-san was ready to begin triumphal performances that would make all the bombing of all cities everywhere by anyone else look small.

One raid at the end of February tested the effect of incendiaries vs. high explosives. The combination was deadly and the destruction rolled like a carpet through the city. A week later the B-29s came again, but no one saw them, they were flying high above the city and above the clouds that hung over it that day, bringing snow on Tokyo. On the B-29s came, bombing by radar through the snow, bombs exploding and shattering houses and buildings, and firebombs setting the roofs aglow, to break out in bright lights that spread, keeping the Kanda district and Azabu lighted all the night long.[19]

On March 9, 324 B-29s took off from the Marianas, carrying 2000 tons of firebombs, bound for Tokyo with instructions to burn the city.

It was a mild day for March, but the winds were very high that day, and as night fell they increased in gustiness. The B-29s arrived at about 11:00 P.M., their coming announced by the picket boats far out at sea and the coastwatcher radar and visual stations. The air raid sirens began roaring, and Radio Tokyo announced the coming of a large force of enemy bombers.

The target to which the American commander led the B-29s was a factory district of Tokyo, the northeastern section of the city, on the plain where factories, houses, and small workshops huddled together. A twenty-five-foot front on a lot in Tokyo was not unusual, the houses and buildings virtually scraped their eaves together, particularly in this old district where the streets were narrow and always crowded.

This section of Tokyo is bisected by the Sumida River, into which then flowed a large number of small canals and drainage ditches. Tokyo's sewer system, such as it was, consisted of narrow sluices running a few feet under the sidewalk level, covered by gratings.

On the west was the Fukagawa dock section, which looked out to Tokyo Bay, and behind it the Mukojima and Honjo districts, which were occupied by factories and the houses of their workers. On the right bank of the Sumida stood Asakusa, Shitaya, Kanda, and Nihonbashi districts, whose eastern sectors had already been blasted by the high-altitude raids.

A handful of "pathfinder" bombers came in first, creating a big circle of fires. Inside this circle the rest of the bombers were to strike.

They came in low, at 4000 and 5000 feet, scattering their incendiaries throughout the area. The tests in Utah had proved that the type of fire-fighting equipment used by the Japanese could not possibly put out such fires as the ones that were being started that night. But even the Americans had not anticipated what did happen. The fires were caught by the high winds, and the heat made the winds whirl faster until a fire storm was created, swirling winds of flame leaping across streets and open spaces; the flames would leap a whole block and then drop down and begin the destruction of that new section. At first many householders tried to get up on their roofs and brush the incendiaries off. Many died that way, burned horribly by the spreading napalm. Others tried to flee, heading for the canals, for the tiny handful of parks and squares and other open spaces, some of them left by previous bombings. But they could hardly move fast enough through the narrow streets. Often the buildings crashed down upon them, or the fire leaped forward and cut them off, to burn in the midst of the blazing wreckage. People in padded kimonos found their clothing on fire. Women running with babies on their backs stopped to discover the babies dead of smoke and flames. Even stronger winds picked up the fires and made glittering whirlwinds of them, the rising heat created vacuums and air rushed in to carry fire back up, out and away to expand the disaster. Whole blocks erupted and went up all at once and in a few minutes had collapsed into rubble, burying more hundreds of people beneath the ash and trash. Firemen at first rushed to try to put out the individual blazes, but as the fires increased and the heat toppled buildings, their water sources broke down; and they hooked up to a hydrant only to find a trickle of water coming out. There was virtually no fire fighting to be done in the ordinary sense. The firemen rushed here and there, trying to save people from trapped buildings, trying to guide them out of the hell that their city had become.

Japan had been planning for raids. Protective clothing had been advertised for fire raids, consisting of heavy fireproof cloth hoods and helmets, and padded clothing. But these were of no use against the napalm, which clung to the cloth and burned right through. Hundreds reached the open spaces, only to have the fire sweep across them and singe them. Hundreds of others reached the swamps and canals and stinking waterways. Some sought the wet safety of the Sumida River, and it was crowded almost from shore to shore. Then the tide rose, and many of the people drowned. The bridges across the river in Asakusa and Honjo were made of steel, and the railings grew red hot; people either fell or jumped into the stream, to be carried off and drowned. Trees burned like matchwood. Temples blazed and their gods toppled into the ash. Even modern buildings were not immune. In Nihonbashi theaters and restaurants went up in the whirling haze of smoke and flame that lapped across the city.

The bombers had come in waves, and they kept the fires burning brightly all night long, the people entrapped within the fiery circle. At five o'clock in the morning the all clear sounded, but the weary fire fighters worked on. They were joined by police and soldiers; any organized force in the area pitched in to try to save the people trapped under the rubble of collapsed buildings.[20]

The Americans went home pleased. The surprise of the low-level raid and the paucity of Japanese night fighters had worked as General LeMay had predicted. The Americans lost only two aircraft that night.

It was a week before the Americans could get through the smoke and haze above the city to photograph their accomplishment. When they saw what they had done, General LeMay called it a "diller" of a raid. The official U.S. Army Air Forces records showed that 83,000 Japanese civilians had died in the bombing that night. Japanese records were never complete because of the flight from the city then and thereafter of so many hundreds of thousands of people, and the constant disruption of Japanese society from this point on. But the facts indicate that 200,000 people died on the night of January 9–10 in General LeMay's pyre, about three times as many as would be killed directly at Hiroshima.[21]

For once Radio Tokyo did not exaggerate in any way in its report on the bombing. The announcer compared the bombing to Nero's destruction of Rome. "The sea of flame which enclosed the residential and commercial sections of Tokyo was reminiscent of the holocaust of Rome. . . ."[22]

They called it "slaughter bombing," and, of course, it was. In the next few weeks, Nagoya was burned out, and then Osaka, and then Kobe, where LeMay was forced to use 500-pound clusters of magnesium thermite bombs because the napalm supply was exhausted. Magnesium thermite will burn through steel. The heat from the Kobe fires was so intense that it very nearly destroyed one of the B-29s flying above a raging thermal fire storm at 4500 feet above sea level.

For days the burned-out area of Tokyo sent up little columns of smoke, and for more than a week the body crews came in to cart off the dead. They found them clustered in air raid holes in the gardens of their property, in the drains and the canals and on the river banks, stacked up like cordwood in the open spaces. Whole streets and alleys were impassable at first because of the bodies.

An area of sixteen square miles had been completely gutted. Only twenty-two factories and installations of military significance had been destroyed, but three hundred thousand houses had burned. The whole area looked like nothing more than the Warsaw ghetto after it had been painstakingly demolished—pulverized—by the Nazis. But even Warsaw could not match Tokyo, for the buildings of Tokyo were paper and wood, and in many places all that was left was a thick covering of ash.[23]

The emperor, sequestered behind his moat, heard from members of the Imperial Household that the raid had been ghastly, and he insisted on going out to see the destruction. Imperial Headquarters and the government tried desperately to dissuade him from making this trip, but he insisted. Finally, about ten days after the event, the emperor's motorcade toured the destroyed area, and he stopped frequently to talk to groups of people, huddled in temporary shelters, or in no shelters at all.

When the emperor returned from this visit of horrors, he was sick and shocked. That is the point at which Emperor Hirohito knew that no matter what his generals and his admirals told him, the war was lost and every effort must be made to bring it to a conclusion as quickly as possible.

The chiefs of the U.S. Army Air Forces were delighted. The firebomb raids had gutted thirty-two square miles of Japanese cities. They must have killed at least half a million civilians and destroyed a million houses. Indeed, the fire raids against Japan represented a mighty military accomplishment of World War II. It is a good thing for General LeMay and the others involved that they won the war, for most certainly they would have been duly tried and executed as war criminals had they lost it, on the grounds of murder of civilians in acts of terrorism without regard to military objectives. LeMay was very pleased. The strong reaction of shocked dismay that was expressed by Radio Tokyo convinced him that he had accomplished a major feat. He called it "strategic bombing."[24]

月に叢雲　花に風

35. "Fortune changes, that's the rule"

f you asked a Chinese what were the worst atrocities of the war, he would say the Japanese Rape of Nanking and the policy of destroying whole village populations in retaliation for warlike acts. If you asked a Briton the same question, he would tell you the rape of Hongkong, the rape of Singapore, and the building of the Thai-Burma railroad that cost so many Allied lives. If you asked an American, he would say the Bataan Death March and the murder of captured Allied airmen. If you asked a Japanese, he would give you a whole litany of Allied war crimes, of which most Westerners are still not aware: the mistreatment of Japanese citizens in America, the wholesale killing of Japanese civilians on the Central Pacific islands, the disrespect shown the Japanese dead in battle, the machine-gunning of survivors of ships by submarines, and, above all, the Allied bombings of the civilian population of Japan.

Beginning with the great Tokyo fire raid, which the Japanese called "The March 10 Terror Raid," that murderous bombing continued, almost without regard for military targets. General LeMay's announced intention was to terrorize Japan by hitting at the civilian population. "We have them cold," he announced gleefully after the great Tokyo raid.[1] Each time Admiral Nimitz asked LeMay to use his B-29s for military tactical or strategic purposes, the general objected and had to be brought into line by General Arnold, as on April 5 when Admiral Nimitz demanded the bombing of the Mitsubishi engine works at Nagoya. The B-29s bombed the military target and destroyed 90 percent of it. So there was no doubt that the military use of B-29s was effective. But what the flamboyant LeMay wanted was visual effect, and there was none greater than a burning city. There was plenty of heroism on the part of the Americans making these bombing raids. Radio Operator Henry E. Erwin won the Medal of Honor on one raid—but that was for saving his aircraft and smothering a phosphorus bomb in the cabin—not for plastering the Japanese.[2] The bombing of Japan was what author Hyoe Murakami termed "the wholesale massacre" of the civilian population. It continued with as much force as LeMay could muster. In April they hit the Tokyo "arsenal area"[3] northwest of the Imperial Palace and burned out another eleven and a half square miles of Tokyo. On April 15 they hit the Tokyo area on the west shore of the bay and Kawasaki, burning out another six square miles of Tokyo and three and a half square miles of Kawasaki. They also destroyed a square mile and a half of Yokohama.[4]

Admiral Nimitz was having a great deal of difficulty in capturing Okinawa, which was attacked late in March. The basic problem was the kamikazes, highly organized by the Japanese navy and army on Kyushu. Their assaults on Allied ships at Okinawa would be a major aspect of the battle, and Nimitz was not at all certain of winning it. After the kamikaze suicide dives on ships began at Leyte in October 1944, the U.S. Navy had established a special office in Boston devoted to search for an "antidote." None was ever found, and at Okinawa, in spite of valiant defenses by the sailors of the ships and increasingly accurate antiaircraft fire, the ship toll climbed day after day. More American ship personnel were killed and wounded in the Okinawa battle than in any of all the other engagements of the U.S. Navy in World War II.[5]

Also, the kamikaze spirit had taken over all the Japanese armed forces. As Admiral Ohnishi said, one did not have to have an airplane to have the kamikaze spirit; the principle was to sacrifice one's life in order to strike an effective blow at the enemy. Thus, soldiers bearing satchel charges threw themselves under tanks, soldiers in small boats from neighboring islands approached the warships at anchor around Okinawa, clambered aboard and went charging along the decks, slashing with swords any and everyone until they were cut down. One-man *kaiten* suicide submarines set out to ram ships. In Japan civilians were being primed to make suicide attacks when the Allied troops hit the beaches.

On April 7, 1945, P-51 fighters from Iwo Jima joined the

B-29s for the first time, and this brought Japanese fighter losses higher than before but caused no slackening of the defense effort. Japanese aircraft production was still proceeding at a very healthy rate. This was one of the matters that bothered Admiral Nimitz.

General LeMay had to slow down his effort to destroy Japan's cities on April 17 when he was ordered by General Arnold to support Admiral Nimitz by attacking the Japanese air bases in Kyushu from which the kamikaze planes were coming. Nearly every day those bases were attacked: Tachiarai, Kokubu, Izumi, and Kanoya, the central base for Vice Admiral Matome Ugaki's Fifth Air Fleet. The Japanese hid their aircraft, sometimes underground, sometimes a mile or more from the airfields. A number of pinpoint raids were carried out against aircraft factories such as the Hitachi aircraft plant at Tachikawa. The result of these factory strikes and the carpet bombing of the airfields was what Admiral Nimitz had needed; the number of Japanese kamikazes was kept down and so was the number of American ship casualties. The Americans did not know it, but their assaults on Japanese cities were not as effective in hurting the war effort as they believed. The pinpoint raids now ordered on aircraft factories did far more to slacken the Japanese effort; the rate of aircraft production took a violent slump. Even so, the growing shortage was not so much of planes as of pilots trained well enough to man them.[6]

In spite of the emphasis on military targets, the civilian slaughter continued. LeMay was allowed to use about a quarter of his force for that purpose, and some of the B-29 raiders assigned to the airfield control used the cities as dumping targets of opportunity.

By the first of April the wholesale destruction of Japanese cities was so great that the cabinet approved a program to turn large areas of Tokyo, Nagoya, and Osaka into agricultural zones. Pumpkins, hogs, and chickens would grow where once children had played. The agricultural workers would be women, children, and the old, who would be housed in temples and other standing public buildings until housing could be constructed. For housing was an enormous problem in the cities, now that General LeMay was destroying the houses by the hundreds of thousands. The bombings destroyed more and more buildings. The authorities destroyed still more, to create broad open pathways around essential buildings and prevent another fire storm. In Tokyo the authorities began issuing extra rations of dried biscuit for emergencies because of the bombing out of markets and restaurants.[7]

Taking note of the invasion of Okinawa, so close to the home islands of Japan, on April 3 the government announced the establishment of the "National Volunteer Force," which would be headed by the prime minister of Japan. It was to be a People's Army, organizing every citizen for the defense of the realm. The old, the very young, and women began learning to drill and use such primitive weapons as the pike and such complicated ones as explosives.[8]

This mobilization was assisted by news from Okinawa, picked up from the reports of American journalists via Lisbon and other neutral centers. One United Press Associations report told of eleven women charging an American position with rifles and machine guns. Another report told of American tanks running over civilians and crushing them. "They would never surrender anyhow," was the justification of one tanker.[9] There were virtually no medical facilities for civilians or soldiers. The instructions went out from General Kurabayashi's defense headquarters: those wounded too badly to fight will kill themselves. Articles in the press and tales on the radio of the no-quarter battle raging on Okinawa strengthened the determination of the civil population. The Americans had shown themselves to be barbarians in Japanese eyes. The barbarians must not triumph over the Japanese people. Americans who continued to marvel at the deadly fear in which enemy civilians held them simply did not understand what had happened elsewhere and how effective the Japanese use of the facts had been. Particularly telling were the unthinking dispatch of Japanese bones back to the United States, as souvenirs, and the wholesale bombing of civilian population. The one was repulsive in spirit; the bloody, mangling results of the other were apparent every day. Americans were monsters and death was far preferable to falling into the hands of the monsters.

The mobilization of all Japan was moving quickly. The national medical association took over the management of all civil hospitals and medical facilities, which included the movement of doctors, nurses, and technicians from one area to another as needed.[10]

The Imperial Rule Assistance Association, established by Prince Konoye so long ago to absorb and supersede the political parties, was now made a vital part of the National Volunteer Force. In the cities two units of the Manhood Corps would be organized in each prefecture. Units of 1000 men each were set up on April 5 in eight

Tokyo prefectures to start building defense positions. The civilian volunteer force was going to take part in the hand-to-hand fighting for the beaches, the fields, and the streets of Japan.[11]

Even university professors of the arts—a notoriously unorganizable group—were organized at a meeting of the All-Japan University Professors Federation. Their task would be to work from a Tokyo headquarters, from which they would be dispatched, particularly to cities raided by the B-29s, to stop rumors and shore up the local will to resist. "They will also work for the thought guidance of war victims and promotion of ideas for decisive war victory."[12]

On the day that these plans were announced the Koiso government collapsed. It was not forced out even by the disastrous news of the invasion of Okinawa. The Japanese were now numbed to disaster and waiting for the attack on the homeland. General Koiso quit because he could no longer even pretend that he knew how to stop the Allied juggernaut. He was replaced by Admiral Kantaro Suzuki, one of the victims of the young officers' corps uprising of February 1936 who had survived. At first Suzuki refused the appointment. He had absolutely no political instincts or sense, he said. He did not know that this was precisely why Emperor Hirohito needed him. The war could be stopped only if the cabinet was in the hands of men inimical to the militarists, who still controlled the army and the navy and posed a constant threat to cabinet government by their right to withhold a war minister or navy minister from service.

"We need you," said Emperor Hirohito,[13] setting a precedent by making a direct request. So Admiral Suzuki assumed the prime ministry and brought into the government a number of civilians, including Shigenori Togo as foreign minister, a Togo whom the Imperial Household knew to be opposed to many of the excesses of the militarists. All the old problems continued to exist, particularly the military's ability to bring down a government. But the antimilitary forces were gathering quietly. Their problem was to establish a situation in which the military could not act to bring down the government.

This spring once again the cherry blossoms came forth, blossomed explosively, to shower Japan with their brilliant falling, then to wither swiftly in death. This spring like no other, the Japanese observed the cherry blossoms as they fell with deep emotion. The kamikazes often likened themselves to cherry blossoms. The newspapers dwelt on the simile, and printed many poems about the blooming and the falling, especially the most famous of all, by Motoori Norinaga:

> Shikishima no
> Yamato gokoro wo
> Hito towaba
> Asahi ni niou
> Yamazakura bana.

> If one should ask you
> What is the heart
> Of Island Yamato,
> It is the mountain cherry blossom
> Which exhales its perfume in the morning sun.[14]

The cherry blossoms were falling thick and fast, but they also took their toll of the enemy. The kamikazes claimed to have sunk or damaged 293 enemy ships off Okinawa. The total was not so high, but it was high enough to worry the Americans, and to give a sense of fatality and acceptance to the Japanese people that the new way of life was death. That was what the militarists insisted upon, and that was the tenor of Japanese home information programs. The army was building its own bastions. General Sugiyama, war minister for so long, was minister no more, replaced by General Anami, who was dedicated to the prosecution of the war, but was not as fanatical as Sugiyama. The latter and General Hata, former commander of the China Expeditionary Army, were set to work to prepare Japan's ultimate defenses of the homeland from the beaches of Kyushu to the Japan Alps. This meant defense of Japan. This meant planning and positioning the 2.5 million soldiers on duty in the homeland, to make the best defense against attacks expected on Kyushu first and then Honshu around the Kanto Plain.

The cabinet, meanwhile, set to work to gain strength. Prime Minister Suzuki, Foreign Minister Togo, and Navy Minister Yonai were now all quiet advocates of peace—quiet because to raise their voices just now would be to court a new violent takeover by the army's militarists. Since 1940 the government of Japan had gone from military in the guise of civilian (Prince Konoye's cabinets) to pure military oligarchy, to Tojo's military dictatorship, and now to civil or peace control in the guise of military. The problem at this point for the Imperial Palace and the peace advocates in the *Genro,* the council of elder statesmen, was to achieve their ends without facing the military directly until the proper hour.

To accomplish this end, Admiral Suzuki had to pretend to support the war effort completely, and in his daily speeches and contact with politicians, soldiers, and the press he did so admirably. The news of the war, of course, dominated all else. The glorious exploits of the kamikazes were honored by Imperial Rescript and by Imperial acknowledgment, and by medals and postmortem promotions. In every way Imperial Headquarters continued to press for victory or death, in the manner of reporting the news. The rapidly failing fortunes of Japan's ally, Germany, in the war on the other side of the world were told in those terms. The picture painted was of a Germany that was going down, but was going down united, with every citizen resisting the Allies to the last.

As the spring of 1945 moved along, the government speeded its efforts to prepare for the defense of the Japanese homeland. In Tokyo the Scientific Mobilization Society made preparations to arm the people with the weapons they would need for fighting on the beaches. Lieutenant General Dr. Reikichi Tada, head of the government-sponsored organization, outlined the problem:

> The type of warfare suited to Japan at this moment is close-range fighting or the so-called bamboo lance fighting. This does not, of course, mean fighting with bamboo lances, but with scientific weapons fit for the people.
>
> These include barricades against tanks, hand grenades, rockets, planes for the Special Attack Corps and many others. The urgent need is to secure increased production of these weapons by every means. They may be easily produced in underground factories or in the establishments transferred to safe localities with domestic materials. The people's weapons, which are the weapons of close-range fighting are best suited to the Japanese temperament.[15]

While the people's militia waited for the "people's weapons," they trained. Emperor Hirohito sent one of his brothers out to discover what was going on, and the prince saw women marching in Yokohama with bamboo spears on their shoulders.[16]

In mid-April, the death of President Roosevelt brought a glimmer of hope to Tokyo. Japanese government spokesman Sado Iguchi indicated it was time the Americans reconsidered their war aims, "because Roosevelt had been the one who had driven the United States into such a meaningless and costly war." It was a bitter disappointment in Tokyo that President Harry S. Truman vowed to go on and change nothing.[17]

On May 8, when Admiral Doenitz as the chief of the German state surrendered to the Allies, there was no banner headline in the Japanese newspapers. The grim news was received grimly by the government. The note about the surrender was terse and had no details.

War Minister General Anami, Army Chief of Staff Umezu and all the rest knew that the war was lost. Now that the Germans surrendered, Japan was all alone against the world.

The Japanese were on the retreat everywhere. In the Philippines General Yamashita's troops were holding out in the wild Igorot Mountain country. Holding out was all that could be said. Nearly all their fieldpieces had been destroyed. The last artillery shell was fired from a mountain gun and then the Imperial Japanese Army in the Philippines was reduced to a force of machine guns and rifles. Haggard from malaria and malnutrition, the Japanese moved about, surrounded by their enemies, but still having plenty of room. Men died every day from hunger and disease. Some began committing suicide.[18]

In Burma the Japanese were retreating steadily eastward. In China the last offensive (west of Hengyang) was given up in May, and the Japanese retreated toward the coast of central and south China. They had been pulling out divisions for a year to strengthen other areas. Now more divisions would move to Korea and Manchuria. There was no further hope of ending the war by victory in China.

From time to time reports came about fighting on Bougainville, and it was true. The Japanese were still there, in the southern half of the island, but they were surrounded and capable only of creating difficulty. Rabaul was totally cut off.

On Okinawa the Japanese had lost fifty thousand men by the end of May. In June another sixty thousand fell, and then on June 21 the final word came from General Ushijima, his regrets to the emperor for having failed. Then nothing more.

The Allies now had Okinawa. They were poised on the front doorstep of Japan. The Japanese had been primed over the past six months to believe that if the Americans conquered Japan the men would be reduced to slavery, the women would suffer unspeakable tortures, and the children would be brought up in foreign ways. The Japanese were not willing to accept that. More and more of them were willing to die instead. Their wish, encouraged by the government with all its might, was that they might die so valiantly and hurt the enemy so much, that he would stop his efforts to kill off the whole population and would give Japan a peace with honor.

戦争 終わる

36. "The battle ends"

When Admiral Suzuki took office as prime minister of Japan
it was with the basic understanding that his real mission was
to find a way out of the war. The emperor and his advisors were
agreed on that. Suzuki was one of the few men who could be used
to this end; he had the ear of the militarists, but having been one of
their victims, he did not share their views. One of his first steps was
to appoint Shigenori Togo as foreign minister. Togo took the job
with the understanding that Togo would seek peace. Togo quickly
discovered that the army was adamant against any negotiation with
the Americans, so he turned to the USSR, hoping to secure Stalin's
assistance as an intermediary. But the Soviets had their own game
to play in Asia, and they refused. The trial balloons sent up by Togo
had been launched very carefully, and it was good that they were
for the reaction in Tokyo was immediate and intense. In London the
Reuter diplomatic correspondent drew the logical conclusion that
Togo's approaches to the Soviets meant he was seeking peace, and
virtually all of the Japanese newspapers leaped upon this statement
with fury. No such thing they said. Japan would never seek peace.
Japan would win the war.[1]

More important, the *Kempeitai* began searching for antiwar sentiment and throwing people into jail if they seemed "defeatist."[2]

Admiral Suzuki then came forth with a number of statements
that indicated he had no thought in mind other than to prosecute
the war to a successful conclusion.

As this fulminating went on in May, Suzuki's chief cabinet secretary was making a realistic survey of Japan's resources for the prime minister, to see just how the country stood in relation to the war. This is what he found:

Japan's steel production was 1,000,000 tons per year, just a third of what was needed.

The all-time high of 2500 planes per month had been steadily going down, because of the B-29 raids on factories and the shortage of materials. Only 500 planes per month were being produced. That did not keep up with losses on the Okinawa level.

Stocks of oil fuel for the ships were so low that the navy was mixing soybean oil with petroleum.[3]

At the rate of destruction of the cities by the B-29s, by the end of September every city of 30,000 or more would have been burned out. On May 29, 500 B-29s bombed Yokohama, killing more thousands of people and reducing a third of the city to rubble.[4]

On June 8, at an Imperial Conference, the army and navy leaders expressed their determination to carry on the war, no matter what.[5]

On June 22, the emperor summoned a meeting of the Supreme War Council, which included the prime minister, minister of foreign affairs, president of the Privy Council, army and navy ministers, and army and navy chiefs of staff.

"We have heard enough of this determination of yours to fight to the last soldiers," said the emperor. "We wish that you, leaders of Japan, will strive now to study the ways and means to conclude the war. In doing so, try not to be bound by the decisions you have made in the past."

The room was completely silent. These men, the leaders of Japan, had just suffered the worst shock of their lives.[6]

The emperor had broken precedent. Never before had he said a word that implied criticism of the military as such. He was invoking his constitutional privilege to rule rather than reign, but it had never been done since the days of Emperor Meiji; these modern men did not know what to do.

None of these leaders was willing to say anything, and the meeting broke up. Prime Minister Suzuki and Foreign Minister Togo went back to their offices, with higher hopes for peace than they had dared to feel before. The emperor had come out on the side of peace in a manner that confounded the militarists.[7]

It was apparent to all who wanted peace that there was very little time.

The Soviet Union, having rebuffed Foreign Minister Togo, was sending huge reinforcements of troops to the maritime provinces. It was apparent that the USSR was preparing to invade Manchuria and Korea soon. From Moscow the Japanese ambassador reported that he could get no answers at all. Would the USSR renew the neutrality pact, which had just expired? He got no answer. Would the USSR accept Prince Konoye as a special envoy to discuss means of finding peace? He got no answer. He reminded Tokyo that the Allies were meeting in mid-July at Potsdam to plan for the future of the war, and the only belligerent left in the opposite camp was Japan. The Soviets were going to the meeting. What position they would take, nobody knew. The Soviet-Japanese neutrality pact had expired. But the generals, knowing their Russians, expected an attack in Manchuria. For many months the army had been moving elements of the Kwantung Army south, to south China, to the Marianas, to Taiwan, as far as Guadalcanal, on the theory that the Soviets would not attack. In recent months, as it became apparent the Germans were being beaten, the army tried to restore more strength to the Kwantung Army by moving new units up, mostly from China.

When the Potsdam meeting ended, the Japanese peacemakers had a shock. The Big Three, the United States, Britain, and China, again demanded unconditional surrender as the only basis on which the war could end. Those terms set back the hopes of Foreign Minister Togo and the other peacemakers, because they played into the hands of the militarists. The official line now was that the Allies intended to destroy Japan and turn the Japanese into slaves. Better death than slavery; the people must be ready to defend their sacred land to the last, and if it meant the death of the Japanese race, so be it.

Against this fanaticism of the army leaders, the emperor's party had to take grave care, for it was much more than possible that the army was now ready to engineer a coup d'état and depose the emperor from the throne if his real aims were known. Marquis Koichi Kido, the Lord Privy Seal, was the emperor's major instrument in getting facts and making his decisions, and had been since January, when Hirohito first realized he could believe nothing his generals said. After the March 9 B-29 fire raid on Tokyo, his mind was made up. The Japanese people were suffering too much in what he knew was a lost cause.[8]

In the inner councils of the cabinet, Foreign Minister Togo argued that they should accept the Potsdam terms, because they could be interpreted as meaning less than was said. The real sticker was the emperor system—could it be retained?

When the Potsdam Declaration was released, early in August, with its call for Japan's surrender, lest the war grow even more punishing, Togo argued for negotiation. The military refused to consider negotiations and forced the public media to an attitude of rejection. Prime Minister Suzuki refused comment, which only gave the wrong impression to the war party and to the Americans.

"The joint declaration on Japan is a one-man show put on by America in order to arouse her people in the war against Japan," said Domei, the official government news agency.[9]

Domei noted that the call for unconditional surrender of Germany had brought forth a last-ditch fight by the Germans, who could not stomach the idea. If the Americans wanted to avoid this in Japan, then they had to take a different tack.

If the Americans really wanted peace, said the statement, "The terms for Japan should be clarified and the approval of their own peoples obtained so that the failure which they had made in their declaration on Germany will not be repeated."[10]

This statement was publicized by the press and on the radio. At various points around the world, American diplomats secured the Japanese newspapers and studied them carefully. They also monitored Japanese radio and studied the transcripts. The apparent Japanese refusal to consider surrender, indicated by Prime Minister Suzuki's "no comment," hardened the American attitude. The army's recalcitrance prevented any further speculation. Even this call for some amelioration of the terms was rejected by the Americans. Some of President Truman's advisors wanted him to announce that the surrender of Japan would not mean the end of the imperial system. This plea failed against the hard line demanded by the military.

By this time, the wheels were already in motion in the United States to drop the atomic bomb, which had just been perfected in the month of July. Some of President Truman's advisors again suggested that he refrain from dropping the bomb, but describe it. The

American military objected, it would give away the American hand, and the Japanese probably would not believe it anyhow.

So the bomb went on its way to the Marianas. On August 6 it was dropped on Hiroshima by B-san. The explosion was enormous, wiping out the center of the city and killing a great number of people. The official figure was around 80,000. Other figures ranged as high as 200,000.[11]

When the news reached Tokyo, the Japanese army was really not dismayed. Even when Dr. Yoshio Nishina, an atomic expert, flew down to Hiroshima and came back to report that an atomic bomb had caused the damage, the generals said they could live with it. Their reasoning was really sound: the atomic bomb had not done as much destruction or killed as many people as the great fire raid on March 9 on Tokyo, and the cumulative effect of all the B-29 fire raids was much worse indeed. B-san threatened every city in the land. The army did not have the benefit of scientific studies on the long-range effects of radiation, but from the short-term point of view, they were quite willing to live with the atomic bomb. They reasoned that the Americans could not have more than one or two more of them. (They were quite right.) So one or two more atomic bombs would be dropped, and there would be more destruction, but the war could go on. No announcement of the bomb or its implications was allowed in the media.[12]

When Prime Minister Suzuki called a special meeting of the Supreme Council for the Conduct of the War for August 9, he said a way to secure peace must be found. He reminded the other members of the Supreme War Council of Emperor Hirohito's statement, asking them to find ways to end the war. The military men were still doing their best to ignore the emperor's words.[13]

At this same time, the Soviets stopped pussyfooting and announced to the Japanese ambassador at Moscow that they were declaring war on Japan. In fact, the Soviets secured revenge for the Port Arthur strike of Admiral Togo in 1904; the Japanese Embassy telephone lines were cut, and the ambassador was unable to let Tokyo know about the war situation until after the Soviets had begun crossing the Manchurian border the next morning.

General Anami, the war minister, was quick to respond. He had gone on the national radio to speak to the new issue raised by the Soviet invasion:

"Now that things have come to such a pass, argument is unnecessary. For there is no other way than to fight out this sacred war determinedly for the defense of Japan."[14]

On August 9, then, the Japanese Supreme Council met in the bomb shelter of the Imperial Palace, for one reason, because B-san had burned out the public rooms of the palace in one of the raids, despite the standing orders of the American high command that the palace was to be left alone. The war council had two grave issues to resolve. The army and the navy raised constant objections to the acceptance of the Potsdam Declaration. No conclusion could be reached. In the afternoon the cabinet had met, and the feeling for peace was almost unanimous. The one holdout was General Anami, the war minister. He still had the power to destroy the cabinet, so the meeting again was inconclusive.[15]

That day, finally, the Japanese public was let in on the atomic secret. That day the second atomic bomb was dropped on Nagasaki. Another 60,000 people were killed, about as many as in one of the great fire raids. The damage to buildings was less. Another atomic bomb. So what? said War Minister Anami, the nation would survive and must fight the battle of Japan on the beaches to so hurt the Americans that they would offer peace with honor.

The army bid for the people's continued support of the war. The people's continued support was indicated in the papers that day. Since June 17, said a statement that originated at Imperial Headquarters, the American enemy had subjected Japanese cities to such intensive bombing that it "has made it plain that his object is to wipe out the Japanese race with its glorious history of over 3,000 years."[16]

> With the start of July the enemy followed up the attacks upon Tokyo-Yokohama area, Osaka, Kobe, and Nagoya with raids on medium and small cities using for the most part incendiary bombs, a fact that suggested that he is chiefly interested in the destruction of the lives of children, women, and perfectly harmless men.
>
> [The raids on these small cities were killing mostly children (30 percent) and women (59 percent).]
>
> In the attack on the city of Okayama, on June 29, the enemy burned twenty-three shrines, forty-four temples, ninety-three hospitals and thirty-one schools, in addition to a large number of places with historic associations. The famous Okayama Castle was set on fire.

The day is near when the 100,000,000 people as one man will be in active resistance to the enemy who does not allow any consideration of humanity and of cultural values to stand in the way of establishing a hegemony over the world.[17]

There, in essence, was the Japanese army's stand. The atomic bomb was just another American weapon designed to do what the B-29s were doing with fire bombs, destroy the Japanese people, men, women, and children. The war must go on, to the death of Japan if necessary.

Admiral Suzuki, however, had another card to play. No decision of the Japanese cabinet could be effective unless it was unanimous. War Minister Anami's refusal to consider the Potsdam Declaration made it impossible for the cabinet to reach a decision. The next step for Suzuki, then, was to call an Imperial Conference, at which the cases would be laid out, and a decision would be made. If the Imperial War Council voted four to three for peace, would the emperor approve of a majority rule? This matter had never really come up before because there had never before been a situation in which the military was totally opposed by the civilian elements of the government. Even in the 1930s, when the militarists were gaining power, and the emperor failed at least twice to take the action that *might* have stopped them, there had been no clear-cut issue. This time, the issue was peace or destruction, and not even the army could water it down or confuse it. This time, too, the militarists did not have the old support. When the prime minister explained the problem and the discussions before the emperor and everyone had his say, the sides lined up: Foreign Minister Togo, Privy Council President Kiichiro Hiranuma, and Navy Minister Yonai for peace; War Minister Anami, Army Chief of Staff Umezu, and Navy Chief of Staff Soemu Toyoda, for war. The prime minister then might have voted and swayed the meeting for peace, but had he done so he might have precipitated another of those "young officers" takeover attempts too common in the past. For the young officers, majors and lieutenant colonels of the general staff, were well aware of the conflict at the top of government and were already talking about a coup. Prime Minister Suzuki did not know that, but he suspected it.[18]

Prime Minister Suzuki then put it squarely up to the emperor:

"We have spent a long time in debate but have failed to reach any conclusion. However we cannot afford to lose a moment. Therefore—without any precedent and with the utmost distress—I would respectfully submit that His Imperial Majesty give the final judgment."[19]

This action was perfectly proper under the Meiji Constitution, for the emperor was head of government and head of the military as well, on separate lines. But for years the military had been acting in the name of the emperor and so had the government, without his express approval. Never in the modern history of Japan had the emperor used the power that was his.

When Prime Minister Suzuki made his move, the military men sucked in their breaths. The old admiral had tricked them. They would be unable to use the stonewall technique of suspending all activity by refusal to participate in a decision. That rule applied to the cabinet but not to the Supreme War Council. The decision had been thrown to the highest authority in the land, and there was nothing they could do about it except cry "foul."

The emperor, leaning forward in his seat, said in his usual mild voice:

"My opinion is the same as that of the foreign minister."[20]

The bombshell had been dropped. The emperor had ruled that they must accept the Potsdam Declaration and surrender.

As the words struck home, all these men realized that the great adventure had ended, the war was over, Japan had been defeated, and now she must expect the consequences of her actions. There was not a dry eye in the room, as the emperor, wiping away a tear, continued. It became clear that in the weeks since the March 9 terror bombing of Tokyo, the emperor had been a busy man. He had recalled all those assurances made him by General Sugiyama in the past, and he had acted accordingly.

"To make things clear, I will tell you my reasons for the decision."[21]

The army and the navy reported that they could mount a decisive battle on the main islands and that they had confidence in their ability to do so; here again I feel worried. What the chief of staff says is seriously at variance with the reports of my aides de camp. In fact, almost no defenses are ready. According to what I hear not all the troops have guns even. [This was true.] What would happen if we embarked on a decisive battle in such a state of affairs? Continue fighting and we will be plunging the entire nation into further devastation and distress. I cannot bear any longer to see my innocent subjects tormented under the cruelties of war. There are certainly conditions that can hardly be accepted: Disarmament of the Imperial Forces by foreign hands for one. But we have to bear it now. I think of the spirit of those who have died for the nation's cause and I reflect on My incapacity to respond to their loyalty. My heart aches as I think of those who have faithfully fulfilled their duties and who now have to bear the disgrace. But this is the time when we must bear the unbearable to restore peace to the nation and to the world.

They sat there, stone, these leaders of Japan, and no one had a thing to say. Suddenly someone began to sob, and soon the room was filled with the sounds of lament. The emperor left. The decision was made. Now it was up to his government to carry it out.

Later in the day the cabinet met again. Admiral Suzuki said he proposed to announce to the enemy that they would accept the Potsdam Declaration with the provisions that no change be made "in the national polity." That meant no change in the form of government. Japan would continue to be an imperial realm. He then looked around and asked if anyone present wanted to go against the will of the emperor. No one spoke. Finally General Anami did speak:

"I want to make sure that in case the enemy doesn't accept our proposal we will fight to the last man."[22]

Prime Minister Suzuki nodded. "You have my word," he said.[23] The cabinet session was over. But as all of them knew, the matter was not yet settled. Anami's words did not necessarily control the army, as these men knew so well from the army behavior of the 1930s. They were sitting atop a powder keg. Someone might try to light it at any moment.

Knowing this, the imperial advisors had taken steps to prevent it. Hiroshi Shimamura, director general of the government information bureau, was summoned to the palace. The one way the emperor could convince the people was to speak to them directly, although this had never before been done by a Japanese emperor. But no previous emperor had radio as a means of general communication, either. This decision was so momentous, and the reaction of the army still so unknown, that the emperor's household felt it was possible the army might try to stage a coup and reverse the action. By going directly to the people, the emperor would make the surrender irrevocable.

There was good reason for concern. After the cabinet meeting, when War Minister Anami returned to his office, he was surrounded by an excited group of young officers. They were talking rebellion, as they had been for several days. "Destroy the corrupt elements who hide underneath the emperor's sleeves," they said. It was always the army way to blame "those around the emperor"; they dare not blame the emperor himself.[24]

But for once they could not play this drama. General Anami informed them grimly that this decision to accept the Potsdam Declaration was the emperor's personal decision.

"From now on the Imperial Army must remain firmly united. You are under no circumstances free to do what you and only you think is right. One disorderly act might upset the whole nation."

A voice spoke up:

"Are you, the war minister, thinking of surrendering to the enemy?"

Anami raised his voice.

"Anyone who intends to disobey this Imperial Order will do so over my dead body."[25]

But the young officers continued to work on General Anami. His loyalties were split down the middle; he understood only too well what these young men faced: they had spent their lives learning that death was to be preferred above dishonor, that was the Imperial Way, the way of the Japanese army since the 1930s. Now these young men were being asked to accept dishonor, not death, as if it were the natural thing to do. But on the other hand, General Anami's emperor was also his God, another aspect of the Imperial Way, and God had told him that the army must submit.

All Anami could do was temporize between the conflicting loyalties, wait, and hope for the best. He issued a statement that indicated that the army was not going to accept the Imperial Will.

"Even if we have to eat weeds, gnaw sand, and sleep in the fields, we are firmly convinced that we can find a way out of the present crisis only by continuing to fight resolutely."[26]

But when the young rebels demanded that he lead them in a coup, he stalled them off.

The message of the emperor had already been transmitted by radio to the Allies. In the very early hours of August 19 came a reply, saying that from the moment of surrender, the authority of the emperor and the Japanese government would be subject to the Supreme Commander for the Allied Powers, "who will take such steps as he deems proper to effectuate the surrender terms." It also said "the ultimate form of the government of Japan shall, in accordance with the Potsdam Declaration, be established by the freely expressed will of the Japanese people."[27]

Gobbledegook. It meant nothing at all. But the fact that it meant nothing at all indicated a new caution on the part of the Americans. As Foreign Minister Togo argued, they could have replied that unconditional surrender meant unconditional surrender, and not have mentioned the emperor at all. By mentioning him, the Allies had indicated that they had at least made no decision on the continuation of the Japanese "polity." If they could be trusted, and if they left the decision to the real will of the Japanese people, then there was no question: the imperial system would be retained.

Once again, the Allies, by their ignorance of Japan and Japanese psychology, had played into the hands of the army, for the gobbledegook of the statement was seized upon by the militants to argue the case that the Americans meant to destroy Japan.

A new meeting of the cabinet was called. General Anami announced that the Americans had rejected the one condition the Japanese had invoked and that Japan must now fight to the death.[28]

Foreign Minister Togo said he had been to the Imperial Palace where he had audience with the emperor, who accepted the Allied reply.

Once again the cabinet discussion dropped off into interminable argument. It was finally resolved by a message from the Japanese minister in Stockholm, who said the Americans were giving assurances that in spite of Soviet demands, there would be no deposing of the emperor.

All day on August 14, the pressure continued on General Anami to fight on, and he was hard put to withstand it because he agreed that fight on, Japan should. Several times during the day he told Admiral Suzuki. Each time, Admiral Suzuki reminded the general of his responsibilities to the emperor. After the last such discussion that day, General Anami went away, tight-lipped.

At the War Office, the young militants proposed to kill Admiral Suzuki, Foreign Minister Togo, and Admiral Yonai, thus emasculating the peace factor. General Anami told them to wait until Tuesday. He indicated that he was inclined to back their coup d'état. Leader and spokesman for the young officers was Major Kenji Hatanaka.[29]

Impatiently, the young officers struggled through Monday, August 14, making their plans. On the morning of August 15 General Anami was to give his approval, and they would act.

But on the morning of August 15 Anami was again called to the Imperial Palace along with an extended group of national leaders, including other cabinet officers, and the army and navy chiefs of military affairs—the men who really controlled the army and the navy. Again they met in the underground bomb shelter.

Once again the military men asked that the emperor wait, letting them make another inquiry of the Allies about the imperial system.

Hirohito stood up, then:

> The argument is impressive. But my attitude has not changed from last Friday. I have given very careful thought to the situation both of the world and Japan and come to the conclusion that we should not continue the war. True, there are certain misgivings about the preservation of the national polity. After studying thoroughly the enemy's offer, however, I cannot but notice their good will. Everything depends, after all, on our people, whom I trust. So I am for the acceptance of the Declaration. I am resolved to do anything that is requested of me. If you think I should appeal to the nation through radio I will do so. No doubt our people, especially the soldiers, will be shocked by Our decision. If necessary I am ready to talk directly to the armed men. I wish the cabinet would start drafting the Rescript of acceptance to the Declaration as soon as possible.[30]

There it was. Final. Final. Final.
There was nothing more to be said.

And that is precisely what Major Hatanaka and his young colleagues had decided. When General Anami returned to the War Office twenty of these young officers descended on him. They were all in advanced stages of hysteria, faces red, fists clenched, breasts trembling, hardly able to speak.

General Anami said that the emperor had personally said that the national polity would be preserved. "We must not do a thing that will harass the Gracious Mind."

Major Hatanaka was already rushing from the room, to find and beard other high-ranking officers and seek their support for his coup d'état. He went into the office of General Shizuichi Tanaka, commander of the Eastern Region of the army (which included Tokyo), to plead for help. The general growled:

"Don't speak to me about that stupid idea of yours. I know before hearing from you. Return home at once!"[31]

But Major Hatanaka did not go home.

In the next few hours the emperor recorded his radio statement for broadcast at noon on August 15, the next day. Radio Tokyo began announcing the imperial event over and over again, all night long.

Once the records were cut, the problem was: what to do with them until morning. For the Imperial Household was expecting some attempt by elements of the army to stop the broadcast and somehow to force Japan to fight on.

The records were placed in the hands of Court Chamberlain Yoshihiro Tokugawa for safekeeping until the morning.

The chamberlain considered where he might hide the records. Finally he took them to the office of the empress's personal secretary, a place most unlikely to hold the emperor's belongings. He opened a small locker, put the records inside, and locked the door. Even as he was doing so, soldiers arrived at the Imperial Palace gate and arrested the NHK (national broadcasting company) recording crew who were just going out of the palace. The soldiers held them in the gate hut near the Double Bridge that faces the Outer Plaza.

The soldiers were surrounding the palace. They were Major Hatanaka's men, at this point. The major, ordered home by General Tanaka, had rushed on to the office of Lieutenant General Takeshi Mori, commander of the First Imperial Guards Division, which had the task of defending the Imperial Palace. Hatanaka had demanded that Mori join him and send troops to occupy the Imperial Palace, imprison the emperor and stop the broadcast. Mori had told him he was mad, and Hatanaka had shot him dead.

Major Hatanaka had then issued a false order to the Imperial Guards to surround the palace, to surround the NHK, and to cut off Imperial Palace communication with the outside world.

Major Hatanaka then went to the palace. The NHK broadcasting team was searched in the hut. They did not have the records. The major decided the records were hidden inside the palace. He entered the sacred precincts and began moving through the Imperial Household, a crime punishable by death, and unthinkable by a loyal subject of the emperor. He tore up one office after another. He did not find the records.

Hatanaka's commandeered troops had surrounded the underground rooms where the emperor slept since the bombing of the palace. Chamberlain Tokugawa was found in the area by one of Hatanaka's lieutenants and supporters.

"We are searching for the minister of the Imperial Household and the records. You must know where they are."

"I know nothing."

The lieutenant put his hand on his samurai sword:

"If you keep saying that, I'll cut you up."

"Do so. But that will not help."

"Chamberlain, don't you have any Japanese spirit?"

"Oh, yes, I have spirit. You are conceited to think the military alone are defending the nation."

"Fool!" The lieutenant struck the chamberlain and knocked him down. But no sword slash followed. The chamberlain lay quiet, the lieutenant and his men rushed off to search somewhere else.

At the same time other members of the Hatanaka conspiracy hurried to the official residence of the prime minister, found it empty except for servants, spilled oil around the floors, and set fire to it. They then hurried to Suzuki's private house to find and kill him. He was not there. They burned the house.

Prime Minister Suzuki, fortunately, was in his office in the Diet buildings. That evening he was visited by General Anami, who apologized for all the trouble he had caused after the imperial mandate had been received. The prime minister accepted the apology gracefully, saying that they were all Japanese patriots together. General Anami gave the prime minister a box of cigars as a gift, saying he did not smoke them, and saluted and withdrew. The prime minister's eyes followed his figure sadly. Suzuki knew he would never see Anami alive again.

The general went home to the patio outside the house. He looked out toward the Imperial Palace, and he composed and then wrote down a poem. Then he knelt down and disemboweled himself.

The conspirators failed to find the records of the emperor's impending broadcast and without Hatanaka there, even they did not have the brass to invade the emperor's privacy. Leaving the guards surrounding the palace, Major Hatanaka went rushing from the palace grounds to the NHK studios. He passed through the line of his own guards stationed there and entered. It was now late in the night, and the studios were virtually deserted. The only person on duty was the night announcer, Maro Tateno. Major Hatanaka pointed his pistol at the announcer.

"I want to speak to the nation."

"You must obtain permission from the army Eastern Region Headquarters."

Hatanaka started. General Tanaka, the man who had so brusquely cast him off.

He blustered, Tateno refused. Hatanaka did not know how to manipulate the equipment. It was impasse.

As dawn broke General Tanaka learned that the palace had been invaded and that companies of the Imperial Guard were lining up in their barracks area, preparing to march on the Imperial Palace. Tanaka went to the headquarters and addressed the troops.

"What you have done is completely contrary to the spirit of the Imperial Army. Follow the Imperial Will and stop this foolishness!"

Tanaka then turned on his heel. The officers behind him told the men to fall out and go back to their barracks.

The general's staff car approached the Imperial Palace. It was stopped at the moat by a soldier with a fixed bayonet.

"Who goes?"

"Your commander." Tanaka signaled the driver, who rolled on through across the bridge, the awestruck sentry suddenly recognized the car of a general officer.

Inside, General Tanaka found the commander of the regiment that had seized the palace, dressed him down, and ordered him to get out immediately. Did he know that Major Hatanaka had murdered his commanding general?

The colonel was shamefaced, crestfallen, and afraid all at once. He rounded up his men and moved out.

At NHK studio, Major Hatanaka was informed that the plot had failed. He stood there, still demanding to be heard on the radio.

"Just five minutes. . . ."

"No."

The major suddenly realized that there was no option. No matter who he killed now, he had failed. He left the NHK studio, called off the guards, and headed back to the Imperial Palace to check out what he had heard. On the way someone told him that General Anami had committed suicide, and that General Tanaka had taken over the palace. Major Hatanaka walked to the Outer Plaza of the palace he had violated. He could not go farther. He was no longer in charge. There he put a bullet through his head. The palace coup was over.[32] At noon the imperial broadcast was made. The emperor had taken care to send some of his relatives around Japan to what might be the worst trouble spots: two air bases and Yokosuka naval base. The broadcast was greeted by tears and silence by the millions, but by attempts at violence by a few. By late afternoon they were under control, and the battle stage of the war was ended.

堪え難きを 堪える

37. "To bear the unbearable"

On the day of Japan's surrender Admiral Suzuki's cabinet re-signed and was replaced by a caretaker government headed by His Imperial Highness Prince Naruhiko Higashikuni, who had served faithfully, if not brilliantly, since the Emperor Meiji's days. For the first time in the history of Japan all cabinet posts except war and navy were given to civilians. Higashikuni kept the war ministry for himself, and Admiral Yonai, one of the peace party, held the navy ministry.

One of the first acts of the Higashikuni cabinet, which was to have enormous impact on the Japanese economy, was to authorize payment to the *zaibatsu* cartels for their unfulfilled contracts for war materiels, knowing that the materiels would now never be delivered. The result was an immediate inflation. In 1941 there were Yen 4,700 million in Bank of Japan notes in circulation. On August 15, 1945, the sum was Yen 28,600 million, quite remarkable in view of the war. But by December the money in circulation had doubled, cre-ating enormous hardship for the ordinary Japanese, but saving the *zaibatsu*.[1]

Japan was in shambles. The Imperial Rescript ending the war told part of the story. (See Appendix D.) The whole economy geared to war had been levered away from food production; until very recently the food had come from the Greater East Asia empire. Now the farmers had no implements, no fertilizer, and millions of their sons were still abroad, stranded prisoners of war. A Ministry of

Health survey showed that the daily calorie level of the average Japanese had dropped from 2400 calories per day at the outbreak of the Pacific War to 1800 calories per day. It would get worse before it got better. Japanese merchant shipping had been decimated by the American submarines and bombers. What ships were left were pressed into service to repatriate Japanese servicemen from all areas save Manchuria, where the Soviets pursued their own course (which resulted in many Japanese being held as prisoners in labor camps for years).[2]

Immediately after the surrender, the newspapers were full of classified ads which indicated the condition to which the middle class was reduced:

> To Exchange: White linen suit, medium size. White linen trousers, one pair white leather shoes, almost new, to exchange for foodstuffs.

> For sale: a bottle of John Haig (pinched bottle) whiskey for sale to the highest bidder or in exchange for oil.

> Woman's bicycle, almost new to highest bidder or in exchange for commodities.[3]

Except for the farmers, who could at least survive on their own produce, the people of Japan's cities and towns were nearing starvation.

Food was the great problem. In that first winter of 1945–46, when the victors were still harboring their hatreds, an average of six people per day starved to death in Tokyo, and three per day in Yokohama. The figures for the rest of the country were not reported by the newspapers, but the agony was enormous. One man, convicted of raping and killing seven women, boasted at his trial that it was easy, because all he had to do was tell them that if they would accompany him to his hideout, he would give them food. They all went willingly to their assignations with death.[4]

Ten days after the surrender the pinch was already being felt. The *Japan Times,* an English-language paper, on August 24 cut its size from eight columns to one tabloid sheet, because it virtually ran out of paper. More was borrowed; it would be deemed useful to keep the English-language press going during the American occupation.[5]

Millions of Japanese soldiers all over the Pacific and Orient were scarcely in better condition than the people in the homeland. On the small atolls of the Central Pacific many had starved. On Bougainville and at Rabaul the vast majority had survived by literally making their swords into plowshares and tilling the ground for crops. The surrender of the military forces began without delay, and without incident. Japanese soldiers manned the airports and handled the enemy planes without a whimper. The commanders met with Allied officers in Hanoi, Taihoku (Taipei), Seoul, and gave formal surrender, although their every fiber resisted. Only where the Japanese did not get the word was there any difficulty.[6] There individuals and small groups tended to hold out, sometimes for years. Late in the 1970s the "last" survivor emerged from the jungles of the Philippines. Yet he was not the last; in 1985 came a report of another Japanese still living with wild tribesmen on Luzon Island.

The Allies had announced that they proposed to punish "war criminals." In some areas such as Taiwan, where the Japanese continued to control the island well into September, the army commanders ordered "war crimes trials" of officers and men who had tortured or beheaded American fliers shot down during the carrier raids on Taiwan. The hope seemed to be that if the Japanese punished their own men, the Allies would lay off.[7]

But the Allies had no intention of curtailing the "punishment of the guilty." Clothed in the moral superiority of the victors, they began "investigations." The first victim was General Yamashita. He came down out of the mountains to surrender and was immediately clapped into New Bilibid prison as a war criminal. General MacArthur then rushed through a "trial," which was no more than a kangaroo court. General Yamashita was duly convicted, sentenced, and ultimately hanged after his American army officer defenders had taken the case to the U.S. Supreme Court, convinced of the general's innocence. Yamashita was a victim of Filipino hysteria and British vengeance. The British could not forgive his defeating them so resoundingly with a vastly numerically inferior force. The Filipinos reacted to the to-the-death defense of Manila by the air force (in defiance of Yamashita's orders), and he was given the blame for the excesses he had forbidden. Thus began a series of trials which included some visitations of justice and some visitations of pure vengeance.

There were war crimes in the Philippines, many of them, and one of the worst was on Palawan Island, where 151 American prisoners of war had been slaving to build an airfield for the Japanese. When an American plane appeared overhead, the garrison commander ordered all the prisoners into their air raid shelters, and then ordered his troops to pour gasoline over the shelters and ignite them. Most of the trapped Americans were burned to death. Those who escaped outside were machine-gunned. Ultimately, only nine men survived, by jumping into the sea and swimming to another island where they eluded the Japanese.[8]

But was Yamashita guilty of this offense, as charged? The atrocity took place on December 14, 1944, and Yamashita was not given command of the air force troops until January 1. The war crime was the responsibility of the local commander. The Americans did not understand, and they did not want to understand, that greatest failing of the Japanese military—that local commanders had almost ultimate tactical control of their areas. What the Allies wanted was blood, and they were determined to get it. General MacArthur set the tone. He had hundreds of eager assistants.

Yamashita was only the first victim of victors' justice. An elaborate procedure was developed for the war crimes trials in Tokyo, starting with the beginning of the occupation.

General Homma, who had been in charge of Japanese forces during the occupation of the Philippines, was charged for the Bataan Death March. The defense tried to show that the basic problem was a lack of transportation for the wounded and sick because the Japanese had no idea so many Americans and Filipinos were on Bataan. The defense attorneys did not have a chance; the Death March had become celebrated in American folklore and had to be regarded as a major war crime. The real culprits, men like Colonel Tsuji, went unpunished. General Homma was convicted and shot by a firing squad at Los Banos.[9]

Had Admiral Yamamoto and his subordinate Admiral Nagumo survived the war, undoubtedly they would have been tried, convicted, and executed as war criminals for the Pearl Harbor attack was, as President Roosevelt said, a "day of infamy" in American history.

Because of the American threat, or because of the heartbreak of defeat, many Japanese officers committed *seppuku* in these first days after surrender. Admiral Ugaki, who had commanded the kamikaze air fleet against Okinawa, flew off to his death after hearing the emperor's message. He had promised his men that he would join them, and he was determined to keep that promise. Admiral Ohnishi committed suicide in his home, paying tribute in his last message to the youth of Japan and the kamikaze spirit.[10]

General Sugiyama, who had led the emperor astray time after time with his predictions of immediate success for Japan's military operations, knew that he would be tried as a war criminal. He was responsible for the execution of the B-25 fliers, which was, indeed, a violation of the rules of war and a real war crime. Sugiyama and his wife committed suicide within hours after the surrender.

One of the first men the Allies wanted to bring into custody was General Tojo. Military police were sent to pick him up. When they arrived, he shot himself in the chest. Unfortunately, although he had marked his heart out with crayon, he missed it and survived, to be tried by the victors.

So were thousands of other Japanese tried. On the lower levels many of these officers were actually guilty of the crimes of which they were accused. But what the Allies were after were bigger fish. Someone—several someones—had to be punished for Japan's militant activity since 1931. Consider first the composition of the Allied "court of justice": Great Britain, United States, Australia, China, USSR, Canada, Netherlands, France, New Zealand, Philippines, and India. Each justice had his own axes to grind. Above all was the feeling that Japan must be punished for undertaking the actions, beginning with the occupation of Manchuria, that seemed to the Allies to have led to the Pacific War. The result was what might be expected; from the vantage point of twenty-five years later a young scholar named Richard H. Minear wrote a book on the trials. *Victors' Justice* was the title, and victors' justice—revenge—was what the trials turned out to be. U.S. Supreme Court Justice William O. Douglas, a rocklike advocate of human rights, noted at the end of the trials that whatever they were they were not justice.[11]

MacArthur and the others of Supreme Command for Allied Powers had their reason, just as the Japanese had their reason, for the Bataan Death March: the Allied reason was to destroy Japanese morale, to bring down the leading political figures of the past, to smear their memories, in the hope that this sullying would change the Japanese character.

And who were the principal defendants of the great Tokyo trials?

General Tojo, of course. General Sugiyama had escaped them by suicide, and so had Prince Konoye, who had been encouraged by MacArthur to participate in the government, and then was betrayed. He took poison as the authorities came to clap him in jail.

General Araki was tried for his part in the "conspiracy" of Japanese leaders to conquer the world. Araki, in fact, had an enormous responsibility for the buildup of *bushido* as a major element of Japanese philosophy. But that was not a war crime. He was convicted of the "overall conspiracy" and of making war against China—scarcely war crimes—but acquitted of all the real war crimes charges.

Of the twenty-five major "war criminals" only two, General Matsui, the commander of the central China forces, and Mamoru Shigemitsu, the career diplomat and sometime foreign minister, escaped conviction on the "conspiracy" charge.

Admiral Asami Nagano escaped "victors' justice" by dying in the middle of the trial, and so did Yosuke Matsuoka. The admiral had been naval chief of staff at the time of Pearl Harbor, so he would have been hanged, most certainly, and so would Matsuoka, who, more than any other man, was responsible for the taking of Manchuria and Japanese expansion there.

The conspiracy charge was something the Japanese simply could not understand. For as this book shows, Japan's whole direction, from the day she was aroused from sleep by Commodore Perry, was to control her own country and destiny. Japan learned from the West that, given her geography, the only way to keep from becoming a victim was to become perpetrator. She learned too well to suit the Western Allies.

That particular blunderbuss charge of conspiracy was virtually inescapable by anyone who had participated in Japanese political life since 1853. Had Lord Hatta not died in the late nineteenth century he would have been on trial for his memorial to the throne in which he suggested the plan Japan had followed in the conquest of Asia. The plan was not a conspiracy, it was a logical progression for a nation learning to do as the colonial powers did. Japan's problem was that she came too late upon the scene, the Europeans resented her successes, and the Chinese were beginning to awaken and produce a nationalism of their own. Had Japan's moves been made between 1840 and 1900 there would have been very little fuss. It was the height of the age of colonialism. But coming between 1880 and 1941, those moves infuriated the Western powers and made war inevitable.

Asia owes a great debt to Japan for the Greater East Asia Co-Prosperity Sphere, for, even though it was a cynical ploy by the army, the establishment of governments for Asian countries by Asiatics was heady stuff, and when the war ended, the Asians were not willing to resume the yoke of colonialism. More than any other nation, Japan caused the end of colonialism in less than two decades after the war.[12]

No one in the West thanked Japan for that boon to the enslaved.

When it came to assess Japan's conduct, the victorious Allies went all the way back to Manchuria. General Doihara, one of the Manchuria conspirators, was hanged for his part in the railway plot. And so were five others convicted, essentially, in revenge for making war. General Tojo did have one real war crime against him: his decision that Allied war prisoners should be used as slave labor caused the death of thousands. Koki Hirota, whose crime was to be foreign minister at the time of the beginning of the war with China, was sentenced and hanged, although it was well known in Japan, and came out at the trial, that Hirota was one of Japan's men of peace, who had done what he could to avoid war, and had tried to stop the China incident. General Itagaki, chief of staff of the Kwantung Army during the conspiracy days, was a soldier doing what he thought was his duty; one of the real charges against him might have been participation in the murder of the old Marshal Chang Hsueh-liang. General Kimura's major crime was to be in charge of the forces that fought the Soviets at Lake Khasan and Homonhom. General Muto was given the blame for the Rape of Nanking although he did not even know about it until after the fact. These six high personages were duly hanged, and lest the Japanese people be able in any way to honor them in future, their ashes were ordered by SCAP to be mixed together and scattered to the winds. But the best laid plans. . . .

Japanese workmen preserved some of the ashes, put them into six urns, and saved them.[13] Later, in a little park in Tokyo a great boulder was inscribed with a simple memorial to these men who had died victims of the Allied revenge, and the wording of the inscription indicates that from the beginning their trial was a mockery and the "justice" was revenge, just as the Americans got their revenge on Admiral Yamamoto by murdering him in the South Pacific. The marker to the six war criminals was placed on the inner side of the boulder, with another more general memorial on the front, and only those who knew what to look for were likely to find it. Over the years the walkway to the inscription showed the marks of many thousands of feet, as Japanese came to consider the price that must be paid for defeat in war.[14]

Had the war crimes trials been conducted on the basis of real crimes, their outcome might have been considered a precedent for international justice.

The fact is that the war crimes trials did not serve the Allied purpose because the Japanese people then, and much of the world now, concluded that the Japanese were being visited with revenge. It was a part of what the emperor had warned them about in his remark that they "must bear the unbearable."

Out of the war also came one great myth, perpetuated by well-meaning people throughout the world who fear an atomic holocaust. That myth is that the atomic bomb caused the surrender of Japan.

The fact is that as far as the Japanese militarists were concerned, the atomic bomb was just another weapon. The two atomic bombs at Hiroshima and Nagasaki were icing on the cake, and did not do as much damage as the firebombings of Japanese cities. The B-29 firebombing campaign had brought the destruction of 3,100,000 homes, leaving fifteen million people homeless, and killing about a million of them. It was the ruthless firebombing, and Emperor Hirohito's realization that if necessary the Allies *would* completely destroy Japan and kill every Japanese to achieve "unconditional surrender" that persuaded him to the decision to end the war. The atomic bomb is indeed a fearsome weapon, but it was not the cause of Japan's surrender, even though the myth persists even to this day.

A s it turned out, Japan could have had no better friends than Douglas MacArthur and the Americans. They might have imposed a military government (as the Americans did in Korea), but instead, MacArthur chose to deal through the Japanese government. He was also adamant against allowing the Soviets any part in the occupation of Japan. This stand, backed by President Truman, saved Japan from fragmentation, probable split into Communist and non-Communist camps, and economic destruction of the sort visited on Germany.

In the beginning, the Supreme Command for Allied Powers set out to eliminate what they believed to be the root causes of Japanese militarism.

What the Americans did not realize (and do not seem to have realized since) was that essentially they were dealing with the people who had ruled Japan since 1868.

They reduced the emperor to the ranks of mortals. They reduced Shintoism to an ordinary religion. But emperor and Shinto remained.

The Americans were on the right track when they sought to remake the Japanese educational system. Control was removed from the hands of the Ministry of Education. An American-type system of local school boards was established, and schools were put on the American 6-3-3 ratio, from grammar school through high school. In the Western democratic tradition, the teachers were instructed to form unions.

Unions soon enough became an enormous problem. As political prisoners were released, the well-organized Communists and Socialists began to draw strength with their talk of the suffering masses—for, indeed, Japan was little but a suffering mass. The number of union members jumped from zero in 1944 to 3.5 million in 1947, and the leftists led them. The left made its bid for power by calling a general strike in 1947. Had not General MacArthur stopped it by dictum, Japan probably would that year have become a Socialist state. In the spring of 1947 the Yoshida government fell and the Socialists formed a coalition cabinet with the assistance of two smaller parties.

By this time relations between the United States and the USSR had gone downhill so far that leftists were anathema to the Americans. Washington and Tokyo panicked. MacArthur had vowed in 1945 to break up the *zaibatsu,* and the process had begun. The Chinese Nationalists demanded Japanese factories as reparations to replace the Manchurian factories carted off by the Soviets at the end of the war. The Australians, British, and the Soviets all wanted reparations. If they got them, Japanese industry would be destroyed. General MacArthur announced that there would be no reparations and no further breakup of the Japanese business system. Instead of repression, Japan was to have American assistance. Thus, under a new constitution, were saved the essential political and economic systems of prewar Japan.

Many changes did come: land reform, fragmentation of police power, and elimination of militarist control. In 1947 the Americans began talking about a peace treaty. China had begun to fall apart in civil war, and relations between the United States and the USSR worsened. Aided by the United States, the Japanese economy began to revive.

In 1949 the Chinese Communists conquered China. In 1950 the Korea war broke, and the Americans suddenly discovered they needed Japan very badly as an arsenal. The Japanese military had never really been disbanded completely, particularly the navy, and it was called into action to sweep for mines. Japanese factories began to produce land mines and other munitions for the Americans.

In 1951 the Americans worked out a peace treaty with Japan. In the spring of 1952, the treaty went into effect. American military forces remained in Japan, but as paying guests who were among other things entrusted with Japan's defense, including atomic.

Japan was then free to accomplish by economic means what she had failed to do by military expansion: make Japan into a prosperous power. In the next twenty years Japan did just that, to the astonishment of the world.

Japan's war against the West, then, began in 1853 when Commodore Perry and his black ships forced the Japanese to enter the modern world. Japan's response was to destroy Western colonialism, assure the equality of the colored peoples of the world, and take the leadership of Asia. She accomplished the first end; political colonialism scarcely exists at all in the world of the 1980s. She accomplished the second end: the single anomaly of South Africa attests to the end of racism as an acceptable political theory. She is now once again seeking world leadership.

APPENDIX A

On July 18, 1944, Imperial General Headquarters issued the following statement regarding the fall of Saipan. This defeat meant the Allies had breached the inner reaches of the Japanese empire, something Tojo's militarists had promised would never happen. The direct result was the fall of the Tojo government, which collapsed in the total lack of confidence now shown by the emperor and the men around him, and many in the military. This communiqué is one of the most important ever issued by Imperial Headquarters. Inherent in its sentences is the story of Japan's war against the Allies, going badly, with virtually no cooperation between army and navy despite all the brave words. And to the careful reader, it was apparent in July 1944 that Imperial Headquarters knew the war was lost, and was warning the Japanese people:

> In the early part of June a powerful task force of the enemy approached east of the Mariana Islands and Saipan Island on June 11 was subjected to air attacks by an aggregate total of 200 and scores of planes, while on June 14 the neighborhood of the Oreai Airfield on the southwestern coast of the island was furiously bombarded with ships' guns. The main force of the enemy that appeared near the place of landing was built up around more than a dozen aircraft carriers, eight battleships and about 70 large transports.
> Before daybreak on June 15 the enemy commenced terrific bombardment with ships' guns and aircraft and at about 7:00 A.M.

under its cover sent more than 300 landing barges over the water in an endeavor to effect a wholesale landing near Oreai on the southwest coast of the island. The Japanese units stationed on the island at once gave battle and more than once bent the enemy back after inflicting heavy losses, but past noon, a part of the enemy force managed to secure a foothold near Cape Susup and afterwards gradually extended it. Braving the razing bombing and gunfire of the enemy, our units continued to counterattack and by sundown set ablaze more than a dozen enemy tanks by attacking at close quarters. Our air force sank one enemy battleship and one cruiser and set ablaze two other cruisers. [Not true, au.] Also in concert with gunfire from on land, it sank or damaged numerous enemy landing barges loaded with troops. Relying on the sheer weight of numbers and volume, however, the enemy came on and his strength now reached a full division.

On June 16, by reason of our terrific attacks, the enemy was almost entirely unable to extend his foothold, while day and night the Japanese units carried out night attacks from the east and north, part of them breaking through as far as Cape Susup, thereby cutting the enemy force in two, south and north, and throwing him into utter confusion but with dawn on June 7 the enemy bombardment became so fierce that the defenders were compelled to withdraw.

Thereafter damage to our side gradually increased under the frenzied bombing of enemy aircraft and gunfire. Beginning on about June 19 the defending force was compelled to adjust its front on the line at the center between the town of Garapan and Laulau Bay. Since June 20 the enemy were using the Oreai airfield and the same day the Aslito airfield, too, fell into enemy hands.

On the other hand a part of our Combined Fleet, which had been waiting for an opportunity to smash the enemy, suddenly commenced operation. Against it, an American fleet in the South Pacific area proceeded north and thus, ours and enemy's task forces met in battle in waters west of the Marianas on June 19 and 20. The situation at this point was already described in a communiqué of the Imperial Headquarters. [That communiqué was one of the typical "victory" communiqués issued by the navy throughout the war until this point. Au.]

By about June 23 or 24 the sources of water on Saipan Island had been completely destroyed. The island being short of water and provided with few wells, it became extremely difficult to obtain any water supply.

Furthermore the enemy, in command of the air and sea supremacy, daily intensified warship bombardments and bombing attacks, which eventually covered the entire island. For over ten days following the enemy landing on the island, the Japanese Forces fought bravely day and night. Unfortunately, however, the losses on our part considerably increased, and the movement of our troops, not to mention night assaults, were rendered difficult by the searchlights from enemy warships and also by flare bombs.

Until the evening of June 25 the Japanese forces maintained the line linking Garapan, the southern foot of Mt. Tapochau and Donnie, but due to the onslaughts of enemy units supported by tanks, the firing line became entangled from about this time. Undaunted in the face of such furious fighting the Japanese troops charged into the enemy, some with bombs under their arms, to the great terror of their opponents.

On the night of June 26, Mt. Tapochau finally fell into enemy hands. Since Mt. Tapochau is the highest peak on Saipan the enemy immediately established a powerful artillery force on the southern side of the height. Thus the war situation became very unfavorable for the Japanese. From June 28 on the enemy attack became further intensified and the Japanese were forced into a state where all the guns were destroyed and all the ammunition exhausted. Despite such predicament, our forces kept on fighting, and a part of our units still holding firmly the important points in the southern and southeastern sectors of Mt. Tapochau prevented the enemy's northward advance. As the war situation became further aggravated the Imperial Japanese Forces, displaying their characteristic bravery, continued their terrific attacks against the enemy. Some of our soldiers had no water to drink for three days while some kept on fighting, eating the leaves of trees and even snails. Especially noteworthy is the fact that the Otsu unit, which had held a key point on the Southwestern area of Mt. Tapochau, surprise-attacked and annihilated an enemy force possessing five or six light trench mortars and also seven or eight enemy flare units. Upon receiving an order to return to the battalion, a group of 15 surviving soldiers of the unit broke through several enemy lines and after killing at least 150 enemy troops and destroying the enemy field headquarters, returned to their battalion headquarters. Such instances of the heroic action of the Japanese soldiers were seen everywhere on the island.

In the meantime the Japanese Air and Sea units, in order to better the situation on land, daily pounded the enemy positions, munitions dumps and enemy airfield from June 21. On the other hand, the same units also attacked the enemy fleet in the waters around Saipan and sank two aircraft carriers and one transport, in addition to damaging one cruiser and one warship of an unknown type as well as blasting some 35 enemy positions.

Since the enemy task force came attacking the Marianas on June 11, the Japanese Air and Sea units gained the following war results:

1. Sank . . . Two aircraft carriers, three battleships, four cruisers, three destroyers, and one submarine, two warships of an unknown type, two transports.

2. Sank or damaged more than five aircraft carriers and over one battleship.

3. Damaged five or six aircraft carriers, one battleship, three cruisers, three destroyers, one warship of unknown type, seven transports.

4. Airplanes . . . shot down. More than 863.

It is indeed regrettable that despite such brilliant war results, we were unable to frustrate the enemy's malicious attempt.

[Au. note. The entire naval claims, above, are untrue. The carrier *Bunker Hill* was hit and damaged during the Battle of the Philippines Sea. A few other ships were hit. But the remarkable aspect of the naval side of the Marianas campaign was the virtual untouchability of the ships. Ashore, the marines and soldiers took terrible casualties in the desperate struggle with the Japanese soldiers who did not expect to survive the battle and so fought all the more ferociously. Also note the malicious statement of the navy that despite their heroic victory, the army was unable to hold the island. If the Japanese navy had managed even half as much as claimed, the army might have been able to hold the island. But the army dared not complain against this attack; the army had failed to hold the island.]

On June 17, the Japanese units on Saipan Island were honored with words of appreciation from the Throne.

Again on June 30 they were honored with another Gracious Message from the Throne.

The officers and men shed tears of gratitude over the Great Imperial Benevolence and vowed to proceed with the annihilation of the enemy to the last.

Twenty days of hard fighting had been experienced. A considerable dwindling in our strength was evident. On the other hand the enemy fire increased in intensity. Their land forces now numbered three divisions. Thus it came about that our positions were pierced.

As a result the front was shortened in the northeastern part of Saipan Island and adjusted, the work being completed by July 4.

By this time not a single gun remained for use against enemy tanks and the Japanese were placed in the worst position where they had to check the enemy attacks with human bullets.

Next day, July 5, it became necessary to shorten the front at last to the area around Mt. Marpi and the northern extremity of the island.

Thereupon, about 3000 wounded men, who could not rise because of their wounds, voluntarily ended their own lives. All important papers were burned and destroyed. At night the same day, the final order to attack was given.

Under this order about fifty groups of raiders who had been selected on the night of July 6 made their stealthy way deep into the enemy positions and blasted their headquarters camps as well as guns and planes. Thus they caused serious disturbance within the enemy positions.

From early daylight the next day, the Japanese, with the entire strength at their command, turned to the neighborhood of Charankanoa, the enemy landing point, a long way, and carried out a final heroic attack.

Thus the Imperial Forces acted, the Army and the Navy as one body, with Vice Admiral Nagumo Supreme Commander of the Japanese forces in the area, Lieutenant General Saito, commander of the Army unit, Rear Admiral Tsujimura, commander of the Navy unit, at the head of their forces.

Carrying out charge after charge, they killed numerous enemy officers and men.

Subsequently they fell back to their cavern defense and kept on battling bravely with the enemy for about ten days, til finally they reddened the soil, of Saipan with their blood.

On July 16 they died gloriously one after another shouting Banzai for His Majesty the Emperor and praying for the prosperity of Japan.

The circumstances of this heroic fight were also confirmed by our planes making reconnaissance.

Concerning the resident Japanese, as has been confirmed by Imperial Headquarters, they cooperated with the Imperial Forces throughout the fighting. Those of them who had the capacity to fight took part and they shared the fate of the officers and men.

To them we express profound gratitude and express our deep condolence.

The enemies on their part have confessed that the fight on Saipan was the most difficult they have ever experienced in the Pacific and that the damage sustained in manpower was the heaviest. It was announced that the casualties sustained in the fight reach more than 15,000 as known up to July 10. Of course this figure is discounted as usual, and it is likely that the real figure will be much larger. [U.S. casualties were 17,000 including 4000 killed. Japanese casualties will never be known. The military casualties were placed at 24,000, but that represents only bodies recovered. Many—perhaps thousands of—other bodies went into the sea or were sealed in caves. Virtually all of the Japanese civilian population also perished, either by joining the battle or by suicide.]

A report to the following in substance was received from the commander on the spot [General Saito] just before the launching of the general attack:

I respectfully offer my apologies that I have lost many trusted fighting men of His Imperial Majesty and have not been able to fulfill my duties well. The brilliant exploits rendered by the Imperial Units which are revealed in the brave fighting of the Otsu unit and which have displayed the quintessence of the Imperial Forces, are too numerous to be mentioned here.

I have no time at command to refer in detail to their exploits here and I lack words of apology to the fallen officers and men. Lastly we all loudly shouted Banzai for His Majesty the Emperor—the shouts of the officers and men who firmly believe in sure victory for the Japanese Empire and who are resolved to live eternally for the cause of the great justice with smiles on their faces.

Yes, in response to the shouts of the officers and men, who sacrificed themselves for eternal justice with the smiles on their faces, believing in sure victory for Nippon, we will without fail display the glorious tradition of the Imperial Forces and profoundly pledge that we will annihilate the enemy if the arrogant enemy approaches the mainland of Nippon.

[That night General Saito ordered out the last of the delicacies he had saved in the command cave, and he and his staff ate canned crabmeat and drank sake. He then excused himself, saying that he wanted to sleep until just before the dawn, when he would personally lead the last *banzai* charge into the teeth of death. But he did not. He went to his secluded spot in the command cave, and there he committed *seppuku*.]

APPENDIX B

As the Pacific War reached its height and one territory after another was overrun, the Japanese people were hard pressed to secure the details of their empire's collapse. Too often, as at Saipan, there were no survivors at all to come home to tell the tales. Thus, the Japanese people clutched at whatever information they could find, and often found themselves relying on American sources. In August 1944, a month after the fall of Saipan, a correspondent of *Asahi Shimbun* in Stockholm filed this following dispatch, which, when published in Japan, created a sensation and played directly into the hands of the Japanese government's encouragement of a new "victory or death" policy. The stilted English of the dispatch does not represent Correspondent Robert Sherrod's writing, but Japanese selection and translation of the article by the *Asahi* correspondent:

By an *Asahi* Correspondent

STOCKHOLM. How the courageous Japanese noncombatants on Saipan Island including women and children, killed themselves before the eyes of American marines, sharing the fate of the heroic members of the Imperial Garrison Forces stationed there was vividly described by Robert Sherrod, war correspondent for the American magazine *Time,* in his article entitled "Enemy's Character," which appeared in the August 7 issue of the same periodical.

Sherrod said that "the self-inflicted deaths of the Japanese noncombatants on Saipan shows that the entire Japanese nation prefers death than to surrender.

"We thought that before the final Japanese attack on Saipan Island was repulsed we had seen in all details the manner in which Japanese officers and men dispose of themselves but this was not true. Still more was to be revealed.

"A detachment of the American marines which set out for mopping up operations aboard an amphibian tank discovered seven Japanese on a coral reef off the beach and proceeded there to capture them. As the amphibian tank approached the coral reef, six of the seven Japanese disposed of themselves and the remaining one, who apparently looked like an officer, dashed forward to the American tank, sword in hand. However the officer met a heroic death before the volleys of lead fired by the Americans. Prior to this incident we had heard the incredible fact that a large percentage of the 20,000 noncombatants on Saipan island had disposed of themselves, helping each other in the act.

"Your correspondent went to the place called Marpi Point at the northern extremity of the island. At this spot was a long expanse of field and the second Japanese airfield. At the end of the plain was a 200-meter precipice overlooking the rugged coral reef, which faced the angry waves of the ocean. At break of day I went to the edge of the cliff across the airfield and there I saw nine members of the interment corps of the U.S. Marines engaged in picking up the corpses of two marines who had died in action the previous day. I asked one of them about a story I had heard about the Japanese.

" 'You will not believe what I tell you unless you see it with your own eyes,' he said. 'Yesterday and the day before yesterday there were several hundred Japanese noncombatants, men, women, and children, on this cliff. All of them, however, either jumped into the sea from the top of the precipice or descended it to walk into the sea. I saw a father plunge into the sea with his three sons in his arms.

"The marine paused, and pointed with his finger.

" 'Look! There is a man about to jump into the sea.'

"There I saw a Japanese youth apparently not older than fifteen walking towards the sea over the rocks. He stopped and bowed low and then went into the water. He was not seen long. Looking down from the top of the cliff I saw seven corpses of Japanese. One of them was of a child apparently about five years old. Wearing a white shirt, the dead body was drifting. I started to leave the place.

"A marine then said, 'That's nothing. There are hundreds like these about a half mile down on the western side.' The correspondent went to the spot and the officer of a minesweeper, whom he met, confirmed the fact.

" 'I came across a woman wearing a white blouse and khaki colored slacks with her black hair floating around her in the water,' replied the officer. Every time I see a woman wearing a white blouse the picture of that woman in the water comes back vividly to me. I also saw a child, probably four or five years old, dead, with his arms tightly encircled around the neck of a dead soldier.'

"The officer told me what he had seen. It can be surmised from all these cases that a Japanese soldier will go to any extreme to avoid surrender. The Japanese noncombatants, too, absolutely did not want to surrender."

The foregoing was the story as vividly narrated by the correspondent. Regardless of sex or age it is an etching in clear profile of the crystallization of the lofty racial spirit that flows in every Japanese breast. What does the picture of a dead child with his arms around the neck of a soldier arouse in those who read this story in Japan?

In all probability, a faint smile must have played around the child's mouth as he met his death without the trace of slightest fear. The child had no doubt become chummy with his soldier friend before the Americans came and had often been carried gleefully around on the shoulders of his big playmate. He had gone to his death in peace and security.

It is not this child alone that met death fully confident that his compatriots at home will surely avenge their deaths. The Japanese on Saipan died with a deep tranquility in their hearts—a tranquility that such words as tragic or courageous fail to adequately describe.

Hot tears sting my eyes as I continue to write the report of the American correspondent for dispatch home. Quoting the report further, "At Mt. Marpi a Japanese sharpshooter had hidden himself in a cave. This Japanese soldier was an excellent shot and two American marines had been killed in attempting to force him out of his shelter. One of the marines had been shot at a distance of 700 yards. A third marine was severely wounded. It took the Americans about one hour to get him out of the cave. They had to resort to even blasting with dynamite.

"The American marines were dumfounded at seeing Japanese women calmly combing their hair on the top of a rock.

"The Americans were evidently ignorant of the well known annal that King Leonidas of Sparta and his gallant men met heroic death in the bloody battle waged against the Persians at Thermopylae. The story refers to the heroic death of King Leonidas and 300 men in battle against the Persian forces, several hundred times larger than the Spartan troops in 480 B.C. At the old battlefield there now stands a monument with the words: Travelers: Go and tell the Spartans that we sleep here as we were ordered.

"With bated breath we screwed our eyes on the Japanese women on the rock. Joining hands they soon quietly disappeared under the surface of the water. In the meantime some one hundred Japanese who were standing on the summit of Marpi Point began to observe a solemn ceremony. When the marines approached the point the Japanese composedly divided hand grenades among themselves and hoisted the Rising Sun flag atop a flat rock in the vicinity.

"On another occasion the marines were stunned upon seeing some 50 Japanese including small children hurling hand grenades at each other as though they were warming up for a baseball game. Suddenly six other Japanese who had been attacking the Americans from their hiding place rushed out and in no time ended their lives before the eyes of the group of fifty.

"Why do the Japanese commit suicide. Why do they take their own lives? Is it that the Japanese believe that the Americans are brutes and will kill anyone coming within their power? The Japanese civilians apparently preferred death to ignominy as captives in the hands of the Americans."

Before closing his lengthy story, Sherrod commented, "American marines anticipated that the Japanese forces would end their lives after having fought to the last because they had read of the heroic deaths of the Japanese soldiers at Attu Island under the command of Lieutenant General Yasuo Yamazaki. However, who could have expected such pathetic deaths of noncombatants? Some of the Americans who attempted to stop the Japanese from taking their own lives were killed by the latter. Saipan Island is the first to be invaded by the Americans, of the numerous others which are inhabited by the Japanese."

APPENDIX C

The following Imperial Rescript, issued on December 8, 1941, was reprinted on the eighth day of each month until September 1945, to remind the people of Japan of the reasons for their war.

IMPERIAL RESCRIPT

We, by grace of heaven, Emperor of Japan, seated on the Throne of a line unbroken for ages eternal, enjoin upon ye, Our loyal and brave subjects:

We hereby declare War on the United States of America and the British Empire. The men and officers of Our Army and Navy shall do their utmost in prosecuting the war. Our public servants of various departments shall perform faithfully and diligently their respective duties; the entire nation with a united will shall mobilize their total strength so that nothing will miscarry in the attainment of Our war aims.

To insure the stability of East Asia and to contribute to world peace is the far-sighted policy which was formulated by Our Great Illustrious Imperial Grandsire and Our Great Imperial Sire succeeding Him, and which We lay constantly to heart. To cultivate friendship among nations and to enjoy prosperity in common with all nations, has always been the guiding principle of Our Empire's foreign policy. It has been truly unavoidable and far from Our wishes that Our Empire has been brought to cross swords with America and Britain. More than four years have passed since China, failing to comprehend the true intentions of Our Empire, and recklessly courting trouble, disturbed the peace of East Asia and compelled Our Empire to take up arms. Although there has been reestablished the National Government of China, with which Japan had effected neighborly intercourse and cooperation, the regime which has survived at Chungking, relying upon American and British protection, still continues its fratricidal opposition. Eager for the realization of their inordinate ambition to dominate the Orient, both America and Britain, giving support to the Chungking regime, have aggravated the disturbances in East Asia. Moreover these two Powers, inducing other countries to follow suit increased military preparations on all sides of Our Empire to challenge Us. They have obstructed by every means Our peaceful commerce and finally resorted to a direct severance of economic relations, menacing gravely the existence of Our Empire. Patiently have We waited and long have We endured, in the hope that Our government might retrieve the situation in peace. But Our adversaries, showing not the least spirit of conciliation, have unduly delayed a settlement; and in the meantime they have intensified the economic and political pressure to compel thereby Our Empire to submission. This trend of affairs, would, if left unchecked, not only nullify Our Emperor's efforts of many years for the sake of the stabilization of East Asia, but also endanger the very existence of Our nation. The situation being such as it is, Our Empire, for its existence and self-defense has no other recourse but to appeal to arms and to crush every obstacle in its path.

The hallowed spirits of Our Imperial Ancestors guarding Us from above, We rely upon the loyalty and courage of Our subjects in Our confident expectation that the task bequeathed by Our forefathers will be carried forward and that the sources of evil will be speedily eradicated and an enduring peace immutably established in East Asia, preserving thereby the glory of Our Empire.

Hirohito
(Imperial Seal)

The 8th day of the 12th month
of the 16th year of Showa.

APPENDIX D

*T*he Imperial Rescript granted by Emperor Hirohito on August 14, 1945, officially ending the war for Japan by surrender:

To Our good and loyal subjects

After pondering deeply the general conditions of the world and the actual conditions obtaining in Our Empire today, We have decided to effect a settlement of the present situation by resorting to an extraordinary measure.

We have ordered Our Government to communicate to the Government of the United States, Great Britain, China and the Soviet Union that Our Empire accepts the provisions of their Joint Declaration.

To strive for the common prosperity and happiness of all nations as well as the security and well-being of Our subjects is the solemn obligation which has been handed down by Our Imperial Ancestors and which We lay close to heart. Indeed, We declared war on America and Britain out of Our sincere desire to assure Japan's self-preservation and the stabilization of East Asia, it being far from Our thought either to infringe upon the sovereignty of other nations or to embark upon territorial aggrandizement. But now the war has lasted for nearly four years. Despite the best that has been done by everyone—the gallant fighting of military and naval forces, the diligence and assiduity of Our servants of the State and the devoted service of Our one hundred million people, the war situation has developed not necessarily to Japan's advantage, while the general trends of the world have all turned against her interest. Moreover the enemy has begun to employ a new and most cruel bomb, the power of which to do damage is indeed incalculable, taking the toll of many innocent lives. Should We continue to fight it would not only result in the ultimate collapse and obliteration of the Japanese nation, but also it would lead to the total extinction of human civilization. Such being the case how are We to save the millions of Our subjects or to atone Ourselves before the hallowed spirits of Our Imperial Ancestors? This is the reason why We have ordered the acceptance of the Joint Declaration of the Powers.

We cannot but express the deepest sense of regret to our Allied nations of East Asia, who have consistently cooperated with the Empire towards the emancipation of East Asia. The thought of those officers and men, as well as others, who have fallen on the fields of battle, those who die at their posts of duty, or those who met with untimely death and all their bereaved families pains Our heart night and day. The welfare of the wounded and the war sufferers and those who have lost their home and livelihood are the objects of Our profound solicitude. The hardships and suffering to which Our nation is to be subjected hereafter will certainly be great. We are keenly aware of the inmost feelings of all ye, Our subjects. However, it is according to the dictate of time and fate that We have resolved to pave the way for a grand peace for all the generations to come by enduring the unendurable and suffering what is insufferable.

Having been able to safeguard and maintain the structure of the Imperial State, We are always with ye, Our good and loyal subjects, relying upon your sincerity and integrity. Beware most strictly of any outbursts of emotion which may engender needless complications or any fraternal contention and strife which may create confusion, lead ye astray and cause ye to lose the confidence of the world. Let the entire nation continue as one family from generation to generation, ever firm in its faith of the imperishableness of its divine land and mindful of its heavy burden of responsibilities, and the long road before it. Unite your total strength to be devoted to the construction for the future. Cultivate the ways of rectitude, foster nobility of spirit, and work with resolution so as ye may enhance the innate glory of the Imperial State and keep pace with the progress of the world.

> Imperial Sign (Manual)
> Imperial Seal

The 14th day of the 8th month
of the 20th year of Showa.

APPENDIX E

THE CONSTITUTION OF THE EMPIRE OF JAPAN
(MEIJI KEMPO)

PREAMBLE

Having, by virtue of the glories of Our Ancestors, ascended the Throne of lineal succession unbroken for ages eternal; desiring to promote the welfare of, and to give development to the moral and intellectual faculties of Our beloved subjects, the very same that have been favoured with the benevolent care and affectionate vigilance of Our Ancestors; and hoping to maintain the prosperity of the State, in concert with Our people and with their support, We hereby promulgate, in pursuance of Our Imperial Rescript of the 12th day of the 10th month of the 14th year of Meiji, a fundamental law of State, to exhibit the principles by which We are to be guided in Our conduct, and to point out what Our descendants and Our subjects and their descendants are forever to conform.

The rights of sovereignty of the State, We have inherited from Our Ancestors, and We shall bequeath them to Our descendants. Neither We nor they shall in future fail to wield them, in accordance with the provisions of the Constitution hereby granted.

We now declare to respect and protect the security of the rights and of the property of Our people, and to secure to them the complete enjoyment of the same, within the extent of the provisions of the present Constitution and of the law.

The Teikoku Gikai shall first be convoked for the 23rd year of Meiji, and the time of its opening shall be the date when the present Constitution goes into force.

When, in the future, it may become necessary to amend any of the provisions of the present Constitution, We or Our successors shall assume the initiative right, and submit a project for the same to the Teikoku Gikai. The Teikoku Gikai shall pass its vote upon it, according to the conditions imposed by the present Constitution, and in no otherwise shall Our descendants or Our subjects be permitted to attempt any alteration thereof.

Our Ministers of State, on Our behalf, shall be held responsible for the carrying out of the present Constitution, and Our present and future subjects shall forever assume the duty of allegiance to the present Constitution.

(His Imperial Majesty's Sign-Manual.)

(Privy Seal.)

The 11th day of the 2nd month of the 22nd year of Meiji.

(Countersigned) Count Kuroda Kiyotaka,
> *Minister President of State.*

Count Ito Hirobumi,
> *President of the Privy Council.*

Count Okuma Shigenobu,
> *Minister of State for Foreign Affairs.*

Count Saigo Tsukumichi,
> *Minister of State for the Navy.*

Count Inoue Kaoru,
> *Minister of State for Agriculture and Commerce.*

Count Yamada Akiyoshi,
> *Minister of State for Justice.*

Count Matsukata Masayoshi,
> *Minister of State for Finance and Minister of State for Home Affairs.*

Count Oyama Iwao,
> *Minister of State for War.*

Viscount Mori Arinori,
> *Minister of State for Education.*

Viscount Enomoto Takeaki,
> *Minister of State for Communications.*

CHAPTER I
THE TENNO

ARTICLE I

The Empire of Japan shall be reigned over and governed by a line of Tenno unbroken for ages eternal.

ARTICLE II

The Imperial Throne shall be succeeded to by Imperial male descendants, according to the provisions of the Imperial House Law.

ARTICLE III

The Tenno is sacred and inviolable.

ARTICLE IV

The Tenno stands at the head of the Empire, combining in Himself the rights of sovereignty and exercises them, according to the provisions of the present Constitution.

ARTICLE V

The Tenno exercises the legislative power with the consent of the Teikoku Gikai.

ARTICLE VI

The Tenno gives sanction to laws, and orders them to be promulgated and executed.

ARTICLE VII

The Tenno convokes the Teikoku Gikai, opens, closes and prorogues it, and dissolves the House of Representatives.

ARTICLE VIII

The Tenno, in consequence of an urgent necessity to maintain public safety or to avert public calamities, issues, when the Teikoku Gikai is not sitting, Imperial Ordinances in the place of law.

Such Imperial Ordinances are to be laid before the Teikoku Gikai at its next session, and when the Gikai does not approve the said Ordinances, the Government shall declare them to be invalid for the future.

ARTICLE IX

The Tenno issues or causes to be issued, the Ordinances necessary for the carrying out of the laws, or for the maintenance of the public peace and order, and for the promotion of the welfare of the subjects. But no Ordinance shall in any way alter any of the existing laws.

ARTICLE X

The Tenno determines the organization of the different branches of the administration and the salaries of all civil and military officers, and appoints and dismisses the same. Exceptions especially provided for in the present Constitution or in other laws, shall be in accordance with the respective provisions (bearing thereon).

ARTICLE XI

The Tenno has the supreme command of the Army and Navy.

ARTICLE XII

The Tenno determines the organization and peace standing of the Army and Navy.

ARTICLE XIII

The Tenno declares war, makes peace, and concludes treaties.

ARTICLE XIV

The Tenno declares a state of siege.

The conditions and effects of a state of siege shall be determined by law.

ARTICLE XV

The Tenno confers titles of nobility, rank, orders and other marks of honor.

ARTICLE XVI

The Tenno orders amnesty, pardon, commutation of punishments and rehabilitation.

ARTICLE XVII

A Regency shall be instituted in conformity with the provisions of the Imperial House Law.

The Regent shall exercise the powers appertaining to the Tenno in His name.

CHAPTER II
RIGHTS AND DUTIES OF SUBJECTS

ARTICLE XVIII

The conditions necessary for being a Japanese subject shall be determined by law.

ARTICLE XIX

Japanese subjects may, according to qualifications determined in laws or ordinances, be appointed to civil or military or any other public offices equally.

ARTICLE XX

Japanese subjects are amenable to service in the Army or Navy, according to the provisions of law.

ARTICLE XXI

Japanese subjects are amenable to the duty of paying taxes, according to the provisions of law.

ARTICLE XXII

Japanese subjects shall have the liberty of abode and of changing the same within the limits of law.

ARTICLE XXIII

No Japanese subject shall be arrested, detained, tried, or punished, unless according to law.

ARTICLE XXIV

No Japanese subject shall be deprived of his right of being tried by the judges determined by law.

ARTICLE XXV

Except in the cases provided for in the law, the house of no Japanese subject shall be entered or searched without his consent.

ARTICLE XXVI

Except in the cases mentioned in the law, the secrecy of the letters of every Japanese subject shall remain inviolate.

ARTICLE XXVII

The right of property of every Japanese subject shall remain inviolate.
Disposal of property necessary for the public benefit shall be provided for by law.

ARTICLE XXVIII

Japanese subjects shall, within limits not prejudicial to peace and order, and not antagonistic to their duties as subjects, enjoy freedom of religious belief.

ARTICLE XXIX

Japanese subjects shall, within limits of law, enjoy the liberty of speech, writing, publication, public meetings and associations.

ARTICLE XXX

Japanese subjects may present petitions, by observing the proper forms of respect, and by complying with the rules specially provided for the same.

ARTICLE XXXI

The provisions contained in the present Chapter shall not affect the exercise of the powers appertaining to the Tenno, in times of war or in cases of a national emergency.

ARTICLE XXXII

Each and every one of the provisions contained in the preceding articles of the present Chapter, that are not in conflict with the laws or the rules and discipline of the Army and Navy, shall apply to the officers and men of the Army and of the Navy.

CHAPTER III
THE TEIKOKU GIKAI

ARTICLE XXXIII

The Teikoku Gikai shall consist of two Houses, a House of Peers and a House of Representatives.

ARTICLE XXXIV

The House of Peers shall, in accordance with the Ordinance concerning the House of Peers, be composed of the members of the Imperial Family, of the orders of the nobility, and of those persons, who have been nominated thereto by the Tenno.

ARTICLE XXXV

The House of Representatives shall be composed of Members elected by the people, according to the provisions of the Law of Election.

ARTICLE XXXVI

No one can at one and the same time be a Member of both Houses.

ARTICLE XXXVII

Every law requires the consent of the Teikoku Gikai.

ARTICLE XXXVIII

Both Houses shall vote upon projects of law submitted to it by the Government, and may respectively initiate projects of law.

ARTICLE XXXIX

A Bill, which has been rejected by either the one or the other of the two Houses, shall not be again brought in during the same session.

ARTICLE XL

Both Houses can make representations to the Government, as to laws or upon any other subject. When, however, such representations are not accepted, they cannot be made a second time during the same session.

ARTICLE XLI

The Teikoku Gikai shall be convoked every year.

ARTICLE XLII

A session of the Teikoku Gikai shall last during three months. In case of necessity, the duration of a session may be prolonged by Imperial Order.

ARTICLE XLIII

When urgent necessity arises, an extraordinary session may be convoked, in addition to the ordinary one.

The duration of an extraordinary session shall be determined by Imperial Order.

ARTICLE XLIV

The opening, closing, prolongation of session and the prorogation of the Teikoku Gikai, shall be effected simultaneously for both Houses.

In case the House of Representatives has been ordered to dissolve, the House of Peers shall at the same time be prorogued.

ARTICLE XLV

When the House of Representatives has been ordered to dissolve, Members shall be caused by Imperial Order to be newly elected, and the new House shall be convoked within five months from the day of dissolution.

ARTICLE XLVI

No debate can be opened and no vote can be taken in either House of the Teikoku Gikai, unless not less than one third of the whole number of Members thereof are present.

ARTICLE XLVII

Votes shall be taken in both Houses by absolute majority. In the case of a tie vote, the President shall have the casting vote.

ARTICLE XLVIII

The deliberations of both Houses shall be held in public. The deliberations may, however, upon demand of the Government or by resolution of the House, be held in secret sitting.

ARTICLE XLIX

Both Houses of the Teikoku Gikai may respectively present addresses to the Tenno.

ARTICLE L

Both Houses may receive petitions presented by subjects.

ARTICLE LI

Both Houses may enact, besides what is provided for in the present Constitution and in the Law of the Houses, rules necessary for the management of their internal affairs.

ARTICLE LII

No Member of either House shall be held responsible outside the respective House, for any opinion uttered or for any vote given in the House. When, however, a Member himself has given publicity to his opinions by public speech, by documents in print or in writing, or by any other similar means, he shall, in the matter, be amenable to the general law.

ARTICLE LIII

The Members of both Houses shall, during the session, be free from arrest, unless with the consent of the Houses, except in cases of flagrant delicts, or of offences connected with a state of internal commotion or with a foreign trouble.

ARTICLE LIV

The Ministers of State and the Delegates of the Government may, at any time, take seats and speak in either House.

CHAPTER IV
THE MINISTERS OF STATE AND THE PRIVY COUNCIL

ARTICLE LV

The respective Ministers of State shall give their advice to the Tenno, and be responsible for it.

All Laws, Imperial Ordinances and Imperial Rescripts of whatever kind, that relate to the affairs of the State, require the countersignature of a Minister of State.

ARTICLE LVI

The Privy Councillors shall, in accordance with the provisions for the organization of the Privy Council, deliberate upon important matters of State, when they have been consulted by the Tenno.

CHAPTER V
THE JUDICATURE

ARTICLE LVII

The Judicature shall be exercised by the Courts of Law according to law in the name of the Tenno.

The organization of the Courts of Law shall be determined by law.

ARTICLE LVIII

The judges shall be appointed from among those, who possess proper qualifications according to law.

No judge shall be deprived of his position, unless by way of criminal sentence or disciplinary punishment.

Rules for disciplinary punishment shall be determined by law.

ARTICLE LIX

Trials and judgements of a Court shall be conducted publicly. When, however, there exists any fear, that such publicity may be prejudicial to peace and order, or to the maintenance of public morality, the public trial may be suspended by provision of law or by the decision of the Court of law.

ARTICLE LX

All matters, that fall within the competency of a special Court, shall be specially provided for by law.

ARTICLE LXI

No suit at law, which relates to rights alleged to have been infringed by the illegal measures of the administrative authorities, and which shall come within the competency of the Court of Administrative Litigation specially established by law, shall be taken cognizance of by a Court of Law.

CHAPTER VI
FINANCE

ARTICLE LXII

The imposition of a new tax or the modification of the rates (of an existing one) shall be determined by law.

However, all such administrative fees or other revenue having the nature of compensation shall not fall within the category of the above clause.

The raising of national loans and the contracting of other liabilities to the charge of the National Treasury, except those that are provided for in the Budget, shall require the consent of the Teikoku Gikai.

ARTICLE LXIII

The taxes levied at present shall, in so far as they are not remodelled by a new law, be collected according to the old system.

ARTICLE LXIV

The expenditure and revenue of the State require the consent of the Teikoku Gikai by means of an annual Budget.

Any and all expenditures overpassing the appropriations set forth in the Titles and Paragraphs of the Budget, or that are not provided for in the Budget, shall subsequently require the approbation of the Teikoku Gikai.

ARTICLE LXV

The Budget shall be first laid before the House of Representatives.

ARTICLE LXVI

Expenditures of the Imperial House shall be defrayed every year out of the National Treasury, according to the present fixed amount for the same, and shall not require the consent thereto of the Teikoku Gikai, except in case an increase thereof is found necessary.

ARTICLE LXVII

Those already fixed expenditures based by the Constitution upon the powers appertaining to the Tenno, and such expenditures as may have arisen by the effect of law, or that appertain to the legal obligations of the Government, shall be neither rejected nor reduced by the Teikoku Gikai, without the concurrence of the Government.

ARTICLE LXVIII

In order to meet special requirements, the Government may ask the consent of the Teikoku Gikai to a certain amount as a Continuing Expenditure Fund, for a previously fixed number of years.

ARTICLE LXIX

In order to supply deficiencies, which are unavoidable, in the Budget, and to meet requirements unprovided for in the same, a Reserve Fund shall be provided for in the Budget.

ARTICLE LXX

When the Teikoku Gikai cannot be convoked, owing to the external or internal condition of the country, in case of urgent need for the maintenance of public safety, the Government may take all necessary financial measures, by means of an Imperial Ordinance.

In the case mentioned in the preceding clause, the matter shall be submitted to the Teikoku Gikai at its next session, and its approbation shall be obtained thereto.

ARTICLE LXXI

When the Teikoku Gikai has not voted on the Budget, or when the Budget has not been brought into actual existence, the Government shall carry out the Budget of the preceding year.

ARTICLE LXXII

The final account of the expenditures and revenue of the State shall be verified and confirmed by the Board of Audit, and it shall be submitted by the Government to the Teikoku Gikai, together with the report of verification of the said Board.

The organization and competency of the Board of Audit shall be determined by law separately.

CHAPTER VII
SUPPLEMENTARY RULES

ARTICLE LXXIII

When it has become necessary in future to amend the provisions of the present Constitution, a project to that effect shall be submitted to the Teikoku Gikai by Imperial Order.

In the above case, neither House can open the debate, unless not less than two-thirds of the whole number of Members are present, and no amendment can be passed, unless a majority of not less than two-thirds of the Members present is obtained.

ARTICLE LXXIV

No modification of the Imperial House Law shall be required to be submitted to the deliberation of the Teikoku Gikai.

No provision of the present Constitution can be modified by the Imperial House Law.

ARTICLE LXXV

No modification can be introduced into the Constitution, or into the Imperial House Law, during the time of a Regency.

ARTICLE LXXVI

Existing legal enactments, such as laws, regulations, Ordinances, or by whatever names they may be called, shall, so far as they do not conflict with the present Constitution, continue in force.

All existing contracts or orders, that entail obligations upon the Government, and that are connected with expenditure, shall come within the scope of ARTICLE LXVII.

THE CONSTITUTION OF JAPAN, 1946

We, the Japanese people, acting through our duly elected representatives in the National Diet, determined that we shall secure for ourselves and our posterity the fruits of peaceful cooperation with all nations and the blessings of liberty throughout this land, and resolved that never again shall we be visited with the horrors of war through the action of government, do proclaim that sovereign power resides with the people and do firmly establish this Constitution. Government is a sacred trust of the people, the authority for which is derived from the people, the powers of which are exercised by the representatives of the people, and the benefits of which are enjoyed by the people. This is a universal principle of mankind upon which this Constitution is founded. We reject and revoke all constitutions, laws, ordinances and rescripts in conflict herewith.

We, the Japanese people, desire peace for all time and are deeply conscious of the high ideals controlling human relationship, and we have determined to preserve our security and existence, trusting in the justice and faith of the peace-loving peoples of the world. We desire to occupy an honored place in an international society striving for the preservation of peace, and the banishment of tyranny and slavery, oppression and intolerance for all time from the earth. We recognize that all peoples of the world have the right to live in peace, free from fear and want.

We believe that no nation is responsible to itself alone, but that laws of political morality are universal; and that obedience to such laws is incumbent upon all nations who would sustain their own sovereignty and justify their sovereign relationship with other nations.

We, the Japanese people, pledge our national honor to accomplish these high ideals and purposes with all our resources.

CHAPTER I. THE EMPEROR

ARTICLE 1. The Emperor shall be the symbol of the State and of the unity of the people, deriving his position from the will of the people with whom resides sovereign power.

ARTICLE 2. The Imperial Throne shall be dynastic and succeeded to in accordance with the Imperial House Law passed by the Diet.

ARTICLE 3. The advice and approval of the Cabinet shall be required for all acts of the Emperor in matters of state, and the Cabinet shall be responsible therefor.

ARTICLE 4. The Emperor shall perform only such acts in matters of state as are provided for in this Constitution and he shall not have powers related to government.

The Emperor may delegate the performance of his acts in matters of state as may be provided by law.

ARTICLE 5. When, in accordance with the Imperial House Law, a Regency is established, the Regent shall perform his acts in matters of state in the Emperor's name. In this case, paragraph one of the preceding article will be applicable.

ARTICLE 6. The Emperor shall appoint the Prime Minister as designated by the Diet.

The Emperor shall appoint the Chief Judge of the Supreme Court as designated by the Cabinet.

ARTICLE 7. The Emperor, with the advice and approval of the Cabinet, shall perform the following acts in matters of state on behalf of the people:

Promulgation of amendments of the constitution, laws, cabinet orders and treaties.

Convocation of the Diet.

Dissolution of the House of Representatives.

Proclamation of general election of members of the Diet.

Attestation of the appointment and dismissal of Ministers of State and other officials as provided for by law, and of full powers and credentials of Ambassadors and Ministers.

Attestation of general and special amnesty, commutation of punishment, reprieve, and restoration of rights.

Awarding of honors.

Attestation of instruments of ratification and other diplomatic documents as provided for by law.

Receiving foreign ambassadors and ministers.

Performance of ceremonial functions.

ARTICLE 8. No property can be given to, or received by, the Imperial House, nor can any gifts be made therefrom, without the authorization of the Diet.

CHAPTER II. RENUNCIATION OF WAR

ARTICLE 9. Aspiring sincerely to an international peace based on justice and order, the Japanese people forever renounce war as a sovereign right of the nation and the threat or use of force as means of settling international disputes.

In order to accomplish the aim of the preceding paragraph, land, sea, and air forces, as well as other war potential, will never be maintained. The right of belligerency of the state will not be recognized.

CHAPTER III. RIGHTS AND DUTIES OF THE PEOPLE

ARTICLE 10. The conditions necessary for being a Japanese national shall be determined by law.

ARTICLE 11. The people shall not be prevented from enjoying any of the fundamental human rights. These fundamental human rights guaranteed to the people by this Constitution shall be conferred upon the people of this and future generations as eternal and inviolate rights.

ARTICLE 12. The freedoms and rights guaranteed to the people by this Constitution shall be maintained by the constant endeavor of the people, who shall refrain from any abuse of these freedoms and rights and shall always be responsible for utilizing them for the public welfare.

ARTICLE 13. All of the people shall be respected as individuals. Their right to life, liberty, and the pursuit of happiness shall, to the extent that it does not interfere with the public welfare, be the supreme consideration in legislation and in other governmental affairs.

ARTICLE 14. All of the people are equal under the law and there shall be no discrimination in political, economic or social relations because of race, creed, sex, social status or family origin.

Peers and peerage shall not be recognized.

No privilege shall accompany any award of honor, decoration or any distinction, nor shall any such award be valid beyond the lifetime of the individual who now holds or hereafter may receive it.

ARTICLE 15. The people have the inalienable right to choose their public officials and to dismiss them.

All public officials are servants of the whole community and not of any group thereof.

Universal adult suffrage is guaranteed with regard to the election of public officials.

In all elections, secrecy of the ballot shall not be violated. A voter shall not be answerable, publicly or privately, for the choice he has made.

ARTICLE 16. Every person shall have the right of peaceful petition for the redress of damage, for the removal of public officials, for the enactment, repeal or amendment of laws, ordinances or regulations and for other matters; nor shall any person be in any way discriminated against for sponsoring such a petition.

ARTICLE 17. Every person may sue for redress as provided by law from the State or a public entity, in case he has suffered damage through illegal act of any public official.

ARTICLE 18. No person shall be held in bondage of any kind. Involuntary servitude, except as punishment for crime, is prohibited.

ARTICLE 19. Freedom of thought and conscience shall not be violated.

ARTICLE 20. Freedom of religion is guaranteed to all. No religious organization shall receive any privileges from the State, nor exercise any political authority.

No person shall be compelled to take part in any religious act, celebration, rite or practice.

The State and its organs shall refrain from religious education or any other religious activity.

ARTICLE 21. Freedom of assembly and association as well as speech, press and all other forms of expression are guaranteed.

No censorship shall be maintained, nor shall the secrecy of any means of communication be violated.

ARTICLE 22. Every person shall have freedom to choose and change his residence and to choose his occupation to the extent that it does not interfere with the public welfare.

Freedom of all persons to move to a foreign country and to divest themselves of their nationality shall be inviolate.

ARTICLE 23. Academic freedom is guaranteed.

ARTICLE 24. Marriage shall be based only on the mutual consent of both sexes and it shall be maintained through mutual cooperation with the equal rights of husband and wife as a basis.

With regard to choice of spouse, property rights, inheritance, choice of domicile, divorce and other matters pertaining to marriage and the family, laws shall be enacted from the standpoint of individual dignity and the essential equality of the sexes.

ARTICLE 25. All people have the right to maintain the minimum standards of wholesome and cultured living.

In all spheres of life, the State shall use its endeavors for the promotion and extension of social welfare and security, and of public health.

ARTICLE 26. All people shall have the right to receive an equal education correspondent to their ability, as provided by law.

All people shall be obligated to have all boys and girls under their protection receive ordinary education as provided for by law. Such compulsory education shall be free.

ARTICLE 27. All people shall have the right and the obligation to work.

Standards for wages, hours, rest and other working conditions shall be fixed by law.

Children shall not be exploited.

ARTICLE 28. The right of workers to organize and to bargain and act collectively is guaranteed.

ARTICLE 29. The right to own or to hold property is inviolable.

Property rights shall be defined by law, in conformity with the public welfare.

Private property may be taken for public use upon just compensation therefor.

ARTICLE 30. The people shall be liable to taxation as provided by law.

ARTICLE 31. No person shall be deprived of life or liberty, nor shall any other criminal penalty be imposed, except according to procedure established by law.

ARTICLE 32. No person shall be denied the right of access to the courts.

ARTICLE 33. No person shall be apprehended except upon warrant issued by a competent judicial officer which specifies the offense with which the person is charged, unless he is apprehended, the offense being committed.

ARTICLE 34. No person shall be arrested or detained without being at once informed of the charges against him or without the immediate privilege of counsel; nor shall he be detained without adequate cause; and upon demand of any person such cause must be immediately shown in open court in his presence and the presence of his counsel.

ARTICLE 35. The right of all persons to be secure in their homes, papers and effects against entries, searches and seizures shall not be impaired except upon warrant issued for adequate cause and particularly describing the place to be searched and things to be seized, or except as provided by Article 33.

Each search or seizure shall be made upon separate warrant issued by a competent judicial officer.

ARTICLE 36. The infliction of torture by any public officer and cruel punishments are absolutely forbidden.

ARTICLE 37. In all criminal cases the accused shall enjoy the right to a speedy and public trial by an impartial tribunal.

He shall be permitted full opportunity to examine all witnesses, and he shall have the right of compulsory process for obtaining witnesses on his behalf at public expense.

At all times the accused shall have the assistance of competent counsel who shall, if the accused is unable to secure the same by his own efforts, be assigned to his use by the State.

ARTICLE 38. No person shall be compelled to testify against himself.

Confession made under compulsion, torture or threat, or after prolonged arrest or detention shall not be admitted in evidence.

No person shall be convicted or punished in cases where the only proof against him is his own confession.

ARTICLE 39. No person shall be held criminally liable for an act which was lawful at the time it was committed, or of which he has been acquitted, nor shall he be placed in double jeopardy.

ARTICLE 40. Any person, in case he is acquitted after he has been arrested or detained, may sue the State for redress as provided by law.

CHAPTER IV. THE DIET

ARTICLE 41. The Diet shall be the highest organ of state power, and shall be the sole law-making organ of the State.

ARTICLE 42. The Diet shall consist of two Houses, namely the House of Representatives and the House of Councillors.

ARTICLE 43. Both Houses shall consist of elected members, representative of all the people.

The number of the members of each House shall be fixed by law.

ARTICLE 44. The qualifications of members of both Houses and their electors shall be fixed by law. However, there shall be no discrimination because of race, creed, sex, social status, family origin, education, property or income.

ARTICLE 45. The term of office of members of the House of Representatives shall be four years. However, the term shall be terminated before the full term is up in case the House of Representatives is dissolved.

ARTICLE 46. The term of office of members of the House of Councillors shall be six years, and election for half the members shall take place every three years.

ARTICLE 47. Electoral districts, method of voting and other matters pertaining to the method of election of members of both Houses shall be fixed by law.

ARTICLE 48. No person shall be permitted to be a member of both Houses simultaneously.

ARTICLE 49. Members of both Houses shall receive appropriate annual payment from the national treasury in accordance with law.

ARTICLE 50. Except in cases provided by law, members of both Houses shall be exempt from apprehension while the Diet is in session, and any members apprehended before the opening of the session shall be freed during the term of the session upon demand of the House.

ARTICLE 51. Members of both Houses shall not be held liable outside the House for speeches, debates or votes cast inside the House.

ARTICLE 52. An ordinary session of the Diet shall be convoked once per year.

ARTICLE 53. The Cabinet may determine to convoke extraordinary sessions of the Diet. When a quarter or more of the total members of either House makes the demand, the Cabinet must determine on such convocation.

ARTICLE 54. When the House of Representatives is dissolved, there must be a general election of members of the House of Representatives within forty (40) days from the date of dissolution, and the Diet must be convoked within thirty (30) days from the date of the election.

When the House of Representatives is dissolved, the House of Councillors is closed at the same time. However, the Cabinet may in time of national emergency convoke the House of Councillors in emergency session.

Measures taken at such session as mentioned in the proviso of the preceding paragraph shall be provisional and shall become null and void unless agreed to by the House of Representatives within a period of ten (10) days after the opening of the next session of the Diet.

ARTICLE 55. Each House shall judge disputes related to qualifications of its members. However, in order to deny a seat to any member, it is necessary to pass a resolution by a majority of two-thirds or more of the members present.

ARTICLE 56. Business cannot be transacted in either House unless one-third or more of total membership is present.

ARTICLE 57. Deliberation in each House shall be public. However, a secret meeting may be held where a majority of two-thirds or more of those members present passes a resolution therefor.

Each House shall keep a record of proceedings. This record shall be published and given general circulation, excepting such parts of proceedings of secret session as may be deemed to require secrecy.

Upon demand of one-fifth or more of the members present, votes of the members on any matter shall be recorded in the minutes.

ARTICLE 58. Each House shall select its own president and other officials.

Each House shall establish its rules pertaining to meetings, proceedings and internal discipline, and may punish members for disorderly conduct. However, in order to expel a member, a majority of two-thirds or more of those members present must pass a resolution thereon.

ARTICLE 59. A bill becomes a law on passage by both Houses, except, as otherwise provided by the Constitution.

A bill which is passed by the House of Representatives, and upon which the House of Councillors makes a decision different from that of the House of Representatives, becomes a law when passed a second time by the House of Representatives by a majority of two-thirds or more of the members present.

The provision of the preceding paragraph does not preclude the House of Representatives from calling for the meeting of a joint committee of both Houses, provided for by law.

Failure by the House of Councillors to take final action within sixty (60) days after receipt of a bill passed by the House of Representatives, time in recess excepted, may be determined by the House of Representatives to constitute a rejection of the said bill by the House of Councillors.

ARTICLE 60. The budget must first be submitted to the House of Representatives.

Upon consideration of the budget, when the House of Councillors makes a decision different from that of the House of Representatives, and when no agreement can be reached even through a joint committee of both Houses, provided for by law, or in the case of failure by the House of Councillors to take final action within thirty (30) days, the period of recess excluded, after the receipt of the budget passed by the House of Representatives, the decision of the House of Representatives shall be the decision of the Diet.

ARTICLE 61. The second paragraph of the preceding article applies also to the Diet approval required for the conclusion of treaties.

ARTICLE 62. Each House may conduct investigations in relation to government, and may demand the presence and testimony of witnesses, and the production of records.

ARTICLE 63. The Prime Minister and other Ministers of State may, at any time, appear in either House for the purpose of speaking on bills, regardless of whether they are members of the House or not. They must appear when their presence is required in order to give answers or explanations.

ARTICLE 64. The Diet shall set up an impeachment court from among the members of both Houses for the purpose of trying those judges against whom removal proceedings have been instituted.

Matters relating to impeachment shall be provided by law.

CHAPTER V. THE CABINET

ARTICLE 65. Executive power shall be vested in the Cabinet.

ARTICLE 66. The Cabinet shall consist of the Prime Minister, who shall be its head, and other Ministers of State, as provided for by law.

The Prime Minister and other Ministers of State must be civilians.

The Cabinet, in the exercise of executive power, shall be collectively responsible to the Diet.

ARTICLE 67. The Prime Minister shall be designated from among the members of the Diet by a resolution of the Diet. This designation shall precede all other business.

If the House of Representatives and the House of Councillors disagree and if no agreement can be reached even through a joint committee of both Houses, provided for by law, or the House of Councillors fails to make designation within ten (10) days, exclusive of the period of recess, after the House of Representatives has made designation, the decision of the House of Representatives shall be the decision of the Diet.

ARTICLE 68. The Prime Minister shall appoint the Ministers of State. However, a majority of their number must be chosen from among the members of the Diet.

The Prime Minister may remove the Ministers of State as he chooses.

ARTICLE 69. If the House of Representatives passes a non-confidence resolution, or rejects a confidence resolution, the Cabinet shall resign en masse, unless the House of Representatives is dissolved within ten (10) days.

ARTICLE 70. When there is a vacancy in the post of Prime Minister, or upon the first convocation of the Diet after a general election of members of the House of Representatives, the Cabinet shall resign en masse.

ARTICLE 71. In the cases mentioned in the two preceding articles, the Cabinet shall continue its functions until the time when a new Prime Minister is appointed.

ARTICLE 72. The Prime Minister, representing the Cabinet, submits bills, reports on general national affairs and foreign relations to the Diet and exercises control and supervision over various administrative branches.

ARTICLE 73. The Cabinet, in addition to other general administrative functions, shall perform the following functions:

Administer the law faithfully; conduct affairs of state.

Manage foreign affairs.

Conclude treaties. However, it shall obtain prior or, depending on circumstances, subsequent approval of the Diet.

Administer the civil service, in accordance with standards established by law.

Prepare the budget, and present it to the Diet.

Enact cabinet orders in order to execute the provisions of this Constitution and of the law. However, it cannot include penal provisions in such cabinet orders unless authorized by such law.

Decide on general amnesty, special amnesty, commutation of punishment, reprieve, and restoration of rights.

ARTICLE 74. All laws and cabinet orders shall be signed by the competent Minister of State and countersigned by the Prime Minister.

ARTICLE 75. The Ministers of State, during their tenure of office, shall not be subject to legal action without the consent of the Prime Minister. However, the right to take that action is not impaired hereby.

CHAPTER VI. JUDICIARY

ARTICLE 76. The whole judicial power is vested in a Supreme Court and in such inferior courts as are established by law.

No extraordinary tribunal shall be established, nor shall any organ or agency of the Executive be given final judicial power.

All judges shall be independent in the exercise of their conscience and shall be bound only by this Constitution and the laws.

ARTICLE 77. The Supreme Court is vested with the rule-making power under which it determines the rules of procedure and of practice, and of matters relating to attorneys, the internal discipline of the courts and the administration of judicial affairs.

Public procurators shall be subject to the rule-making power of the Supreme Court.

The Supreme Court may delegate the power to make rules for inferior courts to such courts.

ARTICLE 78. Judges shall not be removed except by public impeachment unless judicially declared mentally or physically incompetent to perform official duties. No disciplinary action against judges shall be administered by any executive organ or agency.

ARTICLE 79. The Supreme Court shall consist of a Chief Judge and such number of judges as may be determined by law; all such judges excepting the Chief Judge shall be appointed by the Cabinet.

The appointment of the judges of the Supreme Court shall be reviewed by the people at the first general election of members of the

House of Representatives following their appointment, and shall be reviewed again at the first general election of members of the House of Representatives after a lapse of ten (10) years, and in the same manner thereafter.

In cases mentioned in the foregoing paragraph, when the majority of the voters favors the dismissal of a judge, he shall be dismissed.

Matters pertaining to review shall be prescribed by law.

The judges of the Supreme Court shall be retired upon the attainment of the age as fixed by law.

All such judges shall receive, at regular stated intervals, adequate compensation which shall not be decreased during their terms of office.

ARTICLE 80. The judges of the inferior courts shall be appointed by the Cabinet from a list of persons nominated by the Supreme Court. All such judges shall hold office for a term of ten (10) years with privilege of reappointment, provided that they shall be retired upon the attainment of the age as fixed by law.

The judges of the inferior courts shall receive, at regular stated intervals, adequate compensation which shall not be decreased during their terms of office.

ARTICLE 81. The Supreme Court is the court of last resort with power to determine the constitutionality of any law, order, regulation or official act.

ARTICLE 82. Trials shall be conducted and judgment declared publicly.

Where a court unanimously determines publicity to be dangerous to public order or morals, a trial may be conducted privately, but trials of political offenses, offenses involving the press or cases wherein the rights of people as guaranteed in Chapter III of this Constitution are in question shall always be conducted publicly.

CHAPTER VII. FINANCE

ARTICLE 83. The power to administer national finances shall be exercised as the Diet shall determine.

ARTICLE 84. No new taxes shall be imposed or existing ones modified except by law or under such conditions as law may prescribe.

ARTICLE 85. No money shall be expended, nor shall the State obligate itself, except as authorized by the Diet.

ARTICLE 86. The Cabinet shall prepare and submit to the Diet for its consideration and decision a budget for each fiscal year.

ARTICLE 87. In order to provide for unforeseen deficiencies in the budget, a reserve fund may be authorized by the Diet to be expended upon the responsibility of the Cabinet.

The Cabinet must get subsequent approval of the Diet for all payments from the reserve fund.

ARTICLE 88. All property of the Imperial Household shall belong to the State. All expenses of the Imperial Household shall be appropriated by the Diet in the budget.

ARTICLE 89. No public money or other property shall be expended or appropriated for the use, benefit or maintenance of any religious institution or association, or for any charitable, educational or benevolent enterprises not under the control of public authority.

ARTICLE 90. Final accounts of the expenditures and revenues of the State shall be audited annually by a Board of Audit and submitted by the Cabinet to the Diet, together with the statement of audit, during the fiscal year immediately following the period covered.

The organization and competency of the Board of Audit shall be determined by law.

ARTICLE 91. At regular intervals and at least annually the Cabinet shall report to the Diet and the people on the state of national finances.

CHAPTER VIII. LOCAL SELF-GOVERNMENT

ARTICLE 92. Regulations concerning organization and operations of local public entities shall be fixed by law in accordance with the principle of local autonomy.

ARTICLE 93. The local public entities shall establish assemblies as their deliberative organs, in accordance with law.

The chief executive officers of all local public entities, the members of their assemblies, and such other local officials as may be determined by law shall be elected by direct popular vote within their several communities.

ARTICLE 94. Local public entities shall have the right to manage their property, affairs and administration and to enact their own regulations within law.

ARTICLE 95. A special law, applicable only to one local public entity, cannot be enacted by the Diet without the consent of the majority of the voters of the local public entity concerned, obtained in accordance with law.

CHAPTER IX. AMENDMENTS

ARTICLE 96. Amendments to this Constitution shall be initiated by the Diet, through a concurring vote of two-thirds or more of all the members of each House and shall thereupon be submitted to the people for ratification, which shall require the affirmative vote of a majority of all votes cast thereon, at a special referendum or at such election as the Diet shall specify.

Amendments when so ratified shall immediately be promulgated by the Emperor in the name of the people, as an integral part of this Constitution.

CHAPTER X. SUPREME LAW

ARTICLE 97. The fundamental human rights by this Constitution guaranteed to the people of Japan are fruits of the age-old struggle of man to be free; they have survived the many exacting tests for durability and are conferred upon this and future generations in trust, to be held for all time inviolate.

ARTICLE 98. This Constitution shall be the supreme law of the nation and no law, ordinance, imperial rescript or other act of government, or part thereof, contrary to the provisions hereof, shall have legal force or validity.

The treaties concluded by Japan and established laws of nations shall be faithfully observed.

ARTICLE 99. The Emperor or the Regent as well as Ministers of State, members of the Diet, judges, and all other public officials have the obligation to respect and uphold this Constitution.

CHAPTER XI. SUPPLEMENTARY PROVISIONS

ARTICLE 100. This Constitution shall be enforced as from the day when the period of six months will have elapsed counting from the day of its promulgation.

The enactment of laws necessary for the enforcement of this Constitution, the election of members of the House of Councillors and the procedure for the convocation of the Diet and other preparatory procedures necessary for the enforcement of this Constitution may be executed before the day prescribed in the preceding paragraph.

ARTICLE 101. If the House of Councillors is not constituted before the effective date of this Constitution, the House of Representatives shall function as the Diet until such time as the House of Councillors shall be constituted.

ARTICLE 102. The term of office for half the members of the House of Councillors serving in the first term under this Constitution shall be three years. Members falling under this category shall be determined in accordance with law.

ARTICLE 103. The Ministers of State, members of the House of Representatives, and judges in office on the effective date of this Constitution, and all other public officials who occupy positions corresponding to such positions as are recognized by this Constitution shall not forfeit their positions automatically on account of the enforcement of this Constitution unless otherwise specified by law. When, however, successors are elected or appointed under the provisions of this Constitution, they shall forfeit their positions as a matter of course.

Date of Promulgation: November 3, 1946
Date of Enforcement: May 3, 1947.

NOTES

Preface

1. The *Hagakure* is the work of Tsunetomo Yamamoto, a samurai whose daimyo, Mitsushige Nabeshima, died in 1700. In the early years of the shogunate it was the practice of a daimyo's closest retainers to commit *seppuku* when their master died. This practice was outlawed in 1660 by the Tokugawas, so as the next best course, rather than becoming a masterless samurai, or *ronin,* Yamamoto forswore the world and entered the Buddhist priesthood. In the years that followed his thoughts were collected from time to time by a younger samurai who wrote them down. The result was a classic document that details the lives and thoughts of the Japanese warrior class and became a sort of textbook for the revival of the samurai tradition by the Japanese military in the twentieth century.
2. Robert C. Miller, UPI.
3. Prime Minister Yasuhiro Nakasone, in speech to the Diet, Dec. 1984.
4. Reischauer, *Japan Past and Present* (hereafter Reischauer), chap. 2.

1

1. *Nihon Shoki.*
2. Reischauer, chap. 1.
3. *Hagakure,* chap. 8.
4. Borton, *Japan's Modern Century* (hereafter Borton), chap. 2.
5. Craig and Shively, *Personality in Japanese History* (hereafter Craig and Shively), pp. 180–208.
6. Borton, pp. 27–40.
7. Hawks, *Narrative of the Expedition of An American Squadron Under Commodore Perry,* vol. 1, pp. 1–50.
8. Ibid.

9. Craig and Shively, p. 185.
10. Borton, pp. 29–44.
11. Ibid.
12. Lord Hotta Memorial to the Imperial Throne, 1858.

2

1. Borton, chap. 4.
2. Nomura, *Rekishi ni naka ni nihon kaigun* (*Inside History of the Japanese Navy*, hereafter Nomura), pp. 3–5.
3. Craig and Shively, p. 264.
4. Borton, p. 53ff.
5. Ibid.
6. Ibid.
7. Craig and Shively, pp. 302–03, 321–22.
8. Borton, p. 105.
9. Reischauer, pp. 5–7, 156–57.
10. Borton, chap. 6.
11. Ibid., pp. 142–45.

3

1. Borton, pp. 155–64.
2. Ibid.
3. Craig and Shively, p. 318, 330–31.
4. Borton, pp. 200–01.
5. Ibid., p. 230.
6. Craig and Shively, pp. 328–29.
7. Borton, p. 206.
8. Martin, *Russo-Japanese War* (hereafter Martin), chap. 2.
9. Craig and Shively, pp. 318–21.
10. Tolischus, *Through Japanese Eyes* (hereafter Tolischus), p. 58.
11. Hoyt, *Pacific Destiny* (hereafter *Pacific Destiny*), pp. 25–32.

4

1. Borton, pp. 198–99.
2. Blond, *L'Admiral Togo* (hereafter Blond), chap. 1.
3. Ibid., chap. 2; Nomura, pp. 5–17.
4. Blond, pp. 98–100.
5. Martin, p. 40ff.
6. Ibid.
7. Blond, chap. 6.
8. Martin, chap. 3.
9. Hoyt, *Asians in the West*, chaps. 1, 2.
10. Ibid.
11. Blond, p. 243.
12. *Pacific Destiny*, pp. 69–81.

13. Ibid.
14. Borton, pp. 244–49.

5

1. Colegrove, *Militarism in Japan* (hereafter Colegrove), p. 22.
2. Blond, pp. 245–50.
3. Colegrove, chap. 2.
4. Hoyt, *Fall of Tsingtao* (hereafter *Fall of Tsingtao*), pp. 100–130.
5. Hoyt, *Kreuzerkrieg* (hereafter *Kreuzerkrieg*), pp. 180–245.
6. Borton, chap. 6.
7. Hoyt, *Army Without a Country* (hereafter *Army*), chap. 6.
8. *Asahi Shimbun*, Dec. 17, Dec. 23, 1919.
9. *Asians in the West*, pp. 40–49.
10. *Pacific Destiny*, chap. 4.
11. Sunoo, *Japanese Militarism, Past and Present* (hereafter Sunoo), pp. 5–7.
12. *Nichi Nichi*, Nov. 16, 1918.
13. Meiji Constitution, see Appendix.
14. Sunoo, chap. 3.

6

1. Stimson, *The Far Eastern Crisis* (hereafter Stimson), pp. 23, 35.
2. Borton, pp. 301–04.
3. Agawa, *The Reluctant Admiral* (hereafter Agawa), p. 30.
4. Ibid., p. 31.
5. Ibid.
6. Ibid., p. 8.
7. Borton, pp. 308–12.
8. Tanin, *Militarism and Fascism in Japan* (hereafter Tanin), p. 99.
9. Lory, *Japan's Military Masters* (hereafter Lory), chap. 6.
10. Colegrove, p. 22.; Lory, p. 99ff.
11. Liang, *The Sinister Face of the Mukden Incident* (hereafter Liang), p. 26.
12. Lory, p. 136.
13. Ibid.
14. Fujimoto, *Fifty Years of Light and Dark* (hereafter Fujimoto), p. 12.
15. Ibid.
16. Ibid., pp. 12–14.
17. Ibid., pp. 30–33.
18. Yoshihashi, *Conspiracy at Mukden* (hereafter Yoshihashi), p. 26.

7

1. Yoshihashi, p. 35.
2. Liang, pp. 111–12.
3. Ibid.
4. Yoshihashi, p. 33ff.
5. Liang, p. 113.
6. Yoshihashi, pp. 44–45.

7. Ibid., p. 41.
8. Liang, p. 110.
9. Yoshihashi, p. 39ff.
10. Ibid.
11. Ibid.
12. Ibid., p. 156.
13. Ibid.
14. Liang, p. 118.
15. Ibid.
16. *Asahi Shimbun,* June 5, 1928.
17. Liang, p. 119.
18. Fujimoto, pp. 31–32.
19. Ibid.

8

1. Agawa, p. 29.
2. Ibid.
3. Borton, p. 315.
4. *Asahi Shimbun,* Sept. 1930.
5. Borton, pp. 314–15.
6. Liang, p. 124.
7. Agawa, chap. 2.
8. Hayashi, *Kogun* (hereafter *Kogun*), p. 10.
9. Liang, pp. 21–22.
10. Fujimoto, pp. 53–54.
11. Ibid.
12. Yoshihashi, chap. 6.
13. Ibid.
14. Ibid.
15. Liang, pp. 96–98.
16. Yoshihashi, chap. 6.
17. Fujimoto, p. 35.
18. Borton, pp. 330–32.
19. Yoshihashi, p. 154.
20. Ibid., p. 155.
21. Ibid., p. 156.
22. Liang, chap. 3.
23. Yoshihashi, p. 158.
24. Liang, chap. 3.
25. Ibid.
26. Liang, p. 3.
27. Ibid.

9

1. Fujimoto, pp. 33–34.
2. Yoshihashi, p. 198.
3. Yoshihashi, pp. 200–05. Also the Honjo diary goes into considerable detail

about the emperor's behavior in this period. It seems certain that Hirohito did all he could to show the militarists how much he disapproved of their conduct. It also seems obvious that the generals were all determined to carry the Manchuria plot through, once it had been begun.

4. Yoshihashi, p. 192. The author checked Prime Minister Wakatsuke's memoirs carefully for this material and refers to it in footnotes.
5. *Asahi Shimbun*, Sept. 21, 1931. *Nichi Nichi Shimbun*, Sept. 21, 1931. The complacent attitude of the newspapers at this point is inexplicable unless one takes the view that their jingoism was sufficiently aroused to obscure their judgment. Later, in the war years, faced with stringent restrictions, the newspapers managed to convey the truth to the Japanese people in various subtle ways. So it could be done, and, besides, in 1931 the harsh restrictions on the press had not been invoked.
6. Prince Saionji, from this point on, was to be Hirohito's single advisor on the side of peace and conservatism.
7. It seems apparent that the Manchuria incident marked the end of conservative control of the army. It also showed the generals that they could bluff their way past the civil government, and that even the emperor could be bullied. Liang and Yoshihashi and the newspapers of the period are all in accord on the facts.
8. The conspiracy between General Senjuro of the Korea army and the plotters at Mukden is well detailed by Yoshihashi, p. 170ff. What is remarkable is that the prime minister had no way of securing reliable information about what was happening in Seoul.
9. Stimson, p. 32. Secretary of State Henry Stimson's recollection of the Manchurian crisis shows that at least this one American official was under no illusions about the direction in which Japan had begun to move. As the Mukden incident was developing, he and the Japanese ambassador, Katsuji Debuchi, were congratulating each other on the betterment of relations that had occurred in recent months, and Stimson was indicating his hope that in the new atmosphere of friendliness he could bring about U.S. repudiation of its harsh anti-Japanese immigration laws. The chances looked good. But after Mukden, there was no hope.
10. Stimson. The Stimson recollections indicate how hard he tried to show the Japanese the full extent and probable future of American disapproval of the Manchurian grab. They show how little long-range effect the disapproval by one nation of another's policy has had; just as the United States did not "lose China" at the end of World War II, so U.S. diplomacy had no real influence in stopping Japan's militarists in the 1930s. Even then, force would have been the only stopper.
11. *Asahi Shimbun*, Sept. 22, 1931.
12. Ibid.
13. Ibid.
14. Stimson, chap. 3.
15. Yoshihashi, p. 198ff.
16. Ibid.
17. *Japan Times*, Oct. 24, 25, 1931. *Asahi Shimbun*, Oct. 25, 1931.
18. Shiroyama, *War Criminal* (hereafter Shiroyama), pp. 190–200.
19. Yoshihashi, p. 201ff.
20. Ibid.

21. *Asahi Shimbun,* Oct. 25, 1931.
22. Stimson, p. 22.
23. Henry Pu-yi testimony before Tokyo war crimes trials, 1946.
24. Stimson, chap. 1.
25. *Japan Times,* Jan. 20, 1932.
26. *Asahi Shimbun,* Jan. 28, 1932.
27. *Japan Times,* Jan. 29, 1932.
28. *Asahi Shimbun,* Apr. 30, 1932.

10

1. *Japan Times,* Feb. 1932.
2. Ibid.
3. *Asahi Shimbun* and *Japan Times,* March 1932.
4. Colegrove, pp. 36–37.
5. Ibid., pp. 28–29.
6. Zhukov, *The Rise and Fall of the Gumbatsu,* chap. 3.
7. Fujimoto, p. 54.
8. Ibid.
9. Ibid.
10. Murakami, *Japan, the Years of Trial, 1919–52* (hereafter Murakami), p. 46.
11. *Japan Times,* May 17, 1932.
12. *Asahi Shimbun, Nichi Nichi Shimbun,* May 1932.
13. Murakami, p. 53.
14. Murakami, pp. 54–55; *Asahi Shimbun,* Sept. 2, 1932.
15. *Japan Times,* Sept. 2, 1932.
16. *Jiji Shimpo,* Sept. 2, 1932.

11

1. *Asahi Shimbun,* Sept. 25, 1932.
2. Ibid.
3. Lory, p. 40.
4. Ibid., p. 60. These bloodthirsty statements were created by the officer corps to teach the men that death was to be expected, that there could be no honorable surrender in battle under any conditions.
5. Lory, p. 40. Hirohito objected strenuously to the "emperor-organ theory," which was the basis for emperor worship. The theory gained strength in the army in 1934. By 1935 the emperor was firmly established as a god, no matter whether he liked it or not. When he complained, he was told by his advisors that the elevation of his position was essential for the national interest.
6. Lory, p. 63.
7. *Hagakure,* Book I.
8. *Japan Times,* Sept. 24, 1932.
9. Agawa, p. 23.
10. Agawa, pp. 90–94.
11. Honjo, *Emperor Hirohito and His Chief Aide-De-Camp, The Honjo Diary, 1933–36* (hereafter known as Honjo), p. 80. At one point Imperial Prince Chichibu, the emperor's brother, came to the palace to plead with Hirohito to take

personal rule of the country and suspend the constitution to prevent the young officers from seizing power. Hirohito refused. They argued heatedly and Chichibu warned that this way the imperial power would be lost. Hirohito said he would not disgrace the memory of his ancestor (Meiji) by subverting the Meiji Constitution, apparently not realizing that the army was subverting the spirit of the constitution by using that loophole that gave the military power to bring down governments by refusing to participate.

12. Honjo, pp. 26–27. The *kodo ha* controlled the army until 1934. General Tetzusan Nagata was a leader of the *toso ha*, which lamented the lack of army headquarters' control of the Kwantung Army. Soon he became head of the Military Affairs Bureau of the army and then one of his first acts was to purge the followers of General Araki from control positions.
13. Honjo, p. 27.
14. Honjo, Mar. 28, 1934.
15. Brown, *The Last Banzai* (hereafter Brown), p. 49.
16. Honjo, pp. 151–53.
17. Honjo, p. 159.
18. *Asahi Shimbun*, Feb. 15, 1936.
19. Fujimoto, pp. 54–55.
20. Ibid., p. 46ff.
21. Brown, p. 59.
22. Honjo, p. 207ff.
23. Ibid.
24. Fujimoto, p. 61ff.
25. Ibid.
26. Tokyo newspapers, Wednesday, Feb. 26, 1936.
27. *Mainichi, Asahi, Yomiuri Shimbun*, Feb. 27, 1936.
28. Honjo, Part III. As the emperor's military aide, the general was deeply involved in this matter from start to finish, and within the strictures of his prejudices, his account is one of the most accurate available.
29. Ibid.
30. Honjo, pp. 212–13.
31. Honjo, p. 213.
32. Fujimoto, p. 52.
33. Ibid., p. 33.
34. Honjo, pp. 213–14.
35. Ibid., p. 215–16.
36. Ibid., p. 217.
37. Ibid., p. 218.
38. *Asahi, Mainichi Shimbun*, Feb. 28–March 6, 1936.

12

1. Shiroyama, *Rakujitsu Moyu* (*War Criminal*, hereafter Shiroyama), p. 132.
2. Ibid., p. 138.
3. Ibid.
4. Ibid., p. 139.
5. Honjo, pp. 224–25.
6. Murakami, p. 62ff.

7. Ibid.
8. Ibid., p. 67ff.
9. Zhukov, p. 93ff.

13

1. Agawa, chap. 6.
2. Nomura, chap. 7.
3. Brown, p. 60.
4. Ibid., p. 70.
5. Hayashi, p. 9.
6. Brown, chap. 13.
7. Shiroyama, pp. 153–55.
8. Brown, pp. 63–64.
9. Ibid.
10. Ibid., pp. 28–30.
11. Shiroyama, pp. 163–70.
12. Ibid.
13. Murakami, pp. 71–74.
14. Brown, pp. 75–76.
15. Shiroyama, pp. 166–68.
16. Ibid., p. 168.
17. Ibid.
18. Shiroyama, pp. 172–73.
19. Hsu, *History of the Sino-Japanese War* (hereafter Hsu), p. 175ff.
20. Ibid., p. 176.

14

1. Shiroyama, p. 189ff.
2. Ibid., p. 179.
3. Hsu, p. 175ff.
4. Ibid.
5. Brown, pp. 74–75.
6. Hsu, pp. 171–72.
7. Author's observations, west China, 1944–45.
8. Hsu, p. 163ff.
9. *Asahi Shimbun,* Aug. 1, 1937.
10. Shiroyama, pp. 174–75.
11. Ibid., p. 175.
12. *Asahi Shimbun,* Aug. 10, 1937.
13. Hsu, p. 202ff.
14. Shiroyama, pp. 177–81.

15

1. Shiroyama, p. 188.
2. *Asahi Shimbun,* Sept. 2, 1937.
3. War Office communiqué, Sept. 2, 1937.

4. *Asahi, Mainichi Shimbun,* Sept. 3, 1937.
5. *Japan Times,* Sept. 10, 1937.
6. *Japan Times,* Sept. 11, 1937.
7. This photograph, distributed by the Associated Press, won many journalistic prizes that year, and was published by hundreds of American newspapers. It probably did more to crystallize American opinion against Japan's attack on China than any other factor.
8. Shiroyama, p. 190.
9. Personal conversations with the late James R. Young, correspondent for International News Service in Tokyo. He had worked for several years on English-language newspapers in Tokyo. He said he began to notice harassment at about this time. Ultimately he was jailed, tortured, and finally deported from Japan in 1940 for his journalistic writings about Japanese affairs.
10. *Asahi Shimbun,* Sept. 5, 1937.
11. *Japan Times,* Sept. 3, 1937.
12. *Japan Times.* A long article about this war in Shanghai appeared on Sept. 4, 1937.
13. I heard the tale of this famous incident from the late John Allison himself.
14. *Japan Times,* Sept. 10, 1937.
15. Shiroyama, p. 187.
16. *Asahi Shimbun,* Sept. 15, 1937.
17. Shiroyama, p. 195ff.
18. *Japan Times,* Sept. 16, 1937.
19. Ibid.
20. *Asahi Shimbun,* Sept. 17, 1937.
21. *Japan Times,* Sept. 21, 1937.
22. Writings of Chairman Mao.
23. Shiroyama, p. 196.
24. Ibid.

16

1. *New York Herald Tribune,* Oct. 4, 1936.
2. Agawa, p. 169.
3. *Japan Times,* Oct. 15, 1937.
4. Agawa, pp. 103–06.
5. *Asahi Shimbun,* Dec. 1937.
6. Ibid.
7. *Japan Times,* July 15, 1984. This diary was suppressed for many years, but was finally exposed to Japanese public opinion as part of an exhibition organized at Kyoto University in the spring of 1983 to inform the Japanese people of the facts of the war against China so long ago. Until that time most Japanese had never heard of the Rape of Nanking, or of any of the other atrocities committed by the Japanese forces in China.
8. Shiroyama, pp. 193–200.
9. Ibid., pp. 198–200.
10. Imperial General Headquarters announcement, Dec. 12, 1937.
11. Agawa, pp. 133–34.
12. Ibid.

13. Agawa, p. 135; Shiroyama, p. 193ff.
14. *Japan Times,* Dec. 1937, Jan. 1938.
15. The memoirs of Prince Asaka were published at the end of World War II, but the material about the Rape of Nanking became general public knowledge only as part of the revisionist historical studies in Japan in the 1980s.
16. Shiroyama, pp. 196–97.
17. Author's observations.
18. Author's observations. *Asahi Shimbun,* July 1981.
19. Shiroyama, pp. 198–200.

17

1. Agawa, p. 134.
2. Chamberlin, *Japan Over Asia* (hereafter Chamberlin), chap. 15.
3. Shiroyama, pp. 201–03.
4. Brown, chap. 15.
5. *Asahi, Mainichi Shimbun,* Feb. 1938.
6. Agawa, pp. 145–46.
7. Brown, pp. 80–81; Fujimoto, pp. 70–76.
8. Fujimoto, pp. 75–76.
9. Ibid.
10. Ibid.
11. Brown, p. 80.
12. Fujimoto, pp. 72–76.
13. Ibid.
14. Ibid.
15. Ibid.
16. Ibid.

18

1. Agawa, pp. 160–170.
2. Agawa, p. 160.
3. Fujimoto, p. 84.
4. *Asahi Shimbun,* July 12, 1940.
5. Editorial, *Asahi Shimbun,* June 16, 1940.
6. *Mainichi Shimbun,* July 3, 1940.
7. *Japan Times,* July 16, 1940.
8. *Asahi, Mainichi Shimbun,* June, July, Aug. 1940.
9. Hayashi, pp. 18–19.
10. Agawa, p. 188.
11. Ibid., p. 189.
12. Ibid., p. 190.
12. Ibid., p. 191.
13. Report of Imperial Conference, Sept. 19, 1940.
14. Ibid.
15. Ibid.
16. *Mainichi Shimbun,* Sept. 19, 1940.
17. Potter, *The Life and Death of a Japanese General* (hereafter Potter), chap. 3.

19

1. *Asahi Shimbun,* Oct. 7–13, 1940.
2. Imperial Rescript on peace, Oct. 1940.
3. Agawa, pp. 212–14.
4. Ibid.
5. *Asahi Shimbun,* report from Berlin, Jan. 6, 1941.
6. Japanese Imperial Army pamphlet.
7. Yamashita Commission report, 1940.
8. Potter, p. 33.
9. Ibid.
10. Fujimoto, p. 82.
11. Tripartite Treaty, Germany, Italy, Japan, 1941.
12. Potter, p. 34.
13. Potter, p. 35.
14. Potter, chap. 3.
15. Ibid.
16. Yamashita report on German Mission, 1941.
17. Liaison conference, Apr. 18, 1941.
18. Transcript of Imperial Conference, July 2, 1941.
19. Ibid.
20. Ibid.
21. Ibid.
22. Ibid.; Hayashi, chap. 2.
23. Transcript of 38th Liaison conference, July 10, 1941.
24. Transcript of 41st Liaison conference, July 24, 1941.
25. Agawa, chap. 9.
26. Ibid.
27. Agawa, p. 225.

20

1. Brown, chap. 18.
2. Shiroyama, pp. 207–08.
3. Transcript of 50th Liaison conference, Sept. 3, 1941.
4. Ibid.
5. Ibid.
6. Ibid. The emperor's little poem was a reprimand for his officials and they all knew it. But so far had they now gone that there was no turning back for any of them. The war philosophy had developed a life of its own. Knowing that their chances of victory were extremely slim, that the enormous power of the United States had not begun to be unleashed, they still moved forward as if in a trance. No one was willing to break the spell.
7. Ibid.
8. Transcript of Imperial Conference, Sept. 6, 1941. Reference paper prepared by secretary of Imperial Headquarters after consultations between Imperial High Command and government.
9. In the postwar years several Japanese told me that this was the common wisdom, as taught even school children in 1940 and 1941.

10. Agawa, pp. 223–36.
11. Agawa, chap. 9.
12. Ibid.
13. Ibid.
14. Ibid.
15. Ibid.
16. Brown, chap. 18.
17. Imperial statement Sept. 6, 1941, to conference.
18. Brown, chap. 18; *Japan Times*, Oct. 1941.
19. Agawa, chap. 9.
20. *Asahi Shimbun*, Nov. 1, 1941. The unusually long article indicated the importance with which the government regarded this mission.
21. Transcript of 66th Liaison conference, Nov. 1, 1941.
22. *Nichi Nichi (Mainichi)*, *Asahi*, *Yomiuri*, and *Japan Times*, Nov. 1941.
23. Transcript of 67th Liaison conference, Nov. 5, 1941.
24. Transcript of Imperial Conference at the Imperial Palace, Dec. 1, 1941. This was the final conference at which the decision for war was made irrevocable.
25. Agawa, p. 245.
26. Agawa, p. 238.
27. Agawa, p. 246.

21

1. Prange, *At Dawn We Slept* (hereafter Prange), p. 254. Also, Agawa mentions that Admiral Yamamoto was quite familiar with Yoshikawa's efforts.
2. Agawa, pp. 150–51.
3. Agawa, p. 246.
4. Ibid.
5. Agawa, p. 253.
6. Prange, p. 499ff.
7. Prange, p. 536.
8. Ibid., p. 532.
9. Ibid., pp. 426, 543.
10. Prange, p. 544.
11. Prange, p. 547.
12. *Japan Times*, Dec. 8, 1941.
13. *Asahi Shimbun* (and all other Japanese newspapers), Dec. 9, 1941. This rescript was printed on the front page of all newspapers and broadcast over Japanese radio stations. Thereafter throughout the war it was reprinted on the ninth day of every month to remind the Japanese public of the war.
14. *Japan Times*, Dec. 9, 1941.
15. Agawa, p. 265.
16. Radio Tokyo (as monitored by the United States Office of War Information, Dec. 7–15, 1941).
17. Author's observations.

22

1. This material comes from research done for my *How They Won the War in the Pacific*, New York, Weybright and Talley, 1969.

2. Tokyo daily newspapers, Dec. 9, 1941.
3. Ibid.
4. Ochi, *Maree Senshi* (hereafter Ochi), chap. 1.
5. This material is from research for my *The Lonely Ships, The Life and Death of the Asiatic Fleet*, McKay, 1975.
6. Agawa, pp. 265–69. This also depends on research materials from the Admiralty files in the British Office of Public Records, collected for an unpublished history of HMS *Prince of Wales*.
7. Ibid.
8. Agawa, p. 268.
9. Agawa, p. 269.
10. Again this material is from research from the United States Navy's historical files, collected for *How They Won the War in the Pacific*.
11. Ibid.
12. Ibid.
13. Hoyt, *Blue Skies and Blood*, chap. 1.
14. *Boei*, vol 10. Hawaii Operations.
15. Ibid.
16. *How They Won the War*, chap. 2.

23

1. *Japan Times*, Dec. 15, 1941.
2. Imperial General Headquarters communiqué, Dec. 14, 1941.
3. *Asahi Shimbun*, Dec. 15, 1941.
4. *Asahi Shimbun*, Dec. 9, 1941.
5. *Mainichi Shimbun*, Dec. 11, 1941.
6. *Japan Times*, Dec. 12–15, 1941.
7. *Asahi Shimbun*, Dec. 15, 1941.
8. Ibid.
9. *Asahi Shimbun*, Dec. 16, 1941.
10. Cabinet announcement, Dec. 12, 1941.
11. Tojo report to Diet, Dec. 18, 1941.
12. Report of Japan Planning Agency, published by all newspapers, Dec. 18, 1941.
13. Ibid.
14. IGHQ communiqué, Dec. 29, 1941.
15. *Asahi Shimbun*, Dec. 30, 1941.
16. Ibid.
17. Author's observations, particularly following discussions with various CINC-PAC staff officers and Pacific Fleet officer of 1941–42.
18. Fujimoto, p. 108.
19. Tokyo newspapers, Dec. 10–20, 1941.
20. IGHQ communiqué, Dec. 29, 1941.
21. Ibid.
22. *Asahi Shimbun*, Dec. 31, 1941.
23. Tojo in speech to the Diet, Dec. 31, 1941.
24. Carew, *The Fall of Hongkong* (hereafter Carew), p. 210ff.
25. Potter, p. 85ff.
26. Ibid.
27. Ibid., p. 91.

28. Kennard, *Lafcadio Hearn*, p. 342ff.
29. *Fall of Tsingtao*, p. 147.
30. Tojo speeches to Diet, Mar. 1942.
31. Potter, p. 95ff.

24

1. Tojo speeches to the Diet, Mar. 1942.
2. Fujimoto, p. 108ff.
3. Brown, p. 143ff.
4. United Press report, Chungking, Mar. 4, 1942.
5. IGHQ communiqué and statement, Mar. 5, 1942.
6. *Asahi Shimbun*, Mar. 7, 1942.
7. Ibid.
8. *Asahi Shimbun*, Mar. 16, 1942.
9. Imperial Liaison conference, Mar. 7, 1942.
10. Brown, p. 156ff.
11. Ibid.
12. Imperial Liaison conference, Mar. 7, 1942.
13. Ibid.
14. *How They Won the War in the Pacific*, chap. 3.
15. Hayashi, chap. 4.
16. Brown, p. 161ff.

25

1. *Japan Times*, Mar. 2, 1942.
2. Hayashi, chap. 4.
3. *Asahi Shimbun*, Mar. 26, 1942.
4. Ibid.
5. Hayashi, chap. 4.
6. Murakami, p. 128.
7. *Asahi, Mainichi Shimbun*, Mar.–Apr. 1942.
8. Ibid., Apr. 1942.
9. Imperial General Headquarters communiqué, Apr. 6, 1942.
10. Imperial General Headquarters communiqué, Apr. 10, 1942.
11. *Japan Times*, Apr. 14, 1942.
12. *Asahi Shimbun*, Apr. 14, 1942.
13. Murakami, p. 110.
14. *Asahi Shimbun*, Apr. 15, 1942.
15. Bateson, *The War With Japan* (hereafter Bateson), pp. 77–79.
16. *Japan Times*, front pages, Apr. 1942.
17. Glines, *Doolittle's Tokyo Raiders* (hereafter Glines), p. 6.
18. Agawa, p. 300.
19. Glines, chap. 6.
20. Agawa, pp. 301–02.
21. Imperial Headquarters communiqué, Apr. 19, 1942.
22. *Miyako Shimbun*, Apr. 20, 1942.
23. *Nichi Nichi (Mainichi Shimbun)*, Apr. 20, 1942.

24. *Asahi Shimbun,* Apr. 22, 1942.
25. Brown, p. 147.
26. Murakami, pp. 111–12.

26

1. *Japan Times,* Apr. 28, 1942.
2. Brown, p. 173ff.
3. Glines, p. 88.
4. Tokyo newspapers, May, June 1942.
5. Hayashi, p. 49. The Japanese had pinpointed twelve airfields in three provinces that must be destroyed. The whole effort, given top priority by the Japanese high command, was called Operation Chekiang.
6. Glines, p. 47ff.
7. Hayashi, pp. 49–50.
8. Hsu, p. 387ff.
9. Glines, p. 320.
10. Hayashi, p. 51.
11. *Boei,* vol. 14, *South Pacific Ocean Army Operations,* chaps. 1–3.
12. *Boei,* vol. 49, *Guadalcanal Naval Operations,* p. 251ff.
13. U.S. Naval records. Operations of Admiral Fletcher's Task Force, May 1942; Hoyt, *Blue Skies and Blood.*
14. *Boei,* vol. 49, pp. 320–35.
15. Ibid.
16. Imperial General Headquarters communiqué, May 10, 1942.
17. Agawa, p. 288. Biographer Agawa says that Yamamoto could not hear the "Battleship March" without flinching, once the naval section of Imperial Headquarters began its boastful and almost totally inaccurate reporting on the sea battles.
18. *Boei,* vol. 43, *Midway,* pp. 1–76.
19. Ibid.

27

1. *Boei,* vol. 14.
2. Agawa, p. 232ff.
3. Ibid. Also *Boei,* vol. 43, chap. 1.
4. Agawa, p. 209ff.
5. Ibid.
6. Holmes, *Double-Edged Secrets* (hereafter Holmes), p. 90.
7. Agawa, p. 293ff.
8. Ibid.
9. Ibid.
10. Agawa, p. 303.
11. Ibid.
12. Agawa, p. 300.
13. Fuchida, p. 121ff.
14. Fuchida, p. 124.
15. Ibid.

16. Ibid., p. 129.
17. Ibid., p. 142ff.
18. Ibid.
19. Ibid., p. 179ff.
20. Ibid.

28

1. Radio Tokyo broadcasts (as monitored by USOWI) June 7–10, 1942.
2. Fuchida, p. 249.
3. Tokyo daily newspapers; Radio Tokyo.
4. Brown, p. 159.
5. Fujimoto, preface.
6. *Asahi Shimbun,* July 1, 1942.
7. *Boei,* vol. 14, p. 240.
8. Hoyt, *Guadalcanal,* chap. 1.
9. Ibid.
10. Agawa, p. 330ff.
11. Okumiya, *Zero* (hereafter Okumiya), chap. 1.
12. Hayashi, p. 58ff.
13. Agawa, p. 346.
14. U.S. Navy action reports, Fletcher task force, August 1942; *Boei,* vol. 43, p. 549ff.
15. Hayashi, p. 59ff.
16. Ibid.
17. *Boei,* vol. 43, p. 624ff.
18. Agawa, p. 342.

29

1. *Asahi Shimbun,* Sept. 1, 1942.
2. Ibid.
3. *Asahi Shimbun,* Sept. 2, 1942.
4. Tojo press announcement, Sept. 8, 1942.
5. *Mainichi Shimbun,* Sept. 22, 1942.
6. Ibid., Sept. 28, 1942.
7. *Japan Times,* Oct. 10, 1942.
8. Japan Board of Information press communiqué, Oct. 19, 1942.
9. *Asahi Shimbun,* Oct. 24, 1942.
10. Imperial General Headquarters communiqué, Oct. 28, 1942.
11. *Asahi Shimbun,* Oct. 29, 1942.
12. Imperial conference transcript, Dec. 31, 1942.
13. So superbly had the Japanese executed this withdrawal that it was several days before the Americans realized that all of the enemy had abandoned the island.
14. *Asahi Shimbun, Mainichi Shimbun,* Radio Tokyo broadcasts, Feb., March 1943.
15. Fujimoto, p. 208ff.
16. Ibid., pp. 111–12.
17. Yamamoto's prediction had been to General Imamura when Imamura arrived at Rabaul in the middle of 1942.

18. The Imperial General Headquarters order of January 4, 1943, presaged the Japanese rollback to a line of defense that ended at Truk. The reason was the continued lack of cooperation between navy and army. After the February disaster in the Battle of the Bismarck Sea, which proved Allied air superiority over New Guinea, the army knew that it could not count on the navy for sea and air support adequate to protect army troop movements in New Guinea. This was the first time the army had found itself on the defensive (Guadalcanal was a Japanese navy show primarily), and it was an enormous shock. A few more months of trying in New Guinea, and the high command would see that the South Pacific was lost.
19. The ambush of Yamamoto ended all the myths about the Japanese navy. His successor, Admiral Koga, did not have the Yamamoto willingness to risk all. American production was beginning to create an enormous war machine by the spring of 1943, and the Combined Fleet's superiority in strength was dissipated.
20. The Imperial High Command had to live with the remnants of Admiral Yamamoto's Midway plan, with troops in the Aleutians that had become a liability. It was apparent in April 1943 that Japan had to go on the defensive and try to hold as much of the empire as possible. The meetings and Imperial Conference of early April simply put the official stamp of approval on a policy that everyone knew had to come.

30

1. I visited Bangkok in the fall of 1946 and found that broad avenue still there, the street full of weeds and grass, and some of the false fronts tumbling over. The Hotel Ratanakosindh was an impressive piece of architecture but the plumbing did not work. The whole remained for many months after the war.
2. Imperial General Headquarters communiqué, Nov. 12, 1943.
3. De Asis diary introduction.
4. Ibid., July 10, 1943.
5. U.S. Strategic Bombing Survey, 1946.
6. De Asis diary, July 18, 1943.
7. Ibid, July 19, 1943.
8. Tojo speech to Diet, July 15, 1943.
9. *Asahi Shimbun,* various editions announcing various draconian measures, Sept. 1943.
10. *Japan Times,* Sept. 15, 1943. This is the first public mention I could find of "collision tactics" as an authorized method of attack. In the past, many brave Japanese airmen had been praised for sending their crippled aircraft into some target as a "living bomb" but only when either the pilot or the aircraft was mortally wounded.
11. General Araki, army pamphlet, 1935.
12. *Japan Times,* Nov. 6, 1943.
13. *Mainichi Shimbun,* Nov. 7, 1943.
14. Ibid.
15. *Asahi Shimbun,* Nov. 10, 1943.
16. Ibid.
17. *Asahi Shimbun,* Nov. 1, 1943.

18. *Asahi Shimbun,* Nov. 8, 1943.
19. *Asahi Shimbun,* Domei dispatch, Nov. 28, 1943.
20. *Asahi Shimbun,* Dec. 31, 1943.

31

1. Brown, p. 174ff.
2. Okumiya, chap. 4.
3. Brown, p. 174.
4. D'Albas, *Death of a Navy* (hereafter D'Albas), p. 160.
5. Ugaki diary, Dec., 1943.
6. Hoyt, *To the Marianas,* chap. 4.
7. Hoyt, *Submarines at War,* p. 238.
8. Morrison, *Point of No Return* (hereafter Morrison), p. 48ff.
9. Ibid.
10. *Boei,* vol. 78, *Army Air Preparations from 1941.*
11. *Japan Times* files, 1943.
12. Morrison, p. 48ff.
13. Ibid., p. 60ff.
14. Ibid., p. 62ff.
15. *Asahi Shimbun,* July 3, 1944.
16. *Mainichi Shimbun,* July 10, 1944.
17. Imperial General Headquarters communiqué, July 4, 1944.
18. Ibid., July 9, 1944.
19. Ibid., July 12, 1944.
20. See appendix.
21. Imperial General Headquarters communiqué, July 16, 1944.
22. Tojo statement to press, *Japan Times,* July 18, 1944.

32

1. See appendix A.
2. Conversations of the author with various Japanese citizens at the end of the war indicated that almost uniformly their first suspicions about the war were aroused with the fall of Guadalcanal, and their certainty that the war was lost dated from the fall of Saipan.
3. *Asahi Shimbun,* July 29, 1944.
4. Like little pufferbellies, all the cabinet ministers lined up on the day of their appointment and gave such statements to the media, which then dutifully broadcast and printed them verbatim. The result was something like a chorus.
5. De Asis diary, July 19–20, 1944. I used this to show that even as the government of Japan was in crisis, the countryside did not indicate it.
6. De Asis diary notes for July and August, 1944. *Asahi Shimbun* notes, and classified advertisements showed the growing strain on Japan.
7. *Japan Times,* July 20, 1944.
8. Kusanayagi, *Tokko no Shiso (The Kamikaze Idea,* hereafter Kusanayagi), p. 180.
9. Ibid., chap. 1.
10. Okumiya, chap. 1.
11. July 29, 1944, Imperial Rescript.

12. Kusanayagi, chap. 4.
13. Ibid., chap. 6.
14. *Boei*, vol. 19, *Homeland Air Defense Operations*, chap. 3.
15. *Asahi Shimbun*, July 30, 1944.
16. See Appendix.
17. *Asahi Shimbun*, Aug. 5, 1944.
18. Ibid. Such articles appeared over about a two-week period in all major Japanese newspapers.
19. *Asahi Shimbun*, Aug. 10, 1944.
20. *Japan Times*, Aug. 10, 1944.
21. Ibid.
22. *Japan Times*, Aug. 14, 1944.
23. *Asahi Shimbun*, Aug. 16, 1944.
24. *Japan Times*, Aug. 16–18, 1944.
25. *Japan Times*, Aug. 25, 1944.

33

1. *Japan Times*, Aug. 30, 1944.
2. *Asahi Shimbun*, Aug. 30, 1944.
3. *Asahi Shimbun*, Aug. 21, 1944. This attack was announced by Imperial General Headquarters in a special communiqué on August 20, and reported in the papers the next day. U.S. Army Air Forces' records confirm a part of the story.
4. *Asahi Shimbun*, report of exhibition of B-29, Sept. 12, 1944.
5. U.S. Strategic Bombing Survey notes, 1946. That contempt for American bombing held by the Japanese was justified in the early months of the war. But at the Battle of the Bismarck Sea the Americans suddenly unveiled the new technique of skip-bombing, which involved a medium bomber coming in at mast height, and after that, there was no more contempt.
6. Report of Diet session, Japanese daily newspapers, Sept. 8, 1944.
7. Sugiyama was the greatest promiser in Japan. As noted he had promised the emperor that the China "incident" would end in Japanese victory within thirty days after it began in 1937.
8. Makoto, *Kaigun Koku Tobetsu Kogekitai Shi* (hereafter Makoto), chap. 2.
9. Author's observations from 1944, 1945 in China and northern Burma. The rumor that Chiang Kai-shek was negotiating with the Japanese, which saturated Chungking in the fall of 1944 and the spring of 1945, was never pinned down during the war, although later the Japanese records showed that Chiang and the Japanese were in contact several times. Chiang was always more concerned with the Communists than with the Japanese, and if he could have figured out a way to do it, he would have made a deal with them. All this has been confirmed in several postwar books, by Barbara Tuchman, by Sterling Seagrave in his book, *The Soong Dynasty,* and above all, by the Japanese army records in various volumes of the *Boei*.
10. Potter, p. 101ff.
11. Ibid.
12. Ibid.
13. Ibid.
14. De Asis diary, Sept. 7, 1944.

15. *Asahi Shimbun,* Sept. 11, 1944.
16. Imperial General Headquarters communiqué, Sept. 12, 1944.
17. De Asis diary, Sept. 19, 20, 1944.
18. De Asis diary, Sept. 25, 1944.
19. De Asis diary, Oct. 2, 3, 1944.
20. Navy writer Nakajima was a war propagandist for the Imperial Navy. His series of articles appeared in many Japanese newspapers in the middle of September 1944, part of the Japanese navy's preparation of the people for news of "the last great battle," the Sho Operation.
21. *Asahi Shimbun,* Sept. 25, 1944.
22. Japanese press, Sept. 15–25, 1944.
23. *Asahi Shimbun,* Sept. 26, 1944.
24. Ibid.
25. Imperial General Headquarters communiqué, Sept. 26, 1944. American air force records confirmed the raid, but not the enormous damages claimed by the Japanese.
26. During the first week of October 1944, the Japanese newspapers carried a great number of articles about willing self-sacrifice on the home front. It was part of the new campaign to prepare Japan for the battle of Japan, when all would be expected to fight.
27. Almost every day in early October there was some talk in the media about air raid precautions, and indications of the movement of much of Japanese industry out of the cities.
28. The account of Admiral Toyoda's quick visit to the Philippines is contained in the *Boei* volume that deals with the Sho Operation and the Allied invasion. It is mentioned in the biography of Admiral Ohnishi by Kusanayagi.
29. Imperial General Headquarters communiqués, Oct. 11–17, 1944, as published in *Asahi Shimbun.*
30. *Japan Times,* Oct. 19, 1944.
31. Imperial Rescript, Oct. 19, 1944.
32. Inoguchi, Action Report of USS *Franklin,* Oct. 1944.
33. Inoguchi, chap. 2.
34. Ibid.
35. Ibid.

34

1. *Mainichi Shimbun,* Oct. 25, 1944.
2. Imperial Headquarters communiqué, Nov. 1, 1944.
3. Radio Tokyo broadcast, as intercepted by USOWI, Nov. 6, 1944.
4. Imperial General Headquarters communiqué, Nov. 3, 1944.
5. Ibid., Nov. 7, 1944.
6. Ibid., Nov. 24, and U.S. 20 AAF records.
7. Makoto, chap. 4.
8. Morrison, p. 166.
9. Ibid., p. 166ff.
10. Ibid., chap. 15.
11. Ibid., p. 174.
12. *Japan Times,* Dec. 23, 1944.

13. Morrison, p. 178.
14. *Japan Times,* Jan. 14, 1945.
15. Morrison, p. 166ff.
16. Ibid., p. 192ff.
17. Ibid., p. 193.
18. *Boei,* vol. 41, *Shogo Sakusen (Philippine Operations,* vol. 1), p. 456ff.
19. Guillain, *La Guerre au Japan, de Pearl Harbor à Hiroshima* (hereafter Guillain), chap. 14.
20. Ibid., *Japan Times,* Mar. 1945.
21. Guillain, chap. 14.; *Boei, Air Defense of Homeland.*
22. Radio Tokyo broadcasts, Mar. 10, 11, 1945, monitored by USOWI.
23. *Boei, Air Defense of Homeland;* Guillain, chap. 14; Strategic Bombing Survey, 1946.
24. Morrison, p. 228ff.

35

1. Morrison, p. 203.
2. Ibid., p. 206.
3. Ibid., p. 227.
4. Ibid., p. 228.
5. *How They Won the War in the Pacific,* p. 480ff. So deadly was the rain of kamikazes on the American, Australian, and British naval forces off Okinawa that the U.S. Navy established a special unit to try to figure out a way to deal with the kamikazes. By war's end no useful development had been achieved other than the constant vigilance built up by the naval forces around Okinawa.
6. U.S. Strategic Bombing Survey, 1946.
7. *Japan Times,* Apr. 1945.
8. *Asahi Shimbun,* Apr. 4, 1945.
9. *Asahi Shimbun,* Apr. 10, 1945. Throughout the war the Japanese people were far better informed about events in the United States and other Allied countries than the Americans were about events in Japan. The reason: the Japanese were interested enough to follow enemy activity through the neutral press. The American press was not.
10. *Asahi Shimbun,* Apr. 4, 1945.
11. *Asahi Shimbun,* Apr. 5, 1945.
12. *Japan Times,* Apr. 5, 1945.
13. *Japan Times,* Apr. 6, 1945.
14. Virtually every Japanese paper printed the Norinaga poem.
15. *Japan Times,* Apr. 15, 1945.
16. Guillain, chap. 14.
17. Sado Iguchi press communiqué, Apr. 14, 1945.
18. Potter, chap. 10.

36

1. Japanese newspapers, May 1945.
2. Guillain, chap. 15.
3. Ugaki diary, May 16, 1945.

4. Morrison, chap. 23.
5. June 8, 1945, minutes of Imperial Conference.
6. Minutes of Supreme War Council Meeting, June 22, 1945.
7. Brooks, *Behind Japan's Surrender,* chap. 10.
8. Guillain, chap. 15.
9. *Japan Times,* Aug. 1, 1945.
10. Ibid.
11. The figures are still murky. I last visited the Hiroshima museum in the fall of 1984 and found the estimates still the same as they had been twenty years earlier. No accurate figure of people who died later as a result of the bomb will ever be reached, nor the specific effects of radiation on later generations. But the fact remains that horrible as the atomic weapons were, almost equally horrible results had been achieved with conventional weapons, given General LeMay's concept of killing off a whole people.
12. I dealt with this argument in some detail in *Closing the Circle.* The original materials are to be found in the minutes of the Imperial Conferences, and the memoirs of some participants. Feis and Brooks both dealt with the arguments of the militarists to some extent.
13. Ibid.
14. *Japan Times* report, Aug. 9, 1945.
15. *Japan Times,* Aug. 10, 1945. A bare bones report on a cabinet meeting.
16. June 17 communiqué, Imperial General Headquarters.
17. Ibid.
18. Hoyt, *Closing the Circle,* pp. 170–72.
19. Imperial Conference, Aug. 14, 1945.
20. Ibid.
21. Ibid.
22. Supreme War Council meeting, Aug. 14, 1945.
23. Ibid.
24. Murakami, p. 182ff.
25. Fujimoto, p. 188.
26. *Japan Times,* Aug. 15, 1945.
27. *Japan Times,* Aug. 20.
28. Fujimoto, p. 189ff.
29. Ibid.
30. Ibid., pp. 193–94.
31. Ibid.
32. Ibid., pp. 194–96.

37

1. Borton, p. 393.
2. The American enthusiasm for tearing down the Japanese war machine brought trouble very quickly. Within a matter of weeks SCAP had to allocate American ships (mostly LSTs) to the Japanese for the repatriation of Japanese and Koreans from far-flung points of the old empire.
3. *Japan Times,* Aug. 21, 1945.
4. *Japan Times,* Jan. 15, 1946.
5. *Japan Times,* Aug. 24, 1945.

6. I went to Hanoi at the time of the surrender. It seemed odd to arrive at the airfield, to have a Japanese sergeant open the door of our C-47, help us down the steps he provided, and escort us to a truck, which took us to the terminal, and later to the Hotel Metropole in Hanoi. It seemed odder to encounter Japanese soldiers and civilians on the streets. But as soon as the surrender was officially made, the Japanese military disappeared into camps and remained there until repatriated in 1946.

7. On Taiwan, in October 1945, I attended what may have been the first "war crimes trial" to come out of the Pacific War. On trial were two sergeants accused of beheading two American navy pilots shot down over Taiwan during the great Formosa air battle. They were court-martialed by their own army after the surrender. They both admitted their actions; the defense claimed it was not a crime, but an act of war, and they both received brief prison terms, of about five years each. The Americans in attendance, two naval intelligence officers from Admiral Miles' China Rice Paddy Navy (coastwatchers) and I, were not impressed. Obviously, neither were the SCAP powers in Tokyo.

8. Potter, chap. 12.

9. Ibid.

10. Kusanayagi, chap. 6; *Asahi Shimbun,* Aug. 17, 1945.

11. Minear, *Victors' Justice,* pp. 170–72.

12. The Dutch East Indies became Indonesia, the Federated Malay States became Malaysia, Singapore became independent. French Indochina split into two Vietnams. Taiwan became part of China again, and separated again, but was still Chinese. Korea became independent. Manchuria went back to China. The Philippines became independent. So, ultimately, did the old Japanese trust territories, which chose their own forms of government. Samoa advanced from an American territory to the status of commonwealth, but remains the most colonial of all the Pacific lands.

13. The ashes were later offered to the families, but the families were queasy about taking them, particularly since the ashes had been intermingled and thus were not very meaningful.

14. The memorial to the six who died remains in a little park in the middle of Tokyo. Every Tokyo taxi driver knows where it is, although mine thought it odd that a foreigner should even know about the memorial.

BIBLIOGRAPHY

Unpublished

United States Pacific Fleet War Diary, 1941–45.
Papers of Admiral William F. Halsey.

Published

Note: In the interest of brevity I have taken the liberty of listing my own past books
which contain the primary sources of the material used, rather than relisting
all those many sources here since this book is aimed at a general audience, and
many readers will not be interested in the source material.

Agawa, Hiroyuke. *The Reluctant Admiral.* Tokyo: Kodansha, 1981.
Appleman, Roy E. et al. *Okinawa, the Last Battle.* Washington: Historical Division,
U.S. Department of the Army, 1948.
Asada, Teruhiko. *The Night of a Thousand Suicides.* New York: St. Martin's Press,
1970.
Asahi Shimbun (eds.). *The Pacific Rivals.* New York: Weatherhill, 1972.
Axelbank, Albert. *Black Star Over Japan.* New York: Hill and Wang, 1972.
Baker, Paul R. *The Atomic Bomb.* New York: Holt, Rinehart and Winston, 1968.
Bateson, Charles. *The War With Japan, A Concise History.* Sydney: Ure Smith, 1968.
Blair, Clay, Jr. *Silent Victory.* Philadelphia: Lippincott, 1975.
Blond, Georges. *L'Amiral Togo, Samourai de la Mer.* Paris: Librairie Artheme Fayard,
1958.
Borg, Dorothy. *The United States and the Far Eastern Crisis of 1933–1938.* Cam-
bridge: Harvard University Press, 1964.
Borton, Hugh. *Japan's Modern Century.* New York: Ronald Press, 1955.
Brooks, Lester. *Behind Japan's Surrender.* New York: McGraw Hill, 1968.

Brown, Courtney. *Tojo: The Last Banzai, a Biography of Hideki Tojo.* New York: Holt, Rinehart and Winston, 1967.

Brown, Delmer, and Ichiro Ishida. *The Future and the Past.* A Translation and study of the *Gukansho,* an interpretive history of Japan, written in 1219. Berkeley: University of California Press, 1979.

Bryan, J. and W. F. Halsey. *Admiral Halsey's Story.* New York: Da Capo Press, 1976.

Butow, Robert J. C. *Tojo.* Princeton: Princeton University Press, 1961.

Carew, Tim. *The Fall of Hongkong.* London: Anthony Blond, 1960.

Carter, Kit, and Robert Mueller. *The Army Air Forces in World War II, Combat Chronology 1941–45.* Washington: Office of Air Force History, 1973.

Castro, Ferdinando. *I Kamikaze. Stories of Japanese Suicide Pilots.* Milan: Giovanni de Vecchi, 1970.

Causton, E. E. N. *Militarism and Foreign Policy in Japan.* London: George Allen and Unwin, 1937.

Chamberlin, William Henry. *Japan Over Asia,* revised ed. Garden City, N.Y.: Blue Ribbon Books, 1942.

Christopher, Robert. *The Japanese Mind.* New York: Fawcett, 1982.

Clinard, O. J. *Japan's Influence on American Naval Power, 1897–1917.* Berkeley: University of California Press, 1947.

Coffey, Thomas M. *Imperial Tragedy.* New York: World, 1970.

Colegrove, Kenneth W. *Militarism in Japan.* Boston: World Peace Foundation, 1936.

Craig, Albert M. and Donald H. Shively. *Personality in Japanese History.* Berkeley: University of California Press, 1970.

Cutlack, F. M. *The Manchurian Arena. An Australian View.* Sydney: Angus and Robertson, 1934.

D'Albas, Andrieu. *Death of a Navy.* Greenwich, Conn.: Devin-Adair, 1957.

Davis, Burke. *Get Yamamoto.* New York: Random House, 1970.

De Asis, Leocadio. *From Bataan to Tokyo. Diary of a Filipino Student in Wartime Japan, 1943–44.* Kansas: Center for East Asian Studies, 1979.

Dull, Paul S. *A Battle History of the Imperial Japanese Navy.* Annapolis: Naval Institute Press, 1978.

Ebina, Kashiko. *Saigo no Tokko Ki.(The Last Suicide Plane. Biography of Vice Admiral Matome Ugaki.)* Tokyo: Yamashita Mitsuo Tosho Shuppangaisha, 1975.

Emmerson, John K. and Leonard A. Humphreys. *Will Japan Rearm.* Stanford: Hoover Institution, 1974.

Feis, Herbert. *The Road to Pearl Harbor.* Princeton: Princeton University Press, 1950.

Feldt, Eric. *The Coastwatchers.* New York: Oxford University Press, 1978.

Fuchida, Mitsuo, and Masatake Okumiya. *Midway, the Battle That Doomed Japan.* Annapolis: Naval Institute Press, 1955.

Fujimoto, Hiroshi. *Fifty Years of Light and Dark. The Hirohito Era.* Tokyo: Mainichi, 1975.

Glines, Carroll V. *Doolittle's Tokyo Raiders.* Princeton: Van Nostrand, 1964.

Gomigawa, Jumpei. *Kyokugenjyoko ni okeru ningen.* Tokyo: 1973.

Gordon, Gary. *The Rise and Fall of the Japanese Empire.* Derby, Conn.: Monarch Books, 1962.

Grew, Joseph C. *Ten Years in Japan.* New York: Simon and Schuster, 1943.

Griswold, A. Whitney. *The Far Eastern Policy of the United States.* New Haven: Yale University Press, 1938.

Guillain, Robert. *La Guerre au Japon, de Pearl Harbor à Hiroshima.* Paris: Editions Stock, 1979.

Hachiya, Michihiko. *Hiroshima Diary.* Chapel Hill: University of North Carolina Press, 1955.

Hane, Mikiso. *Emperor Hirohito and His Chief Aide De Camp. The Honjo Diary, 1933–1936.* Tokyo: University of Tokyo Press, 1982.

Hara, Tameichi. *Japanese Destroyer Captain.* New York: Ballantine Books, 1961.

Harada, Katsumasa. *Showa no Seso.* Tokyo: Dai Nihon Insatsu Kabushiki Kaisha, 1983.

Harrison, B. J. and K. W. Palmer. *China and Japan Between the Wars.* Sydney: William Brooks, undated.

Hart, Robert A. *The Great White Fleet.* Boston: Little, Brown, 1965.

Hattori, Takushio. *Daitoa Senso Zenshi (The Complete History of the Pacific War),* 4 vols. Tokyo: Matsu, 1953.

Hawks, F. L. *Narrative of the Expedition of an American Squadron in the China Seas and Japan, Performed in the Years 1852, 1853, and 1854, Under Command of M. C. Perry of the U.S. Navy,* 3 vols. Washington: A. O. P. Nicholson, 1856.

Hayashi, Saburo. *Kogun, The Japanese Army in the Pacific War.* Quantico: The Marine Corps Assn., 1959.

Hess, William N. *Pacific Sweep.* New York: Zebra, 1974.

Holmes, W. J. *Double-Edged Secrets.* Annapolis: U.S. Naval Institute Press, 1979.

Hoyt, Edwin P. *Army Without a Country* (The Czechoslovak Legion in Russia in World War I). New York: Macmillan, 1962.

———. *Asians in the West.* Nashville: Thomas Nelson, Inc., 1974.

———. *Blue Skies and Blood, The Story of the Battle of the Coral Sea.* New York: Eriksson, 1975.

———. *Closing the Circle.* New York: Van Nostrand, Reinhold Co., 1982.

———. *Fall of Tsingtao.* London: ur Barker Ltd., 1965.

———. *Guadalcanal.* New York: Stein & Day, 1981.

———. *How They Won the War in the Pacific, Nimitz and His Admirals.* New York: Weybright and Talley, 1970.

———. *Kreuzerkrieg.* New York: World Publishing Co., 1963.

———. *Pacific Destiny.* New York: W. W. Norton and Co., 1981.

———. *Submarines at War.* New York: Stein & Day, 1983.

———. *To the Marianas.* New York: Van Nostrand, Reinhold Co., 1980.

Hsu Long-Hsuen and Chang Ming-Kai. *History of the Sino-Japanese War 1937–45.* Taipei: Chung Wu Pub. Co., 1971.

Ienaga, Saburo. *The Pacific War.* New York: Pantheon, 1980.

Ike, Nobutaka. *Japan's Decision for War. Records of the 1941 Policy Conferences.* Stanford: Stanford University Press, 1967.

Inoguchi, Rikiheio and Tadashi Nakajima. *Kamikaze; Tobetsu Kogekitai.* Tokyo: Nihon Shuppan Kyodo Kabushiki Kaisha, 1951. Published by Naval Institute Press, Annapolis, under the title *The Divine Wind* with translation and notes by Roger Pineau.

Ito, Masanori, with Roger Pineau. *The End of the Imperial Japanese Navy.* New York: W. W. Norton, 1962.

Ito, Masashi. *The Emperor's Last Soldiers.* New York: Coward McCann, 1967.

492 · BIBLIOGRAPHY

James, David H. *The Rise and Fall of the Japanese Empire*. London: George Allen and Unwin, 1951.

Japan Defense Agency (*Boei Senshishitsu*) (History of the Pacific War), compiled by the Japan Defense Agency, vol. 1–101. Tokyo: Japan Defense Agency War History Room, 1955–70.

Jones, F. C. *Japan's New Order in East Asia: Its Rise and Fall, 1937–45*. London: Oxford University Press, 1954.

Kaiser Company, the. *The Kaiser Story*. Oakland: the Kaiser Corporation, 1960.

Kase, Toshikazu. *Journey to the Missouri*. New Haven: Yale, 1950.

Kato, Masuo. *The Lost War*. New York: Knopf, 1946.

Kawasaki, Ichiro. *Japan Unmasked*. Tokyo: Tuttle, 1969.

Kennard, Nina H. *Lafcadio Hearn*. Port Washington, N.Y.: Kennikat Press, 1967.

Kodama, Yoshio. *I Was Defeated*. Tokyo: Booth and Fukuda, 1951.

Konnichi no Wadaisha. *Kamikaze Tokkotai Shutsugeki no Nichi* (Japanese Special Attack Unit Sorties). Tokyo: Konnichi no Wadaisha, 1970.

Kusanayagi, Daizo. *Tokko no Shiso* (*The Kamikaze Idea*). *Biography of Admiral Takejiro Ohnishi*. Tokyo: Bungei Haru Aki, 1972.

Kuwahara, Yasuo and Gordon T. Allred. *Kamikaze*. New York: Ballantine Books, 1957.

Lattimore, Owen. *Manchuria, Cradle of Conflict*. New York: The Macmillan Co., 1932.

Lee, Chong-sik. *Counterinsurgency in Manchuria, the Japanese Experience, 1931–1940*. Santa Monica, Calif.: The Rand Corp., 1967.

––––––. *Revolutionary Struggle in Manchuria. Chinese Communism and Soviet Interest 1922–45*. Berkeley: University of California Press, 1983.

Liang, Chin-tung. *The Sinister Face of the Mukden Incident*. New York: St. John's University Press, 1969.

Livingston, Jon, Joe Moore, and Felicia Oldfather. *Japan Reader*. New York: Pantheon, 1973.

Lory, Hillis. *Japan's Military Masters. The Army in Japanese Life*. Washington: Infantry Journal, 1943.

Lum, Peter. *Six Centuries in East Asia*. New York: S. G. Phillips, 1973.

Madej, W. Victor. *Japanese Armed Forces of Battle, 1937–45*. Allentown, Pa.: Game Marketing Co., 1981.

Maki, John M. *Japanese Militarism, Its Cause and Cure*. New York: Knopf, 1945.

––––––. *Conflict and Tension in the Far East: Key Documents, 1894–1960*. Seattle: University of Washington Press, 1961.

Makoto, Ikuta. *Kaigun Koku Tobetsu Kogekitai Shi* (History of the Navy Aviation Special Attack Units). Tokyo: undated.

Martin, Christopher. *Russo-Japanese War*. New York: Abelard Schuman, 1966.

Mayo, Lida. *Bloody Buna*. New York: Doubleday and Co., 1974.

McWilliams, Carey. *Prejudice: Japanese-Americans, Symbol of Racial Intolerance*. Boston: Little, Brown, 1944.

Millot, Bernard. *Divine Thunder*. New York: Pinnacle Books, 1970.

Minear, R. H. *Victors' Justice, The Tokyo War Crimes Trial*. Princeton: Princeton University Press, 1971.

Minichiello, Sharon. *Retreat from Reform*. Honolulu: University of Hawaii, 1984.

Moore, Frederick. *With Japan's Leaders*. New York: Scribners, 1942.

Morison, Samuel Eliot. *History of United States Naval Operations in World War II*, 14 vols. Boston: Atlantic Little Brown, 1948–58.

———. *Old Bruin, Commodore Mathew C. Perry*. Boston: Atlantic Little Brown, 1967.

———. *The Two Ocean War*. Boston: Atlantic Little Brown, 1963.

Moriya, Tadashi. *No Requiem*. Translated by Geoffrey Kishimoto. Tokyo: Hokuseido Press, 1968.

Morris, John. *Traveler From Tokyo*. New York: Sheridan House, 1944.

Morrison, W. H. *Point of No Return, The Story of the 20th Air Force*. New York: Times Books, 1979.

Murakami, Hyoe. *Japan, The Years of Trial, 1919–52*. Tokyo: Japan Culture Institute, 1982.

Naemura, Naro. *Bansei Tokkotai En no Issho (Writings of the Eternal Rest Suicide Squadron Crewmen)*. Tokyo: Gendai Hyoronsha, 1978.

Nagatsuka, Ryuji. *I Was a Kamikaze*. London: Abelard Schuman, 1972.

Nihon Kyosanto. *Fukkutsu Suru nihongun shugi*. Tokyo: Nihon kyosanto chuo iinkai shupanbu, 1966.

Nomura, Minoru. *Rekishi no naka no nihon kaigun (Inside History of the Japanese Navy)*. Tokyo: Genshobo, 1978.

Norman, E. H. *Soldier and Peasant in Japan*. New York: Institute of Pacific Relations, 1943.

Ochi, Harukai. *Maree Senshi*. Tokyo: Yorochiki Kaisha, 1973.

Ogawa, Taro. *Koza: Gunkokushugi Kyoiku*. Tokyo, 1970.

Ogawa, Tetsuro. *Terraced Hell, A Japanese Memoir of Defeat and Death in Northern Luzon, Philippines*. Tokyo: Charles E. Tuttle, 1972.

Okumiya, Masatake, and Jiro Horikoshi (with Martin Caidin). *Zero*. New York: Ballantine Books, 1956.

O'Kane, Richard. *Clear the Bridge*. Chicago: Rand McNally, 1977.

Okumiyo, Masatake. *Rabauru Kaigun Kokutai (Rabaul Navy Air Force)*. Tokyo, 1976.

Orita, Zenji, and Joseph Harrington. *I Boat Captain*. Canoga Park: Major Books, 1973.

Pacific War Research Society. *Japan's Longest Day*. New York: Ballantine Books, 1972. First published in Tokyo as *Nihon Ichiban Nagai* by Bungei Shunju sha, 1965.

Perry, Hamilton Darby. *The Panay Incident*. New York: Macmillan, 1969.

Potter, John Deane. *The Life and Death of a Japanese General* (Biography of General Tomoyuke Yamashita). New York: Signet Books, 1962.

Prange, Gordon W. *At Dawn We Slept, the Untold Story of Pearl Harbor*. New York: McGraw-Hill, 1981.

Quigley, Harold S. *Far Eastern War 1937–1941*. Boston: World Peace Foundation, 1943.

Reischauer, Edwin O. *Japan Past and Present*. New York: Alfred A. Knopf, 1964.

Sansom. G. B. *Japan a Short Cultural History*. New York: Appleton Century, 1962.

Sehai bunsha. *Nihonjin no Hyakunen, Gunkoku no Ashioto*. Tokyo: Sehai bunsha, 1973.

Shilloney, Ben-Ami. *Revolt in Japan, The Young Officers and the February 26, 1936 Incident*. Princeton: Princeton University Press, 1973.

Shirer, W. L. *The Rise and Fall of the Third Reich*. New York: Simon and Schuster, 1960.

Shiroyamaa, Saburo. *Rakujitsu Moyu (War Criminal, The Life and Death of Koki Hirota)*. Tokyo: Shinchosa, translation into English by John Bester as *War Criminal, The Life and Times of Hirota Koki*, Japanese edition, 1974, English edition, Kodansha, International, 1977.

Silberman, Bernard S., and H. D. Harootunian. *Japan in Crisis*. Princeton: Princeton University Press, 1970.

Stefan, John J. *Hawaii Under the Rising Sun. Japan's Plans for Conquest after Pearl Harbor*. Honolulu: University of Hawaii Press, 1984.

Stimson, Henry L. *The Far Eastern Crisis*. New York: Howard Fertig, 1974.

Sunoo, Hakwon. *Japanese Militarism, Past and Present*. Chicago: Nelson Hall, 1975.

Takeyama Michio. *Showa No Seishinshi*. Tokyo, 1956.

Tanekawa Tosha. *Nihon Kaigun Sento Butai, Tsuku: Esu Retsuden* (Japanese navy fighter squadrons, with capsule biographies). Tokyo, 1978.

Tanin, O., and E. Yohan. *Militarism and Fascism in Japan*. New York: International Publishers, 1934.

Terai, Shun. *Shippu Tokko Furutake Tai (The Story of a Fighter Squadron)*. Tokyo: Hara Shobo, undated.

Thomas, David A. *The Battle of the Java Sea*. New York: Stein and Day, 1969.

Thorne, Christopher. *Allies of a Kind. The U.S., Britain and the War Against Japan 1941–45*. London: Hamish Hamilton, 1978.

———. *Tokyo Record*. New York: Reynal and Hitchcock, 1943.

Tolischus, Otto D. *Through Japanese Eyes*. New York: Reynal and Hitchcock, 1945.

Turnbull, S. R. *The Samurai. A Military History*. New York: Macmillan, 1977.

Ugaki, Matome. *Dai-Toa Senso Hiki (Great East Asia War Secret Diary)*. Tokyo: Gensho Moshi, 1950.

Wheeler, Gerald F. *Prelude to Pearl Harbor*. Columbia, Mo.: University of Missouri Press, 1963.

Willmott, H. P. *Empires in the Balance*. Annapolis: Naval Institute Press, 1982.

Willoughby, Westel W. *Japan's Case Examined*. Baltimore: Johns Hopkins University Press, 1940.

Workers Party of Korea. *Reminiscences of the Anti-Japanese Guerillas*. Pyongyang: Foreign Languages Publishing House, 1970.

Yamamoto, Tsunetomo. *Hagakure. The Book of the Samurai*. Translated by William Scott Wilson. Tokyo: Kodansha, 1979.

Yoshihashi, Takehiko. *Conspiracy at Mukden. The Rise of the Japanese Military*. New Haven: Yale University Press, 1963.

Yutaka Yokata, with J. D. Harrington. *Kamikaze Submarine*. New York: Leisure Books, 1962.

Zhukov, Y. M. *The Rise and Fall of the Gumbatsu*. Moscow: Progress Publishers, 1975.

Newspapers

Asahi Shimbun
Asahi Evening News
Japan Times
Mainichi Shimbun (formerly *Nichi Nichi Shimbun*)
Miyako Shimbun
Yomiuri Shimbun

INDEX